Forest and Range Policy

McGraw-Hill Series in Forest Resources

Avery: Natural Resource Measurements
Boyce: Forest Pathology
Brockman and Merriam: Recreational Use of Wild Lands
Brown and Davis: Forest Fire: Control and Use
Chapman and Meyer: Forest Mensuration
Dana and Fairfax: Forest and Range Policy
Daniel, Helms, and Baker: Principles of Silviculture
Davis: Forest Management
Davis: Land Use
Duerr: Fundamentals of Forestry Economics
Guise: The Management of Farm Woodlands
Harlow, Harrar, and White: Textbook of Dendrology
Heady: Rangeland Management
Knight and Heikenen: Principles of Forest Entomology
Panshin and De Zeeuw: Textbook of Wood Technology
Panshin, Harrar, Bethel, and Baker: Forest Products
Rich: Marketing of Forest Products: Text and Cases
Sharpe, Hendee, and Allen: An Introduction to Forestry
Shirley: Forestry and Its Career Opportunities
Stoddart, Smith, and Box: Range Management
Trippensee: Wildlife Management
    Volume I—Upland Game and General Principles
    Volume II—Fur Bearers, Waterfowl, and Fish
Wackerman, Hagenstein, and Michell: Harvesting Timber Crops
Worrell: Principles of Forest Policy

Walter Mulford was Consulting Editor of this series from its inception in 1931 until January 1, 1952.

Henry J. Vaux was Consulting Editor of this series from January 1, 1952, until July 1, 1976.

Forest and Range Policy

Its Development in the United States

Second Edition

Samuel Trask Dana
Late Dean Emeritus
School of Natural Resources
University of Michigan

Sally K. Fairfax
Professor of Conservation and
Resource Studies
University of California, Berkeley

Assistance from
Mark Rey and
Barbara T. Andrews
on Chapters 9 and 10

McGraw-Hill Book Company

New York   St. Louis   San Francisco   Auckland   Bogotá   Düsseldorf
Johannesburg   London   Madrid   Mexico   Montreal   New Delhi
Panama   Paris   São Paulo   Singapore   Sydney   Tokyo   Toronto

FOREST AND RANGE POLICY

4 5 6 7 8 9 0   DODO   8 9 8 7 6 5 4

This book was set in Times by Phoenix Publishing Services.
The editor was Marian D. Provenzano and
the production supervisor was Diane Renda.
R. R. Donnelley & Sons Company was printer and binder.

Library of Congress Cataloging in Publication Data

Dana, Samuel Trask, date
    Forest and range policy, its development in the
United States.

    (McGraw-Hill series in forest resources)
    Bibliography: p.
    Includes index.
    1. United States—Forest policy. 2. Range policy—
United States—History. I. Fairfax, Sally K. II. Title.
SD565.D3 1980   333.7'4'0973   79-13652
ISBN 0-07-015288-8

Samuel Trask Dana
1882–1978

There is an understandable tendency to regard Dean Dana's death in 1978 as ending an era in the forestry profession. The loss of his insight, experience, and wisdom leaves resource managers without their most respected and durable sage. But it is a tribute to his vision that Dean Dana's era is in many ways just getting underway. The lessons he taught generations of students are not old or gone by; they are the very heart of modern land management professionalism.

Rather than ending something, Dean Dana's death should remind us how close we are to the beginning. His career spanned almost the entire history of American conservation and resource management. The effort to institute multiple-use land stewardship is a relatively new undertaking. If we are inclined to be dismayed by present conflict and uncertainty, we can take pride and inspiration from the tremendous accomplishments of Dean Dana's career. What was achieved in his lifetime is both a challenge and a promise to us all.

to Roy Feuchter
U.S. Forest Service

and George Lea
Bureau of Land Management

Their hopes and efforts should remind us that, among the bureaucrats, there are public servants. They need attentive critics; but they have also earned respect, support, gratitude, and affection.

Contents

Preface

It is difficult to undertake a revision of this text, which has been long considered a classic, without feelings of humility. My major goal has been to update Dean Dana's work without introducing errors. In order to make room for new material, it has been necessary to eliminate some of the detail of the first edition. These revisions and eliminations have been guided by four basic principles. The first was a strong belief that it was desirable and appropriate to maintain the historical, chronological approach Dean Dana used. Knowing how we got to where we are today will help us understand where we are and what we have to carry us into the future. The editing of the existing text was also guided by a desire to have the text provide a background for current issues. For example, Dean Dana gave very little treatment to the wilderness movement. When he wrote, it was not clear that wilderness was going to become the major issue it is today. I have, therefore, felt obliged to go back and admix wilderness policy with Dean Dana's discussion starting about 1920. Third, I believe that the book is appropriately backend loaded. There is more detail on the legislative history and the provisions of the most recent legislation than there is on earlier and perhaps more important legislation because the impact of the earlier acts is easier to understand now. Finally, I have taken the Dean's appendix on developments in related fields and integrated it into the copy where appropriate. Water management, minerals development, and wildlife management are important parts of forest and range policy in the 1970s and should not, in my opinion, be treated as "related." This is a view which I am certain that he shared, although I am not sure that he would have wanted to eliminate the appendix.

There are several other points at which my own interests are reflected in the text. Many of these Dean Dana and I had in common. I believe that I depart significantly from Dean Dana's attitudes, however, in that I do not share his teleological approach to the development of forest and range management. If there is a major shift in the focus of the text, it is that I have attempted to put a veneer of interpretation on the procession of events and facts which have previously been assumed to be progress.

The second edition focuses on policy as a process of evolving compromises. The text will, therefore, emphasize explicitly and by implication a number of factors which appear to be major influences on the development of forest and range policy. First, policy is discussed as a series of negotiated settlements resulting from interaction among competing interest groups, among competing regions, and among agencies competing for the support, interest, and attention of the public. This view of policy as an unending process of negotiation should mitigate against the all too familiar view of conservation history as a crusade of the forces of enlightenment against the forces of darkness. There are very few good guys and bad guys in this story. There are simply decent people with different views trying to do a difficult job. At the turn of the century, resource management was only fleetingly a moral crusade, and even then it was an intensely politicized and tactically sophisticated morality which fueled its energies.

A second major influence on policy is institutional. Policy is negotiated in a variety of arenas. Each arena has different access points and negotiating styles and, therefore, affects the outcome slightly differently. The legislature, the courts, and the executive agencies all have great strengths and weaknesses as arenas for debate, and these are clearly visible in the development of policy. It is also apparent that different institutions are dominant influences in the policy process at different points in history. Too frequently, we look to Congress or the President for initiatives and direction in policy matters. Important leadership in forest and range policy has come from citizens, state governments, and federal agencies as well. In the present era, it is also far too common to assume that the bureaucracy is a faceless, even malevolent, group that only responds when kicked hard. Hopefully, what follows will suggest that different institutions have strengths and weaknesses in terms of access, process, and characteristic outputs and each suits the needs of various policy advocates and decision makers under different circumstances.

A third major influence on forest and range policy has been what might be characterized as exogenous factors: two world wars, several major economic crises, the energy crisis, the civil rights movement, and the political turbulence of the late 1960s. The impact of some of these events on the forest and range policy debate has been more direct or immediate than others, but forest and range policy does not develop in a vacuum.

In addition to these three major factors, three lesser influences also shaped the development of forest and range policy. First among these is simply chance. Why did the Forest Service develop in the Department of Agriculture rather than in the Department of Interior? Simple happenstance, at least in the first instance. The funding measure authorizing the initial forestry investigations by Franklin D. Hough passed in 1876 as a rider to an appropriations measure supporting a seed distribution program. Secondly, personality factors can occasionally become quite important. How can we assess the irascible magnetism of a man like Gifford Pinchot in a rigorous way? We cannot. We simply have to recognize that occasionally there is going to be a Pinchot, a Harold Ickes, or a Wild-Horse Annie who by force of will can change the course of events. These returns to individual personality and effort can be just as inspiring as they are frustrating. Finally, and fortunately infrequently, public policy is influenced by simple blunders: errors in judgment or execution for which there is no deeper explanation than that it is simply as dumb as it looks.

These basic influences on public policy are durable and relatively constant. However, it is clear that in the last thirty years there has been a gradual change in values. The center around which the debate turns has clearly shifted from a dominating concern for commodity production and economic development toward increasing attention to preservation and amenity values. This gradual evolution of the new values regarding resource management and land allocation has largely defined the issues through which the more durable factors are expressed. Readers should be aware of these themes to help make sense out of the myriad detail presented.

It might also help the reader to be aware of some decisions that I made regarding footnotes. Dean Dana and I have a disdain for cluttering things up with endless citations and scholarly references. Unfortunately, however, Dean Dana did not use any references at all in his text. Therefore, when I went to include some of his quotations in the second edition, it was extremely difficult to identify where they had come from. Because I do not want to leave that problem to the author of the third edition, I have adopted the following strategies: unidentified references from the first edition are noted in the text in parentheses with Dana and the page number from which the reference was taken. All other references in the text will be noted in a similar fashion, that is, with the name of the author or source and the page number from which it was taken. Full citations of all materials, including those cited in the first edition, are contained in a bibliography at the end of each chapter. In addition, in lieu of the Dean's appendix on related subject matters, I have prepared a bibliographic essay on the literature which has burgeoned around this field in the last twenty years. His widely praised chronology remains, updated and slightly revised.

Acknowledgments

I used to think that the lengthy and flowery expressions of gratitude which grace the front of most books, and which indeed are the liveliest part of many, were simple vanity. Now I see otherwise.

First, there is a strong temptation to want to implicate as many people as possible. I am aware that I do not know thoroughly a fraction of what occurred between 1609 and 1979 in forest and range policy. It is comforting to have as many recognized experts as possible as named co-conspirators. That does not, however, explain the urge, apparently irresistible among authors, to include so many others—to divide and spread the satisfaction of having completed the process of writing a book. I now believe that the length and fervor of acknowledgments is simply a recognition of the special joy of the collegial relationship. The labor is lengthy, tedious, and frequently conflicts with most human impulses—"I can't; I have to work on the book." The best reason I know for working on a book is the pleasure of finding people who are willing to give their ideas, their information, and their time to guide and inform the author. There is no cast party when a book comes off the presses when you can strike the sets and revel in the pleasure of sharing an endeavor. Therefore, people write windy acknowledgments. So be it. This is the passionate part of an otherwise analytical and hopefully objective study.

Mark Rey and I started this together. His efforts form the backbone of Chapter 9. Barbara (Bebo) Andrews's research and writing are the only reason Chapter 10 is not still on the drawing boards. Gail Achterman has read, reread, edited, rewritten, and debated with me about virtually every page except this one. Her blue pencil stands between the first "draft" and the first official draft, and all subsequent readers who oppose hyperbole and fuzzy generalities suffer less because of her efforts. Gail is responsible, as well, for my first introduction to Peffer, Gates, Rolvaag, Cather, and, incredibly, John Wesley Powell. Working with her on her thesis was the beginning of my education in the politics of the Bureau of Land Management (BLM) and the settlement of the arid West. Although Gail, Mark, and Bebo were all in my classes at one time or another, I cannot bring myself to say that *they* were *my* students. The opposite is equally true, which is, of course, the way it is supposed to be.

Two other associates from the University of Michigan, Lois Witte and Nancy Saylor, endlessly combed the library to locate much of the material on which I have relied. Becky Bruce and Don Buder have ably assisted in the same effort since I came to the University of California. Jan Goldman, Merry Tuten Schutt, Brigid Flynn, Lois Witte, Bill Rockwell, and Bruce Fox have also been an important part of my education in general and specific aspects of what follows. They also helped me through a series of long, cold winters, for which I am deeply grateful.

Dick Behan took up with a red pencil where Gail left off and has read, edited, criticized, and improved every page. Nina Bunin of the Heritage Conservation and Recreation Service (née BOR) also edited the whole first draft for sense and syntax and has been especially helpful in making me clarify points that would be obvious only to someone who has just read Peffer a half dozen times. Roy Feuchter read and commented upon this draft and, I am pleased to say, the draft of almost everything else I have ever written. Keith Argow also took great pains to direct my frequently breezy style onto the high ground of well-considered, moderate, *short* sentences. Hank Vaux has also been through the draft twice and has led me to add much-needed material on state programs. He, Keith, Roy, Dick, and Nina have saved me from many errors of omission, commission, and overstatement. Christopher Lehman also read the entire manuscript as it neared the finish. He made excellent suggestions for clarifying and expanding many of the discussions for which I am most grateful.

George Lea and Thad Box took on the unenviable task of showing a nice kid from New York "which end of a cow gets up first." Any shortcomings in the range management aspects of what follows reflect the near total ignorance I started from, not the enormity of their efforts. I am also grateful to the BLM folks, their families, and the public lands users who patiently talked to me about range management. I am particularly grateful to Bob Buffington, the Kincades, Paul Rigtraup, Gary McVickers, Gene Nodine, Dave Walters, Carroll Leavitt, George Fraser, Wayne Boden, Bob Bainbridge, Paul Leonard, Jerry O'Callaghan, Eleanor Schwartz, Joe Dose, George Lea, George Turcott, Frank Gregg, and Mrs. John Neal. Pictures of my visits to BLM offices tell the age-old tale of a greenhorn going west: Sally and the cactus thorns; the chewing tobacco; and that charming conveyance Wood Tick, a horse. I will always be a tenderfoot from New York, but I have been shown much about the public lands and have tried to reflect what I have seen.

I did not harass anyone in the Forest Service specifically for the purpose of preparing this text. I am, however, grateful for the many opportunities that Andy Gilbert, Stan Adams, Russ Dahl, and Roy Feuchter have made available for me to learn my trade. I never met a Forest Service person I did not like. I have argued with many, however; and if one or two should recognize conversations in the following pages, it probably is not entirely coincidental. Frank Smith and William D. Hurst, formerly Forest Service rangemen, were helpful in explaining the Forest Service range program, especially in the postwar period.

Jim Giltmier and Susan Schrepfer noted, bravely perhaps, that the text was a bit dull in places and could use a bit of brightening. I have not been able to include all the local color that I would like in order to give a human dimension to this very human story. However, they emboldened me to mention details such as the fact that George Perkins Marsh was a philologist and Carl Schurz was run out of Germany as a revolutionary. I have especially enjoyed learning more about the people involved in the process and am grateful for their encouragement. Susan also led me to reconsider many of my generalizations—especially about the Park Service. To meet her criticisms, I have had to do a lot more reading and thinking about the traditions of the Park Service than I was originally inclined to do. I hope the text reflects some of her efforts and my learning. I have no doubt that my treatment of the Park Service suffers from its association with Harold Ickes—who emerged from my inquiry as less than lovable in spite of my best efforts—but the two are, of course, intimately related.

Several friends have been kind enough to review parts of the manuscript that were particularly in need of criticism. Mike Miskovsky and Bill Hyde made detailed comments on the first and last chapters that tremendously altered and improved them both. If I was not appropriately grateful at the time, I certainly am now.

Secretaries generally get credit for typing the manuscript. In my experience, this contribution, though necessary and gratefully acknowledged, is really almost beside the point. I was most fortunate to be working with Diane Voss while preparing the bulk of this manuscript. During the most hideous year of my life, she kept everything at the office sufficiently under control so that I could work on the book. She was also the first one not to laugh out loud at the first draft and to assure me that it was improving during the lengthy rewriting process. Typing is only one of the things for which I am grateful to Diane.

Many other fine folks have labored long over the three lines of scribbles stuck between two lines of typed copy which wound up into the margin at the top of the page. They have also translated my generally phonetic spelling into more familiar forms. Joan Grier and her jovial staff patiently responded to rush job after rush job. Ikuko Takeshita has remained admirably calm while I mother-henned throughout the preparation of the final copy. I am grateful to her and to Mary Beebe, Francis Hammond, Amor Nolan, Robert Muller, Stacey Yamagiwa, Gertrude Halpern, and Nola Leong for their reliable good spirits and assistance.

Writing a book, I have found, is not what it is cracked up to be; but it has its compensations. Most of the good times were shared with the people who helped me. I cherish their friendship far too much to try to palm my errors off on them. If such there be, and for love of Sam I have labored to keep them few, they are mine.

Sally K. Fairfax

February 12, 1979

Chapter 1

Conservation from the Broad Arrow Policy Through the Disposition of the Public Domain

Since the earliest days of settlement in the American colonies, resource policy has been a major concern. Although the colonists, and then the new nation, soon laid claim to unprecedented natural diversity and wealth, the cornucopia of the North American continent was frequently more a matter of vision than of reality. By its very nature, the concept of resources—abundance, scarcity, exploitation, development, and conservation—evolves as the society evolves and reflects its needs and values. Policy regarding the management of resources —including forest and range policy—is both a major influence on and an expression of the social, economic, and political structure of the United States. Ideas regarding the appropriate approach to wild lands resources have changed and developed as the nation has changed and developed.

The familiar concept of resource conservation which dominates the events discussed in this book did not emerge until the early 1900s. Ideas popularized then by Theodore Roosevelt and Gifford Pinchot emphasized comprehensive development programs and "wise use" of resources to provide "the greatest good for the greatest number for the longest time." This utilitarian or use-oriented approach to conservation has been definitive in resource policy until quite recently; however, it has never been unchallenged. John Muir represents a different concept of conservation, emphasizing aesthetics and nonuse, which developed almost simultaneously with the first. He energetically advanced his ideas, frequently in opposition to Pinchot and Roosevelt. Resource professionals and policymakers have long attempted to blend these two opposing concepts by identifying conservation as a careful balance among complementary and competitive "multiple uses" of land, but the emphasis has traditionally been decidedly utilitarian. The environmental era of the 1960s and 1970s has, however, occasioned increasing emphasis on the aesthetic and nonuse component of the conservation spectrum.

Confronting the confusion inherent in these distinct, frequently conflicting approaches to conservation, the theorist may be tempted to seek clarity in definitions such as: "Conservation comprises a conscious, individual or public response to a certain perceived condition—usually one of *scarcity*—of a particular component of the natural environment which is known as a *resource,* so called because it is exploited for its material usefulness to some phase of human life or activity" (Ciriacy-Wantrup, 28). This definition is bland and does not indicate a particular end result such as "preservation" or "use." Worse, it does not explain the fervor with which advocates have long embraced their particular positions. Nevertheless, the abstraction is instructive. It shows clearly that the idea of conservation—a function of personal and social perspective as well as physical realities—relies on other key concepts which resist precise definition. *Scarcity* is not an objective condition based on the material availability of resources but varies with the needs and views of society, with the technological and economic system which responds to those needs, and with the political and legal forces acting either in support of or in opposition to intensified resource exploitation. The concept of *resource* varies along similar lines and does not apply to some immutable or exactly defined entity.

Resources, scarcity, and, hence, conservation are dynamic concepts which permit a variety of definitions and must be understood in a particular context of time and place. The settlement decades, both the colonial and post-Revolutionary period, were not, as is sometimes suggested, characterized by a completely haphazard or unrestrained exploitation of natural resources. The British, Colonial, and American governments adopted policies which, although not resource management measures in the modern sense, were directed at conserving resources in response to specific shortages or needs. An array of factors—physical resource availability, the society's perceptions of the environment, the material demands of a developing nation, the primitive state of technology, and the period's prevailing economic and institutional systems —shaped policies for resource use. These policies were unique to the times as well as significant in setting precedents which have continued to influence the nation's forest and range programs.

The conservation measures adopted by the British government probably contributed to the movement for independence. Americans were especially irritated by the Crown's reservation of trees valuable for ship masts. After the Revolution severed formal political ties with the United Kingdom, Americans continued to live largely as before. The nation was, however, confronted with a situation which represented both a unique problem and inestimable opportunity. Through cessions from the states and acquisition by purchase, treaty, and conquest, the federal government acquired a vast domain of land extending westward from the Allegheny and Appalachian mountains. Throughout its first century, the social, political, and economic life of the United States was dominated by questions surrounding the public domain. Decisions regarding the use and disposition of the land shaped the institutions of government and molded the character of the new nation. In a world that gave philosopher John Locke's theorizing about the state of nature the appearance of prophecy, the westward movement expressed and developed national ideals concerning freedom, equality, and the right of every individual to pursue material prosperity with the aid of whatever natural wealth the land could be made to yield.

THE COLONIAL EXPERIENCE

The North American continent is richly endowed with a variety of natural resources. Particularly important during the colonial period were the renewable resources—fish, wildlife, forests, grasslands, and water. On the eastern seaboard, the expanse of virtually untouched forest was the dominant feature of the landscape, covering nearly 100 percent of the land area between Maine and Georgia. In area, variety of species, and size of individual trees, the forests of the New World were a phenomenon far removed from the experience of the European immigrant.

Colonists' Perspective

To the American settlers, the forests of the New World were a mixed blessing. On the one hand, wood provided an indispensable material for fuel, home construction, fences, and ships and in the manufacture of furniture, farm implements, shingles, and posts needed to support a growing society. In addition to their widespread domestic use, forest products were the basis for a profitable international trade. Together with fish, fur, and tobacco, forest products provided foreign exchange and permitted purchase of manufactured goods not available on American shores. To these ends, the colonial forest resources—inexpensive due to their abundance—were liberally and extensively applied. There was nothing ruthless or reprehensible about this process of resource utilization. It was nothing more or less than a sensible way for the colonists to make the most effective use of the factors at their disposal.

On the other hand, forests were both frightening and a nuisance to the

American settler. Forests were a hazard, an impediment, and a liability. They had to be removed wherever anyone wanted to start a farm, establish a settlement, or build a road. The wilderness also appeared a godless, fearful place to most colonists; it was unknown and threatening, containing a storehouse of potential dangers. Forests had to be removed to make way for civilization, and clearing the trees served a multiplicity of functions on the colonial scene; it provided raw materials, eliminated hiding for beast and foe, and conformed with the biblical injuction to subdue the earth (Nash, passim). Contemporary Americans' ambivalent attitudes toward the natural world are rooted partly in the early settlers' simultaneous dependence on and fear of forests.

The fact that natural resources were plentiful, cheap, and used with abandon in the coloinal period tells only part of the story. Resources were abundant, yet access to them was limited. Labor, capital, and technology—the human, economic, and manufactured resources necessary for development—were in short supply in the colonies. When the first federal census was conducted in 1790, the population of the colonies totaled four million—about half the present size of New York City. The scattered settlers possessed few tools, and equipment was invented or imported and distributed only gradually. Communications and transportation were slow to develop, and it took time for the colonists to reach and open up new areas where the available natural wealth could effectively be exploited.

Early Colonial Policies

Further tempering present-day assumptions regarding colonial abundance is the fact that local shortages frequently occurred on the settled seaboard and became a growing problem throughout the colonial period. Depletion tended to occur in the desirable product classes, such as oak for ship construction; mulberry for silk production; and pitch pine or tar trees for naval stores. Responding to these local supply problems as well as to related adverse impacts such as soil erosion and the threat of fire, colonial governments passed regulations to control timber access, cutting, trespassing, burning, and grazing. It is important to recognize that these regulations were neither widespread nor incorporated into a public program to achieve broad conservation goals. The measures do, however, indicate that resource depletion was viewed as a problem even during the seventeenth and eighteenth centuries and that the colonists attempted to deal with the issue in accordance with the economic realities of the times.

The first forest legislation in the colonies came only six years after the landing at Plymouth Rock and was caused by anxiety concerning available timber. In 1626, Plymouth Colony—to prevent the "inconvenience which might befall the plantation by the want of timber"—forbade the sale or transport of any timber whatsoever out of the colony without the approval of the governor and council. In 1681, William Penn became the first government leader to forbid clear cutting in the East. The document governing the establishment of a colony in "Penn's Woods" provided that 1 acre of trees must be left for every 5 acres cleared and that special care must be taken to preserve oak for shipping and mulberry for silk. Forest parks were also a feature of many colonial settlements. The Boston Common, purchased in 1634 by residents of the area, continues to this day as a public open space within the city.

Policies aimed at controlling fire were also common during the colonial period. By the time of the Revolution, some type of fire-control legislation existed in eight of the thirteen colonies. Most of the measures dealt with the time of year, month, or week when fires might or might not be set and required owners to notify their neighbors before burning on their land. Penalties included whippings, imprisonment, commitment to the county workhouse, and fines in addition to the payment of damages for any losses inflicted on other property owners.

British Government Attitude

The British attitude toward the substantial natural wealth of North America was somewhat different from that of the colonists. While the settlers were attempting to develop a new life for themselves in a new world, the British government thought in terms of its own interests, markets, and need for raw materials. The United States, accordingly, began its economic history as a supplier of primary, unprocessed materials to the British Crown. Restrictions on colonial manufacturers, regulation of trade, and control of credit were the major tools the Crown used to achieve its economic ends. One of the most important British policies relating to the colonies' resources arose from the urgent need of the King's navy and merchant marine for an adequate and steady supply of mast timber.

The British government soon discovered that even with the overall abundance of forests in America, good trees for mast purposes were not common. They were highly valued for a number of uses and were thus subject to localized scarcities. The Crown decided to take action to ensure that the suitable timber which remained would be put to its highest and best use—providing masts for British naval ships. In 1691, a new charter granted to the Province of Massachusetts Bay reserved to the British government all trees which could be used for masts. The trees were not to be cut without a license from the Crown, and any violation carried a penalty of £100 per tree illegally removed. This measure soon became known as the Broad Arrow Policy since trees reserved for masts were marked with three blazes to represent the broad arrow—symbol of the British navy. The original provisions of the policy were extended in 1711 to include all white pine or other trees in New England, New Jersey, and New York which were fit for masts and were not located on private property.

The Broad Arrow Policy might be viewed as a forward-looking attempt by the Crown to provide its navy and merchant marine with essential material needs. However, while the measure had the objective of prolonging the available supply of timber, it was not a conservation measure in the Pinchot tradition of promoting programs to achieve long-term resource productivity through enlightened scientific management. The Broad Arrow Policy was, rather, a practical measure taken by the Crown to restrict assess and establish a priority of use to safeguard for the immediately foreseeable future a valued resource in danger of depletion and vital to national economic goals and defense interests. From the British perspective, the policy was thoroughly justified on both legal and practical grounds. The colonists, in contrast, felt they had a moral right to the use of all the natural resources of the continent. It was they, not the British government, who were bearing the risks and hardships of subduing the wilderness and taming the land.

The Broad Arrow Policy failed because of vigorous and widespread colonial opposition which the distant British government was unable to overcome. The policy led to a continuing and often bitter struggle between the King's officers, who were trying to enforce the laws, and the colonists, who were anxious to evade them. It is interesting to speculate that the British timber agents were among those whom the signers of the Declaration of Independence had in mind when they complained that the King "has erected a multitude of new offices and sent hither swarms of officers to harass our people, and eat out their substance." For all of their vociferous protestations against British interference, the early supporters of the fledgling U.S. government would encounter similar resistance to their own attempts to administer the distant lands of the public domain. Throughout the nineteenth century, these attempts would be ignored, flaunted, and disdained in the hinterlands, where individual enterprise reigned supreme and government regulation was regarded as an unwarranted intrusion.

ACQUISITION OF THE PUBLIC DOMAIN

Cession by the States

After the Revolution, the thirteen states claimed ownership of the former Crown lands not already in private ownership. Massachusetts, Connecticut, New York, Virginia, North Carolina, South Carolina, and Georgia claimed large areas of land on the basis of colonial boundaries which were generally vague and often overlapping. Even before the end of the war, the other six colonies, under the leadership of Maryland, started a movement to force the cession of these western lands to the central government. The objective was threefold: to bring about greater equality in land resources among the states, to provide tangible assets to the central government with which to meet the overwhelming national debt, and to strengthen the Union by the increased feeling of political and economic solidarity which would be fostered by common ownership of such an extensive and potentially valuable territory. In 1780, the Continental Congress resolved that lands ceded to the United States should be used for the common benefit of all the states. Promises of land bounties to induce enlistments in the Continental Army had been made as early as 1776 in the expectation that land for this purpose would be available.

The proposed cessions were made by all seven states between 1781 and 1802. New York, which had by far the smallest area at stake, was the first state to take action, and Georgia was the last. Four of the states accompanied their cessions by certain reservations of which Connecticut's "western reserve" and Virginia's "military lands"—both in Ohio—are the best known. North Carolina's cession of the area that is now the state of Tennessee was so encumbered with reservations and claims that the United States in 1806 and 1846 relinquished whatever rights it might have had under the original grant. Altogether the cessions comprised a total area of 233 million acres and embraced the present states of Ohio, Indiana, Illinios, Michigan, and Wisconsin; that part of Minnesota lying east of the Mississippi River; and all of Alabama and Mississippi lying north of the 31st parallel of latitude.

Other Accessions

The next addition to the public domain came in 1803 when Louisiana was purchased from France. In view of the strategic importance and natural wealth of the territory, this purchase of 523 million acres at a cost of less than 5 cents per acre was a bargain. In 1819, Florida was purchased from Spain at about 16 cents an acre for 43 million acres. The "Oregon Compromise" of 1846 added another 181 million acres in the Pacific Northwest without cost and settled an issue that had threatened to lead to war with Great Britain. In 1848, the treaty ending the war with Mexico transferred nearly 335 million acres in the Southwest to the United States in return for $16,300,000, again, about 5 cents per acre.

In 1859, Texas—which had retained title to all public lands within its borders on it admission to the Union in 1845—sold the federal government an irregularly shaped piece of land comprising nearly 79 million acres in what are now the states of Oklahoma, Kansas, Colorado, Wyoming, and New Mexico for nearly 20 cents an acre. Another 19 million acres on the southern borders of Arizona and New Mexico were acquired in 1853 by the Gadsden Purchase from Mexico at a cost of about 53 cents an acre. Finally, more than 365 million acres in Alaska were purchased from Russia in 1867 for a little over 2 cents an acre.

Original Public Domain

These various cessions and acquisitions constitute the original "public domain" which has played such an important part in virtually every phase of U.S. development. It included all land, exclusive of that already in private ownership, acquired by the United States by the cessions, purchases, and treaties described above, approximately 1804 million acres of land and 33 million acres of water. It thus included all land which was subject to disposal under a variety of general land laws passed by Congress since the late eighteenth century. The public domain does not, however, include land subsequently purchased by the federal government for specific purposes such as post office or customhouse sites, military reservations, national parks, or national forests purchased under the Weeks Act. Accordingly, lands obtained in exchange for public lands or timber were subject to legislation applying to the original public domain, but acquired lands—those subsequently purchased—were not.

The public domain has always been subject to complete control by the Congress of the United States under Article IV, Section 3, Paragraph 2 of the Constitution: "The Congress shall have Power to dispose of and make all needful Rules and Regulations respecting the Territory or other Property belonging to the United States." This paragraph has repeatedly been interpreted by the Supreme Court as giving Congress full power to sell, give away, or retain the public domain for such purposes and by such methods as it sees fit. During most of the nation's history, Congress attempted to foster orderly settlement of the continent by selling, giving away, or otherwise disposing of the land. At present (omitting Alaska, which did not become an important issue until the mid- 1900s), only about 411 million acres, or 29 percent of the original public domain, is still in federal ownership.

The terms "public domain" and "public land(s)" are frequently confused, and their meaning often has to be determined from the context in which they are used. In this volume, the two terms will be used as follows: Public lands consist of all those federally owned lands which are or were once part of the public domain and are still in federal ownership plus the acquired lands contained in national parks, forests, game refuges, and areas administered by the federal public land-managing agencies. Public domain lands are those unentered,* unreserved unoccupied lands of the original public domain which were or are still in public ownership and were subject to disposition under the general land laws until 1976 and are managed by the Bureau of Land Management (BLM). The public lands thus include the public domain lands plus lands reserved for national monuments, parks, forests, and other specified special uses.

Table 1-1 and Figure 1-1 summarize the major factors concerning the location, area, and initial cost of the original public domain. They show that in seven decades, the population of the United States swept across the continent so that by the middle of the nineteenth century the United States controlled 1441 million acres of land lying between the Atlantic and the Pacific and between Canada and Mexico. More than three-fourths of this vast area

*Entered in this context means to go upon the land in order to take possession of it.

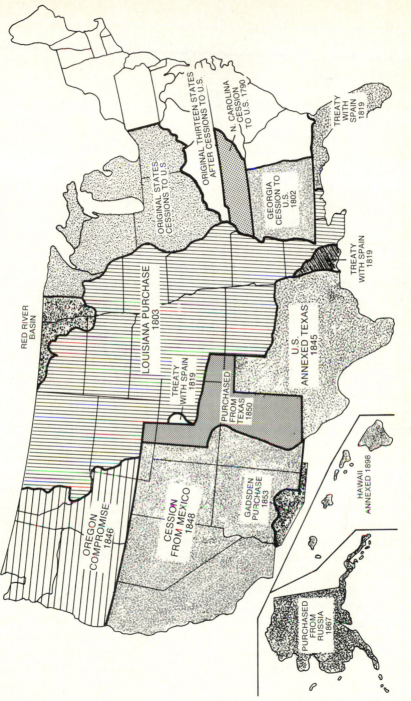

Figure 1-1. Dates, sources, and areas of land acquisition of the territory of the United States. (Prepared by the Bureau of Land Management. Reproduced from Gates, 1968, p. 76.)

9

was at one time or another in federal ownership as part of the public domain. The forest and range policy of the country—like so many of its other policies —is inextricably interwoven with the disposal and management of these lands.

DISPOSITION OF THE PUBLIC DOMAIN: 1775–1891

Public land policy can be divided into three periods: disposition, reservation, and management. A period of disposition in which Congress disposed of the public domain lasted from about 1776 until 1891. It was followed by a brief period in which lands were reserved or withheld from disposition and lasted until 1905. The period of management dating from 1905 marks the beginning of government programs to manage actively rather than simply retain the public domain. These periods are useful analytic concepts because they characterize many statutes, conflicts, and policies into a generally accurate structure. However, the periods overlap considerably. For example, although the disposition era technically lasted until 1976, when Congress finally enacted legislation providing for retention and management of the unreserved, unentered public domain, disposition actually ended in 1934 with the passage of the Taylor Grazing Act. Even before 1934, of course, the government reserved public domain lands for specified purposes, such as parks or forests, and established management systems for the reserved lands. It is most useful analytically to date the end of the period of disposition in 1891, when Congress authorized the President to proclaim forest reserves, even though the first reserves were made in the 1790s. In spite of this clear overlap, the three dominant themes —disposition, reservation, and management—usefully identify periods of public land management.

One of the most difficult and persistent problems faced by the young nation was deciding what to do with the public lands. For years, this question occasioned more oratory and more legislation than any other subject. Everyone agreed that title to the lands should not be retained permanently by the federal government but should be passed to the states and to private owners as rapidly as was consistent with orderly development. On all other points, there was heated controversy in which broad national policies and interregional rivalries played a prominent part. The early debates dealt chiefly with the purpose and terms of disposal. For example, should the lands be given away to promote settlement or be sold to provide revenue? Should surveys precede or follow disposal? Should surveys be done by the rectangular system or by metes and bounds? What price, if any, should be charged for the land; and should sales be made only for cash or on credit? Should there be any maximum or minimum limit on the area one person could acquire? Should sales be made at the seat of the government or at local land offices? All these questions were debated. Decisions about the public domain were typically

Table 1-1 Acquisition of the Original Public Domain

Origin	Year	Land area	Total cost	Average cost	Public domain	Land area of U.S.
		Million acres	Million dollars	Cents per acre	Percent of total	
State cessions	1781–1802	233	6.2*	2.7	16	12
Louisiana Purchase	1803	523	23.2	4.4	36	27
Red River Basin†	–	29	–	–	2	2
Florida Purchase	1819	43	6.7	15.6	3	2
Oregon Compromise	1846	181	–	–	13	10
Mexican cession	1848	334	16.3	4.9	23	18
Texas Purchase	1850	79	15.5	19.6	6	4
Gadsden Purchase	1853	19	10.0	52.6	1	1
Total		1,441‡	77.9	5.4	100	76
Alaska Purchase	1867	363‡	7.2	2.0		

* Payment to Georgia.
† Drainage basin of the Red River of the north, south of the forty-ninth parallel. Authorities differ about the method and date of its acquisition. Some hold that it was a part of the Louisiana Purchase; others, that it was acquired from Great Britain.
‡ Inland waters comprise an additional area of 20 million acres in the continental United States and 10 million acres in Alaska.

Source: U.S. Department of the Interior, Bureau of Land Management.

related to such issues as states' rights, federal trade, slavery and free soil, free land, tariffs, and labor-capital relations.

The disposition of the public domain is frequently confusing and frustrating to modern land managers because physical aspects of the land are not a major factor in disposition policies. Land was merely a means of implementing revenue, states' rights, or social policy. The first approach to public domain policy was to sell the land to generate revenue to retire Revolutionary War debts. The policy failed because land was so plentiful that no one would buy it. Land sold for $2 or 2 cents an acre because that was all it was worth on the market of the day.

By 1840, the government supplemented the sales system by adopting a policy of giving the land away in order to encourage "internal improvements" and settlement. The states and the railroads were the primary beneficiaries of this policy. The enduring notion that large amounts of valuable land were available for free to individual settlers under the homestead laws is false (Gates, 1936, passim). By the time the Homestead Act passed in 1862, most of the valuable agricultural land was already taken, and homesteaders were left with the least desirable areas.

The disposition era is widely described as a debacle, a period of waste and destruction, a source of national shame. It is true that congressional policies failed, but not because we did not conserve valuable resources. The resources were not valuable, and we were not attempting to conserve them. The first stated goal was to raise money, and it failed. The subsequent goal, to provide for the orderly development of the country by actual settlers, was thwarted by stunning graft and chicanery in administration of the statutes. The nation was indeed settled and the frontier closed at the end of the disposition era, but that accomplishment was not the result of congressional wisdom in defining goals and policies for the public domain during the nineteenth century. Many of the disposition statutes appear to be invitations to fraud, and other programs quickly became tools of land speculators. Settlement occurred in spite of rather than in accord with congressional policies.

Military Land Bounties

Long before issues about the public lands were formally discussed in Congress, the first system of land disposition, although not a sales system, was in the making. Military land bounties began during the Revolution. In lieu of paying soldiers with money, which was not available, land bounties were offered, first to encourage soldiers to enlist and later to reward soldiers for their service. It was hoped that land bounties would reduce the possibility of rebellion by an unpaid army and help populate the frontier with particulary vigorous settlers. Most of the soldiers, however, were not interested in migrating to the western wilderness, and they sold their warrants. This led to lively trade and speculation in military bounty warrants, which at one time were quoted on the New

York stock exchange. The system continued until the late 1800s. In 1855, the bounty system was liberalized to give 160 acres to every soldier who had participated for at least fourteen days in any way since the Revolution. During some postwar periods, bounty warrants were a major medium of land transactions.

General Ordinance of 1785

The General Ordinance of 1785 passed by the Continental Congress was the first comprehensive public land statute enacted and perhaps the most significant legislation of all time in terms of impact on the land. The ordinance established the rectilinear system of public land surveys with townships 6 miles square divided into thirty-six sections of 640 acres each. The decision to divide the nation into a checkerboard "for the sole purpose of making available easily identifiable and saleable tracts" (Johnson, 116) has had a tremendous but frequently unnoticed effect on the way we think about and use land. For example, the grid system for land disposition led to a similar pattern of straight lines in field borders and furrows. Farmers simply plowed along the boundary lines of their property. Following the dust storms of the 1930s, we turned away from the grid pattern of plowing in favor of contour plowing, which adapts to the contours of the land (Johnson, 193). Moreover, political organization followed the same grid as the survey and plowing. The effort to manage irregularly shaped watersheds proposed by reformers in the 1880s floundered on county, township, and state boundaries, which were based on rectangular surveys. Thus, the first sales policy—the decision to divide the land into little blocks and sell it—had a critical influence on everything that followed.

General Sales

The General Ordinance of 1785 also provided that after survey, the lands would be sold at auction for cash to the highest bidder at not less that $1 an acre. Half the townships were to be sold in their entirety, the other half in sections of 640 acres each. Section 16 in each township was reserved for schools, and four additional sections were reserved for later disposal by the government.

The 1785 ordinance aimed to promote settlement *and* to provide revenue. Unfortunately, the financial hopes which led to its passage were never met. The first patent was issued in 1788, but sales were slow. Even $1 per acre was expensive compared to the price of lands offered by the states. In addition, few immigrants could raise the $640 in cash needed to purchase federal land. The ordinance of 1787 provided that one-third of the sale price could be paid in cash and the balance in three months, but this did little to relieve the situation. Many did not buy the land at all; they simply "squatted" on it without paying and without obtaining legal title in spite of the prohibition against the practice.

During this early period, public lands were also sold in large blocks to private companies and individuals. The theory was that the federal government could get substantial immediate income by selling several townships to a single buyer at considerably reduced rates. The buyer would then actively promote the resale of the land to actual settlers. The practice, however, involved so much speculation and other difficulties that it was soon abandoned.

Credit Sales

The system of land disposal embodied in the General Ordinance of 1785 proved unsatisfactory in practice. The immigrants who wanted to settle the land simply did not have the money to buy it. Acts passed in 1796, 1800, and 1804 attempted to solve the problems by allowing delayed payments, although they also raised the minimum price of public lands to $2 an acre.

Endless difficulties followed the adoption of the installment plan of payment for public land. Many people never paid some or most of their debt. Theoretically, the government could evict a delinquent and confiscate the land, but frontier sentiment made this step a practical impossibility even if the government had tried to adopt that drastic a course of action. Many relief acts were passed to meet the needs of settlers whose intentions were honest and who were obviously an asset to the country but who simply could not meet the obligations they had assumed. Sales increased dramatically under the credit system, but payments lagged. By 1820, delinquent purchasers owed the government more than $21 million.

Return to Cash Sales

In 1820, the general sales policy was revised almost to its final form. The installment plan was abolished, and both the minimum price and the minimum area were reduced. Public lands were to be sold at auction to the highest bidder in half-quarter sections of 80 acres at not less than $1.25 per acre with full payment at time of sale. In 1832, the minimum area was further reduced in private sales to 40 acres, which has remained the standard unit of measure in the sale of public lands. Lands offered for sale were not classified, and no restriction was placed on the maximum area that one person could purchase.

"Squatting"

Squatting on public lands was a practice that originated in colonial times and increased in frequency after the Revolution. It was defended because the government was slow to survey and open land to use, and there seemed to be no end to the growing public domain. Although a few members of Congress championed the squatters from the very beginning, the practice was slow to receive legislative approval. The majority of representatives, who were from the original thirteen states, felt that squatting should be forbidden in the interest of orderly procedure and in order to obtain the maximum price for land. They also wanted to avoid the confusion in land title which would certainly arise from simply occupying Indian lands to which Indian tribes held recognized rights. When it became evident in 1807 that little attention was being paid to the provisions of the early land legislation prohibiting settlement prior to survey and sale, Congress adopted an antitrespass law with teeth in it. This law authorized the President to take measures, including the employment of military force, to remove anyone attempting to settle on the public domain unless authorized by law.

In practice, the law did little to stop squatting. Surveys and sales proceeded so slowly that the Western lands had to be occupied illegally if they were to be occupied at all. Although the act of 1807 was never formally repealed, Congress recognized the facts of frontier life by repeatedly passing special laws which, in effect, legalized occupation by squatters in specific cases. On the frontier, the squatters were not classed with other lawbreakers but were referred to as "a very respectable class of citizens," "a sturdy class of pioneers," "the hardy yeomanry," and "meritorious and industrious citizens."

By 1828, the number of representatives from recently admitted states began to change the composition of Congress. The Public Lands Committee of the House of Representatives expressed the new view that squatting was both inevitable and desirable. An illustration of this enterprise was the presence in 1838 in what is now Iowa of an estimated 20,000 to 30,000 squatters on land that had never been offered for sale. The committee pointed out that the pioneer settlers—although technically trespassers—were actually benefactors, not malefactors, whose enterprise and contribution to the development of the country should be regarded by permitting them to buy without competition the land on which they had settled.

Claim Associations

Under the understanding eye of Congress, squatters formed "claim associations" in order to protect themselves from subsequent surveys and sales. These associations had their own rules and regulations for making land claims and for seeing that justice was done between original claimants or squatters and intruders and between rival claimants. When a sale was to be held, the association would register the location of each claim and the name of the squatter on a plat and would appoint a "bidder" to bid off the lands so registered in the names of the respective claimants. The Commission of the General Land Office in 1836 complained that receipts from sales of public land had been cut down by some millions of dollars due to suppression of prices by these "unlawful organizations."

Experience in the settlement of the agricultural lands demonstrated repeatedly that laws must have support to be effective. A vigorous people bent on occupying a rich territory were not deterred by legislation unsuited economically, socially, or psychologically to the conditions of the westward expansion. An editorial in the *Chicago Democrat* of June 4, 1835, referring to an approaching sale of the public lands, voiced the spirit of the times:

"Public opinion" is stronger than the law, it has been well said, and we trust . . . that the strangers who come among us . . . will not attempt to commit so gross an act of injustice as to interfere with the purchase of the quarter section, on which improvements have been made by the actual settler. We trust for the peace and quietness of our town that these local customs, to which long custom has given the force of law . . . and which are so strongly sustained by the principles of justice and equality, will not be outraged at the coming sale.

Preemption and the End of the Sale System

Growing pressure to legalize squatting led in 1830 to passage of an act granting preemption rights for one year to settlers on the public lands. Those who could prove that they had settled and improved the land were allowed to purchase not more than 160 acres at the minimum price of $1.25 per acre. Approval of preemption as a basic policy came in 1841 with passage of the "Log Cabin Bill." It authorized every head of a family, widow, or single man over twenty-one years of age, who was a citizen, to settle upon and purchase at $1.25 per acre not more than 160 acres of surveyed, unoccupied, unreserved, nonmineral public lands, subject to certain restrictions. In order to have a right to preempt, settlers were required to inhabit and improve the land and erect a dwelling on it. They also had to swear that the land was being taken up for their own exclusive use and benefit. As might have been anticipated, it was impossible to limit preemption to surveyed lands. In 1853 and 1854, the privilege was therefore extended to unsurveyed lands in six states and to unsurveyed land in all states in 1862.

The Preemption Act was a victory for the West,* which had consistently struggled to curb speculation and to facilitate actual settlement of the public lands. It was a defeat for the East, which feared that preemption would reduce government receipts, lower the price of lands already sold, and, by attracting immigrants to the West, deplete the supply of labor and increase wages in the East. The act emphasized settlement rather than revenue as the primary objective in the disposal of the public domain. It also tried to favor the settler rather than the speculator and to encourage the establishment of many small

*The "West" at this time included the land between the thirteen original states and the Mississippi River.

farms. Unfortunately, the act was often used for fraudulent acquisition of land.

LAND GRANTS TO THE STATES

The sales system represents the attempt of the original thirteen states to retire the debt incurred in fighting the Revolution and to support eastern economic development. As the territories became states and sent representatives to Washington, disposal policies became increasingly more generous to the new states.

Grants for Education

The General Ordinance of 1785 reserved Section 16 in every township for later donation to the states for the support of education. The first grant was made to Ohio on its admission to the Union in 1803. In 1848, when Oregon was first organized as a territory, section 36 was also reserved for the same purpose. Still later, two more sections were added to the grants to new states. The escalating generosity reflects the increasing political power of the West. Altogether, twelve states received grants of one section per township, fourteen states received grants of two sections, and three states received grants of four sections. If the granted sections were not available because of previous occupation or reservation, the state was ordinarily allowed to select any other available public lands. These were called "in lieu" selections.

Several states have still not selected all the lieu lands due them under these provisions, but the most interesting situation exists regarding Nevada. Shortly after being admitted to the Union, numerous citizens of Nevada—noting that most of the land the state was to receive to benefit education was worthless desert—requested that Congress grant them money instead. Congress complied, but recently Nevadans, unhappy with federal landownership and management in their state, have argued that the state was inadequately compensated and are demanding its original selection rights. In other states, where designation of forest reserves antidated completion of state land selection, the state's continuing rights in sections 16 and 36 have clouded title to national forest lands.

Because these grants were to benefit public education, state sale of school lands was prohibited. In 1826, Ohio was permitted to sell its land if the sale was approved by the township concerned and the proceeds were permanently invested in some productive fund. The same privilege was later extended to the other states, often with a set minimum price at which sales could be made. The proceeds from these grants, which totaled nearly 78 million acres, assisted in the support of public schools in all of the public land states. In some states, they are still a significant source of income. Unfortunately, the state grant system was also an invitation to land fraud in many areas.

Grants for Permanent Improvements

Beyond its early commitment to development of public education, Congress also provided that the public lands and receipts therefrom could be used to assist the states in constructing transportation facilities and other permanent improvements. Acts in 1802 and 1803 provided for the establishment of the state of Ohio and granted the state 3 percent of the net proceeds from all sales of public lands within the state for the construction of roads. This precedent gradually led to the distribution to the public land states of 5 percent of the net proceeds from the sale of public lands within their borders.

Many similar grants of public land to assist in the construction of specific internal improvements were made from 1823 to 1871. These included donations to various states of 3 million acres for construction of wagon roads, 4 million acres for the construction of canals, and 1.5 million acres for river improvement.

500,000-Acre Grants

During the early 1800s, proposals to cede the public lands outright to the states were almost continuously before Congress, particularly after 1826. President Jackson favored the proposal, which was commonly linked with states' rights; and in 1837, Senator Calhoun of South Carolina introduced a bill providing for the cession to the states of all the public lands within their borders.

Although no general cession was ever approved, the idea undoubtedly influenced the inclusion in the Preemption Act of 1841 of a provision granting 500,000 acres of public domain to each of the existing states and to each new state. Grants already received from the federal government were to be deducted from the 500,000 acres. The lands were to be sold by the states for not less than $1.25 per acre and the proceeds used only for the construction of internal improvements. In practice, these revenues were also used for many other purposes. Approximately 8 million acres passed to the states under this grant.

Swampland Grants

Louisiana had a profound interest in a very particular type of internal improvement. Because nearly a third of its land was swampy and unsuitable for cultivation, Louisiana representatives led a long effort to have the swamplands of the public domain donated to the states. If Congress could donate land for schools, highways, and canals, why not for swamp drainage? The campaign succeeded in 1849, when Congress granted to Louisiana "the whole of those swamps or overflowed lands which may be, or are found unfit for cultivation." Proceeds from the sale of the lands were to be used exclusively, as far as necessary, for the construction of levees and drains. In 1850, similar grants were made to Alabama, Arkansas, California, Florida, Illinois, Indiana, Iowa, Michigan, Mississippi, Ohio, and Wisconsin and, in 1860, to Minnesota and Oregon.

These acts resulted in much fraud and little reclamation. Most states determined which of the public lands within their borders were "swamp and overflow." Extensive agricultural and timber lands found their way into the hands of the states, and later private owners. In Florida, whole townships classified as swamp proved on investigation to be substantially dry land; and, at two places in California, irrigation works were subsequently found on areas claimed as swamps.

Land-Grant Colleges

A substantial expansion of federal aid to education took place with the passage of the Morrill Act of 1862, which made liberal grants of public land for the establishment of colleges of agriculture and the mechanic arts. Grants under this act totaled about 10 million acres and provided important support for the "land-grant colleges," as the institutions benefiting from it came to be called. The Second Morrill Act in 1890 provided further support for the colleges from cash grants to be paid out of the proceeds from the sale of public lands. An amendment in 1903 authorized the use of other funds in case these proceeds were inadequate to meet the full amount of the appropriation.

RAILROAD LAND GRANTS

Land grants to aid in the construction of railroads greatly overshadowed all other grants for permanent improvements not only in area but in economic and political importance. From 1835 on, Congress frequently granted railroads free rights of way through the public lands, and this privilege was made general in 1852.

The need for better transportation facilities to connect the rapidly developing Midwest and Far West with the Eastern states was generally recognized, but there was much opposition to large grants of public lands to aid in their construction. This opposition came largely from the South, which feared that the proposed railroads would link the agricultural West and the industrial East more closely together, to the South's detriment. It further feared that the increased accessibility of Western lands would strengthen pressure for the enactment of homestead legislation, to which it was also vigorously opposed.

The first large grant was made in 1850 to assist in the construction of the Illinois Central Railroad from Chicago to Mobile. The act granted Illinois, Alabama, and Mississippi (the three public land states through which the road would pass) a right of way not over 200 feet wide; free use of construction material; and every even–numbered section of land in a strip six sections wide on each side of the road, with the right to make lieu selections in place of alienated lands to a distance of not more than 15 miles from the road.

The alternate sections retained by the federal government were to be sold at not less than $2.50 per acre, double the normal price, reflecting the enhanced value created by the railroad. This, it was argued, would double the receipts received from the lands so that the donation of the other sections would actually result in no loss to the government. This rationale did not work out in practice, but the needed railroads were built. The alternate sections pattern persists today, commonly referred to as "checkerboarding." Privately held sections are admixed with sections never patented and therefore retained and managed by the federal government. Especially in the arid West, where this condition is most frequently encountered, the ownership pattern makes it extremely difficult to administer the federal holdings. In return for the land granted, the railroads agreed to transport the property and troops of the United States free, and the mails were to be carried at such rates as Congress might fix. Although the grant was actually made to the states, it was understood that the road might be built by a private company, which would be subsidized by the proceeds from the sale of the lands.

The first transcontinental grants were made in 1862. The Union Pacific and the Central Pacific railroads were then given alternate sections of public land, at first to a distance of 10 miles and later 20 miles, on each side of the road. Mineral lands were excluded, but an amendment in 1864 specified that coal and iron were not to be classified as minerals. In 1864, the Northern Pacific Railroad received a grant of alternate sections to a distance of 40 miles on each side of the road in the territories through which it passed and of 20 miles in the states, again with the exclusion of mineral lands. Similar grants were made in 1866 to the Atlantic and Pacific, the Southern Pacific, and the Oregon and California railroads.

The liberality of these grants removed large areas of accessible land from the operation of the Homestead Act and aroused criticism from the settlers. As a result of mounting opposition, the last railroad grant was made in 1871. An act passed in 1890 provided that all grants adjoining rights of way on which railroads had never actually been constructed should be forfeited to the United States and restored to the public domain. The total area received by the railroads amounted to more than 132 million acres, of which about 94 million acres went directly to railroad corporations and the other 37 million acres to states for the benefit of the railroads (Gates, 1968, 385, 803).

THE HOMESTEAD ACTS

Demand for Free Land

Efforts to obtain public lands free of charge date from 1797, when settlers along the Ohio River asked for a grant of 400 acres per family in return for an agreement to remain on the land for three years before receiving title. From then on, petitions for donations reached Congress regularly. In 1828, the Public Lands Committee of the House, in the same report in which it urged legalization of preemption, recommended the grant of 80 acres "to the heads of such families as will cultivate, improve, and reside on the same for five years." Four special "donation" acts, passed between 1842 and 1854, resulted in the granting of about 3.1 million acres to frontier settlers in Florida, Oregon, Washington, and New Mexico, with certain residence and cultivation restrictions.

Free land was always favored in the West, but at first it was generally opposed in the East, particularly in the South. As the population of the public land states increased, the pressure on Congress for free land also increased so that, during the twenty years preceding the outbreak of the Civil War, it was one of the hottest political issues of the day. The West received strong support from the Northeast, where increased federal receipts from the tariff and an increased labor supply had largely removed the region's former objections to cheap or free land. Rapid development of the West became a desirable objective as a means of expanding the market for eastern manufactures. The South, on the other hand, remained opposed because of the conviction that the plantation system, which depended on slave labor, could not compete with small farms operated by their owners. Conflict over the extension of slavery was a critical aspect of the debate.

Although the terms "free land" and "free soil" are not synonymous, during debate the two ideas were interwoven. The free soil concept was advocated by those who opposed slavery and did not want to see the practice extended into the developing territories. Free land refers to giving land, without charge, to the "landless." Because Westerners generally advocated free soil, the South opposed free land, afraid that if the territories entered the Union as states where slavery was not permitted, Southern representatives would quickly be outnumbered and outvoted in Congress.

Homestead Grants

In 1862, in the absence of most of its members from the Southern states, Congress overwhelmingly passed the Homestead Act of May 20, 1862. The act provided that any family head or anyone over twenty-one years of age who was a citizen of the United States or had declared an intention to become a citizen could enter up to 160 acres of land for cultivation. Free patent to the land could be secured by settlers when they paid certain fees and proved that they had resided upon and cultivated the land for five years. Thus began one of the most durable and destructive myths in American folklore.

It is widely believed that the West was opened and settled by homesteaders who gained valuable free land by their honest toil. Reverence for this bucolic myth stalled for decades the reform of disastrous land disposition statutes. There is, to be sure, nobility and inspiration in the lives of homesteaders chronicled by such great American authors as Willa Cather *(My Antonia, O Pioneer!)*, O. E. Rölvaag *(Giants in the Earth)*, and Mari Sandoz *(Old Jules)*. These stunning tales of human endurance are harshly at variance with the land-of-milk-and-honey versions of early American abundance. They speak tragically of the waste in human and physical resources begotten by land policies made in disregard for the productive capacity of the land. Most of the lush American land was occupied well before 1862, and successful homesteading took place primarily in the upper Midwest. The incredible toil of the Great Basin homesteader was frequently rewarded by drought, blizzard, dust storm, and financial and physical ruin.

Liberalization of the Homestead Act

Unfortunately, the act was based on experience in the humid parts of the East and was not suited to the semiarid conditions in the prairie states and Far West, where 160 acres was inadequate to support a family. Congress tardily tried to remedy this defect in two acts passed in 1909 and 1916. The Enlarged Homestead Act of 1909 enabled acquisition of homesteads of 320 acres anywhere in the nine Western states and territories of Arizona, Colorado, Montana, Nevada, New Mexico, Oregon, Utah, Washington, and Wyoming but forbade commutation. The lands entered had to be nonmineral and nonirrigable and could not contain merchantable timber. The provisions of the act were later extended to Idaho, Kansas, North Dakota, South Dakota, and California. The 1916 Stockraising Homestead Act provided for 640-acre homesteads on nonirrigable land.

Experience also showed that in the semiarid regions, five years was too long a period of residence to require of the settler. Critics pointed out that the Homestead Act was in effect a wager in which the government bet homesteaders 160 acres that they could not live on it for five years, and the government was too often the winner. Congress finally recognized this situation when it passed the Three-Year Homestead Act of June 12, 1912, which provided that patent could be obtained after three years of residence during at least seven months per year. The act also set minimum cultivation requirements. These reforms were not effective; 640 acres were no closer to adequate for subsistence agriculture in the arid West than the 160 acres had been. The new laws simply

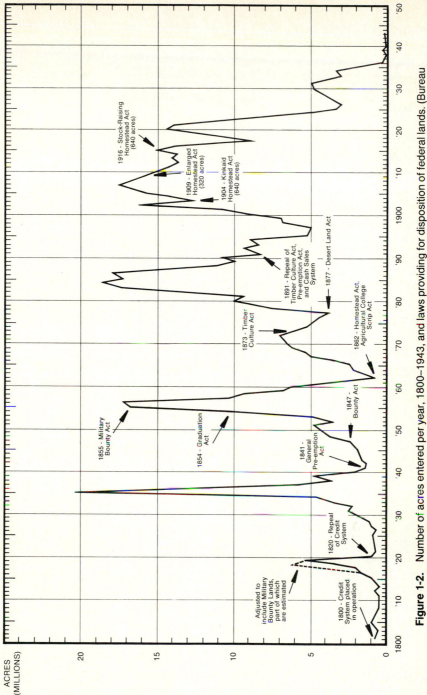

Figure 1-2. Number of acres entered per year, 1800–1943, and laws providing for disposition of federal lands. (Bureau of Agricultural Economics, U.S. Department of Agriculture. Reproduced from Gates, 1968, p. 496.)

23

provoked one last desperate effort to farm the Great Plains. Figure 1-2 shows the number of land entries per year under the various disposition programs and the importance of twentieth century statues and settlement in the alienation of the public domain. The soil uprooted by the homesteaders' efforts to "prove up" their claim blew all the way to Washington during the dust storms of the 1930s.

Abuses

The economically inadequate homesteads virtually required land abuse, and the results are now familiar. It is frequently overlooked, moreover, that the Homestead Act was also the focus of fraudulent land operations. One of the most abused features of the Homestead Act was the commutation provision, which permitted entrymen to purchase title to their claim for $1.25 per acre at any time after six months rather than occupying the land for the designated period. This provision was commonly used, particularly after 1880, by large stock operators or lumber companies in consolidating enormous landholdings. Phony entrymen would enter the land, remain there for six months, purchase the land for $1.25 an acre with cash provided by unscrupulous operators, and then turn the land over to them. Cowhands were frequently required to "homestead" in this way as a condition of employment.

The General Revision Act of 1891 extended the period required before commutation to fourteen months, but this was not long enough to stop the practice. For example, in North Dakota alone in the ten years between 1900 and 1910, 5.7 million acres were commuted while final proof was made on only 5.6 million acres. The problem of preventing abuse of the privilege, without being unfair to the actual settler who had a legitimate reason for wishing to purchase before the end of the period required to obtain free title, was never solved.

Actual fraud took many forms. The "twelve-by-fourteen" house required to prove occupancy might be a dry-goods box, with the dimensions measured in inches instead of feet. A "shingle roof" might consist of two shingles. A house that from a distance looked habitable might lack a floor or have a wooden chimney. "Dummy" entrymen were hired to stake false claims on land and transfer title to speculators, who were thus able to block up large holdings. There is no way of knowing how many of the 285 million acres patented under the Homestead Act were acquired fraudulently, but the figure must be sizable. Land office officials were too few and far between for effective enforcement of the laws, and public opinion commonly tolerated or even supported the illegal practices.

INTERNAL IMPROVEMENT THROUGH SETTLEMENT

Two programs, the Timber Culture Act and the Desert Land Sales Act, combine the internal improvement and homesteading themes. Congress tried to encourage settlers to plant and irrigate by rewarding their efforts with gifts of land.

Timber Culture Act

Commissioner Wilson of the General Land Office, in his annual report in 1866, suggested that tree planting should be required of all homesteaders in localities where timber was scarce. Settlers on the fertile soils of the Middle Western plains and prairies were seriously handicapped by lack of wood and water. Trees were scarce except along the river bottoms so that practically all of the wood needed for construction had to be imported, largely from the lake states. Moreover, precipitation was often so low that farming without irrigation was a hazardous enterprise. Tree planting was advocated as a means of meeting both needs. Forests would obviously produce wood, and at that time it was believed by many that they would also increase rainfall in addition to protecting watersheds by preventing floods and siltation.

In 1873, Congress passed the Timber Culture Act, which offered to donate 160 acres of public land to any person who would plant 40 acres of it to trees and keep them growing and healthy for ten years. Amendments to the act were necessary almost immediately. The offer to grant land to "any person" was too liberal, while the requirement that the entire 40 acres must be planted in one year was too strict. The acreage was soon reduced to 10 acres, the length of time allowed for planting was extended, and the "healthy trees" requirement was shortened to eight years. The title of the act, "to encourage the growth of timber in the Prairie States," indicates the region where Congress expected it to be operative. Tree planting in the prairies is a difficult and expensive undertaking which the early settlers had neither the knowledge nor the money to handle successfully. Parts of the region are too dry for forest growth; and even where conditions are favorable, successful planting demands considerable technical skill.

As with most of the other land laws, both the terms and the spirit of the Timber Culture Acts were widely violated. Entries were made for speculation to sell relinquishments at substantial profits to actual settlers. Dummy entrymen were used to acquire large tracts for wheat and cattle ranges.

The Timber Culture Act is one of Congress' first attempts to respond to the growing public concern with conservation and propagation of forests. Unfortunately, the policy was doomed to failure from the outset; and until it was repealed in 1891, the *Congressional Record* was full of discussions regarding amending, deleting, or improving the program.

Desert Land Sales Act

Congressional attempts to encourage private individuals to irrigate the public lands also failed. The 1877 Desert Land Sales Act authorized the government to sell 640 acres of land unfit for cultivation except by irrigation at $1.25 per acre to settlers who would irrigate the land within three years after filing. Irrigating land is even more arduous and demanding of skill and investment than silviculture. Unfortunately, congressional recognition of the need for irrigation was no more productive than its attempt to encourage tree growing with the Timber Culture Act. Speculation was rife, and collusive entries were common. Large areas primarily valuable for grazing or for the production of hay without irrigation were taken up. Also, control over grazing land to which title was not acquired was obtained by making desert entries on land including or bordering on water. Over 10 million acres were patented under the act, chiefly in Montana, Wyoming, Colorado, Idaho, and California. In spite of repeated recommendations for its repeal, the law remains in effect.

MINERAL LANDS

Congress was generally reluctant to classify lands according to their physical attributes or productive capacity, preferring to emphasize instead the home-steader theme and the idea that all lands should be open to cultivation by actual settlers. In spite of this dominant idea, Congress always recognized the special value of mineral lands. Nevertheless, it was slow to provide clear-cut legislation for their disposal and use. The Ordinance of 1785, which established the rectangular survey, reserved "one-third part of gold, silver, lead, and copper mines, to be sold or otherwise disposed of as Congress shall hereafter direct." A similar act in 1796 reserved all salt springs and licks and the section in which they were located. The saline lands, aggregating a few hundred thousand acres, were later turned over to the states when they were admitted to the Union. But a definite mineral land policy was slow in developing. Legislation passed between 1807 and 1846 provided first for the lease and later for the sale of specified mineral lands, but administration of the provisions was inadequate. In 1850, the lands were opened to sale and preemption in the same manner as other public lands.

The discovery of gold in California in 1848 and the subsequent rush of immigrants to California and later to the Rocky Mountain states created new problems. "Possessory rights" to mineral claims were universally respected. Hundreds of local associations similar to the old claim associations were organized, and they promulgated regulations which became the law of the land. The miners were in the saddle; all attempts to control their activities other than by their own regulations were vigorously resisted.

General Sales System

Congress finally took action in 1866, when it made the public domain mineral lands, both surveyed and unsurveyed, "free and open to exploration by all citizens of the United States, and those declaring their intention to become citizens, subject to such regulations as may be prescribed by law" and "subject also to the local customs or rules of miners in the several mining districts so far as the same may not be in conflict with the laws of the United States." Patents to lode mines could be bought for $5 an acre if the claimant had occupied them according to local rules and had expended as much as $1000 in labor and improvements. In 1870, Congress authorized the survey and sale of placer mining lands at $2.50 per acre.

In 1872, Congress passed the General Mining Act. As a result, mineral lands became a distinct class subject to sale under prices and requirements materially different from those for other lands. Congress provided that any person finding a valuable mineral deposit anywhere on the public lands was entitled to the mineral without paying the government any royalty or rent. Until 1976, the claimant was not even required to report the discovery to the federal government. Simply staking a claim—literally driving stakes into the ground and reporting their location to the appropriate local officials—was sufficient to establish title to the minerals. Miners wishing to take full title to the land surrounding their claims also could do so under the 1872 act. The prices of $5 per acre for lode claims and $2.50 per acre for placer claims were retained in the 1872 statute. In order to get title to the land, claimants were required to spend not less than $100 per year on labor and improvements, and the total expenditure required before patent could be obtained was reduced to $500.

When compared with much of the legislation pertaining to the public domain lands, the 1872 act seems relatively enlightened since it recognizes the special value of a particular land for particular purposes. At the time, it seemed reasonable to encourage private entrepreneurs to undertake the physical and financial risks involved in locating and developing mineral resources necessary for national growth and settlement. However, mineral law has not kept pace with changes in land policy. The law remains essentially unchanged. The net result has been that hard rock mining is statutorily defined as the highest and best use of all federal lands and the government is still committed to a policy of encouraging mining. The government cannot claim even a royalty for the resources extracted or prevent the miner from acquiring the land itself for a nominal fee. This policy has led to many abuses, and valuable scenic or timber resources have been taken under the guise of a gravel "mine." Efforts to manage the public lands have been complicated by priorities codified in the 1872 act ever since they were initiated at the beginning of the twentieth century.

Extent of Disposals

Figure 1-3 and Table 1-2 present the basic information regarding land disposition as of 1976, when the disposition policy was ended except for mineral entry under the 1872 act, desert land entry, and homesteading in Alaska.

Table 1-2 Area of Public Lands Disposed of Under the Public Land Laws as of 1974

Method	Area	Percent of	
		Total disposals	Original public domain
	Million acres		
Public, private, and preemption sales, mineral entries, and miscellaneous disposals	300.0	29	20
Homestead grants and sales	285.0	28	19
Grants to states for:			
Support of common schools	77.6	8	5
Reclamation of swampland	64.9	6	4
Construction of railroads	37.1	4	3
Support of miscellaneous institutions	21.7	2	1
Purposes not classified elsewhere	14.3	1	1
Construction of canals	4.6		
Construction of wagon roads	3.3	1	1
Improvement of rivers	1.5		
Total	223.8	22	15
Grants to railroad corporations	91.3	9	6
Grants to veterans as military bounties	61.0	6	4
Confirmed private land claims	34.0	3	2
Sales under timber and stone laws	13.9	1	1
Grants and sales under timber culture laws	10.9	1	1
Sales under desert land laws	10.0	1	1
Total	1,029.9	100	70

Source: U.S. Department of the Interior, Bureau of Land Management.

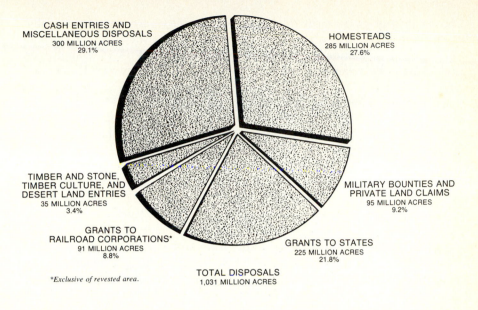

Figure 1-3. Approximate area of the public domain disposed of under the public land laws. (Reproduced from Clawson and Held, 1957, p. 26.)

Altogether, title to 1030 millin acres or more than 70 percent of the original public domain has been transferred from the federal government to other owners. Of this total, some 69 percent has gone to individuals and institutions, 22 percent to the states, and 9 percent to railroads. Public, private, and preemption sales and homestead grants comprise nearly three-fifths of all disposals. Grants to aid in the construction of permanent improvements and to support education also occupy a place of major importance.

RESERVATION, WITHDRAWAL, AND CLASSIFICATION

The disposition era of public land management ended in 1891, when Congress authorized the creation of forest reserves. The public movement leading to that legislation and the era of reservation will be discussed in the next chapter, but three concepts are essential to understanding the transition from disposition to management: reservations, withdrawals, and classification.

Reservation was the earliest tool employed by the government to conserve particular lands or resources for government use. The Crown reserved all mast timber for use by the British navy. John Quincy Adams reserved numerous sites in the South to protect live oaks needed for ship timber by the nascent American navy. A reservation is a declaration that the designated property will be retained in government ownership for specified purposes. Occasionally, other uses of the land which do not conflict with the stated federal purpose are allowed to continue. For example, the Mining Law of 1872 applies on national forests because mining is not viewed as inconsistent with forest management, but it is generally forbidden in national parks. The President has considerable authority derived both from specific statutes and from the power inherent in the office to reserve public domain lands. Reservations have been made for military purposes, wildlife refuges, and a host of public purposes in addition to forests.

Withdrawals are similar to reservations, and occasionally they produce a similar result; however, they are not the same. Withdrawal is the removal of land from the applicability of a particular disposition statute. The land is not necessarily reserved for a particular activity. Typically, lands which are valuable for dam sites or mining were withdrawn from homestead entry. This was done to prevent unscrupulous operators from monopolizing, under the guise of homesteading, resources needed for settlement and development of the nation. Subsequently, many lands with high timber, wildlife, or aesthetic values were withdrawn from mineral entry to prevent destruction of the higher values. Again, the President and his designee, the Secretary of the Interior, have broad discretion to make withdrawals from the public domain.

Classification connotes assessing the physical attributes, productive capacity, and appropriate utilization of the lands. One might think that classification would necessarily precede withdrawal or reservation. Frequently, however, that has not been the case. Large areas have been inappropriately reserved for forest purposes or withdrawn from homestead entry to protect nonexistent mineral values. Many reserves and withdrawls were made with little or no factul informtion. Classifiction, by itself, does not alter the legal status of the land.

SUMMARY

The century following the American Revolution marked the occupation and development of a virgin continent at an unparalleled rate. This development depended on the rich agricultural, timber, and mineral resources contained in the billion and a half acres of public domain. The apparent inexhaustibility of these resources made it inevitable that they were used freely, often wastefully, by present standards.

The government's policy during this period was to encourage settlement by transferring public lands to state, corporate, and private ownership. Sometimes this was done by grants to the states chiefly for the support of education and the construction of permanent improvements. More often, the transfer of title was direct to individuals or corporations with general sales, preemption sales, homestead grants, and railroad grants as the principal means of disposal.

In retrospect, much of the legislation was unsound and administration was ineffective.

Land was not scarce and was not treated as a resource until late in the nineteenth century. However, this does not reflect as ill upon the government and people as is frequently alleged. Labor and capital were scarce, and they were the factors of production appropriately conserved. Land disposition went forward as a means of achieving related economic and social goals.

The sectionalism apparent in discussions of public land management is ample testimony to the point that scarcity precedes conservation. Rather early in our history, resource scarcity was a local problem in the East around major population centers. Efforts of the Eastern states to manipulate the westward expansion for their own benefit received the same short shrift on the frontier which had greeted Britain's Broad Arrow Policy a generation before. As the public lands became territories and states, their representatives altered the federal policy from one of sale to one of general largesse.

The mythology of the hardy yeoman which developed during the nineteenth century is a double tragedy. It is tragic first because the hardy yeoman really never participated fully in the land disposition program. Even the grants to states for internal improvements and education were surrounded by fraud, and statute after statute was passed which virtually assured that corrupt land speculators and corporations would get the cream of the American land. More tragic for the land, of course, were the disastrous impacts wrought by the hardy yeomanry's attempts to make a living on the droughty, untillable land left to them. The land disposition statutes were based on experience in the eastern watersheds, where 160 acres would support a family. They were not appropriate to the arid West and virtually required settlers to destroy their allotments. And so they did.

The public domain was a treasure for the new nation unique in the history of the world and had a profound influence on the nation's economic, social, and political life. Free and abundant natural resources of every description promoted material prosperity, broke down barriers between classes, and bred a sturdy individualism that rebelled at governmental restraints. Soil, timber, forage, wildlife, and minerals were to be had for the taking; evasion of laws attempting to control their disposal and exploitation was easy and respectable. However, even as the settlers rushed to subdue and settle the territories, concerned citizens in the East began to agitate for conservation, husbandry, and efficient use of the lands. Toward the close of the nineteenth century, the laissez-faire philosophy of the frontier was seriously challenged. Then came the crusade for "conservation" and the retention in public ownership of other natural resources. Gradually, the national policy with respect to the public domain changed from one of almost complete disposal to one of reservation. Particularly inspired by the rapid liquidation of the American forest, the growing movement focused first and succeeded most spectacularly in the area of forest conservation. Yet the legacy of individualism and unconcern for the future bequeathed to us by free land still colors our attitudes and has influenced every subsequent effort to conserve and live in the natural world.

REFERENCES CITED

Albion, Robert G. *Forests and Sea Power*. Cambridge, Mass.: Harvard University Press, 1926.

Cameron, Jenks. "American Forest Influences—Sea Power." 32 *American Forests* 707 (1926).

———. "An Anchor to Forestward." 34 *American Forests* 199 (1928).

———. *The Development of Governmental Forest Control in the United States*. Baltimore, Md.: Johns Hopkins Press, 1928.

———. "President Adams' Acorns." 34 *American Forests* 131 (1928).

———. "Who Killed Santa Rosa?" 34 *American Forests* 263 (1928).

Ciriacy-Wantrup, S. von. *Resource Conservation*. Berkeley: University of California Press, 1952.

Clawson, Marion. *Uncle Sam's Acres*. New York: Dodd, Mead & Company, 1951.

Gates, Paul W. "The Homestead Law in an Incongrous Land System." 41 *American Historical Review* 652 (June, 1936).

———. *History of Public Land Law Development*. Written for the Public Land Law Review Commission. Washington, D.C.: Government Printing Office, 1968.

Greeley, William B. *Forests and Men*. New York: Doubleday and Company, 1951.

———. *Forest Policy*. New York: McGraw-Hill Book Company, 1953.

Hibbard, Benjamin H. *History of the Public Land Policies*. New York: The Macmillan Company, 1924.

Huth, Hans. *Nature and the Americans*. Berkeley: University of California Press, 1957.

Ise, John. *The United States Forest Policy*. New Haven, Conn.: Yale University Press, 1924.

Johnson, Hildegard B. *Order Upon the Land: The U.S. Rectangular Land Survey and the Upper Mississippi Country*. New York: Oxford University Press, 1976.

Kinney, Jay P. *Forest Legislation in America Prior to March 4, 1978*. Ithaca, N.Y.: Cornell Forest Experiment Station Bulletin 370, 1916.

Lillard, Richard G. *The Great Forest*. New York: Alfred A. Knopf, Inc., 1947.

Nash, Roderick. *Wilderness and the American Mind*. New Haven, Conn.: Yale University Press, 1967.

Peffer, E. Louise. *The Closing of the Public Domain*. Stanford, Cal.: Stanford University Press, 1951.

Robbins, Roy M. *Our Landed Heritage*. New York: Peter Smith, 1950.

Chapter 2

First Awakening: Forest Reservations

The evolution away from the commitment to disposing of the public domain to states, corporations, and individuals was gradual. Before the nation could be convinced of the need to conserve resources, those resources had to become valuable; and for that to happen, they had to be recognized as scarce. Before that could occur, settlers and developers had to subdue and even destroy much of the continent's natural bounty. This happened slowly during the nineteenth century, accelerating after the Civil War. Gradually the idea developed that the government should retain parts of the federal lands to achieve general public purposes. The theory of retention developed first in the East, where local shortages of specific resources had caused concern in the early 1600s. Westerners have, with some justification, accused Easterners of fouling their own nest and attempting to conserve Western resources both in order to expiate their guilt and to suppress competition from the developing Western states. This was clearly part of the rationale. However, after the Civil War, a number of scientific studies, notably George Perkins Marsh's *Man and Nature* and John Wesley Powell's *Report on the Arid Regions of the United States,* pointed out the destructive impact of human activity on the productive capacity of the earth. This awakening was accompanied by growing fears of scarcity. As the century passed, the nation saw the logging industry play itself out in the Northeast, the lake states, and the South and move into the Northwest. The threat of shortages began to look real. Public concern was also aroused by events such as the decimation of buffalo herds. The scientific inquiries, vanishing wildlife, and threat of shortages stimulated an expanding national movement among prominent citizens to halt waste and protect land and resources. Associations and societies were formed and actively "memorialized" Congress to take action.

Forestry was the focus of much of this growing concern for two reasons. First, the destruction of forests and the fire that almost inevitably follows were emotionally charged issues which attracted diverse public attention. The loss of the scenic beauty and natural heritage aroused as much concern as did the threat of timber famine. Both issues were overshadowed by concern for water supply in the West and the widespread belief that forests cause rain, prevent floods, and retain moisture. Second, forest management was one of the only resource fields in which there was an established science, literature, and profession. Forest management had long been practiced in Europe, and its techniques were enthusiastically discussed by the newly concerned Americans. German-born foresters such as Bernhard Fernow emigrated to the United States and provided early and decisive leadership in the burgeoning forestry movement. Most of our early foresters were either born in Germany or educated in Europe, and the impact of German assumptions on American land management has been interesting and profound.

Toward the end of the nineteenth century, the small but growing number of trained foresters provided the insight and political force behind the evolution of the third major era in public land policy. The idea of federal land retention developed almost unquestioned out of the German experience in state ownership of forested lands. To the foresters, however, land retention was necessary but insufficient. Fernow failed to convince a reluctant Congress that the retained lands should be actively managed to increase and perpetuate the resources of the forests. His successor, Gifford Pinchot, effectively developed both the idea of management and the institutions to achieve it.

In the 1870s, the learning, teaching, and political activities of the new groups led to important government action. John Wesley Powell in 1878 made his famous *Report on the Lands of the Arid Regions* to the Secretary of the Interior and Congress. By 1879, there was sufficient concern with resource problems for Congress to authorize a Public Lands Commission to study the situation and make recommendations. In 1886, Congress authorized the Secretary of Agriculture to establish a Division of Forestry within the department to study the situation and make recommendations regarding forest issues. From beginnings such as these developed the vision required to transform public land policy completely.

EARLY RESERVES, SALES, AND TIMBER TRESPASS

Naval Timber Reserves

The birth of the United States Navy led to the first federal forest reserves in this country. Unfortunately, the reserves did not prevent unauthorized use of the timber, and the experience demonstrated many of the difficulties the young nation would have in protecting its resources.

In 1799, Congress appropriated $200,000 for the purchase of timber or timberlands in order to preserve timber suitable for naval construction for future use. Eighteen years later, Congress further authorized the Secretary of the Navy, with the approval of the President, to reserve from sale public lands containing live oak and red cedar for the sole purpose of supplying timber for the United States Navy.

The frontier spirit differed little from that of pre-Revolutionary days. Merely placing a law on the statute books did not stop the settlers from using the reserved timber. But, because the navy continued to obtain the timber it needed in spite of heavy illegal cutting, interest in the reserves gradually waned. In 1843, some of the reservations of live oak lands in Louisiana were opened to settlement, and from then on the reserved acreage continued to dwindle. Iron and steel came into use for shipbuilding in the 1850s, and the destruction of the wooden ships of the federal fleet by the Confederate ironclad *Merrimac* marked the end of wood as an indispensable material in ship construction. In 1879, the bulk of the naval reservations in Florida, where most of them were located, were restored to the unreserved public domain. The naval timber policy, ineffectual as it was, constituted an important landmark in the development of this country's resource policy. It underscored the value of the public lands as a source of raw materials and the right of Congress to exercise complete control over those lands in the national interest. Unfortunately, it also demonstrated the impossibility of effectively preventing trespass on publicly owned resources regarded by the locals as inexhaustible.

Timber Trespass

The problems of the naval reserves were encountered more generally in all efforts to deal with public resources. Until about 1840, it was government policy to sell the resources to retire the Revolutionary War debt, and therefore it was necessary to exclude nonpaying persons from the public lands. Prevention of trespass was always the formal policy, but not even Congress was particularly interested in enforcing its own prohibitions.

For nearly a century after the Revolution, no general legislation dealt with the enormous area of forestland included in the public domain. Until 1878, the only legal way to acquire either timber or timberlands from the federal government, except incidentally by agricultural entry, was under statutes providing for auction sales. This was a cumbersome process, and it became accepted practice simply to take the timber or to acquire the timberlands by fraudulent entry under one of the agricultural land disposition statutes. The concept of "lands chiefly valuable for timber production" would have completely perplexed most early pioneers. The men and women who settled the wilderness which once was Pennsylvania, Ohio, Michigan, and the Northwest Territory feared trees and labored hard to remove them. The question therefore arose early regarding whether the 1807 General Trespass Law even applied to timberlands.

In 1821, the Attorney General ruled that it did, and the government could remove timber trespassers by military force and subject them to fine and imprisonment. A few weeks later the Commissioner of the General Land Office instructed all registers, receivers, and district attorneys to prevent trespass and to advertise in the local papers that persons guilty of "intruding on the lands of the United States and of committing waste of public timber" would be "prosecuted to the utmost rigor of the law." The old Broad Arrow Policy was thus enlarged to include every species on every acre of the public lands. However, no money was appropriated to protect the public timber until 1872.

Isaac Willard of the Lake States

One exceptional agent employed by the General Land Office did not take the hint, and his sad tale illustrates the attitude of his contemporaries toward resource exploitation. In 1853, Agent Isaac Willard seized a large quantity of timber stolen from federal lands in the Great Lakes area where he was stationed. Most of it was burned or restolen by the original thieves. He then obtained warrants to arrest the leading offenders, who promptly escaped or were rescued by violent mobs of their friends. Not until Willard obtained assistance from the warship *U.S.S. Michigan* did he succeed in holding his prisoners in custody. Although most of those finally brought to trial were convicted, the penalties—small fines and jail sentences ranging from one day to one year—did not seem appropriate to the charges, which had included trespass, armed resistance, and the death of federal officers.

The Congress was no more supportive than the courts had been. Representative Eastman of Wisconsin was incensed that government agents should be "persecuting" enterprising individuals and warned that "open revolt" might result. He argued that the forests of the public domain should be thrown open for unrestricted use. Heeding the tone of the times, in 1855, the Secretary of the Interior decided to delegate the timber trespass enforcement duties to local land district officers. In other words, special timber agents were eliminated, and their duties were taken over by the local land officers, who were already fully occupied. For the next twenty years, trespassers on the pineries of the lake states and other public timberlands were undisturbed by government agents.

In 1877, the department tried to charge a uniform fee for federal timber rather than attempting to recover it as stolen property. This "stumpage" charge differed in several important ways from the fees later collected in national forest timber sales. No attempt was made to appraise the true value of the timber; the operator, not the government, decided where and how much to cut; and no supervision was exercised to make sure that the cutting was done properly. Under these lenient conditions, leniently enforced, the problem of timber trespass abated temporarily.

Alternative Policies

In evaluating the policy of the General Land Office during this early period, it must be remembered that, as noted above, there was no way settlers could legally acquire either public timber or timberland except at auction sales. Such auctions were designed primarily for the disposal of agricultural lands and became increasingly infrequent after the passage of the Preemption Act of 1841 and the Homestead Act of 1862. There was simply no way to build a house or a fence without stealing timber.

The government did not, however, have many alternatives in attempting to establish a more constructive policy. Clearly, the public timber could not be reserved or witheld from use, nor was there any motivation to do so. Wood, which could only come from the public lands, was essential to the nation's economy and development. To protect the forests, the government could have classified the lands according to their best use and exempted nonagricultural lands from the operation of the settlement statutes. Timberlands, for example, could have been either retained or sold for settlement only after the timber had been sold separately. This would have increased government receipts substantially; and, if the timber had been sold alone, this procedure would have permitted a later choice as to whether the lands involved should be retained permanently. However, classification depends on inventory and survey data, which were not available at the time. Sales rely, as previously noted, on sufficient force and motivation to exclude the nonpaying resource users.

The government was understandably reluctant simply to ignore the wholesale, frequently fraudulent, usurpation of public resources for private gain. Speculators monopolizing large tracts of public land and resources undercut the orderly settlement and development of the country which was the goal of congressional programs. However, a classification or reservation policy was not only impossible to administer due to lack of data but was also literally inconceivable until well after the middle of the nineteenth century because most people were not thinking of resource conservation. This was due to three factors. First, the forest seemed inexhaustible. Until about 1850, our small, chiefly agricultural population had made only insignificant inroads on the more than 600 million acres of virgin forest. Second, new roads, canals, and later railroads constantly opened new supplies of timber. As transportation facilities pushed back the frontier, the supply of accessible timber increased more rapidly than the cutting of the forests in the older settlements.

Finally, a widespread belief in economic freedom dominated thinking and was especially significant in westward expansion. Laissez-faire left little room for government landownership or management.

Late in the century this situation began to change. By the 1870s, many and various proposals for propagation, reservation, classification, and sale of public timber were introduced in Congress with increasing frequency. Citizens were developing an awareness and understanding of the waste and devastation inherent in the attitudes and public land policies of the period. From a very small whisper of early scientific interest in the forests, the concern grew into a small but effective chorus by 1880.

THE BEGINNINGS OF INTEREST IN RESOURCE MANAGEMENT

Early scientific interest in the forest was limited but keen. At first it was concerned chiefly with research in dendrology, especially focusing on determining the characteristics and distribution of the amazing number and variety of trees of the American forests. Prominent among the earliest students of the subject were two Frenchmen: Andre Michaux and his son, Andre Francois Michaux. The elder Michaux explored the forests of North America west to the Mississippi and north toward Hudson's Bay from 1785 to 1796 for the French government. He was concerned chiefly with the oaks, reflecting the government's concern with oak for naval construction. The work was carried on by his son and resulted in the classic *North American Sylva,* published in 1819. The Michaux family also left a legacy which became available in 1870 to support forestry lectures, publications, and botanical gardens (Kirkland, 73). Thirty years later, another botanist/explorer, David Douglas, kindled great interest in the West with his trips to California, Oregon, British Columbia, and Hudson's Bay. A Scotsman, he was a collector for the British Horticultural Society. Douglas first described over 150 native American species and gave his name to the redoubtable Douglas fir.

GEORGE PERKINS MARSH: MAN AND NATURE

Two later, broader-gauged scientific inquiries put the growing interest in the resources of the American West explicitly into the context of land management policy. In 1864, George Perkins Marsh published his famous book, *Man and Nature.* It was republished in 1874 under the title *The Earth as Modified by Human Action* and was reissued many, many times thereafter. His book discussed the unintended and destructive consequences of human activity in modifying the environment. Marsh was typical of many of the late nineteenth-century forebears of the conservation movement. His scientific interests were only a small part of his wide-ranging activities, and in the nascent field of ecology he was largely self-taught. Marsh was a lawyer, a congressman, a professor of philology and etymology, and an ambassador to Turkey and Italy under Presidents Zachary Taylor and Abraham Lincoln. During his travels in the Mediterranean, he observed the long-term destructive impact of human activities which he described in his innovative work.

Man and Nature was an immediate success, selling more than a thousand copies in the first few months after publication. In its day, that constituted a best-seller, and the work was frequently cited in public and congressional debates on public land policy. Marsh argued effectively that society has a right to use, not abuse, nature's bounty and advocated both caution in intervening in nature's "spontaneous arrangements" and a vast program to rehabilitate the harm already done to the earth. Marsh occupies an interesting place in present resource discussions because he is so widely misinterpreted. Those who think of Marsh as a wilderness preservationist are in error. Marsh was indeed appalled by society's destructive impact on magnificent and beneficial natural systems. However, he strongly advocated careful but exhaustive manipulation of the natural world for the sustained benefit of humanity. He was among the first to speak in terms of the balance of nature, but he also advocated building a canal to fill the Dead Sea. Marsh dealt in great detail with the evil effects of forest destruction on climate and the water supply, particularly in the Mediterranean region, and greatly influenced thinking on these subjects. His book captured the imagination of thousands of readers over a forty-year period, and Marsh is appropriately honored as the first great voice of American conservation (Randall, passim).

JOHN WESLEY POWELL: REPORT ON THE LANDS OF THE ARID REGION

John Wesley Powell was another great observer of the critical relationship among people, land and water (Petulla, 193). Powell was a self-taught scholar in many fields and is perhaps best remembered as the one-armed Civil War veteran who led the first daring exploration of the Colorado River and the Grand Canyon. In addition, he was an accomplished student of Indian language and culture and served as the first director of the U.S. Geological Survey from 1881 to 1892. Powell's contributions to ethnology, geology, and the development of government institutions for scientific inquiry would earn him a place in history (Stegner, passim). His major work, *Report on the Lands of the Arid Region of the United States,* contends with Marsh's work for the distinction of being the most significant document in American conservation history.

Powell was the first to observe that the lands of the arid West differed dramatically from those east of the 100th meridian and should not be treated as had the earlier frontiers. The climate, soils, topography, and ubiquitous shortage of water mandated a completely different approach to the land. Powell proposed that all the public lands be classified according to their best use—mineral, coal, irrigated agriculture, timber, and pasturage—and disposed of accordingly. In some areas, he argued that homesteads of 2560 acres would be required to support a family adequately. To allocate less was to require that settlers destroy the land in trying to live on it. Moreover, he advocated a form of watershed settlement that would lead to a communal or cooperative approach to water development and allocation.

Powell's call for land classification according to physical characteristics was a radical departure from the grid system which had been imposed on the land by the rectangular survey. Watersheds, rather than 640-acre square sections, were Powell's basic planning unit. His cooperative settlement ideas were also a variance with the concept of the hearty individual settler. Although he had a long and varied career in government service, Powell's ideas were never accepted. Because he did not advocate federal land retention, he was frequently at cross-purposes even with the forest protection movement, which was developing out of the successful German experience with state ownership. Nevertheless, in emphasizing land classification and irrigation as the basis for land use, he was thirty to eighty years ahead of his time. His work was an important catalyst in the gradual development of a whole new way of thinking about land and land management in the United States.

THE EARLY MOVEMENT TO SAVE THE FORESTS

The first evidence of growing interest in resource use is the repeated warnings, voiced by persons both in and out of government from the Civil War on, about the dangers of mounting forest destruction. Annual reports of the Secretary of the Interior and the Commissioner of the General Land Office recognized the threat to the economy. Commissioner Wilson in 1866 felt that the supply of timber in the lake states was already "so diminished as to be a matter of serious concern." In 1868, he predicted that in forty or fifty years our own forests would have disappeared and those of Canada would be approaching exhaustion. In 1869, a committee appointed by the Michigan legislature to look into the matter of forest destruction reported: "Generations yet unborn will bless or curse our memory accordingly as we preserve for them what the munificent past has so richly bestowed upon us, or as we lend our influence to continue and accelerate the wasteful destruction everywhere at work in our beautiful state" (Dana, 77).

The Arbor Day Movement

The first public response to concern about forest destruction was manifest in simply planting trees. The first Arbor Day was celebrated in Nebraska in 1872 at the instance of J. Sterling Morton, a prominent citizen who was later Secretary of Agriculture. The purpose was to stimulate interest in tree planting; and the idea proved so popular that the celebration of Arbor Day, proclaimed by state governors, soon became a national fad. Forestry movement leader Bernhard Fernow was among those who questioned the relationship between forestry and tree planting: "I am not sure," he noted, "but this otherwise interesting and beautiful idea has had a retarding influence on practical forestry by misleading people into thinking that tree planting was the main issue instead of a conservative management of existing forests" (Dana, 79). Nevertheless, Fernow was active in urging not only state but also national observance of Arbor Day; and there can be little question that the effort, however tangential to issues of forest management, was a major manifestation of growing public concern with forest destruction. The Timber Culture Act discussed above (p. 25) is a congressional response to the same sentiments.

Forests and Water

Although Powell's overriding concern with the arid West was out of harmony with the dominant opinions of the day, the special relationship between the concern for water and the concern for forests must be noted. Water has been at the heart of national concern about forest destruction from the very beginning of the conservation and preservation movement. Fear of timber famine was a factor, aesthetic and scenic preservation was a factor, but water was the center of it. It was believed that destruction of forest cover led to both floods and droughts, and the forestry movement was fostered by the occurrence of either in the second half of the nineteenth century. The belief that forests cause rain is frequently encountered in the literature and public debates of the day. Preservation of forest cover was, thus, tantamount in the minds of many to assuring an adequate water supply for western development. The common notion that forest preservation was opposed in the West must always be weighed against the importance of water to the arid states and the belief that forests would alleviate the water problem. Eastern activists might have been bent on scenery or forest management, but for every Westerner opposed to the forest protection movement there were thirsty Westerners, many with thirsty livestock, who believed, at some level of analytical sophistication, that water grew on trees.

AAAS Takes a Hand

The American Association for the Advancement of Science (AAAS) was among the most prestigious national groups to rally to the cause of forestry. Initial interest developed within the AAAS in 1873, when Franklin B. Hough presented a brief but forceful paper at their twenty-second annual meeting. "On the Duty of Governments in the Preservation of Forests" stressed the need to educate both the general public and forestland owners about the importance of forests to climate, erosion, runoff, and timber supply and indicated several ways in which such educational activities might be conducted. At Hough's urging, the association passed a resolution "that a committee [shall] be appointed by the association to memorialize Congress and the several State legislatures upon the importance of promoting the cultivation of timber and the preservation of forests, and to recommend proper legislation for securing these objects" (Dana, 80).

The committee's distinguished membership included Franklin B. Hough and such eminent natural scientists as George B. Emerson and Asa Gray. Hough and Emerson, acting in behalf of the committee, formulated the views of the association in a statement which was transmitted to Congress by President Grant in February 1874. After pointing out the great public injury likely to result from the rapid exhaustion of the country's forests, the memorial requested the creation of a commission of forestry which would report directly to the President. The support of the AAAS was vital to the conservation movement for the next several decades, and Hough's efforts bore fruit a scant two years later.

Formation of the American Forestry Association

In addition to attracting the interest of established groups, forestry, timber famine, and forest protection became the focus for a number of new groups in the 1870s. Today's American Forestry Association (AFA) was formed during that decade out of a number of regional groups concerned with forest issues. John A. Warder, an Ohio physician, pomologist, landscape gardener, and amateur forester, was typical of the citizen activist at the time. He prepared a comprehensive report on European forestry which was published in 1876 as a document. In this report, he stressed the fact that forestry, "though quite unknown as an art in our country," must receive greater attention (Dana, 87). In 1875, he was a major figure in calling the first meeting of a small group called the American Forestry Association. He also was a leader in the subsequent formation of the American Forestry Congress, into which Warder's American Forestry Association merged in 1882.

The first meeting of the new and enlarged group was held with fanfare, which indicates the enthusiasm for forestry matters at the time. Some 30,000 invitations were distributed; there was a parade of 60,000 schoolchildren, and Ohio celebrated its first Arbor Day during the meeting. This spectacular portion of the program was supplemented by the presentation of eighty-seven technical papers. The congress decided to perpetuate itself as a permanent organization and met in Atlanta in 1888 to merge with the Southern Forestry Congress. In 1889, they joined to form a new group called the American Forestry Association. Under that name it has since continued to be a popular and effective conservation organization, with membership open to anyone interested in the conservation and wise use of the nation's resources. In 1883,

Bernhard Fernow became corresponding secretary of the AFA and subsequently served as chairman of the executive committee and the editor of the Proceedings. He occupied these positions simultaneously with being Chief of the Division of Forestry, which put him in a strategic position to exercise great influence in the development of forest policy during this critical period. The American Forestry Association was virtually alone for fifty years as an enlightened, politically active and astute group advocating a broad range of conservation goals. It continues to occupy a critical center position in resource policy debates, advocating an intelligent balance between preservation and wise use.

Early Forestry Education

The numerous groups which flourished and were combined to form the American Forestry Association reflect growing popular concern with forest resources. This development was spurred by the initiation of forestry education. In 1880, the Chamber of Commerce of St. Paul, Minnesota, petitioned Congress to grant 300 sections of public land to the state of Minnesota for the establishment of a school of forestry; and proposals to start a forestry school in the Dakota Territory were regularly introduced in Congress in the 1880s. The measures were never acted on, and schools of forestry eventually developed without direct support from the government. Special lectures and courses in forestry were, however, given at a number of institutions prior to the inauguration of professional instruction in forestry in 1898. William H. Brewer's lectures at Yale in 1873 were perhaps the first. In 1882, Volney M. Spalding offered a course in forestry required for a degree in political science at the University of Michigan. By 1887, instruction in forestry was also being offered at the New Hampshire, Massachusetts, Michigan, Iowa, and Missouri agricultural colleges, the University of Pennsylvania, and the University of North Carolina. These early efforts did not constitute comprehensive professional education. Young Americans desiring forest management training were, like Gifford Pinchot, obliged to go to France or Germany. However, many generalists and self-taught naturalists, such as Muir, Marsh, Warder, and Hough, were actively interested and developed an impressive background in the area.

FROM TALK TO ACTION

During the 1870s, growing public concern about the conservation and preservation of the nation's resources led to many important state and federal actions.

New York Takes Early Action

New York was the first to establish state forests. In 1872, it appointed a commission to study the advisability of establishing a state forest preserve in the Adirondacks. The commission submitted a report recommending the prohibition of further sales of state land, which was pigeonholed by the legislature. Ten years later, in 1883, the legislature prohibited further sales of some 600,-000 to 800,000 acres of state land and appointed a second commission to study the situation further.

As a result of the commission's recommendations, the legislature in 1885 designated all the state lands in fourteen counties in the Adirondack and Catskill regions a "forest preserve." The move was motivated by a number of factors, including a growing concern with maintaining wilderness areas for aesthetic and recreational purposes. The dominant theme, however, was watershed protection. New Yorkers were concerned about floods and water for agriculture. They were also concerned with maintaining an adequate flow of water in the Erie Canal (Nash, 116–121). In 1894, the new state constitution was passed providing that all lands in the preserve shall forever be kept as wild land and forbidding the cutting of any timber, dead or alive, on state-owned land within its boundaries. This proviso, which treats reserves literally as preserves, precluded forest management and typified a major vein in the early movement toward land reservations.

Early Federal Reservations for Park Purposes

New York's forest reserve was part of a national movement which developed in the late 1800s to preserve a portion of our national resources by withholding land from use altogether. In the 1800s, the difference between parks and forests was not widely appreciated. All the early forest reserves in this period were, in fact, made to preserve scenic wonders and watersheds rather than to promote forestry. Most were entirely closed to management.

In 1864, Congress took the first step toward the present extensive system of federal land reservations by ceding Yosemite Valley and Mariposa Big Tree Grove to the state of California to be held for purposes of public recreation. State administration of the lands was not acceptable, and the land was receded to the federal government in 1906. The first reservation for park purposes was made in 1872, when Congress enacted legislation reserving 2 million acres in Montana, Wyoming, and Idaho as a "park or pleasuring ground for the benefit of the people." The reservation of Yellowstone could be viewed as the major departure point from the disposition orientation in public land policy. It was, however, an idiosyncratic response to the truly spectacular natural phenomena found in the area. It was not a land classification scheme, as had been suggested by Powell. It was not, moreover, a commitment to management of the reserved lands. Having excluded private exploitation of the reserved lands, Congress lost interest and the task of protecting and administering the areas was left by default to the army (Hampton, passim). The idea of a national park *system* was not even mentioned in Congress.

John Muir and the Early Preservationists

The early reserves, although innovative, are not indicative of a thorough redirection of the disposition policy but, rather, the beginning of new thoughts on the issue. They also represent the successful emergence of a set of land values which was not always consonant with the concepts of forest management. Although the two ideas cannot readily be separated, the preservationist impulse represented by the parks movement emphasized reservations in order to preserve areas of natural beauty from use, rather than to establish efficient management and wise use of natural resources favored by the conservationists. The preservation movement is usually associated with John Muir. John Muir, like John Wesley Powell, was the self-taught product of a hard-scrabble youth on a Midwestern homestead. Born in Scotland, he migrated to Wisconsin as a youth with his family and spent much of his lifetime exploring and chronicling the beauties of the Sierra Nevadas. When the Sierra Club was founded by a group of California hiking enthusiasts, he became its first president. Until his death, he used that position to promote the preservation of scenic wonders and wilderness areas. At first an active and effective supporter of the forest reservation movement, Muir broke with the use-oriented conservationists first over the issue of grazing in the reserves, which Muir took to be preserves, and then over the question of dam building in national parks (Rakestraw, chap. 4).

Muir is an appropriate symbol of the preservationist movement, but he inadequately represents the broad intellectual and cultural roots of the preservationist approach to natural policies. It was a philosophical movement rooted in transcendentalists such as Thoreau and Emerson. It was reflected in art, poetry, religion, and politics. Muir was a major influence on the movement, but it is broader and deeper than his wilderness life-style and concern for the Sierras suggest.

Conservation and Preservation in the 1880s and 1890s

The conservationists and preservationists were almost indistinguishable in their early efforts to stop despoilation and destruction of nature's gifts. They shared the assumption that the essential first ingredient of a proper wild lands policy was retention of the land by the government. When the common ground was won, the alliance came under stress, and the conflict between the goals of the two movements was increasingly apparent. In the 1870s, however, the land reserves were supported by all those generally concerned with despoilation of public resources, and the distinction between forest conservation and park preservation had not emerged.

Public Land Commission of 1879

The early land reservations of the 1870s are part of the rethinking of land policy. A more comprehensive approach was taken by the first Public Land Commission. This was the first inquiry of its kind, though there have been numerous ones since then, and it was the first explicit congressional recognition that a comprehensive public lands policy might be necessary or appropriate. As such, it constitutes a significant departure from previous attitudes.

Congress established the Public Land Commission to codify existing laws and to recommend the best methods for the disposal of the public lands. The commission visited all the Western states and territories and in 1880 submitted a constructive report which included the draft of a comprehensive bill "to provide for the survey and disposal of the public lands of the United States." One of its major recommendations was that the public domain be classified by government surveyors into arable lands, mineral lands, irrigable lands, pasturage lands, and timberlands and that land in each class be disposed of under laws and regulations suited to its particular character. The influence of John Wesley Powell was clearly evident in the commission's report.

The proposed bill provided that "all lands, excepting mineral, which are chiefly valuable for timber of commercial value shall be classified as timber lands." The phrase "chiefly valuable for timber of commercial value" was then and continued to be intended to exclude arable, irrigable, and pasture lands suited for homesteading. The commission pointed out that "timber lands, as thus defined, comprise a comparatively small area and consequently the classification will probably only include lands in the Territories and Pacific States." This analysis of the situation reflected the prevailing view that forest lands, in the lake states and the South were essentially agricultural in character. The commission recommended that all timberlands be withdrawn from sale or other disposal and the timber on even-numbered sections be sold for cash. Settlers would be allowed free use of timber for building, agriculture, mining, and other domestic purposes but not for sale, commerce, or export. The commission expressed the view that these provisions would "result in the maintenance and reproduction of the forest" and suggested that "the experiment is at least well worth trying" (Dana, 66).

Congress took no immediate action on any of the commission's recommendations, but the sales system proposed continued to be debated until the general Land Law Revision of 1891, which provided general authority for the establishment of forest reserves. More important than any influence the inquiry might have had on specific legislation, its major significance lies in its recognition of the need for a public land policy adapted to different physical attributes, productive capacities, and resources of the land. It marks the beginning of the end of the all-land-is-the-same, 160-acre-parcel approach to resource management. The nation still awaits full and effective implementation of management programs embodying these new principles, but the basic ideas were well developed in the commission's report.

Interior's Efforts to Enforce Existing Laws

In the atmosphere of concern which created the Public Land Commission, a most extraordinary man became Secretary of the Interior. Carl Schurz fled from Germany to this country after taking an active role in the revolution of 1848–1849. He became an active antislavery Republican and served both Lincoln and Johnson in high appointive capacities. He was also a Civil War general, leading troops at Bull Run, Chancellorsville, and Gettysburg, and a United States senator for one term. He broke with the Republicans over what he viewed as intolerable corruption in the Grant administration, but returned to become Rutherford B. Hayes's Secretary of the Interior. Schurz was friendly with John Wesley Powell and was an important leader in the growing reconsideration of land policy (Payton, passim).

Secretary Schurz approached public land problems with strong convictions about the value of rigorous law enforcement. His efforts to achieve his goals through application of existing statutes were unrelenting and unavailing. His attempts to protect public lands by enforcing the old timber trespass statutes in fact created such a strong reaction that two very unfortunate timber laws were hastily passed by Congress. Legislation forbidding private fencing of the public lands by the livestock operators was similarly ineffective. The failure of Schurz's tremendous efforts underscored the need for a whole new approach to public land management.

In 1877, Schurz rescinded the previous secretarial order delegating timber trespass responsibilities to local land officers and returned enforcement responsibilities to employees acting directly for the Commissioner of the General Land Office. This marked the beginning of a new campaign of law enforcement unprecedented in the history of the department. For the first time, the timber agent system brought substantial results, in spite of the constant complaint of the department that inadequate funds for effective prosecution of the campaign were appropriated by Congress. The enforcement progam was only effective in reducing timber trespass, but Schurz's actions focused public and congressional attention on the huge timber resources of the nation which were not legally obtainable (see above, p. 35–36).

Congress reacted by simultaneously passing the Free Timber Act and the Timber and Stone Act. Both acts were designed to encourage settlement and development rather than specifically to protect the federal timber, although they reflect Congress' intense concern with monopoly and fraudulent entry of timberlands. These two bills rely on the vain hope that if timber were readily available for mining, agriculture, and domestic use, theft and destruction of the resource might be abated. Various versions of the two bills had been debated throughout the decade of the 1870s as part of the growing concern with public land policy. The general scheme of making public timber available to settlers at no charge was adopted rather than numerous items designed to establish special treatment for the sale of timber and timberland. Even as the sale and free timber measures were debated, however, proposals to reserve forestland from entry and use altogether were increasingly introduced, usually to protect a preferred species, a specific watershed, or watersheds generally. Legislative attention to forest matters grew with public recognition of the problem. Unfortunately, like the Timber Culture Act, the two 1878 enactments failed to achieve congressional hopes.

The Free Timber Act

The Free Timber Act provided that U.S. citizen residents of Colorado, Nevada, New Mexico, Arizona, Utah, Wyoming, Dakota, Idaho, and Montana could cut timber on mineral lands for building, agriculture, mining, or other domestic purposes. On its face, the act was a well-intentioned attempt to provide timber without charge for bona fide settlers and miners to develop their farms and mineral claims. Yet it was simultaneously so broad and so restrictive that effective administration was impossible. For example, cutting was limited to mineral lands; but, as the Public Land Commission pointed out in 1880, "perhaps not one acre in 5,000 in the states and territories named is mineral and not one acre in 5,000 of what may be mineral is known to be such" (Dana, 64). In 1891, the act was extended to permit the free cutting of timber anywhere on the public domain in all of the Rocky Mountain states except Arizona and New Mexico. Cutting was allowed not only for mining, agriculture, and domestic purposes but also for manufacturing. In 1893, these liberalized provisions were extended to Arizona and New Mexico and, in 1901, to all the public land states.

Sale of Timber and Stone

The Timber and Stone Act authorized the sale of 160-acre tracts of unoccupied, surveyed, nonmineral land in Washington, Oregon, California, and Nevada, chiefly valuable for timber or stone and unfit for cultivation. The land which could have been offered at public sale previously was sold for not less than $2.50 per acre. Purchasers had to swear they were not buying the land for speculation but in good faith for their own exclusive use and benefit. These provisions differ from those which make timber available free to Rocky Mountain West settlers, and the goals behind the differences in the two acts are not clear. If the primary object were to provide actual settlers with a supply of wood in addition to that on their preemption or homestead claims, it is odd that they were not simply offered free timber, as was done in the Free Timber Act for the Rocky Mountain states, or that residents of the latter states were not given the opportunity to acquire wood lots. Congress believed that the large timber on the Pacific Coast was so much more valuable than that in the Rocky Mountains that a charge should be made for it. However, if the object were to make timber legally available to the lumber industry for manufacture and sale in the open market, the maximum area of 160 acres that could be acquired by any one person was too small. Why timber was lumped with stone in the act also remains a mystery.

Whatever the intent, bona fide settlers made little use of the act since they were usually more concerned with clearing the heavy stands of timber already on their claims than in acquiring more. The act was used chiefly by commercial timber operators to acquire large holdings of valuable timberlands. Speculation and fraud were greatly facilitated by a Supreme Court decision that a person who planned the immediate sale of a timber claim to another party was nevertheless taking it up "for his own exclusive use and benefit," unless collusion to sell prior to entry could be proved (Dana, 65). This was exceedingly difficult. Original purchasers from the government did not even have to await the issuance of patents. They could sell immediately upon receipt of a certificate of entry, and thereafter any number of subsequent transfers were possible.

Neglect of Range Lands

Public and congressional concern for protection of timberlands did not extend to the untimbered areas more suitable for stock raising. John Wesley Powell's concern was not shared, and no legislation dealing with the range or the use of grazing lands was passed by Congress prior to 1916. Until that time, stock raisers either obtained patent under legislation dealing with other classes of land, notably the preemption, homestead, timber culture, and desert land laws, or made free use of the range with no attempt to establish title except to the water holes that were the key to its successful utilization. Although such use was unauthorized and constituted trespass against the government, no steps to prevent it were taken until some of the larger owners in effect turned immense areas of open range into private preserves by building hundreds of miles of illegal fences. This followed the invention of barbed wire. The smaller owners and prospective settlers then complained, and the government was forced to take action.

In 1885, Congress passed an act forbidding enclosure of the public domain and authorizing fence destruction. Passage of the act by itself had little effect, so President Cleveland issued a proclamation calling attention to violations of the act and enjoining all persons to obey it. In spite of episodic efforts to have the fences removed, they remained and were accepted by the government as evidence of historic range use following the passage of the Taylor Grazing Act in 1934.

The Department of the Interior's efforts to protect public resources within the framework of existing policies and statutes gained little; but by 1876, steps were being taken to alter the framework. By happenstance, the reorientation of forest policy began in the Department of Agriculture.

THE DIVISION OF FORESTRY

Several proposals to appoint a commission or a commissioner to study the timber situation were introduced in Congress during the early 1870s. Finally, Representative Dunnell of Minnesota, recognizing that chances for enactment of a specific authorizing statute were slim, added an amendment to the section of the sundry civil appropriation bill for 1877 which provided for the free distribution of seeds for experimental purposes. This rider, which remained in the act as approved by the President on August 15, 1876, authorized the Secretary of Agriculture to spend $2000 to hire "some man of approved attainments, who is practically well acquainted with methods of statistical inquiry, and who has evinced an intimate acquaintance with questions relating to the national wants in regard to timber," to study the present and future demand "for timber and other forest products, the probable supply for future wants, the means best adapted to their preservation and renewal," and to file a report on his inquiry with Congress (Dana, 81).

Thus, the study of forestry became a function of the Department of Agriculture through a rider attached to an appropriations bill. This initiated a division of responsibilities wherein the land was administered in the Department of the Interior but the foresters were located in the Department of Agriculture—which became a source of controversy twenty-five years later. Franklin B. Hough, who had earlier advocated such a study before the AAAS, was appointed to undertake the task outlined by Congress. Hough was granted $2000 to cover all expenditures for salary and other costs. The federal government embarked on its first venture in the field of forestry with one employee on a shoestring budget.

The Division Under Hough

Hough tackled his assignment with energy and enthusiasm. Without funds for travel or hiring assistants, he had to compile his report by reading and correspondence. He was a tireless letter writer and succeeded in collecting an amazing amount of information from knowledgeable people both at home and abroad. The result was the monumental *Report Upon Forestry* published in 1878. This report is a comprehensive collection of miscellaneous forestry information, varying from the trivial to the highly significant but representing a variable compilation of contempoary understanding of the subjects treated. A second *Report Upon Forestry,* published in 1880, focused primarily on U.S. exports and imports of forest products and the timber trade of Canada. Hough's third and final report in 1882 focused on forest fires. With respect to timber on the public lands, he strongly endorsed the concept of a reservation policy. The report also vigorously urged the establishment of forest experiment stations in various parts of the country. Hough's efforts contributed to public appreciation of the importance of the country's forest resources. In addition to his official reports, Hough wrote a book entitled *The Elements of Forestry* in 1882, the first American textbook on the subject.

Fernow Takes Over

In 1886, Congress statutorily recognized the Division of Forestry. That same year, Bernhard Edward Fernow became its chief. His arrival at that critical point was significant; he was probably the only man in the country qualified for the office. He was the first professionally trained resource manager to engage in the practice of forestry in this country.

Fernow was trained at the well-known school of forestry at Muenden in Western Prussia. Several years of practical experience followed in the diverse forests of Silesia, Brandenburg, and East Prussia. He came to the United States in 1875 and married a woman to whom he had become engaged while she was visiting Germany. He became a citizen of the United States in 1883.

Prior to his appointment in the federal service, Fernow had managed 15,000 acres of hardwoods supplying charcoal for an ironworks; he also traveled extensively to study American forest conditions. He first came to the attention of the growing group interested in forestry matters at the American Forestry Congress at Cincinnati in 1882, when he read a paper. He later served as secretary to the congress for several years.

With Fernow's advent, the work of the Division of Forestry took a new slant. While the division continued to be primarily a bureau of information and investigation, the fact that its activities were now under the direction of a professional forester changed its tone. In particular, Fernow stressed forest management as a much broader set of concerns than forest "culture," which had come to mean little more than reforestation by tree planting.

Under Fernow's direction, the research work of the division intensified. It covered all of forestry, which he described as resting on three main bases: (1) scientific, including forest biology, timber physics, soil physics, and soil chemistry; (2) economic, including statistics, technology (applied timber physics), and forest policy; and (3) practical, including forest organization, management, regulation, and harvest. An important innovation was the inauguration of research in "timber physics," which Fernow defined as comprising "not only the anatomy, the chemical composition, the physical and mechanical properties of wood, but also its diseases and defects and knowledge of the influences and conditions which determine structural, physical, chemical, mechanical, and technical properties." The new field, he pointed out, had economic as well as scientific utility since "the properties upon which the use of wood, its technology, is based should be well known to the forest manager if he wishes to produce a crop of given quality useful for definite purposes" (Dana, 85). These endeavors are so familiar to modern forestry professionals that it is difficult to imagine a forestry movement that excluded them. Fernow, however, spent much of his career proselytizing for a concept of management that included more than merely growing trees.

German Influence on American Resource Management

German ideas were extremely influential in this country during the last half of the nineteenth century. American universities and the civil service are two familiar institutions in which German concepts were formative. German experience is also reflected in American forestry and resource management. Although Bernhard Fernow led the early movement in behalf of professional forestry, he was not alone. Carl Schenck, Carl Schurz, Gifford Pinchot, and the second chief of the Forest Service, Henry A. Graves, were also trained in Germany.

Sustained yield is the basic idea which characterized Fernow's approach to forest management. It continues to be so unquestioningly accepted by contemporary American foresters and citizens alike that it is difficult to view the concept as a product of nineteenth-century German social and economic conditions. The assumptions which were the cornerstone of German forest management were brought here and personified by Fernow and institutionalized by Pinchot, Graves, and generations of their followers and students.

The basic facts of German forestry when Fernow, Pinchot, Schurz, Graves, and others studied were threefold: Land was scarce, trees were correspondingly scarce, and yet they appeared to be virtually indispensable to the nation's life, economy, defense, and survival. Further, Germany was a densely populated country with a clear social hierarchy and plentiful labor. These circumstances led to several assumptions concerning criteria for forest management: scarcity, stability, and certainty.

> 1 As the product of a limited land base, wood is *scarce;*
> 2 wood is a necessity for which there will always be a demand, and because of unchanging social patterns and consumption patterns, the demand for wood is *stable;*
> 3 because wood is scarce and demand is stable, the appropriate standards for forest management are *certain:* limit the consumption of wood to the growth potential of the forest [Bennett, 5–20].

German foresters developed a technique for managing forests under conditions of scarcity, stability, and certainty. When their techniques were brought to this country, the prevailing social and economic conditions were radically different from those of the Continent. Land was not scarce, timber was not scarce, the social structure was fluid, and new sources of supply were constantly being brought within economic reach. Moreover, consumption patterns, utilization, and technology were constantly changing.

The most enduring and destructive residue of these misplaced assumptions is the physical-volumes approach to forest resource allocation. Even today this preoccupation fosters inappropriate concern with the depletion of material—saw logs, Douglas fir, or "virgin" timber. Moreover, it leads us to think in terms of annual physical production and consumption without regard to price. The forestry profession has always emphasized simply growing more trees without sufficient emphasis on the costs involved, the utilization of the growth, or the use-life of the products (Olson, 190–91). Nontimber uses of the forests have been covered by parity of logic or force of necessity, but the basic preoccupation with physical supply and unrelenting demand remains. These erroneous assumptions were introduced uncritically as part of a wholly laudable effort to bring order out of the chaos that characterized American public land policy. However, the assumptions must be recognized as such and their current validity and utility questioned. Interestingly, Fernow was among the first to recognize the limitations of German forestry in the American setting. Discussing the issue of whether or not forestry could be profitable for private American landowners, Fernow reflected on experience in his homeland and concluded:

> If, then, in a country with dense population, where in many places every twig can be marketed, with settled conditions of market, with no virgin woods which could cheaply be exploited and come into advantageous competition with costlier materials produced on managed properties, with the cost of labor low and the prices for wood comparatively high—if under such conditions the returns for the expenditure of money, skill, intellect in the production of wood crops is not more promising, it would seem hopeless to develop the argument of profitableness in a country where all these conditions are the reverse, and a businessman considers 6 percent investment no sufficient inducement [Fernow, 21]

Fernow suggested that entrepreneurs in fields such as mining, paper, or charcoal manufacture or the railroads, which were dependent for their main business on a constant flow of timber, would be the only nongovernment groups which could afford an investment in silviculture (Fernow, 22–23).

FORESTRY AND PRIVATE OWNERS

Fernow's analysis is in harmony with contemporary private landowners' and loggers' assessment of the German assumptions. With one small but much discussed exception, forest management found little support among private landowners.

The small exception is, of course, Gifford Pinchot's work on the Vanderbilt estate in western North Carolina in the early 1890s. Gifford Pinchot, the enthusiastic and charismatic son of a wealthy and prominent Pennsylvania family, was encouraged by his father to study forestry in Europe after he graduated from Yale. He then embarked on one of the most notable careers of public service in American history. Pinchot studied forestry in Nancy, France, and then engaged in extensive field studies in Germany. In spite of this training, Pinchot's consummate skills were political. Immediately upon returning from his studies abroad, he secured a position as forester on Cornelius Vanderbilt's North Carolina Biltmore estate and began his prodigious efforts to demonstrate the virtues of forest management.

Pinchot's work at Biltmore, and later on the much larger Pisgah Forest, included the management of the forest itself, establishment of forest plantations, building up a forest nursery and an arboretum, and the preparation of a forestry exhibit for the Chicago World's Fair of 1893. All trees to be removed in either harvest cuttings or improvement cuttings were marked prior to cutting, and special attention was paid to conducting logging operations with the least possible damage to young growth. "Thus," wrote Pinchot,

> Biltmore Forest became the beginning of practical forestry in America. It was the first piece of woodland in the United States to be put under a regular system of forest management whose object was to pay the owner while improving the forest. As Dr. Fernow wrote me on July 20, 1893, forest management has not been put into operation on any other area in this country except Biltmore! [Dana, 94].

Pinchot's characteristic enthusiasm for his own endeavors notwithstanding, the general assessment of "practical forestry" among loggers was less positive.

The limited success of the forest management movement on private lands is indicative of general attitudes within the lumbering and woodworking industries. Apart from an understandable interest in fire control and other methods of protecting standing timber, there was little interest. J. E. Defebaugh, editor of *The Timberman,* assessed the situation bluntly at an American Forestry Association meeting in 1893. He stated that lumbermen and woodsworkers had no interest in forest preservation and culture. The reasons he cited were economic. Defebaugh argued that it was useless to accuse lumbermen of destroying the forests: "The invective is misdirected and wasted, because the lumberman, as such, is . . . but a part of a commercial and industrial system the blame for which must be divided among the fifteen millions of our voting population . . ." (Dana, 75). Defebaugh reminded his listeners of the economic law that controls the proportioning of the factors of production: "Where men and not materials are the chief resource of a country, there men are cheap; where natural resources are abundant in proportion to population, there these resources are cheap and men are dear." Forest culture in this country, in his judgment, would become feasible only when "the forest area is small in proportion to population" (Dana, 75). The wisdom of Defebaugh's analysis has become apparent. It preordained that forestry for the next sixty years would be essentially a government undertaking.

FOREST RESERVES: ACTION AND CONFUSION

Diverse government and public concern with the rapid and frequently wasteful depletion of the nation's natural resources led to the first decisive action in the field of forestry in the 1890s. In 1891, Congress enacted a measure which established a comprehensive policy for retaining public land under public control. This was the earliest indication that the federal government would continue to hold significant amounts of land to accomplish broad public goals.

Early Proposals for Forest Reserves

The first general bill on forest reserves was introduced in 1876 by Representative Granberry Fort of Illinois "for the preservation of the forests of the national domain adjacent to the sources of the navigable rivers and other streams of the United States." Nothing came of this measure or similar ones introduced during the next ten years. However, congressmen annually introduced and debated a growing diversity of proposals to amend the Timber Culture Act; to expand the Free Timber Act; to establish schools of forestry; or to establish classification, sales, or reservation systems for timberlands in general or specifying for special timber species, watersheds, or other areas. Well over 200 bills were proposed and numerous ones passed before the Reserve Act of 1891 was agreed to.

Several major proposals were extensively debated and give an indication of the concepts current at the time. A detailed plan for the reservation and administration of the public timberlands was prepared in 1887 by Edward A. Bowers, a lawyer who later became Commissioner of the General Land Office. He became intimate with Fernow and other leaders in the forestry movement and served for a while as secretary of the American Forestry Association. He recommended the withdrawal from entry of "all the public lands valuable in any degree for timber or their forest growth." The reservations would then be administered by a Forestry Bureau, an elaborate agency established to administer an equally elaborate system of timber licenses at an initial annual cost of $500,000 (Bowers, 2). Bowers's plan was transmitted to Congress at its request in April, 1888, but was not seriously considered.

Subsequently, Fernow in collaboration with Bowers and others had prepared a bill for the protection and administration of forests on the public domain. The bill, which became known as the Hale Bill, resembled Bowers's earlier proposals. It provided for the classification of public timberlands into those primarily valuable for agriculture (which should be opened for home-steading) and those more valuable for forest purposes than for cultivation and suitable for commercial utilization. It also called for a category of areas primarily valuable as "protection forests" which would be reserved from all utilization. The timber-management-oriented schemes were simply too grandiose to find favor in Congress, though numerous proposals for protecting watersheds, timber, and forests generally were introduced annually.

However, even as the passage of the Forest Reserve Act came closer to reality, Congress was taking related steps in other areas which seriously confuse the meaning of the term "forest reserve." Developments involving the 1864 cession of Yosemite Valley to the state of California provides a case in point. In 1890, Congress established federal reserves which ultimately became parts of Sequoia, General Grant, and Yosemite national parks. The bill was debated and passed as a "forest reservation" in California, but the reserve it created surrounded lands ceded to the state for state park purposes. The land is explicitly labeled as a forest reservation, but it required the Secretary to make rules necessary to "provide for the preservation from injury of all timber, mineral deposits, natural curiosities or wonders within said reservation, and their retention in their natural condition." Thus, it is not clear that in passing the Forest Reserve Act of 1891 Congress was contemplating forest management as we now know it. It is probable, in fact, that forest reservations were intended to establish parklike preserves (Miller, 290–98).

Forest Reserve Act of 1891

In the closing days of the 1891 legislative session, both houses passed lengthy revisions of the general land laws which they had been considering for many years. When the two bills went to a conference committee where differences between them were to be ironed out, neither referred to forest reservations. When a final bill emerged from the conference committee, its final section contained the following provision:

> Section 24. That the President of the United States may, from time to time, set apart and reserve, in any State or Territory having public lands wholly or in part covered with timber or undergrowth, whether of commercial value or not, as public reservations, and the President shall, by public proclamation, declare the establishment of such reservations and the limits thereof.

The conference report reached Congress on February 28, 1891, four days before final adjournment. In the Senate, Senator Plumb of Kansas insisted on speedy consideration and the bill passed with little comment. In the House, Representative McRae of Arkansas objected to section 24 on the ground that it gave the President too much power and that no one could foresee its consequences. Representative Dunnell of Minnesota, long an advocate of forest protection measures, insisted that the bill should be held until it could be studied in print. Representative Payson of Illinois assured the House that there was no danger of the President's going too far and that, if he did, Congress could easily pass a joint resolution or a bill opening to settlement any lands which the President reserved. That ended the discussion. The bill did not come before the House again until the closing hours of the session on March 2, when it was passed without further debate. It was signed by the President on March 3.

Section 24 authorizing the President to set aside forest reserves was attached to the bill in violation of the rule forbidding the inclusion of any new material in a conference committee report. It is unclear how it came about because the legislative history is, like the history of many bills discussed above, skimpy by comparison with present-day standards. Historians have combed the records trying to identify the author of section 24 to little avail. Secretary of the Interior Noble, Fernow, Bowers, John Muir, and numerous congressmen and senators who worked on forestry matters for long years would all seem to deserve recognition for their efforts. The section was prepared in considerable haste, as is reflected in the fact that it is not even a complete sentence. The verbs "set apart and reserve" are not followed by any objects. This grammatical slip has not led to any question as to the validity of reserves made under power granted to the President by the act, but the intent of Congress in authorizing the reservations continues to be problematic (Fairfax and Tarlock).

Confusion Surrounding Meaning of the Act

One of the obvious problems in assessing the intent of section 24 is that it passed as the least-discussed segment of a complex array of other provisions. The 1891 Land Law Revision repealed the much lamented Timber Culture Act and the Preemption Act. That and section 24 constituted important progress in forest protection. On the other hand, the 1891 act also extended the provisions of the Free Timber Act and the Timber and Stone Act to all public land states (Kirkland, 71), which clearly spread opportunities for graft and destruction. On balance, therefore, the legislation is mixed—a typical congressional compromise—and it is difficult to read into the bill as a whole any clear commitment to conservation, preservation, parks, or forest management.

Furthering the confusion about section 24, this major step in the redirection of public land policy was taken by Congress with less discussion and debate than one might anticipate. Because section 24 emerged in the conference committee report immediately prior to passage, many have assumed that the measure passed accidentally, unintentionally, or without full appreciation in Congress of the ramifications of the enactment. Such conclusions have been cited and accepted in almost every major discussion of the issue since 1920. However, in the light of more recent investigations of the subject, these conclusions seem sweeping and unsupportable. The concept of forest reservations, though tacked onto the 1891 bill by the conference committee, was a familiar and much discussed issue. Congress frequently made reservations from the public domain for numerous purposes, and the President had long been recognized as having independent executive authority to make reservations apart from any specific authorization from Congress. Section 24, then, merely puts congressional encouragement behind a *general* reservation program that had, in fact, been going forward on a piecemeal basis for twenty years.

The idea that section 24 was thrust upon an unwilling Congress is usually bolstered with another set of assertions which have also crept into the store of "common knowledge" on the forest reserves: that when the President began to exercise the authority formalized in section 24, the West "declared war upon the reserves" (Ise, 130). Exactly the opposite is true. The contemporary press was apparently as comfortable as was Congress with section 24; it excited almost no comment, in the West or elsewhere, when it passed. There were no recriminations or dire forebodings about the disastrous implications of the law. Most of the reserves established between 1891 and 1897 were, in fact, created upon petition from the citizens in the area of the reserves to do so (Kirkland, 166–167). Moreover, in spite of the fact that two presidents had set aside nearly 13 million acres of reserves by 1893, Congress made no move to rescind the reserves or the authority granted in section 24 through subsequent legislative action.

President Harrison issued the first proclamation under the 1891 act less than a month after it passed. He set aside the Yellowstone Park Forest Reservation and thereby achieved the long-sought enlargement of Yellowstone National Park. During the next two years he proclaimed fourteen additional reservations in various parts of the West, bringing the total gross area to more than 13 million acres. Before the end of 1893, President Cleveland set aside another 4.5 million acres, but thereafter he took no further action because of the lack of any provision for the protection or administration of the reserves.

Toward Forest Administration

In the absence of any specific authorization for their management, Secretary of the Interior Noble believed that creation of the reservations withdrew them not only from sale and entry but from any form of utilization. In the 1891 Annual Report of the Department of the Interior, the Secretary "urgently recommended that Congress take proper action to have the reservations . . . established as national parks or granted to the states to be preserved unimpaired and used for the benefit of the public only" (Report, p. xiv). Congress had not, however, provided for protection from fire and trespass. Establishment of forest reserves therefore did not inaugurate the protection of forest management which is now frequently and erroneously associated with the passage of section 24. On the other hand, withdrawing the land from *all* use was opposed by settlers, miners, stock raisers, and lumbermen who wanted access to the reserved lands. The situation satisfied no one.

Numerous proposals that would meet the legitimate complaints of both supporters and opponents of the reserves by clarifying their status and purposes were discussed in Congress and among interested public groups. Between 1891 and 1897, no less than twenty-seven bills dealing with forest reserves were introduced. The most frequently heard proposal was to authorize the army to protect the reserves, as had been done in Yellowstone National Park. Charles Sargent, one of the most important citizen/scientists active in the debate, suggested that a forestry curriculum be established at West Point to inform young officers about the fundamentals of forest protection and management. Several bills introduced by Representative McRae of Arkansas received the most attention. After several years of intense discussion of the use or nonuse of the reserves, Congress had resolved most of the basic issues in favor of protective regulation of limited forest use. The basic goal of the carefully wrought compromise was to authorize the Secretary to regulate limited use of the reserves without altering their basic purpose, which was watershed protection. In 1895, slightly different versions of McRae's bill passed in both houses of Congress. Unfortunately, McRae was called away due to illness in his family; and, without his leadership, conference committee efforts to resolve the differences between the two bills before the congressional session ended were not successful.

Forest Commission of the National Academy of Sciences

The following year, Secretary of the Interior Hoke Smith requested recommendations regarding forest policy from the National Academy of Science. The academy had been formed in 1862 to bring together outstanding scientists for the purpose of advising government. Smith asked for the academy's "official expression" on three key points: (1) the practicality of preserving forestland; (2) the influence of forests on climate, soil, and water; and (3) specific legislation which would resolve the existing ambiguous situation. The Secretary wanted the information within two weeks, before Congress adjourned, but it took that long for President Gibbs of the academy to respond that time and money were required to establish a commission to study the matter. He appointed a committee, commonly known as the Forest Commission, to make an inquiry and report to Secretary Smith. Congress provided $25,000 to defray expenses, and the whole undertaking delayed legislative action for another year.

President Cleveland urged the commission to concentrate on legislative recommendations which he could include in his Annual Report to Congress. The National Academy of Science and the commission's chairman, Charles Sargent, were not, however, to be rushed. After a three-month tour of the West and several months of delay due to Sargent's house having burned down, the commission decided to delay legislative proposals and recommend instead that Cleveland designate thirteen new forest reserves before leaving office in March 1897 (Kirkland, 221–27). Many advocates of forest management believed that the new reserves would generate pressure which would force Congress to act on the matter. Since Congress had been on the verge of enacting a measure and delayed further action pending receipt of the commission's report, this tactic seems questionable.

The commission studied and dallied so long that its recommendations arrived too late to be influential in congressional consideration of reserve administration. The major importance of the AAAS effort, aside from the thirteen Cleveland reserves, is probably its contribution to the emergence of Gifford Pinchot in the politics of forestry. Headstrong, impatient, and self-assured, Pinchot was intensely frustrated by the ponderous pace of the committee's activities. Being a member of the commission did, however, give him experience, exposure, and an opportunity to begin efforts to build the forest reserve into a national system of managed forests.

Cleveland Celebrates Washington's Birthday

Just prior to the close of his days in office, President Cleveland adopted the tactics of the Forest Commission. On February 22, 1897, he issued proclamations creating thirteen new reserves with a gross area of 21.3 million acres, which more than doubled the existing area of reserves. His action came without warning and was not accompanied by a proposal, from the commission or the administration, for the administration of the reserves. Moreover, the proposals were made on the basis of inadequate studies by eastern academics (Pinchot being a partial exception to this characterization) and without consultation with a single governor or elected representative from the affected areas. Five of the recommended forests had not even been visited by the commission (Rakestraw, 65). The prophesied reaction materialized immediately and perhaps more violently than anyone had anticipated.

Angry Reaction to Cleveland Reserves

President Cleveland's action set off a virtually unanimous burst of anger in Congress. An amendment was added to an appropriations bill then under consideration in the Senate which would restore the February 22 reservations to the unreserved public domain. This amendment was promptly approved, but the House failed to concur and requested a conference. During the debate on the conference committee report, Representative Lacey of Iowa offered an amendment which included several features of the 1895 McRae bill plus a provision giving the President power to modify or revoke any executive order establishing any forest reserve. Much of the antagonism to the Cleveland reserves stemmed from the fact that, unlike the previous reservations, Cleveland's final thirteen were hastily and improvidently drawn, including not only numerous towns, cities, and important developments, but millions of acres of land suitable for agriculture. Granting the President authority to modify the reserve boundaries could lead to elimination of these unfortunate inclusions. Reserve defenders hoped that this possibility would mollify the angry critics. Surprisingly, it did. The rider which passed omitted all reference to revoking the reserves and simply authorized the President to modify or abolish forest reserves. In this form, it passed both houses of Congress. However, as President-elect McKinley rode toward the White House to be inaugurated, Cleveland refused to sign the appropriations measure. His pocket veto created a double crisis for the new President: Not only was the forest reserve conflict reignited, but Cleveland had left the government without funds with his appropriations bill veto.* Consequently, soon after the inauguration, President McKinley called a special session of Congress to provide funds for the operation of the government. At this special session, the legislation which those seeking protection and administration of the public timberlands had been urging for twenty years was finally passed.

Bills for Administration of the Reserves

Early in the special session, Senator Pettigrew of South Dakota introduced an amendment to the sundry civil appropriations bill incorporating most of the features of the McRae bill, which had passed in 1895. Major opposition to the bill came from western irrigation interests. They believed that any use of the forests undercut their primary purpose which, they thought, was to protect watersheds. Watershed interests were particularly hostile to grazing and timber harvesting uses of the reserves. Western representatives supportive of commodity uses of the forests were joined by forest management advocates and many preservationists, who feared the reserves would be lost entirely unless provisions which recognized the legitimate aspirations of western settlers were made. Unfortunately, the act, which had almost passed in 1895, did not pass again until the Cleveland reserves were suspended and a "lieu lands" provision was added. The lieu lands provision, which will be discussed below in detail, gave settlers in designated reserves the opportunity to select other land parcels outside the reserve and gave rise to some of the most spectacular land frauds in history. This provision, plus the temporary reopening of the Cleveland reserves to settlement, might leave one wishing that Cleveland had not vetoed the relatively innocuous provisions which passed in the first blush of anger over

*Most of the early forestry legislation was indeed passed just before the end of the session in *March*; McKinley was also inaugurated in March. In 1933, the Twentieth Amendment to the Constitution changed the nation's political calendar and made noon, January 20, inauguration day for presidential terms of office. By the same amendment, opening day for Congress was set on January 3.

the 21-million acre additions. On the plus side, however, congressional action in 1897 also resolved some of the confusion regarding the nature, purposes, and administration of the forest reserves.

After disagreements between the two houses had been ironed out by a conference committee, the bill was approved by the President and became law on June 4, 1897. In its final form, it is the main statutory basis for national forest management by today's Forest Service.

Purposes of the Forest Reserves

The major accomplishments of the act were that it defined the purpose of forest reserves and authorized the Secretary of the Interior to establish rules for their utilization. Three basic purposes of the forest reserves are defined in the act: (1) to "preserve and protect the forest within the reservation"; (2) "for the purpose of securing favorable conditions of water flows"; and (3) "to furnish a continuous supply of timber for the use and necessities of the people of the United States." The basic theme of the legislation is a compromise between preservation and use, protective administration of the reserves through regulation of use and occupancy.

Two types of questions have arisen about the purpose of the reserves. Generally, when the Forest Service has undertaken new programs such as recreation management, which are not specifically mentioned in the statute, the agency has had to find statutory authority for its expenditures. Second, the question of federal purposes behind the reservation has recently become central in determining the extent of water rights attaching to the reserved lands. In defending itself against the charge that an activity was unwarranted by the law, the agency has typically pointed to the broad grant of authority inherent in the first purpose, to "preserve and protect the forest within the reservation."

Regulation of Occupancy and Use

The Forest Service also points to the fact that the Secretary was granted broad authority "to make such rules and regulations and establish such services as will insure the objects of such use, namely, to regulate their occupancy and use and to preserve the forests thereon from destruction." The agency maintains that the rule-making authority granted to the Secretary is comprehensive. Those seeking to curtail Forest Service activities maintain that the authority to make rules did not expand the purposes for which the forests were established and, hence, for which rules could be made. The question was first raised regarding regulation of grazing use of the forests.

Timber Sale Provision

A separate section of the act authorizes the Secretary to sell timber. The Secretary can make sales "for the purposes of preserving the living and growing timber . . . under rules as he shall prescribe. . . ." Congress specifically limited cutting to "the dead, matured or large growth of trees found upon such forest reserves as may be compatible with the utilization of the forests thereon." The timber, having been "marked and designated" prior to sale, must then be "cut and removed under the supervision" of a secretarial designee. The section also provides for advertising sales and prohibits export of the timber from the state or territory in which the reserve is located. All the words about the sale of timber—mature, dead, large growth of, marked and designated, cut and removed—were uncontested for nearly eighty years. Not until 1973 in the critical Monogahela litigation did the courts focus on the meaning of those words.

Three other sections—the right-to-access provision, the law enforcement authority grant, and the infamous lieu lands provision—precipitated immediate problems. The act maintained state authority over violation of state law on the reserves by providing that civil and criminal jurisdiction within forest reserves should remain unchanged except as regarding the punishment of offenses against the United States. The intent was that states should not lose jurisdiction nor state inhabitants their rights, privileges, and duties because of the establishment of the reserves. However, the act did not provide any means for the arrest of persons violating the laws or regulations for the protection of the reserves. In 1897 and subsequently, Congress saw constitutional objections or feared that the power might give rangers "additional means of annoyance and irritation." Finally, in February 1905, Congress passed an act authorizing the arrest by any officer of the United States, without warrant, of any person taken in the act of violating the laws or regulations relating to the forest reserves and the national parks. This was the first authorization for a civil officer to make an arrest without a court warrant. It greatly facilitated protection of the reserves.

Lieu Lands

A second provision, providing free access to settlers within the reserves, seemed fair and necessary at the time of passage but has become controversial in recent years. Full access includes construction of roads and other improvements necessary for settlers to reach their homes and utilize their property. The Forest Service must presently allow roads to be built to provide access to forest homesteads, mining claims, and various inholdings. Just how much access is required by this provision if the homestead of 1897 is converted into a vacation resort or condominum in 1977 is frequently hotly contested.

The lieu lands provision was even more destructive, and it became controversial immediately. The provision seemed reasonable; it authorized the settler or owner of a tract in a designated forest reserve to relinquish it to the government and in lieu thereof to select a tract of vacant land open to settlement outside the reserve. Unfortunately, this effort to protect settlers and solidify the forest reserve title proved to be a bonanza for land grabbers. An unpatented claim within a reserve could be exchanged for clear title to land outside the reserves. In order to capitalize on this "opportunity," unscrupulous land speculators successfully urged the creation of reserves simply because they contained worthless lands claimed by the speculators, which were then traded for clear title to valuable properties on the unreserved public domain. Within a year, the Secretary of the Interior and the Commission of the General Land Office were urging its repeal.

Congress was slow to act. In 1900 and 1901, it limited lieu selections to vacant, nonmineral, surveyed public lands subject to homestead entry. These acts improved the situation but fell far short of stopping abuses under the privilege. Outright repeal of the provision did not come until March 3, 1905, about a month after the transfer of the reserves to the Department of Agriculture.

Obviously, the 1897 legislation was not perfect. Legislation never is, particularly when Congress is attempting to reach a compromise acceptable to the representatives of divergent interests. For the third time, a major forward step in the development of a national forest policy had been taken by attaching a rider to a bill with an entirely different primary purpose. Although the Organic Act represented a compromise, it has proved in practice to be quite a serviceable piece of legislation. Its really undesirable provisions—those permitting lieu selections—were repealed shortly thereafter. Other problems were slow to arise and, until the late 1960s, were handled administratively. The major victory, establishing the principle of retaining and administering parts of the public domain for public purposes, was never threatened by the inadequacies of the act.

Early Management of the Forest Reserves

Within a month of the passage of the act, the Department of the Interior issued rules and regulations for the administration of the forest reserves. The first rules pertained to the exclusion of all sheepherding except in Washington and Oregon. No enforcement funds were available, however, since the act had not provided anything specifically for their protection and administration. Congress appropriated $75,000 for this purpose for the fiscal year 1899. The principles defining early management of the reserves are familiar to all those who have knowledge of the present-day Forest Service.

Each forest reserve was placed in the charge of a forest supervisor, under whom the fieldwork was handled by forest rangers. The reserves were grouped into districts, each in the charge of a superintendent through whom the supervisors reported to the General Land Office in Washington. Forest officers were promptly given specific instructions to prepare detailed reports on fires, sheep grazing, timber sales, timber trespass, and areas proposed for reservation.

On November 8, 1901, Secretary Hitchcock sent the Commissioner of the

General Land Office a detailed outline of the principles and practice which, he had concluded, should govern the administration of national forest reserves. Hitchcock's plan included such items as the following:

> every effort should be made to create an *esprit de corps* among the forest officers. . . .
> [Grazing] permits should run for five years. Residents should have precedence in all cases over tramp owners and owners from other states. . . .
> Local questions should be decided on local grounds and on their own merits in each separate case. . . .
> The sale of mature live timber whose removal will benefit the forest should be encouraged. . . .
> The cutting of unmarked timber should be absolutely prohibited. . . . [Dana, 110–11].

Secretary Hitchcock instructed Commissioner Hermann to "note carefully the plan submitted and take such steps as may be necessary to carry the same into effect." The reason these principles and policies have a familiar ring to them is not hard to discover. Working behind the scenes to control the reserves, with the full cooperation of the Secretary of the Interior, Gifford Pinchot wrote the plan. Pinchot had succeeded Fernow as head of the Bureau of Forestry in 1898, and he began a strenuous campaign to institute use-oriented management of the reserves. His position in the Department of Agriculture, while the reserves were managed in the Department of the Interior, required that his influence be indirect. However, he soon enlisted the aid of the Secretary of the Interior in supporting a transfer of the reserve to Agriculture.

Weaknesses in Administration

The intentions of the Department of the Interior were good, and the policies which they established were written by Pinchot himself. Why then was Pinchot so adamant that the reserves be transferred out of Interior? The best argument to be made in behalf of the transfer rested on inadequacies of the General Land Office. Inevitable difficulties encountered in establishing effective administration of the forest reserves were compounded by the excessive red tape and emphasis on paperwork of the General Land Office and its susceptibility to political influence. Interior Secretary Hitchcock was aware of the imperfections in the administration of the forest reserves. In an attempt to remedy the situation, he decided in 1901 to create a Forestry Division in the General Land Office to handle the reserves. A number of foresters, including some from the Bureau of Forestry in the Department of Agriculture, took positions with the General Land Office. All was not smooth sailing, however. Politics and inertia

made thoroughgoing reform difficult, but the real barrier to Interior's effectiveness was Pinchot's insistence that the reserves be transferred.

Pinchot began advocating transfer of the reserves almost immediately
after he was made Chief of the Division of Forestry in the Department of
Agriculture. His unrelenting efforts to have the administration shifted to where
they would be managed under his formal supervision were strengthened by his
ability to secure Secretary of the Interior Hitchcock's strong endorsement of
the proposal. In 1901, just as Interior's Division of Forestry was getting
underway, Hitchcock noted that "the presence of properly trained foresters in
the Agricultural Department, as well as the nature of the subject itself, makes
the ultimate transfer, if found to be practicable, of the administration of the
forest reserves to the Department essential to the best interests, both of the
reserves and of the people who use them." With their own Secretary on record
for transfer, the General Land Office's Division of Forestry floundered.

SUMMARY

The first century of American independence was marked by steadily accelerating use of forest resources, with little effort on the part of either public or
private owners to check the destruction of the forests or to adopt methods of
forest management that would assure their perpetuation. Except for a few men
with professional training, such as Fernow, Sargent, Hough, Warder, Schurz,
and Schenk, even the meaning and the practical possibilities of forestry were
unknown to most of the population, including timberland owners and lumbermen. In general, the period was one of education and preparation. Through
the efforts of these relatively few devoted men, public interest was aroused; and
the way was paved for the adoption of a constructive federal forest policy. The
establishment and activities of the American Forestry Association and the
Division of Forestry in the Department of Agriculture led to even broader
concern with forest problems.

In 1891, a conference committee addition to general land law revision
authorized the President to establish forest reserves and began sweeping
changes in public land policy. Presidents Harrison and Cleveland promptly set
aside large areas as forest reserves, but confusion regarding the purposes of the
reserves and the failure of Congress to provide for their protection and administration created a situation that satisfied no one. Between 1891 and 1897,
Congress and the public debated numerous proposals for the future of the
reserves. Cleveland's precipitous reservation of 21 million acres during the
closing weeks of his administration ended the discussions with a crisis. Congress passed the generally constructive Forest Reserve Act on June 4, 1897.

It has become common practice to view the 1891 legislation as the start
of forest management and the national forest system. Subsequent events, rather
than conscious purpose or observable consensus at the time of passage, make

this a legitimate interpretation. Forest preservation for park and watershed protection was more clearly on people's minds than silviculture. The concern for watershed protection also belies the myth that the move toward conservation was a holy war between East and West or between the forces of good and evil. Many Westerners and Easterners wanted the forests preserved, not managed; and grazing interests shut out of the reserves shared the forestry movement's enthusiasm for opening and managing the reserved lands. Running through and dominating congressional concern for these conflicting priorities is concern for homesteaders and actual settlers. Sincere and legitimate congressional efforts to keep land and resources available to settlers became, perhaps inevitably, the source of continuing land fraud, speculation, and monopoly.

From the start, the reserve policy was defended as a way to hold the lands away from unscrupulous operators so that all the people would benefit. At first, this appeared to imply that the land might eventually be opened to homestead (Miller, 24) or, conversely, held forever inviolate as a source of water. The reserve system, however, survived confusion and conflicting goals intact, and the stage was set for subsequent clarification of their ultimate purposes.

REFERENCES CITED

Behan, R. W. "Foresting and the End of Innocence." 81 *American Forests* 16 (1975).
————. "Political Popularity and Conceptual Nonsense: The Strange Case of Sustained Yield Forestry." Address, Northwestern School of Law Symposium on Federal Lands Policy, Portland, 1978.

Bennett, John David. "Economics and the Folklore of Forestry." Ph.D. dissertation, Syracuse University, 1968.

Bowers, Edward A. *Report Submitting a Plan for the Management and Disposition of the Public Timber Lands.* U.S. House of Representatives, 50th Congress, 1st Session, Executive Document 242. Washington, D.C.: Government Printing Office, 1888.

Cameron, Jenks. *The Development of Governmental Forest Control in the United States.* Baltimore, Md.: Johns Hopkins Press, 1928.

Fairfax, Sally K. and A. Dan Tarlock. "No Water For the Woods." 15 *Idaho Law Review* 89 (1979).

Fernow, Bernhard E. *Report Upon Forestry Investigations, 1877–1898.* Washington, D.C.: Government Printing Office, 1899.

Gould, E. M. "The Future of Forests in Society." Address, C. I. F. Annual Meeting, Toronto, 1964.

Greeley, William B. *Forests and Men.* New York: Doubleday and Company, 1951.

Hampton, H. Duane. *How the U.S. Cavalry Saved Our National Parks.* Bloomington: Indiana University Press, 1971.

Hough, Franklin B. *Report Upon Forestry,* vol. 1. Washington, D.C.: Government Printing Office, 1878.

Ise, John. *The United States Forest Policy.* New Haven, Conn.: Yale University Press, 1920

Kirkland, Herbert D. III. "The American Forests, 1864–1898: A Trend Toward Conservation." PhD. dissertation, University of Florida, 1971.

Miller, Joseph A. "Congress and the Origins of Conservation: Natural Resources Policy, 1865–1900." Ph.D. dissertation, University of Minnesota, 1973.

Nash, Roderick. *Wilderness and the American Mind,* Rev. ed. New Haven, Conn.: Yale University Press, 1973.

Olson, Sherry. *The Depletion Myth.* Cambridge: Harvard University Press, 1971.

Petulla, Joseph M. *American Environmental History,* preliminary ed. San Francisco: Boyd and Fraser Publishing Company, 1976.

Peyton, Jeannie. "Forestry Movement of the Seventies, in the Interior Department, Under Schurz." 18 *Journal of Forestry* 391 (1920).

Pinchot, Gifford. *Breaking New Ground.* New York: Harcourt, Brace and Company, 1947.

Rakestraw, Lawrence. "A History of Forest Conservation in the Pacific Northwest, 1891–1913." Ph.D. dissertation, University of Washington, 1955.

Randall, Charles E. "George Perkins Marsh: Conservation's Forgotten Man." 71 *American Forests* 20 (1965).

Robbins, Roy M. *Our Landed Heritage.* New York: Peter Smith, 1950.

Rogers, Andrew Denny III. *Bernhard Edward Fernow: A Story of American Forestry.* Princeton, N.J.: Princeton University Press, 1951

Smith, Henry Nash. *Virgin Land: The American West as Symbol and Myth.* Cambridge, Mass.: Harvard University Press, 1950.

Steen, Harold K. *The U.S. Forest Service: A History.* Seattle: University of Washington Press, 1977.

Stegner, Wallace. *Beyond the Hundredth Meridian: John Wesley Powell and the Second Opening of the West.* Boston: Houghton Mifflin Company, 1953.

Chapter 3

Conservation in Practice and Politics: The Golden Era of Roosevelt and Pinchot, 1898–1910

The period between 1898, when Pinchot took charge of the Division of Forestry, and 1910, when he was dismissed from his position as head of the Forest Service, constitutes the Golden Era of American Conservation history (Ise, chap. 4). Resource management issues were the touchstone of Theodore Roosevelt's vigorous presidency. Gifford Pinchot was the most prominent of the uniquely gifted and dedicated group of scientists, visionaries, and managers who surrounded the President and defined his administration's conservation program. After forty years of westward expansion accompanied by growing awareness of resource waste and depletion, the nation embarked on a series of bold new initiatives in resource management.

Conservation was part of, and perhaps the best expression of, the Progressive movement with which the Roosevelt administration is frequently associated. Social and political themes of the progressive era—reverence for scientific organization, technical competence and nonpartisan good government, and a strong commitment to supporting citizens against the trusts and monopolies—found their way into every aspect of conservation rhetoric and programs . The consistent underlying theme of Roosevelt's conservation rhetoric was to build homes on the public lands. In spite of this commitment, however, a major legacy of Roosevelt's administration is the large amount of public domain land reserved or withdrawn from entry by homesteaders or developers. Withdrawals and reservations were part of the conservationists' program that did not, in most instances, require congressional approval. Roosevelt's view of his executive authority was expansive, and the withdrawals and reservations satisfied his predisposition toward vigorous presidential activity.

Because Pinchot dominated the era, it is common and reasonable to view forestry matters as the heart of Roosevelt's undertakings, but forestry was just one aspect of the crusaders' dreams. They envisioned a self-supporting system of planned resource development on the federal lands. Following the recommendations of the Second Public Land Commission, established in 1903, Roosevelt supported vast developments for water power, irrigation, grazing, forestry, recreation, and wildlife resources. Although all their programs and principles still have not been adopted, the basic contours of resource management policy in the twentieth century were first embraced by Roosevelt and his conservationist associates.

Forestry was the area in which the movement achieved its most conspicuous and durable success. Under Pinchot's dynamic leadership, a profession was built and an organization established to bring scientific management to the federal forests. Although as head of the Division of Forestry Pinchot expressed concern with forestry on private lands, after the forest reserves were transferred to the Department of Agriculture in 1905, he put all his time and attention into building the Forest Service and its programs. His accomplishments were legendary. It is often overlooked, however, that the main users of the newly named national forests were stock raisers. Most of the important conflicts in early Forest Service history were over grazing issues. Nevertheless, the aura of the forester as planter and defender of stately forests was firmly established and became the crowning glory of Roosevelt's diverse conservation program.

Pinchot's success has led subsequent generations to view the Golden Era as a period of unbroken accomplishment and unmitigated enthusiasm for the administration's conservation initiatives. Nothing could be further from the truth. Conservation became a great national cause; but many, especially in the West, remained opposed to either the substance or the tactics of Roosevelt's ardent supporters (Ise, chap. 5, 8, and 9). Pinchot, the Forest Service, and the conservationists suffered severe setbacks in 1907, for example, when the President's authority to designate forest reserves in six Western states was withdrawn and the revolving fund which supported Forest Service activities without congressional review and appropriations was ended. The famous Governor's Conference of 1908 was less an expression of public support for Roosevelt's programs than an attempt to build public enthusiasm following the debacles of 1907. The meeting was an unqualified success, and the hoped-for support was forthcoming. Nevertheless, Roosevelt, Pinchot, and their programs continued to engender widespread controversy and suffered frequent setbacks and defeats.

The aura of the period is to be found less in its achievements than in the coherence of its vision. For the only time in American history, the executive branch of the federal government espoused an integrated program for the allocation and development of public resources. The interagency competition that has compromised subsequent administrations' efforts had not yet developed. Roosevelt's team was, in fact, a team, and they approached their tasks with the passion and devotion of true believers. Their vision was golden, and it is to their credit that so much of it has come to pass.

Unfortunately, the coherence of Roosevelt's administration did not survive the transition to his hand-picked successor, William Howard Taft. Taft was, among many other things, a federal judge both before and after his White House days; he served as chief justice of the Supreme Court for the decade before his death in 1930. Taft's view of the President's powers differed sharply from Roosevelt's. Where Roosevelt found means to justify the broadest conceivable exercise of presidential power, Taft interpreted his authorities narrowly, acting only where specifically authorized to do so. The freewheeling Roosevelt men immediately ran afoul of the new President. Angrily they charged that Taft had deserted his predecessor's standard. The facts do not seem to support the charges made by the dismayed Pinchot and his allies; but, in a series of heated controversies, the Progressive conservation leaders left the federal government. Dramatizing the collapse of the cooperation which had characterized Roosevelt's administration, Pinchot was forced to resign as Chief of the Forest Service after a protracted and divisive offensive against Taft's new Secretary of Interior failed to cause the Secretary's dismissal. The Ballinger-Pinchot controversy, as the unfortunate episode has become known, constitutes the opening round in the hostilities between the Departments of Agriculture and Interior that continue to complicate integrated management of federally administered resources.

THE VISION OF THE GOLDEN ERA

The Pinchot-Roosevelt Team

The marked progress toward management of the nation's resources that occurred during the first decade of the present century was due largely to effective teamwork on the part of two remarkable men—Gifford Pinchot and Theodore Roosevelt. Seldom has there been a more productive relationship between two people in high public office. Both loved the outdoors, preached and lived the strenuous life, enjoyed a fight, and were guided by high ideals of public service. They saw natural resources as assets to be used for the benefit of all the people, both present and future. To them, the struggle to stop destruction and waste and to prevent monopoly was much more than a resource management issue; it was a moral crusade. Their enthusiasm was so contagious that it inspired an almost fanatic devotion among their followers, both to the men themselves and to the causes they espoused.

The partnership was formed in the fall of 1901, shortly after Roosevelt became President following the assassination of McKinley. Pinchot and his friend Frederick H. Newell, an engineer in the Geological Survey, called on the new President to enlist his interest in the forest and water resources of the country. So successful was their mission that the President asked them to let him have some material on these subjects for inclusion in his first message to Congress.

That message proposed federal government construction of irrigation works for the reclamation of arid western lands and urged that the forest reserves be expanded and transferred from the Department of the Interior to the Department of Agriculture. Pinchot rapidly became one of Roosevelt's closest personal friends and most trusted advisers. Along with Newell, Secretary of the Interior James Garfield, Secretary of Agriculture James Wilson, W J McGee, and a host of less well known enthusiasts, Pinchot and Roosevelt brought resource issues to the forefront of national concern.

"Conservation" Acquires a New Meaning

It is impossible to define conservation in all its permutations and applications; yet, its underlying philosophy was clear to Roosevelt and his associates. It was not only preservation; it was wise use for the benefit of both present and future generations. What constituted wise use must be determined by economic, social, aesthetic, and moral considerations. Its goal was frequently stated in the vague slogan adopted by Pinchot: "the greatest good for the greatest number for the longest time" (Pinchot, 48). It dealt with all natural resources, recognized that each resource has a relation to every other resource, and aimed at developing an integrated program that would give each resource its proper place and its proper treatment in the large picture. The great strength of this view of conservation is that no one can disagree with its broad objectives. Its major weaknesses are understanding and applying the concept and agreeing upon priorities as theory is put into practice. It too readily may mean all things to all people. Roosevelt's conservation philosophy was expressed in a number of proposals to establish a system for planning and funding comprehensive federal resource development.

Reservations and Withdrawals

The basic building block of Roosevelt's conservation program was public domain retention. Through reservations and withdrawals, he attempted to secure federal ownership of all but the most obviously tillable lands. This policy of retention is superficially at variance with his commitment to building homes for the homesteader. All those who opposed Roosevelt made much of the homesteader theme. However, Roosevelt countered that the disposition statutes had been manipulated by fraudulent operators to the point that reservations and withdrawals actually protected the long-term interests of potential homesteaders. Resources that would be stolen by land speculators or destroyed through inappropriate development would be held in federal custody until they could be dedicated to uses serving the best interests of all the people.

Between 1905 and 1909, some 80 million acres of public lands thought to contain workable deposits of coal were withdrawn from entry by the Secretary of the Interior under instructions from President Roosevelt. The purpose was to protect the genuine prospector and to prevent monopolization of coal lands through fraudulent use of the homestead and other land laws to obtain valuable mineral lands. About half of the withdrawals were restored to entry when it was discovered through the classification process that they did not actually contain coal. In addition, Secretary of the Interior Garfield withdrew approximately 4.7 million acres of public lands in Wyoming, Utah, and Idaho from entry which were suspected of containing potash valuable for fertilizer. Under President Roosevelt, 4 million acres of oil lands were withdrawn from entry, and President Taft withdrew an additional 3 million acres during his first two years in office. At the very end of the Roosevelt administration, Secretary Garfield withdrew from entry nearly 3.5 million acres because of their potential as sites for the production of water power (Robbins, 366–368). Finally, by the time Roosevelt left office, large areas of public land had been reserved for national forests, national parks, monuments, and game refuges. These reservations and withdrawals were frequently made without explicit congressional authority and were the major focus of Roosevelt's critics.

Independent Funding

The second fundamental component of the conservationists' program was a financing system that would make resource development programs self-supporting. Oil, gas, coal, phosphate, and other valuable mineral lands would be leased to entrepreneurs for long-term development. Grazing districts would be established and allotments leased to stock raisers for a fair price. Timber would be managed for sustained production and sold to the highest bidder. In all instances, revenues generated by sale or lease of public resources would be used to fund administration and further development of the federal lands. Although this funding system may have appeal as a matter of frugality, its more significant aspects are political. Programs with independent funding are not subject to the appropriations process and can proceed unhampered by congressional machinations.

Scientific Management

The third characteristic of Roosevelt's approach was its emphasis on scientific management. In an era which valued technical competence and efficiency, the political independence of the resource programs was viewed as essential (Hays, chap. 8). Roosevelt's conservationists did not wish to deal with political boundaries or variables. This is not to suggest that Pinchot and his colleagues were apolitical. Quite the contrary; Pinchot was a master manipulator of public opinion and the political process. Rather, the leaders of the day saw technical questions as entirely separate from political ones, and their goal was scientific management of the nation's resources. They espoused comprehensive multipurpose resource planning. Frequently, the watershed was viewed as the basic planning unit, and all the resources within the watershed were to be managed as an interdependent system.

Second Public Lands Commission

One of the earliest and most comprehensive statements of Roosevelt's concerns regarding federal resource management came in the report of the Public Lands Commission which Roosevelt appointed in 1903. It was the commission's responsibility to report upon the condition, operation, and effect of the existing land laws and recommend needed changes.

The commission submitted two partial reports together with an extensive and informative appendix. It stated bluntly that "the present laws are not suited to meet the conditions of the remaining public domain" (Dana, 131). With respect to the theory that the major purpose in the disposal of the public lands was to place them in the hands of actual settlers, it stressed the fraudulent practices rampant under the disposition statutes and noted the obvious fact that the number of homes being built was vastly exceeded by the number of patents being granted. The commission proposed some specific reforms which were designed to eliminate fraud in land disposition and assure that the optimum use was made of public resources.

The commission recommended that the remaining public lands should be studied to identify those chiefly valuable for agriculture. Pending such classification, provision should be made for the government to hold the lands likely to be developed by actual settlers. Echoing the concerns of John Wesley Powell and the first Public Lands Commission, they urged that a homestead should be large enough to support a family, which meant that its size should vary in different localities.

The commission offered a comprehensive program for the unreserved public domain as well, recommending that the President should be authorized to establish grazing districts by proclamation. The proposed grazing districts should be administered and managed by the Secretary of Agriculture under rules including a moderate fee for grazing permits. The commission also recommended that provisions be made for the sale of timber on the unreserved public domain for which there was then no legal authority (Dana, 132).

Only two recommendations were made with respect to the forest reserves: (1) that lands primarily valuable for agriculture be opened to homestead entry with no opportunity for commutation and (2) that the lieu land provision of the act of 1897 be repealed. The government always lost under the latter provision which had given rise to speculation, scandal, and consolidation of timber holdings in the hands of large holders. Unscrupulous operators went so far as to attempt to have their worthless or denuded lands proclaimed forest reserves so that the owners could exchange them for valuable lands elsewhere. Fraudulent manipulation of the lieu lands provision contributed to western hostility to the forest reserves. In its place, the commission recommended that the government be authorized to buy private lands within the reserves which were needed for public purposes or that owners of such lands be permitted to exchange them for specified tracts of equal area and value outside of the reserves.

Action on Recommendations

Four of the commission's major recommendations were enacted into law—one of them after a lapse of fifty years. The lieu land provision was repealed in 1905 and a general exchange authority defined in 1922 (see p.125); forest homesteads were authorized in 1906, grazing districts were established in 1934, and authority to sell timber on the unreserved public domain was granted in 1955. Although immediate results were not spectacular, the commission did dramatize the administration's overriding concern with public land management.

ROOSEVELT'S WATER POLICY

Water management inevitably became the initial focus of Roosevelt's concern with public resources. Most of the public lands are located in the West, and their productivity is largely dependent on water management. There were two basic components of early water management policy: irrigation and navigation. The reservation of hydroelectric power sites was also a major concern, but the development of those sites was generally regarded as a private undertaking. Relatively early on it was recognized that irrigation and navigation required federal investment and direction. Irrigation, or the reclamation of arid lands, is the most important of these in the context of forest and range policy.

Before 1900, irrigation and reclamation policy consisted mainly of programs to encourage private parties or states to irrigate their lands. In 1866, Congress granted water owners free rights of way over public lands for the construction of ditches and canals. A decade later the Desert Land Act of 1877 was passed to encourage individuals to irrigate lands. In 1888, Congress instructed the Geological Survey to determine the extent to which the arid lands could be reclaimed by irrigation. The Geological Survey was authorized to reserve all lands that might be selected as sites for reservoirs and irrigation canals and all other lands capable of being irrigated as a result of the construction of such reservoirs and canals. John Wesley Powell, director of the Geological Survey, took advantage of this authority to withdraw 127 reservoir sites and more than 30 million acres of irrigable land. His action aroused so much protest that, in 1890, Congress restricted withdrawals to reservoir sites and, in 1891, to land actually needed for the construction and maintenance of reservoirs. The opportunity for comprehensive planning on the public domain was lost temporarily, but the concern for irrigation of dry lands remained (Stegner, chap. 5).

In 1894, the Cary Act was passed. It recognized the limitation of an irrigation program dependent upon the uncoordinated and underfunded effort of individual landholders and attempted to lure states into the field by promising them land in return for irrigation efforts. This program met with only limited success (Peffer, 20–21); and, by the end of the nineteenth century, it was clear that most irrigation projects which could be developed by individuals, private corporations, or even the states had already been undertaken. If further progress were to be made, the federal government would have to participate. Pressure from the Western states to do so was great, and Roosevelt notes in his autobiography that reclamation was the first concern of his new presidency (Peffer, 32). Support from the White House led to passage of the Reclamation Act of 1902, often known as the Newlands Act in honor of one of its major architects—Representative Francis G. Newlands of Nevada. It was the basis of all future government irrigation activities. The Reclamation Service was first organized in 1903 as a division of the Geological Survey, but in 1907 it was made a separate bureau. Frederick H. Newell, a close collaborator of both Roosevelt and Pinchot, was in charge of both organizations and continued to be the major force behind the irrigation movement for many years.

The provisions of the Newlands Act illustrate the major themes of Roosevelt's conservation program. Irrigation projects were to be funded initially with receipts from the sale of public lands. The Secretary of the Interior was authorized to withdraw lands which were to be irrigated by federal projects from all entry but homesteading. Homesteaders in the project area were limited to acquiring 160 acres of federally irrigated lands. This provision was intended to prevent wealthy speculators from buying up large blocks of irrigated lands. The limitation was never effectively enforced and provided impetus to many lawsuits in the 1960s and 1970s. The homesteaders were to be assessed for a share of the cost of the project and were to repay the government within ten years. This would free the original federal funds for further projects, and a revolving self-supporting fund was established to finance reclamation programs on the public domain (Peffer, 32). Irrigation was a major part of the comprehensive watershed development planning which Roosevelt espoused.

Inland Waterways Commission

Later in his term, Roosevelt expanded his water resource focus to include navigation. Under its constitutional power to regulate foreign and interstate commerce, Congress has always been concerned with the use of both coastal and interior waters for navigation. Since 1824, when Congress definitely assigned responsibility for the handling of internal improvements to the Army Corps of Engineers, development of rivers and harbors has been the major civilian activity of the corps. President Roosevelt took a broader approach to navigation in 1907 when he appointed an Inland Waters Commission. The commission was to prepare a comprehensive plan for the coordinated use of the water resources of the country, which would take into consideration "the relations of the streams to the use of all the great permanent natural resources and their conservation for the making and maintenance of prosperous homes" (Dana, 361–62).

The following February the commission reported, again echoing John Wesley Powell, that every river system is a unit from its source to its mouth and that it should be managed as such. Local interests should be considered in relation to regional and national interests. "Hereafter plans for the improvement of navigation in inland waterways, or for any use of these waterways in connection with interstate commerce, shall take account of the purification of the waters, the development of power, the control of floods, the reclamation of lands by irrigation and drainage, and all other uses of the waters or benefits to be derived from their control" (Dana, 362). The commission viewed water resource development comprehensively. It also struck the characteristic progressive note of warning against monopoly in the control of natural resources.

National Waterways Commission

In 1909, Congress created a National Waterways Commission to continue the work of its predecessor on questions pertaining to water transportation and the improvement of waterways. Its final report of March 1912 dealt at length with such subjects as impounding reservoirs, forest influences on waterways, and control of water power. After careful consideration of the many factors involved, the commission decided that "whatever influence forests may have upon precipitation, run-off, and erosion, it is evidently greatest in the mountainous regions where the rainfall is heaviest, slopes steepest, and run-off most rapid" (Dana, 362). It favored the protection and perpetuation of forests in such regions both for the influence they might have on runoff and erosion and for the production of timber on lands not suited to other purposes. It is also interesting in the light of subsequent developments to note that the commission concluded that the federal government "has no power to regulate the methods of farming or the cutting of timber on private lands" (Dana, 362). Any responsibility which the public may have in this area must be exercised by the states under their police power. Federal cooperation with states in the prevention of forest fires and the introduction of scientific methods were endorsed.

The commission took a crimped view of federal authority, recommending reliance on the state and private efforts favored by the Taft administration in which the commission reported. Nevertheless, the integrative view of water resource management is characteristic of Roosevelt's approach. The commission pointed out that the government had already undertaken to control water power development through its ownership of the public lands in two ways: (1) by withdrawing water power sites from entry and (2) by authorizing the Department of the Interior and the Department of Agriculture to make rules for the use of public lands.

Because water development was the way to western economic growth and to utilization of most of the public lands in the West, water policies and watershed management are the central focus of Roosevelt's conservation program. A number of other significant programs evince the diversity of concerns in the period.

PRESERVATION UNDER ROOSEVELT

Antiquities Act of 1906

Use rather than preservation dominated the Roosevelt approach to conservation, but the Antiquities Act was oriented toward preservation of cultural artifacts and objects of scientific importance. The act established a new type of federal reservation and authorized the President to establish national monuments by proclamation in order to protect areas of historic, prehistoric, or scientific interest. The reservations were to be limited to the smallest area compatible with the proper care and management of the objects to be protected. The Secretary of the department already having jurisdiction over the lands in question was to continue to administer the monuments. Because the monuments were administratively rather than congressionally established, the Antiquities Act provided a way rapidly to extend protected status to Indian ruins and other archeological sites which were being vandalized at a distressing rate. By 1910, twenty-three national monuments had been reserved in eleven states and Alaska, several of which were subsequently expanded to form national parks.

Preservation of Wildlife

Federal wildlife protection programs were also instituted during the Roosevelt years. The federal government's first recognition that it had any responsibility in connection with wildlife was directed at research. In 1871, Congress authorized the President to appoint a Commissioner of Fish and Fisheries to study the causes of the decrease in the supply of coastal and inland lake food fish. In 1886, similar concerns in a different field led to the establishment of the new Division of Economic Ornithology and Mammalogy. In 1896, this division became the Division of Biological Survey and, in 1905, the Bureau of Biological Survey. This group was primarily concerned with the economic impact of birds and mammals on agricultural crops.

Two major events of the Roosevelt era broadened that focus considerably. First, the Lacey Act of 1900 laid the foundation for active federal involvement in wildlife conservation. It was aimed primarily at prohibiting interstate trade in wild animals or birds which were taken or held in violation of the laws of the state from which or to which they were shipped. This statute was intended to protect plumage birds and bison, both of which were being harvested by market hunters, frequently to the point of extinction (Trevethen, chap. 11). More significantly, Roosevelt used both the 1891 forest reserve authority and the 1906 Antiquities Act to initiate a national system of game refuges.

These preservationist concerns notwithstanding, the major focus of the times was on the wise use of natural resources. Waste was deplored, and scientific management and sound development were everywhere encouraged. Nowhere in the Roosevelt years or subsequently did these conservationist themes enjoy more complete expression than in the development of forestry and the U.S. Forest Service.

BIRTH OF AN AGENCY

Prelude

On July 1, 1898, following Fernow's resignation to become director of the newly established New York State College of Forestry at Cornell University, Pinchot took charge of the Division of Forestry. He used the title of Forester, not Chief. "In Washington chiefs of division were as thick as leaves in Vallombrosa," according to his view, but there was only one Forester spelled with a capital letter (Dana, 119). He found an organization that was desperately poor in terms of money, equipment, and personnel. The original appropriation of $2000 in 1876 had gradually increased to $33,520, but it was reduced to $28,520 in 1898. Three years later, under Pinchot's aggressive leadership, the budget rose to $185,440 for fiscal year 1902. During the same period, the employees in the division grew from 11—of whom only two aside from Pinchot had any technical training—to 179 persons. Of this total, 81 were student assistants and about 25 were collaborators. The student assistants were young men studying to become foresters who were employed at $25 a month plus expenses to assist in the fieldwork of the division; the collaborators were scientists with permanent positions elsewhere who were employed at a salary of $300 a year to conduct special studies. These two groups bolstered the division's personnel at relatively low cost.

On July 1, 1901, the Division of Forestry became the Bureau of Forestry. The name did not change the activities of the organization, but it did perhaps marginally raise its standing in the Washington government hierarchy. As head of both organizations, Pinchot had two major objectives: (1) to get forestry (always referred to as "practical" forestry) actually practiced in the woods, particularly on private lands, and (2) to get the administration of the forest reserves transferred from the Department of the Interior to the Department of Agriculture.

Pinchot's emphasis on practical forestry put an effective end to any remaining debate over the utilization of the forest reserves. It was also a useful means to distinguish himself and his administration of the Division of Forestry from his predecessor, for whom he had neither respect nor affection. Fernow's preoccupation with research and the scientific basis of silviculture and wood utilization was not an appropriate vehicle for the movement Pinchot wished to build. However, it must be noted that the silvicultural approach to wood supply which dominated forestry thought for decades is one of Pinchot's least constructive legacies. Planting and harvesting trees is not the only route to a stable timber supply. For example, extending the use life of wood has the effect of increasing the supply. Pinchot, in attempting to discredit Fernow, overemphasized silvicultural aspects of forestry and, unfortunately, narrowed the young profession in its formative period (Olson, chap. 9).

Pinchot was disappointed in the results of his attempts to interest forest-land owners in practical forestry. In spite of increasing requests for technical assistance, little progress was being made. His annual report for 1903 lamented that "practical forest work in the woods was better in quality and greater in amount than ever before. But great though the progress was in comparison with other years, actually it was small. The saving of the forests by wise use is but little nearer than it was a year ago, except for the wider spread of knowledge of the nature and objects of forestry" (Dana, 121). Pinchot argued with characteristic confidence that only the lack of money and personnel in his bureau program prevented the adoption of scientific forest management practices. "If this Bureau can be equipped to meet the demands before destruction has gone too far, the extensive protection of woodlands by the practice of forestry will certainly be attained. The only obstacle is present inability to handle the work" (Dana, 121). Fifteen years later, in his bitter battle to secure federal regulation of private cutting practices, Pinchot was to revise dramatically his assessment of the readiness of forest owners to practice forestry if they only had the necessary knowledge.

Pinchot and the Forest Reserves

If his efforts toward his goal of practical forestry proved frustrating, progress toward his second major objective was slow but encouraging. Pinchot was in the Department of Agriculture administering a technical assistance-oriented bureau while the forest reserves were being held for management by the Department of the Interior's General Land Office. Transfer of the forest reserves to the Department of Agriculture was not a new idea. Fernow had argued strongly for the transfer in his final report on the activities of the Division of Forestry. What was new was widespread support for the proposal and the vigorous skill with which Pinchot pursued his goal.

Oregon Land Frauds

Pinchot's zeal in building support for the transfer was unrelenting, but the most important support for his cause probably came inadvertently from the General Land Office. During the early 1900s, the country was shocked by the exposure of widespread frauds affecting the public lands. The best-known schemes were described by Stephen A. Douglas Puter, "king of the Oregon land fraud ring," in a book written while he was in jail. The extent of the land frauds is indicated by the fact that a federal grand jury was in session for eleven months between 1903 and 1905. It brought in twenty-six indictments affecting over one hundred people. Among those convicted were a U.S. senator, a congressman, a former U.S. district attorney, and a member of the Oregon legislature. A second U.S. senator escaped indictment only because of the statute of limitations. The trials, publicity, and public dismay at what Puter characterized as *The Looters of the Public Domain* did much to undermine confidence in the General Land Office's ability to protect the forest reserves effectively.

Transfer of the Reserves

The long-sought transfer was accomplished shortly after Roosevelt's landslide election to a full term of office in 1904. The Transfer Act passed in February 1905, and two provisions are of paramount importance. First, it transferred the administration of the forest reserves from the Secretary of the Interior to the Secretary of Agriculture, effective immediately. Second, it provided that all receipts from the forest reserves for a period of five years be put into a special fund to be expended as the Secretary of Agriculture might direct for the protection, administration, improvement, and extension of the reserves.

The act constituted the crucial step in the reservation and management of public forests in the United States. Unlike its predecessors of 1891 and 1897, which were passed as riders attached to bills dealing with entirely different subjects, this measure was approved as an independent piece of legislation. The foresters and the government forestland were brought together under one administrative head. Roosevelt, Secretary of Agriculture Wilson, and Pinchot were in a position to demonstrate the advantages of the combination which they had advocated so long and so vigorously.

On the very day that the act was signed, Secretary Wilson addressed a

letter of instructions to Pinchot, written by the recipient himself, stating suc-
cinctly but comprehensively the principles to be followed in the management
of the reserves:

> In the administration of the forest reserves it must be clearly borne in mind that
> all land is to be devoted to its most productive use for the permanent good of the
> whole people, and not for the temporary benefit of individuals or companies. All
> the resources of the reserves are for *use,* and this use must be brought about in
> a thoroughly prompt and businesslike manner, under such restrictions only as will
> insure the permanence of these resources. The vital importance of forest reserves
> to the great industries of the Western States will be largely increased in the near
> future by the continued steady increase in settlement and development. The
> permanence of the resources of the reserves is therefore indispensable to continued
> prosperity, and the policy of this department for their protection and use will
> invariably be guided by this fact, always bearing in mind that the *conservative use*
> of these resources in no way conflicts with their permanent value.
>
> You will see to it that the water, wood, and forage of the reserves are
> conserved and wisely used for the benefit of the home builder first of all, upon
> whom depends the best permanent use of lands and resources alike. The continued
> prosperity of the agricultural, lumbering, mining, and livestock interests is di-
> rectly dependent upon a permanent and accessible supply of water, wood, and
> forage, as well as upon the present and future use of their resources under business
> like regulations, enforced with promptness, effectiveness, and common sense. In
> the management of each reserve local questions will be decided upon local
> grounds; the dominant industry will be considered first, but with as little restric-
> tion to minor industries as may be possible; sudden changes in industrial condi-
> tions will be avoided by gradual adjustment after due notice; and where conflicting
> interests must be reconciled the question will always be decided from the stand-
> point of the greatest good of the greatest number in the long run.
>
> These general principles will govern in the protection and use of the water
> supply, in the disposal of timber and wood, in the use of the range, and in all other
> matters connected with the management of the reserves. They can be successfully
> applied only when the administration of each reserve is left very largely in the
> hands of the local officers, under the eye of thoroughly trained and competent
> inspectors (Dana, 142–43).

The themes which were sounded in the Pinchot-Wilson letter continue to
be major components of Forest Service management philosophy: a system of
decentralized administration emphasizing local exercise of discretion to fit
local conditions, a sound technical basis for directing the conservation and use
of the forests, and a strong commitment to the economic stability of the
surrounding communities. In the turbulent 1960s and 1970s, every one of these
fundamental ideas would be challenged. At the outset, however, the commitments seemed responsive both to the progressive assumptions regarding scien-

tific management and to the political situation in which the Forest Service sought to maintain itself.

Administrative Reorganization

Almost immediately after the transfer of the reserves to the Department of Agriculture, Pinchot began to reorganize the Bureau of Forestry. The major theme in the reorganization was placing responsibility for the administration of the national forests as far as practicable in the hands of local and regional officers. Three, and later six, inspection districts were established. This led in 1908 to the transformation of the inspection districts into administration districts. Each district was placed in charge of a district (now regional) forester with technical and executive experts in charge of the various lines of work.

From then on, the bulk of the national forest business previously referred to Washington was handled on the forests and in the districts. Only questions of large importance and matters involving the general administration and policy of the Forest Service were submitted to the Forester for decision. The arrangement was intended to avoid the problems of bureaucratic centralized administration while maintaining effective national direction. It was the first, and one of the most successful, moves in this direction by the federal government.

A second characteristic of the new agency was that, from the very beginning, it was permeated with the messianism of its leader. Pinchot wrote, "Every member of the Service realized that it was engaged in a great and necessary undertaking in which the whole future of their country was at stake. The Service had a clear understanding of where it was going, it was determined to get there, and it was never afraid to fight for what was right" (Dana, 144). While such confidence has occasionally caused the Forest Service to seem self-righteous and impervious to criticism, the pride of the organization has greatly contributed to its unbroken record of effective, honest resource management. The Forest Service was soon recognized as one of the most efficient bureaus in Washington with an unmatched esprit de corps. A lively demand developed for the young foresters who were beginning to graduate in goodly numbers from the recently established schools of forestry.

BIRTH OF A PROFESSION

Rapid development of the Forest Service, with the personnel requirements inherent in its dual commitment to decentralized administration and scientific management, would not have been possible without the simultaneous emergence of forestry profession. Among the characteristics of a profession are the existence of a technical literature, the conduct of research and the application of the findings of research in actual practice, the development of specialized

education institutions, and the establishment of an association of trained practitioners with the maintenance of high standards of professional ability and
ethical conduct as one of its objectives. Judged by these criteria, forestry
emerged as a profession in this country at the beginning of the present century.

Society of American Foresters

If a single date were to be selected for the birth of the profession, it might well
be November 30, 1900, when a group of foresters met in Pinchot's office to
organize the Society of American Foresters (SAF). The early members of the
organization included Gifford Pinchot, Henry Graves, Overton Price, Bernhard Fernow, Carl Schenck, and Filibert Roth. Full membership in the society
has until quite recently been limited to trained American foresters. Such
luminaries as Grover Cleveland, Benjamin Harrison, John W. Noble, Theodore Roosevelt, Charles S. Sargent, and James Wilson were only permitted to
become associate members. The object of the society, as stated in the constitution, was to "further the cause of foresting in America by fostering a spirit of
comradeship among foresters; by creating opportunities for a free interchange
of views upon forestry and allied subjects; and by disseminating a knowledge
of the purpose and achievements of forestry" (Dana, 138).

In subsequent years, Pinchot's personality and preferences dominated the
society and frequently embroiled the organization in heated internal and public
controversy. At the outset, however, his leadership was essential to the society's success. The Washington members of the society held frequent meetings
at Pinchot's home at which the standard refreshments were baked apples,
gingerbread, and milk—hence the name the "Baked Apple Club," by which
the society was commonly known. Not every young group can attract the
President of the United States to its meetings; but in 1903, Roosevelt broke
his custom of not making speeches at private houses by addressing the society.
It must have been a heady experience indeed for Pinchot's zealous young
followers to sit and listen to the President of the United States expound on the
virtues of their nascent profession.

During his 1903 visit to the society, Roosevelt remarked on the emergence
of a group of American trained foresters. "We have," he noted, "reached a
point where American foresters trained in American forest schools are attacking American forest problems with success. That is the way to meet the larger
work you have before you. You must instill your own ideals into the mass of
your fellow men and at the same time show your ability to work with them
in practical and business fashion [sic]. This is the condition precedent to your
being of use to the body politic" (Dana, 138).

Professional Education

Truly professional education in forestry started in 1898 with the establishment
of the New York State College of Forestry at Cornell University. Fernow left

the Division of Forestry to become its director. In addition to Fernow, the original Cornell faculty included Filibert Roth, who later became dean of a new School of Forestry at the University of Michigan in Ann Arbor. Almost simultaneously came the opening of the Biltmore Forest School under Carl A. Schenck at Biltmore, North Carolina. The Biltmore Forest School was unique in the history of forestry education in America. It was essentially a one-man "master" school emphasizing field training and participation in activities involved in the management of a large forest property. The Society of American Foresters has never recognized forest technicians trained along the lines of Schenck's nonacademic school as having full professional standing. However, Schenck's program and many similar schools have turned out many leaders in the profession.

Another approach to professional education in forestry was tried in 1900 with the establishment of a School of Forestry at Yale University. Only men with a bachelor's degree were admitted to the two-year program of studies which led to a master of forestry degree. Funds for the support of the school were provided by an endowment from the Pinchot family. Henry S. Graves left his position as assistant chief of the Division of Forestry to become director of the new school. Its purpose, according to Gifford Pinchot, who "had small confidence in the leadership of Dr. Fernow or Dr. Schenck," was to provide a supply of "American foresters trained by Americans in American ways for the work ahead in American forests" (Dana, 136). Thus, within three years, professsional education in forestry, hitherto conspicuous by its absence, was represented at three important distinctive institutions. By 1910, seventeen schools, primarily in the East and Midwest, were offering programs of study.

Research in Forestry

Scientific investigations continued as an activity of the Federal Division of Forestry and Bureau of Forestry under Pinchot's administration, but they received less attention than they had in Fernow's time. After the Transfer Act, forestry research increased in line with the government's active commitment to managing the national forests. In 1908, the research work of the service was decentralized. Fort Valley, Arizona, was the site of the first forest experiment station. It was soon followed by others in Colorado, Idaho, California, Washington, and Utah. Most of the early work of the stations was intended to provide a sound technical foundation for the management of the national forests in the area.

Two features of the experiment stations distinguished them initially from the agricultural experiment stations. They were completely financed and controlled by the federal government, and they were organized by regions rather than by states. The Forest Products Laboratory, established at Madison, Wisconsin, in 1910, is an exception to this generalization. Forests themselves must be studied where they occur, but their products can be brought to a central laboratory. Nongovernment forestry research was stimulated by the development of the forestry schools. Although funding was limited, early research programs were undertaken at Yale, Purdue, Washington University (in St. Louis), and the University of Washington.

Forestry Literature

With the advent of a readership and findings to report, forestry literature of scientific integrity and professional significance began to develop. The foresters' need for a technical journal was met first in 1902 when the students of the New York State College of Forestry at Cornell established the *Forestry Quarterly*. The journal started as an official publication of the college; but after the school was disbanded, Fernow continued to edit it. Three years later, in May 1905, the first issue of the *Proceedings of the Society of American Foresters* made its appearance. This publication was issued at irregular intervals until 1914, when it became a quarterly. In 1917, the *Proceedings* were joined with the *Forestry Quarterly* to create the *Journal of Forestry*. The Department of Agriculture contributed technical literature in the form of bulletins and circulars. These publications, issued with increasing frequency, presented the results of the Department of Agriculture investigations and other activities and contributed substantially to the growing body of forestry literature.

The birth of the profession, its schools, society, and journals were the essential ingredients in the development both of the Forest Service and the practice of scientific forest management. Without research findings, trained professionals, and a system of communicating the findings to the professionals, foresters would not have developed, as they certainly did, into the near perfect embodiment of the progressive ideal of nonpartisan, technically competent public servants (Kaufman, 1952, 1962). The political strength inherent in a tightly knit organization with dedicated members has been an equally significant factor in professional and agency growth. It never hurt the foresters that, in their formative years, their leader was the President's best friend. In times of challenge, the Forest Service could count on prompt and effective demonstrations of support from the SAF and its growing membership.

THE LIVESTOCK INDUSTRY AND THE FOREST SERVICE

In spite of the growing professionalism emphasizing forest management, the Forest Service met its first and most important challenges not from timber barons but from livestock operators. The attitude of the operators toward federal reserves and the Forest Service has a long and confusing history. Similarly, though the Forest Service often needed the support of the livestock interests, its attitude toward grazing use of the forests has ranged from ambivalent to hostile. The SAF was absolutely intransigent on the subject, refusing for many years to accept stock grazing as a legitimate use of the national forests. When the new agency took charge of the forest reserves in 1905, the livestock operators first challenged their authority to regulate use of the forests. It was also, however, the operators who gave initial support to the Forest Service's beleagured programs. Since the very beginning, the operators have been a critical influence on forest as well as range policy.

The reason for this is simple: The national forests are in the West, and the earliest, most numerous settlers of the West and users of the national forests were livestock operators. The early dominance of grazing can be illustrated by noting that, in spite of the fact that range fees were scandalously low, grazing receipts exceeded timber receipts from 1906 to 1910; approximately equaled timber receipts from 1911 to 1917; and substantially outstripped timber receipts until 1921. Livestock was a major foundation of the western economy and western way of life. Range management may be a minor forest use now; but in the early years of the Forest Service, range problems constituted the bulk of the foresters' daily tasks (Greeley, 1955, passim). The operators were the users to be reckoned with.

The operators were not, however, a coherent or single-interest group. They were divided along lines made familiar by some the bloodiest tales of the American West. Livestock operators can be distinguished from the squatters and homesteaders. Because operators were using the unreserved public domain as their own, they opposed settlers and settlements that would close the range to their use or block cattle drives from winter to summer range. Beyond this point of fundamental agreement, the operators were divided among themselves: sheep versus cattle operators. The former were nomads, frequently without a home base, wandering the range widely. They interrupted the more stationary operations of the cattle operators, who regard the public land around their base properties as their own and violently resisted the sheep operators. The attitude of the stock operators toward the national forests was initially mixed. As long as the reservations prevented homesteaders from cutting up the range with homes, fences, and settlements, the operators were supportive. However, their support waned when the foresters impeded or regulated their use of what they considered to be their own range.

The first regulation of the livestock industry followed the invention of barbed wire in the 1880s. Although fencing of public land by private persons was illegal, the fences did establish a rudimentary indication of who was using what land and allowed for control of livestock grazing patterns. These rudimentary allocations of the range stabilized the industry under the control of the large cattle operators. Initially, it provided a system which, backed by occasional bloodshed, excluded the sheep operators. Gradually, however, it became apparent that regulated range use improved the quality of the range and benefited the users.

This is not to suggest that the stock operators were early and enthusiastic supporters of Pinchot's scientific management schemes for the national forests. To the contrary, the cattle operators, especially the more prosperous ones, were among the earliest critics of the Forest Service; and their influence in Congress was significant. The new agency moved cautiously to allay the concerns of its detractors and establish minimal regulation of range use. After an initial rash of hostilities and several crucial court tests of their authority to do so, the Forest Service succeeded in imposing minimal fees for range use and eventually in winning the grudging support of the stock operators.

Grazing allocations were carefully drawn to protect the water supply, tree growth, and the range itself. Permits were issued to applicants; and early in 1906, official recognition was given to advisory boards from the livestock associations. These boards did much to reduce friction between the stock operators and the Forest Service. Fees for grazing permits constituted a particularly thorny problem. Operators were unenthusiastic about paying for a privilege that was formerly free. Their influence in Congress was sufficient to prevent approval of the repeated requests of the Department of the Interior for legislative authority to charge a fee and to block the attempted inclusion of such authorization in the Transfer Act.

Pinchot was, however, so thoroughly convinced that a fee was desirable both on general principles and as a means of swelling forest reserve receipts that he decided to bypass Congress and approach the matter from a different angle. He asked the Attorney General whether the necessary authority to charge fees could be inferred from power already granted to the Secretary in the act of June 4, 1897, which authorized him to make rules and regulations for the occupancy and use of the reserves. In a series of well-planned maneuvers, Pinchot became one of the only people successfully to outflank the livestock industry's congressional supporters.

In May 1905, Secretary of Agriculture Wilson sent a letter to the Attorney General which made no reference to grazing but asked important questions with respect to an application for the use of forest reserve land in Alaska for a fish saltery, oil, and fertilizer plant. Did he have legal authority to grant a permit or lease for such use; could the permit be for a period longer than one year; and could he require reasonable compensation or rental for such permit? The Attorney General, having been properly educated not only by Pinchot but by the President himself, replied in the affirmative to all three questions. With respect to fees, the key sentence in his reply was as follows: "I have to advise you that, in my opinion you are authorized to make a reasonable charge in connection with the use and occupation of these forest reserves, whenever, in your judgement, such a course seems consistent with insuring the objects of the reservation and the protection of the forest thereon from destruction" (Dana, 145).

This opinion was couched in sufficiently broad terms to authorize the charging of a fee not only for the fish saltery but for grazing or other use of the reserves. Beginning with January 1, 1906, a charge was made for all livestock grazed on the reserves except for a limited amount of free use by actual settlers. This action caused a storm of protest and the Attorney General's opinion was challenged by the stock operators all the way to the Supreme Court.

Up to the time of the Supreme Court decision in 1911, efforts to control grazing on the national forests had been handicapped by a uniform line of lower court decisions. They held that the provision in the Forest Reserve Act of 1897 authorizing the Secretary to establish rules and regulations was invalid because it was an unconstitutional delegation of legislative power to an administrative officer. Supreme Court decisions in two separate 1911 cases reversed the lower court decisions. In the cases involving alleged illegal occupancy of the range, *Grimaud* v. *United States* and *U.S.* v. *Light,* the Supreme Court unanimously upheld the Secretary's authority. The two cases established a number of points critical to Forest Services programs generally and the grazing question specifically.

First, the Court found that congressional authority over the public lands is plenary and that the 1891 and 1897 acts passed by Congress providing for the reservation and administration of the national forests were constitutional. Second, the court held that the authority given the Secretary to regulate use of the forest reserves was not, as the stockmen had argued, an unconstitutional delegation of legislative power. Third, the Court concluded that the authority to charge for a grazing permit is implied both in the 1897 act and in other acts disposing of revenues from national forests. Finally, the Court held that any previous implied license to graze stock on public lands did not confer any vested right on the users, nor did it deprive the United States the power of recalling such licenses.

Definite settlement of these important points established beyond question the constitutionality of the national forests management and greatly strengthened the hand of the Secretary of Agriculture in administering not only grazing but all other activities. With these points clearly established, the Forest Service was able to move ahead, slowly, cautiously, but firmly in establishing a set of fees and regulations for administering the public range on the national forests. The stock operators gradually turned away from their initial hostility toward the Forest Service, in part because they began to see advantages in regulated range use even if they had to pay for it and in part because they shared the Forest Service's antipathy toward homesteading.

HOMESTEADING ON THE NATIONAL FORESTS

The Forest Homestead Act of 1906 authorized the Secretary of Agriculture to open for homestead entry forest reserve lands chiefly valuable for agriculture "which, in his opinion, may be occupied for agricultural purposes without injury to the forest reserves, and which are not needed for public purposes" (Dana, 147). The 1906 legislation simply authorized the opening of national forests to homestead entry; it did not require it. Pinchot and the Forest Service were predictably reluctant to relinquish forested lands or to encourage private intrusions within natural forest administrative boundaries. They proceeded very slowly with the suggested program. The Forest Service recommended the opening of lands to entry only in response to specific applications. Lands needed for administrative purposes or suitable only for grazing were not listed for entry. Lands suitable for cultivation but having heavy stands of timber were not listed until after sale of the timber. By June 1910 the total area listed for entry was only 632,412 acres. The Forest Service used every subterfuge available to prevent and delay homestead entries. However, the homesteader mystique was so powerful that, even during the heyday of Pinchot's administration, it proved an unstoppable threat to the forests.

EARLY SETBACKS FOR THE NATIONAL FORESTS

Problems with the stock operators and the homesteaders constituted a real and continuing challenge to the Forest Service in its early years. However, the young agency could anticipate some difficulty in accommodating established interests and expectations. Over time these problems were resolved. A more serious challenge to the Forest Service came in a series of altercations about the allocation of Forest Service receipts. The hostility of Westerners to the reserves peaked in the Agricultural Appropriations Act of 1907, and the Forest Service was permanently and profoundly impaired by the legislation.

Contributions to Counties

The first move against the fledging agency came in June 1906. During the appropriations process, Congress provided that 10 percent of the gross receipts from forest reserves during any fiscal year, including 1906, should be turned over to the states or territories for the benefit of the public schools and public roads of the counties in which the reserves were located, not to exceed 40 percent of the localities' income from other sources.

This was the first blow to the Forest Service's independent funding, a major component of Roosevelt's scheme for self-supporting resource development and administration. Although the amount lost was only 10 percent of gross revenues, it did not augur well for continued agency independence. Legislation passed in 1908 increased the payment to the states for the benefit of county schools and roads to 25 percent of the gross receipts, eliminated the 40 percent limitation, and made the legislation permanent. This arrangement continued for many decades in spite of numerous suggestions that contributions should be based on the value of national forest lands rather than on receipts. These arguments came most frequently from towns and counties neighboring eastern national forests where land values are relatively high and the receipts from the timber sales are generally quite low. This was not an issue in 1908 because eastern national forests, though they had been proposed, did not exist. Nor was the increased payment to countries specified in the 1908 act actually a blow to the Forest Service. The agency had already lost control of receipts in the 1907 Appropriations Act.

Agricultural Appropriations Act of 1907

The hostility to the forest reserves which existed in parts of the West and among certain members of Congress was expressed in the Agricultural Appropriations Act of March 4, 1907. This broad legislation dramatically altered the future of the Forest Service. Although the bill changed the name of the forest reserves to "national forests," other provisions relating to the agency were profoundly negative.

The act abolished the special fund consisting of receipts from the forest reserves which was created by the Transfer Act of 1905. In 1906, Congress had started to restrict the use of the fund. Now it did away with it entirely and, in addition, required the Forest Service to submit a classified and detailed report of receipts and estimate of expenditures annually.

The Forest Service's reliance on receipts could have tempted the agency to permit overutilization of the resources of the reserves in order to obtain funds for administration. However, the 1907 act cut at the heart of the Roosevelt conservation programs by abolishing the fund. The fund had dramatically increased the resources at the disposal of the Secretary of Agriculture and the Forest Service and provided complete freedom in determining the purposes for which they should be used. Flexibility of this sort is always attractive to an administrative office, especially since the Congress was viewed as a reluctant participant in conservation programs during this period. In retrospect, the abolition of the special fund may appear to have been wise from the standpoint of political responsibility and the long-term good of the reserves themselves. At the time, however, it was a crushing defeat for the agency and a telling expression of the western congressional delegation's general hostility to Roosevelt's conservation program.

Limitations on New National Forests

In addition to changing the basis for funding Forest Service programs, the 1907 act also forbade the further creation of forest reserves except by act of Congress in the states of Washington, Oregon, Idaho, Montana, Wyoming, and Colorado. The prohibition was particularly serious because these six states contained by far the heaviest stands of timber in the West. This put Roosevelt and Pinchot in a difficult position. The President could not veto the appropriations bill, but he did not want to foreclose prematurely the opportunity for adding to the national forests. This resulted in the famous 1907 reservations. The Forest Service already had plans to add a large area to the reserve system. These plans were hastily put in shape and rushed to the President. Roosevelt signed proclamations adding 16 million acres of forest reserves just before he approved the appropriations act forbidding him to do so. Irate senators complained vigorously that he could not take such action. The President gleefully replied that he had already done it.

This exercise of executive authority in clear contravention of the express intent of Congress is frequently cited as the ultimate example of the Roosevelt-Pinchot genius. That interpretation is shortsighted and limited in perspective. Hostility engendered by the flouting of congressional policy continued to haunt the Forest Service for decades.

GOVERNORS CONFERENCE OF 1908

The 1907 appropriations bill was a debacle for Roosevelt and his conservation program. It served notice that he had gone as far as he could with executive action and would have to rely on public support in order to deal with opposition in Congress in the future. In order to build that support, Roosevelt, Pinchot, and Frederick H. Newell conceived a conference of state governors and others to discuss the conservation of the nation's natural resources. Governors' conferences are rather common occurrences today, but Roosevelt's was the first gathering of governors ever held to discuss national issues. This highlights the ingenuity of its instigators and the severity of the crisis they confronted.

Invitations went out in November 1907, requesting the governors of all the states and territories to a conference at the White House on May 13 to 15, 1908, to confer with the President and each other upon the conservation of natural resources. The gathering was one of the most distinguished ever to assemble in Washington. In addition to the governors and the three advisers by whom each was accompanied, the roster included many members of Congress; the Supreme Court; the Inland Waterways Commission; representatives of scientific, professional, and other organizations; and the press. There were also numerous special guests, including William Jennings Bryan and Andrew Carnegie. Arrangements were made by the chairman, Gifford Pinchot, and the conference was an overwhelming success. It focused national attention on the vital importance of natural resources and the urgent need for their conservation to an extent that would probably have been impossible otherwise. More pertinent to Roosevelt's immediate goals, the conference passed resolutions and established committees that endorsed and supported his conservation programs.

The conference made recommendations requesting the President to call future conferences to continue cooperation between states and nations and urging that each state appoint a commission on the conservation of natural resources to cooperate with each other and with any similar commission of the federal government. Other resolutions endorsed federal forest policies and urged that they be continued, extended, and that laws leading to the protection and replacement of privately owned forest lands be enacted. The governors also urged Congress to pass laws fostering the conservation of water resources for irrigation, water supply, power, and navigation and the prevention of waste in mining and the protection of human life in the mines.

Creation of National Conservation Commission

In accordance with the recommendation of the governor's conference, President Roosevelt appointed a National Conservation Commission on June 8, 1908, to advise him on the condition of the country's resources and to cooperate with similar state bodies. The executive committee of the conference promptly proceeded to prepare an inventory of the natural resources of the United States—the first ever to be made. In this herculean task it was assisted by employees from various agencies, each of which was instructed by the President to secure, compile, and furnish data to the commission.

Joint Conservation Conference

In December 1908, the report of the commission was presented to a Joint Conservation Conference attended by members of the commission, governors of twenty states and territories, personal representatives of eleven governors and governors-elect, members of twenty six state conservation commissions, and presidents and representatives of sixty national organizations. President-elect Taft presided at the first session. The joint conference unanimously adopted a resolution approving the report of the National Conservation Commission. It especially commended the principle of cooperation among the states and between the states and the federal government, favored the maintenance of conservation commissions in every state, and expressed the advisability of maintaining a national commission on the conservation of natural resources. More specifically, it urged adoption of a number of specific proposals which constituted the unfinished agenda of the waning Roosevelt presidency: the policy of separate disposal of the surface rights and mineral rights on the remaining public lands; the disposal of mineral rights by lease only; treatment of all watersheds as units; approval of the broad plan recommended by the Inland Waterways Commission for waterway development under an executive board or commission appointed by the President; and the enactment by states of laws regulating the cutting and removal of timber and slash on private lands. These issues, formulated in the closing days of Roosevelt's administration by the men who had made it great, continued to dominate resource management debate for the next fifty years.

Pickett Act of 1910

The success of the conference in building public support for conservation programs can be read in the Pickett Act, which passed in 1910 over a storm of protest from the Western states. Taft's views about the inherent power of the President to take action without specific authorization from Congress were much narrower than Roosevelt's. He therefore asked Congress to validate the withdrawals already made and to authorize further withdrawals. Spurred by a vast outpouring of support, Congress acceded to Taft's request and passed the bill promptly in June 1910. It authorized the President to make temporary withdrawals and reservations of public lands for water development or other public purposes. To make sure that the Pickett Act could not be interpreted as repealing the ban on presidential establishment of national forests in six Western States, Congress reenacted that provision of the 1907 act.

It is doubtful whether this statutory definition of presidential authority significantly augmented the President's withdrawal and reservation powers. Following the passage of the act, the validity of pre-1910 withdrawals was challenged in court. In the famous Midwest Oil case (*United States* v. *Midwest Oil*, 236U.S. 459 [1915]), the Supreme Court upheld the withdrawals, citing not the Pickett Act but the President's traditional authority over the public lands. The Supreme Court concluded that Presidents' authority to withdraw public lands from entry has been so long exercised and recognized by Congress that it was equivalent to a general grant of power. The specificity of the Pickett Act has been, in fact, a barrier to withdrawals and reservations in the decades since it passed. It is frequently seen as a limitation on a previously recognized presidential power rather than a grant or confirmation of executive authority, because the withdrawals authorized by the Pickett Act are only temporary and must be for specific public purposes. The possibility of this interpretation was not overlooked during debate on the bill, but the press and the public insisted that it was a conservation measure and demanded its enactment. The ambiguities raised by the Pickett Act have been most troubling regarding mineral withdrawals. Forest and range management, except as they are affected by mineral locations, were not seriously confounded by the conservationists' error (Peffer, 16–18, 324–325).

THE BALLINGER-PINCHOT CONTROVERSY

The famous feud between Roosevelt's old confidante and Forester and Taft's new Secretary of the Interior brought an unfortunate end to the Golden Era. The specific dispute involved some alleged improprieties on the part of Ballinger and the Department of the Interior regarding coal claims on withdrawn lands in Alaska. The actual issue was created by the Roosevelt conservationists' frustration at having lost their access and influence in the White House. The coal claim incident provided the opportunity for them, particularly Pinchot, to give full voice to their dismay and bitterness. More than half a century after the outbreak of hostilities, it is still impossible to find agreement on the charges against Ballinger. Neither Taft nor Ballinger was guilty of all the sins of omission and commission attributed to him. Ballinger, in fact, appears as a decent, honorable, capable citizen who went to Washington reluctantly and with high ideals of public service (Richardson, passim). Public land fraud and chicanery involving mineral lands were pervasive both when Ballinger was Commissioner of the General Land Office and then when he was Secretary of the Interior. It seems reasonable to argue that, if all the allegations and the investigations of his affairs failed to produce any decisive evidence of wrong doing, Ballinger must have been unusually honest. Pinchot, however, was looking for a way to discredit both Ballinger and Taft and was dismissed from office by Taft for publicly discussing the affair. In his letter dismissing Pinchot, Taft noted his

> improper appeal to Congress and the public to excuse in advance the guilt of your subordinates before I could act, and against my decision in the . . . case before the whole evidence on which that was based could be considered . . . if I were to pass over this matter in silence, it would be most demoralizing to the discipline of the executive branch of the Government.

> By your own conduct you have destroyed your usefulness as a helpful subordinate of the Government, and it therefore now becomes my duty to direct the Secretary of Agriculture to remove you from your office as the Forester [Dana, 168].

Although most of the newpapers regarded Taft's dismissal of Pinchot as justified, and under the circumstances inevitable, Pinchot supporters feared its impact on the Forest Service and the conservation movement generally. Taft requested Henry Graves, one of Pinchot's closest associates and dean of the Yale Forestry School, to return to the Forest Service as Forester. This appointment was appropriately interpreted as a sign of Taft's continuing commitment to the Forest Service.

Pinchot's departure from office in January 1910 did not, unfortunately, end the controversy. Both Congress and the press continued the discussion for almost a year. The congressional investigation of Ballinger's conduct was dominated by partisan politics, and its findings were inconclusive. Congress took no action; and in March 1911, Ballinger resigned against the wishes of the President, who continued to express complete confidence in his integrity. The most important result of the fracas is the hostility engendered between the

Departments of Agriculture and the Interior. The era of coherent federal leadership in forest and range policy was ended.

Long after Pinchot was fired, he remained—until his death in 1946— active, highly visible, and articulate in conservation causes. His singleminded participation was interrupted by two terms as governor of Pennsylvania (1923– 1927 and 1931–1935), but it was always characterized by the adamant self-righteousness of his Forest Service days. Unfortunately, over the years his commitment to the Forest Service and the Department of Agriculture led him to oppose many important measures which were aimed at implementing the Roosevelt conservation program simply because they would have been administered in the Department of the Interior. Any assessment of Pinchot's contribution to conservation and the nation must weigh the destructive partisanship of his mature years against the vigor, vision, and accomplishment of the Golden Era.

SUMMARY

The Roosevelt-Pinchot years constitute a major revolution in conservation history. New or unique ideas were not developed, but old ideas and often-made suggestions were combined, elaborated, and advocated as a comprehensive scheme for managing public resources. Conservation expressed the social and economic philosophy of the Progressives. A group of inspired and inspirational leaders made conservation their special cause and captured the public imagination with their energy. Their vision has been written in laws, policies, and programs implemented over the past sixty years and is reflected in our most basic assumptions about resource management. Gifford Pinchot and the Forest Service were the zenith of Roosevelt era thought and accomplishment. Under Pinchot's leadership, the agency began its long history as the epitome of technical competence and scientific management.

Even at its peak, however, the conservation movement had critics. Although Roosevelt talked eloquently in terms of homes for homesteaders, the most prominent features of his programs were reservations and withdrawals. Millions and millions of acres of the most valuable remaining public domain lands were withdrawn from entry in order to protect their potential development value for all the people. Except for the Forest Service reserves, very little arrangement was made for opening the withdrawn lands to use and development. Great hostility developed in the West and was expressed in the disastrous Appropriations Act of 1907. Roosevelt recovered spectacularly by staging the governor's conference the following year to build public support for his conservation goals. The support was forthcoming and the stage set for decades of conflict over the great visions of the Golden Era.

REFERENCES CITED

Cameron, Jenks. *The Development of Governmental Forest Control in the United States.* Baltimore Md.; Johns Hopkins Press, 1928.

Conference of the Governors of the United States, *Proc.,* 1909.

Gates, Paul Wallace. *History of Public Land Law Development.* Written for the Public Land Law Review Commission. Washington, D. C.: Government Printing Office, 1968.

Greeley, William B. *Forests and Men.* New York: Doubleday & Company, 1951.

————. "The First 25 Years." 61 *American Forests* 12 (March, 1955).

Hays, Samuel. *Conservation and The Gospel of Efficiency.* Cambridge: Harvard University Press, 1959.

Kaufman, Herbert, *The Forest Ranger.* Baltimore, Md.: The Johns Hopkins Press, 1959.

Olson, Sherry. *The Depletion Myth: A History of Railroad Use of Timber.* Cambridge: Harvard University Press, 1971.

Peffer, E. Louise. *The Closing of the Public Domain.* Stanford: Stanford University Press, 1951.

Pinchot, Gifford. *Breaking New Ground.* New York: Harcourt, Brace and Company, 1947.

————. *The Fight for Conservation.* Garden City, N. Y.: Doubleday, Page & Co, 1911.

Puter, S. A. D. *Looters of the Public Domain.* Portland: Portland Printing House, 1908.

Richardson, Elmo. *The Politics of Conservation: Crusades and Controversies, 1897–1913.* University of California Publications in History Vol. 70. Berkeley Ca.: University of California Press, 1962.

Robbins, Roy M. *Our Landed Heritage.* Princeton: Princeton University Press, 1942.

Rogers, Andrew Denny, III. *Bernhard Eduard Fernow: A Story of North American Forestry.* Princeton, N. J.: Princeton University Press. 1951.

Roosevelt, Theodore. "Forestry and Foresters." 1 *Soc. Amer. Foresters Proc.* 3–9 (1905).

Stegner, Wallace. *Beyond the Hundredth Meridian: John Wesley Powell and the Second Opening of the West.* Boston: Houghton Mifflin Co., 1953.

Trefethen, James B. *An American Crusade for Wildlife.* New York: Winchester Press and Boone and Crockett Club, 1975.

Chapter 4

Conservation After Roosevelt: Beyond Reservations, 1910–1920

Although Roosevelt and Pinchot emphasized development and wise use of resources as the essential ingredient in their programs, federal reservations were the main focus of early conservationists' attention. By the end of the Roosevelt-Pinchot regime, over 150 million acres were reserved for national forests; and extensive mineral and water resources had been withdrawn. With the exception of the 1897 Organic Act, no authority existed for allowing utilization of the reserved and withdrawn lands by either the government or private enterprises. Many Westerners vociferously opposed withdrawals and reservations. Several of the Western states had only recently joined the Union, Arizona being the last in 1912. Everywhere in the West the pressure for settlement, and economic growth was tremendous. Westerners' concern with the development of federal land holdings was understandable given their distribution. Even the contempory array of federal lands shown in Figure 4-1 is heavily concentrated in the West. Natural resources development on the public lands was the key to western growth, hence the root of most conflicts. Forest and range policy in the post-Roosevelt years was defined largely by the human aspirations and political imperatives of the Western states.

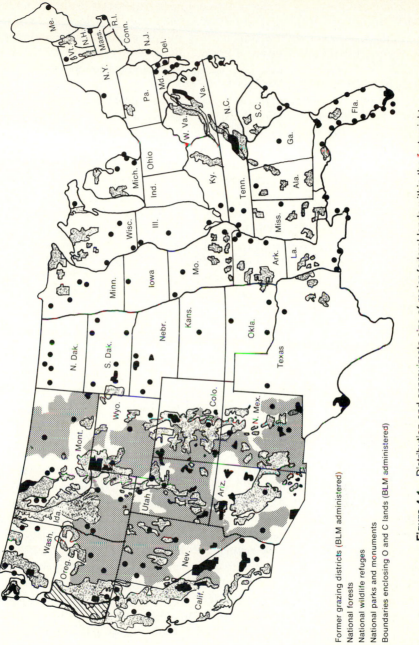

Figure 4-1. Distribution and approximate size of major federal lands within the forty-eight contiguous states. (Reproduced from Clawson, 1971, p. 44.)

Former grazing districts (BLM administered)
National forests
National wildlife refuges
National parks and monuments
Boundaries enclosing O and C lands (BLM administered)

The mystique of the homesteader continued as a major factor in public land management. Homesteading endured much later than most people believe, although the era of "free land" in this country was quite short and most of it occurred in the first quarter of the twentieth century. Between 1910 and 1920, reverence for the homesteader was as much an antimonopoly theme as a prosettlement one; but it was clearly the dominant chord in the prodevelopment rhetoric. Many present-day land management problems—most notably numerous in-holdings on national forests and severed title to minerals—were created during the last tragic refrain of the paean to hardy yeoman.

Forest and range policy was significantly different from previous decades. The objectives of the conservation movement were defensive—to hold on to the reserves in the face of development pressures and to solidify support for the Forest Service. The circumstances of Pinchot's departure did not help the Forest Service's relationship with the White House. Henry Graves returned to the agency from the Yale School of Forestry to serve with distinction as chief Forester during these turbulent troubled years. However, the privileges and opportunities inherent in the Forest Service's position as the special focus of presidential attention were gone forever.

The national forests faced two major threats during the Graves years. First, homesteading continued to be the dominant theme in public land management. The national forests were threatened with homestead entry and consequent confusion in ownership patterns and management programs. Second, there was continuing pressure to cede the public lands, including the national forests, to the states. The forests, like all other federal lands, were often viewed as locked-up resources in need of development. Westerners were frequently hostile to the Forest Service and its programs and repeatedly attempted to gain access to all or part of the forests.

In addition to these immediate threats to the federal reserves, institutional changes within the federal government have had a major influence on forest and range policy. After Theodore Roosevelt and his band of conservationists left Washington, the commitment to cooperation between the Departments of Agriculture and Interior broke down. The preservationist approach to resource conservation, downplayed or ignored by Pinchot and his followers, found support and institutional expression in the National Park Service. The Park Service, housed in the Department of the Interior, represented not only a different philosophy of resource management but a strong competitor for land, appropriations, and public attention. It was established despite the strenuous opposition of Forest Service leaders, who wanted to manage the park reserves themselves. A second omen of future challenge to the Forest Service was the decision to revest the valuable O & C timber lands to the Department of the Interior for management. These were not major defeats; but the era of a uniform federal wild lands policy was over, and forces to challenge the Pinchot forces from within the government were created.

However, not all of the developments during this period were threatening to the foresters. Perhaps the most significant forestry legislation ever written, the Weeks Act, passed in 1911. This critical law authorized purchase of national forests in the East and made rudimentary steps toward cooperative federal-state fire control programs. Less familiar is the breakthrough achieved in the 1912 Appropriations Act, which gave the Forest Service authority and dollars to build roads for management and fire protection. In addition, the Forest Service made significant strides toward defining recreation and research programs. Important steps were also made toward institutionalizing the nascent forestry profession. Although the Forest Service personnel and forestry professionals were virtually identical at the time, professional progress is not always synonymous with agency development. Quite apart from government action, the Society of American Foresters grew significantly during the period; and the number and quality of professional training programs, journals, and societies evinced the growing importance of the young profession. Forestry and forest management survived the troubled times not in small measure because of the growing number of competently trained professionals who advocated its application. Finally, range protection began in earnest during the years after 1910. Even a meager assertion of management authority provoked angry response from some stock operators. Others, however, noting that orderly allocation and use of the range was necessary to the long-term viability of the industry, welcomed the regulation and supported the agency. Although two key homesteading bills—one in 1909 and the other in 1916—implicitly recognized the land abuse inherent in the disposition system, it was continued and expanded; and no progress was made toward protecting the public domain lands.

A CHANGE IN EMPHASIS

In his first annual report issued in 1913, President Wilson's Secretary of the Interior, Franklin K. Lane, summed up the attitude toward conservation that characterized the post-Roosevelt years:

> There has slowly evolved in the public mind the conception of a new policy—that land should be used for that purpose to which it is best fitted, and it should be disposed of by the Government with respect to that use. To this policy I believe the West is now reconciled. The West no longer urges a return to the hazards of the 'land is land' policy. *But it does ask action.* It is reconciled to the Government making all proper safeguards against monopoly and against the subversion of the spirit of all our land laws, which is in essence that all suitable lands shall go into homes, and all other lands shall be developed for that purpose which shall make them of greatest service. But it asks that the machinery be promptly established in the law by which the lands may be used. And this demand is reasonable [Dana, 178.]

The administrative machinery that the West demanded had, of course, been in existence so far as the forests were concerned since passage of the Forest Reserve Act of 1897. The Westerners were not, however, generally supportive of the Forest Service. Even as the nation struggled to develop means for managing mineral, grazing, and water resources, the Forest Service was under constant attack.

EARLY NATIONAL FOREST PROBLEMS: HOMESTEADING, STATES RIGHTS, AND LIVESTOCK MANAGEMENT

When Henry S. Graves became Forester in 1910, he found two major threats to the integrity and permanence of the national forests—wholesale opening to homestead entry and cession to the states. The homesteading arguments were inevitably put forth in the context of "the little people" and the homesteader-settler cult. Graves called attention to the real threat behind the homesteading motif:

> Experience has amply proved that the elimination, under pressure, of national forest lands locally considered or alleged to be of agricultural value but in point of fact more valuable for other purposes has led to their early acquisition by timberland speculators, great lumber interests, water-power companies, livestock companies, and others who desire the lands for other ends than agriculture. . . . It is necessary that the country should understand the manner in which bona fide settlement is being brought about in the national forests, and also the motive of those who are trying to break down the system of forest conservation under the guise of promoting settlement [Dana, 179.]

Homesteading on the National Forests

Given the inadequacies of the information on which many of the national forests were proclaimed, especially in Roosevelt's last-minute 1907 reservations, agricultural lands were inevitably included—sometimes when they were not necessary to form a cohesive management unit. The Forest Homestead Act of 1906, which gave the Secretary authority to classify such lands for entry, was an initial attempt to deal with the situation. The Forest Service response had been, as previously noted (see p. 89, above), desultory; and Congress, favoring rapid homesteading, was not satisfied. Prohomesteading forces within Congress subsequently tried to secure legislation instructing the Secretary of Agriculture to open for entry all agricultural lands on the national forests regardless of their value for other purposes. That effort failed, but a rider in the 1912 appropriations bill *directed and required* the Secretary of Agriculture "to select, classify and segregate, as soon as practicable, all lands within the boundaries of national forests that may be opened to settlement and entry under the homestead laws. . . ." The Forest Service was thus obliged rather than simply permitted to identify and segregate the lands in national forests which were agricultural in character and which could pass into private ownership (Ise, 256–259).

By 1919, the classification work was practically completed except in Alaska. Altogether, more than 20,000 separate tracts with an area of about 2.5 million acres were listed for entry. Some of these were later withdrawn; a few were never entered; and still others were abandoned after homestead entry. The total area patented amounts to about 1.8 million acres. In addition to the individual tracts which were opened to entry, some 12 million acres were eliminated from national forests by changes in boundaries.

Two Final Homestead Acts

Homesteading threats to the national forest reservations were intensified by a fad in agriculture known as "dry farming," which was in its heyday from about 1905 to 1910. The concept was promoted by railroads, real estate developers, and business interests. It created the misimpression that semiarid lands could be successfully farmed if the right techniques were used. Many dry farm experiments succeeded remarkably due to above-average rainfall (Gates, 503); and many believed that if the 160-acre limitation were lifted from the Homestead Act to allow for larger farms, settlers could enter and cultivate previously untillable lands. In 1909, the enlarged Homestead Act provided that qualified entrymen could claim up to 320 acres of nonmineral, nonirrigable land. Eager dry farmers entered 18 million acres between 1909 and 1910–the largest area of land entered in any year under homestead legislation (Peffer, 142–148). By 1912, the hardships wrought by the 1909 act were clear. Not only was the soil cover on many millions of acres destroyed, but two years of drought bankrupted many hopeful industrious families and finally proved the adage, "Dry farming succeeds best in wet years" (Peffer, 155).

In spite of the failure of the 1909 act, Congress still refused to think beyond the homestead concept as the major tenet of public domain policy. Even though Congress was confronted with clear evidence of disastrous impacts of the homesteaders' largely futile efforts, the demand for land was so great that homesteading was continued and expanded. In an effort to resolve the human and resource problems created by the 160- and 320-acre land parcels, Congress passed the Stockraising Homestead Act of 1916. This act provided for homesteads of 640 acres, which Congress hoped would be sufficient to support settlers in the arid West. Since the land could not be farmed in the traditional eastern sense, they attempted to provide for ranch homesteads. Entries under this act were delayed by the outbreak of World War I. However, the pace accelerated after the war and 32 million acres were ultimately patented under this one act alone (Peffer, 167). Years later, in the 1960s and 1970s, these lands would be especially troublesome to federal managers, since entries under the 1916 act did not grant title to the minerals, only to the surface resources. Although this was well known at the time, no one anticipated that the subsurface minerals would ever be valuable. In the late 1960s, the government began leasing the publicly owned coal beneath the 640-acre homesteads, thus creating great problems for the surface owners. In 1916, however, the most obvious weakness in the legislation was that it extended rather than solved problems created by efforts to farm too small units of untillable arid land. The public domain was being broken into units too small to support a family, and overexploitation of the land was virtually required.

Confronted with these difficulties and ultimately recognizing the fairness and benefits of Forest Service retention and management of the range lands, many stock operators became agency supporters. Their repeated efforts to secure a leasing system on the public domain failed, but one success story is indicative of the Forest Service's growing support in some western circles. Range conditions were so obviously unacceptable on 400,000 acres in California that cattle and sheep growers joined to convince Congress to add the area to the Modoc National Forest. Passage of that bill set off a flurry of similar requests from all over the West (Achterman, 28).

Cessions to the States

In spite of the growing respect that the Forest Service was earning, the overall tenor of the times was inauspicious for the agency. The same 1912 appropriations bill rider which required that the Forest Service open the forests to homesteading also proposed granting the national forests to the states. Although the proposal was ruled out of order, it attracted a great deal of support. Especially in the West, the idea of states' rights in resource development was and is a powerful political force. The underlying purpose of such proposals was generally, as Chief Graves stated it, "not to substitute State for Federal control, but rather to substitute individual for public control" (Dana, 180). This and subsequent efforts to gain cession to the states failed, but the idea surfaced constantly as a solution to land management problems. Many specific complaints regarding the Forest Service accompanied the widespread western campaign to gain access and title to the national forests.

First there was general and understandable disgruntlement toward the rather high-handed tactics and self-righteous attitudes of Pinchot's crusading young followers. The vision of a zealous but inexperienced Yale-trained forester arriving to preach the gospel of Pinchot in many turn-of-the-century western boom towns is amusing in retrospect. At the time, it created problems. Many of the ardent eastern foresters did not accept the plain fact that forestry on western public lands could not succeed until privately owned timber was scarce and no longer available at "give away" prices (Roberts, 38). The sense of mission in the agency is usually seen as the Forest Service's greatest asset. However, all of the assumptions behind the messianism—scarcity, stability, and certainty—made little sense in the rapidly developing West. The zealous foresters engendered much hostility. Moreover, the foresters themselves were nonplussed to find that range management rather than forestry occupied most of their time and attention. Many became hostile to range use of the national forests, which did not endear them to local residents.

Second, the Forest Service was criticized because so many resources other than trees were "locked up." Water, minerals, and power sites which had been available in Eastern states for development were being denied to Westerners. Representative Taylor of Colorado, who would subsequently change his position and lend his name and support to the Taylor Grazing Act, began his career as an eloquent opponent of the "lock ups." "Resources," he intoned in 1911, "are the property of the people who go there to develop them. If you want a share of them, come to our country and help us reclaim the forest and the desert land and develop the water power. We will extend you a hearty greeting and you are welcome to your share of it. But you have no right to remain cozily in the east and put a tax upon one industry in trying to build up those great Western states" (cited in Ise, 272).

Taxes were a third major source of antagonism toward the Forest Service. Beginning in 1906, arrangements were made to return a percentage of Forest Service receipts to the counties in which the forests were located. Nonetheless, one ubiquitous feature of forest policy discussions in 1910 and today is the complaint that removing valuable land from settlement, development, and the tax rolls of local communities imposes an unfair burden on the region.

Conservation progress was slowed but not halted by these criticisms. There was sufficient support in the East and in many quarters of the West for building on Roosevelt's initiative. The revesting of the O & C lands and the formation of the National Park Service are major achievements in wild lands management, but hostility toward the Forest Service discussed above is manifest in both. The O & C lands revested to the General Land Office, not the Forest Service; and the Park Service was established over the strenuous objections of the Forest Service.

THE OREGON AND CALIFORNIA RAILROAD GRANT LANDS

The revestment of the O & C lands, as they are commonly called, is a long and complicated story. It began in 1866 with a fairly typical grant of federal land to a railroad, and did not end until the 1950s. The first unusual turn took place with the federal government's effort, beginning in 1912, to get the land back from the railroad. This revesting of the land, returning it to federal ownership, was achieved in 1917, but management of the area caused problems for another forty years.

In 1866, Congress granted to the Oregon and California Railroad Company all of the odd-numbered sections of nonmineral public land to a distance of 20 miles on each side of a proposed railroad from Portland, Oregon, to the California border. Three years later the grant was amended to provide that the lands granted just be sold only to actual settlers in quantities not greater than 160 acres to any one purchaser and at a price not exceeding $2.50 per acre. These additional provisions were intended to ensure that in selling the land to pay for railroad construction, the company would assist Congressional homesteading and settlement policies. Unfortunately, timber prices in the Northwest began to rise in the 1890s, and the company found it more advantageous to hold the land than to sell it. All three of the conditions were flagrantly violated. In 1903, the Southern Pacific Company, of which the Oregon and California Railroad Company had become a subsidiary, for all practical purposes withdrew the remaining lands from the market. The total area involved was nearly 3 million acres containing some of the finest timber in Oregon.

In 1908, Congress authorized the Attorney General to initiate proceedings which would lead to the forfeiture of the grant. Suit was accordingly brought against the railroad company and also against some forty-five purchasers who had each bought more than 1000 acres from the company. In the main suit against the Southern Pacific Company, the federal district court in 1913 declared the lands forfeited to the government on the ground that the grant was made "on condition subsequent" and therefore forfeitable if the conditions were broken. Two years later the Supreme Court reversed this ruling, finding that the terms of the grant did not constitute a "condition subsequent" but a covenant. Therefore, the court held that the remedy for the violation of congressional direction could be rectified only by act of Congress, not by a court-ordered forfeiture of the grant. In 1916, Congress passed the Chamberlain-Ferris Act, which revested in the United States title to all unsold lands which the Oregon and California Railroad Company owned and all lands for which it was entitled to receive patent.

Disposal of Revested Lands

Given the unusually valuable timber involved in the O & C lands, it is surprising that the lands were not turned over to the Forest Service. The O & C lands were checkerboarded with Forest Service lands and intermingled management has been a continuing source of difficulty. However, revestment implies that the land reverted to its former status, unreserved public domain lands under the General Land Office. While proximity and the obvious forest potential indicated Forest Service administration was most appropriate for the area, the lure of the homesteader and disinclination in the West to lock up any more land precluded Forest Service involvement. Instead, the Secretary of the Interior was ordered to classify the lands into three classes for disposition. Class I was to include only lands chiefly valuable for waterpower sites. These lands were subject to withdrawal, use, and disposition as was provided by previous laws pertaining to similar public lands.

Class II was a temporary category including timberlands having not less than 300 M board feet of timber on each 40-acre subdivision. The timber on these lands was to be sold under competitive bidding as rapidly as reasonable prices could be secured in a normal market. After the timber had been removed, the cutover lands were then to become subject to disposal in the same way as class III lands, except that no payment was required.

Agricultural lands, class III, included all lands not falling into either of the other classes, regardless of their actual character. These lands were opened to entry under the general provisions of the homestead laws, except that a charge of $2.50 per acre was made and commutation was not allowed. All lands except power-site lands were to be open for exploration, entry, and disposition under the mineral laws. During the passage of the revestment bill, the Oregon delegation insisted that the federal government pay to the counties all of the back taxes which the railroad company refused to pay while the status of the land was being litigated. After this sum had been repaid and the railroad company had been compensated for its equity in the lost land, the remainder was allocated according to the following formula: 25 percent to the state for its school fund, 25 percent to counties for schools and transportation facilities, and 40 percent to the reclamation fund. The other 10 percent went to the general fund of the U.S. Treasury. The Forest Service was at the time returning only 25 percent of receipts to the counties, the remaining going to the general fund. This generous return to counties and the state may partially explain the Oregon congressional delegation's enthusiasm for General Land Office rather than Forest Service administration of the lands.

Handling of the Revested Lands

The basic weakness of the Chamberlain-Ferris Act lay in its assumption that practically all of the revested lands were agricultural in character. The three disposition classes are a clear example of Congress' tendency to define land uses without particular regard for the characteristics of the land in question. Mountainous land with thin soil, marginal climate, and a heavy concentration of old growth forest cover is not transformed by act of Congress into agricultural land suitable for homesteading. Both the land and many hapless settlers suffered mightily in the attempt to make it otherwise. However, less than 500,000 acres were ever patented. The total area of revested lands was reduced, by transfer to private owners and by transfer to national forest status, to about 2.5 million acres, which continued under the jurisdiction of the General Land Office. The lands contained some 50 billion board feet of timber. This constituted about a sixth of the total sawtimber stand in the Douglas fir region of Oregon at the time; but, because of the erroneous assumption that the lands would eventually be cleared for agriculture, no attempt was made to manage the timber.

The O & C revestment was a major step forward, but failure to turn the land over to the Forest Service was a lost opportunity for the agency as well as the nation. A more direct and generalized challenge, to both the assumptions of forestry and the Forest Service, was manifest in the formation of the National Park Service.

THE NATIONAL PARK SERVICE

Beginning in 1864, when Congress ceded Yosemite Valley and Mariposa Big Grove to the state of California for public recreation purposes, Congress occasionally reserved from entry public land areas of unusual natural or scenic importance for preservation as national parks. Thirteen areas had been designated before specific provision for their administration was made. For many years before the National Park Service was established, protection and supervision of the parks was provided by the United States Cavalry (Hampton, passim.). After sustained and vigorous pressure from influential park advocates in the East, Congress passed an authorizing statute for the National Park Service in 1916.

The Hetch Hetchy Controversy

Controversy over the building of a dam in the Hetch Hetchy Valley in Yosemite National Park in California was a critical factor in finally achieving passage of the long-sought Park Service bill. It clearly identified preservation as an effective political force distinct from conservation. The conflict was a long and bitter debate lasting fifteen years and pitting John Muir and those interested in resource preservation against the utilitarian conservationists. The conflict frequently is misrepresented as a "battle of the Titans"—Muir versus Pinchot. There is some accuracy in this caricature because Pinchot was a leading conservationist and because he did end a long and productive cooperative relationship with Muir over the issue. However, neither Pinchot nor the Forest Service was a leading advocate of the project. Whatever voice Pinchot raised in behalf of the Hetch Hetchy Dam was simply one in a chorus of San Franciscans who needed a water supply, western developers who sought electric power, irrigationists who saw rivers and dams as the key to prosperity in the West, and advocates of public as opposed to private water and power development. That combination was insurmountable, and the dam was built. Outcry against the dam—particularly in the East—was sufficient, however, to focus public and congressional attention on management of aesthetic resources. Freed from the battle over Hetch Hetchy, the preservationists turned their attention to establishing an administrative system for park areas. In 1916, their efforts were successful in spite of a long-standing effort by the Forest Service to block the move (Steen, 114–118).

Purposes of the Parks

The Park Service was created to regulate the use of the national parks and similar reservations. The purpose of the agency was stated primarily by the great landscape architect and park planner, Frederick Law Olmstead, who contributed to the most familiar portion of the bill: "To conserve the scenery and the natural and historic objects and the wildlife therein and to provide for the enjoyment of same in such manner and by such means as will leave them unimpaired for the enjoyment of future generations" (Dana, 200). The National Park Service was organized in 1917 with Stephen T. Mather as its first director. In a gesture reminiscent of the Secretary of Agriculture's 1905 letter of instruction to Gifford Pinchot regarding the conduct of the national forests, the Secretary of the Interior wrote Mather in May 1918, admirably stating the three broad principles on which the administration of the parks was to be based:

> First, that the national parks should be maintained in absolutely unimpaired form for the use of future generations as well as those of our own time; second, that they are set apart for the use, observation, health, and pleasure of the people; and third, that the national interest must dictate all decisions affecting public or private enterprise in the parks. Every activity of the Service is subordinate to the duties imposed upon it to faithfully preserve the parks for posterity in essentially their natural state [Dana, 200].

Mather saw his responsibilities, once the Park Service had been established, in terms of expansion (Everhart, 17–18). Mather was every bit as zealous a crusader for the parks as Pinchot was for Roosevelt's conservation program. He saw that to expand the park system, he needed more money. To increase appropriations, he needed supportive citizenry, which meant he had to lure people to the parks. This emphasis on visitor days led to a decision to emphasize hotels, roads, concessions, and a massive campaign to encourage tourism in the national parks. The central position in park management afforded to the development-oriented concessionaires during the sustained period of Park Service boosterism has been a troubling barrier to the agency's recent efforts to implement a more ecologically sensitive management regime.

Mather was neither insincere nor foolish. He recognized that his fledgling agency was threatened by the same pressures for western development that challenged many Forest Service programs. His problems in establishing and promoting the Park Service were in many ways more acute than those the Forest Service confronted. First, it is harder to establish a park than a forest. National forests were designated by presidential proclamation. Before the major reaction in the 1907 appropriations bill, more than 150 million acres had been reserved as national forests by this relatively uncomplicated process. Except for the national monuments, which are also established by proclamation in accordance with the provisions of the 1906 Antiquities Act, creation of each national park still requires a separate act of Congress. The process is slow, arduous, and polarizing and requires much public effort. Mather had to build the necessary public support. In many instances, the effort to secure passage of requisite designating legislation required park advocates to compromise their goals. Moreover, each park has a slightly different mandate; and confusion and inconsistency frequently result.

Second, until the early 1960s, the Park Service was not authorized to purchase land for park purposes except under highly constrained special circumstances. The Park Service was dependent on donations from states and private individuals to secure lands outside the public domain states. The Forest Service, as shall be discussed below, was authorized in 1911 to purchase forest land in the East.

Third, with exceptions occasionally required to achieve designation of a park, the preservationists were supporting a very restrictive management scheme. The Forest Service was accused of "locking up" resources; yet timber harvesting, mining, grazing, hunting, and water management projects were encouraged in national forests. All were disallowed in parks. The limited use of parks appealed to the preservationists, but it was frequently difficult to sell the idea to the local population.

Finally, there was no provision in the Park Service mandate for returning a percentage of the receipts to the counties. The Park Service has never generated much revenue. They had to attract visitors and, therefore, the agency was—and continues to be—reticent to charge fair market value for use of the recreation facilities. The absence of a return to the counties to compensate for the lost tax base was not an asset in attempting to convince locals to support parks. It was necessary to curry local favor by promoting the parks as tourist bonanzas which would be contributions to the local economy.

Mather was in a difficult position in defending Park Service programs, especially in the development-oriented West. Moreover, his commitment to vast expansion of the system required more support than could be garnered by strict adherence to the Secretary of the Interior's basic guidelines for park administration. The preservation mandate so eloquently stated in the Park Service organic act was replaced by a commitment to tourism. In this, Mather had three major allies. The railroads rapidly became partners in transporting tourists to the parks and in publicizing their scenic wonders. The American Automobile Association (AAA), just founded to promote the interests of the rapidly expanding number of motorists in the country, played a similar role. Motorists found in Mather a staunch ally of road building in the parks (Shankland, 145–150). Finally, the parks were supported by the concessionaires—

individuals encouraged to invest in visitor facilities in the parks. Because the Park Service did not have the budget to provide the "grand hotel" type of visitor facilities which Mather believed necessary and appropriate, the resorts were built by private concerns, which became major supporters of the parks and their further development.

Mather is the Park Service's Pinchot. He lacks Pinchot's stature in conservation history only because his effort was directed at one agency and one aspect of resource management in a period which was not the critical epoch in initiating the conservation movement. Mather was, however, much less irascible than Pinchot and was extremely effective in building congressional and public support for his fledgling agency.

EASTERN LAND ACQUISITIONS

The movement to establish national parks was an important aspect of an increasing concern for conservation of wild lands resources in the East. Interestingly, at the same time that cession of public lands to the states was being strenuously advocated and enthusiasm for the Forest Service programs was low in many areas of the West, the national forest concept was being significantly expanded in the East. Beginning in about 1880, the idea of protecting large blocks of eastern lands through government purchase steadily gained ground. There seems to be considerable confusion in the public mind about the difference between a park and a forest. A proposal for acquiring forested lands in the southern Appalachians for a park was soon followed by agitation for the purchase of forest reserves in the White Mountains of New Hampshire. Several bills were introduced in the early 1900s in Congress but got nowhere. Then New England and the South decided to join forces, and in 1906 a bill providing for the acquisition of lands in both the southern Appalachians and the White Mountains passed the Senate but stalled in the House.

Interest in the purchase of lands for national forests also developed in other regions. Between 1905 and 1908, bills were introduced in Congress providing for such purchases on the watershed of the Potomac River, in the Ozarks, at the head of the Mississippi and Red rivers, and in the Hudson River highlands. A bill appropriating $5 million for the purchasing of forestlands without geographic limitation was nearly enacted in 1909 but was killed by a filibuster by a few western senators in the closing days of the Sixtieth Congress.

Western opposition to extending the reservation concept is relatively uncomplicated: The concept of national forests was controversial; and, when in doubt, they preferred that federal effort and dollars for resource management be spent on developing water and other resources in the West. Eastern support for the concept came from many quarters, three of which are worth mentioning because they continued to be important aspects of forest policy formulation for several decades.

First, eastern loggers, having cut their lands, wanted to move to more promising harvest areas. They naturally preferred to sell the lands rather than to abandon them. They encouraged the federal acquisition program because it created a market for lands thought to be worthless otherwise.

Second, eastern acquisition programs were supported by eastern conservation, preservation, and naturalist's clubs. The National Academy of Sciences and the Appalachian Mountain Club were typical of the strong coalition of interested citizens that urged the acquisition of national forests in the East as a preservation measure.

Third, these same cutover lands were a tremendous fire hazard. It is difficult for people raised after the forest fire threat had been largely subdued to credit the reports of fires in the first third of this century. Smokey Bear was not born until the 1940s; but from its earliest days, Forest Service support in the East was closely tied to the agency's reputation as a fire fighter. The hazards of fire and the need to control the menace were all too clear in the Forest Service's first three decades. The agency became so committed to putting out fires that, until recently, it suppressed information regarding many clear benefits of fire in the forest ecosystem (Schiff, passim.). Reeducating both the agency and the public has been a problem in the 1970s; but, at the time, commitment to fire suppression made political and empirical sense.

Constitutional Issues Regarding Acquisition

As frequently happens when powerful alliances line up to debate, much of the discussion of acquisition centered on an issue unrelated to the merits of the program—in this instance, its constitutionality. Opponents of the Weeks Act argued that the constitution does not give the government the authority to buy land for purposes of forest protection. Advocates countered that the constitution does give Congress power "to regulate Commerce among the several states" and that the purchase of forests would improve the flow of navigable streams that might be used in interstate commerce. The debate marks the end of the long-standing assumption that forests control flood, drought, siltation, climate, and water supply. After careful consideration, the House Committee on the Judiciary in May 1908, with one dissenting vote, adopted a critical resolution on the subject. The committee regarded the proposed purchase program as constitutional if it would, in fact, exert a beneficial influence on the flow of navigable streams. The committee did not believe that forests had any substantial effects on stream flow or, even if they did, that change in ownership would substantially alter that effect.

The situation was complicated by radical disagreement among alleged experts about the issue. Foresters and geologists claimed that forests in hilly country markedly reduce surface water runoff and therefore regularize stream flow. Meteorologists and many engineers vigorously disputed this claim. Unfortunately here, as in the fire program, the Forest Service fit its science to the political exigencies of the day. The claims made by foresters and their political allies regarding the impact of forest cover on stream flow and navigability were exaggerated, occasionally demonstrably false (Schiff, chap. 4). The field was young, many of its truths were speculative, and no one is exempt from the need to deal with political realities. However, the discussion was undignified at best and continued to be so for many years before the record regarding the influence of forest cover on stream flow and flooding was set straight. The Weeks Act was passed in the interim.

Passage of the Weeks Act—1911

How many votes were changed by the scientific and pseudoscientific arguments about the influence of forests on stream flow is open to question. More than likely, members of Congress chose to believe the experts who agreed with their own positions. The decision was a political rather than a technical one. The Weeks Act blazed two new trails of major importance in the development of forest policy in this country.

First, it appropriated $200,000, to be available until expended, to enable the Secretary of Agriculture to cooperate with any state or group of states in protecting from fire private or state forestlands on the watersheds of navigable streams. The limited funds appropriated undercut the potential importance of this provision. However, the gesture encouraged many states to adopt effective fire control legislation and established fire control organizations and focused attention on fire control activities throughout the country.

Second, the Weeks Act authorized appropriations for the survey and acquisition of "lands located on the headwaters of navigable streams or those which are being or which may be developed for navigable purposes." There was no geographic limitation on where acquisition could take place, although it was generally understood that the first purchases would be in the southern Appalachians and the White Mountains. This provision made it possible for the Forest Service to extend its activities beyond the public land states in the West and become a truly national organization. The Secretary of Agriculture was authorized to recommend the acquisition of lands which were, in his judgment, necessary for regulating the flow of navigable streams and to purchase such lands.

The Secretary was also authorized to organize acquired lands to be administered as national forests. Purchase boundaries are established by the Secretary, and when acreage within the purchase unit is sufficient, the area is designated as a national forest. In most eastern national forests, a program for acquisition of private "inholdings" continues to this day within the designated purchase units (Shands and Healy, passim.). No purchases were to be made until the U.S. Geological Survey (USGS) reported that control of the lands would promote or protect the navigation of streams on whose watersheds they lay and until the legislature of the state in which the land was located consented to United States acquisition of the land. These provisions were designed to check any exaggerated ideas the Forest Service might have about the influence of forests on stream flow and to observe the rights and wishes of the states. The act also created a National Forest Reservation Commission to review areas recommended for purchase and fix the price at which purchases should be made.

Field studies soon convinced the USGS that forest cover affected stream flow in the southern Appalachian Mountains. More extensive studies in the White Mountains, where the relationship was less clear, led USGS to the same conclusion. No tract which the Forest Service wished to buy has been turned down because of an adverse USGS report. Most of the states in which purchases were contemplated also gave their consent promptly and enthusiastically. Maryland first gave its consent but some years later withdrew it. Some states in other regions limited consent to a specific part of the state, as in Pennsylvania, and in others to a maximum area, as in Wisconsin. In general, the requirement of state approval has not interfered with the acquisition program.

Related Legislation and Appropriations

Funds appropriated for the land purchases varied greatly from year to year after June 30, 1915, when the original appropriations ended. On the whole, they were disappointingly small, and the erratic fluctuations made it difficult to maintain an effective purchase organization. Purchases were limited chiefly to cutover areas and were made at extremely reasonable prices. In the 1920s, dissatisfaction with the slow progress of the program became so acute that a vigorous drive for increased appropriations began. It resulted in the McNary-Woodruff Act of 1928, which will be discussed subsequently.

In 1913, the acquisition provision of the Weeks Act was broadened to permit the purchase of lands having rights of way, easements, or reservations as long as they do not interfere with the use of the lands purchased. Sellers of land were permitted to retain minerals or merchantable timber on the purchased lands under terms specified in the deed. The amendment facilitated the acquisition of needed lands which might not otherwise have been available for purchase. However, it subsequently created hostility in some quarters. Citizens who did not understand that the title to the land had been severed from the mineral estate or the merchantable timber were sometimes confused when the Forest Service was unable to control mining or harvest operations on national forest lands.

Funding for road building in the national forests was achieved through the same 1912 appropriations bill which obliged the Forest Service to divest itself of agricultural lands. The fund made 10 percent of the annual receipts from national forests available to the Secretary of Agriculture for the construction of roads and trails within national forests in the states from which the receipts were derived. This legislation was made permanent the next year. It constituted a partial reversion to the 1905 policy of placing all receipts from national forests at the disposal of the Secretary of Agriculture, but differed in two respects. Only a small part of the total receipts was involved, and this part had to be used for a specific purpose. The road building program was critical to fire protection and many other management programs. To have the funds available for necessary construction on a continuing basis has proved most helpful in making forest resources more available and in improving their administration.

With major legislation in 1911 and 1912, Congress had come to the end of a long and creative period of attention to forest matters. Conservation receded from the center of public concern. Although resource issues continued to be debated, most of the innovation in the next six or eight years was undertaken primarily within the Forest Service. Critical among these internal efforts was the development of the Branch of Research.

Research Branch

The research activities of the Forest Service were greatly strengthened by the establishment on June 1, 1915, of the Branch of Research as part of a reorganization which had two major purposes. One was to bring about more effective correlation of all investigative work by placing it under a single administrative head. With research in so many different fields (forest management, range management, forest and range economics, forest influences, and forest products) conducted by the Washington office, the district offices, and the forest experiment stations, the need for such correlation was clear. The second purpose was to give the research work and personnel fullest recognition by developing and strengthening research as a coordinate division of the service with the same organizational status as administrative activities. Under the imaginative and aggressive leadership of Earle H. Clapp, rapid progress was made toward attaining the desired objectives. Coordination, expansion, and above all the successful conduct by competent personnel of studies yielding fruitful results gradually brought the Branch of Research recognition as one of the most useful and important parts of the Forest Service.

In 1921, the first regional forest experiment station in the eastern United States was established with headquarters at Asheville, North Carolina. Others followed until the entire country was covered by a network of regional stations. Both the value of the research and the growing interest of private landowners in forestry are illustrated by the fact that pressure for the establishment of the eastern stations came largely from timberland owners in the East. At all the stations, in both the East and West, research activities are oriented to meet the needs of public and private owners alike. Many of them have established advisory committees made up of local citizens to guide in policy formulation.

PROFESSIONAL DEVELOPMENTS

The early years of forestry and forest policy are so dominated by federal programs and the Forest Service that it is easy to overlook significant developments in other areas. Professional development and forestry education burgeoned during this period. It is true that Pinchot and the Forest Service were preeminent, and that the profession was held together initially by the passion of true believers. Growth and development in the early years did, however, provide various centers of influence within the profession which led rapidly to necessary diversification.

Forestry Education

The success with which forestry is practiced obviously depends on the ability of its practitioners. By 1910, technical training in forestry was offered at fifteen schools, of which one was in the South and only four in the West. The establishment of so many schools in so short a time, with widely varying curricula and quality of instruction, led Pinchot, then Chief of the Forest Service, to call a conference of forest schools. The primary purpose was to consider standards of education in forestry. The conference met and recommended the organization of an association of forestry schools and appointed a committee to formulate a standard of forest education.

That committee submitted a provisional report at a national conference on forest education held in Washington in December 1911. It presented in detail the contents of each technical subject that in its judgment should be included in a four-year curriculum and the minimum number of hours that should be devoted to each subject. The totals came to 1500 hours, of which it was recommended that 585 hours be in classwork and 915 hours in field or laboratory work. For nearly a decade, these standards continued to serve as a guide to the schools of forestry. The standardization could not and did not last. However, the careful, collective consideration given to education in forestry during a critical period in its development helped create high standards of competence in the profession.

Society of American Foresters

Another major influence in any profession is the standing of its national organization. The Society of American Foresters, established in 1900 with a handful of members, grew steadily in numbers and in strength. Its influence was felt most strongly in raising the standards of technical competence and in establishing an exceptionally strong esprit de corps throughout the profession.

One weakness, the practice of holding all meetings of the society in Washington, where they could be attended by only a few members, was remedied in 1912 by the establishment of a Northern Rocky Mountain Section at Missoula, Montana. This precedent was followed in other parts of the country until there are now numerous regional sections, subsections, and working groups reflecting the diverse interests of its many members. An important move was made on January 1, 1917, when the society assumed responsibility for publishing the *Journal of Forestry,* a periodical formed by amalgamation of the *Forestry Quarterly* and the *Proceedings of the Society of American Foresters.* First published eight times a year, it became a monthly in 1935.

WORLD WAR I

The benefits of the growing management profession were beginning to be felt on forests and, to a much lesser extent, range lands when World War I began. The entrance of the United States into the war had immediate and far-reaching effects on both industry and government resource management programs. The material requirements of the army and navy had to be met on a time schedule that brooked no delay. The situation was not one to encourage even the more progressive owners to improve their forest practices. Range resources were less protected than the forests and were overexploited accordingly.

So far as the Forest Service was concerned, the national forests had to be managed with a greatly reduced force; but the heaviest impact was felt in the research field, in which all investigations not concerned with war problems were soon halted. The Forest Products Laboratory became an invaluable part of the war machine not only through the conduct of fundamental research but also by assisting military and civilian agencies in every phase of the selection, purchase, and utilization of wood for the countless purposes for which it was used. Hardly less valuable were the field studies conducted by other parts of the Forest Service to locate adequate supplies of timber of the species, size, and quality essential for aircraft, ships, vehicles, gunstocks, tanning materials, wood distillation, cooperage, containers, and other products. Forest research, especially in the field of wood technology, suddenly assumed an urgency previously unknown.

LOGS AND LABOR

One of the major difficulties faced by the lumber industry in meeting wartime needs arose from its relations with labor. The efforts of the Industrial Workers of the World during the preceding decade to organize lumberjacks and mill workers, raise starvation wages, decrease long hours of work, and improve disgraceful working conditions had accomplished little but to stir up occasional violence. The coming of war, with its urgent demands for wood supplied without delay, gave the "Wobblies" an opportunity of which they were quick to take advantage.

The situation was particularly critical in the Pacific Northwest, where strikes seriously endangered production of adequate supplies of Sitka spruce for airplane construction and of heavy Douglas fir timbers for a wide variety of purposes. Government and industry found an answer in the establishment of the Loyal Legion of Loggers and Lumbermen. The "4 L" sought to promote understanding and cooperation in the war effort by including equal numbers of workers and employers throughout the organization, from a camp committee to the board of governors. It succeeded not only in maintaining production at the necessary level but in effecting a substantial increase in wages, reduction in working hours, and betterment in living conditions.

FOREST ENGINEERS IN FRANCE

Efforts to keep our troops and our British and French allies supplied with wood is one of the most colorful chapters in forestry history. A shortage of shipping virtually precluded the export of lumber and other forest products from the United States to the war zone, with the result that 75 percent of the timber used by the American army had to be cut from French forests by our own troops. At the request of the War Department, first one and then a second regiment were formed to handle the necessary logging and milling. The regiment included skilled woodsworkers and mill operators from all the main lumber regions of the country, while about half of the officers were trained foresters. By the date of the armistice, the forestry section numbered some 12,000 engineer troops and 9000 service troops. Their accomplishments were tremendous in providing the wood needed by the army for lumber and railroad ties; large timber for docks, barges, trestles, and bridges; piling, telephone, and telegraph poles; fuel; and small material. By the end of the war, there were about ninety active operations, most of them with sawmills.

EXPLOITATION OF THE RANGE

The story of range management during the period is less colorful and uplifting. On the unreserved public domain, there was no barrier to overgrazing. There was a great demand for meat, no charge for the range, and accelerated production was encouraged by loans from the War Finance Corporation. The Forest Service was forced to abandon its policy of removing excess stock from the range. They were, in fact, obliged to issue many "temporary" permits to increase use of the range. The results were easily foreseeable and disastrous. Range management deteriorated under pressure for unrestricted use during the war. Worse still, the livestock industry, having overexploited the productive capacity of the range and expanded itself beyond the potential peacetime market on war loans, went into a severe depression when hostilities ceased. The economic stress within the industry made subsequent regulation all the more difficult.

SUMMARY

Material requirements of the war led to overexploitation of both forest and range resources. However, even under the pressure of war, the nation's basic commitment to resource reservation and management was not broken. A rethinking and sorting out of the many Roosevelt-Pinchot initiatives was inevitable and necessary. Although the Forest Service was criticized and challenged, the overall direction of the period was forward.

Passage of the Weeks Act of 1911 established two new federal policies of major importance—cooperation with the states in the protection of forests from fire, and acquisition of forest lands for the protection of the watersheds of navigable streams. The creation of the National Park Service is appropriately viewed as a mild rebuke to the Forest Service, but it constitutes a major expansion of the conservation program to include aesthetic preservation. The O & C revestment with its unrealistic reiteration of the homesteading concept reflected a continuing problem which was manifest in two other equally unsatisfactory laws of the period. The Enlarged Homestead Act of 1909 and the Stockraising Homestead Act of 1916 exacerbated the crisis in range occupancy and did nothing to alleviate range deterioration. Confronted with this deterioration situation, many stock raisers became supportive of the Forest Service and its range management programs.

REFERENCES CITED

Achterman, Gail L. "Judicial Control of Administrative Discretion in the Development of BLM Land Classification Policy." Unpublished masters thesis, Ann Arbor: The University of Michigan, 1975.

Cameron, Jenks. *The Development of Governmental Forest Control in the United States.* Baltimore: Johns Hopkins Press, 1928.

Everhart, William C. *The National Park Service.* New York: Praeger Publishers, 1972.

Gates, Paul W. *History of Public Land Law Development.* Written for the Public Land Law Review Commission. Washington: Government Printing Office, 1968.

Greeley, William B. *Some Public and Economic Aspects of the Lumber Industry.* Washington: Report 114, Office of the Secretary of Agriculture, 1917.

Hampton, H. Duane. *How the U. S. Cavalry Saved Our National Parks.* Bloomington: Indiana University Press, 1971.

Ise, John. *The United States Forest Policy.* New Haven: Yale University Press, 1920.

Lillard, Richard G. *The Great Forest.* New York: Alfred A. Knopf, Inc., 1947.

Peffer, E. Louise. *The Closing of the Public Domain.* Stanford: Stanford, University Press, 1951.

Robbins, Roy M. *Our Landed Heritage*. New York: Peter Smith, 1950.

Roberts, Paul H. *Hoof Prints on Forest Ranges*. San Antonio: The Naylor Company, 1963.

Schands, William E. and Robert G. Healey. *The Lands Nobody Wanted*. Washington: The Conservation Foundation, 1977.

Shankland, Robert. *Steve Mather of the National Parks*. 3d ed. New York: Alfred A. Knopf, 1970

Schiff, Ashley L. *Fire and Water: Scientific Heresy in the Forest Service*. Cambridge: Harvard University Press, 1962.

Steen, Harold K. *The U. S. Forest Service: A History*. Seattle: University of Washington Press, 1977.

U.S. Department of Commerce and Labor, Bureau of Corporations. *The Lumber Industry, Part I: Standing Timber*. Washington: Government Printing Office, 1913.

Woolsey, Theodore S., Jr. *Riding the Chuck Line. A Forester in Peace and War*. New Haven: The Tuttle, Morehouse and Taylor Company, 1930.

Chapter 5

Diversification, Disagreement, and Cooperative Programs, 1920–1932

The period between World War I and the New Deal is critical in the development of wild lands policy. Frequently dismissed as a quiet interlude between the two titans, Theodore and Franklin Roosevelt, these years actually mark the beginning of many of our contemporary wild lands management programs. The time for messianism, crusading, and bold new initiatives was over. Forestry was less a movement than a maturing, diversifying profession.

The period is appropriately viewed in terms of the Chief of the Forest Service, William B. Greeley, who served from 1920 to 1929. Greeley did not dominate an era as did Pinchot, but he presided with firmness and finesse over intense internal debate which emerged within the profession. With both the forestry profession and the concept of national forests on firm footing, the solidarity and singularity of foresters disappeared. Greeley's effort was focused on rethinking the goals of forest management, and concern shifted away from forest reservations to extending forest practices to private lands. This part of the forestry agenda had been all but forgotten after Pinchot pushed Fernow aside in the 1890s and riveted attention on the crusade for national forests. In the 1920s, the issue resurfaced, with Pinchot a central figure in the discussion but frequently at odds with the Forest Service leadership. In the debate over government regulation of private lands management, the profession went through its first, most prolonged, and divisive family fight.

Vigorous internal debate was augmented by the beginnings of external strife as well. The formation of the National Park Service was both a rebuke and a threat to the Pinchot utilitarian conservationists who underestimated the importance of aesthetic conservation. He and his followers were unconvincing in their argument that the Forest Service should manage the national park reservations. The Park Service was established over their protests in 1916 and found its feet during the 1920s largely through the leadership and keen political sensitivities of Steven Mather, its first director. The birth of the Park Service partially stimulated the inevitable diversification of forestry. Recreation emerged as an important forest use, and wilderness was recognized as an appropriate category of national forest management. Other important factors also contributed to the maturation of the profession. Range policy again became a contested management and political issue for the Forest Service in the mid-1920s, and the wildlife concerns began to emerge as a minor but visible component of the forester's responsibilities. This did not alter, or even seriously challenge, the predominant silvicultural bias of the profession and the Forest Service, but these new and durable issues were arising.

During these debates, Congress was a source of leadership and direction in forest and range management in a way that has never been repeated. The name of Charles McNary, Senator from Oregon, figures prominently in much of the legislation, particularly the Clarke-McNary Act of 1924 and the McSweeney-McNary Act of 1928. Two bills enacted in 1930—the Knutson-Vandenberg Act and the Shipstead-Nolan Act—round out the roster of major legislation. Congress built on the cooperative programs begun under the Weeks Act of 1911. Federal assistance in fire control, reforestation, and forest protection was extended and intensified and a major federal leadership role in research and education initiated. During the 1920s, the groundwork for most of what constitutes the present federal forestry program was established.

Unfortunately, similar developments did not occur in range management. Both the open range and the Forest Service grazing areas were destructively overstocked during World War I. The imbalance was not wholly righted when peace came. In the mid-1920s, the situation deteriorated further. The Forest Service was trapped in a controversy over setting grazing fees that undercut their grazing program. The forestry profession and conservation groups unnecessarily and foolishly alienated the strong allies within the livestock industry that the Forest Service had been winning since 1905. The result of the unfortunate conflict was that it virtually guaranteed that the Forest Service would never be authorized to manage the public domain lands.

The period is a nadir of sorts for the public domain lands. A major presidential public land study late in the decade concluded that the policy toward the unreserved public domain should be to turn the lands over to the states. Governors throughout the West roared complaints that the federal government was trying to burden them with a useless administrative headache, and the idea was dropped. No other meaningful proposals were put forward regarding public domain management. Many hoped that the precedent for leasing public domain resources which was embodied in the long-sought Mineral Leasing Act of 1920 would carry over to the range resources, but it did not happen during this decade.

The accomplishments of the 1920s are thus mixed: tremendous diversification, redirection and extension of forest management concepts and programs, and costly setbacks in range policy. Because these years lack the invigorating sense of new beginnings of the Pinchot years and the trauma and drama of the Depression, they tend to be overlookeld as insignificant. This is wholly inaccurate. The decades between the Roosevelts, most especially the 1920s, are among the most important and creative in American conservation history (Swain, passim).

INTERNAL DEBATE: THE QUESTION OF FEDERAL REGULATION AND STATE COOPERATION

The regulation controversy was probably inevitable. Foresters, having achieved their initial goals in federal forest reserves and forest management, needed new fields to conquer. The privately held forest lands were not being managed in accordance with sound forest practices and constituted an irresistible challenge and opportunity to the burgeoning new profession. The conflict, which began in earnest in 1919 and raged until the early 1950s, was a professional and political battle over how and to what extent the Forest Service should bring scientific forestry to the private forest lands. At one extreme, Pinchot and his followers advocated an unflinching policy of federal regulation of private cutting practices. Frequently opposing Pinchot, the Forest Service position varied over time depending on who was Chief. In the 1920s, the agency was the primary supporter of state and private cooperation and federal leadership as a means of preventing destructive private practices. At various times, the question of federal regulation was confused with efforts to expand federal forest ownership, but the initial stage of debate was largely focused on federal regulation versus state and private cooperation. As such, it pitted Pinchot against the Forest Service and severely divided the profession.

The conflict was more tactical and ideological than technical. Chief Greeley was inclined to accept a cooperative program emphasizing fire control rather than risk the stalemate which he feared would result from Pinchot's impatient all-or-nothing advocacy of federal control. Greeley also recognized that Pinchot's definition of "sound forest practices" was based on the idealogy of German forestry. Managing every acre for maximum productivity is reasonable only when land scarcity is assumed. Greeley was more sensitive than Pinchot to the capital scarcity that the private forest managers were experiencing. Their plea that they could not afford to grow trees until they could be sold for more than the cost of growing them seemed merely a delaying tactic to Pinchot's zealous crusaders (Greeley, 102–106).

Committee for the Application of Forestry

The first major debate came over the report of the SAF's Committee for the Application of Forestry. Pinchot was the head of the group established in 1919 to recommend programs for preventing devastation on privately owned timberlands. The substance of the committee report, *Forest Devastation: A National Danger and How to Meet It,* was dictated by the preferences of the ever-crusading head. Although there was significant dissent within the committee, the report was pure Pinchot (Ise, 395). It emphasized the nation's requirements for wood, the danger of a serious timber shortage resulting from the devastation of privately owned forest lands, and the consequent need to keep all forest lands in continuous production. The plan which it proposed to achieve this goal was based upon nine fundamental principles, including the idea that "the national timber supply must be made secure by forbidding the devastation of private forestlands and by promoting the conditions necessary to keep these lands permanently productive." The report continued, "national legislation to prevent forest devastation should [provide] such control over private forestlands . . . as may be necessary to insure the continuous production of forest crops. . . . and to place forest industries on a stable basis in harmony with public interest . . . [with] transfer of control back to the forest industries as soon as they become able and willing to assume responsibility for respecting the public interests" (Dana, 211).

The plan itself was most comprehensive. With respect to the central issue of regulation, it recommended the creation of a federal commission with authority "to fix standards and promulgate rules to prevent the devastation and provide for the perpetuation of forest growth and the production of forest crops on privately owned timberlands operated for commercial purposes, except upon farm wood lots and other areas which might be exempted." The commission would also be authorized "to control timber production in the public interest in times of economic stress." Pinchot, in a personal statement accompanying the report, expressed himself with his usual vigor:

> The fight to conserve the forest resources of our public domain has been won. . . .
> Another and a bigger fight has now begun, with a far greater issue at stake. I use the word fight, because I mean precisely that. Forest devastation will not be stopped through persuasion, a method which has been thoroughly tried out for the past twenty years and has failed utterly. Since otherwise they will not do so, private owners of forest land must now be compelled to manage their properties

in harmony with the public good. The field is cleared for action and the lines are plainly drawn. He who is not for forestry is against it. The choice lies between the convenience of the lumbermen and the public good [Dana, 212].

Forest Service Position

The official position of the Forest Service during the 1920s was that the problem of forest devastation is a national one in which federal leadership is necessary but in which regulatory measures should be handled by the states under their police powers. William B. Greeley, who became Chief Forester in April, 1920, following Graves's resignation, was the major advocate of cooperative programs. He was convinced that the first order of business in establishing responsible management practices on industry holdings was to prevent fire. In his first annual report, he emphasized that "both Federal leadership and a large measure of Federal aid are obligatory. There is practical unanimity of agreement that the first and most essential step is nation-wide protection from forest fires, applicable to all classes of forest land and borne jointly by the landowner and the public."

Capper Report

Both sides of the controversy, the federal regulation advocates and the exponents of cooperative and state regulation schemes, sought congressional support for their position. Senator Arthur Capper of Kansas was one of Pinchot's most effective allies in Congress. In February, 1920, he managed to get the Senate to request the Secretary of Agriculture to submit information on *Timber Depletion, Lumber Exports, and Concentration of Timber Ownership.* The Forest Service responded to the request in behalf of the Secretary, as is customary. Although the report is commonly known as the Capper Report, it reflects its authorship and endorses the Greeley position rather than the Capper-Pinchot line. Throughout the report, emphasis was placed on the extent and seriousness of forest depletion, the remedy for which lay in a "national policy of reforestation." Among the many measures recommended to stop forest devastation and to restore idle land to timber production, the report laid special stress on "the immediate urgency of legislation . . . which will permit effective cooperation between the Federal Government and the several states in preventing forest fires and growing timber on cut-over lands. . . ." (Dana, 218).

The General Exchange Act of 1922

The first legislative achievement of the campaign for an expanded program of forestry was the passage of the General Exchange Act of 1922. After the lieu land provision of the 1897 Organic Act was repealed in 1905, the only way exchange of private and public lands within national forests could occur was by specific act of Congress. The General Exchange Act, as the name implies, grants a general authority to the Secretary of the Interior to exchange nonmineral national forestland or timber for private or state-owned lands of equal value within the forest. The law has proved critical to Forest Service efforts to consolidate federal ownership of the national forests.

The 1922 law resembles the repealed lieu land law which was widely considered a disaster. The major difference between the two provisions is that under the 1922 legislation, the basis of exchange is equal *value* rather than equal area. Moreover, land-for-timber exchanges have enabled the Forest Service to expand as well as to consolidate its holdings.

Capper and Snell Bills

Although the report provided the Forest Service with an opportunity to justify its position, Senator Capper was not pursuaded by the report bearing his name. In May, 1920, he introduced a bill which incorporated practically all of the recommendations of Pinchot's Committee for the Application of Forestry, including the creation of a Federal Forest Commission with direct administrative control over cutting on privately owned forest lands. The bill was supported by Pinchot and by the National Conservation Association, which he founded to support his views on conservation programs. It was opposed by the Forest Service. Actually, there were three versions of the Capper Bill. Constitutional problems were raised by the first two regulatory schemes he proposed, and the final version was not introduced until 1924. No hearings were ever held on any of the bills because of the evident preponderance of opinion in favor of state regulation.

Congressman Bertrand Snell of New York introduced a number of his own bills reflecting the Greeley position. The Snell bills emphasized federal encouragement of state regulation. One key section authorized federal financial assistance to states passing legislation which required private owners to handle their forestlands so as to keep them continuously productive. The one outspoken opponent of the bill was Gifford Pinchot. He was certain that state legislation would never be effective because, in the heavily timbered states, the legislatures would be controlled by the timberland owners and lumbermen. He also feared that passage of this part of the bill would do more harm than good by giving the public the impression that nothing more was necessary, when actually the federal government alone was big and strong enough to take effective action. Pinchot's influence in Congress was not sufficient to achieve passage of the Capper Bill, but he did block the Snell Bill.

Clarke-McNary Act of 1924

When it became clear that the struggle between the state regulationists and the federal regulationists was likely to result in a stalemate, Greeley recommended that that regulation issue be sidestepped and attention concentrated on obtaining favorable action on the cooperative programs proposed in the Snell Bill. Bills incorporating that approach were introduced in the Senate by Senator McNary and in the House by Representative Clarke. These bills resulted in the Clarke-McNary Act of June 7, 1924.

The contours of the Clarke-McNary Act are so familiar to present-day foresters that it is difficult to appreciate the congressional leadership it exemplifies. Several of its themes are extensions of the Weeks Act, and the issue of private forest regulation was left unresolved. Nonetheless, the bill is undoubtedly the major accomplishment of a period of unprecedented congressional creativity in the forest management area. Three major features of the legislation continue to be vital parts of our national forestry program: fire control, reforestation and education, and land acquisition.

Cooperation in Fire Control   Reflecting Greeley's personal crusade and the nation's horror at the continuing threat and devastation of forest fires, the Clarke-McNary Act significantly enhanced the potential for effective fire control. First, the act authorized the Secretary of Agriculture to recommend systems of forest fire prevention and suppression for each forest region in the country. Standards were established pursuant to this provision by which the effectiveness of fire control activities under the widely varying conditions in different parts of the country could be fairly appraised. Second, the act authorized the Secretary to cooperate with states in forest fire control programs that meet federal standards and objectives. Finally, it authorized an annual appropriation of not more than $2,500,000 to enable the Secretary of Agriculture to cooperate with the states in fire control activities. Part of the appropriations could be devoted to studies of forest taxation and forest insurance. The purpose of these studies was to devise "tax laws designated to encourage the conservation and growing of timber, and to investigate and promote practical methods of insuring standing timber on growing forests from losses by fire and other causes." Of more immediate practical importance was the sizable authorization for cooperative forest fire protection which permitted federal participation to a degree previously not possible given the relatively small appropriations available under the Weeks Act.

Cooperation in Reforestation and Management   In addition to strengthening the existing forest fire programs, the Clarke-McNary Act initiated small but important new programs in two critical areas. First, a $100,000 annual appropriation was authorized to enable the Secretary of Agriculture to cooperate with the various states in providing nursery stock for windbreaks, shelterbelts, and farm wood lots on denuded or nonforested lands. The funds were available to states on a fifty-fifty matching basis. Although the authorized appropriation was small, it extended federal cooperation with the states into

a new and important field. A similarly small but important provision authorized cooperative education and assistance programs. The Secretary was authorized to cooperate with the various states in bringing educational assistance
and technical advice to the owners of farms in establishing, improving, and
renewing wood lots, shelterbelts, windbreaks, and other valuable forest
growth. Again the fifty-fifty matching device was used to stimulate development of state programs. This provision extended federal cooperation to still
another new field.

Liberalization of Acquisition Program   Finally, the Clarke-McNary Act
amended the Weeks Act by authorizing the Secretary of Agriculture to recommend for purchase forested, cutover, or denuded lands within the watersheds
of navigable streams which were necessary for the regulation of the flow of
navigable streams *or* for the production of timber. This provision removed
restrictions in the Weeks Act that confined purchases to the "headwaters" of
navigable streams, and it permitted the purchase of lands for timber production as well as stream flow protection. The proviso that purchases must be
"within the watersheds of navigable streams" was retained, as a constitutional
safeguard, but it has not significantly curtailed purchases. A more serious
problem was the fact that the new purchase authorities were not initially
supported by authorization to spend money.

Two provisions for further expanding the national forests have had little
impact. The Secretary of Agriculture was authorized to identify unreserved
public domain lands valuable to stream flow protection or for timber production which could be economically administered as parts of national forests. He
located considerable acreage which he recommended adding to the national
forests. Because of predictable opposition from the Secretary of the Interior,
who was then responsible for the lands, no action was taken on the suggestions.
Another provision of the Clarke-McNary Act authorized the President to
establish national forests on military reservations. This effort also failed.
Within a year, thirteen military reservations in the eastern United States
totaling some 210,000 acres were established as national forests and five additional military reservations totaling some 144,000 acres were added as districts
to adjoining national forests. However, the arrangement did not work out as
satisfactorily as had been hoped; and by 1929, all but two of the first group
of reservations had been removed from national forest status. Military uses and
timber production often proved to be incompatible.

Significance of the Act   The Clarke-McNary Act failed in directing that
public domain and military lands chiefly valuable for forest products should
be managed by the Forest Service. No agency would give up programs or
responsibilities without a fight; in these instances, the Forest Service did not
seriously attempt to prevail. In other areas, the act was a tremendous success.

It greatly strengthened Weeks Act programs in the fields of forest acquisition and cooperative forest fire protection, and it extended the principle of federal financial cooperation with the states to the important areas of reforestation and forest management.

The critical dimensions of the act are those which encouraged the diversification of the forestry profession. By this act, the Forest Service was authorized to develop extensive cooperative programs at the state and local levels for fire prevention, reforestation, and forestry education. This marks the take-off point for Forest Service activities beyond the boundaries of the national forests. As the agency was authorized to do more things in more places, it enlarged its support base with Congress and the public. Moreover, as forestry embraced more and different activities and emphases, the profession grew and diversified.

McSweeney-McNary Act

In 1928, the profession and the Forest Service were enhanced further by the passage of a research oriented bill. During 1925 and 1926, a thorough study of the current status of forest research was made by a special committee of the Washington section of the Society of American Foresters headed by Earle H. Clapp, Chief of the Branch of Research in the Forest Service. This exhaustive report served as the basis for a bill authorizing a comprehensive program of forest research which was introduced by Representative John R. McSweeney of Ohio in March 1927 at the close of the Sixty-ninth Congress. The proposal was lost in the shuffle as Congress prepared for the 1928 elections, but it focused discussion and educated the public. The bill was reintroduced in the next Congress by Representative McSweeney and Senator McNary in December 1927 and was enacted into law in less than six months, a remarkable record for speed. The broad scope of the act is indicated by its instructions to the Secretary of Agriculture:

> to conduct such investigations, experiments, and tests as he may deem necessary . . . to determine, demonstrate, and promulgate the best methods of reforestation and of growing, managing, and utilizing timber, forage, and other forest products, or maintaining favorable conditions of water flow and the prevention of erosion, of protecting timber and other forest growth from fire, insects, disease, or other harmful agencies, of obtaining the fullest and most effective use of forest lands, and to determine and promulgate the economic considerations for the management of forestland and the utilization of forest products [Dana, 225].

The bill further encouraged the geographic dispersion of Forest Service and forestry activities by funding research activities at regional forest experiment stations established in the legislation. This provision reflects the understandable desire of representatives and senators to have federal dollars go to their districts, but it was also of critical importance to the Forest Service. The McSweeney-McNary Act focused attention on the fundamental importance of forest research in providing the basis for effective forest management and utilization and laid a solid foundation for the further elaboration of Forest Service and forestry research programs.

McNary-Woodruff Act

A third legislative initiative of the 1920s proved to be somewhat of a disappointment. In 1924, a bill was introduced to remedy the lack of authorization for the national forest acquisition program expanded by the Clarke-McNary Act. After frustrating delay, the McNary-Woodruff Act passed four years later, but the proposal had been trimmed from a heady $40 million to only $8 million over a three-year period. The actual appropriations amounted to only $5 million. Moreover, the McNary-Woodruff Act limited the total acquisition program to one million acres in any state, except for protection of navigable streams and flood prevention. Although the legislation aroused considerable interest in eastern national forests, the acquisition program did not gain momentum until the Depression.

Knutson-Vandenberg Act

The fourth major legislative initiative of the period was the Knutson-Vandenberg Act of June 9, 1930. It was the outcome of an effort to speed up reforestation and improve silvicultural practices in the national forests. It set up a fiscal program for national forest planting by authorizing appropriations for the operation of nurseries and the establishment and maintenance of plantations. The act also authorized the Secretary of Agriculture to require purchasers of national forest timber to make deposits for tree planting, seed sowing, or forest improvement work on cutover areas. This provision has permitted much desirable silvicultural work on cutover areas that would otherwise have been impossible. The Knutson-Vandenberg Act is, of course, the origin of the familiar "K-V" terminology: K-V funds, K-V deposits, K-V practices.

These three major pieces of legislation—Clarke-McNary, McSweeney-McNary, and Knutson-Vandenberg—form the backbone of contemporary forestry programs at the state and federal levels. They were critical in the development of the diversification—both geographic and intellectual—of the profession. They do, however, reflect the predominantly silvicultural bias of the profession and the German assumptions which dominated its early years. Throughout the private lands regulation battle and underlying all of the legislation discussed above, there is the specter of a timber famine, the assumption of scarcity, and a belief that every available acre must be used for growing trees, regardless of the investment necessary. These assumptions continue to be major influences within the profession; but, starting in the late teens and

1920s, forestry diversified to include a healthy recognition of noncommodity forest uses.

Recreation in the National Forests

Much has been written about Pinchot's insensitivity to aesthetic and recreation values (Cate, 31–37). Much of what is said is true—foresters generally, their professional training, and the legislation which authorized Forest Service activities all emphasize timber production in the national forests. It is easy to overdraw this caricature, however. The agency's concern with timber production is real, but it should not obscure the fact that the fundamental emphasis of forestry and the Forest Service has been on wise *use* of the national forests. Recreation has always constituted an important use of forest resources, and the Forest Service has always recognized it as such. The Waugh Report, a 1918 study of *Recreation Uses on the National Forests,* is an early and extensive expression of Forest Service recreation policy. Written by landscape architect Frank A. Waugh, the report describes the recreation potential of the forests and the Forest Service commitment to coordinated management of all forest resources (Cate, 47–49). Throughout the 1920s, interest in recreation burgeoned within the agency. A small group of recreation advocates in the late teens developed into a group that demanded recognition and administrative attention for recreation as a major forest use by the early 1930s. These enthusiasts were not unchallenged in Forest Service circles. Within the agency, many forest managers were concerned that recreationists caused fires and sanitation problems and diverted them from their main tasks. Nevertheless, it is also true that early agency recreation programs were hampered less by lack of internal support than by the efforts of outsiders to prevent the Forest Service from mounting an effective recreation program.

In the years after World War I, the rapidly increasing use of the automobile brought "hoards of outdoor pleasure seekers" to the public lands. In 1920, outgoing Chief Forester Henry Graves called for a national recreation policy which would enable public and private land managers to meet the public's growing demand for outdoor recreation facilities. Newly appointed Chief Greeley continued the initiative but was unable to secure congressional appropriations for recreation programs. Park Service advocates and commodity users of the forests made a strange alliance but successfully argued that recreation programs on national forest lands were redundant and a misuse of the forests (Cate, chap. 4). The Forest Service was able to secure funding only for the sanitation and fire prevention aspects of recreation use. Yet in 1924, more than eleven million recreationists visited the national forests. The money for personnel and facilities to deal with the rapidly increasing visitation was diverted from other budgets where possible. Thus while the Washington office was struggling to meet the growing demand, many field managers became hostile to a program which produced tremendous management problems and brought no financial support.

Forest Service hostility to the Park Service did not begin in the 1920s. It is well known that Pinchot and Graves both opposed the authorization of a separate land management agency and believed the Forest Service could manage the scenic resources which were to form the backbone of the national park system (Steen, 113–122). Park Service efforts to thwart Forest Service recreation management efforts during the early 1920s did not, however, do anything to allay the tensions in the inherently competitive relationship between the two agencies.

National Conference on Outdoor Recreation

The need for a national policy regarding recreation which Graves noted in 1920 was widely acknowledged among concerned citizens. The Izaak Walton League, the Boone and Crockett Club, and similar organizations urged President Calvin Coolidge to convene a national conference on recreation. The 1924 conference focused public attention on the nation's recreation potential and requirements. Following the conference, Coolidge established a permanent committee to assist in implementing the conference's resolutions. Ultimately, it functioned primarily as an informal arbiter on the forest-to-park land transfers which were increasingly proposed toward the close of the decade.

WILDERNESS POLICY

The problems between Interior and Agriculture were relatively minor in the 1920s. The conflict was real, but it was not a major factor in forest policy until the Depression. In the 1920s, most of the debate concerning both recreation as an aspect of forest management and the designation and administration of wilderness took place almost entirely within the Forest Service.

In the early 1920s, Aldo Leopold—a forester on the Gila National Forest in New Mexico—began agitating for formal recognition of roadless areas in the national forests. Leopold was dismayed by the rapid penetration of roads into previously inaccessible areas. He argued that a large section of the Gila National Forest should be designated and managed as a permanent roadless area. He also urged that a wilderness area of at least 400,000 acres be set aside in every Western state. Leopold was joined in this cause by many foresters who shared the belief that motorized access and intense recreation developments, such as those favored by the Park Service management philosophy, were spoiling the remaining places of wild beauty. Arthur Carhart, the first landscape architect in the Forest Service, began emphasizing roadless, undeveloped recreation in 1916. In 1926, he drew up a recreation management plan for Superior National Forest that prohibited roads, timber harvest, or recreation developments along the area's major canoe routes (Cate, 88–98).

Despite this effort within the Forest Service to gain recognition for wilderness reservations, there was little public support for the idea. Moreover, among Forest Service personnel and potential commodity developers, there was a great deal of hostility to withholding resources from management. Carhart's plan for the Superior National Forest was adopted in spite of the Forest Supervisor's intention to develop recreation in the area by building roads and summer facilities in especially scenic places (Carhart, 144–146). During the late 1920s, however, support for the wilderness program began to develop in the Forest Service Washington office, in Congress, and, to a lesser extent, among the public. Two major events signaled the beginning of a formal national wilderness system.

Shipstead-Nolan Act

In 1930, Congress passed the Shipstead-Nolan Act which legislatively supported Carhart's 1926 recreation plan for the Superior National Forest. The Forest Service had had difficulty implementing Carhart's plan due to developments on private lands within the forest that the agency could not control. Moreover, the forest was threatened by a proposed dam which would have altered the level of water in the lakes. Congress passed the legislation at the urging of the Izaak Walton League, then primarily a fishing and sporting club. It required the Forest Service to preserve the natural beauty of the lakes and to refrain from cutting timber on the shoreline. A provision that the lake and stream levels could not be altered without consent of Congress eliminated further dam problems (Gilligan, 130–131).

L-Regulations of 1929

The Shipstead-Nolan Act is the first legislative recognition of the wilderness concept, but it was confined to a specific area facing a specific threat. The Forest Service L-regulations of 1929 constitute a first, albeit imperfect, attempt to establish wilderness as a general classification for land use with established management goals and directions. The L-20 regulations eschewed the name wilderness, defining instead criteria and procedures for establishing primitive areas. There was considerable confusion about the precise meaning of "primitive" under the L-regulations both within the Forest Service and elsewhere.

Basically, the program urged regional foresters to locate and define areas in which primitive conditions would be maintained. Special use occupancy was prohibited in designated areas; special management plans were required; and the Chief's concurrence was required for the construction of any permanent "improvements." It was not clear, however, whether timber, forage, and water resources were withdrawn from use or whether the designation was permanent or merely temporary. Chief Greeley and Assistant Chief L. E. Kneipp fought hard to strengthen and clarify the L-20 restrictions, but the hostility within the agency engendered by the first major steps prevented any further action. In spite of the efforts of Leopold, Carhart, Kneipp, and like-minded agency personnel, many foresters strongly opposed the wilderness concept. Although many areas were designated under the L-regulations, clarification of the program awaited the development of strong public support and Park Service pressure, which began in the mid- to late 1920s.

Mineral Leasing System

Wilderness policy was not the only major new concept to emerge in forest and range management during the period. Early in the 1920s, there was strong evidence to suggest that Congress was at last willing to consider a leasing system for distribution of valuable commodities on the public domain. The Mineral Leasing Act of 1920 culminated twenty years of sustained debate in Congress regarding management of oil, coal, gas, phosphates, and other sedimentary mineral deposits on public lands. The 1920 act does not apply to metallic ores nor does it represent a complete break with the theories implicit in the Mining Law of 1872, which continued to control mining of metallic ores. The fundamental commitment to private exploitation of public mineral resources was not altered. In fact, Congress rejected many proposals which would have authorized a government agency to exploit public mineral resources. However, the turnabout in other major aspects of mineral policy was dramatic and critical and augured well for similar developments in other areas of public domain management.

The most significant barrier to instituting a leasing system involved the issue of private ownership. A major goal of public land policy for 150 years had been disposal of the public domain, passing the land into private hands for settlement and development. The idea of federal reservations for parks and forests was not completely accepted even in 1920. Moreover, many people who supported the general public purposes of forest and park reservations were unalterably opposed to the idea of the government retaining land for purposes of revenue production. The myth of the homesteader combined with distrust of government programs and hostility to proliferating government agencies stalled the passage of a general leasing system on the public lands for decades. Finally, in 1920, an initial breakthrough was achieved in the Mineral Leasing Act.

The first major innovation of the 1920 act is that development of sedimentary deposits takes place at the discretion of the Secretary of the Interior. Prospectors were required to have a permit, which the Secretary could refuse to grant, in order to search for deposits in areas where minerals were not known to exist. In areas of known geologic activity, mineral development could take place only after the area had been designated for leasing by the Secretary and a competitive lease auction had been held. Unlike the system established in 1872 for hardrock minerals, sedimentary deposit development is not presumed to be the highest use of the land, and it does not proceed automatically at the instigation of the discoverer. A prospector who found a valuable deposit had a right to a lease. However, the claimant could not take title to the mineral or the mining claim under the 1920 act as could be done under the 1872 act. Developers could lease the land they wanted to mine, but it remained public property. The miner also had to pay a nominal rental fee, and the Secretary was authorized to write a lease with conditions which would protect the resources and the public interest. Finally, the minerals were taken from the land; but, again in contrast to the 1872 system, the developer was required to pay a return to the government, normally 12.5 percent of the proceeds annually.

The leasing provisions were among the most controversial issues in the long debate over the 1920 bill. The western representatives voiced the familiar complaints about the Easterners' denying them their rights, their property, and their opportunity for economic development. This objection was ultimately met by provisions for distributing the royalty income: Forty-five percent of the revenues were to be given to the states where they were generated for school developments and 45 percent were to be used to supplement the reclamation fund, which was by then financially troubled. Thus, 90 percent of the minerals proceeds were to stay in the West with only 10 percent earmarked for the federal treasury. This system remained in place until 1976, when extensive amendments to the 1920 act eliminated prospecting permits and required that all leases be awarded through competitive bids.

The 1920 act was not perfect from a land management standpoint. Chief among its problems from the foresters' view was that the General Land Office was responsible for implementing the leasing. The Forest Service continues to this day to have only limited authority to control oil, coal, and other mineral development on national forestlands. This division of management responsibilities is always inconvenient and occasionally leads to conflict. However, the Mineral Leasing Act was a tremendous step forward because it authorized the government, through the General Land Office, to exercise some control over development of phosphates, coal, gas, oil, and other sedimentary mineral deposits. More important here, it established the principle of leasing—government retention of land and supervision of private use of public resources—as a means for managing the public lands. It was a major and fundamental reorientation of attitudes toward public domain. Efforts to extend this major rethinking of minerals policy to metallic ores still covered by the 1872 act have been unavailing.

RANGE MANAGEMENT IN THE 1920s

Developments in the mineral leasing field led many to hope that a similar system for management of grazing on the public domain would be instituted. Unfortunately, the time was not auspicious for initiating range-use regulation.

The stock raising industry, after a flurry of prosperity during the war years, went into a serious recession in the early 1920s which was exacerbated by an extended period of severe drought. Stock operators were politically active during the 1920s, preventing the imposition of fees and regulations which they feared would drive them out of business. The Forest Service range program was subjected to severe and constant criticism whenever the agency tried to raise grazing fees. The fine working relationships between the stock operators and the Forest Service eroded to the point that efforts to extend regulation to the public domain lands were set back another decade.

Trouble on the range began, as has become familiar, with the managing agency caught in a cross fire on raising grazing fees. Forest Service grazing fees were initially set quite low since, prior to the creation of the national forests, range use was free. In 1916, the Secretary of Agriculture announced a plan to increase the very low fees in order to bring them more nearly in line with the fair market value of the forage. The gradual fee increase was accompanied by the inception of a policy of granting multiyear permits to the operators. In 1919, for the first time, many permits were issued for a period of five years, with the understanding that grazing fees would not be increased again during the five-year period.

Unfortunately, just as the Forest Service was making these commitments, the House Committee on Agriculture and Forestry began to insist on dramatic fee increases to help offset the World War I debts. In 1920, a rider requiring the Forest Service to impose charges equal to commercial rates was almost inserted in the agricultural appropriations bill. The Forest Service was opposed to having the fees set by the legislature. They did not want to break the commitments made in the five-year permits just issued. Moreover, they did not want to alienate the support they had built with the stock operators. The Department of Agriculture and the Forest Service were also engaged in a struggle with the Department of the Interior over which department should manage the unreserved public domain. The Forest Service's good standing with the grazing interests was a valuable asset. Confronted with strong pressure from the House committee to raise rates dramatically, the agency stalled. Finally, the Forest Service was authorized to undertake an intensive study of grazing fees, with the expectation that any further increases which might be found justifiable would be put into effect in 1924 when the report was finished.

The study was made by C. E. Rachford, the Forest Service Chief Range Inspector. The Rachford report showed that national forest grazing fees would have to be raised 60 to 70 percent to equal comparable commercial rates. Unfortunately, this report was published when the stock industry was in the middle of a severe recession. The threat of raised fees set off a storm of protest. The uproar caused the Secretary of Agriculture to have Dan Casement, a prominent stock operator, review the Rachford report. Casement found, predictably, that Rachford's proposed fee increases were exorbitant. He recommended that increases totaling approximately one-quarter of the Rachford recommendations be phased in over a four-year period between 1927 and 1931 (Voight, 63–65).

The Forest Service was in a difficult dilemma. The agency was trying to abide by commitments it had made to the stock operators in the multiyear permits. It was anxious not to alienate its staunchest western allies, but its own studies proved that grazing fees were less than one-third of the value of the forage. It was under pressure from the House Committee on Agriculture and Forestry to raise grazing fees drastically, yet it was being excoriated by a peculiarly vindictive group of western senators and stock operators for its range management efforts.

The operators were also in a difficult situation brought on by drought, economic depression, and range deterioration. Soon the debate transcended the fee question and the very idea of range management was challenged. The operators were virtually obsessed by the idea that they needed even more security than that afforded by multiyear permits. Many insisted on permanent allotments to existing permittees, and they wanted full access to defined areas rather than permission to put a specified amount of stock in specified places. Emotion as well as economics played a prominent part in the thinking of the more radical elements in the industry, who took the lead in pressing these demands.

The controversey soon resulted in a Senate investigation of public land management. The investigating subcommittee, under Senator R. M. Stanfield of Oregon, held hearings throughout the West. Malcontents were not only permitted but actually encouraged to air their grievances, real and imaginary, against the Forest Service. Senator Stanfield himself had a grievance since his stock grazing permit had been canceled because of misrepresentation in obtaining it.

Unfortunately, the stage-managed senatorial attack on Forest Service grazing policies provoked vitriolic counterattack on livestock operators generally by forestry and conservation organizations. The American Forestry Association and the Society of American Foresters conducted a vigorous publicity campaign opposing grazing use of the forests and equating all stock operators with the most extreme agency critics. The SAF complained that "the effect of the constant contact with grazing as an industry and as a user of a resource contained within the national forests has produced, from the [chief] forester down, a tolerance for grazing and a desire to adjust to forest production which in effect has already elevated it to the dignity of a coordinate use with forestry and an end in itself" (Peffer, 195). The SAF wanted the grazing areas removed from national forests and advocated establishing a separate agency within the Department of Agriculture to handle grazing matters. Ovid Butler, Secretary of the American Forestry Association—a leading and influential conservation organization—entered the fracas at a high emotional pitch. He traveled the country, writing editorials, press releases, and thousands of letters attacking the livestock industry (Peffer, 195–197). The stock operators were incensed, and neither side in the dispute made much effort to debate the issues rationally. Perhaps our heritage of the wild West preordains that discussions of range policy will be unusually tumultuous and bitter. The tendency was certainly well established by the mid-1920s.

This was not a propitious time to extend the concepts of the Mineral Leasing Act to range allocation. With the financially desperate stock operators making unreasonable demands for secure range rights and the SAF and conservationists in the hustings decrying the evil industry, the moment was lost. Even before Senator Stanfield's subcommittee completed its investigation, he introduced a bill applying both to the national forests and to the unreserved public domain, which included virtually all of the provisions recommended by the most radical of the operators. The chief items relating to national forests provided legal recognition of grazing as a subordinate use, continued regulation of grazing along existing lines, charging of fees that are reasonable in view of all the circumstances affecting use of the range, issuance of ten-year permits having a contract status, preference to certain classes of present permittees with opportunity for the admission of new qualified applicants, and establishment of local grazing boards to cooperate in administering the act and in deciding appeals from decisions of forest officers. The counterattack by the SAF and other forestry and conservation groups halted the bill. In the East, citizens were so aroused by the declamation of the stock operators' selfish demands that it became virtually impossible to secure legislation regarding range management because any such legislation would appear to benefit the stock raising interests. Management of the public rangelands was thus delayed another ten years. Worse still, the setting in which subsequent debate occurred was tragically and irreparably altered by the rift which had been created between the Forest Service and its former supporters in the stock industry.

FEDERAL-STATE RELATIONS

The public rangelands were steadily deteriorating, with no prospect of improvement as far as Congress was concerned, when Herbert Hoover became President in the spring of 1929. The Secretary of Agriculture and the Secretary of the Interior were in full agreement about the basic principles that should underlie the leasing system which they repeatedly urged on Congress. Each believed, however, that jurisdiction over the lands should be placed in his department, and this difference of opinion was a key factor in Congress' failure to take action.

Hoover, in the recognition that something had to be done, supported a proposal to transfer the public domain lands to the states. He believed such a move could not make the situation worse than it already was and might improve it. He proposed a commission to study the whole problem of the disposal of the remaining unreserved public lands. In 1930, Congress authorized Hoover to appoint a Committee on the Conservation and Administration of the Public Domain. The committee consisted of twenty members, with James R. Garfield, Secretary of the Interior under Theodore Roosevelt, as chairman and the Secretaries of the Interior and of Agriculture as ex-officio members. W. B. Greeley was the only forester on the committee. The committee made twenty special recommendations. Its most memorable proposal was the recommendation that Congress pass an act granting all the unreserved, unappropriated public domain within their respective boundaries to the public land states, subject to the reservation to the United States of all mineral rights. Bills embodying the recommendations of the committee were promptly introduced in Congress and extensive hearings were held, but no legislation was ever seriously considered. Opposition to the Hoover proposals was virtually unanimous.

Probably to the surprise of President Hoover, reaction to the proposed grant of lands to the states was unenthusiastic even in the West. Opposition from the Eastern states was to be expected because of their stake in the lands as a national resource. Conservationists feared that state ownership would lead to private ownership and would result in even more serious deterioration than was taking place under federal ownership. This fear was intensified by a hint from Hoover's influential Secretary of Interior Ray Lyman Wilber, for whom the committee's report is named, that the same treatment might later be applied to the national forests.

That the West should be inclined to look a gift horse in the mouth was hardly to be anticipated, particularly in view of prior and present efforts to obtain state control of public lands. Opposition was based primarily on three grounds. First, the lands were so run down that they were more of a liability than an asset. Second, the mineral rights were not to be included in the grant. Finally, the grant would reduce the substantial contributions to the states from the federal government for the building and maintenance of highways which were apportioned on the basis of the amount of land in each state in federal ownership. As Governor Dern of Utah put it, "The States already own, in their school land grants, millions of acres of this same kind of land, which they can neither sell nor lease, and which is yielding no income. Why should they want more of this precious heritage of desert?" (Dana, 233). Reaction to the Wilber report constitutes a low point in public domain history. The Forest Service's management efforts were jeopardized both by stock operators' hostility and the myopia of the SAF regarding grazing. The Forest Service had experience in range management but could not rally sufficient support to extend their efforts to the unreserved public domain. The Department of the Interior was eager to have the land, but there were no land managers in Interior. The conservationists argued heatedly that the operators were trying to steal a national treasure for personal gain; but when Hoover tried to give the treasures to the states, he was accused of trying to burden them with a white elephant.

SUMMARY

The gloomy situation surrounding range management is not, fortunately, the appropriate note on which to leave the 1920s. The conflicts which emerged during the decade were real and enduring, but they are the inevitable and healthy tensions resulting from diversification of the forestry profession. Dissent and disagreement is not always productive—in retrospect the 1920s SAF position on grazing seems foolish and counterproductive. The opportunity to extend the leasing concepts of the Mineral Leasing Act to other public resources was lost. However, the same dissention brought growth and new strains of thought to forest management.

Shortly after the First World War, the Forest Service and the Society of American Foresters espoused conflicting directions for the future development of forestry. Both groups proposed vastly expanded programs and both emphasized the previously overlooked lands in private ownership. However, the SAF proposal for federal regulation of cutting on private lands was opposed by the Forest Service, which emphasized fire control and argued that regulation was the responsibility of state governments. The result was a stalemate on that issue. However, under the leadership of an active and attentive Congress, three major pieces of legislation were enacted—the Clarke-McNary Act of 1924, the McSweeney-McNary Act of 1928, and the Knutson-Vandenberg Act of 1930. These acts strengthened the programs for the acquisition of national forests and for cooperation with the states in forest fire control initiated by the Weeks Act of 1911, extended federal cooperation with the states to the field of reforestation and forest management, and established a sound and comprehensive program for forest research.

The major progress of the period in wild lands management is represented by these acts of Congress, but significant agency leadership in the areas of recreation and wilderness program development was also apparent. Underlying these efforts, perhaps undermining some of them, were initial flurries of competition between the Park Service and the Forest Service. Hostility between the two agencies was inevitably played out as part of the department-level conflict seen in the jostling for management authority over the public domain. It was not yet serious, however, compared to the bitter battles of the 1930s.

REFERENCES CITED

Cameron, Jenks. *The Development of Governmental Forest Control in the United States.* Baltimore: Johns Hopkins Press, 1928.

Carhart, Arthur H. *Timber in Your Life.* Philadelphia: J.B. Lippincott, 1955.

Cate, Donald. *Recreation and the U. S. Forest Service.* Unpublished Ph.D. dissertation, Stanford: Stanford University, 1963.

Clepper, Henry. *Professional Forestry in the United States.* Baltimore: John Hopkins Press, 1971.

Committee on Conservation and Administration of the Public Domain (James R. Garfield, Chairman). *Report.* Washington: Government Printing Office, 1931.

Gilligan, James P. *The Development of Policy and Administration of Primitive-arid Forest Service Administration of Wilderness Areas in the Western United States.* 2 vols. Unpublished Ph.D. dissertation, Ann Arbor: University of Michigan, 1953.

Graves, Henry S. "A Policy of Forestry for the Nation," 17 *Journal of Forestry* 901, 1919.

Greeley, William B. *Forest Policy.* New York: McGraw-Hill Book Company, Inc., 1953.

Hosmer, Ralph S. "The National Forestry Program Committee, 1919–1928," 45 *Journal of Forestry* 627, 1947.

Ise, John. *The United States Forest Policy.* New Haven: Yale University Press, 1920.

Peffer, E. Louise. *The Closing of the Public Domain.* Stanford: Stanford University Press, 1951.

Pinchot, Gifford. "The Lines are Drawn," 17 *Journal of Forestry* 899, 1919.

Steen, Harold K. *The U. S. Forest Service: A History.* Seattle: University of Washington Press, 1976–77.

Swain, Donald. *Federal Conservation Policy, 1921–33.* Berkeley: University of California Press, 1963.

Society of American Foresters, Committee for the Application of Forestry (Gifford Pinchot, Chairman). "Forest Devastation: A National Danger and a Plan to Meet It," 17 *Journal of Forestry* 911, 1919.

U. S. Department of Agriculture, Forest Service. *Timber Depletion, Lumber Prices, Lumber Exports, and Concentration of Timber Ownership* (Capper Report). Report on S. Res. 311, 66th Cong., 2d Sess. 1920.

Voigt, William, Jr. *Public Grazing Lands: Use and Misuse by Government and Industry.* New Brunswick: Rutgers University Press, 1976.

Chapter 6

Resource Management Under the Second Roosevelt, 1933–1945

Franklin Roosevelt's years as President, like those of his cousin Theodore, are characterized by an intense concern with resource management. FDR was perhaps better prepared for leadership in the field than his forebear. Even after his crippling bout with polio, he was an avid outdoorsman and he had long practiced forestry on his estate at Hyde Park. For *Who's Who in America,* he described himself as a "tree grower." Franklin Roosevelt did not, however, preside over a period of burgeoning self-confidence and economic expansion such as dominated Theodore Roosevelt's presidency. He took office on March 4, 1933, with the country in a state of widespread and acute economic distress. The banks were closed, unemployment was at an all-time high, and agriculture and industry faced bankruptcy. When he died in office thirteen years later, the nation was engaged in the Second World War. In the context of those national crises, resource management was for the second time in the century a major focus of government and public attention.

The underlying theme of the attention was importantly different from the TR-Pinchot conservation movement. Theodore Roosevelt's program arose from a need to protect watersheds, a fear of timber famine, and a desire to halt destruction and waste of the nation's natural bounty. Thirty years later, these goals persisted; but the main concern was not the resources themselves, but the human dimensions of their use. Forest and range policy during the Depression emphasized the contribution that those resources could make to rectifying social and economic dislocations. Renewable resources could provide jobs for the unemployed and a stable base for a national economy, and they were managed with those goals in mind. Similarly, during the Second World War, resource management was directed toward supplying the needs of the armed forces. Thus, the land stewardship approach to land management typified by the pre-Depression Forest Service of Graves and Greeley was redirected during the economic recovery and war effort of the Roosevelt years.

Under the pressure of economic crisis, the Roosevelt administration pressed for the protection and utilization of resources on a number of fronts. Soil conservation, wildlife management, multiple purpose dams, and state parks and forests all received tremendous attention during the 1930s. A multitude of new goals, values, institutions, and employment opportunities sprouted and flourished in the resource management field that was once almost the exclusive domain of foresters and the Forest Service. The Soil Conservation Service, the Tennessee Valley Authority, the Grazing Service, and an early version of the Fish and Wildlife Service all were established in the 1930s; and the Forest Service had to compete with new agencies for attention, funds, and authority.

Forestry and the Forest Service entered this increasingly complex resource management arena without the advantage of the strong charismatic leadership of Gifford Pinchot. Franklin Roosevelt's Secretary of Interior, Harold Ickes, wielded commensurate skills and resources frequently against the Forest Service. Ickes heightened the competition and distrust between the Departments of Agriculture and Interior. His persistent but unsuccessful efforts to return the Forest Service to Interior have had lasting expression in Park Service-Forest Service rivalry and durable hostility to similar reorganization efforts. Pinchot himself participated with characteristic vigor in the discussions of the 1930s, but he more than met his match in the irascible, powerful Ickes.

This does not mean, however, that forest management was ignored during this critical period. On the contrary, many important steps were taken. In the near-replay of 1920s debates, major battles were fought over the appropriate extent of federal forest land ownership and the place of government regulation in increasing productivity on private lands. Sustained yield forestry was defined in a new law passed to bring coherence to the management of the O & C revested lands. State and federal legislation was passed to encourage reforestation of cutover lands. Cooperative federal-state efforts in fire and insect control, reforestation, and management were boosted by the rapid development of state forest systems. The state efforts were aided by reversion of extensive forest acreage to the states for nonpayment of taxes during the economic collapse. The movement to protect large areas of national forests as wilderness began in earnest and industrial forestry began to emerge during the Depression as a major force within the profession and the national economy.

Ickes's strong hand was clearly evident in the passage of the Taylor Grazing Act in 1934. This is clearly the most significant development in forest and range policy during FDR's administration. Before this point, there was no widespread or coordinated effort to manage, conserve, or improve the public domain lands. Ickes fought hard to have the Grazing Service established in Interior and he prevailed. His victory was costly, however, since the bargains he struck set patterns which continued overgrazing for four more decades. Although the Tayor Grazing Act was an important first step, it was an inadequate base for establishing effective management of the public domain lands.

Franklin Roosevelt's emphasis on development of natural resources was dictated by the social, economic, and political exigencies of his presidency. The Depression and the war preordained and probably required an emphasis on the fullest exploitation of forest and range resources. However, excesses of those years prompted criticism of dominant assumptions regarding resource development and use; and by the end of the Roosevelt era, the limits of this policy were beginning to be recognized.

DIVERSIFICATION OF RESOURCE MANAGEMENT

Franklin Roosevelt believed that improving and developing the land was a key to relieving unemployment. Many of his economic recovery programs were oriented to resource management and conservation. Extensive funding and personnel were made available for forestry and other conservation activities through the Emergency Conservation Act of March 1933; the Federal Emergency Relief Act of May 1933; the National Industrial Recovery Act of June 1933; and the Works Relief Act of April 1935. Special legislation was also passed authorizing new programs in soil erosion control, water resource development, and rural development.

The Civilian Conservation Corps

The most famous of Roosevelt's conservation initiatives was the Civilian Conservation Corps (CCC). Less than three weeks after his inauguration, Roosevelt asked Congress for legislative authority to proceed with a program of land improvements and unemployment relief. Ten days later the Emergency Conservation Act had become law. The act authorized the President to employ unemployed citizens on works of a public nature for the purpose of relieving the acute condition of widespread distress and unemployment then existing in the United States, and in order to provide for the restoration of the country's depleted natural resources and the advancement of an orderly program of useful public works" (Dana, 245). The program was to be conducted on federal or state lands but could be extended to county, municipal, and private lands for the control of fires, insects, disease, and floods. Research in forest management and wood utilization was also authorized. The duration of the act at first was limited to two years, after which it was continued by annual appropriations until 1937. The CCC was then formally established for a period of three years by the act of June 28, 1937. Although many proposals were considered for making it permanent, the CCC was discontinued in 1943 after the war had solved the unemployment problem.

The CCC was among the most popular and successful of the New Deal programs. Its initiation is unparalled for speed. The first camp, on the George Washington National Forest in Virginia, was occupied on April 5, 1933, five days after the authorizing statute was passed. Actual work in the woods started twelve days later. When the program was at its peak, in 1935, there were 520,000 enrollees in 2652 camps, about half of which were forestry camps. The camps were primarily on state and federal lands, and to a lesser extent on private lands. Altogether the Corps gave employment to approximately three million men at a cost of some $2.5 billion. The CCC programs were comprehensive. More than 150 major types of work were defined under the general headings of reforestation, forest protection and improvement, soil conservation, recreational developments, range rehabilitation, aid to wildlife, flood control, drainage, reclamation, and emergency rescue activities. In forestry alone, the Forest Service estimated that 730,000 person-years were devoted to such activities as reduction of fire hazards, construction of firebreaks, actual fire fighting, timber stand improvement, tree planting, and the building of roads, trails, bridges, telephone lines, lookout towers, and other permanent improvements. Similar results were accomplished in other fields.

The occasional complaint that the quality of the work was not always top-notch (Dana, 249) is probably justified. However, it was an emergency program, directed largely by inexperienced supervisors and carried out by unskilled youths, many of whom had never been in the woods before. Its primarily aim was relief of unemployment. The marvel is not that the program had its shortcomings, but that they were not more serious. Even more impressive was the human success of the program. Young men who had become unemployed through no fault of their own but simply because there were no jobs to be had were given an opportunity to support themselves and their families. The quality of the work is not really a significant issue. In retrospect, a better question is whether some of the work should have been done at all. In the rush to use wild lands resources as a source of employment, planners gave very little consideration to whether roading, campsite development, and construction within parks and forests were desirable. It is probably not coincidental that the wilderness movement, an effort to protect forestlands from roads and development, took on major proportions during the CCC days.

Another important by-product of the CCC was enlargement of the purchase program for the acquisition of national forests. Two months after taking office, in order to make available more federal land in the eastern United States on which the CCC could usefully pursue its activities, President Roosevelt allocated $20 million of emergency funds for the purchase of forest lands under the Weeks Act and the Clarke-McNary Act. Subsequent allocations in 1934 and 1935 brought the total made available for land purchases to $44.5 million in those three years. This sum resulted in the establishment of nearly sixty new purchase areas and the acquisition of 7.7 million acres, or two and a half times that amount acquired during the preceding twenty-two-year period.

Rural Development Programs

Developing publicly owned resources was only part of Roosevelt's recovery effort. The New Deal also included a number of programs for alleviating rural poverty by manipulating the utilization of private lands. The assumption of the period was that too much land was under cultivation. This led to overproduction, resulting in low crop prices and economic distress. The Roosevelt administration attempted to solve these problems in a number of ways.

The shelterbelt project is one of the best remembered Depression era efforts to provide employment and reduce adverse impacts of erosion caused by uninterrupted acres of plowed fields. The original scheme of planting strips of trees 10 rods wide in a belt 100 miles deep from Texas to Canada across the prairie states was designed to intercept the prevailing winds. Its rigid formula was modified to encourage tree planting where soil and climatic conditions indicated trees might survive. In 1942, the project was terminated after 18,600 miles of trees had been planted in cooperation with some 30,000 farmers. Under the severe economic pressure of the 1970s, many farmers have begun removing the shelterbelts in order to plant additional crops. There is some concern that we may be inviting a repetition of 1930s Dust Bowl conditions.

The shelterbelt system was one method for getting land out of production and into a rehabilitation program. A second approach to the same goals was directed at tax lost land and resulted ultimately in the National Grasslands. The National Industrial Recovery Act of 1933 provided initial authority for federal acquisition and rehabilitation of tax delinquent lands, most of it 160-acre parcels of unsuccessfully homesteaded land. Under the series of statutes enacted between 1935 and 1953, a program was established for permanent federal management of the rehabilitated lands. Under the Emergency Relief Act of 1935 purchase boundaries were established to focus such acquisitions into land utilization projects. In 1938, these "LU lands" were further consolidated under the management provisions of the Bankhead-Jones Farm Tenant Act. In 1953, much of the acquired acreage was turned over to states or converted to national forest status. About 3.8 million acres selected for permanent federal ownership was transferred to the Forest Service for management as national grasslands (Argow, passim).

Another straightforward program attempted to improve the lot of farmers simply by subsidizing efforts to bring electricity to rural America. The Rural Electrification Administration (REA) was established by executive order in May 1935, and authorized by Congress in 1937. Approximately nine out of every ten American farms were without electricity in 1933. Private power companies had been reluctant to extend transmission lines and other necessary facilities to rural areas because they constituted such small markets that the anticipated returns would not justify the investment.

The Rural Electrification Administration without question succeeded in its mission to bring electricity to rural areas. The program was humanitarian and political, apparently unaffected by such questions as whether electricity actually improves the quality of life or whether the government should subsidize or encourage the consumption of "cheap" electricity. Resource policies of the 1930s, no less than those of the previous century, relied on unmistakable assumptions regarding both the abundance of resources and the appropriateness of consuming them. By bringing electricity and modern technology to rural America, the REA program caused great changes in life-styles and land use in America. Broad swaths were cut from farm, park, and forest to make room for transmission wires. Hydroelectric generators and other facilities claimed even more land. Objections on aesthetic grounds were barely voiced, and reservations concerning misallocation of productive lands to dam sites or transmission corridors were rare and ineffective. The whole way of life in rural America was radically altered by the REA program in an unfettered flourish of unquestioned economic development.

The Tennessee Valley Authority

The assumptions and motivations behind the REA program received an even clearer expression in the creation of the Tennessee Valley Authority (TVA). One of Roosevelt's earliest proposals called for the unified development of all of the resources of the Tennessee River Valley. In a special message to Congress proposing the project, he said:

> Many hard lessons have taught us the human waste that results from lack of planning. Here and there a few wise cities and counties have looked ahead and planned. But our Nation has just grown. It is time to extend planning to a wider field, in this instance comprehending in one great project many States directly concerned with the basin of one of our greatest rivers.
>
> This in a true sense is a return to the spirit and vision of the pioneer. If we

are successful here we can march up, step by step, in a like development of other great natural territorial units within our borders [Dana, 253]

Roosevelt's vision contained a concrete proposal which for the first time incorporated the admonitions of John Wesley Powell and many others that every river system should be developed as a unit.

The TVA was directed to bring about in the valley: (1) the maximum amount of flood control; (2) the maximum use of the Tennessee River for navigation purposes: (3) the maximum generation of electric power consistent with flood control and navigation; (4) the proper use of marginal lands; (5) the proper method of reforestation of all lands in the drainage basin suitable for reforestation; and (6) the economic and social well-being of the people living in the river basin. It would be difficult to imagine a more comprehensive program. The authority paid special attention to navigation, flood control, power development, and fertilizer production but did not overlook other aspects of land and water utilization and industrial development.

The TVA was one of the show pieces of the New Deal. The government corporation format has, however, been both praised and criticized. Perhaps the best assessment is found in the fact that Roosevelt's dream that the TVA might set a precedent for marching on, "step by step, in a like development of other natural territorial units" has not been fulfilled. Bills subsequently introduced to create a Missouri Valley Authority, a Columbia Basin Authority, and even to divide the entire country into nine resource development regions have not been debated since the early 1950s. Although the TVA model has not been followed, the idea of multiple-purpose dams and intensive watershed development is now a familiar if controversial part of American resource management. Moreover, the many accomplishments of the TVA highlight the urgent need to substitute unified planning for piecemeal development of regional and national resources.

Wildlife Management and the New Deal

At least in part because of its emphasis on dam construction, the impact of the Roosevelt administration on wildlife management is also difficult to assess. There is very little doubt that the development programs and massive federally sponsored dam programs contributed directly and indirectly to the destruction of millions of acres of fish and wildlife habitat. This destruction cannot be offset by habitat protection aspects of national forest acquisition, by CCC programs in habitat improvement, or by Roosevelt's extensive efforts in expanding the federal game refuges. More than $8.5 million was spent to acquire game refuges during the 1930s. However, as wildlife enthusiasts have noted with some irony, the CCC boys were busily building water fowl habitats while hundreds of thousands of acres of marsh were drained for mosquito control (Trefethen, 230). Nor can the negative impact of the work relief projects be considered mitigated by such nostrums as the Fish and Wildlife Coordinating Act. That 1934 legislation required dam builders to consult with the Secretary of the Interior prior to construction to attempt to mitigate harm to fish. It led to the construction of fish ladders on some of the larger dam projects.

On the other hand, it is easy to be too harsh in assessing Depression era progress in federal wildlife management programs, especially when viewing them in comparison with federal efforts in other resource areas such as forestry. Until the 1930s, federal wildlife programs were confined largely to a concern for migratory birds based on the federal power to make treaties and an extensive effort to eradicate coyotes and other predators in the western range. Federal wildlife conservation efforts were restricted during the Depression in part because there was little base to build on. In 1940, the Fish and Wildlife Service was organized in the Department of the Interior by bringing together the Bureau of Fisheries from the Department of Commerce and the Bureau of Biological Survey from Agriculture. The new agency was not able to break rapidly with its past, but it did elbow its way into the proliferating group of government bureaus seeking funds and programs.

A more important reason for the marginal federal role in this area is that wildlife management has been traditionally viewed as the responsibility of state governments. Most State Fish and Game Commissions are quite territorial about their prerogatives, and the major progress of the New Deal era in wildlife management was made at the state rather than the federal level. The Pittman-Robertson Act of 1937 provided funding, standards, and encouragement for state programs and continues to this day to be the sine qua non of state wildlife management. Under this act, receipts from the federal tax on firearms, shells, and cartridges were allocated to the states on the basis of their size and the number of licensed hunters. The funds were made available for research and for the purchase and development of game refuges and public hunting grounds. States accepting grants were required to provide that all receipts from the sale of hunting licenses would be used for the State Fish and Game Department, to submit all proposed projects to the Fish and Wildlife Service for approval, and to contribute from state funds at least 25 percent of the total cost of all approved projects.

In the 1970s, the emphasis on hunting and consumptive wildlife uses inherent in these provivions has become the target of much criticism. Bird-watchers, wildlife photographers, and defenders of the gene pool believe that the hunters have ready influence in state wildlife management programs because their fees and special taxes pay for most of them. At the time, however, in most states "PR funds" (as they are known) made the difference between having a wildlife management program or not having one. This is the singular accomplishment of the New Deal era against which the habitat destruction must be weighed.

The Soil Conservation Service

The Dust Bowl is as important a symbol of the Depression as is the TVA. The Soil Conservation Service (SCS) was established in 1935 in response to massive farm soil erosion. Although originally established in the Department of the Interior as the Soil Erosion Service (SES), it was transferred to Agriculture in 1935. This is one of the few transfers of responsibility for resources out of Interior during the 1930s. Secretary Ickes was considerably agitated by the move, which was accomplished by the President while Ickes was out of town, especially since he had established the SES himself. He was, however, forced to concede that soil was an agricultural problem primarily (Ickes, 1953, 259, 339, 343, 398). The first SES director, Hugh Hammond Bennet, waged a national campaign against erosion which finally resulted in the SCS enabling legislation. Legend contends that Bennet was testifying in behalf of the bill before the Senate Public Lands Committee "when the Capitol building itself was almost blacked out by a dust storm which had originated two thousand miles away" (Smith, p. 249).

The need for remedial action was obvious and in 1935 Congress passed the Soil Erosion Act. The primary objective was to protect the nation's soil and water resources by helping landowners carry out desirable practices which they otherwise would not adopt to the needed extent. The bill authorized technical assistance and cash subsidies to farmers. The Secretary of Agriculture was authorized to "coordinate and direct all activities" concerning soil erosion, to conduct research, demonstration projects, and preventive operations. The Secretary was also empowered to establish the Soil Conservation Service (Morgan, 2–25). In order to implement the comprehensive new programs, Hugh Bennet set about at once to organize the nation into soil conservation districts. This was accomplished in 1936 (Morgan, chap. 2), and a third Department of Agriculture agency with strong state and county level organizations appeared. Both the Agricultural Extension Service and the Forest Service cooperative state and private forestry programs had long been providing soil conservation information and education (as opposed to the SCS's subsidies and technical assistance). Neither was enthusiastic about the field level hierarchy of soil conservation districts. They believed the new agency threatened their authority and support. The concern with soil erosion and the clear political need to do something about it practically required that a new and separate agency be established. Given the disasters then taking place, existing agencies were in an awkward position if they tried to assert that soil erosion was their responsibility alone. Nonetheless, there is clear duplication among the old and new agencies.

INTERAGENCY CONFLICT: AGRICULTURE
AND INTERIOR

The proliferation of agencies with overlapping interests was characteristic of FDR's approach to administering the federal bureaucracy. By creating competing agencies in the same fields, Roosevelt gave himself alternative personnel, policies, and approaches to choose from. His masterful balancing of the ambitions and capabilities of the various agencies did not result in a tidy organizational chart, but much was accomplished.

This approach was tailor-made for the talents and ambitions of Harold Ickes. He occupied a number of key positions; and in the administrative and programmatic confusion of the New Deal, he proved to be an effective and creative empire builder. Ickes is best remembered as Roosevelt's Secretary of the Interior, a position he held from 1933 to 1946. He was simultaneously head of the Public Works Administration for eight years, during which time he administered millions of dollars worth of miscellaneous recovery programs, many of which impacted forest and range policy. Ickes also spent six years as head of the National Resources Planning Board, a position which he frequently used to further his plans for a Department of Conservation which he envisioned including the Forest Service. The idea of such a department was at least thirty-five years old when Ickes adopted it, and the thought has continued to be a favorite dream of reorganization-prone Presidents and Interior Secretaries.

That the proposal has merit and appeal can be read, in part, from the frequency with which it is proposed and the broad support it continues to command. Ickes's efforts were in principle part an attempt to achieve programmatic and institutional goals of the Theodore Roosevest era conservationists. Ickes was, in fact, a progressive Republican with warm affection for Pinchot, at least when he took office (Ickes, 1953, 17). The old friends split over Ickes's reorganization goals which ultimately were thwarted by two major forces. First, Pinchot and his supporters were suspicious of Interior, loyal to Agriculture, and would not tolerate the suggestion of moving the Forest Service. Pinchot, the Forest Service, the Department of Agriculture, and their supporters within Congress and throughout the nation, although frequently unable to beat Ickes on lesser points, successfully rallied support for the Forest Service on this emotionally charged issue. Second, Ickes was his own worst enemy. "He was vainglorious, self-righteous, and suspicious; and these traits left him few close friends either in the New Deal bureaucracy or along the other avenues used to evoke favorable public opinion needed to support the empire-building within the Interior Department which became his goal" (Smith, 265). Ickes's unfortunate personal style turned understandable but probably surmountable partisanship between the two departments into a bitter and frequently personal feud. It soon became apparent that achieving the transfer of the Forest Service would be difficult at best and Ickes's attention turned to subtler maneuvering. Hostility engendered by Ickes' tactics continues to be evident in discussions of moving the Forest Service to Interior.

1933 Park Service Reorganization

The first volley in this prolonged conflict was fought over an Executive Reorganization Order promulgated in June 1933. It changed the name of the National Park Service to the Office of National Parks, Buildings, and Reservations. The newly named agency was given jurisdiction, which it had been seeking since 1917, over all national monuments. It was also given responsibility for military parks, historic sites, and a number of cemeteries; a number of public buildings, mostly in Washington, D.C.; and the George Washington Memorial Parkway. The number of Park Service administered areas doubled and the scope of its mission was broadened and confused by the reorganization order (Lee, 136–148). Although an act of Congress in 1934 reinstated the Park Service name, the Park Service idea of preserving natural wonders unimpaired for future generations was diluted beyond repair. Buildings, battlefields, highways, and developed recreation distorted the Park Service agenda and almost nothing was beyond the range of its new mission. The situation exacerbated Ickes's empire building tendencies dramatically.

A critical feature of the reorganization gave the Park Service authority over sixteen national monuments previously administered by the Forest Service, several of which were completely surrounded by national forest land. Thus the transfers broke up administrative units and gave the Park Service a major foothold in several national forests. Several of these areas later served as a basis for urging further Forest to Park Service land transfers. This in itself would have generated ill will between the two agencies. However, the transfers were mishandled in a way that contributed immeasurably to interagency mistrust and hostility. During a sixty-day review period following the Executive Order, the two agencies agreed orally that only four of the sixteen Forest Service administered national monuments should be transferred. Toward the end of the review period, however, the Park Service simply announced that all national monuments were thereafter under its jurisdiction (Cate, 123).

Forest Service partisans were rightly annoyed at the Park Service perfidy, but the real importance of the event is not its uniqueness but the animosity it generated. Bureaucratic games are unrelenting and the victories achieved must be weighed against the hostility provoked. As noted in Chapter 3, Pinchot's high-handedness in creating the 1907 national forests had unfortunate repercussions for decades following. In 1933, Ickes's manipulation of the monument transfers worked to the benefit of the Park Service. Since then, however, cooperation between the two services has been conditioned by Forest Service wariness of the Park Service's constant search for land to administer.

National Resources Board Report

Harold Ickes also served as chairman of the National Resources Board, a group established by Roosevelt to inventory resources and land use in the United States. As chairman, Ickes assigned to the National Park Service responsibility for compiling a survey of national recreation resources. The report, issued in 1934, was a bold and provocative argument for transferring large amounts of national forest land to the Park Service. It concluded that

> If the recreation values of a superlative area are to be realized, the area must be dedicated to that end alone. Otherwise it will be impaired. You cannot conduct banking in a temple and keep it a place of worship. Neither can you graze sheeep and cattle in a superlative forest and keep the forest superlative . . .
>
> It is evident that administration of great scenic areas, for appropriate recreational use, under two departments of government is an unwarranted duplication of expenditure and effort. Moreover, the administration of national parks and monuments by the Forest Service would be inconsistent with the purposes for which it was created . . . [National Park Service, 210–211].

Continuing in that vein, the report identified ten Forest Service areas which ought to be added to existing national parks and four new national parks which should be created out of national forestland. Like the monument transfers, the report heightened the tension between the two agencies.

Park, Parkway, and Recreation Area Study
Act of 1936

The first victim of the hostility generated by Park Service coveting of Forest Service lands was comprehensive national recreation planning. The Department of the Interior tried to prevent the director of the CCC from undertaking any recreation development except under the direct supervision of the National Park Service (Cate, 120–121). That move failed, but it was rapidly followed by a Park Service-supported bill which would have established its position as the sole government recreation planning agency. Fearing Park Service ambitions, the Forest Service successfully opposed the bill until it was amended to preclude Park Service planning on Department of Agriculture lands. With that limitation, the Park, Parkway, and Recreation Area Study Act of 1936 authorized the Park Service to undertake a nationwide survey of recreation needs and resources and to cooperate with other federal agencies, states, and localities in implementing the plan. However, the law did not apply to national forests, and recreation planning proceeded with the leading land management agency absent from the process. This was not simply a defeat for the Park Service; it was an unfortunate dislocation in land management that was not rectified for thirty years.

Alteration of National Park Standards

A second result of the Park Service-Forest Service hostility was the decline of the preservation component of the Park Service mandate and a dilution of their management criteria. Steven Mather had emphasized recreation and tourism to gain public recognition and support for his new and struggling agency. He actively fought, however, to keep less than superior areas of national significance out of the system (Shankland, chap. 14). The idea of national preserves persisted in spite of the tourist developments. Under Ickes, the Park Service emphasized recreation, explicitly lowering standards for selecting and managing park areas in order to get more land into the system.

In the late 1930s, Park Service Director Arno Cammerer and former Director Horace Albright stated quite clearly the need to lower standards in order to expand the park system. Albright wrote:

> In any case, in order to create a new National Park, we must overcome the objections to the inclusion of forest areas, grazing areas, mining claims, hunting territory and other commercial and popular uses. . . . The net result of applying the unmodified territory theory is that those who advocate it are in fact aligning themselves with other national park objectors to prevent any more areas from being incorporated into the system. . . . [Gilligan, 160–164].

In addition to lowering admission standards, Ickes fought hard in the 1930s to establish new management criteria for additions to the park system. He wanted to establish "recreation areas" so that the Park Service could compete with the Forest Service for the management of multiple-use lands. He wrote in his diary:

> I think this is the best way to meet some of the opposition we are having in the West. People are more and more reluctant to give up prospecting and hunting rights. They can both prospect and hunt in national forest areas . . . there will be a loud outcry. If we take them over as national recreation areas, there ought not to be so much opposition. This will be outflanking the Forest Service. . . . [Ickes, 1955, 160.]

By allowing hunting and mining in areas administered by the National Park Service, Ickes hoped to facilitate further Forest-to-Park Service land transfers.

When Ickes failed to achieve the goal of outright transfer of the Forest Service into Interior, he adopted an explicitly stated policy of incorporating the national forests into Interior acre by acre through the National Park Service (Ickes, 1955, 624–625). The many forest-to-park land transfers of the 1930s were accompanied by charges and countercharges concerning alleged Forest Service mismanagement of the lands in question. Ickes did not initiate Park Service-Forest Service rivalry, nor did it cease when he passed from the scene; but the constant involvement of the Secretary accentuated the inevitable competition and created hostilities that continue to influence the undertaking.

FOREST SERVICE RECREATION PROGRAMS

Ickes's goals for the Park Service and a Department of Conservation were clear. Just as clear, however, was Roosevelt's tendency to divide responsibility for any programmatic area among several competing agencies. The President was a great supporter of the Park Service and its ambitions. Nevertheless, the Forest Service also rightly regarded FDR as a champion. The Forest Service recreation program received a great deal of support from the administration during the Depression. The CCC did much to develop National Forest recreation facilities and many of the programs which were thwarted in the 1920s were encouraged in the 1930s. Obviously, a major component of the Forest Service recreation program resulted from the efforts of recreation advocates within the agency who had been working since about 1917 to gain support for Forest Service recreation programs. With high-level external support and expanded funding, those early efforts bore fruit. In 1932, the Chief issued a memorandum classifying recreation as a major use of the national forests equal to others (Cate, 114–115).

The Wilderness Debate Continues

No aspect of the Forest Service recreation program or of Forest Service-Park Service confrontation has proved so durable a public issue as wilderness designation and management. In the 1930s, the Forest Service set the stage for the legislative debate of the 1950s and 1960s and the roadless area controversy that has continued to be a focus of concern and controversy. The wilderness concept was not widely recognized or supported during the 1930s, and most of the people actively working to establish a system of wilderness preserves were employed by the Forest Service. They succeeded moderately during the 1920s, when the wilderness idea received limited, perhaps grudging, recognition in the L-regulations discussed above (see p. 133–134). In the 1930s, the idea took fire because of the Park Service threat. Wilderness supporters within the agency were able to capitalize on Park Service predations to win support for their cause.

By far the most effective spokesperson the wilderness movement ever had was Bob Marshall. Marshall was energetic, wealthy, and totally dedicated to wilderness preservation. He was a founder of the Wilderness Society and a major financial supporter of their programs and publications. In May, 1937, he was transferred from the Bureau of Indian Affairs and appointed chief of the Recreation and Lands Division in the Forest Service. His was a highly unusual appointment made by Chief Silcox; Marshall is one of very few Forest Service officers ever to attain high rank without working up through the organization. In the two turbulent, frantic years that he held that position, Marshall proselytized endlessly to build support for wilderness designations.

Wilderness advocates made three general points in behalf of wilderness designations. First, they argued that wilderness designations were necessary to demonstrate to Congress that the Forest Service had a well-developed management approach to scenic and recreation resources and that transferring land to the Park Service was unnecessary. Second, they suggested that it would be several decades before the resources in many of the areas could be exploited and that they ought to be protected from intrusion until they were needed. Third, they urged, quite apart from the first two points, that the recreation, research, and preservation purposes inherent in wilderness designation were suitable uses for the superlative national forestlands in question. Wilderness advocates recognized the first two points as expedient rather than fundamental (Sax, 115). If the only points that wilderness areas had in their favor were that they were temporarily inaccessible and that the Park Service wanted to manage them, most of the areas would be gone now. However, until the public was ready to support wilderness designations and the Forest Service was generally ready to accept the third point, the first two were critical.

None of the three arguments went unchallenged in the internal agency discussions. Many Forest Service officials feared that, far from being an appropriate way to prevent Park Service takeovers of Forest Service lands, wilderness designations were invitations to Park Service intrusions. They feared that if the Forest Service identified land as having primarily scenic or recreational values, it would facilitate Park Service acquisition of the areas. In January, 1939, the Park Service seemed to justify these fears when they asked for a map of all national forest primitive areas. Many believed that the first step in another round of Park Service usurpations. Marshall and his allies apparently won this phase of the internal discussions—almost every area in which the Park Service had evinced an interest, including some areas of less than 10,000 acres which Marshall had not lobbied for, were designated primitive (Gilligan, 199).

Forest Service officials were also leery of the second point made by wilderness advocates. If wilderness was a way to avoid spending money to manage something inaccessible until it was needed, they were not opposed. If, however, the designation was a preliminary to park or parklike status in which none of the resources could be used, then many foresters were against the designation. Moreover, the "bank" argument for wilderness, the idea that the best way to conserve our resources is not to use them until we really need them, does not always ring true. In many areas where basic inventory and exploration has not been completed, the "lock it up till we need it" theory is tantamount to putting a safe deposit box into the vault without first learning what is in it. This is especially true regarding mineral resources for which we still do not have much of the necessary inventory data. Moreover, though many wilderness opponents tolerated the designations because the land in question was inaccessible and could not be managed in any event, they were well aware that the designations were not temporary in the eyes of their advocates. The bank theory tends to be a ploy since land designated to a special use is very difficult to reallocate at a later date.

Finally, many in the Forest Service believed that wilderness was not an appropriate use of national forest lands. They pointed to the fact that national forests were established for purposes of protecting and improving the forests, timber production, and water flow. They claimed that the agency did not have authority to withhold large tracts of the public lands and concern itself with wilderness recreation when so many in the nation were in such dire economic straits.

The U-Regulations

Discussion of principles and tactics raged within the agency throughout the 1930s. In 1939, the Secretary of Agriculture promulgated a new set of regulations defining Forest Service wilderness policy. The new regulations, known as the U-regulations, were much more precise and restrictive than the L-series of regulations that they replaced.

The U-regulations established three categories of roadless areas: wilderness, wild, and recreation. Regulation U-1 described wilderness areas as tracts of not less than 100,000 acres in which no roads, timber harvesting, motorized transportation, or occupancy under special use permits would be permitted. Established grazing, water storage projects, access to inholdings, and administrative and emergency access was permitted subject to such restrictions as deemed necessary by the Chief. Smaller areas, 5000 to 100,000 acres, were called "wild" areas in Regulation U-2 and were to be treated the same as wilderness areas. Recreation or roadless areas defined in Regulation U-3 were to be managed for recreation use "substantially in their natural condition." Areas of 100,000 acres or more could be included, and management would permit timber harvest, roads, and other activities at the discretion of the Chief.

The process for designating the wilderness and wild areas was also clarified by the new regulations. Wilderness areas were to be designated by the Secretary of Agriculture and wild areas by the Chief. Any alteration, modification, or designation required a public hearing, ninety-day posted notice, and a decision by the Chief or the Secretary. As a result of these clarifications, the wilderness program was no longer an ad hoc or informal undertaking left to the discretion of Regional Foresters and Forest Supervisors. The new regulations required that the primitive areas defined under the haphazard 1924 L-regulations be studied for reclassification under the new program. During the review period, the agency's policy was to manage all primitive areas as if they were under the U-regulations until the new management plans were developed. Thus, areas which were originally identified as "primitive" on the assumption that their status might be altered by the Chief as economic demand indicated became semi-permanent reserves. The U-regulations defined a Forest Service program of permanent, unchangeable areas.

Robert Marshall died at the age of thirty-eight only two months after the new wilderness management scheme was adopted. Marshall's death was a tremendous setback for preservationists, wilderness enthusiasts, and his Forest Service supporters. The loss of his strong and effective voice within the agency allowed his dissenting colleagues to question the Forest Service commitment to the wilderness program. The fears of the wilderness proponents were exacerbated by the very slow progress made in reclassifying the primitive areas for protection under Marshall's U-regulations.

Ultimately, the desultory pace of reclassification led preservationists to seek legislative protection of wilderness areas. During the late 1930s, however, that effort was embryonic; and the major focus of discussion was the competition between the Departments of Agriculture and Interior. Although the wilderness movement owes much to the devotion and effort of many preservationists less well known than Robert Marshall, the hostility between the two agencies was without question a major factor in the development of a national wilderness system.

It is strange how often we decry in government the same competitive forces that are the essential and revered component of the American free enterprise system. Competition, which is seen in business as the appropriate and necessary means of assuring adequate quality and choice among toothpastes, cars, and universities, is typically reviled in government as confusing, wasteful, and inefficient. The competition between the Park Service and the Forest Service frequently is manifest in partisanship or rooting for the "home team." Occasionally, it is petty and destructive. In the case of recreation policy and wilderness preservation, however, we see a clear instance of creative competition. The Forest Service was motivated in part by the fear of land transfers to develop and implement a far-reaching program in land preservation. The competition between the two agencies resulted, moreover, in a much broader and more inclusive spectrum of recreation activities than would have been available to the American people if one agency had been exclusively in charge. In the chaos of proliferating New Deal programs, Roosevelt never allowed either agency to subdue the other. Ickes's effort to take over the Forest Service was unsuccessful; however, during the 1930s, the Park Service grew and took its place next to the Forest Service, the SCS, and the other New Deal conservation agencies as a major and important factor in wild lands policy.

PUBLIC DOMAIN LANDS AND THE
TAYLOR GRAZING ACT

The Depression era attempts to deal with the unreserved public domain lands reflect less positive consequences of interdepartmental competition. Ickes's determination that the lands should remain in Interior for administration was understandable. However, the deals that he made in order to achieve his goal compromised subsequent efforts to achieve regulation and conservation of the public range.

Two related issues were paramount in the public domain management debate. The first was the obvious problem of range abuse. Much of the public land in the arid West was simply being destroyed by unregulated use. This overuse was, as was noted in Chapter 3, encouraged by the inappropriate land disposition policies of the late nineteenth and early twentieth centuries. The second was chronic economic instability in the livestock industry. The competition between cattle raisers and sheep raisers, the economic necessity to raise more stock on a limited land base, and the prolonged fluctuation in stock prices all mitigated against wise utilization of the public domain lands. These problems had long been recognized and many efforts had been made to resolve them. Legislation to regulate range use was introduced every year between 1899 and 1934.

Problems in Securing Legislation

Problems on the public domain were everywhere apparent. Solutions to these problems were not, however, obvious or readily agreed to. Three major factors stand out as perennial barriers to remedial action. The nature of the land involved was a major stumbling block. The public domain was unoccupied, unreserved, unentered, and therefore retained in public possession precisely because nobody could think of anything useful to do with it. As noted above, when Hoover's Secretary of the Interior tried to give it away to the states, they would not take it. Second, because the land seemed useless and unattractive, the public paid very little attention to its fate. The preservationists who supported the wilderness concept and the Park Service were interested in mountain and forest recreation. By default, the main group of people paying attention to the issue was the livestock industry. Their attention was undivided, and therefore their perceptions defined the issues. The lands, their use and management, were viewed exclusively in terms of the domestic livestock industry. The public domain became grazing districts, and public domain issues became grazing issues because no other uses and no other issues were raised. Third, even if grazing were accepted as the appropriate exclusive or dominant use of the public domain lands, Congress had very little knowledge upon which to draw in setting up a scientific range management program. Unlike the forestry profession, which was centuries old and steeped in science and tradition when it was introduced in this country, the science of range management was almost nonexistent when the Taylor Grazing Act passed.

In spite of the long-standing difficulties, the time for achieving range regulation seemed auspicious in the early 1930s. The idea of range management gained support from an experimental grazing district established in 1928 at the initiative of a group of Montana stock operators. Congress passed a bill which permitted federal and state assistance to stock operators in the Mizpah-Pumpkin Creek Basin. The range improved dramatically and the leasing scheme was so well received that other regions were soon pressing for congressional authorization to create their own grazing districts (Achterman, 25-28). The depression, the drought, and the Dust Bowl which accompanied it, and the acute economic upheaval which it caused, proved to be the necessary catalyst to congressional action.

Debate on the Taylor Grazing Act

It was inevitable that the Taylor Grazing Act emphasized use regulation rather than scientifically based land management. Nobody demanded more, the stock operators would not tolerate more, and the professionalism and technique were simply unavailable to accomplish more. Suboptimal though the Taylor Grazing Act was, it did constitute a start on a major refocusing of public domain activities. Even this modest beginning was stymied by the battle waged over authority to manage the grazing lands.

At the time the act was being debated, the General Land Office of the Department of the Interior, which recorded patents and titles under the myriad of disposition statutes, was nominally in charge of the public domain lands. In line with his ambition to create a Department of Conservation, Ickes battled to retain control within his department. Opposing him, of course, was a significant proportion of the Pinchot conservation movement, which fought to have the lands transferred to Agriculture. Many foresters were not enthusiastic about grazing use of the national forests and favored a separate Grazing Service within the Department of Agriculture. Others within the Forest Service were aware of the opportunities inherent in public domain management and wanted to administer them as part of the national forests. Gifford Pinchot returned to fight one last battle in behalf of his cherished Forest Service.

On the merits, there is probably no question which department was better qualified to manage the lands. In contrast to the Department of the Interior, the Forest Service had an extensive staff, well-deployed field organization, and thirty years' experience in dealing with range management problems. However, the Forest Service had alienated many in the livestock industry by trying to raise the grazing fees in the mid-1920s.

Astutely, Ickes exploited this weakness in the Department of Agriculture position. He not only wanted to retain the public domain lands in Interior, he also wanted to build his position with the stock operators in order to win their support for his Department of Conservation. Therefore, Secretary Ickes made a number of unwise commitments to the stockmen: (1) He promised that no extensive bureaucracy resembling the Forest Service would be established to manage, protect, and regulate the use of public domain lands. (2) He promised that fees for use of public forage would be tied to the cost of administering the lease program rather than to the fair market value of the forage. (3) He grossly misrepresented the cost of administering the lease program. The Forest Service estimated that the cost of administering the proposed program on 80 to 160 million acres would be at least $1.5 to $2 million. Ickes alleged Interior could do the job for about $150,000 annually (Gates, 612). This low estimate would ensure both low grazing fees and a very weak agency to collect them.

Provisions of the Act

Ickes's preferences and promises were reflected in the bill which passed. The purpose of the legislation was to "stop injury" to the range by "preventing overgrazing" and to "provide for orderly use, improvement and development" of the grazing land. In order to accomplish these goals, the Secretary of Interior was authorized to establish as grazing districts not more than 80 million acres of vacant, unappropriated, and unreserved public lands which in his judgement were chiefly valuable for grazing and raising forage crops. The 80 million acres were subsequently expanded to 142 million acres because of a ruling that public domain lands outside of the grazing districts were ineligible for CCC assistance. The forage resources were to be leased to established operators for ten-year periods under a system to be defined by the Secretary. Finally, the Secretary was authorized to make rules and regulations regulating the use of the range.

The act provided that the Secretary *could* "cooperate with local associations of stockmen" in the implementation of the act. This provision was made mandatory in an amendment adopted in 1939, which provided for the establishment within each grazing district of an advisory board of five to twelve local stock operators elected by the users of the range and subsequently appointed by the Secretary of the Interior. Symbolically, the Secretary was authorized to appoint to the Grazing Advisory Boards one person to speak for wildlife interests on the public domain lands. These advisory boards became the vehicle for domination of the Grazing Service by the livestock users. The advisory boards virtually controlled the approval of grazing permits in their districts and offered "advice" on all other matters affecting the administration of the Taylor Grazing Act within their respective districts. Except in an emergency, the Secretary of the Interior had to request the advice of the advisory board prior to the promulgation of any rules and regulations affecting the district.

All of these provisions were undercut by the phrase "pending final disposition," which was inserted in the section of the act defining the Secretary's authority. The Taylor Grazing Act was superimposed on top of the myriad of disposition statutes and altered the existing pattern only temporarily. The lands were not to be retained and managed by the federal government but leased to stock operators until they passed into private ownership or were otherwise disposed of.

Implementation of the Act

In one sense, the Taylor Grazing Act can fairly be called a conservation measure because the Taylor Bill ended the period of free access to the public domain. One major study of the legislation has appropriately marked 1934 as "the closing of the public domain" (Peffer). Following passage of the legislation, President Roosevelt withdrew from homestead entry all remaining public lands in the contiguous forty-eight states. From 1934 forward, entry and use of the public domain lands was regulated by the federal government. No longer would it be possible for stock operators simply to use public range. As long as the lands remained in public ownership, operators must have a permit, pay for it, and graze their stock in a manner prescribed by the Department of the Interior to protect and revitalize the public domain lands. Although the Taylor Grazing Act entailed an unmistakable commitment of 142 million acres of public land to a single use, it did represent a potential and urgently needed assertion of public regulation over the public lands, albeit pending their disposition.

Unfortunately, three major factors doomed this initial assertion of authority to failure. First and most significant were the attitudes and power of the stock operators themselves. The graziers had been on the land using it and treating it as their own for at least sixty years before the passage of the Taylor Grazing Act. Through three generations of chaos, the operators had evolved their own systems for allocating rangeland. These schemes relied on practices which evolved from early use of force in controlling water supply, illegal fencing, and physical violence to minimize intruders (Scott, passim). Those operators who had come to dominate the industry in a period of might makes right were not inclined to give up "their" land or prerogatives under a federal regulatory scheme. Through the concerted efforts of their congressional delegations, that powerful minority within the industry gained control of Taylor Grazing Act implementation.

The most obvious manifestation of the authority of this group was in the priorities devised for allocating grazing permits. Because there were too many users on the public range, some had to be eliminated in the permit granting process (Calef, 60–62). Two criteria were established: commensurate property and prior use. The act requires that preference be given to historic range users. The prior use requirement was designed to assure that traditional range users would not be displaced by the federal regulatory program. The commensurate property requirement was administratively imposed. It required permittees to own sufficient private property to support their herds when they were not on public lands. The manipulation of these two apparently reasonable requirements stabilized the stock industry. It did so, however, to the absolute advantage of one segment of the industry and virtually assured the elimination of all others.

The original scheme for allocating permits proposed that first priority be granted to those with adequate base private property *and* a history of range use. Second priority would go to traditional users, and third priority would be given to those with base property who had never before made use of the range. Following a meeting of representatives of all established grazing districts, the order of priorities two and three was reversed: Landowners with no history of use were given preference over traditional users who did not own base property. Sheep grazers, whose operations tend to be nomadic and frequently distant from or without a base property, were virtually excluded. Furthermore, the prior use requirement was defined to mean those who had actually grazed stock on the public domain between June 1929 and June 1934. Because those years were a period of drought as well as economic collapse, many operators who had been on the range for generations had recently cut the size of their herds or liquidated them. Because they had made limited or no use of the range during the crucial period, they were given slight consideration or none at all in the distribution of grazing permits. Thus, only the most prosperous of the traditional users were eligible for permits under the Taylor Grazing Act. Quite apart from anything required by the act, powerful interests were consistently able to define its implementation to their own advantage.

The second major difficulty encountered in implementing the Taylor Grazing Act was the total absence of groups or institutions to counter the power of the stock operators. The Grazing Service needed support and funding which were not forthcoming. By design and default, the Grazing Service was weak, ineffective, and vulnerable. The power of the stock operators in and out of Congress maintained the Grazing Service at a level sufficient to enforce the advantage gained by the dominant grazers under the Taylor Grazing Act without permitting any serious regulation or interference with their activities. The conservation groups were either anti-Grazing Service because they followed Pinchot's lead in refusing to support any effort, however laudable, that was not administered by the Forest Service, or they were preoccupied with the forest-to-park land transfers. The public domain lands became grazing lands, and the Grazing Service was literally run by the stock operators who controlled the Grazing Advisory Boards.

The problems presented by lack of outside support were compounded by Ickes's unwise promises, made during debate on the bill, regarding low level of administration and funding. Neither the money nor the personnel was available to promulgate or enforce the necessary regulation of the grazing districts. In accord with Ickes's promise, grazing fees were tied to the cost of administering the program rather than to the fair market value of the forage, and personnel was kept at a minimum to keep the costs down. As a result, Grazing Service fees were typically one-third of what the Forest Service charged for grazing permits and in 1936 there was one Grazing field employee for every 4.9 million acres of grazing district land (Calef, 59). With no money, no personel, and no source of income for range improvements, it is little wonder that the Grazing Service was unable to make headway in controlling use and reversing degradation of the public range.

The final factor in the continuing degradation of the public domain lands was the unfortunate phrase "pending final disposition" which was added with almost no discussion at the final phase of congressional review of the bill. All subsequent efforts to manage the public domain lands or to invest in their use or future productivity have been hampered by this cloud on their status. Although President Roosevelt promptly withdrew the lands from homestead entry, their ultimate utilization was uncertain. Since the homesteading acts were temporarily deactivated by President Roosevelt's withdrawals, the nature of the disposition which awaited the lands was entirely unspecified. Predictably, self-interested schemes were promoted by numerous groups over the years, creating a series of unresolved minicrises. Until 1976, it was not clear that the lands would be retained in federal ownership. Exacerbating all the weaknesses in the act and its implementation, that phrase kept the public domain lands under a fog of uncertainty for forty more years.

Forest Service Grazing Lands and Programs

In spite of the obvious shortcomings apparent in early administration of the act, only eighteen months passed before Ickes began overt efforts to have the Forest Service-administered grazing areas transferred into the Grazing Service. This transfer was a component of the major reorganization of the federal government proposed by the noted Brownlow Committee Report on Administrative Management (Gates, 616). The Forest Service countered almost immediately in a 1936 report of the Agriculture and Forestry Committee of the Senate entitled *The Western Range*. Briefly stated, its message was that the Forest Service-administered range was in excellent condition, that all range could benefit from Forest Service attentions, and that as an agricultural undertaking grazing should be located in the Department of Agriculture. The volume, which has become known as "The Green Book," is appropriately compared with the Park Service study of recreation resources referred to above (p. 153). Underneath the Forest Service efforts to discredit the Department of the Interior, there is much valuable data regarding range conditions in the 1930s which provide the only rough benchmark for purposes of establishing trends and making time series comparisons with present conditions (Box, 20–22). However, the Forest Service goal of transferring the grazing districts to the Department of Agriculture was never seriously considered.

It was nevertheless a propitious time for the Forest Service to assert the virtues of its range management effort. In contrast to the drastic upheaval of policy with respect to the handling of unreserved public domain lands brought about by the Taylor Grazing Act, little change in the administration of grazing on the national forests took place during the 1930s. The major Forest Service range management tactic, reduction of the stock on the range, was tragically abetted by the drought, the Depression, and the consequent number of livestock operators who went bankrupt under the adverse conditions. Although there was a steady undercurrent of criticism on the part of certain members of the livestock industry, most attention was focused on Grazing Service developments. Enjoying relative calm and success, the Forest Service met Ickes's predations directly with The Green Book and the Interior Secretary's transfer requests were soon forgotten.

FOREST MANAGEMENT ISSUES

Public domain and wilderness/recreation seem to be the most critical wild lands issues of the 1930s by hindsight because they have continued to be hotly debated in subsequent decades. There were a number of other issues, in forest management particularly, that seem less important now because they do not continue to be problems. They deserve attention, however, because they constituted the major focus of forest policy debate in the 1930s and because their resolution was significant. It is important to note that many of the things which seem natural or unquestioned today were divisive national issues only thirty or forty years ago. Two issues stand out. First, sustained yield forestry received an impressive endorsement in the congressional reconsideration of the O & C revested lands question. Once again Ickes and the Forest Service squared off, but no land changed hands and the undisputed victor was sound land management. While the O & C issue was far from closed, the management scheme mandated for the lands was a tremendous step forward. Second, forest regulation and ownership continued to be a contentious issue through the war years. The debate is an important indicator of three important developments in the profession—the impact of New Deal ideology on forest management, the first stirrings of industrial forestry, and tremendous progress in state forestry.

O & C Lands

In 1937, Congress made attempt to resolve the controversy surrounding the O & C revested lands. The goal of the Chamberlain-Ferris Act of 1916 was to dispose of the lands. Very little thought was given to the suitability of the land for family farming or the need to protect the land by regulating the sale and harvesting of the timber. The results were disastrous. Unrestricted exploitation and destruction of the most productive timberlands in the Northwest was encouraged by the act. The most obvious problem was fire caused by unregulated slash burning by both loggers and homesteaders. Steadily mounting public dissatisfaction with the O & C situation finally led to passage of the act of August 28, 1937, which completely reversed the previous policy. The new act provided that the lands should be managed

. . . for permanent forest production, and the timber thereon shall be sold, cut and removed in conformity with principal [sic] of sustained yield . . . providing a permanent source of timber supply, protecting watersheds, regulating stream flow, and contributing to the economic stability of local communities and industries, and providing recreational facilities [sic] [Dana, 266].

Predictably, the Forest Service believed that establishing a forest management agency in the Department of the Interior was unwise and inefficient. Similarly, Ickes was determined to hold onto the O & C timberlands. He saw the revested lands as a toehold in the forestry area which would strengthen his case for reuniting Interior and the Forest Service. Following an inevitable flare-up of hostilities, Interior retained control. An Oregon and California Revested Lands Administration was established in the General Land Office, and the O & C lands were placed under sustained yield management for the first time in their troubled history.

The contrast between Grazing Service management of the grazing districts and the treatment afforded to the O & C lands is an informative one. Although O & C management efforts are not funded anywhere to the level that Forest Service programs in the same area, O & C managers, unlike the Grazing Service, have never lacked support for their tasks. This is attributable to the resource involved—50 billion board feet of Douglas fir saw timber as opposed to 140 million acres of degraded range country. Money was also partially accountable for lodging O & C land management in Interior rather than in the Forest Service. Fifty percent of the timber sale dollars are returned to the counties under the O & C statutes and another 25 percent of the receipts is "plowed back" into land management. The Forest Service payment to counties is 25 percent of the receipts. This considerable differential probably accounts for much of the Oregon Congressional delegation's pro-Interior enthusiasm.

This same factor, however, contributed to an unfortunate continuation in the O & C saga in the 1950s. Although the 1937 legislation took the crucial step of putting the O & C lands on a sustained yield management footing, it stirred up a considerable controversy over the intermingled lands which the Forest Service had been managing. At the time O & C lands revested in 1916, there were some 465,000 acres which caused confusion. These lands were included in odd-numbered sections within the railroad grant limits. The railroad company had, however, never received a patent for the lands, no patents were pending, and they had been included in national forests by various presidential proclamations between 1892 and 1907. After the Chamberlain-Ferris statute passed in 1916, the Forest Service inquired whether the lands had revested into the General Land Office along with the other railroad lands or whether they had stayed with the Forest Service. The Commissioner of the General Land Office in 1919 and the Assistant Secretary of the Interior in 1923 both found that since the lands had never belonged to the company and therefore did not revest, the 465,000 acres should remain where they had been —in the national forests.

Ickes, however, tried to reopen the issue and take control of the Forest Service-administered areas. Following the passage of the act of 1937, the Department of the Interior proceeded to make three sales of timber on the lands over which both departments claimed jurisdiction. Shortly thereafter, the Forest Service advertised a sale of timber on one of the controverted sections; and the Department of the Interior promptly challenged its right to do so. These actions created a difficult situation, which led to an agreement between the two departments that the Forest Service would continue to administer the lands but that all receipts from them would be placed in a special fund until the status of the lands should be definitely determined. A year later (1940), the Attorney General ruled that in his opinion "disturbance of the continued administration of these lands by the Department of Agriculture as part of the national forest reserves would not be warranted under existing law" (Dana, 268). The matter was reopened again with a new Attorney General, who declined to withdraw the opinion rendered by his predecessor. The Secretary of the Interior and the eighteen Oregon counties in which the lands are located then attempted to obtain legislation effecting the desired transfer of jurisdiction. Their efforts finally resulted in the act of 1954, which will be discussed in the next chapter.

Sustained-yield Forest Management Act

Believing that it would contribute to the stability of communities dependent for their economic livelihood on the manufacture of forest products, Congress passed the Sustained-yield Forest Management Act in March 1944. It authorized the Secretary of Agriculture and the Secretary of the Interior to establish either (1) cooperative sustained-yield units consisting of federal forest land and private forest land or (2) federal sustained-yield units consisting only of federal forest land, whenever the stability of communities primarily dependent upon federal stumpage could not be maintained through the usual timber sale procedures.

In such cases, the Secretaries could enter into agreements with private forest landowners, with each other, and with other federal agencies to provide for the coordinated management of forest lands. Provision was made for the sale of federal stumpage in sustained-yield units to cooperating landowners or to others in the dependent community without competitive bidding. In the case of cooperative sustained-yield units on private land, the agreement reached can run for as much as one hundred years. Only one cooperative sustained-yield unit has ever been established. The agreement is with Simpson Logging Company and aims to stabilize the towns of Shelton and McCleary, Washington. Altogether, 111,466 acres of federal land and 158,760 acres of company land are included in the unit. Smaller operators and some labor groups vigorously opposed the scheme, and no other units have ever been established.

Federal Forest Regulation

The regulation controversy of the 1930s was fought over basically the same issues as were reflected in the Snell and Capper bills of the 1920s. However, the economic crisis of the times put a slightly different emphasis on the more recent debate. A great many businesses and farms were lost for unpaid taxes or available for purchase at reduced prices and there was considerable pressue to expand federal ownership as well as regulation of forest lands. Moreover, unlike Graves and Greeley who preceded them, the Depression Chiefs of the Forst Service (Stuart, Silcox, and Acting Chief Clapp) were increasingly vociferous and adamant in their espousal of federal forest regulation. Three major events dominate the period: the Copeland Report, the NIRA code developed in 1934, and the Joint Congressional Committee on Forestry, which was established in 1938 and reported in 1941.

Copeland Report

The Copeland report, formally titled *A National Plan for American Forestry* and published in 1933, was the most extensive and comprehensive inquiry into the forest situation made up to that time. The data amassed in that study was impressive even by today's standards. Nonetheless, it was considered striking more because of the scope of its recommendations than because of its impressive volume and charts. Two major themes stand out among the report's proposals: a huge increase in public ownership of forest and more intensive management of public woodlands (Clepper, 146). Principal authors of the report include Robert Marshall and Earle Clapp, the most adamant advocate of regulation to occupy the Chief's office.

The Copeland Report is based on ideas about the social utility of forests and forest management which are a very important part of the Progressive era lineage of the profession. However, the ambience of the New Deal and the stridency with which government ownership is espoused makes the report sound somewhat radical. The Copeland Report is a forceful reminder that many of the traditions foresters now seek to conserve were quite revolutionary at the time of their inception. "What we are after is human happiness," wrote Robert Marshall, a principal author of the report. "Our problem then is to find how we may manage our forests to realize their highest potentialities for the well being of mankind" (Marshall, 79).

The Copeland Report demonstrated that private forestry had not, even with the assistance and cooperation of federal and state governments, made an adequate contribution to human happiness and welfare. Therefore, the report recommended a massive federal-state cooperative effort in planning and managing the forests for a variety of uses. Its proposals included public acquisition of 224 million acres of forestland. These included 32 million acres of abandoned farmland to be reforested and 30 million acres of noncommercial forests. One hundred seventy-seven million acres were to be acquired in the East.

These proposals were controversial, and many viewed them as socialistic. What was involved was a massive reallocation of landownership and the imposition of extensive federal land use planning. These concepts reflect important themes of the New Deal era and were built on a compelling argument about the inadequacies of private forestry derived from a massive array of data. The land acquisition proposals never were funded to the recommended level, but the report provided a strong empirical base for the assertion of the federal role in private foresty (Gates, 598).

NIRA and the Lumber Code

The forest industry was not in a strong position to resist regulation during the 1930s. In fact, the situation was so chaotic that many industrial leaders welcomed the stabilization, clarification, and support inherent in regulation and actively cooperated in developing codes under the National Industry Recovery Act (NIRA) of June, 1933. The NIRA had diverse goals and provisions. It included the Public Works Administration under which Harold Ickes spent $3–5 billion annually on roads, highways, housing, and dams. It also required industry trade associations to develop codes which would fix wages and hours of labor, control production, and impose fair trade practices in industry (Petulla, 270–271).

Another declared purpose of the National Industrial Recovery Act was "to conserve natural resources." The Code of Fair Competition for the Lumber and Timber Products Industries approved by the President on August 19, 1933, contained a critical statement headed "Conservation and Sustained Production of Forest Resources." This famous Article X committed the industry to developing rules of forest practice in cooperation with government agencies. It provided that each division and subdivision of the industry having jurisdiction over forest utilization operations should establish an agency to formulate rules of forest practice and to exercise general supervision over their application and enforcement.

The rules of forest practice were to include

> practicable measures to be taken by the operators to safeguard timber and young growing stock from injury by fire and other destructive forces, to prevent damage to young trees during logging operations, to provide for restocking the land after

logging if sufficient advance growth is not already present, and where feasible, to leave some portion of merchantable timber (usually the less mature trees) as a basis for growth and the next timber crop [Dana, 256].

After approval by the Lumber Code Authority, the rules were to become effective on June 1, 1934. Thereafter violators were subject to punishment by fine and imprisonment. In order to permit flexibility, all operators were encouraged to submit a specific plan of management for their own property, which, if approved by the agency, could be followed instead of the standard rules. Each agency was also instructed to encourage the application of sustained yield forest management wherever feasible.

There was great variation in the speed with which rules of forest practice were adopted and put into effect in the different regions. More seriously, the government undermined the program by refusing to prosecute violators, thereby putting those who were complying with the requirements at a serious competititve disadvantage. The whole program was, in fact, falling apart when the Supreme Court on May 27, 1935, unanimously invalidated the whole NIRA program (Loehr, chaps. 6–8). The Court held that the industry-backed codes involved an unconstitutional delegation of legislative power, that the concept exceeded the power of Congress to regulate interstate commerce, and that the program invaded the powers reserved exclusively to the states. The decision abrogated not only the rules of forest practice but also the provisions of the Lumber Code relating to hours of labor, minimum wages, control of production, cost protection, and fair trade practices.

The NIRA experiment in self-regulation of cutting practices did not last long enough to give any fair indication of how effective it would have been. The idea itself was so new and the practices recommended so foreign to the experience of most operators that considerable time would have been required to attain the goal of sustained production. After legal compulsion to do so had been removed by the Supreme Court decision, several regional associations continued their efforts to formulate workable rules of forest practice and to obtain their adoption by private owners. Economic conditions during the period were not conducive to general improvement in forest practice by private owners.

Although Article X of the Lumber Code proved to be an abortive attempt to effect a revolution in forest practice on private lands, it was undoubtedly an educational influence of great value in hastening the evolution of forestry as a private enterprise. The Forest Service, which had cooperated actively in the formulation of the rules of forest practice, also continued its efforts to be helpful under the voluntary setup. Moreover, the industry learned the benefits of self-regulation from the exercise both as a stabilizing factor and as an antedote to calls for strong and potentially burdensome government regulation. Many of the state forest practice acts of the 1940s were based on that experience and were encouraged rather than opposed by the regulated industries.

Joint Congressional Committee on Forestry

The last major volley in the regulation battle centered on the Report of the Joint Congressional Committee on Foresty. The Copeland report and Article X of the NIRA fostered discussion and education but very little action. On March 14, 1938, President Roosevelt sent a special message to Congress recommending the appointment of a joint committee to conduct a study of the forest problem which he hoped would form the basis for essential legislation at its next session. His remarks reflect the New Deal attitude toward resource management:

> Forests are intimately tied into our whole social and economic life. . . . The forest problem is therefore a matter of vital national concern, and some way must be found to make forest lands and forest resources contribute their full share to the social and economic structures of this country, and to the security and stability of all our people. . . . The public has certain responsibilities and obligations with respect to private forest lands, but so also have private owners with respect to the broad public interests in those same lands. . . .

Among the specific items that the President asked Congress to consider was "the need for such public regulatory controls as will adequately protect private as well as the broad public interests in all forest lands" (Dana, 275-76).

Under the vigorous leadership of Acting Chief Earle Clapp, the Forest Service supported federal as opposed to state regulation and offered a compromise plan to the joint committee. Clapp suggested that the states be given five to seven years in which to develop and administer reasonable regulations, after which the federal government would intervene. He endorsed the proposition that the federal government should contribute on a fifty-fifty basis to the cost of such state administration. He also recommended that the state legislation and standards of enforcement should be satisfactory to the federal government, with mandatory provision that federal financial assistance in regulation be withdrawn if enforcement proved unsatisfactory.

In the view of the joint committee, the management of commercial forest lands in private ownership constituted the nation's major forest problem. Many of the committee's recommendations concentrated on creating an economic environment in which environmentally sound forestry on private lands would be economically feasible. These included such specifics as provision for a forest credit system to make long-term loans at low interest rates to private forest operators and encouragement of farm-forest cooperatives, including federal financial aid in building and operating forest industries and woodworking plants.

The committee report disappointed many by not calling for a strong federal regulatory program. Its failure to do so marks the end of federal regulation as a major and divisive issue within the profession. some effort was made to use the wartime timber requirements as the occasion for imposing broad scale federal regulation, but the momentum was by then in the opposite direction. The war material needs were overwhelming. The debate was not without impact, however, since during the years 1940–1950 thirteen states passed forest practice acts; and many federal programs have incorporated inducements to achieve the regulation advocates' goals. This sufficed until the early 1970s, when regulation of private land management practices emerged as an important aspect of federal air and water quality programs and environmental protection and land use regulation in several states.

The decline of the federal regulation issue after the joint committee's report also marks the emergence of an effective forest products industry and lobby. With the outbreak of World War II, they emerged from the Depression and were able to oppose regulations which might have hindered contribution to the war effort (Clepper, 156–162). The industry became an effective entity during the war after evolving slowly throughout the Depression.

The 1930s marks the first point at which industry began to hire foresters in any appreciable numbers. Until then almost all the professional foresters were employed by the government. The Copeland report noted in 1933 that only 146 technically educated foresters were employed privately. By 1941, the number was 650; and by 1951, it was 4400 (Clepper, 207–208). In the 1920s, the regulation battle was a disagreement among government foresters. Up to the 1930s, forestry and the Forest Service were virtually synonymous. By the Second World War, there were sufficient professional foresters within industry to give the Forest Service an external challenge. Although this diversification of the profession was first manifest in the area of forest regulation, its importance far transcends that issue and will be discussed in subsequent sections of this and later chapters.

New Directions in State Forestry

Although several state forest programs were begun in the late 1800s and were diverse and impressive well before the 1920s, most gained state ownership and management of forest lands was not extensive; and most state programs focused on education, fire fighting, and cooperative services.

Interestingly, during the period in which the most comprehensive proposals for federal forest ownership and regulation were being put forward, state forestry was making its most significant gains. Many components of these advances have already been discussed. Tremendous investment of dollars and labor in state lands was made possible through the CCC. Tragically, state programs were also abetted by much tax-lost land made available for inclusion in burgeoning state forest systems. These factors notwithstanding, a characteristic development of the Roosevelt years is the emergence of the states as major actors in the regulation of silvicultural practices on private lands.

Pressure from both federal and state agencies to enlarge federal aid programs continued throughout the New Deal. In 1935, the Fulmer Act was passed, partially as a result of the recommendations of the Copeland report. The Fulmer Act provided aid to participating states to purchase tax-delinquent lands and to hire professionally trained foresters. No money was ever appropriated to implement this program. However, pressure continued to build as economic reversals caused states to curtail their spending on forest programs and a number of measures passed which expanded the scope and financing of the Clarke-McNary Act. Attention began to focus explicitly on the problems encountered in bringing sound forest management practices to the small woodlot owner. The Cooperative Farm Forestry Act of 1937 authorized the Secretary of Agriculture to work through state universities and forestry agencies to bring technical advice to forest farmers. The cooperative programs in fire protection were enhanced by the provisions of the act.

The most comprehensive initiative in this area was a federal bill which did not pass. Senator Bankhead introduced legislation following the report of the Joint Congressional Committee on Forestry so broad in scope that it was called the Omnibus Forestry Bill. The legislation followed the lines of Forest Service acting Chief Clapp's proposals outlined above (p. 171). It would have required states to submit plans for adopting rules of forest practice, approving working plans for individual properties, and preventing forest destruction and deterioration. States failing to submit adequate plans within three years would lose their Clarke-McNary assistance. The Bankhead omnibus bill did not pass. However, the concept and the experience gained under Article X of the NIRA provided precedent for a flurry of activity in state legislatures. The forest products industry was initially unable to resist this regulation boom; but as the Depression passed, it made considerable gains and began to defend itself politically.

Industry Development

The Depression was not a good time for the forest products industry. Production shrank from 39 billion board feet in 1929 to 14 billion board feet in 1932, a decrease of 64 percent. Much of the land that went into federal and state forest systems, especially in the East, was holdings on which timber companies could not pay taxes during the early Depression years. In many instances, the companies harvested the timber and then requested the government to relieve them of the denuded land. Hence the 1930s can be seen as the last gasp of cut-and-get-out logging. If the Depression was the nadir of the logging industry, it was also the birth of industrial forestry. Greeley has described the 1930s as the period of transition from "timber mine to forest crop" (Greeley, 1953, 201). A number of factors combined to make it economically prudent for private landowners to think in terms of holding land, not simply for the standing timber but for the subsequent stands which could be produced. Technological changes and economic developments combined to make industrial forestry a possibility.

Southern Pineries

One of the major factors in the birth of industrial forestry was the gradual disappearance of virgin timber in the Southeast. Although old growth remained in the Northwest in commercial quantities, the eastern forests had a competitive advantage due to the transporation costs involved in bringing Washington and Oregon products to the eastern markets. Second-growth timber in the East became valuable because of its location, and this simple fact encouraged the management of land for continued forest production.

A second major factor in the emergence of industrial forest management was the technological breakthroughs achieved in the pulping process, which led to the development of the paper products industry. The combination of available second growth in the Southern pineries and a market for it in the growing paper industry changed utilization patterns nationwide. These developments in the pulping process, made possible by long-term government investment in research on wood utilization and forest product development, have probably done more than any other government program to encourage the practice of sound forest management activities on private holdings. When there is a market and a profit involved, private landowners will take the necessary risks and make the necessary investments. When there is not, no amount of government cheerleading on the virtues of forest management will achieve the desired goals.

The burgeoning paper industry was also representative of a third major factor encouraging sound industrial timber management. Industry, having invested in wood processing plants at an increasing rate, could justify investment in timber growing to keep the expensive mills producing profitably. Finally, the tremendous efforts made by government and private groups to conquer the fire menace were an important component in the emergence of the forest products industry. It simply was not possible for private firms to make large investments in landownership and reforestation when the chances of literally burning up the capital were quite high. Particularly in the South where deliberate woods burning was an integral part of the agricultural way of life, fire protection was an important prerequisite to forest investments.

World War II

It is true that very little progress was made toward economic recovery prior to World War II. However, the New Deal programs made possible tremendous advances in forest and range policy. Economic prosperity resulting from the war advanced and solidified the gains made by industrial forestry. In general, however, the effect of the war years on forest and range policy was negative. Understandably, the emphasis was on meeting the needs of the war effort, but the results on the land were devastating.

Given the technological intensity of modern warfare, the amount of wood products required was amazing. Far more wood was needed than steel. Wood and wood derivatives were needed for housing, ships, wharves, airplanes, trucks, boxes and crates, paper and paper products, explosives, and a host of other products. Colonel F. G. Sherrill, Chief of the Materials and Equipment Section of the Army Corps of Engineers, said that lumber was "the most vital material for the successful prosecution of the war" and that the lumber industry "was therefore the most important war industry in the country" (Dana, 280).

Civilian consumption of wood was substantially curtailed, and the combined efforts of federal and state agencies and private industries were required to meet military needs. Research by the Forest Products Laboratory, the Timber Engineering Company, and other agencies was stepped up to a new high. All of this wood was necessary at a time when trained woodsworkers were otherwise occupied. The government established dozens of programs to assist both public and private forestry in meeting the war requirements; and, on numerous occasions, prisoners of war confined in this country were employed in harvest and salvage operations.

Pressure for more and more wood on a time schedule created conditions unfavorable to adherence to high standards of forest practice. Moreover, the public forests, which had been withholding timber from market during the Depression to avoid competing with the struggling timber industry, were not ready to meet the overwhelming demand. The Forest Service spent most of the war years rushing to get into production while industry, motivated both by patriotism and profit seeking, vastly overcut its own lands. The impact of the overcutting would not be felt for several decades, but the result of the situation for federal forestry was immediate. The Forest Service was, at the close of the war, thoroughly oriented toward production forestry in a way that it had never been previously.

The forests, however, emerged from the war in far better condition than public domain lands. The Forest Service made a tremendous effort to prevent a repetition of the World War I overgrazing calamity on lands that they managed; but on Grazing Service lands, range abuse went virtually unchallenged. To meet the intense demand for meat, wool, and hides, the stock operators expanded their herds without restraint. Moreover, the war emergency was exploited as an excuse for not raising grazing fees, as had been proposed slightly before Pearl Harbor. Range deterioration was further exacerbated by growing conflict between wildlife and livestock. In the absence of hunters who normally cropped the wildlife populations, game species multiplied rapidly during the war. Because their stock competed with wildlife for forage, the stock operators did everything they could to get rid of the wildlife. While they fought with the wildlife advocates, the range continued to deteriorate. The war, and the markets it created for livestock, was as beneficial to the industry as it was hard on the land. The industry emerged from the war stronger than ever and increasingly less willing to tolerate any interference with their use of "their" range. The Grazing Service, having proven itself to be totally inadequate to the task of range protection, became a virtual adjunct of the industry.

SUMMARY

President Roosevelt's inauguration in 1933 was followed by a burst of conservation activities unequaled since early in the century. The programs undertaken were emergency measures designed to relieve unemployment and to spur economic recovery. Notable among these activities were the CCC, the TVA, the REA, and the initial attempt to formulate rules of forest practice under the NIRA.

Progress in state forestry resulted largely from the activities of the CCC on state lands and the increased assistance to farmers made possible by the New Deal public works and education programs. The genesis of the SCS and the passage of the Cooperative Farm Forestry Act were central in the growing recognition of small woodlots as an important issue in forestry. Many New Deal programs also sought to relieve rural poverty while addressing the management problems of the forest farmer.

Other important measures that were more the result of the normal evolution of forest and range policy than of the economic emergency included the inauguration of range management on the unreserved public domain under the Taylor Grazing Act of 1934 and the application of sustained yield forest management to the O & C revested lands under the 1937 legislation.

The passage of the Taylor Grazing Act should have been the major achievement of the period. However, the potential of the act was compromised from the outset by the phrase "pending final disposition," which obscured the status of the lands for another forty years. Moreover, implementation of the Taylor Grazing Act gave significant control over range use to a prosperous and aggressive segment of the livestock industry. Finally, commitments to low fees and minimal range management and regulation made by Secretary of the Interior Ickes were successful in keeping the public range out of the Department of Agriculture, but they hampered future efforts to regulate range use. This competition between Agriculture and Interior was probably productive in terms of developing recreation and wilderness programs, but the public domain lands continue to suffer from having been a pawn in the game.

Because Franklin Roosevelt's term of office was dominated by the worst economic collapse in American history, it is interesting to note that one of the major results of the New Deal era was the emergence of stable and powerful industries. Forest and range policy would no longer be the exclusive domain of government conservationists. The implementation of the Taylor Grazing Act's priority provisions was decisive for the stock operators. In the timber field, forest mining gave way to cropping for a variety of reasons: technological developments in the pulping process, disappearance of old growth, and the growing need to amortize heavy capital investments. These trends were accelerated by the economic opportunities created by the war emergency.

The emphasis on use and exploitation of the Roosevelt years is understandable. It is, in fact, the last era of virtually unchallenged exploitation of wild lands resources for human consumption and profit. The war brought prosperity to the industries involved in resource policy, but it also significantly altered the lives of the American people. The postwar years in forest and range policy are dominated by the emergent industries, but the tendency to view wild lands resources predominantly as a source of income, commodities, and employment did not survive the war. New ideas and changing life-styles typified by Robert Marshall and the wilderness movement, which were relatively minor influences in the Roosevelt era, began to assume large proportions thereafter. The trauma of the Depression began a gradual undermining of our preoccupation with resource development and commodity production which was to transform forest and range policy in the next forty years.

REFERENCES CITED

Achterman, Gail L. "Judicial Control of Administrative Discretion in the Development of BLM Land Classification Policy." Unpublished Masters thesis. Ann Arbor: The University of Michigan, 1975.

Argow, Keith A. "Our National Grasslands: Dustland to Grassland." 68 *American Forests* 10 (1962).

Box, Thadis W. "The Arid Lands Revisited: 100 Years After John Wesley Powell." Address, 57th Annual Faculty Honor Lecture, Logan, Utah: Utah State University, 1978.

Butler, Ovid. *Youth Rebuilds—Stories from the C.C.C.* Washington, D.C.: American Forestry Association, 1934.

———. "The Oregon Checkmate." 42 *American Forests* 4.156 (1936).

Calef, Wesley. *Private Grazing and Public Lands: Local Management of the Taylor Grazing Act.* Chicago: University of Chicago Press, 1960.

Cate, Donald. *Recreation in the U.S. Forest Service.* Ph.D. dissertation, University of Michigan, 1963.

Clepper, Henry. *Professional Forestry in America.* Baltimore, Md.: Johns Hopkins Press, 1971.

"Conference of Lumber and Timber Products Industries with Public Agencies on Forest Conservation." 40 *Journal of Forestry* 275 (1934).

Gates, Paul W. *History of Public Land Law Development.* Written for the Public Land Law Review Commission. Washington, D.C.: Government Printing Office, 1968.

Gilligan, James. *The Development of Policy and Administration of Forest Service Primitive and Wilderness Areas in the United States.* Ph.D. dissertation, University of Michigan, 1954.

Greeley, William B. *Forest Policy.* New York: McGraw-Hill Book Company, 1953.

—— *Forests and Men.* New York: Doubleday & Company, Inc., 1951.

Ickes, Harold L. *The Secret Diaries of Harold Ickes,* 3 vols. New York: Simon and Schuster, 1953, 1955.

Lee, Ronald F. *Family Tree of the National Park Service.* Philadelphia: Eastern National Park and Monument Association, 1972.

Loehr, Rodney C. *Forests for the Future: The Story of Sustained Yield as Told in the Diaries of David T. Mason, 1907–1950.* St. Paul: Minnesota Historical Society, 1952.

Marshall, Robert. *The People's Forests.* New York: Harrison Smith and Robert Haas, 1933.

Morgan, Robert J. *Government Soil Conservation: Thirty Years of the New Decentralization.* Baltimore, Md.: Johns Hopkins Press, 1965.

Peffer, E. Louise. *The Closing of the Public Domain.* Stanford, Cal.: Stanford University Press, 1951.

Petulla, Joseph M. *American Environmental History,* preliminary ed. San Francisco: Boyd and Fraser Publishing Co., 1976.

Robbins, Roy M. *Our Landed Heritage.* New York: Peter Smith, 1950.

Sax, Joseph, "Towards a Philosophy for Land Management." In S. K. Fairfax, ed. *Legal Aspects of Wildlands Management.* Ann Arbor, Mich.: Natural Resources Law Monograph No. 1, 1977, pp. 106–111.

Scott, Valerie Weeks. "The Range Cattle Industry: Its Effect on Western Land Law." 28 *Montana Law Review* 155 (1967).

Shankland, Robert. *Steve Mather of the National Parks,* 3d ed. New York: Alfred A. Knopf, Inc., 1970.

Smith, Frank E. *The Politics of Conservation.* New York: Harper & Row, Publishers, 1966.

Trefethen, James B. *An American Crusade for Wildlife.* New York: Winchester Press and Boone and Crockett Club, 1975.

U.S. National Park Service. *Report of the Land Planning Committee of the National Resources Board, Park XI: Recreational Use of Land in the United States.* Washington, D.C.: Government Printing Office, 1938.

Chapter 7

The Postwar Years: Transition to New Values, 1945–1960

It is common to characterize the postwar years, particularly during the presidency of Dwight Eisenhower, as dull or uninteresting. It was probably necessary that we as a nation take a breather after two turbulent decades of crises and crusades. Going from the Crash in 1929, through the Depression, the CCC and Roosevelt's recovery programs, Pearl Harbor, Hiroshima, and into the cold war in twenty years left people winded. We were not ready at mid-century, as we had been at the turn of it, to become embroiled in bold new initiatives in conservation or anything else. The changes that took place in those years were gradual. Yet there were fundamental, and the impact of the reorientation in forest and range policy which began to emerge then has been profound.

The basic changes that concern us began in society rather than in government programs. To summarize rapidly the familiar aspects of this transformation, we can think of the war babies. They were born in the mid-1940s and entered kindergarten in the early 1950s. They needed homes, schools, food, clothing, recreation, health care and eventually jobs. The 1950s were years of unprecedented population growth, economic expansion, urban and suburban sprawl. It is true that the social and environmental problems exacerbated by this period of rapid development were largely unheeded. However, the seeds of change and emerging new attitudes were clearly in evidence in the 1950s discussions of resource management issues.

The issues debated after the war were not radically different in substance from those of previous decades. The basic conflicts in the resource area were concentrated, as before, on questions of allocating publicly owned lands to specific uses—timber production, grazing, recreation, wildlife. Characteristic issues of the 1950s include three specific concerns: public domain management, minerals development, and, most important, recreation. Two crucial developments occurred in the years surrounding and including the decade of the 1950s. First, there was a clear evolution away from the assumptions, actors, and goals of pre–World War II days. Second, the new actors and values emerged at a time when demand for all wild lands resources was increasing and it became obvious that for the first time all users could not be accomodated on the existing land base without conflict.

It is probably not too much of a simplification to note that for the first half of the century the conservation movement had been, with a few notable exceptions, government defined and government led. Interest groups involved in conservation arrayed themselves around the accepted leadership of government agencies and supported their programs. In the 1950s, new groups not easily accommodated in the established pattern began to form. We see the inception of the third great wave of conservation in which initiative ultimately slipped from the government and new directions were defined by the demands of new interest groups.

By far the most obvious of the new concerns in resource management was the emphasis given to recreation in the 1950s. If anything approached a crusade during that period, it was that mounted by the millions of increasingly affluent and mobile Americans who spread out in all directions seeking activities, destinations, and diversions to occupy their leisure time. Forest lands particularly had been used for recreation before; but in the 1950s, recreation emerged as a major land use rather than a residual category to be restricted to areas unneeded or unsuitable for commodity production. Recreation users entered the traditional debate about land allocation with new values and priorities backed by new and well-organized political support.

Industrial forestry contributed another new component to the discussions. It may surprise some to learn that the forest products industry did not emerge as a major political force until these same years. Before the Second World War, the industry was primarily a logging operation. Thereafter, industrial foresters comprise a new and different force and their goals regarding management of the national forests were major factors in forest policy. Recreation, however, stands out as the major theme of the 1950s because it was critical then and because the contemporary elaboration of those recreation ideas and groups dominate the popular definition of public land management issues today.

The public domain lands were a second focus of intense debate during the post war years. Management of these lands was traditionally discussed solely in terms of grazing. This pattern did not change during the 1950s, but the new interest groups began to be felt and broader aspects of public land management were recognized. These questions were not resolved until the mid-1970s, but it was during the postwar period that they were initially raised.

The third major area of development during this period was in minerals management on federal lands. Basic relationships between surface and subsurface management of wild lands were defined in the 1955 Multiple Use Mining Act. This legislation reflects an early recognition by renewable resource managers that surface and subsurface values must be managed in harmony.

If the changes of emphasis and value which occurred in the 1950s were gradual and evolutionary in nature, it is not surprising that public and private resource management professionals responded slowly. In a number of major battles with the new conservationists, the resource establishment took a traditional orientation. The managers' response to new values was really one of containment, defining and limiting the assertion of new goals. This strategy is illustrated by the Multiple Use and Sustained Yield Act of 1960. The Forest Service initiated legislation which attempted to recognize and placate new groups while maintaining the traditional priorities of the agency. The bill is a fitting monument to the gradual changes in value and perspectives regarding resource management that found their political feet in the postwar years.

PUBLIC DOMAIN ISSUES

The first stirrings of controversy following the war centered on the administration of the public domain lands. These management issues are difficult to understand because the actors are hard to identify and assess. Alliances formed and shifted rapidly and the vitriol of the debate was vaguely reminiscent of the range wars. These difficulties were exacerbated by caricatures of the actors and their interests—the robber cattle baron, the hardworking homesteader—which continued to color public perception of the issues.

While the debate was hard to follow, the basic issues were rather clear. Owing to the unfortunate phrase "pending disposition" in the Taylor Grazing Act, the question of allowing the public domain to pass into state or private ownership was constantly debated. A second and related debate concerned rights, as opposed to privileges, involved in grazing use of the public domain. Does a person with a permit to graze cattle or sheep in an area gain property rights therein? How much authority does the government have to charge for and regulate grazing and other uses of the public domain? These issues were held in abeyance during the war; but almost before the cessation of hostilities, the controversy raged anew. The Grazing Service was summarily destroyed and replaced by the Bureau of Land Management. That agency inherited all the problems of the Grazing Service and was further undercut by confusion surrounding the scope and nature of its mission.

"Grazing Fee Controversy"—An Oft-Told Tragedy

The final blow to the Grazing Service was the same kind of grazing fee cross fire that had confounded the Forest Service range program following the 1924 Rachford report (see p. 136–137 above). In a nearly identical fashion, the Grazing Service was caught between two segments of Congress (Foss, chap. 8).

The problems began in 1944 when Clarence Forsling, newly appointed director of the Grazing Service, suggested that grazing fees be tripled, from 5 to 15 cents per animal unit month (A.U.M.). This suggestion was based on a study conducted by the Grazing Service in 1941 and not implemented because of the war. The proposed 15 cent fee must have looked reasonable to Forsling, who had transferred to his new position from the Forest Service, which was then charging an average of 31 cents per A.U.M. The response from Congress, particularly Senator Pat McCarran of Nevada, head of the Senate Public Lands Committee and chief advocate of the stock operators' position, was immediate and harsh: "attack, postpone, investigate" (Peffer, 264).

McCarran Subcommittee Report

McCarran extracted a commitment from the Department of the Interior that no fee increase would be imposed until his subcommittee made a report on its investigation, then in progress, of the agency. This subterfuge enabled him to delay the imposition of an increase for almost three years—the investigation was begun in 1941 and the report was delayed until 1947. During these years, field hearings were held frequently throughout the Western states. The investigation was more like a stage-managed inquisition. It stirred up and gave voice to the most disgruntled and reactionary of the Western cattle raisers. McCarran's handling of the investigation constituted a lightning rod by which discontent among the grazers was conveyed as a threat to the Grazing Service.

> McCarran's 1947 report caps the lengthiest, most concerted, and in some respects, the most successful attempt made in the twentieth century by one person to force a reinterpretation of land policy more in accordance with the wishes of the using interests. Senator McCarran was not without support once his grievances were known. Around him rallied the scattered remnants of the states' rights factions of the West. Senator McCarran was at the same time both the general formulating tactics and the most belligerent fighter in the seven year war of attrition which he waged, and was responsible for the most violent attacks upon the Department of the Interior and its grazing policies (Peffer, 248).

By the time McCarran filed his final report in 1947, the Grazing Service had, in fact, been disbanded. Its budget had been virtually eliminated by the refusal of two powerful congressional committees to take a consistent approach to range management and grazing fees in particular. The House Appropriations Committee wanted the Grazing Service to charge a higher fee for publicly owned forage, and the Senate Public Lands Committee favored lower charges for use of the public range. While congressional committees could not agree on the proper approach to be taken by the Grazing Service in managing the grazing districts, or setting fees, they were equally insistent on the rectitude of their respective positions. The Appropriations Committee cut the Grazing Service's budget because of the low fees. The Public Lands Committee, led by McCarran, allowed the cuts to go unchallenged because of the threat of higher fees. The result of an 85 percent reduction in the services' budget was that it virtually ceased to exist. In 1946, the remnants of the Grazing Service were joined with the General Land Office by an executive reorganization. Thus without any money or any mission, the Bureau of Land Management was born in the wreckage of the Grazing Service.

The problem of grazing fees is a continuing, persistent one. The Grazing Service was, however, much more vulnerable to the political pressures than the Forest Service had been twenty years earlier. There are two components to this greater vulnerability. Grazing was the sole aspect of the Grazing Service's activities. It was the creation and servant of the stock operators; and if it lost their support, it had no nonrange programs with which to attract and develop alternative support groups. The Forest Service, in contrast, had diverse programs and public support. Despite the emphasis of the Forest Service on silviculture, Gifford Pinchot took the position that any use which was not prohibited was to be encouraged. Grazing Service programs lacked the diversity and widespread popularity necessary for balanced, reliable support.

Second, the Grazing Service was handicapped by promises made by then-Secretary of Interior Ickes during the debate over the Taylor Grazing Act. As was noted above, Ickes "underbid" Agriculture by $350 to $750 thousand and also promised that the grazing fees would be tied to the cost of range administration rather than to the market value of the use of the range. These promises guaranteed that the Grazing Service would be underfunded and weak. When the BLM was created by executive reorganization without any remedial legislation, it was, as shall be discussed below, similarly hamstrung. However, the Forest Service's relative strength in both the budgetary and constituency areas did not guarantee it immunity from the stock operators.

FOREST SERVICE GRAZING PROGRAMS AND THE "GREAT LAND GRAB"

The Forest Service ran afoul of the stock industry, as they had in 1924 and as did the Grazing Service, over the issue of grazing fees. The controversy peaked in an effort by extremists in the stock industry to take title to the public domain in what is frequently referred to by its opponents as the "great land grab." In 1945, Forest Service permits were due for a decennial review. The agency was planning to reduce the number of livestock on the range, shorten the grazing season, and exclude stock altogether in some areas (USFS, 20–23). This proposal rekindled the hostility of the stock operators toward the Forest Service. In October 1946, a specially formed Joint Livestock Committee on Public Lands developed a legislative program from ideas that had been circulating among the stock operators for about a year. The proposals were subsequently adopted at the Convention of the American Livestock Association in 1947. The program called for legislation that would allow permittees to purchase the property allotted to them under the Taylor Grazing Act. Moreover, the operators wanted Forest Service administered grazing lands transferred to the Department of the Interior for disposition under the same scheme. It is possible that if the Forest Service lands had been omitted from the proposed land sale, the scheme would never have been noticed outside the West. The threat to Forest Service lands was, however, a national conservation issue, "the stick which broke the hornet's nest" (Peffer, 281). Within months, opposition to the idea was so great that it was withdrawn and the few senators and representatives who had backed it were denying that it had ever existed (Voight, 115–116). In fact, the proposal was such an obvious raid that it probably never had a chance of success. Still, the land grab fracas of 1946–1947 left some important residue.

Most obvious was its contribution to mythology; it gave occasion for some of the most vitriolic conservation literature of the century. Bernard DeVoto, a noted western historian, used his famous *Harper's* magazine feature column, "The Easy Chair," to spread the news of the land grab. Some of the bitterest attacks on stock operators ever printed were published in "The Easy Chair" between 1947 and 1954. DeVoto's attack was followed by articles in *Collier's, The Nation, Atlantic Monthly, Reader's Digest,* and hundreds of daily newspapers. The imagery of the thieving cattle baron was again abroad in the land. Understandably, it angered the vast majority of stock raisers, who had absolutely nothing to do with McCarran or the alleged land grab. Only the most prosperous permittees supported the sale idea, for only they could afford to buy their allotments (Gates, 624–625).

Repeated unfair personal attacks on stock operators generally were not in the interests of the conservationists, the Forest Service, or the public lands. If the land grab stirred up the conservationists, and it surely did, their overreaction stirred up the operators. Attacking stock operators irrationally or unfairly was not conductive to resolution of public domain problems. Ranchers' attention to the issues is not intermittent, as is the general public's. It does not require recharging by publicists like DeVoto. They are on the land, dependent on it, and their attention does not wander. Even the most attentive citizens required the spector of a major debacle, a "land grab," before they paid even slight attention to the public domain. When the scheme waned, the conservationists had a sense of victory; but they had set the stage for another traveling investigation of range policy, this time aimed at the Forest Service.

Barrett Committee Investigation

In May 1947, Rep. Frank Barrett of Wyoming successfully introduced a resolution authorizing an investigation of Forest Service range programs. All accounts indicate that the extreme fringe of the stock operators and their congressional representatives, envisioned a replay of McCarran's cacaphony of criticism which had killed the Grazing Service. Although few who testified at the hearings embraced the Forest Service without reservation, it became quite evident that the large grazing interests which opposed regulation and favored disposition of the public lands to states or individuals were not alone on the range. Many operators saw the benefits of the federal presence and advocated extension and diversification of federal programs. The Idaho State Legislature went so far as to pass a formal resolution opposing disposition of the public domain (Peffer, 289).

Instead of providing the desired occasion for legislation clamping down on Forest Service range programs, the Barrett hearings particularly reveal the growing support for reclamation and recreation in the Western states (Peffer, 288). These new voices would be heard increasingly in subsequent years. Unfortunately, however, in spite of the emergence of these important new interests, the discussion of the public domain continued to be trapped in rhetoric of the sins of the cattle barons and the excesses of their congressional representatives for the next several decades.

Granger-Thye Act of 1950

The Barrett Commission report did not, as had been hoped by the stock operators, initiate a round of congressional activity in support of their goals. Many important prostock industry proposals were defeated. Although the Granger-Thye Act of 1950 is considered to be the legislative response to the Barrett report, its major provisions simply codify preexisting Forest Service policy. The act was, however, somewhat controversial because it gave legal status to the grazing advisory boards on each forest. Well aware of the abuses perpetrated by the grazing advisory boards established for the grazing districts under the Taylor Grazing Act, many were opposed to extending such legitimacy to the national forest boards. McCarran had introduced a similar provision in 1944–1946, but it had not passed. In 1950, the boards were authorized and stock operators achieved the recognition they had long sought. They have not, however, been as strong as the Taylor Grazing Act advisory boards have been. This is probably because the Forest Service is, as noted above, less vulnerable and more diverse than was the Grazing Service. The act also authorized the Secretary of Agriculture to issue grazing permits on the national forests for ten-year terms. This had been done for years and the act simply gives specific recognition to a long-recognized practice.

Although the act did not change either the basic purposes for which the national forests were established or the general scheme for management of the forest ranges, there is no doubt that the bill strengthened the position of the grazing permittees. This cannot, however, be seen as a great legislative victory, as numerous proposals which were of far greater importance to the stock operators did not pass. Most of the defeated provisions would have enhanced the ever-troubling assumption made by BLM permittees that theirs is a *right* rather than a privilege to graze the public domain. The Forest Service was also successful in forestalling such proposals as (1) making the renewal of a permit mandatory if the permittee had a bank loan for which livestock was pledged as security and (2) granting the permittee title to any range improvements made on allotments.

The most odious proposals were eliminated during the development of the Granger-Thye Act. The stock operators won codification of their position on the national forest ranges and the conservationists could claim some success. The obvious disasters were prevented and firm funding for Forest Service range management programs was established. The issue did not, however, rest there. Operators continued their legislative initiatives well into the Eisenhower years. If success is measured only in terms of legislative enactments, they failed. In spite of the fact that the Eisenhower administration was clearly supportive of many of their aims, their major bills did not pass. In the administrative area, however, they were more successful. The events of 1945–1950 had amply demonstrated that the congressional supporters of the reactionary cattle operators were quite prepared to destroy an agency that did not meet their peculiar set of goals—through budget cuts, legislative enactment, and simple harassment. Obviously, the ability of a McCarran or a Barrett to hold "hearings" year after year and to tie up the time of BLM and Forest Service officials testifying, gathering data, and defending themselves is a tremendous weapon that members of Congress used to bring recalcitrant officials into line.

THE NEW BUREAU OF LAND MANAGEMENT

This ambience, and the recent memory of the fate of the Grazing Service, did not constitute an auspicious start for the Bureau of Land Management. In addition to the generally negative atmosphere, the BLM suffered from a number of specific handicaps which left it in a distinctly unenviable position.

First, it did not commence activities on the basis of an authorizing statute enacted by Congress. Rather, it was the offspring of Executive Reorganization No. 3 of June 6, 1946, in which the Grazing Service was merged with the

Gereral Land Office (GLO). Thus, the bureau had no coherent mission, no authority, and no statutorily defined existence. It was rather like the lands it managed, a residual category, assigned to administer the loose ends of over 3500 statutes randomly enacted over the previous 150 years.

Second, BLM had almost no personnel. Following the Grazing Service budget debacle, only eighty-six people remained to supervise grazing on 142 million acres. The financial crisis for the new agency was so acute that the grazing boards, recognizing the benefits to be gained by maintaining the weak regulation of their activities, actually contributed monies from their portion of the grazing fees to pay BLM salaries. This did not auger well for effective regulation of stock operators' activities, nor did it provide a strong basis for recruiting top young land management professionals for a BLM career.

Finally, the nature of the reorganization, the combination of the Grazing Service with the GLO, was unfortunate and apparently ill considered. The personnel, proclivities, and responsibilities of the GLO were not appropriately responsive to the grazing problems. Nor was the grazing orientation which dominated the BLM appropriate for much of the new agency's mission. When the GLO was combined casually with remnants of the Grazing Service, the entire mineral leasing program and all of the public domain lands in Alaska went with them. To understand the confusion created by this hasty expedient, a brief look at GLO background and the responsibilities is necessary.

The General Land Office figures prominently if not proudly in several major events in forest and range history. The GLO originally had jurisdiction over the forest reserves. Gifford Pinchot worked for the GLO early in his career and led a successful fight to have the reserves transferred from the GLO to the Department of Agriculture. His unflattering assessment of the GLO fueled the transfer movement. His criticisms were familiar and at least partially accurate. The Department of the Interior owes much of its turn-of-the-century reputation for graft and corruption to early patterns established in the General Land Office. Pinchot fueled the fire with his charges against Richard A. Ballinger, a former head of GLO, ultimately Secretary of Interior. The controversy is famous and need not be recounted except to note that GLO suffered enormously during the scandal and was not at the time of Executive Reorganization No. 3 in 1946 a vigorous, assertive agency.

Nevertheless the GLO had important responsibilities which BLM inherited. Established in 1812 to conduct land surveys and to process and record sales, entries, withdrawals, and reservations and leases on the public domain, the General Land Office had primary jurisdiction over the entire public domain. GLO was mainly a record-keeping organization responsible for land disposals under a variety of statutes. Though it sporadically attempted to prevent trespass pending disposition, it was not a land managing agency. After the passage of the Mineral Leasing Act in 1920, the GLO role increased in importance. Issuing prospecting permits and auctioning mineral leases is discretionary, and GLO exercised the discretion on behalf of the Secretary of the Interior.

The BLM inherited all the GLO's responsibilities for real estate functions on the entire public domain and for all mineral leasing. BLM responsibility in this area was further expanded when it was given responsibility for administering mineral leasing on the Outer Continental Shelf. This happened in 1953, when Congress passed first the Submerged Lands Act and then the Outer Continental Shelf Act. The first bill resolved a long-standing dispute between states and the federal government regarding jurisdiction over land under water along the coast. States were granted title up to 3 miles out. The seabed beyond the 3 miles and extending to the border of the nation's claim was added to the unreserved public domain. Later that year Congress passed the Outer Continental Shelf Lands Act, which established an oil and gas leasing system roughly similar to the one set up in 1920 under the Mineral Leasing Act. Overextended, underfunded, dominated by grazing interests, BLM's responsibilities were extended to the limits of the nation's territorial waters. At the time of the reorganization, very little thought was given to the minerals aspect of the transfer. This is probably because the grazing issue was so hot and there had been, moreover, relatively little previous interest in federal coal and oil. The GLO also had responsibility for nearly all of Alaska, since it was still federally owned, and for the revested O & C railroad lands in western Oregon. Commercially valuable timber in the area led Congress to support intensive management of the O & C lands, but the problems of Alaska were not to be addressed until the 1960s and 1970s.

The effect of the reorganization was to grant authority over most of the federal lands and all of the federal mineral estate to an uneasy collection of Grazing Service range managers and political hacks and the GLO's Washington-based clerks, bookkeepers, and paper shufflers. It was not designed to usher in an era of effective land stewardship. The reorganization was preeminently the handiwork of congressional supporters of the large livestock operators. Their goal was quite clearly to maintain the weak and easily manipulated range regulations programs which characterized the late Grazing Service. The BLM fared little better in the appropriations process than had its predecessor. The stock operators were well pleased that the BLM imposed the minimum regulation necessary for the conduct of orderly business without imposing costs or restraints on an industry which was enjoying virtually unopposed control over the public domain lands.

BURGEONING INTEREST IN THE FEDERAL MINERAL ESTATE

The stock operators', success in maintaining a weak BLM abetted the interests of a newly burgeoning group of public domain users—those interested in mineral development on federal lands. The 1950s was a period of intense interest in federally owned minerals. Much important legislation was passed during the early 1950s and several bills had significant impact on forest and range management.

In 1955 Congress made a minor but significant alteration in the Mining Law of 1872. The change had relatively little impact on legitimate mining operations, but considerably simplified the tasks of both BLM and the Forest Service. The major purpose of the legislation was to clarify the Mineral Leasing Act of 1920. Congress wrote the leasing provisions such that hardrock mining was prohibited on an area leased for oil or gas. Because of this oversight, a gold vein could not be mined if it happend to occur next to an oil well. Congress rectified the error in 1955 by passing the Multiple Use Mining Act. More significantly for present purposes, this act also has a "common varieties" provision which was of tremendous importance to both BLM and the Forest Service. This provides that the Secretary of Agriculture or Interior "may dispose of mineral materials (including sand, stone, gravel, pumice, pumicite, cinders and clay) and vegetative materials (including yucca, manzanita, mesquite, cactus, and timber or other forest products) on the public lands of the United States. . . . " By this provision, Congress established a third category of minerals in addition to the locatable hardrock minerals governed by the 1872 Mining Act and the leasable sedementary deposits managed under the 1920 Mineral Leasing Act. It authorized a sale program to dispose of common or construction minerals. The advantage to the land manager is clear. Sand, gravel, and pumice mines were frequently "located" under provisions of the 1872 act by fraudulent operators in close proximity to extremely valuable stands of timber or scenic recreation sites. Under the location system, Forest Service or BLM officials were powerless to prevent the patenting of such claims. The 1955 legislation removed the common varieties of minerals from the operation of the 1872 act by authorizing the managing agency to sell common varieties at their discretion. This provision in the 1955 law was of double significance to BLM. Not only did it prevent the loss of valuable public land to specious miners, but it also gained authority to sell timber from the public lands which it had not had until 1955. Finally, the act clarified the jurisdiction of the federal government to manage the nonmineral resources on unpatented mining claims. Congress clearly established the responsibility of federal land managers to protect the surface resources of claimed areas until title actually passed to the locator.

Although the 1955 legislation eliminated some of the most obvious problems in minerals management on the public lands, many equally difficult problems remained. BLM, created and dominated by grazing interests, was made responsible for management of *all* federal mineral resources, including those on Forest Service lands. This presents obvious problems for a long-term, multiple-use management of the national forests. Moreover, BLM has been quite restricted in its ability to limit or control mineral leasing. Their authority in that area came to them, as has been noted, without much thought on the part of Congress. For almost twenty years after the reorganization which created BLM, that agency was ignored by the public and dominated by the commodity interests.

RECREATION BOOM OF THE 1950s

Recreation stands out among post–World War II developments in forest and range policy as one which is characterized by spontaneous public activity. Obviously the concern was not entirely new. There had been a long-standing group articulately interested in developing recreation opportunities as typified by Mather and Olmstead. But the movement was aimed at preserving areas of outstanding scenic grandeur as pleasuring grounds for the wealthy adventurers who could afford to travel to such extravagant facilities as Yellowstone's Old Faithful Inn. Recreation in the 1950s was significantly different. By the end of the Second World War, expanding population combined with rising disposable income, longer paid vacations, retirement programs, and increased mobility ushered in an era of *mass* recreation.

This new emphasis had at least two significant components. The first and most important was sheer numbers of people involved. Demand for recreation facilities in every category expanded dramatically at the end of the Second World War and continued to grow at an increasing rate for nearly two decades. Mass recreation implied, first and foremost, a literally overwhelming number of bodies. Second, the new users demanded motorized access and developed facilities in the recreation areas. Mass recreationists do not extoll the virtues of spartan wilderness travel. They want ski resorts, tramways, scenic highways, and developed water-based recreation. In the 1950s, we developed a national system of freeways, throughways, and highways. Gas rationing ended, cars were readily available, and they began to flood into parks and recreation areas.

Recreation management had been up until that time a relatively casual undertaking. The emphasis of the National Park Service and its supporters was on extending a protective administrative status category to particular pieces of especially cherished land. Insofar as it was necessary to be concerned with visitors, much of the pre–World War II effort focused on luring enough users to a site to justify the designation and the expenditure for administration. The Forest Service was less inclined to consider recreation users as part of their management task. Until the war, there was plenty of Forest Service land for every use. There were occasional skirmishes over a piece of ground particularly coveted by competing user groups; but there was land enough for all, and the recreationists were generally satisfied with their allocation.

In the 1950s, demand increased dramatically for all categories of forested land use. Cities and towns sprawled into the countryside. Timber was needed to build the cities and towns. The pressure for recreation lands became intense. Recreationists were no longer satisfied with being a residual use. Moreover, they themselves began to require management in an explicit and unprecedented fashion. As they came in droves, they trampled the vegetation; jammed the transportation, parking, and sanitary facilities; and began to get in each others' way. Providing for the hunter and the hiker; the swimmer, the fisherman, the canoeist, and the motorboater; the motorist, the skier, and the wilderness buff became management concerns of pressing importance.

The major response to this burgeoning new aspect of wild land management was administrative rather than legislative. Generally this was not a period of great congressional leadership regarding outdoor recreation. Public pressure was beginning to organize effectively, but the major responses to that pressure came from the executive agencies. The activities of the Park Service, the Forest Service, the BLM, and the Corps of Engineers were obviously motivated by rational calculation regarding their future well-being. All the agencies saw recreation as a new source of support and funds which they could tap. The agencies moved to fill the gap. That they did so largely on their own traditionally defined terms is not surprising; this is a period of transition rather than revolution, but the change quite clearly had begun.

The Postwar Plight of the National Park Service

Although Park Service programs include many variations on its basic mission, the agency is appropriately viewed as a single-use agency. As such, it is subject to the vicissitudes of public and congressional attitudes toward that one use, recreation. During the war, recreation and scenic beauty were not particularly marketable items. In a guns or butter budget, the Park Service was fat to be trimmed. Most of the schemes for utilizing the resources in the parks during both World Wars were motivated by commodity interests who wanted to use the war to establish precedent for opening up the national parks for commodity production. Thinly disguised raids did not generally succeed. However, the Park Service budget suffered mightily during and immediately after the war.

Because the number of national park visitors and the number of employees dropped off dramatically during the war, it is not suprising that the budget also plummeted. After the war ended, however, the number of visitors skyrocketed. Recreationists arrived at the national parks to find facilities built during the 1930s by the CCC to accommodate the 1930s and 1940s levels of use and not maintained during the war. The national parks were a shambles. Attention was first focused on the tenementlike conditions in national park campgrounds: crowding, long lines for dilapidated outhouses, inadequate supervision and interpretation of the sites, and, very shortly, evidence of damage being done to the national treasures ostensibly being preserved in the parks. The condition of the parks appropriately came to be viewed as a national scandal.

Even under these circumstances, the agency experienced considerable difficulty in getting its appropriations restored even to prewar levels. In the cold war, fiscally conservative Eisenhower years, it was difficult to argue for appropriations or, indeed, to find available dollars for the Park Service. Allocations did not therefore rise dramatically, and public indignation was exacerbated by apparent government inattention to the deterioration of our national treasures.

Conrad Wirth became National Park Service (NPS) director in 1951 and his incumbency was extremely controversial. Some think Director Wirth saved the Park Service by establishing a program which attracted increasing congressinal support and funding. Others consider the Wirth years to be a scourge of inappropriate construction, tourist development, and agency aggrandizement, a Disneyland era in the national parks. Wirth's administration was characterized by very successful planning and implementation of a massive program of park rejuvenation known as "Mission '66." His success demonstrates that although park lovers and careerists correctly insist that the NPS be staffed by trained professionals as opposed to politicians, there is considerable utility in having ranking agency officials familiar with the Washingtin, D.C., political climate. Among NPS directors, Wirth was uniquely able to deal with the various pressures and demands of close contact with Congress, the President, and the national interest groups. Only Mather excelled Wirth in his devotion to tourism and his ability to achieve his goals.

Wirth began by directing an intense and frequently secretive servicewide effort to inventory agency needs, formulate a program to meet those needs, and develop cost data for the program. Mission '66 was unveiled in 1956. Legend has it that in a highly unusual special audience with the President, Wirth won Eisenhower's support for the program with a slide show including a photo of a long line of unhappy campers awaiting their turn at a solitary outhouse (Everhart, 34–37).

Mission '66 was a ten-year rehabilitation and development program for the national parks. The effort was packaged so as to culminate in 1966, the fiftieth anniversary of the Service. Such hokum is a characteristic aspect of the public relations effort that often accompanies an administrative initiative such as the Park Service was mounting. The end result, however, was positive: The Park Service needed more money and got it. In the appropriations process, Congress responded to public dismay over park conditions and its demand for outdoor recreation oportunities. The Park Service had successfully capitalized on the opportunity of the moment. NPS appropriations rose dramatically during the Mission '66 decade. The expenditures in many instances continued to be controversial because of the heavy emphasis on tourist development in the parks; nonetheless, Mission '66 does constitute an aggressive and successful agency response to clear public demand.

Forest Service Recreation in the Postwar Period

The recreation user pressure experienced in the national parks occurred with equal severity in the national forests. The national forests have always constituted a much larger component of federal recreation opportunities than have the parks in terms of user days. This intense recreational use occurs in spite of considerable agency bias against it. Although many people within the agency have long struggled to secure recognition of and appropriations for recreation use of the forests, the program was a residual one. Foresters were not opposed to forest recreation; however, the forester was less likely than other people to see recreation as incompatible with timber production and more likely to view recreation as a less important use of forest lands. Recreation was always encouraged by the Forest Service if it harmonized with overall management plans. In that spirit, the agency repeatedly sought money and specific authorization for its recreation programs. These efforts were thwarted by three major forces. The National Park Service, engaged as it was in trying to acquire extensive Forest Service acreage for recreation management, fought very hard to deny money and recognition to Forest Service recreation programs. Many preservation groups that accused the Forest Service of being too timber oriented in the 1960s and 1970s supported the Park Service in this effort. Second, the diversity of the agency mission, frequently referred to above as a source of strength and security, in the present context is seen as a bit of a disadvantage. Traditional user groups are not going to welcome another "mouth to feed" at the Forest Service table. Grazing interests were as threatened by the recreationists as they had been by the homesteaders. Any Forest Service move to welcome the recreationists to what the permittees considered to be their own land was not encouraged. The timber industry responded to the recreation issue in a more sophisticated way. Many of the industrial landowners were making a public spirited public relations effort to open their own lands to recreationists. However, the industry did not support the diversion of funds, land, or effort from timber management. As shall be discussed below, the timber industry was engaged in a vigorous program to gain greater recognition of its own needs.

Third, support from the preservation and recreation groups was not forthcoming to the extent which one might expect. Although traditional conservation groups continued to support the same "wise use" conservation concept championed by the Forest Service, other newer groups found the agency's approach to conservation antithetical to their own goals. Conservation to them meant not wise use but, in many instances, no use. In the 1950s the long fight for legislative recognition of the wilderness concept was beginning. The preservationists were therefore pitted against the Forest Service at two very significant points. First, continuing Park Service drives of the 1920s and 1930s, they initiated and spearheaded numerous efforts, frequently successful, to have land management responsibilities for extensive acreage transferred from the Forest Service to the Park Service. Second, they were engaged in a serious attempt to secure passage of a wilderness bill. These efforts obliged them to assert that Forest Service management of recreation and wilderness areas was inadequate, so they were in no position to support the agency's recreation efforts.

Operation Outdoors

"Operation Outdoors" was the Forest Service response to recreationist, Park Service, and wilderness enthusiast pressures. Although the Forest Service issued essentially the same press releases and public relations brochures as did the Park Service, their budget requests were much smaller. This was both because the Forest Service allocates its basic infrastructure expenses (roads, housing for rangers, personnel training programs) across a wide variety of expenditure categories, rather than putting them all in one "mission" as the Park Service must, and because the Forest Service concept of recreation was more primitive, less construction intense, and therefore less capital investment oriented than was the Park Service approach.

Operation Outdoors did not attract the public attention Mission '66 enjoyed. Conventional wisdom, that Operation Outdoors was a pale imitation of its highly successful competitor, is in error. The Forest Service actually obtained a higher percentage of the budget request than did the Park Service. Moreover, through Operation Outdoors, the Forest Service recreation budget achieved what might be called "critical mass." The program became identified and recognized and it was no longer necessary to "bootleg" the costs of administering the recreation program from other budget items. Operation Outdoors took the recreation program out of the charity category in forest managers' budgets. This slight change in dollar allocations thus made a tremendous impact on the stature of the program within the agency.

Early BLM Recreation Efforts

The Forest Service recreation problems were minor compared to those faced by the Bureau of Land Management. BLM was in dire straits when the recreation rush started and was largely unable to get public support or gain recognition during the 1950s. Its difficulties stemmed from the sloppy reorganization which created it. As noted above, no legislation defined a mission for BLM or its authority to act. The major statute under which the bureau operated, the Taylor Grazing Act, authorizes the Secretary of Interior to establish grazing districts and administer grazing pending disposition of the land. This is hardly a firm basis for a comprehensive land planning and management scheme.

The problem of insufficient authority is amply demonstrated by BLM problems regarding recreation. The BLM had attempted, more or less unsuccessfully, to gather authority for achieving public purposes on the public domain lands from a variety of other statutes, but this required stretching. Authority for a BLM recreation program was based primarily on a section of the Taylor Grazing Act authorizing the Secretary to make land available for public purposes and to erect improvements on the land. In addition, the Antiquities Act of 1906 required the BLM to protect archeological sites; and the O & C Act of 1937 authorized recreation development on the O & C lands. The only comprehensive recreation authority granted to the BLM was in the 1926 Recreation and Public Purposes Act, which permitted them to sell or lease land to local governments for recreation development. (Clawson, 112–120).

Without explicit authority to act, the Bureau was unable to get recreation-oriented appropriations. They were having considerable difficulty obtaining appropriations for their most basic missions. The stock operators were hostile to any bureau expansion, and they viewed recreation as particularly undesirable. Moreover, because the lands were being held pending disposition, Congress was reluctant to invest in bureau programs, for recreation or otherwise.

Those conservation, preservation and recreation groups which generally did not support Forest Service recreation programs did not pay any attention at all to BLM's efforts. When some ranchers pushed for disposition of the grazing districts, conservationists asserted in anguish that the public domain belonged to all the people; but when the crisis passed, there was no residual of support for BLM's underfunded efforts to manage or protect the national treasure. Occasionally the conservation groups noted that BLM was not performing well, but they paid scant attention to BLM's effort to secure the necessary dollars and personnel. BLM tried to build public support with a meager recreation program in the late 1950s but made little headway.

The Echo Park Controversy

The pressure groups' failure to support Forest Service and BLM recreation programs can be explained by the fact that their attention was focused elsewhere. The famous Echo Park controversy culminating the 1956 was in fact the symbolic issue around which many of the new recreation and preservation groups rallied and organized. The controversy developed around a proposed Bureau of Reclamation dam which would have flooded an obscure national monument in Utah.

A broad range of regional economic and development interest were supported behind the project. Opposed, in addition to the newly vocal conservationists, were the National Park Service, the Army Corps of Engineers,

California water interests who stood to lose if water were held in the upper basin, and budget balancers who did not approve of subsidizing irrigation projects with high-cost electricity and no interest charges. It was a confusing but classic face-off, in many ways similar to the Hetch Hetchy fight half a century before. The critical difference is that whereas Hetch Hetchy was built, Echo Park was not. Faulty Bureau of Reclamation data supporting the economic benefits claimed for the project probably were the decisive factor in its defeat. Nevertheless, Echo Park symbolizes tipping of the scales (Stratton and Sirotkin, passim). Moreover, in the Echo Park battle a cadre of new interests groups, lobbyists, and organizers became hardened and experienced their first major victory.

THE OUTDOOR RECREATION RESOURCES REVIEW COMMISSION

The success of the new conservationists groups in making a national issue out of Echo Park was a clear indication of the political punch which they could muster. In 1958, Congress responded again and even more directly by establishing the Outdoor Recreation Resources Review Commission (ORRRC) to study problems and opportunities in future recreation management. The commission was almost unanimously supported in Congress among all parties, factions, and interests groups.

The ORRRC was to inventory recreation resources and the demand for recreation in light of population, mobility, and income trends and to offer a program for meeting recreation needs in 1976 and 2000. Few "blue ribbon" panels appointed to study a problem have been more notable. Lawrence Rockefeller chaired a panel which included such luminaries as Samuel T. Dana of the University of Michigan, Bernard Orell of Weyerhaeuser, Joseph Penfold of the Izaak Walton League, Senators Anderson of New Mexico and Neuberger of Oregon, and Representative Saylor of Pennsylvania.

Only the National Park Service was tepid in its support of the undertaking. They believed that they had authority to study national recreation needs under the Park, Parkway and Recreation Act of 1936. Correctly, the NPS interpreted the commission as a threat to their position as *the* federal recreation agency and their power to control future recreation development by making the initial studies and recommendations. Aside from Park Service grumblings, the only other criticism of the ORRRC was that it might become, like so many congressional studies, a device for defusing the demand for action. True, the study placed an informal moratorium on further recreation legislation. Interest groups pushing pet projects were frequently frustrated when their bills were shelved pending a review of the ORRRC's report. Many projects were sidelined for those years, the most important of which was the wilderness bill. Unfortunately, the ORRRC Report was delayed several times and its recommendations were not aired until the early 1960s. Congressional interest in the deference to the activities of the commission is significant evidence of growing political awareness of the new ideas and groups developing in the forest and range policy arena.

The Wilderness Movement in the 1950s

An interesting anomaly surrounding the emergence of mass recreationists in the 1950s is the support that this hoard of motorized pleasure seekers gave to the wilderness preservation movement. Although the two groups have much in common—they both, for example, tend to oppose stripmining or clearcutting of pristine areas—their definitions of recreation and recreation goals are frequently incompatible. The wilderness advocate has little sympathy for the increased development and motorized access to wild places which the motor recreationists demand. This split was, however, less apparent in the 1950s than it was twenty years later; and the undifferentiated howl of public dismay over the condition of the federal recreation lands redounded to the clear benefit of the well-organized wilderness advocates. They needed and welcomed numerical support, for they were engaged in a profound struggle with the Forest Service over reclassifications of primitive areas.

As noted in Chapter 6, reclassification required that lands classified as primitive under the 1920 L-20 regulation be studied again before being classified under the 1938 U-regulations. The more elaborate procedures for defining areas to be designated—including public hearings and Washington office review—opened the process but slowed it down considerably. Moreover, the process became more controversial as many commodity users objected to the tighter use restrictions of the U-regulations. Their protests made reclassification all but impossible in many areas; and in 1940, the forest supervisors were instructed to manage the areas as if they were already under the new regulations until they could be studied for reclassification. This instruction was reiterated in 1947 and expanded with the stipulation that when *any* modification of an existing primitive area was contemplated, a public hearing was advisable (Gilligan, 205).

The Forest Service reclassification program was the focus of intensified postwar controversy. Areas that had seemed "safe" for wilderness status in the 1920s and 1930s became commercially valuable through rising prices, expansion of road systems, and technological advances in mineral extraction and harvest and utilization of forest commodities. The Forest Service was under tremendous pressure from industry not to "lock the resources up." The commodity-oriented groups were joined by such developed recreation enthusiasts as downhill skiers and ski resort developers. All of the resource use conflicts exacerbated by the postwar prosperity were apparent in the wilderness reclassification debates. The Forest Service removed many acres from wilderness areas because they were privately owned, roaded, included in new highway development, or contained mining development. More were removed because they contained merchantable timber. Although almost every acre "lost" was replaced with substitute acres, the wilderness movement was achieving full voice politically and refused to be mollified (Gilligan, 204–226).

Probably the most contentious of the reclassification disputes centered on the Three Sisters Primitive Area in western Oregon. The Forest Service announced in 1954 that it would eliminate 53,000 acres of merchantable timber from the area and classify the remaining 200,000 acres as wilderness. In addition, they proposed to classify two smaller nearby areas as wild areas. The excluded area contained approximately 1.5 billion board feet of timber. The Forest Service decision represented a compromise of sorts: Industry had insisted on excluding 70,000 acres containing approximately 2.3 billion board feet. A number of recreation groups would have been satisfied by a compromise in the other direction, a reduction of only 40,000 acres; but preservationists wanted the whole area protected. The charge that the Forest Service was carving all of the timber out of the wilderness areas was overstated, as the Three Sisters case illustrated. Approximately 2.5 billion board feet remained in the Three Sisters under the Forest Service proposal. The wilderness advocates wanted the entire area retained. For three years, the controversy continued while the Forest Service studied, reviewed, and pondered. The final decision was made by the Secreaty of Agriculture, but he acceded to the agency's original suggestion. The Forest Service, under continuing pressure, never implemented the decision. In 1977, the area was added to the wilderness system still unlogged.

Wilderness Bill Proposed

Experiences such as the Three Sisters controversy convinced wilderness advocates that legislation was required to protect the wilderness values they espoused. They believed that the Forest Service was too susceptible to the special pleadings of the development-oriented interests to be the custodian of wilderness lands. Wilderness advocates also sought additional authority for protecting the designated areas beyond that which the Forest Service was able to recommend. This included the authority to exclude mining operations and water reclamation projects from wilderness areas.

The first legislative effort to protect wilderness was clearly aimed at the reclassification problem. Introduced in 1956, the proposal covered all of the lands then administered under the Forest Service U-regulations. Most Park Service lands and game refuges administered by the Bureau of Sport Fisheries and Wildlife (now Fish and Wildlife Service) were also mentioned, but the clear priority was on reclassification. The proposal would have prohibited nonconforming uses in the designated areas. Such uses included timber harvest, grazing, prospecting, mining (including gas and oil leasing), water projects, and roads (except as minimally required to administer the area). Finally, the bill proposed a National Wilderness Preservation Council to advise Congress on administration of the areas. Any changes in the area boundaries were to be submitted to Congress and could not take effect if either house opposed the change within four months.

Before wilderness legislation passed eight years later, many of the basic aims of the early bill were altered. The immediate result of the widely publicized proposal was to redouble the problems in reclassifying primitive areas. Mining and grazing operators who had not been affected by the U-regulations had been realtively inattentive to the wilderness issue until the legislation was introduced. If the bill had been passed as first proposed, those uses would have been excluded. Thereafter, they took a very active interest in all the proceedings and immediately intensified the debates.

THE POSTWAR FOREST PRODUCTS INDUSTRY

It is a surprise to many to learn that the forest products industry, practitioners of industrial forestry, did not emerge as a major political force until after the Second World War. When it did reach lift-off in the postwar boom, it confronted the new groups' values and assumptions, which were contending for a place in public land management. Although the Forest Service neither harvests nor processes timber, its position as the manager of the largest area of commercial forest land and standing timber inventory makes the agency a major factor in private timber management. During the war, a number of significant developments occurred which radically altered the timber industry and its relationship to the federal holdings.

The most obvious change was the increased demand for forest products. From the stock market crash in 1929 to the end of World War II, consumption was at a low ebb. The forest products industry generally pressured the Forest Service to withhold public timber from market to avoid competing with the struggling private enterprise. In the postwar years, pent-up consumer demand was released in a period of unparalled prosperity and population expansion. All of this translated into an increased demand for wood products, especially for housing. A less obvious but more important change in the timber industry was that investment in long-range forest management became viable economically. This development is attributable to improved fire control, new taxation methods, and technological innovations.

Fire control is the most dramatic contribution to economically viable forestry. Until an adequate system of fire control existed, it was literally gambling to invest money in forests. In 1941, 30 million acres burned in 208,000 fires. By 1954, if 2 or 3 million acres burned, it was considered a bad year. A nationwide fire control system evolved to the point that investing in reforestation was a reasonable undertaking.

In 1944, a small but critical amendment was made in the Internal Revenue Code. Before the amendment, timber had to be sold unprocessed in order to qualify for the capital gains taxation rate. The amendment allowed all increases in value over the timber purchase price to be taxed as capital gains, rather than at the higher personal income rate. The timber industry points to a rapid increase in forest management investments after the amendment passed to support their contention that capital gains taxation is a prerequisite to investment in forest management (Gregory, chap. 10).

Finally, long-range investment in forest management became attractive because of innovations in the technolgy of timber management and utilization. Equipment and processes developed to increase the efficiency of the wood products industry; heavy harvesting and roading equipment such as skidders, tractors, crawler tractors, and chain saws were adapted from military equipment. New processes enabled the industry to use more and more of what was previously considered waste materials to create such new products as particle board, Kraft paper, and insulation. New management techniques also contributed to greater efficiency; and industrial integration began, so that a saw mill, veneer, or plywood operation could be coordinated with a pulp or particle board mill in order to reduce waste and increase returns on investment. Forest management, as opposed to harvesting standing timber, became profitable in the years after the Second World War. The huge amounts of capital required inevitably committed the industry to intensive sustained yield forestry which would supply sufficient wood and fiber to permit amortization of investment in equipment and processing plants.

Understandably, the industry became increasingly interested in the management of the national forests. Industry encouraged the Forest Service to sell timber on the open market and to manage its lands for timber production. These were new positions for industry, since during and after the Depression industry had urged the Forest Service not to compete with the private sector by selling timber. After the war, as demand for forest products grew, many processing plants were established without any land base or timber ownership at all; and many businesses became largely or totally dependent on federal timber.

THE MULTIPLE USE SUSTAINED YIELD ACT

It is quite clear that the recreationists and wilderness advocates were but one of the new groups demanding that their special requirements be met by the Forest Service. The timber industry pressed diligently for more intensive national forest timber management. None of the demands were new, but the Forest Service could no longer meet the increasing demands on the available land. Before the war, management of the national forests had been a matter of careful but relatively simple allocation of benefits. In the postwar boom, it became necessary for the agency to assess, weigh, and balance the competing interests.

The agency's difficulties were exacerbated by the constant marauding of the National Park Service, which continued to seek management authority over Forest Service administered lands. The Park Service often promoted public discontent with Forest Service policies. Given that situation, the Forest Service was especially anxious to meet the needs of the vociferous recreationist groups.

The Legislative Solution

Confronted by the timber industry pressures, the stock operators, the recreationists, the wilderness advocates, and the spector of Park Service land takeovers, the Forest Service decided to request a congressional clarification of its mission. It hoped to strengthen its hand in attempting to balance the various single-use advocates and clearly to establish its legislative authority in the recreation area. The Forest Service wrote the bill and lobbied for it. Congress acceded to the agency request without any evidence of grass-roots interest in the bill (Bergoffen, passim).

The Forest Service position in pressing the legislation was quite awkward. On the one hand, they had to convince Congress that the need for legislation was real and haste was necessary in passing the act. On the other hand, they were required to assert that the proposed legislation was nothing new; the agency had all the authority required to practice multiple use management of the forests and had been doing so for over fifty years. Clearly, the agency did not want to be left, if their legislative initiative failed, with the implication that they had no authority to provide recreation facilities on the National Forests. Actually, the agency's statutory authority for the recreation programs relied more on implied congressional support in the form of increasing appropriations for recreation programs than on any specific statutory language authorizing them.

During its two-year attempt to achieve legislative imprimature for a traditional view of its programs, the Forest Service applied the long-range planning concept of Operation Outdoors to its whole operation. "Operation Multiple Use" was a forty-year plan presented to the Congress in the form of "A Program For the National Forests." It contained budget requests for over $1 billion to meet the multiple-use needs of all contending groups from 1960 to 2000. Although the Forest Service was beginning to see that long-range, integrated, fully documented budget requests were well received by Congress, this particular plan was highly problematic due to the billion dollar price tag. Some members of Congress thought the Multiple Use Sustained Sustained Yield (MUSY) Act was connected to the "Operation Multiple Use" expenditures.

Passage of the MUSY Bill

After the brief flurry of confusion was cleared up, the Multiple Use Sustained Yield Act passed rapidly and nearly unanimously. Basically the act accomplished what the Forest Service proposed. As the name implies, it authorized and directed the Secretary of Agriculture "to develop and administer the renewable surface resources of the national forests for multiple use and sustained yield of the several products and services obtained therefrom." Sustained yield did not become an important issue for fifteen years. Multiple Use created controversy from the start.

Section 4(a) of the bill defines multiple use in the now familiar passages:

> Multiple Use means the management of all the various renewable surface resources of the combination that will best meet the needs of the American people; making the most judicious use of the land for some or all of these resources or related services over areas large enough to provide sufficient latitude for periodic adjustments in use to conform to changing needs and conditions; that some land will be used for less than all of the resources; and harmonious and coordinated management of the various resources, each with the other, without impairment of the productivity of the land, with consideration being given to the relative values of the various resources, and not necessarily the combination of uses that will give the greatest dollar return or the greatest unit output.

This definition of multiple use is interesting and problematic for a number of reasons. In subsequent years, its lack of clarity and failure to set standards has been increasingly difficult to deal with; but at the time, it was clear that the major Forest Service goal was to respond to recreationist and Park Service pressure. That the Park Service posed a threat was clearly underscored during debate on the bill. The Park Service attempted to insert language stating that the proposed legislation would not effect subsequent transfers of national forest land to their jurisdiction. This was modified in conference to read, innocuously, that the bill did not "affect the use or administration of lands not within the national forests." The Forest Service priorities in seeking the legislation can be observed in the way the agency strained to have recreation mentioned first when the multiple uses were listed in Section 1 of the bill: outdoor recreation, range, timber, watershed, and wildlife and fish. If there was any doubt that the Forest Service was pushing to emphasize recreation, this litany resolved it. In order to get recreation first on the list, they had to modify it with "outdoor," change fish and wildlife to "wildlife and fish," and call forage "range" (of which the stock interests justifiably complained on the grounds that range was a resource with no use implied and certainly no necessary connection to grazing of domestic livestock). Those alterations having been accomplished, Forest Service personnel repeatedly asserted straight-faced that the order of mention was insignificant. It did not represent a ranking of priorities; it was simply alphabetical.

This alphabetical listing was, moreover, augmented in a separate section of the bill which stated that "the establishment and maintenance of areas of wilderness are consistent with the purposes and provisions of this Act." Some observers believe that the wilderness supporters, frustrated in their attempt to have Congress legislatively protect the wilderness areas, insisted on this passage to assure that they would not be altogether cut out of multiple use. Others have insisted that the Forest Service inserted the phrase, indeed, insisted on the whole bill, in an attempt to blunt the wilderness movement's legislative initiative. Irrespective of the machinations behind the phrases, their combined impact was to create intense concern among traditional commodity users of the national forests. It caused reclamation interests and the forest products industry to insist upon insertion of a passage in section 1 noting that "The purposes of this Act are declared to be *supplemental to, but not in derogation of,* the purposes for which the national forests were established as set forth in the Act of June 4, 1897." They were trying to maintain their position as the primary users of the forests, although it is unclear why they thought such additional nebulous phrases would accomplish that purpose. Throughout the hearings, they assiduously attempted to create a legislative history supporting their reading of the phrase to which courts could subsequently turn in interpreting the act. The Forest Service led the opposing forces in constant reiteration of the position that no priorities were established, all uses were equal, and the list was alphabetical. Of such maneuverings are subsequent lawsuits frequently made.

The forest products industry and water users reluctantly accepted mere equality in the hope of warding off a worse setback. Livestock interests scored a minor victory in gaining equal statutory recognition, though they had been major users of the forests since their inception. These issues of what was mentioned where, in which order, and in derogation of what original purposes have not been significant. They simply illustrate the problems that the actors perceived and how they attempted to resolve them. The continuing difficulty with the term "multiple use" is that it does not give any guidance or set any standards.

The Forest Service extensively promoted the concept as a standard or guiding principle by which the forest had always been managed. Like many ideas, however, it has meaning primarily in the context of its counterproposition. Multiple use came to prominence in the Forest Service lexicon as a concept to emphasize the virtues of the national forest management as distinguished from Park Service management. Forests were, following the Pinchot theme, to be used rather than locked up. Use involved many things—timber, recreation, watershed protection, grazing, wildlife, and wilderness—and not just the single use of tourism. Juxtaposed with the Park Service mission of "locking up" valuable resources, multiple use made tactical sense at least as a slogan.

As a guide to decision making or as a standard for evaluating programs of performance, however, multiple use has almost no meaning at all. Rereading the definition found in section 4(a) of the act will underscore this fact. The bill offers only two guides for setting priorities. First, it is not necessary to produce every good or service on every acre. Second, economic maximization is not the sole criterion for evaluating competing uses. Congress established no basis for assessment of the various uses and gave no direction to the Forest Service for deciding what priority to attach to the various resources.

The Sierra Club complained early and often of this lack of statutory standards. It was the only major group that did not support the bill. They noted that the discretion granted by the Multiple Use Act to the Forest Service for establishing priorities on the national forests was nearly absolute. The group noted that the act granted foresters almost unreviewable authority to make policy determinations which frequently lie beyond their capabilities as technically trained foresters. The Sierra Club argued that foresters, predisposed as they were to manipulating the environment for maximizing fiber production, were not qualified to make value decisions concerning which and how many acres should be set aside and left unmanaged (McCloskey, passim).

The Sierra Club did not prevail in 1960. The passage of the Multiple Use Act was an important victory for the Forest Service, which thereby maintained its discretion over the national forest management. Indeed, their authority and discretion were clearly expanded by the act. However, problems in the definition of multiple use were recognized at the time and reached crisis proportions very shortly. Even though the questions raised by the Sierra Club were ignored by others in 1960, their challenge to Forest Service assumptions about conservation dominated the discussion of forest and range policy in the next fifteen years.

SUMMARY

The Multiple Use Act was an appropriate culmination of the transitions taking place in the postwar years. While it recognized new uses and new pressures, it did so in a traditional way. In initiating that legislation, the Forest Service sought to protect its discretion to continue managing the forests in line with a concept of conservation enunciated at the turn of the century. That philosophy was personified in Gifford Pinchot and institutionalized in the Forest Service. The idea never went unchallenged—Muir and the original Park Service supporters represented a strongly dissenting faction—but it dominated resource management and public thinking about resources until the close of the Second World War.

In the 1950s, the dominance of wise-use conservation started to recede. The wilderness movement represented an explicit philosophical challenge mounted by increasingly well organized activists. The wilderness movement was probably the best early statement of the emergent counterconcerns which argued for nonuse instead of use and espoused a nonanthropocentric reverence for the natural world. The impact of this group was greatly enhanced by the existence of a less well organized and articulate mass movement of recreationists on the nation's wild lands. The recreationists were not preservationists. Skiers, boaters, and motorists were as development oriented in their own way as the traditional commodity users. They were not, however, production oriented. The combination of massive new recreation demands and well-organized preservationists forced a fundamental reconsideration of priorities in the wild land allocation process.

The new wave of preservation and recreation interests was not the only force to be fueled during the postwar years. The timber industry was significantly altered, strengthened, and stabilized by technological and economic changes which turned long-term land management operations into a reasonable investment opportunity. As a result, in the 1950s, the industry pressed increasingly ardently for more intensive management of all forestland holdings. The simple fact is that after the Second World War there was no longer sufficient land to accommodate all uses without conflict.

In all of these developments, the public domain lands were almost completely ignored. Congress continued to allow the issues, and their resolution, to be defined almost exclusively by the grazing interests. The fate of the Grazing Service and the subsequent chronic underfunding of BLM were the result of a clear design on the part of the large cattle interests and their congressional representatives. They desired a weak range administration which was strong enough to maintain the order that was to their advantage without actually regulating private exploitation of public range, which they viewed as their own. This goal was readily achieved with the unwitting aid of the conservationists. The latter groups' interests were focused on relatively tangential but symbolically important fights like Echo Park. Few noticed when responsibility for all the mineral leasing programs, Alaska and, incredibly, the Outer Continental Shelf, fell to the management agency most tragically dominated by the commodity interests.

The Multiple Use Act provided the legislative capstone to this period of gradual change. It was, in fact, one of very few pieces of legislation of any weight that passed in those years. The legislation recognizes the new actors and the new values which emerged in the postwar years. But the inadequacies of the bill clearly demonstrate the failure of the traditional land managing establishment to grasp the significant changes that were taking place. What was happening in the 1950s was the initial public awakening to the idea that there is more to conservation than wise use, technically defined.

REFERENCES CITED

Bergoffen, Gene S. *The Multiple Use-Sustained Yield Law.* M. A. thesis, Syracuse University, College of Forestry, 1962.

Clawson, Marion. *The Bureau of Land Management.* New York: Prager Publishers, 1971.

DeVoto, Bernard. *The Easy Chair.* Boston: Houghton Mifflin Company, 1955.

Everhart, William C. *The National Park Service.* New York: Praeger Publishers, 1972.

Foss, Philip D. *Politics and Grass: The Administration of Grazing on the Public Domain.* Seattle: University of Washington Press, 1960.

Gates, Paul W. *History of Public Land Law Development.* Written for the Public Land Law Review Commission. Washington, D. C.: Government Printing Office, 1968.

Gilligan, James. *The Development of Policy and Administration of Forest Service Primitive and Wilderness Areas in the United States.* Ph.D dissertation, University of Michigan, 1954.

Gregory, G. Robinson. *Forest Resource Economics.* New York: The Ronald Press Company, 1972.

McCloskey, Michael J. The Multiple Use-Sustained Yield Act of 1960. 41 *Oregon Law Review* 49 (1961).

Peffer, E. Louise. *The Closing of the Public Domain.* Stanford, Cal.: Stanford University Press, 1951.

Stratton, Owen, and Sirotkin, Philip. *The Echo Park Controversy.* ICUP Series No. 46. University: University of Alabama Press, 1959.

U.S. Forest Service. *Report of the Chief.* Washington, D. C.: Government Printing Office, 1945.

U.S. Outdoor Recreation Resources Review Commission. *Outdoor Recreation for America.* Washington, D.C.: Government Printing Office, 1962.

Voight, William, Jr. *Public Grazing Lands: Use and Misuse by Industry and Government.* New Brunswick, N. J.: Rutgers University Press, 1976.

Chapter 8

Conflict and Confrontation: Real and Avoided Issues of the 1960s

Subtle shifts in emphasis apparent in the postwar years became new norms in the 1960s. A gradual pace of change continued until, as the decade ended, the debate broadened, deepened, and became rancorous. The 1960s were years of profound questioning and resisting of the established order. Techniques of political activism developed in the civil rights movement and refined in the antiwar movement were employed in the environmental cause. Compared with the first two intensely painful movements of the 1960s, the environmental crusade at first seemed benign, a cause which would unite rather than divide people. Subsequently, it became apparent that the environmentalists were raising fundamental questions about the nature and substance of human existence in the postindustrial world. The debate has yet to become as profoundly anguished as the peace and civil rights movements, but resource issues have never been discussed with such emotional intensity as they were in the late 1960s and early 1970s.

In the area of forest and range policy, as in almost all other areas, the changes emerging from the 1960s were incremental, elaborations of the postwar themes discussed previously. The residue of the ostensible revolutionary rhetoric mainly affected the tone of discussions, polarizing the debate and increasing suspicion and hostility. The traditional land managing agencies, especially the Forest Service, experienced the trauma of self-doubt. For almost a century, the conservation movement had been defined and led by government idealists. In the 1960s, the agencies were not leading the movement; and toward the end of the decade, they were being attacked by it. Particularly in the controversy surrounding clear-cutting, foresters were unable to tell their story effectively and they took a drubbing in every public forum.

The response of the resource management professionals was predictable, understandable, and unfortunate. In the face of criticism and the growing recognition that many resource management decisions were matters of values rather than technique, the managers indignantly pointed to their history, their expertise, and simply asserted their authority to make decisions about wild lands matters. The upshot was a series of minimovements to "save" wild lands from resource professionals and from management. Issues that managers tried to avoid continued to haunt them well into the 1970s. Nonetheless, by the end of the decade, the message of the times began to penetrate. Land managers began to understand that public resource management is a political undertaking as much as it is a technical or biological problem, and they began to respond to public concerns. The cost of their original intransigence was loss of credibility and loss of discretion to manage specified categories of land.

At first the movement focused on preserving areas of unique natural beauty or recreation potential and Congress responded promptly. The legislators faced the clearly defined agenda developed in the previous decade and they were supported and cajoled by a well-focused, cohesive movement. Congressional enactments were numerous and far-reaching. Completion of the report of the Outdoor Recreation Resources Review Commission opened the floodgate on legislation delayed for four years pending circulation of their findings. Both Congress and the public found the natural beauty and preservation concepts easy to deal with compared to the pollution issues raised later in the decade. In many ways, Congress appears to have been sidestepping the profoundly important questions of life-style and economic growth inherent in the environmental movement by embracing scenic wonders and avoiding the implications of environmental quality.

Congress and public interest groups also continued to avoid critical issues surrounding the need for comprehensive management of public domain. Interestingly, the question did receive an initial and important airing. This came not at the insistence of the conservationists and preservationists, for they were still focused on wilderness preservation, but at the behest of one very powerful, commodity oriented Congressman, Wayne Aspinall. The Public Land Law Review Commission was chartered in 1964 to study the morass of public land laws and make revisions. Their report and recommendations were in accord with Aspinall's commodity orientation and did not occasion a great surge of public or congressional attention to public domain lands. Thus, although the issues were raised, they were ignored. The National Environmental Policy Act, intended as a gesture of good will to the growing environmental movement, is an appropriate terminus for this chapter. The bill passed without much thought or discussion, and its hortatory phrases accurately reflected the general level of understanding of the ramifications of environmentalism.

EARLY "ERA OF GOOD FEELING"

The 1960s began in an era of good feeling. The administration of the newly elected President, John Kennedy, did not focus on resource management issues; but new people in Washington took a fresh look at the matter. They alleged, probably without much basis in fact, that after eight years of Republican "giveaways," they were going to preserve and protect our resources. In this atmosphere, the Secretaries of Agriculture and Interior sent a letter to the President which became known as the "Treaty of the Potomac." The letter announced a "new era of cooperation" between the two departments, recognizing the unique contributions that agencies in each make to resource management in America. More to the point, the Secretaries agreed that except for existing administration proposals and routine boundary adjustments, "jurisdictional responsibility will not be disturbed among the agencies of our two departments" and that neither department would unilaterally initiate new proposals to change the status of land under the jurisdiction of the other. The causes of hostility between the two departments have already been alluded to. Between 1902 and 1960, 4,950,000 acres of national forestland were transferred to the Park Service administration in seventy separate actions. The nearly 5 million acres transferred to the national parks comprised slightly less than one-third of the total area of the national parks. During that same period, 451,000 acres were transferred from the Park Service to the Forest Service. Although the treaty's procedures for defining park boundaries were not binding on Congress, they would, if acceded to, significantly reduce the bureaucratic infighting on a broad range of issues. The treaty confronted a serious problem, however: Secretaries and other presidential appointments, Presidents themselves, in fact, are transients. The exchange of letters superficially altered some procedures, but it did not affect the underlying competition between the two agencies. Nevertheless, Congress was again attentive to issues of wild lands management; and optimism regarding meaningful progress on many pressing issues was widespread.

REPORT OF THE ORRRC

The long-awaited report of the Outdoor Recreation Resources Review Commission was stimulus and focus for public and congressional action. A virtual flood of proposals and initiatives had been pending and gathering support for the four years the commission met. With its publication, the starting gun was fired and the new preservationists and recreationists moved out in dozens of directions.

The Report is unexceptional. It recounted the obvious facts that recreation demand was increasing; that most national parks are located far from population centers; and that coordination of federal, state, local, and private efforts would be needed to meet projected demand. Much data was gathered and many useful reports were written, but most of the research findings were familiar or obvious. The report is typical of the genre: dull and noncontroversial. It sets no priorities and is vague about specific proposals and programs. Nevertheless, the report is significant in the history of recreation management. The timely infusion of support for recreation research constituted "seed money," and a cadre of trained, skilled professionals developed to lobby for its continuation and expansion. The inquiry also brought the issue to public attention. The commission held hearings throughout the country, involved the interested public, and created a strong public demand for remedial action. Though many groups were disappointed that the commission did not endorse their own particular causes, still its efforts alienated none. If the commission failed to define specific priorities, its goal was the long-term development of state-level capabilities in recreation management. The ORRRC succeeded brilliantly where other similar commissions had failed because it was not doctrinaire or partisan.

The ORRRC recommendations endorsed planning, coordination, and funding. The report concluded that the federal level of government, aside from preserving nationally significant areas and emphasizing recreation in management of federal lands, should assist the states in recreation planning. Similarly, the report recommends that the states, while managing state and regionally significant recreation areas, should help the local governments plan. The localities should concentrate on creating recreation opportunities in urban areas. To aid the planning and development program, the ORRRC made four important recommendations, all of which were ultimately enacted.

First, the ORRRC proposed that a new bureau be established within the Department of the Interior to coordinate federal recreation programs and give technical and financial assistance to the states. This proposal evinces the commission's dismay at the institutional tangle surrounding government recreation programs. It also reflects the desire of recreation groups for a special agency to minister to their needs. Most special interest groups have not considered the plight of the Grazing Service when they urge the creation of a single interest agency or the amount of effort it takes to support and defend such an agency once founded. The commission recognized that it was politically impossible to give a new bureau responsibilities already assigned to existing agencies. The ORRRC recommendation for the bureau was, therefore, a dilution of its original scheme to establish an independent and authoritative recreation coordinator within the federal government. The Bureau of Outdoor Recreation as proposed was not to be a superagency but a planning and funding organization.

The second ORRRC recommendation was a funding scheme for recreation. The new bureau was to lead in recreation planning by administering a proposed grants-in-aid program. The ORRRC recommended that the federal government establish a matching fund program in which it would pay up to 75 percent of the cost of state recreation planning and 40 percent of acquisition and development expenses.

The third recommendation was to institute a series of comprehensive state outdoor recreation plans. States would be required to complete a plan before they could qualify for federal matching monies for acquisition and development. The combined effect of the grants-in-aid and the planning program would be increased state attention to recreation programs, and to facilitate hiring state recreation planners who would reach into the localities in order to prepare a statewide plan.

Finally, the commission urged that enhancing recreation opportunities should be considered in the planning of federal programs, particularly water developments and highway construction. Although the idea has obvious merits and has been adopted in a number of important programs, there is some irony in the concept. Regarding highways, the contribution of transportation developments to overcrowding in the national parks has already been noted. Moreover, the tendency of the Federal Highway Commission to take park and forestlands for use as road rights-of-way has been a serious problem in many areas. These lands were "cheap" because they were already in public ownership. Thousands of acres of recreation and forestland were lost to road builders as we developed our extensive public highway system. One of the earliest and most familiar environmental lawsuits was instituted in Tennessee to prevent the Secretary of Transportation from taking a city park for a federal highway *(Citizens to Preserve Overton Park* v. *Volpe)*. The commission's suggestion that highways could be designed to provide recreation may strike some, on balance, as ironic.

So too is its recommendation that water development projects should proceed with emphasis on enhancing recreation opportunities. The commission was correct in its assessment of the important contribution water impoundments make to regional recreation, but the dam builders had already built dams on most of the sites where construction could be justified for irrigation, flood control, or hydroelectric power generation purposes. Many projects that were marginal or indefensible became cost effective when the recreation "benefits" were calculated into the cost-benefit ratio.

In addition to these four general themes, the report also contained proposals on specific issues. First, it endorsed the wilderness bill. Second, it urged that rivers with aesthetic, scientific, or recreation value should be "allowed to

remain in their free-flowing state and natural setting without man-made alterations." Finally, the commissioners supported increased attention to and funding for urban recreation.

The urban recreation focus harbingers a growing and important idea in
recreation management. Recreation management was traditionally resource
oriented; the opportunity to recreate was defined by the availability of appropriate scenic or recreation resources. The commission focused attention on the
idea that the need for recreation rather than the availability of the land resource must be determinative. If there were no suitable recreation sites in
urban areas, as there often were not, the commission suggested that we must
be prepared to create them.

The Bureau of Outdoor Recreation

Given the congressional activism of the period, it is somewhat surprising that
the legislation required to implement the commission's recommendations was
not immediately forthcoming. The Bureau of Outdoor Recreation was therefore established within the Department of the Interior by a secretarial order.
The Secretary of the Interior simply redelegated a number of the Park Service
programs, principally those defined in the Parks, Parkways and Recreation
Act of 1936, to the new group, which was named the Bureau of Outdoor
Recreation (BOR). This shift authorized BOR to engage in cooperative efforts
with states, localities, and other federal agencies in doing recreation research
and planning (Cate, 129–131) and to formulate a nationwide outdoor recreation plan. This was not an executive reorganization such as the one which
established BLM. Executive reorganizations require congressional review. It
was accomplished entirely within the Office of the Secretary, and the BOR was
initially funded with money diverted from the Park Service. That this expedient was employed to establish BOR is indicative of the fierce territoriality of
the established agencies and their congressional allies. None of the agencies
providing recreation opportunities at the federal level wanted to be coordinated by a new group. Most particularly, the Park Service did not want to see
the BOR established. Nevertheless, the authority delegated to the Secretary for
recreation coordination was clarified and expanded by legislation in May,
1963.

Even this legislation did not constitute an "organic" act; and in spite of
the public relations fanfare which surrounded BOR's debut, it did not start
auspiciously. It had no land to manage, no programs to administer, no matching money to grant to the states, and limited credibility with the established
federal and state recreation agencies. Its major significance was that it ended
National Park Service efforts to present itself as "the" federal recreation
agency. National recreation planning was, moreover, no longer the responsibility of a particular land managing service. Agencies that had been reluctant to

participate in previous planning efforts for fear of Park Service predations were willing to cooperate with BOR. By 1964, early versions of the land and water conservation fund added the promise of supplementary funding to BOR's appeal as a recreation planner.

Land and Water Conservation Fund Act of 1964

The Land and Water Conservation Fund Act (LWCF), which passed Congress in 1964, has contributed to the development of state and local park systems throughout the nation and to the expansion of federal land acquisition programs in every land management agency. The precise formula and level of funding has been changed several times, but the end result of the LWCF has been to bring thousands of privately owned acres into public ownership for recreation purposes.

The financing of the Land and Water Conservation Fund reflects the congressional policy that recreation users should pay their way. It authorized the President to charge user fees at developed recreation facilities on federal lands or at federal water project sites. It also authorized the President to charge entrance fees at designated federal recreation areas and to establish an annual sticker fee of not more than $7 which would permit automobile access to all designated areas. The user fees were to be the basic component of the fund. Additional monies were to come from three diverse sources: proceeds from surplus property sales; proceeds from a motorboat fuel tax; and congressional appropriation of $60 million annually for its first eight years. The appropriations were strictly aimed at getting the fund operating and had to be repaid starting in the tenth year of the fund's existence.

The fund was to be split sixty-forty between state and federal agencies. The federal share of the LWCF money was designated for acquisition of recreation acreage in national forests, parks, recreation areas, or game refuges. The state portion was to be allocated for planning, acquisition, and development of recreation facilities on a 50 percent matching basis. Only limited planning funds were available to the states, however, until a statewide comprehensive outdoor recreation plan (SCORP) was prepared and approved by the Secretary of the Interior. Once the plan was accepted, state acquisition and development programs also had to be approved. Responsibility for coordinating and directing the state planning efforts was delegated to BOR.

The user fee and permit provisions of the LWCF Act created considerable controversy. Several federal agencies, most notably the Army Corps of Engineers, refused for several years to charge entrance fees in areas they administered. They promoted new dam projects on the basis of "free" recreation and did not wish to charge for it. The Park Service was similarly reluctant to charge fees, although they did not follow the corps in refusing to cooperate with the program. The public was confused by the existence of "free" and "fee" federal recreation areas and was generally hostile to paying entrance fees for tax-supported attractions.

The annual permit known as "Golden Eagle Passport" was not a success either. Many people thought that having purchased the passport, they were not required to pay camping fees or hunting and fishing license charges. The Congressional Record of the late 1960s was, moreover, full of anguished speeches decrying the discriminatory features of the Golden Eagle system; the elderly and the poor, it was frequently alleged, could not afford a $7 entrance fee. The passports were temporarily dropped and the fee program was "clarified" to exempt most day uses. The result of this congressional vascillation on the fee question was a persistent shortfall in the Land and Water Conservation Fund. The fund was based on high expectations regarding user fee income, and Congress simply refused to follow through and make recreation users pay even a small fraction of the costs. The fund achieved slightly better than half of anticipated levels by 1968.

This shortfall was especially troublesome since Congress rapidly was designating new park areas. The eighty-ninth Congress alone approved twenty-three new federal recreation areas requiring the acquisition of approximately 250,000 acres. The acquisition problems were exacerbated by rapidly increasing land costs. Typically, after the lengthy process of congressional debate leading to designation and purchase authorizations for an area, an average of sixteen months elapsed before the first appropriations were made. Land costs frequently increased by 75 to 90 percent during this period (McCloskey, 1968, 19). With its massive purchase authorizations, Congress increased the pressure on an inadequate fund while simultaneously refusing to support the user fee system that was supposed to provide almost half of the fund's revenues.

In 1968, the LWCF was significantly altered. The amendments established a much broader financial base for the fund. The land sale and fuel tax revenues for the fund were augmented by direct appropriations which would not have to be repaid. Further, it provided that if the total from those sources did not reach $200 million annually, proceeds from federal oil and gas leases on the Outer Continental Shelf would be used to achieve a $200 million level. Two years later the upper limit was raised to $300 million, although the full amount authorized has not always been appropriated and frequently Presidents have impounded appropriated funds. By 1978, the fund was authorized to a level of $900 million annually. In an effort to expedite land acquisition in advance of the price escalation that federal designation almost inevitably sets off, the amendments also authorized the agencies to contract for up to $30 million worth of land annually before appropriations were made.

Thus amended, the LWCF became the touchstone of the nation's enhanced commitment to recreation development. Two profound problems are, however, only partially obscured by LWCF's popularity. The first is the persistently troubling issue of users' fees. Congress is infinitely more willing to impose charges on industrial users than on recreation users. Timber purchases, grazing permittees, and mineral leaseholders pay fair market value for goods received or confront the constant assertion that they should do so. When numerous voters are involved as users, however, the propriety of paying for the use is apparently less obvious. The result is a federal subsidy to those who frequent tax-supported recreation areas. Many of the recreationists and wilderness buffs who complain about federal largess benefiting commodity users fail to observe the federal support of their own activities. Meanwhile, urban emphasis of the ORRRC was largely ignored by Congress; and even after the rioting in central cities in the mid-1960s, Congress continued to put the national recreation dollar into scenic beauty projects.

A second and less frequently noted impact of the LWCF program is the massive commitment of funds to public acquisition of private lands for recreation purposes. Figure 8-1, indicating a recent expansion of the public domain after nearly one hundred twenty-five years of disposition, reflects in part the LWCF acquisition program. Even at inflated land prices, that constitutes an enormous acreage—forests, farms, seashores—annually removed form pro-

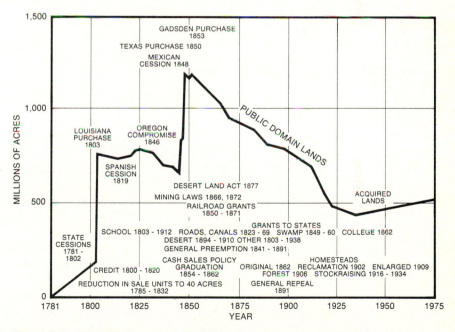

Figure 8-1. Approximate area of federal lands in the states, 1781–1975, with dates of important acquisitions and laws providing for their disposal. (Adapted from graph originally supplied by U.S. Department of the Interior, Bureau of Land Management.)

duction and economic development. The question of how much land appropriately should be owned by the government and dedicated primarily to recreation purposes was not seriously aired during the early 1960s. The recreationists and preservationists dominated the debates of the period; and with the passage of the LWCF funding measures, the legislative response to their pressure was only beginning.

NATIONAL PARK SERVICE EXPANSION

The major beneficiaries of congressional activism were the National Park Service and its advocates. In spite of the two setbacks discussed above, the loss of planning authority to BOR, and the agreement not propose unilaterally converting Forest Service lands to parks, the decade of the 1960s was a period of tremendous Park Service expansion. During that time, Park Service responsibilities were extended to cover ten new natural areas, forty-seven historical areas, one recreation area, eleven lakeshores and seashores, eight recreation reservoirs, three scenic rivers, one scenic area, and one cultural area (Lee, passim). In addition to the specific area designations, Congress granted two important new authorities to the Park Service.

Land Acquisition Authority

The Park Service was not authorized to spend appropriated funds to acquire private lands for parks until 1954. This lack of authority partially explains the Park Service's intense interest in Forest Service and other public lands. All of the parks had to be designated from the existing public lands or donated by a state or private citizens. For example, hoping to reap the economic benefits of tourist development without incurring maintenance and development costs, North Carolina "bought" from its citizens and donated Cape Hatteras National Seashore, the Blue Ridge Parkway right-of-way, and Great Smoky Mountains National Park to the Park Service. When the state appropriations for the latter fell approximately $10 million short, the Rockefeller family donated money to make the park possible. Their private fortune has also been responsible in large part for many other park projects and areas, including Acadia, Grand Teton, and Rocky Mountain National Parks.

In 1954, Congress began to relieve this dependence on private donations and state actions. The Secretary was authorized to spend appropriated funds to acquire lands for the Fort Union National Monument but only to the extent of matching donated funds. The idea of using appropriations to acquire substantial acreage of recreation lands first received congressional support in 1961 legislation establishing the Cape Cod National Seashore and it has been expanded since (Lee, 59). These various provisions do not constitute a general authority to acquire land with appropriated funds comparable to the Forest

Service power conferred by the Weeks Act in 1911. Separate congressional action is required to establish each Park Service area, and the acquisition provisions vary. Nevertheless, simply establishing the idea of acquiring private lands for public recreation purposes has made possible many of the national lakeshores, seashores, and parks established during subsequent years.

National Historic Preservation Act of 1966

A second significant expansion of Park Service programs is found in 1966 legislation amending the Historic Sites Act of 1935. The thirty-year-old program was an attempt to inventory and register archeological sites and historic American buildings. It enabled the Secretary of the Interior to designate "National Historic Landmarks." Section 106 is of most relevance to forest and range policy. It requires that all federal managers of federally assisted programs take into account any impact which they might have on the historic sites. Any project with a potential for disrupting a historic site must be reviewed by the Advisory Council on Historic Preservation, which was part of the National Park Service. Thus attention was focused, a constituency created, and a separate review procedure established to assure the protection of cultural artifacts. Public land managers are required and private landowners are pressured not to disturb archeological sites in their activities.

The programs discussed above—the LWCF fund, the BOR's planning role, the expansion of Park Service areas and authorities—can all be characterized as extensions of traditional agency activities. Congress granted more money and more authority to enable federal and state agencies to respond to public demand for recreation facilities. In contrast to these expansions of existing programs and authorities, a number of the 1960s congressional enactments specifically limit agency authority. Three bills particularly affecting the Park Service and the Forest Service constitute unprecedented congressional participation in the management of public lands. In the Wilderness Act, the Trails Act, and the Wild and Scenic Rivers Act, certain categories of land were identified for which the management regime was specifically defined by Congress rather than the managing agency.

CONGRESSIONAL PRIORITY SETTING

Wilderness Act

The Wilderness Act of 1964 was the only one of these enactments that engendered significant or prolonged controversy. The 1956 proposals discussed in the previous chapter were altered significantly before agreement was finally achieved. Nine years of deliberation saw sixty-five different bills introduced, twenty of which passed in one house at one time or another. Eighteen hearing were held, two-thirds of them in the field; and thousands of pages of hearings records, transcripts, and documents were compiled (McCloskey, 1966, 298). Agreement on the principle involved, the desirability of establishing a national policy of preserving wilderness areas, was never really contested except by extreme advocates of commodity interests and die-hard opponents of permanent special use designations. The controversy very soon focused on two major issues having to do with the discretion of the managing agencies involved: By what procedure would wilderness areas be established and what uses would be permitted in designated wilderness areas?

Designation Issues The designation issue was twofold: What areas would be included initially in the system, and who would be authorized to modify or add to that system? The original 1956 proposals, as noted in Chapter 7, were heavily oriented toward designating an enormous wilderness system within ten years. The proposed system would have immediately included all wilderness, wild, and roadless areas administered under the 1939 U-regulations (1–3a). Primitive areas and the remaining L-regulation areas were to be added to the system within ten years following studies by the Secretary of Agriculture to determine necessary modifications. In addition, the early bills would have included forty-eight national parks and monuments and nineteen wildlife refuges and game ranges in the system in their entirety, with the proviso that the Secretary of Interior could, prior to inclusion, designate areas needed for roads, trails, administrative facilities, buildings, and visitor centers. If the Secretary did not act within ten years, the whole unit was to have gone automatically into the wilderness system.

The bill that passed in 1964 was modified considerably. Only national forest wilderness areas designated under the U-1 and 2 regulations were included as "instant" wilderness. The primitive areas and the national park and Fish and Wildlife Service lands were left for subsequent study. Within ten years, the appropriate Secretary was to study the potential wilderness areas, hold hearings, and make recommendations to the President. The President could alter the recommendations, but the areas would only be included in the wilderness system by specific act of Congress. Finally, a National Wilderness Preservation Council originally recommended by the preservationists was eliminated from the bill. The differences between the two bills are dramatic. In the original bill, extensive areas would have been automatically included in the system. Additions were to be made by the President or Congress and modifications could be made by the Secretary of Agriculture or Interior. Under the act that passed, very few of the areas were initially designated; and additions were to be made only by act of Congress.

This clear assertion of congressional prerogative to direct the management of the public lands fit the preservationists' goals as well as the congressional activism regarding the recreation issue. The preservationists initiated the legislation because they believed that congressional protection was more secure than administrative designation. Their clear goal was to make wilderness designations permanent, but they paid a price to achieve it: The original system was a mere fraction of what they desired, and additions to that system could only be achieved by cumbersome congressional action. Ten years after the act had passed, all the primitive areas still had not been reclassified because many recommendations had been stalled in Congress for almost a full decade. Park and Fish and Wildlife Service studies were way behind schedule and the wilderness system continues to be primarily a Forest Service program.

Although preservationists specifically sought congressional protection of wilderness areas in pressing for the bill, within the legislature it was opponents of the idea who insisted on such full congressional participation in wilderness designations. Most significant among the congressional wilderness opponents was Colorado Representative Wayne Aspinall, who was Chairman of the House Committee on Interior and Insular Affairs during most of the period in which the Wilderness Act was debated. Aspinall supported both full and wise utilization of resources and congressional prerogatives. He viewed early versions of the wilderness bill as attacks on both wise resource use and congressional authority to manage the public lands. He insisted that only Congress should make such important determinations. In this he agreed, in principle, with the advocates of the bill. Aspinall anticipated that subsequent growth of the wilderness system would be subject to review by the committee he chaired. His long-term program for minimizing the wilderness system was truncated by a primary defeat in 1972. Nevertheless, the Wilderness Act was not cleared for floor action until it met Aspinall's numerous requirements.

Permitted Uses   In the second area of major controversy—what uses are allowed in the wilderness areas—the product of nine years of congressional compromise was again very different from the original proposal. Although Aspinall was personally intransigent regarding designation procedures, he was not alone in his reluctance to constrain economic development in wilderness areas. The 1956 proposals were specific and thorough. Established grazing and motorboat use could continue only until they could be equitably terminated. Further, no lumbering, prospecting, mining (including oil and gas production), grazing by domestic livestock, water diversions, water management practices involving manipulation of the plant cover, water impoundment or reservoir storage, any form of commercial enterprise, roads, or any use of motor vehicles or aircraft would be permitted in wilderness areas as originally proposed.

The act that passed is far less restrictive. Established motorboat and aircraft use is continued. Measures necessary to the control of fire, insect, and disease are allowed, as are roads and facilities needed for administration. The President may approve any water development in a wilderness area, and prospecting and mineral exploration can continue until 1983. Claims staked before 1983 can be worked thereafter, although patents will convey title only to the minerals. However, all mineral claims must be worked so as to protect the wilderness values and the Secretary may require reclamation as necessary. The Secretary of Interior was, in fact, instructed to survey mineral values in wilderness areas on a planned, continuing basis.

The Wilderness Act is no more restrictive regarding permitted uses than the Forest Service regulations of 1939. In the quest for congressional designation of wilderness areas, the preservationists compromised many of their primary goals. Although the long-sought passage of the bill was immediately hailed as a victory by preservationists, a careful reading of its provisions may leave the observer wondering what all the fuss was about. Legislative protection of wilderness is not necessarily more permanent than administrative designation. Legislation can be repealed or amended and is not necessarily more permanent than administrative action. Programs can be authorized in glowing language, only to be undone in the implementation and appropriations process. Congress is but one of the several arenas available to special interests at any point. After thirty fairly successful years of pushing their cause within administrative agencies, wilderness enthusiasts felt the need for statutory protection of their gains. The preservationists went to Congress and, in spite of the unavoidable compromises noted above, achieved several important goals.

First, the long and well-publicized legislative effort gave national popular recognition to the wilderness concept. Wilderness preservation became an apple pie issue, an appropriate part of our national ideals and our national agenda. Second, wilderness areas are much easier to defend as part of a recognized national system than as isolated tracts in isolated areas. An important lesson of the Echo Park controversy was that if a system is established and accepted, encroachments can be resisted as a matter of principle rather than on the merits of a particular piece of land (Scott, 193–195).

A third significant accomplishment of the Wilderness Act was that it extended the Forest Service wilderness designation and administration system to national parks and wildlife refuges. The Park Service had long maintained that *all* its areas were administered as wilderness and required no additional protection. The Wilderness Act reminds Park Service officials that their business is partially preservation, not simply the mass recreation characterized by scenic highways, visitor centers, observation towers, and curio shops.

Fourth, the Wilderness Act made important inroads on the Mining Act of 1872. It placed a time limit on filing claims, although in the nineteen years provided, every available inch of land can be claimed. The act provided for strict regulation of the mining activity, which must be in keeping with the wilderness setting, and limits the right of patent to the minerals alone. The miner cannot acquire title to the land and must return the surface to its original condition when mining is finished. It was a terrible defeat to the wilderness advocates to have mining allowed at all; however, the modifications of the 1872 law are significant.

In spite of these achievements, the Wilderness Act did not at first appear to alter the general pattern of land allocation between preservation and multiple-use management. Park and Fish and Wildlife Service lands were not open to commodity production anyway, and the Forest Service lands scheduled for potential inclusion in the system had been managed as wilderness for the most part at least since 1940. The impact of the act has been expanded by a combination of court decisions and administrative action.

Growth of the Wilderness System

The Forest Service lands covered by the act were first expanded by the decision of a Colorado District Court in 1969. In the Parker Case, 405 U.S. 989 (1971), the Forest Service was enjoined from selling timber in an area contiguous to the Gore Range-Eagle's Nest Primitive Area in Colorado. The court held that the Wilderness Act authorizes the President to make final recommendations regarding which contiguous areas should be added to the wilderness system. The court found that allowing the sale would preempt the President's authority to recommend additions to the area. Thus, all roadless areas contiguous to wilderness, wild, or primitive areas were to be protected until the President indicated otherwise (Haight, 290–294).

The Forest Service further expanded the protected acreage with a combination of judicial and administrative action by undertaking a roadless area review study. In *Sierra Club* v. *Hardin,* the Court flatly rejected the plaintiff's assertion that the Wilderness Act required the Forest Service to study wilderness potential of roadless areas. Their responsibilities under the act were explicitly limited to areas previously administered as wilderness, wild, or primitive. Although the law did not require the Forest Service to undertake review of areas in addition to those mentioned, it permitted such activity. The agency has done so in its roadless area review and evaluation program (RARE), to be discussed in Chapter 9. Every roadless area of 5000 acres or more under the agency's jurisdiction was studied for its wilderness potential. In an out-of-court settlement of a suit focusing on the agency's failure to prepare an Environmental Impact Statement on the study, the Forest Service agreed not to permit any activities in "de facto" areas until their status has been resolved through the full Forest Service unit planning and impact statement preparation.

Thus, although the Wilderness Act itself affected only specified areas of the national forests managed since 1940 as wilderness, the act's coverage has been greatly expanded by agency action and judicial interpretation. It is frequently asserted by wilderness opponents that these interpretations went far beyond the Wilderness Act's original purpose. There does not seem to be much question that neither the bill's sponsors nor its opponents envisioned this expansive reading of the act (Keane, 40). However, in assessing the complaints about the "stretching" of the 1964 legislation, a number of factors must be considered. First, Congress can and frequently does ignore the procedures and limitations it established in the act by adding wilderness areas to the system entirely on its own, irrespective of the former status of the land, Forest Service recommendations, or the procedures in the act. Congressional authority to designate wilderness areas is not limited by the Wilderness Act. The complaints seem to focus on delays. Many acres have been "locked up" simply because their best use has not been determined through planning. This delay, the randomness of the procedures, and the uncertain time frame for making final decisions creates real hardships for many groups of forest users. However, all the courts have required is that areas not be altered until they are studied and evaluated in the context of normal land use planning. It is true that delay and uncertainty impose costs that may not be justifiable. However, requiring that the public lands be managed in the light of careful planning and evaluation is not unreasonable.

Land Management Under the Wilderness Act

The act and its elaboration have also created extremely difficult management problems in connection with administering designated or pending areas. A congressional wilderness designation cannot eliminate from an area existing water developments; landing strips; roads; hordes of campers, hikers, and off-road vehicles; fire; insects; disease; or the management problems they entail. All of the agencies involved, most particularly the Forest Service, have been accused of taking an inappropriately narrow view of the definition of wilderness. The agencies say they are trying to achieve a *true* wilderness system that can be reasonably managed as such. Preservationists counter that the agencies are trying to keep the system small by considering only absolutely pristine areas for inclusion. The act itself gives little guidance on such problems as how to deal with a "wilderness" area that attracts so many backpackers that designated campsites and outhouses are required. However both courts and Congress have so far resolved all ambiguities in the direction of a more, rather than less, inclusive wilderness system.

National Trail System Act

Like the Wilderness Act, the National Trails System Act is part of Congress's assertion of its authority to designate specific management regimes to achieve congressionally defined priorities in particular areas. The legislation was initiated in the early 1960s as an effort to protect the Appalachian Trail. When it passed in 1968, it mandated an extensive trail system including three management categories and an elaborate trail planning program. The bill encourages states and localities to protect the scenic trails outside of federal landholdings but provides no funds. State and metropolitan trails will also be recognized as part of the "system" by the Secretary of the Interior, but they are entirely the financial and management responsibility of the states and localities. The recognition of urban recreation needs is included, but it is a marginal, no-budget item. The act also briefly mentions national recreation trails. They are on federal or state lands but short and relatively less spectacular. Congress was primarily interested in the scenic grandeur aspects of outdoor recreation and public land management and the national scenic trails were obviously the heart of the program.

Adopting the Wilderness Act model, the bill provides for two "instant" and fourteen "study" national scenic trails. The two instant trails, the Appalachian and the Pacific Crest, were already complete or nearly so and enjoyed wide regional support. The list of fourteen study trails was an increase from eight originally proposed by the administration. It included a number added to satisfy particular representatives. Federal agencies are urged to cooperate with the trail program and to adopt management practices which will maintain the trail environments. Public agencies are urged to use LWCF monies to acquire trail rights-of-way.

Again adopting the Wilderness Act model, the trails bill does not transfer the jurisdiction of any federal land: Whatever agency is administering trail land will continue to do so under the congressionally defined trail management regime. Old rivalries were recognized in the balancing of lead responsibility for the two instant trails: The Forest Service has overall charge of the Pacific Crest and the Park Service was made responsible for the Appalachian Trail, in spite of the fact that the Forest Service administers the vast majority of federal land traversed by both.

National Wild and Scenic Rivers

The National Wild and Scenic Rivers Act is appropriately considered a companion measure of the Trails System Act. They passed during the same week in 1968 and the structure of the two acts is quite similar. The act provides three categories of rivers: wild, scenic and recreational. Wild rivers are undeveloped and accessible only by trail. Scenic rivers are predominantly undeveloped but are accessible in some places by roads. Recreational rivers are generally open to road access and may have been dammed or developed. The act created eight "instant" rivers, twenty-seven study rivers, and an open-ended authority for BOR to study additional rivers for inclusion. Passage of this bill was achieved with a ploy just opposite to the Trails Act approach. Rather than adding something for everyone, the rivers bill passed only after all the rivers unacceptable to particular members of Congress were eliminated. This different tactic was probably necessary because the provisions of the rivers system were seen, appropriately, as much more restrictive than those in the Trails Act.

The wild and scenic rivers system was established primarily to restrain the dam builders. All but two rivers were exempted from the provisions of the Federal Power Act. The bill also provides for preservation of a strip of land at least one-quarter mile wide on both banks of designated rivers. Federal lands in the strip were withdrawn from mineral entry and up to 100 acres per mile of private lands within the strip could be acquired, but not condemned, to achieve the preservation goal.

Both the Trails Act and the Wild and Scenic Rivers Act give some support to the concept of outdoor recreation in urban and developed areas. It is quite clear, however, especially in the case of the trails bill, that the major concern, financial support, and protective management schemes are aimed at the scenic beauty end of the spectrum.

The model utilized is also significant. The division of the systems into "instant" and "study" provides a way for Congress to strike a compromise. They can establish a system which would be opposed if originally presented at its fullest application. Subsequently, with the principle recognized and the BOR out "studying" and building a constituency for including controversial units, it becomes easier to round out the system gradually, Friction was also reduced because legislation does not require transfer of land from the jurisdiction of one agency to another. The trails Act and the Wild and Scenic Rivers Act build on the insights achieved in the long Wilderness Act debate. All three bills evince congressional initiative and creativity in responding to the recreation boom. Confronted by tremendous public pressure, Congress took unprecedented steps in giving the land managing agencies specific directions for managing designated areas of the public lands.

OVERALL RECREATION PROGRAM

All of these legislative efforts—the Wilderness Act, the LWCF, the Trails Act, the Wild and Scenic Rivers Act, authorization of forty-eight new national park and recreation areas, accelerated state recreation land acquisition, and expansion of Forest Service recreation programs—represent a clear response to the recreation and preservation values that emerged in the 1960s. The victories and gains achieved during the early 1960s are not surprising, given the changes that took place during the 1950s. Recreation and preservation groups emerged as a strong political force; their demands were apple pie issues and were largely met.

What is striking about the period is the callowness with which resource issues were approached. Given growing recognition of the diverse and interrelated nature of environmental problems, it is disappointing that the Kennedy and Johnson administrations continued their paeans to scenic preservation as long as they did without facing the hard questions of resource availability and allocation. Our political leaders in the 1960s saw urban problems—air pollution, water pollution, urban sprawl, and land use control—as something distinct from forest and range policy. The wild lands management discussions of the period were dominated by preservationists. Urban problems were something different and different groups were active in their resolution. The two realms were not seen as related except that the former could provide respite from the latter. The finitude of the earth's resources and the need to allocate them justly and manage them wisely for a multitude of public purposes did not strike home until the oil crisis of 1974. The problem of the 1960s is not that Congress set up an extensive system of land preserves. The problem is that preservation and recreation were accepted as the appropriate frame of reference for discussing all forest and range management issues. The merits of removing so many acres from production were not debated and the costs of the preserves were essentially ignored.

One of the unfortunate aspects of the extreme polarization our country experienced in the 1960s is the widespread public acceptance of the good guys and bad guys theory. Government agencies and corporations were bad guys. Environmentalists and preservationists were good. Industry representatives wanting to harvest timber or develop minerals were dismissed as selfish special interests. Information regarding the impact of repeated reduction of productive acreage on employment, consumer prices, or housing prices was dismissed as the propaganda of industrialists. The Forest Service entered the discussion on the side of "wise use" of resources and was tarred with the same brush as was industry. Preservationists managed to avoid the opprobrium of being a "special interest" both because they cast themselves in the role of outsiders, challenging the established order, and because their efforts were aimed at cost avoidance rather than at profit making.

Given the tone of the times, resource users, "exploiters," would have had difficult going in the 1960s no matter what they said or did. However, both government and private resource managers did a rather poor job of telling their story in the 1960s. Foresters, more than any other profession in the resource management field, became the focus of public skepticism and ire. They were simply unable to make a compelling case for their goals, their practices, and their achievements. The clear cutting controversy is the most obvious example of this serious breakdown in communications.

THE CLEAR CUTTING CONTROVERSY

Even age management, the practice of removing the forest cover from designated areas in order to regenerate a relatively homogenous stand of preferred species, became the focus of public hostility to resource management in the late 1960s and 1970s. Clear cutting on the Monongahela National Forest in West Virginia and the Bitterroot National Forest in Montana occasioned the most intense and publicized disputes in the widespread controversy. During the conflict, forest management became, as it had not been since the days of Gifford Pinchot, a popularly discussed policy issue. Public passions were not, however, aroused in support of government management of public resources. Rather, it was widely assumed that the Forest Service had been unduly influenced by the timber industry to ignore its multiple-use mandate and emphasize timber production on the national forests. Clear cutting symbolized the "sellout," the mismanagement, the warped priorities, and the inappropriate preoccupation of foresters with timber production.

It is true, of course, that the Forest Service did intensify its timber management programs after World War II. Harvesting, like all other uses of the national forests, increased in the 1950s and 1960s. It was brought into a number of areas that had never been harvested before for reasons that the Forest Service never adequately explained. Problems on Monongahela National Forest were a major expression of the controversy engendered by the accelerated Forest Service timber management programs. When the Forest Service began acquiring lands for national forests in the Appalachian Mountains, they were generally in deplorable condition—deserted farms, denuded, cutover, repeatedly burned, abandoned lands. For about thirty years, there was little or nothing to harvest, and the Forest Service enjoyed the status of heroic conservationists who had returned the trees to the scarred landscape. Harvesting programs consisted primarily of stand improvement cuts. A small experimental clear cut on the Monongahela in 1954 had caused a local outburst of criticism, but the outcry did not adequately warn the Forest Service of what was to come.

By 1964, regeneration throughout the forest justified a more intensive timber management effort, and the plan promulgated in that year declared even age management to be the primary timber management system. This change was too abrupt for concerned local citizens; and the Forest Service was not, in spite of the obvious public concern for aesthetics, prepared to deal with the angry, emotional response to the ugliness of clear cutting (Wessling, 1976). The reaction was not long in coming. by 1965, West Virginia citizens were sufficiently angered to have successfully petitioned their state legislature to intervene. The House of Delegates established a group of resource managers to study clear cutting. Their report was critical of Monongahela management but did not stimulate the desired change in Forest Service practices. Twice more, in 1967 and again in 1970, the increasingly annoyed West Virginians demanded that their representatives take action to halt clear cutting. The 1967 study group consisted, significantly, not of resource managers but of legislators. They concluded bluntly that the Forest Service should "cease and desist" clear cutting on West Virginia national forests. In 1970, the West Virginia Forest Management Practices Committee was established by joint resolution of both houses of the state legislature. It included legislators, citizens, and two professional foresters. Their report included fifteen recommendations, two of which urged that uneven age management and selective cutting practices be employed as the primary silvicultural techniques on the national forests in West Virginia (Fairfax and Achterman, passim).

Obviously, the public pressure required to elicit such repeated response from the state legislature was sustained and intense. West Virginians were aroused by what they viewed as Forest Service mismanagement and insensitivity and created a local storm of such magnitude that it attracted national attention. Everywhere that clear cutting was introduced, the Forest Service became the target of bitter criticism. In the heat of the controversy, everything they said or did was suspect.

Contrary to widespread belief, the Forest Service was not, on the Monongahela or elsewhere, intransigent. At first, however, their response was defensive. In the Pinchot tradition, foresters have a calling as well as a profession. Many believed that they knew what was best for the forests and that they were doing quite well without public interference. They failed to recognize that land management decisions were frequently matters of value or preference rather than technique and that being a forester does not necessarily qualify one to decide what are appropriate goals for public land management. They got into trouble by failing to prepare the public adequately for a change in management regime; and then, under severe and unfamiliar attack in the 1960s, they responded with dismay and hostility.

Belatedly, the agency did respond. Nationally and locally it began to reconsider the priorities of its land management program, giving fuller attention to public perceptions of forest values. The Forest Service admitted error in cases where clear cutting had been improperly employed. On the Monongahela, a new multiple-use plan was drawn up, all the timber sales were withdrawn and redesigned, and clear cuts were limited in size and range (Fairfax and Achterman, passim). The agency accepted thirteen of the West Virginia Forest Management Practices Committee's fifteen recommendations, demurring only in the matter of eschewing clear cutting as a management option.

Unfortunately, by the time the Forest Service and the profession began to admit and correct mistakes and explain their practices more adequately and sensitively, clear cutting had become a national issue and the national mood was such that the critics refused to be mollified. The conflict which began in the early 1950s in West Virginia towns and valleys became a major national issue in the early 1970s. Attention shifted to the Bitterroot National Forest in Montana, where the Forest Service clear cut and then terraced the exposed hillsides to improve regeneration. Criticism of the practice led Montana Senator Gale McGee to ask the University of Montana School of Forestry to investigate. The findings from the investigation were published as a Senate document and widely discussed in the popular press. *A University View of the Forest Service,* renamed the "Bolle Report" for dean of the Montana School of Forestry Arnold Bolle, was intensely critical of agency management goals and assumptions. However, the committee's criticisms were directed less at specific harvest techniques than at the expenditure of public funds to regenerate stands on sites where the investment in a new crop of trees was so high that it could not be recovered from the sale of the trees. As was noted in Chapter 2, the commitment to growing trees on every acre can only be justified under the circumstances which prevailed in eighteenth-century German resource management: land scarcity and abundant labor and capital. The Montana group argued forcefully that even timber mining, harvesting trees without any intention of replanting them, was preferable, under American conditions of land abundance and labor and capital scarcity, to incurring unreasonable, unrecoverable regeneration costs.

Journalists and the general public misinterpreted the committee's reference to "timber mining" and read the report as a searing indictment of the Forest Service's timber management and clear-cutting practices. The opportunity to discuss the broader issues was lost in the renewed attack on clear cutting (Popovitch, 793). Six months before the Bolle report was issued, a Forest Service analysis of Bitterroot management specifically discussing the silvicultural systems employed was published. Although it was every bit as critical as the Bolle report, it was ignored by the press and the public. The Forest Service was somewhat dismayed by the fact that outsiders were "pointing with alarm" to problems already recognized by agency analysts. It is not, however, surprising that the public was suspicious of even critical self-evaluation: Admissions of error and action plans to improve practices were not acceptable to the angry activists, who wanted clear cutting, if not timber harvesting, banned altogether.

Enterprising politicians introduced legislation to halt clear cutting pending further studies. Senator Church of Idaho began an extensive Senate investigation of clear-cutting practices on the national forests. Experts from many disciplines testified lengthily and disagreed intensely, and angry citizens decried the Forest Service management. The Forest Service explained and defended its activities. Three volumes of published hearings were amassed in April, May, and June of 1972. In the end, the subcommittee recommended no legislation, issuing instead nonbinding recommendations known as the "Church Guidelines," urging moderation, care, and environmental protection in clear cutting. These guidelines were accepted by the Forest Service as an agency "action plan." The Forest Service's discretion to select silvicultural techniques was not severely restricted, and the congressional guidelines could be used to defend its practices. The matter did not rest there, however. Litigation which brought the clear cutting fight to an uneasy truce will be discussed in Chapter 11.

It could be argued that the clear cutting controversy was a step forward over the recreation-preservation-natural beauty discussion because there was potential for raising important questions. It is also true that the intensity of the public rage engendered by clear cutting forced positive changes in forest management concepts and practices. However, the technical aspects of clear cutting are so complex that it was not an effective focus for meaningful debate on land management goals.

Three things are obvious about clear cutting: It is ugly; it is a commercial harvest method; and it has a sudden impact on the environment. It was possible to "demonstrate" that the Forest Service had sold out to industry simply by printing a picture of a recent, ugly clear cut. The line of attack was clear and effective. What made the debate unfortunate was that the line of defense is complex and controversial. The factors to be weighed in selecting a harvesting regime vary with the region, the species, the slope and elevation, the soil type, the incidence of insects and disease, the exposure of the site, and a host of other factors that are difficult to follow and do not fit well into a punchy *New York Times* editorial. Irrespective of the merits of their case, the technicians' discussions, couched in the language and cadence of science, were no match for a picture and the obvious assertion that it was ugly.

Much of the rage and hyperbole that characterized the clear cutting controversy was probably inevitable, given the volatile mood of the country during the period. However, the effort that went into the confrontation was in an important sense misallocated. The public attempted to debate a complicated question of technique and failed to address the antecedent issues of land management priorities: The effort was misplaced because although the technical training is of marginal relevance to setting priorities for public land management, it is essential to understanding the complexities and ramifications of alternative harvesting regimes. Public attention was aroused to a fever pitch over issues that are probably best resolved by the experts while the bedrock issues in which public values and preference are the critical factor of decision making were essentially untouched.

THE PUBLIC DOMAIN LANDS CONTINUE TO BE IGNORED

The preoccupations of the 1960s are well expressed in the clear cutting episode. It was the aesthetics of the matter rather than the resource management priorities which aroused concern and interest. This same misallocation of effort is manifest in the enduring obscurity of the Bureau of Land Management. In spite of all the public outcry and congressional attention to parks and wilderness, the management of public domain lands continued to be underfunded and essentially unattended to. Although the BLM made some progress, to be discussed below, the best index of the stature of the BLM during this period is probably to be found in the Wilderness Act. The act omitted the public domain lands and did not mention the Bureau. This was not the result of special pleadings or policy but simply an oversight. Four hundred sixty-five million acres of public domain lands were simply forgotten.

This inattention to BLM matters is surprising given the dollar value of the resources involved. Its programs vastly exceed the Forest Service in terms of revenues returned to the Federal Treasury. BLM manages the highly productive O & C timberlands and administers the mineral leasing programs on all public lands and the Outer Continental Shelf. In the case of the O & C lands, BLM returns large amounts to the counties as well. BLM's apparent invisibility and the lack of public concern for the public domain lands was, and continues to be, a serious problem for the Bureau. It is also, however, a rather telling comment on forest and range land policy in the 1960s. General problems of land management or resource allocation received very little attention. The issues were defined largely by vocal and well-organized preservation and recreation groups. Congressional interest in the public lands consisted, with very few exceptions, of meeting the new groups' vociferous demands.

The failure of Congress and the public to deal with BLM-related issues is especially troublesome because by the 1960s the agency was beginning to recover from the Grazing Service debacle. In spite of the BLM's orphan status, a hardy band of professionals was attracted to the agency by the magnitude of its tasks and the responsibilities and opportunities which they presented. These dedicated souls were willing to endure low pay, low prestige, and public indifference or outright hostility in order to live on and manage the public lands of the arid West. After the war, a pool of professionally trained range managers began to develop. The number of universities offering range management programs jumped, and the programs themselves were strengthened. In 1948, the Society for Range Management was formed and began publishing a journal. All the professional developments which proved so important to foresters and forestry for a half a century *began* for range managers in the late 1940s. By the 1960s, there was a strong core of competent professionals moving up in the BLM ranks. They continued to be beset by political and financial problems. The Bureau continued to suffer from deadwood accumulated during the Depression and to show signs of the chasm that never healed after the outrageous marriage of the Grazing Service and the General Land Office. Its responsibilities were enormous while its statutory authorities were uncertain and inadequate. However, by the early 1960s, the bureau was trying to assert itself as a land management agency.

In 1960, the first of many BLM attempts to gain management authority was presented to Congress. Forest Service success in procuring the Multiple Use Act emboldened the Bureau to submit a similar piece of legislation. Hearings were never even held. Similarly imitating both the Park Service and the Forest Service, the BLM launched a comprehensive management program for the public domain lands called "Project 2012." The year 2012 will be the two hundredth anniversary of the founding of the GLO and the proposal was a fifty-two-year program for achieving multiple-use land management. The brochure is handsome, the proposals vague—a perfect copy of Mission '66,

Operation Outdoors, and Operation Multiple Use—and nothing was accomplished. Its existence does indicate, however, that the bureau was on its feet, ambitious, and attempting to become a land managing rather than a temporary land holding and disposal agency.

Although BLM efforts went almost totally unnoticed, in 1964, the agency benefited from a windfall related to Wayne Aspinall's machinations regarding the Public Land Law Review Commission (PLLRC). The Classification and Multiple Use Act and the Public Land Sale Act passed as companion measures to the PLLRC authorizing statute. Pending the PLLRC report, the two acts gave BLM temporary authority to classify and dispose of public lands under prescribed circumstances.

The PLLRC report was, as shall be discussed below in detail, less successful than the ORRRC. The most constructive result of the commission's efforts may have been that it occasioned the other two measures. The new authorities only lasted until the PLLRC made its report, but they started BLM on some important new paths.

The Public Land Sale Act gave the government interim authority to sell lands classified for disposal if they were required for the growth of a community or for residential, agricultural, or commercial purposes. For the first time, this allowed BLM to sell land for fair market value and to engage in normal real estate transactions, albeit on a restricted basis.

More important, the Classification and Multiple Use Act granted the BLM authority to classify the public lands for either disposition or retention. The bill directed the Secretary of the Interior to develop criteria to be used in deciding which lands should be retained and which disposed of and also authority to study the land in the light of the criteria and decide which should be maintained in federal ownership. This statute was the *first* authorization the BLM ever received to inventory or gather information about the land and other resources under its jurisdiction. It was also an initial indication that some of the BLM lands might be retained. The authority to classify lands for retention expired six months after the PLLRC issued its report. In spite of the tenuous legal status of its position, BLM relied on classifications made under the act to prevent further alienation of the public domain and establish land evaluation and planning. Thus although the authorities granted in the act nominally expired in 1971, its provisions continued to be critical until the Congress again turned to the question of public domain management in 1976.

THE PUBLIC LAND LAW REVIEW COMMISSION

The Classification and Multiple Use Act, even with the sustained stretching and broad interpretation BLM employed in reading it, did not remedy the crazy quilt of 3500 statutes defining public land management. The Public Land Law Review Commission was established by Congress to review federal policies, laws, and regulations pertaining to the public lands and to recommend appropriate revisions. The PLLRC constitutes the only major effort of the 1960s to rethink and clarify land management priorities. Unfortunately, the report did not have the influence of the earlier ORRRC recommendations. There are a number of reasons for this difference, but it is at least partially due to the origin and nature of the inquiry. The PLLRC was authorized in 1964 as part of a package deal arranged with the powerful House Interior and Insular Affairs Committee Chairman Wayne Aspinall. The two BLM oriented measures mentioned above were part of the negotiations, but the major hostage was the Wilderness Act. Aspinall allowed a wilderness bill through his committee on the condition that a land law review be undertaken.

Many early versions of the wilderness bill contain provisions for "Land Use Commissions" clearly designed to meet Aspinall's requirements. The final PLLRC bill was separate from the Wilderness Act. It established a federal commission composed predominantly of members of Congress to study laws and policies pertaining to all public lands except Indian reservations. The commission was authorized to hire a staff to conduct the necessary investigations and ultimately spent over $4.5 million on the project. Aspinall was, in a surprise to none, elected chairman.

Problems with the PLLRC

The PLLRC, because of its origins, was in trouble before it began. The studies were conducted and the hearings held with the traditional hoopla of a blue ribbon investigation, but there was no public support of or interest in the effort. Unlike the ORRRC, which was the response to a huge outcry of public demand, the PLLRC was purely Aspinall's idea. He could assure that it would be established and funded, but he could not make the public pay attention. There was, as has been repeatedly noted, no general interest in the public lands. Moreover, the origins of the PLLRC alienated the citizens groups potentially supportive of a rethinking in public lands matters, while the traditional commodity users were concerned to maintain the status quo.

The conduct and the focus of the PLLRC's investigations were not conducive to building extensive citizen support for the commission's recommendations. Public land law was a morass and studying it was a lawyer's game. Few citizens groups were involved or consulted. Those knowledgeable enough to participate were largely from industry. All of these factors preordained that the PLLRC was not going to be a "popular" success like the ORRRC had been. Finally, the commission's report reflects the biases of the chairman to the extent that they engendered hostility from the start.

PLLRC Recommendations

The commission made 137 specific recommendations which were widely circulated in an attractive book and which can be discussed in terms of four dominant themes. First and most characteristic, the report emphasizes the need for Congress to reestablish and assert its constitutional authority for management of the public lands. All of the report's recommendations evince this basic premise, but it is especially apparent in the lengthy discussion of withdrawals and reservations. According to the commission, the executive and the administrative agencies had exercised far too much discretion in withdrawing and reserving public lands without sufficient criteria or time frame. The commission recommended that Congress define clear standards, review their application frequently, and exercise final authority over large-scale or long-term segregations.

Second, the report is disposition oriented. The PLLRC concluded that all federal lands not specifically set aside by Congress for a particular use were eligible for disposition. Wilderness areas, national parks, national trails, and wild and scenic rivers would be protected since they were congressionally established; but national forests, national monuments, and all BLM administered lands were available for disposition in the commission's view. All executive reservations or classifications ought to be reviewed by Congress to see which lands should be retained for federal management and which should pass into state or private control. This recommendation shocked citizens, many of whom did not know that federal lands *could* be disposed of, let alone that it was being contemplated. Even those aware that disposition was an issue were amazed to see the national forests and monuments subject to review. In addition to this inclusive view of potential disposition, the commission appeared to favor disposition over retention wherever justifiable. These themes alarmed more than they pleased.

A third major motif of the report was its orientation toward commodity users. Although the commissioners recommended that environmental protection should be one of the "uses" for which the public lands should be managed, (PLLRC Report, 68), the commission emphasized commodity use and, in fact, considered all uses to be commodities (PLLRC Report, xi). Regarding forest management, the commission adopted a position long endorsed by industry, that timber production should be financed by appropriations from a fund generated by receipts from timber sales. The report simultaneously called for the end of "back-door financing," such as Knutson-Vandenberg reforestation work, that is funded directly from sales receipts rather than through the congressional appropriations process.

The report treats different commodities quite dissimilarly. Timber management decisions should be made "primarily on the basis of economic factors so as to maximize net returns to the federal treasury, but grazing permittees should not have to pay for market value. Forage policies are to be "flexible, designed to attain economic efficiency" and to support regional economic growth (PLLRC Report, 106). The commission in fact recommended the adoption of almost every provision contained in the livestock industry backed bills introduced in the early 1950s. Moreover, the PLLRC recommended that limits on the number of animals per allotment be replaced with a stipulation that the permittee maintain the range in a specified condition. Regarding mineral development, the commission asserted that "mineral exploration and development should have a preference over some or all other uses on much of our public lands" (PLLRC Report, 122).

This strong emphasis on the commodity production aspects of public land management was exacerbated by the commission's firm commitment to the concept of dominant use. This is particularly evident in the timber resources section, where the commission recommends that "there should be a statutory requirement that those public lands that are highly productive for timber be classified for commercial timber production as the dominant use . . ." (PLLRC Report, 92). Dominant use was embraced as an alternative to the ambiguities of multiple-use management and as a means of stating a clear commitment to timber production. The commisson's view was that public lands should be zoned for the particular use to which they are best suited. Since we have allotted areas to livestock, wilderness, and other recreation purposes, we ought to zone some areas for timber production.

Although there is considerable logic and appeal in the idea that good timber production sites ought to be used for growing timber, many questionable assumptions lie behind the dominant use concept. The first, largely untested as yet, is that production of a chosen commodity can be significantly expanded by more intensive management in defined areas. Implicit in such an assumption are the ideas that intensively managing an area for commodity A necessarily precludes intensively managing the area to produce B, and that intensifying the management of B will reduce the production of A. The dominant use concept also implies a clear ecological distinction between timberland and land that is more suitable for other uses, and that the distinctions occur in large, easy to identify and manage areas. This concept is at odds with reality, in which many values—fish, wildlife habitat, minerals, or cultural resources —frequently appear in close proximity with each other and "high timber value." Understandably, the concept of dominant use is an anathema to many. Even if it were adopted by Congress, however, it is also not a promising route to achieving the PLLRC's goal of limiting executive agency discretion in land use allocations.

The final problem with the PLLRC's recommendations was that they were internally incompatible. Many of the specific suggestions conflict with each other or with the basic goals which the report espouses. For example, the commission advocated flexibility for the agencies establishing grazing fees so as to reflect the quality of the local range and the need for economic development in the area. This conflicts with the commission's desire to have Congress assert strict control over the details of public land management.

Response to the PLLRC

The PLLRC report received the traditional attention when it appeared in 1970: press conferences, many reviews, discussions, and speaking engagements for the principals. Along with the perfunctory expressions of gratitude for a job well done, there was a brief cry of horror from most conservationists and preservationists, and then silence. It was unnecessary to criticize the report or to elaborate its themes because the recommendations were being ignored by almost everyone. The commission's discussions of disposition and commodity utilization were sorely out of tune with the times. Its bland generalizations about environmental quality were a thin veneer over recommendations that were unacceptable to the Congress, which Aspinall insisted should impose clear direction on public land management. By 1970, Congress was devoted to making environmental noises. As President Nixon signed the National Environmental Policy Act (NEPA) in January, 1970, he heralded the inception of the "environmental decade." That was perhaps hyperbole, but the political climate that produced NEPA preordained that the PLLRC Report would play to an empty theater. Its recommendations were not even shouted down—they were simply ignored. Some of the basic generalizations found in the Report are also seen in some subsequent legislation, but the connections are not at all clear. In 1972, a young attorney running on an environmental platform defeated Wayne Aspinall in a primary campaign. Although the victor was himself beaten in the general election in November, Aspinall's defeat signaled the end of an era and the rise to power of new values in public land management.

THE ENVIRONMENTAL MOVEMENT

The PLLRC report was stillborn because its recommendations were inconsistent with the growing environmental movement. As expressed in such media events as Earth Day in 1970, the movement was an important elaboration of the back-to-nature impulses reflected in the early 1960s wild lands policy. It reflects a recognition that wilderness and the national parks are a small and relatively insignificant aspect of the natural world. For the millions of people who had never backpacked and never would, environmental degradation reached them in air and water pollution, chemical toxicants, unplanned urban sprawl, and exponential population growth.

Although many conservationists and preservationists share the concerns of the environmentalists and are also active in the environmental movement, the focus of this most recent wave of public alarm differs importantly from previous orientations. As the name implies, the environmental movement is less concerned with use or nonuse of specific areas or commodities—timber, wildlife, scenic wonders—than it is with the overall quality and support capacity of the earth's natural systems. Air and water quality, population growth, agricultural land conversion, and reduction of the gene pool characterize the issue orientation of the environmentalists. This can be distinguished from previous efforts, which were largely, though not exclusively, focused on federal programs involving specific commodities or the use of specific parcels of federal land for specific purposes. The environmentalists' concerns had a clearly urban-industrial focus which is reflected in many of the environmental statutes that passed in the ensuing years. The concern for environmental quality had its most obvious early impact on forest and range managers in public hostility to clear cutting.

A less clear but equally important impact of the environmental activism of the late 1960s was a growing impatience with technology, its products and its unintended consequences. Yankee ingenuity, long a touchstone of American progress and national self-image, seemed to many to have gone sour. Detroit's magnificent cars were strangling cities and fouling the air. Miracle laundry products were killing fish, polluting streams, and producing a head of bubbles on drinking water. Convenience foods and throwaways were clogging streets, landfills, and oceans with garbage. Technology was no longer seen as a cornucopia of consumer goods. Progress itself was suspect and conquering nature was suddenly absurd. In a neo-Luddite reaction to the trinkets and profound problems of industrialized democracy, many who saw technology as a cause became suspicious of technology as a cure. The authority of science and technique, so long unchallenged in American society, was severely diminished. In this period of "do your own thing," the wisdom of impulse and intuition was valued above the wisdom of training and experience. Forestry, particularly the Forest Service, constitute the apogee of technique and scientific management (Hays, passim). In the environmental movement of the late 1960s, ironically, the very basis of their authority was challenged.

Congressional attitude toward the environmental movement is aptly summarized by the passage of NEPA. This law was intended to be symbolic, a "gesture of Congressional concern" (Liroff, 5) for the environment. There was almost no public or congressional discussion of the proposal: It went from the original idea into law in less than a year. The legislative history of the bill is brief and largely irrelevant to its subsequent impact. The major points of dispute were among presidential aspirants in the Senate, who were striving to enhance their proenvironment profile for the 1972 presidential elections and protect the agencies under their committees' jurisdiction.

The bill that passed Congress in 1969 has three basic components. The first was a statement of policy regarding the environment. This hortatory page and a half recognized "the profound impact of man's activity" on the natural environment and declared the federal government's policy to "promote conditions under which man and nature could exist in productive harmony." The act's second section contained a number of general provisions regarding an analysis of environmental impacts which must accompany all proposals for "major Federal action significantly affecting the quality of the human environment." A Council on Environmental Quality was established in the third major part of the bill. The Council was to be part of the Executive Office of the President and assist the President in evaluating programs and policies of the government in the light of the policy statement in the first section.

These provisions were not controversial and were probably not even read by most legislators as the bill passed in the rush for Christmas adjournment. The broad possibilities for litigation raised by the provision for environmental impact analysis was apparently not recognized even by the bill's sponsors. It was certainly not debated in Congress. For several years, public response to the bill focused almost exclusively on the proposed Council on Environmental Quality, its powers, its staffing, its funding. The environmental impact statement did not become a major factor in environmental planning until several years later, when the movement entered a primarily litigious phase.

SUMMARY

The 1960s began and ended with symbolic gestures. The decade opened with the passage of the Multiple Use Sustained Yield Act, which the Forest Service hoped would give it sufficient authority to contain the controversy surrounding conflicting forest uses. This was not to be. The recreation-preservation interests that rose in the 1950s dominated the decade, and both public and private foresters were unable to defend their wise use conservation philosophy against the amenity oriented interest groups that proliferated during the period. Industry generally suffered heavily from public distrust and hostility, and government agencies faired little better in the general disaffection surrounding the war in Vietnam. Forest managers encountered their professional Waterloo in the clear cutting debacle of the late 1960s.

Congress looked at wild lands issues in terms of parks and preservation of natural beauty for most of the decade. It was a pleasant topic in harsh and trying times, and it was a less difficult approach to resource management than taking up hard issues of economic growth, resource allocation, and productivity. Given the tone of the times and the complex technical questions involved, there was probably no way to focus the discussion effectively on issues such as priority of uses, fiber supply, or management of the public range. Eventually the National Environmental Policy Act proved to be a significant piece of legislation. As such it was sharply in contrast with congressional intent and most congressional efforts of the period.

The clear cutting controversy stands out in a decade of avoided issues because it does contain aspects of broader and more significant questions waiting to be raised. Hidden in the cry simply to "spare the tree" and a far too narrowly focused concentration on the aesthetics of the issue is the possibility of an important discussion of relationship between forest practices and environmental quality. Discussion of these larger issues has been complicated by the residuum of the caricatures which resulted from the emotional intensity of the earlier controversy. However, the broader questions were emerging; and land managers, though shocked and hostile, were also rethinking their assumptions and procedures in significant ways.

REFERENCES CITED

Cate, Donald. *Recreation in the U.S. Forest Service.* Ph.D. dissertation, University of Michigan, 1963.

Fairfax, Sally K., and Achterman, Gail L. "The Monongahela Controversy and the Political Process." 75 *Journal of Forestry* 485 (1977).

Haight, Kevin. "The Wilderness Act: Ten Years After." 3 *Environmental Affairs* 275 (1974).

Hays, Samuel P. *Conservation and the Gospel of Efficiency.* Cambridge, Mass.: Harvard University Press, 1959.

Keane, John. "The Wilderness Act as Congress Intended." 77 *American Forests* 40 (1971).

Lee, Robert. *Family Tree of the National Park Service.* Philadelphia: Eastern National Park and Monument Association, 1972.

Liroff, Richard. *National Policy for the Environment: NEPA and Its Aftermath.* Bloomington: Indiana University Press, 1976.

McCloskey, Michael J. "The Wilderness Act of 1964: Its Background and Meaning." 45 *Oregon Law Review* 289 (1966).

————. "Refinancing The Land and Water Conservation Fund." 55 *Sierra Club Bulletin* 16 (1968).

Popovitch, Luke. 74 "Forestry News: The Bitterroot, Parts I and II." *Journal of Forestry* 39 (1976).

Scott, Doug. "Preservation Through Classification." In S. Fairfax, ed. *Legal Aspects of Wildlands Management.* Ann Arbor, Mich.: Natural Resources Law Monograph No. 1, 1977, pp. 191–200.

U.S. Outdoor Recreation Resources Review Commission. *Report: Recreation in America.* Washington, D.C.: Government Printing Office, 1963.

U.S. Public Land Law Review Commission. *One Third the Nation's Land.* Washington, D.C.: Government Printing Office, 1970.

U.S. Senate. S. Doc. 115. *A University View of the Forest Service.* (Bolle report). 91st Cong. 2d Sess., Washington, D.C.: Government Printing Office, 1970.

U.S. Senate. Hearings before the Subcommittee on Public Lands of the Senate Committee on Insular and Interior Affairs. "Clearcutting Practices on National Timberlands." 92 Cong. 1st Sess., Washington, D.C.: Government Printing Office, 1971.

Weisling, Jack. "Monongahela . . . From the Beginning." 82 *American Forests* 28 (1976).

Chapter 9

Environmental Quality and Forest and Range Policy in the 1970s

The clear cutting controversy which erupted in the 1960s reached its peak in the 1970s, and forest management practices were broadly criticized for adversely affecting the quality of the environment. Environmental quality became a new focus of public concern with the nation's resources. In earlier years, conservationists and preservationists had concentrated on particular wild lands uses of commodities such as timber, water, forage, wildlife, recreation, or wilderness; and they concentrated mainly on publicly owned land. The environmental movement of the 1970s, however, focused attention not on particular uses or lands, but on the general quality of the environment. Old issues, such as air and water pollution, were attacked with new urgency; and new threats, such as the proliferation of carcinogenic or toxic chemicals, the disturbing rate of extinction among plant and animal species, and radioactive wastes, were identified. The environmental movement defined and began to defend numerous values that appeared increasingly threatened, scarce, or impaired.

Just as Congress had responded to public demand for enhanced recreation opportunities and natural beauty in the previous decade, the coherence of environmentalists' goals and the tremendous public outcry that supported them produced striking legislative action. Beginning with the Clean Air Act Amendments of 1970, these laws included the Federal Water Pollution Control Act, the Federal Environmental Pesticide Control Act, and the Endangered Species Act and related special wildlife legislation. The air, water, and pesticide laws were all based on preexisting statutes which were substantially amended, indeed transformed, to meet the requirements of the times. Congress also passed important regulatory legislation in other fields such as noise pollution, drinking water supply, and resource recovery and solid waste control. These acts were not, however, as pertinent to wild lands as was the legislation governing air, water, pesticides, endangered species, and other special categories of wildlife.

Whereas clear cutting critics had attacked forestry professionals directly on the basis of their allegedly destructive practices, the environmental regulations of the 1970s affected management activities on wild lands more obliquely. This indirect relationship arose from the fact that the laws, especially the air and water quality acts, were passed to deal with primarily urban problems. Their provisions were extended to other areas mainly as a result of court suits challenging narrow administrative interpretations of the legislation. Thus, although the new laws have had important implications for forest and range management, these were revealed only gradually and in relatively obscure forums. Hence, professionals in the field were sometimes slow to realize their significance. The new laws also reflected a strong regulatory approach which replaced the discretion of the land manager with specified numerical standards, strict deadlines, and required levels of performance. Land managers in the 1970s were thus caught in an uncomfortable bind caused by a failure to attend to key regulations as they evolved and the reality of having to deal with a new breed of constraints on wild land management practices.

The passage of the major environmental laws was accompanied by two other developments of importance to forest and range policy in the first half of the decade. The first of these was a period of intense government reorganization activity at the federal level. During this time many foresters were preoccupied with the recurrent proposal to transfer the Forest Service to the Interior Department and with plans to amalgamate a variety of federal agencies in a new Department of Environment and Natural Resources. The reorganization activity diverted foresters' attention from the rise and creation of the Environmental Protection Agency (EPA), which was charged with administering the air, water, and pesticide acts. Forest and range professionals were thus initially unfamiliar with EPA and its authorities, although that agency became increasingly relevant to wild land activities as the decade progressed.

Second, the 1970s saw a sharp rise in litigation by increasingly militant and outspoken citizens groups. The appearance of new environmental organizations, the growing aggressiveness of existing conservation groups, and the citizen suit provisions of the major environmental laws all coalesced in the courts in an activist effort which dominated the early 1970s. Citizen efforts became a potent force for redirecting land management activity. While this resort to the judicial forum was spurred by tactics evolving out of the environmental impact statement requirements of the National Environmental Policy Act, it became the means whereby federal environmental regulations were expanded beyond the urban perimeter and made applicable to forest and rangelands. Litigation continues to inject a major element of uncertainty into analyses of the environmental laws' ultimate impacts on wild land management activities and options.

ENVIRONMENTALISM AND NEPA

As discussed briefly in the preceding chapter, Congress mandated consideration of the environmental impacts of major federal activities, through the requirements of the National Environmental Policy Act of 1969. In the ensuing years, NEPA came to be considered the cornerstone, or at least an important point of departure, for the environmental movement's participation in governmental decision making. Significantly, and unexpectedly, environmental litigation became a major avenue whereby that participation was expressed. Although some commentators have questioned the effectiveness of NEPA as an environmental protection mandate, the statute is generally accepted as a pivotal development in the history of the environmental movement (Anderson, vii).

Perhaps because much of the initial focus of public attention regarding NEPA was directed at the newly formed Council of Environmental Quality, that body was successful in promulgating detailed guidelines for the development of environmental impact statements (EISs) required by the act. Featured in these guidelines was a strong commitment to public review of EISs and to public participation in the EIS development process. Although public involvement was not a NEPA innovation, NEPA may be associated with intensifying and institutionalizing the public involvement process. Furthermore, so-called "sunshine provisions," opening government operations to the light of public scrutiny, were written into each of the succeeding pieces of environmental legislation passed in the 1970s. Accordingly, resource management agencies were further forced to reexamine the role of the public in natural resource decision making.

The Council of Environmental Quality guidelines were also important in that they gave rise to a dramatic increase in environmental litigation surrounding NEPA. The amount of litigation surrounding NEPA has been enormous. This litigation has been directed largely at agency procedures in filing EISs and the adequacy their contents.

Although litigation under NEPA originally focused on large development projects such as dams and highways, it rapidly expanded to include routine land management activities such as timber harvesting plans and grazing allotment practices. Agencies such as the Forest Service, required by other statutes to account for environmental and multiple-use values, generally considered themselves already in compliance with NEPA. Considering the resource agencies' self-image as defenders of the natural world, their reaction was perhaps understandable, certainly predictable. However, many environmentalists considered such a posture smug and reacted to it aggressively.

Citizen activity in the courts and the courts' concentration on EIS procedural requirements entailed particular consequences for the form of NEPA as a tool for environmental and resource management reform. One consequence was that the development of the environmental impact statement has become almost entirely separated from the activity which the statement is meant to address. Court orders have simply required improvement in an existing environmental impact statement rather than a substantive change in the activity that the statement described. Accordingly, while the progress of environmental litigation surrounding NEPA has been a conspicuous development in the 1970s, court-imposed requirements have not always altered individual forest and range management practices on the ground. In this respect, NEPA seems to have had a less important long-range operational impact than have the other major environmental laws passed in the 1970s.

FEDERAL REORGANIZATION

Almost every new administration tries its hand at reorganizing the federal government to bring it in line with executive leadership and the public desires of the times. The reorganization efforts culminating in 1970 were no exception to this general rule. Reorganization was almost inevitable in view of the widespread call for greater federal attention to environmental issues, the fragmented nature of the various federal environmental regulatory agencies, and the ascendance of an administration that held high the values of efficient managerial skill and executive agency responsiveness.

The President's Advisory Council on Executive Reorganization, better known as the Ash Council after its chairman Roy Ash, was appointed in 1969. The council considered three major alternatives for federal reorganization of natural resources and environmental-related agencies. One alternative involved the creation of a Department of Environment and Natural Resources (DENR) that would include the existing Department of Interior; the water-planning functions of the Corps of Engineers; the Rural Electrification Administration; the Soil Conservation Service; the Forest Service from the Department of Agriculture; the oceanic and atmospheric agencies of the government; and the environmental monitoring, research, standard-setting, and enforcement functions of the various federal pollution abatement programs. A second option was the creation of a Department of Natural Resources (DNR) which would have encompassed all of the preceding agencies and functions except those pertaining to pollution abatement.

The Ash Council also considered a third alternative, that of creating an independent EPA to encompass the pollution monitoring, research, standard-setting, and enforcement activities. Specifically, EPA was to include the Federal Water Quality Administration from Interior, the National Air Pollution Control Administration from the Department of Health, Education and Welfare (HEW), the Environmental Control Administration from HEW, the Pesticide Registration Program from the Agricultural Research Service of the Department of Agriculture, and elements of the radiation protection standards function from the Atomic Energy Commission.

The lobbying and jockeying between existing federal agencies concerning these alternatives was familiar to those who recalled Harold Ickes's maneuverings thirty-five years prior (see Chapter 3). Secretary of Agriculture Clifford Hardin objected to the removal of the Soil Conservation Service and the Forest Service from the Department of Agriculture. Secretary of Interior Walter Hickel strongly favored the larger Department of Environment and Natural Resources alternative built, of course, around the existing Department of Interior. It was also suggestive of subsequent debates over President Carter's proposed reorganization. In 1978, President Carter started slowly in natural resources reorganization by returning to the Park Service most of the recreation site-evaluation functions administered by the Bureau of Outdoor Recreation. BOR, renamed Heritage Conservation and Recreation Service, has floundered since the reorganization, attempting to identify a new mission. Carter's 1979 proposals for reorganization were much more comprehensive, resembling the Nixon package in many respects. Carter's effort like Nixion's, floundered and the Forest Service remained in the Department of Agriculture. Unlike Carter, however, Nixon had a fall-back position of tremendous consequences.

The rejection of Nixon's DENR option was at least partly caused by conflict between the President and Interior Secretary Hickel. It is likely, too, that he wanted to avoid upsetting the farm vote by moving a good deal of the Department of Agriculture into a DENR. Once the DENR proposal was rejected, the alternative of creating an EPA was pressed more strongly. This support also resulted from the rather fragmented nature of federal pollution control efforts at that time: Forty-four such agencies located in nine separate departments suggested the need for better coordination of pollution control within the federal government (Whitaker, chap. 3).

The EPA reorganization plan was submitted to Congress in July, 1970. Congress lodged no strong objection, and the new agency came into being on

December 2, 1970. What was not immediately obvious was that a major new actor in forest and range policy had been born. This critical development had taken place, however, with little consultation or attention from forest and range managers. Land managers had been preoccupied with the implications of reorganization for the Forest Service and other land managing agencies. At the time, there was little apparent reason for them to be concerned with EPA. Moreover, they were not, in general, sensitive or receptive to the new environmental values of the time, which demanded a new structural arrangement for environmental protection at the federal level.

At about the same time that EPA was founded, the various oceanic and atmospheric agencies in the government were also reorganized and consolidated into the National Oceanic and Atmospheric Administration (NOAA). NOAA had little if any direct effect on natural resource land managers until the passage of the Coastal Zone Management Act of 1972 (see Chapter 10). Reorganization by itself, therefore, did not become significant or the dimensions of its impact on land management revealed until the various pieces of federal environmental legislation passed in the 1970s.

ENVIRONMENTAL LEGISLATION OF THE 1970S

Certainly a notable achievement of Congress in the early 1970s was the passage of a series of major environmental acts designed to protect the quality of air and water, regulate the use and abuse of pesticides, and preserve threatened and endangered plant and animal species and their habitat. In most cases, the ramifications of these laws for natural resource management were not at all obvious at the time of passage. Furthermore, as emphasized above, the acts represented an entirely new regulatory approach to wild land management activities. Rather suddenly, land managers were forced to reassess road construction procedures which increased sediment loads and caused water quality problems, slash and prescribed burning practices which could degrade air quality in otherwise unpolluted areas, the use of pesticides which were toxic to nontarget fish and wildlife, and a wide variety of other traditionally unchallenged tools of the land manager. Although they have other important dimensions, the air and water quality, pesticide, and endangered species and related wildlife statutes are reviewed below primarily in light of their relevance to forest and range management and policy and their significance for the interaction between forest and range managers and the society at large.

Air Pollution Control: The Clean Air Acts of 1970 and 1977

On December 31, 1970, President Nixon signed the Clean Air Act Amendments of 1970. The legislation totally recast federal air quality programs first established in 1955. It was, perhaps, the starting gun for a general movement by Congress to strengthen environmental quality laws in terms of regulation and enforcement rather than simply research and development. The Clean Air Act required EPA to set national primary and secondary air quality standards. The former were set to protect public health and have to be met by certain deadlines, while the latter only after the primary standards had been attained. EPA was also given the power to review and approve state implementation plans that would assure compliance with these standards.

Initially, EPA's top priority in the air pollution field was to control emissions from automobiles and from individual "point," industrial sources. However, as a consequence of the EPA's authority to set national air quality standards, many states have adopted regulations controlling open burning in wild land areas. Those regulations bear directly on timber harvest and slash burning activities.

For forest and range management, the most important impact of the 1970 clean air legislation occurred through an interpretation of language in the act pertaining to the "prevention of significant deterioration" of air quality. This interpretation was forced upon EPA by litigation under the citizen suit provisions of the act. On May 30, 1972, the Sierra Club sued EPA and obtained a court ruling that the agency could not approve any state implementation plan that permitted, in clean rural areas, air quality degradation exceeding the national standards (*Sierra Club* v. *Ruckelshaus,* 344 F. Supp 253 [D.D.C. 1972]). In response to the court order, EPA issued regulations establishing three categories of clean air regions: Class I areas could tolerate no change in air quality and had to be retained as pristine; class II areas would be permitted to undergo a moderate degree of air quality deterioration; and class III areas would be allowed to absorb new development to a point which equaled but did not exceed the secondary national standards. The Secretary of the Interior was given the responsibility of identifying those areas appropriate for class I designation (Proctor, 64).

When amendments to the 1970 Clean Air Act passed in 1977, one of their outstanding provisions was the reaffirmation and strengthening of the prevention of significant deterioration (PSD) concept. Congress not only retained the designation of the classes prescribed in the EPA regulations, but also went a step further in mandating that all international parks and all wilderness areas, national memorials, and national parks larger than 5000 acres be automatically classified as class I areas. All other areas were classified initially as class II. The states retained their right to reclassify any such areas as class I. Federal land managers through the Department of the Interior could recommend to Congress that certain federal lands be reclassified as from class II to class I, but only after first consulting with the states. In addition, the new amendments authorized the Secretary of the Interior to identify certain class I sites as "scenic visibility" areas warranting additional protection for aesthetic purposes. Many wild lands areas, including parts of national forests and wilderness areas, fall into this category.

Despite the broad potential impact of the nondeterioration requirement on rural land use, EPA's major emphasis has been on regulating point sources of industrial air pollution. Forest products manufacturing facilities rather than forest and range management activities were the initial focus of attention. However, the potential impact of the nondeterioration provisions on management activities is substantial. For example, "fugitive dust" arising from woods roads or cultivated areas may be regulated under the definition of "major emitting facility" in section 169 *(l)* of the 1977 Clean Air Act. This would require imposition of corrective practices to remedy the air quality problem in class I areas. Moreover, the overlay of mandatory class I designation with the 1964 Wilderness Act and the 1973 Eastern Wilderness Act provides an interesting illustration of environmental quality and land management legislation working synergistically to control land use. The implications of wilderness areas' status as class I air quality areas, with the attendant potential for regulation of land use in the region surrounding the wilderness, has become an important consideration in wilderness legislation.

Water Pollution Control: The Federal Water Pollution Control Act of 1972 and the 1977 Clean Water Act

By far the most important piece of environmental legislation of the 1970s in regard to its impact on forest and range management is the Federal Water Pollution Control Act of 1972 (FWPCA). In spite of this significance, the act was passed with little input from, or understanding by, professional resource managers. Again, this situation arose largely from Congress's apparent emphasis on industrial water pollution in urban areas, municipal sewage, and oil spills in the marine environment. The statute, in fact, requires the governor of each state to identify water pollution problem areas in the state for which special planning is required. Paralleling the developments under the Clean Air Act, the broad applicability of FWPCA for wild lands was not revealed until citizen action in the courts forced EPA attention beyond industrial enclaves and metropolitan limits.

FWPCA is one of the most complicated measures ever passed by Congress. Structurally, FWPCA is similar to the air legislation and requires a series of actions by federal, state, and local governments and the private sector, under tight and relatively inflexible deadlines. States are assigned primary responsibility for water pollution control and enforcement. However, EPA is the administering agency and the states function within the framework of a national program guided by national water quality standards and goals. The two broad goals established by the act were the elimination of discharges into navigable waters by 1985 and the interim attainment of fishable and swimmable waters wherever possible by 1983.

Point versus Nonpoint   Critical to the basic structure of FWPCA, to the types of control strategies which the act requires, and to the particular way in which the act has affected forest and range management is the distinction between point and nonpoint sources of water pollution. Point sources are clearly defined by the act and are, essentially, "discernible, confined and discrete" individual sources of polluting discharges of various types. The control of point sources is described under section 402 of the act and involves a complicated "National Pollution Discharge Elimination System (NPDES)" regulating discharging facilities by strict permit requirements. EPA, in its early enforcement efforts, concentrated on addressing point sources of pollution under section 402 and paid little attention to the control problems associated with the nonpoint category.

Control of nonpoint sources falls under section 208 of the act and was to be addressed by unspecified methods and "to the extent feasible" in areawide waste management plans to be prepared by designated regions within each state. However, while nonpoint sources presumably included important aspects of wild land management activity, they were never defined in the act. This situation posed problems for EPA, the states, and land managers alike.

Section 402 Exemptions   EPA's initial effort to address forestry and agricultural sources occurred in December, 1972, when the agency proposed to designate such sources as point sources and thus as requiring a permit. This determination served mainly to illustrate EPA's lack of appreciation of the nature of land management and was a first indication to the forestry and range communities that their activities might be severely impacted by FWPCA implementation. In response to objections from land managers and to indications evident in the legislative history of the act, EPA withdrew its 1972 proposal. In so doing, however, the agency did not then designate forestry and agricultural sources as nonpoint. Instead, EPA continued to consider such sources as point but decided to exempt them from the permit requirements of section 402.

This discretionary action offered an obvious target for environmentalists under the citizen suit provisions of the Water Pollution Control Act. The Natural Resources Defense Council (NRDC), a citizens' litigating organization established in 1970, took EPA to court and challenged the point source exemption. In March 1975, the court ruled in favor of NRDC (*NRDC* v. *Train,* No. 1629–73, D.D.C., 1975) and required EPA to promulgate new regulations to control the activities which the agency had previously exempted from the 402 permit requirements. Accordingly, in June 1976, EPA published final regulations which recognized most water pollution from forest and range management as nonpoint sources. Four "silvicultural" activities—rock crushing, gravel washing, log sorting, and storage facilities—were classified as point sources. EPA did not define nonpoint pollution, but it provided a list of silvicultural activities which it considered to be nonpoint sources. EPA is, however, still authorized to review the point-nonpoint categorization of any specific activity and the administrator's decision is reviewable in court. Thus, although the 1976 regulations were satisfactory to most land managers in terms of the flexibility they provide, the matter cannot be considered fully resolved.

Nonpoint Source Control Under Section 208   The litigation and rule making surrounding the distinction between point and nonpoint sources of pollution excluded most silvicultural and rangeland sources from FWPCA permit requirements. Seeking more appropriate ways to address wild land, nonpoint sources of pollution, EPA began to pay greater attention to section 208 of the legislation. Developments surrounding "208 planning" have revealed fundamental conflicts between traditional land management techniques and federal regulations for water pollution control purposes.

Section 208, the broadest and most far-reaching provision of FWPCA, authorizes the allocation of federal funds to the state for comprehensive, regional planning. Carried out under the close supervision of EPA, the state planning effort must achieve compliance with and coordination of the various provisions embodied in the act. EPA has authority to disapprove any state 208 plan and thereby withhold grant money for sewage works construction purposes. However, the individual states and regions are theoretically free to develop whatever types of control most reasonably yet effectively solves their water quality problems. Consequently, states are authorized to opt for voluntary measures to address wild land pollution problems if EPA and the state agree that such a program is likely to be effective in controlling nonpoint source pollution (Krivak, 1978).

Section 208, as initially interpreted by EPA, emphasized the control of point rather than nonpoint sources and concentrated on the development of pollution control programs for urban rather than rural areas. Once again the NRDC challenged EPA's decision to require 208 planning for metropolitan or water quality "problem areas" only. In June, 1975, the federal district court ordered EPA to promulgate new section 208 regulations requiring the preparation of plans for *all* areas within a state (*NRDC* v. *Train,* No. 74–1485, D.D.C., 1975). As a result, outlying wild land areas were explicitly brought under the aegis of the section 208 planning effort which was just barely getting underway at that time.

Proposed State Forest Practices Act   About a year prior to the decision in the NRDC court suit, EPA turned its attention to devising provisions which it might recommend to the states for controlling nonpoint sources. In November, 1974, EPA proposed a model forest practice act patterned after strict legislation already passed by the Pacific Coast states (see Chapter 10). In short, EPA's suggested act was based on broad policy statements recognizing the importance of timber and forestlands and the necessity of regulating activities undertaken on those lands. Moreover, the provisions were predictably most applicable to West Coast conditions. The response of the forestry profession, particularly the elements of the forest industry operating in states without regulatory practices acts, was singularly vehement in its opposition to the EPA proposal. While EPA was clearly surprised by this reaction, the agency learned quickly that control of the silviculture nonpoint source category had to be based on better coordination with existing governmental units, private groups, and professionals knowledgeable in the forestry field (Train, 22).

EPA's experience with its proposed forest practice act was a sobering one, but it was also the beginning of a long and ultimately successful dialogue between EPA and the forestry community concerning the nature of control programs for silvicultural nonpoint source pollution under section 208. It is interesting to speculate, in passing, that the heart of the nonpoint source control conflict did not lie in the extent to which forest managers should be held accountable for the water quality implications of their activities. Rather, much of the conflict was created by the interface between distinct professional groups, each interpreting its responsibilities according to its professional backgrounds and biases.

EPA, at that time, was largely dominated by lawyers and civil engineers. Water pollution control agencies have been oriented toward point source permit programs with specific and clearly defined means of both ascertaining compliance with the law and measuring the success of program implementation. Forestry professionals, on the other hand, found EPA's regulatory and permit-issuing posture in regard to section 208 unsatisfactory. This situation was probably less attributable to factors relating to the water quality impacts of silvicultural activities than to EPA's advocacy of strict regulatory programs. The history of cooperative forestry, in contrast, had stressed voluntary and cooperative compliance with the goals of better forest management. Foresters had, furthermore, grown accustomed to thinking that good forest management also entailed as a by-product acceptable levels of water quality.

The vituperative interchange surrounding the model state forest practice act was followed by a period of getting acquainted between EPA and the forestry community. This developing spirit of cooperation was manifested in several forms, perhaps the most significant of which was a series of workshops held across the country by the American Forestry Association in cooperation with EPA and the Forest Service. Among a number of important points which emerged from the workshops, the AFA final report emphasized the fundamental conclusion that regulation of forestry activities on private lands to achieve water quality goals must be compatible with measures to achieve improved timber production goals of landowners (American Forestry Association, passim). A further sign of EPA's growing recognition of its need for information and advice originating from the forestry community was the fact that it contracted with the Forest Service to help produce certain nonpoint source control guidelines which it was then in the process of reformulating. This growing dialogue between EPA and land managers was important in shaping the character of the new section 208 regulations which the court required EPA to issue by June 5, 1975.

Best Management Practices   The salient feature of the new regulations was their endorsement of the concept of "best management practices" (BMPs) as an appropriate tool for nonpoint source control. EPA defined BMPs as "a practice, or combination of practices, that are determined by a state, or designated areawide planning agency, after problem assessment, examination of alternative practices, and appropriate public participation, to be the most effective, practicable (including technological, economic and institutional considerations) means of preventing or reducing the amount of pollution generated by nonpoint sources to a level compatible with water quality goals." Furthermore, according to guidelines issued by EPA in mid-1977, the agency determined that it would accept, for the purposes of compliance with section 208, voluntary nonpoint source control programs if, in the view of the regional administrators, such programs were adequate to achieve desired water quality goals.

This hard-won compromise has not, however, resolved matters. EPA accepted the voluntary BMPs concept but may press for regulatory programs to control certain wild land water quality problem areas. Furthermore, EPA has not determined the relevance of numerical criteria and standards of water quality to nonpoint sources of pollution. If the agency judges the efficacy of BMPs according to specific numerical water quality rather than broader water quality goals, land management activities could be severely restricted. This is because a numerical standard has not yet been developed which can account for the importance of background sediment, the variability of levels of discharge, the vagaries of climatic events, and the differences in individual site characteristics, all of which influence how nonpoint sources affect water quality. The constraints generated by reliance on inflexible water quality criteria would, in addition, be exacerbated by the adoption of an inflexible statewide antidegradation policy which EPA has yet to define but which the new 208 regulations nonetheless require the states to develop and implement (Miskovsky and Van Hook, passim).

The actual impacts of 208 nonpoint source control on forests and rangelands are determined at local and regional levels as the states continue their comprehensive planning processes. Still, EPA retains authority to issue control guidelines and to disapprove any 208 plans which are judged to be inadequate. Accordingly, reasonable 208 control programs can only be achieved through continued and sincere interaction of forestry professionals with EPA and in the section 208 planning process at the state and local levels. Fortunately, the outlook for developing workable section 208 programs based on full involvement of forest and range managers is good. As will be discussed below, Congress ratified EPA's approach to section 208 planning and controlling nonpoint source pollution during congressional consideration of the Clean Water Act of 1977.

Section 404 and Regulation of Dredge and Fill Activities in Navigable Waters and Wetland Areas   Perhaps the most striking controversy surrounding forestry activities to evolve from the Federal Water Pollution Control Act of 1972 has been the regulation of certain forestry activities—primarily drainage ditches for lowland forested tracts, forest and logging road construction in areas defined as wetlands, and stream crossings—by the U.S. Army Corps of Engineers through a permit program administered under section 404 of the act. The Corps was involved in the program because of its traditional responsibilities for navigation and navigable waters.

The Corps's section 404 permit program became vulnerable to litigation due to an apparent expansion of the traditional concept of "navigable waters" found in section 502 of the FWPCA. This situation arose when the FWPCA congressional conference committee had, under section 502 of the act, apparently broadened the definition of "navigable waters" to include "all the waters of the United States." The Corps's 404 permit program was based upon a narrower, more traditional definition of navigable waters. It was not long, therefore, before NRDC appeared on the scene once again, this time to take the Secretary of the Army to court. NRDC wanted the Corps to assert fully its authority under 404 and 502 and thereby provide regulation of dredge and fill activities in the nation's wetlands. The ensuing court decision, reached in March, 1975, ordered the Corps to bring its section 404 regulations in line with the expanded definition of navigable waters found in section 502 of the act (*NRDC* v. *Calloway,* 392 F. Supp. 685, D.D.C., 1975).

In July of 1975, the Corps promulgated what it called "Interim-Final Regulations" to implement the new court-mandated section 404 program. The Corps's definition of navigable waters went beyond truly navigable waters to include all tributary streams, as well as all coastal and freshwater wetlands adjacent or contiguous to such waters. The Corps's definition of "wetlands" was, in fact, sufficiently broad to cover some lands which had merely a high water table. Particularly significant to forest industry was the fact that many commercial forestlands in the southern United States could be defined as wetlands under the Corps's new definition. The regulations were also problematic for forestry interests because the Corps decided that certain activities which EPA had defined as nonpoint under section 208 were—to the extent that they involved discharges of dredge or fill material—to be considered point sources for the purposes of section 404.

The response of the forestry profession, and in particular the forest industry, was predictable, rapid, and vehement. The industry maintained that private forest landowners alone constructed or reconstructed approximately 45,000 miles of road a year with stream crossings averaging four per mile. Presumably, a large percentage of these 180,000 stream crossings per year would require a section 404 permit. Permit requirements of this dimension would be extremely costly, would cause excessive delays in land management operations, and were in general considered to be unworkable under conditions required to maintain forestry and agricultural management efforts.

In the view of environmentalists, in contrast, strong control under section 404 was a desirable development which promised at last to achieve strong federal control over wetland areas and, perhaps, some intensive forestry practices. This belief was especially applicable to the Southeast, where, unlike the Northwest, private forestry had escaped any significant measure of government regulation for environmental protection purposes.

Amendments under the Clean Water Act of 1977   In the heat of the controversy over section 404 regulation, rural landowners howled louder than environmental protectionists. The extensive objections to a broad section 404 permit program became a major force supporting a midcourse congressional review of the FWPCA. The Clean Water Act, emerging from House and Senate oversight hearings held during the summer of 1977, contained important amendments to both section 208 and 404 of the 1972 FWPCA.

With respect to section 208 planning for the control of nonpoint sources of pollution, Congress ratified the concept of mandatory statewide planning which EPA had been ordered to specify in its new 208 regulations. In addition, Congress passed a funding authorization providing $600 million to support cost-sharing programs with rural landowners for the control of nonpoint sources of pollution. These funds would be particularly helpful to small rural land holders of farms and privately owned woodlands. Existing soil conservation districts found in almost all areas of the country were authorized as the delivery agency for the programs. Congress thus recognized that rural nonpoint sources of pollution could be most effectively controlled through cooperative and voluntary, cost-sharing means and that the conservation districts with local credibility and expertise were the proper agencies to carry out the authorized programs.

The Clean Water Act amendments were most significant in terms of their treatment of the controversial section 404 program. Basically, Congress agreed not to restrict the scope of the Corps's authority over all the waters of the United States and endorsed the importance of a federal regulatory program to protect wetlands within the context of the 1972 FWPCA. However, the 1977 amendments exempted most normal farming, forestry, and ranching activities —including minor drainage activities and forest road construction—from section 404 permit requirements.

While these amendments significantly clarified the situation, the potential for considerable impact on wild land management activities remained. First, the amendments did not exempt all drainage activities associated with agriculture or forestry from 404 regulation. Second, portions of the legislative history provide some controversy as to whether or not clear cutting in eastern mixed hardwood forests is a "normal silvicultural activity," qualifying for an exemption if it involves a discharge of dredged or fill material. Third, road construction was exempted only if undertaken in accordance with best management practices. The Corps's BMPs for road construction have not yet been defined and they may not be the same as the best management practices required by EPA in its section 208 regulations (Haeussler, passim).

Additional, confusing overlap between sections 404 and 208 seemed apparent in the 1977 amendments' provisions for transferring certain federal 404 authority to the states. The Clean Water Act allowed the states to assume control over dredge and fill activities in inland waters. These programs, however, must be permit programs and may not take effect until approved by EPA. Once a state has its 404 program approved, it may exempt certain activities from 404 preview and transfer them to control through "best management practices" under a newly enacted section 208(b)(4) dredge and fill program. It remained unclear, however, whether or not these 404/208 "best management practices" are the same as those found in either the section 208 regulations *or* those pertaining to determining road construction exemptions from 404 permit requirements. The 208/404 overlap problem provided an instructive example of how two completely different control programs, even if housed under the same major environmental statute, may act synergistically to increase regulation of land management activities.

It is ironic that during the prolonged struggle between environmental groups and forestry, farming, ranching, and rural landowner interests over the nature of 404 exemptions, environmentalists were unable to stop Congress from removing major federal water projects, including dredging activities, from the requirements of the section, provided that such activities were performed in accordance with an environmental impact statement prepared according to the requirements of NEPA. In this sense, the interpretation of section 404 had essentially come full circle. Originally, 404 was developed to provide EPA some control over federal dredging activities. Subsequently, the section was extended by citizen litigation to control a wide variety of public and private activities. During the ensuing controversy, however, the major activities for which section 404 was originally intended escaped regulation through exemption. Section 404 thus offers an important illustration of how legislating, litigating, and rule-making activities may interact to produce substantial program changes in a relatively short period of time.

One final provision in the 1977 amendments of interest to forestry and ranching activities required full federal facility and land management compliance with the procedures and substance of state water pollution laws. As a consequence of the rather aggressive wording in section 313 of the new statute, it is conceivable that state agencies could require compliance from both the Forest Service and federal timber purchasers with state water pollution control statutes, including forest practice acts, best management practices, nondegradation policies, and water quality standards.

Summary   It should be clear that the 1972 and 1977 federal water pollution control acts have had the largest impact on forestry and range management activities of any of federal environmental statutes. Furthermore, their impacts on forestry and range management activities have occurred both at the federal level and on a state-by-state basis as a consequence of planning provisions and delegation of authority to state agencies in various portions of the 1972 FWPCA. The FWPCA has also illustrated the power of citizen suit provisions in environmental legislation. Sections 208 and 404, having strong implications for the control of forestry and range management activities, both derived their present form from litigation initiated by the Natural Resources Defense Council.

Pesticide Regulation: The Federal Insecticide, Fungicide, and Rodenticide Act of 1947 and the 1972 Federal Environmental Pesticide Control Act

Although litigation, lobbying, and planning pursuant to the air and water quality acts were extensive, two less familiar acts, known together as FIFRA, were also emerging as important aspects of forest and range policy. One important consequence of the Ash Council and the environmental reorganization movement of the early 1970s was the transfer of existing federal authority over pesticide use from the Department of Agriculture to the EPA (Whitaker, chap. 3). EPA, in its new role, quickly became aware of the regulatory shortcomings of the 1947 FIFRA in controlling the use and adverse effects of pesticides. A movement to revise FIFRA substantially developed out of EPA's dissatisfaction with the act and widespread public concern over the impacts of toxic chemicals used in pest control. In 1972, the Federal Environmental Pesticide Control Act (FEPCA) passed Congress and was signed by President Nixon.

The 1972 act constituted a major overhaul of FIFRA and provided the first instance of strong federal control over the application of pesticides. It also changed the balance of pesticide regulation, placing authority for implementation with EPA, an agency without a constituent relationship with pesticide users. This situation, combined with EPA's aggressive implementation of the act, resulted in a call from the agriculture community for an amendment of FEPCA. Accordingly, in 1975, the act was amended again to make several important provisions. First, EPA had to advise the Secretary of Agriculture before taking any action with respect to a pesticide; second, the Department of Agriculture retained the authority to comment on pesticide regulations; and third, EPA must assess the economic impact of any action proposed or undertaken against a pesticide. The 1975 amendments thus ensured a degree of coordination between the Department of Agriculture and the Environmental Protection Agency.

In general, the impact of the FIFRA legislation is more dramatic in the farming community than on forest and range managers. However, there were several provisions in the act, as amended, which affect the what, when, how, and where of pesticide use on wild lands. Although FIFRA allowed for state control over significant phases of the act's implementation, the provisions of importance to wild land managers would be determined largely at the federal level.

One key aspect of FIFRA was its requirements for the classification and reregistration of some 40,000 existing pesticide formulations. To achieve that goal, EPA has developed a review process called "Rebuttable Presumption Against Registration" (RPAR, pronounced are-par). It is instigated against existing formulations deemed to be especially hazardous. This intensive process involves a review of all data on a pesticide to determine whether or not the pesticide should be reregistered. The review was to be a nonpolitical process dependent entirely upon data available on the pesticide at the time of the RPAR. A number of pesticides of importance to forest and range managers have been proposed for or undergone RPAR review. These include 2,4,5-T and related compounds, which are herbicides used in plant control and site preparation; endrin, which protects seed from rodent predation in direct seeding operations; and lindane and benzene hexachloride (BHC), which are occasionally used against woodboring beetles on forest lands but more commonly against such insects as they attack drying hardwood at lumber manufacturing sites.

A chemical which is subjected to the RPAR process is not automatically "guilty." Rather, an RPAR identifies a pesticide as potentially hazardous and then allows proponents of its continued use to "rebut" any incriminating evidence against it. Consequently, although the loss of a number of RPARed compounds would significantly affect certain forest and range operations, not all pesticides will be deregistered. Moreover, an unregistered pesticide is not completely eliminated from use; FIFRA does provide exemptions for federal and state agencies to use unregistered chemicals if they are needed in emergency situations. A good example of how this provision actually operates in a forestry emergency occurred in 1974 during the Pacific Northwest's Douglas fir tussock moth outbreak. In that case, the Forest Service and the states of Oregon and Washington requested an emergency use permit for DDT, which had been banned under FIFRA in 1972. EPA refused to issue the permit in 1973, claiming enough time had not passed to judge whether or not a natural virus would cause the collapse of the outbreak. By early 1974, it seemed that the effect of the virus was minimal. EPA granted the permit for DDT use over intense objections from environmentalists. By the summer of 1974, approximately 800,000 acres of Douglas fir in Oregon and Washington had been defoliated by the moths, and the Forest Service estimated that $59 million in timber after salvage had been lost. Although FIFRA's emergency use provisions resulted in a permit for DDT, the permit process was complex, lengthy, and wrought with conflict. DDT use, once granted, was too late to prevent the loss of large volumes of valuable timber. Moreover, when the tussock moth outbreak subsided, it was apparent that, as the environmentalist had argued, the DDT had nothing to do with the population reduction. Thus the FIFRA process satisfied no one; it did not prevent the application of DDT but merely assured that it would be done in an untimely fashion.

Of all of FIFRA's provisions, the one of greatest concern to the forestry community in particular pertains to the development and availability of new, as opposed to existing, chemicals. The source of this concern is section 12, which converts the product label of a pesticide from a guide to its use into a binding legal document. It is, accordingly, unlawful for any person to use any registered pesticide in a manner inconsistent with its label. Any damage caused while a pesticide is used in accordance with label instructions is attributable to the manufacturer, who is held liable.

This manufacturer liability has particularly serious impacts for forestry, which is considered, in comparison with the vast agricultural market, a "minor user" of pesticides. To ensure protection against label liability, a manufacturer must test for the effects of each pesticide in the context of each of its separate uses. There is little motivation for the manufacturer to conduct the extensive test needed to add to the label a minor use such as forestry, which has only a small revenue potential. As noted below, Congress took steps to solve the minor use problem through 1978 amendments to FIFRA.

1978 Amendments to FIFRA   In October, 1978, Congress passed another set of amendments to the 1972 FIFRA. Many of the 1978 amendments influence the availability of pesticides for "minor uses" such as forest tree nurseries, seed orchards, and greenhouses. The 1978 act required EPA to issue simplified regulations for the registration of all pesticides. The law also provided EPA with the authority to issue conditional registrations and to define "use inconsistent with the label" (that is, a minor forestry use of a pesticide registered for agriculture) in a flexible manner. Finally, the statute required "minor use" registration standards that are consistent with the anticipated use of the product and gives the states greater autonomy for registering pesticides for "special local needs."

Additional Sources of Pesticide Regulation   As significant as the FIFRA legislation is, it is not the sole source of pesticide regulation on wild lands. A chemical widely used against coyotes known as "1080" was banned not by FIFRA but by an executive order regulating predator control on the public lands. On forestlands, publicly visible chemicals such as 2,4,5-T have become the focus of a variety of citizen litigation and local government actions against their use. Suits under NEPA, for example, prohibited the Forest Service from using 2,4,5-T on the Siuslaw National Forest until an adequate environmental impact statement was filed.

Procedures or data generated by FIFRA may not result in chemical deregistration by EPA. The RPAR controversy does, however, highlight a chemical in the public eye and invites litigation under environmental statutes such as NEPA. In response to broad public protest, the Interior Department banned the use of certain registered but controversial chemicals on the lands which it administers. Although the Department of Agriculture did not institute such stringent measures, the Forest Service policy is to avoid or postpone the use of problem pesticides and the department as a whole is committed to developing pest control policies which deemphasize reliance on chemical methods.

Other avenues of environmental control additionally affect pesticide use on forests and ranges. Both public and private landowners are required to handle registered chemicals with ever-increasing care to prevent harming or inadvertently "taking" an endangered or threatened plant or animal species protected by the Endangered Species Act. Private land managers in states with comprehensive forest practice acts may encounter restrictions on pesticide use to minimize toxic run-off and stream pollution. For example, in December, 1978, the California North Coast Regional Water Quality Control Board banned the use of 2,4,5-T on forestlands in northern California. It acted under its authority to develop waste discharge permits for forestry operations through the California state water pollution control act.

FIFRA is not a piece of legislation which acts in isolation. It potentiates or acts in concert with direct and indirect pesticide provisions contained in other environmental statutes. The land management impacts of FIFRA underscore the complexity of environmental regulation.

Special Provisions for the Protection of Wild Horses, Burros, Eagles, Endangered Species, and Other Wildlife

Like pesticide regulation, concern for wildlife developed in the 1970s from a traditional but minor wild lands management concern into a hotly debated public issue. Federal forest and rangelands have been managed under the guiding concept of multiple use since the 1950s. Despite this fact, wildlife management on forests and ranges has not been of central concern to public or private land managers, with the exception of state game professionals and employees of the U.S. Fish and Wildlife Service. Furthermore, although wildlife management is probably more integral to land management than are many of the environmental issues discussed in this chapter, most forest and range managers had little experience with wildlife problems and needs prior to the early 1970s.

Development of Federal and State Roles in Wildlife Management The main reason for this rather interesting disjunction between wildlife and land management is rooted in the development of wildlife law in the United States. Control over wildlife has traditionally been the responsibility of state government. This legal tradition originated early in English history. After the signing of the Magna Carta, common law vested ownership of wildlife in the Office of the King, to be held in sacred trust for all people. After the American Revolution, the newly independent colonies adopted much of England's common law and many of the English statutes in force at that time. As a result, it has usually inferred that the states have acquired the authority of the King and, in this sovereign capacity, hold game in trust for their citizens. In addition, regulations governing the taking of wildlife are often supported by the police power of the state, which entitles the state to take certain actions warranted to protect the public health, safety, morals, and welfare of its citizens.

As a result of this legal tradition, the management of wildlife resources on all lands—no matter what their ownership—developed as a function of state agencies (see Chapter 3, p. 149). The federal role in wildlife management was never as well defined as that of the states. Becasue of this minimal federal activity, and because large federal land ownerships played an important part in shaping the development of forest and range policy in the early part of this century, wildlife issues were never of paramount importance to the majority of federal land managers.

Sources of Federal Authority As wildlife law has developed at the federal level, it was shaped by the kinds of authority allocated to the federal government through the Constitution. This constitutional authority has its basis in three principal sources. The first is the federal power to make treaties with foreign governments. In the case of wildlife, this power enabled the federal government to enter into treaties with other nations to protect migratory birds. The Migratory Bird Act of 1913 was a key product of the federal treaty-making power. The second constitutional source of federal authority for wildlife management emanates from the power to regulate interstate commerce. There is at present, however, no specific court decision which spells out the exact scope of the federal wildlife regulatory power conferred by the commerce clause. The third source of federal authority over wildlife is the property clause of the Constitution. This provides the federal government with the powers necessary to protect and regulate federally owned lands. Although the states retain primary responsibility for wildlife on federal lands, the property clause allows the federal government to control wildlife on public lands when such control is exerted in the paramount interest of the people of the United States (Council on Environmental Quality, 1977).

Most of the federal government's active involvement in the area of wildlife management has occurred as a consequence of legislation emanating from the treaty-making power and the commerce clause. However, a body of litigation revolving around the property clause over the past two centuries has resulted in a broad outlining of federal discretion over wildlife management on federal lands. The federal land managing agencies have reacted in different ways to this evolving interpretation of their management discretion. The Park Service, for example, asserted broad authorities to regulate wildlife in the national parks very early in its history. In 1964, the Office of the Solicitor of the Interior Department issued an opinion asserting that both the Park Service and the Fish and Wildlife Service have the authority to issue regulations to control hunting on lands which they administer.

The Forest Service, in contrast, has taken a much more limited view of its authority concerning the regulation of wildlife on the national forests. One of the reasons for this reaction originates with an opinion rendered by then Attorney General Knox in November, 1901. The "Knox opinion" grossly underestimated the scope of the Forest Service's authority over wildlife on its lands. One result of this narrow interpretation has been that the Forest Service has maintained the precedent of allowing the state fish and game agencies to set hunting limits on the national forests and has confined its role in wildlife management to one of habitat manipulation. The Bureau of Land Management, having even less explicit management authority than the Forest Service, has taken basically the same view of federal-state wildlife responsibilities on BLM lands.

Wild and Free-Roaming Horse and Burro Act   The passage of the Wild and Free-Roaming Horses and Burros Act of 1971 was among the first major developments requiring specific responsibility on the part of forest and range managers for the well-being of a wildlife species. The act was passed as a result of intense public concern over the well-being of wild horses and burros roaming public lands, particularly in areas administered largely by the Bureau of Land Management. The legislation was unique in several respects. First, it was the first specific mandate for federal land managers to become involved in wildlife management. Second, it established and defined an entirely new use of the public lands—that of providing habitat for particular wildlife species. Third, the act specified certain techniques to be used in managing the wild horses and burros. The act also contained numerous management requirements designed to protect the animals but which in fact made proper management of the wild animal herds extremely difficult.

The restrictions on management of wild horse and burro herds were followed by rapid population increases as a result of almost total protection. This set the goals of the 1971 act on an apparent collision course with BLM's long attempt to improve range conditions on the public lands. This conflict was not addressed until legislation passed in 1978 which amended the 1971 act to allow BLM to use motorized equipment to control horse and burro population levels.

Importantly, the act also raised the question of the extent of federal control over wild animal populations on federal lands. This question was addressed in litigation (*Kleppe* v. *New Mexico,* 426 U.S. 529, 1976) in which the Supreme Court held that the property clause provided sufficient power for the federal government to control all wildlife species on its lands. As a consequence of this decision, the stage was set for a new role for federal forest and range managers regarding wildlife. Furthermore, the ramifications of the decision warranted a new and heightened integration of wildlife with the management of other wild land resources.

Sikes Act Extension   The Sikes Act Extension, passed in 1974, adds to the fallout from the wild horse and burro litigation. It required coordination between public land management and state agencies regarding their fish and wildlife conservation efforts. This legislation required Agriculture and Interior to develop comprehensive plans for wildlife conservation on the lands under their respective jurisdictions. The act also provided that state fish and game agencies may enter into cooperative agreements with the Secretaries better to integrate fish and wildlife conservation and wildlife habitat management programs. While the Sikes Act has been described as the most ambitious attempt to encourage wildlife management on the federal lands, it was unclear how much impact the legislation would have. This confusion resulted from a lack of specificity in the act concerning the plans which it requires. Substantial funds were not appropriated until 1978.

Golden and Bald Eagles   At the same time that Congress was concerned with the protection of wild horses and burros, a controversy arose in the West concerning the poisoning of golden and bald eagles. In response to this issue, Congress amended the Bald Eagle Protection Act in 1972 to prohibit the poisoning of bald and golden eagles and to include language allowing for the prosecution of both intentional and inadvertent violations of the act. The ramifications of these provisions were extended in January, 1977, when the Fish and Wildlife Service published draft guidelines forbidding any activity resulting in the disturbance of bald or golden eagles. There was some concern among forest managers, in the Pacific Northwest in particular, that literal interpretation of these regulations would preclude timber management activities in the proximity of the affected animals or their nest sites.

Endangered Species Act   The potential impact on wild lands management of the Bald Eagle Protection Act was but a prelude to a much larger issue that developed out of the Endangered Species Act of 1973. The legislation combined all three of the constitutional authorities enabling federal control over wildlife and clearly mandated the most aggressive federal role to date in wildlife management. Because the act preempted what have historically been state wildlife responsibilities, its consitutionality remained a question.

The major premise of the act was that endangered plant and animal species "are of aesthetic, ecological, educational, historical, recreational, and scientific value to the nation and its people." In view of the national significance of endangered species, the act forbade their exploitation in international and interstate commerce. The act declared the further policy "that all federal departments and agencies shall seek to conserve endangered species," and, in so doing, shall pursue "all methods and procedures which are necessary to bring any endangered species or threatened species to the point at which the measures provided pursuant to the Act are no longer necessary." Such protection of endangered species must include, importantly, "a means whereby the ecosystems upon which they depend may be conserved."

From the point of view of forest and range managers, the Endangered Species Act seemed to constitute an uncompromising piece of legislation which threatens management activities, invites court action, and fails to allow for a balancing of other considerations which warrant weighing against the necessity of protecting a species. Land managers' apprehensions in this regard have resulted from several important, specific provisions of the legislation. First, the Fish and Wildlife Service has interpreted the act's prohibition of "taking" endangered species to include activities which inadvertently harass or harm such species. Land management activities such as timber harvesting could easily fall within the realm of this interpretation. Accordingly, any such management activity somehow harming or "taking" an endangered species could be cited as a violation and hence essentially forbidden under the act.

The "taking" prohibition is important since it extends the purview of the Endangered Species Act to private as well as public lands. The most controversial provision of the act, however, involves the designation and protection of "critical habitat" for endangered species and applies strictly to federal lands or to federal activities undertaken on lands of other ownership. The latter condition could conceivably be extended to include as wide-ranging a circumstance as private lands operating under an EPA-approved section 208 water quality management plan. Thus, the coverage of critical habitat requirements could, in the broadest interpretation, be almost as extensive as that of the "taking" prohibition.

Once a critical habitat has been officially designated for a species, federal agencies are required to consult formally with the Fish and Wildlife Service whenever any of their activities has the potential to harm an endangered species or destroy or modify its critical habitat. The result of this consultation process is a "biological determination" by the Fish and Wildlife Service, concerning the activity in question and the nature of its impact on the endangered species and its habitat. The action may proceed with the proposed activity or some altered form of it even if the Fish and Wildlife Service renders an unfavorable biological judgment. In so doing, however, the agency merely makes itself vulnerable to litigation. Several major suits over critical habitat conflicts have been decided, but they have been fought over large federal water development or construction projects—not forest or rangeland management operations.

For forest and rangeland managers, the conflicts between their activities and critical habitats have been localized and fairly minimal. The experience of the Forest Service offers an instructive example in this regard. Of the 200 animal species listed as endangered, the agency has identified some 16 as having significant impacts on the national forests. Only three of these species, however—the bald eagle, the red-cockaded woodpecker, and the grizzly bear—are truly problematic, since they combine the qualities of being wide-ranging in distribution and interfering substantially with management operations. With regard to plants, the Forest Service reports most of the several hundred proposed species as occurring in remote areas where little commodity-oriented management takes place. Still, an occasional "problem" species is found; for example, one plant in the Six Rivers National Forest caused 9 million board feet to be withdrawn from a Douglas fir timber sale contract.

Perhaps the most striking characteristic of the impacts of the Endangered Species Act is the wide difference of opinion which the land management community expresses concerning them. Some professionals point in despair to the statistics: By November, 1978, the Fish and Wildlife Service had listed 672 animals as endangered or threatened with almost 30,000 nominated for such classification; in addition, 1850 plants were proposed for listing as threatened or endangered, for which 33 critical habitats had been designated with 73 more proposed. While some species are bound to "recover" through intensive protective measures, in all likelihood the endangered and threatened species lists will continue to grow rather than diminish. Should preservationists continue their battle in the courtroom, some land managers fear a complete cessation of forest or rangeland activities in certain areas because of endangered species alone.

Other land managers have taken a more moderate posture on the dimensions of potential conflicts under the Endangered Species Act. First, they view the true "problem" species as being few in number. Second, they are hopeful that, as ecological knowledge of endangered species and their needs improves, special management techniques may be devised to enable harvesting, grazing, or other activities to occur in or near critical habitat areas. Finally, they point to evidence which indicates that management activities may in certain cases actually enhance rather than destroy a species' living space.

The Endangered Species Act Amendments of 1978   As might be expected from the above discussion of the impacts of the 1973 act, the major impetus for amendment came from outside the wild lands management community. On June 15, 1978, the Supreme Court ruled that work on the 90 percent completed Tennessee Valley Authority Tellico Dam in Tennessee had to stop because the dam would destroy critical habitat for the snail darter fish and thus be in violation of section 7 of the act. This decision bolstered what was then developing support for amending the act in Congress. In October 1978, during the final moments of the Ninety-fifth Congress, the Endangered Species Act of 1978 was passed. The views of wild lands managers were represented during congressional deliberations on the 1978 act.

Among the important provisions of the new act is the requirement that a species' status and its critical habitat are to be listed concurrently if at all possible. This will ensure that land managers know that a species is listed and are also aware of those parts of the species' range which are sensitive and require special attention. The new law also defined "critical habitat" as those essential specific sites within a species' range which require special consideration. This definition will avoid difficulties similar to those posed by the Fish and Wildlife Service's 1975 proposal to designate the entire range of the grizzly bear as critical habitat. The new statute also required the secretary of the Interior to use economic and other relevant data in the determination of critical habitat.

To reconcile "irreconcilable conflicts" between federal projects and the well-being of endangered species, the new statute created a cabinet-level committee to weigh the costs and benefits of proceeding with the project and the availability of alternatives. Under certain circumstances, the committee can grant the project an exemption from the provisions of section 7 even if the species is to be destroyed. In January 1979, the new cabinet-level committee decided not to exempt the controversial Tellico Dam from the act's requirements.

Despite the wide-ranging ramifications of the act, it passed with little legislative consideration and with almost no input from forest and range managers or user groups. While that situation may have prevailed in 1973, it certainly did not exist in 1978. The Endangered Species Act raised wildlife protection in the minds of wild land managers to a level that the issue had never achieved before.

SUMMARY

Throughout the early and mid-1970s, a strong interest in protecting the quality of the environment dominated many aspects of a variety of policies pursued at the federal level. Widespread citizen agitation against the growing manifestations of environmental degradation led to demands for comprehensive congressional mandates to protect the threatened ecosystem. Accordingly, several major pieces of single-purpose legislation passed Congress between 1970 and 1973 and were significantly amended in the closely ensuing years. In general, these laws were fashioned by the Nixon administration's particular concept of federalism. They relied on the states, with the aid of federal funding, to carry out the bulk of the required regulatory functions. The administration apparently believed that this strategy was a means to move the center of control closer to the people at the state and local levels. However, the clear provisions for federal overview of state programs, as well as the creation of a powerful federal Environmental Protection Agency, prevented regulatory authority from being delegated entirely to the individual states.

Of the environmental laws important to forest and range management, by far the most extensive in impact was the 1972 Federal Water Pollution Control Act. Successful citizens' litigation made section 208 of the act applicable to wild lands and subjected forest and range operations to potential regulation for their capacity to cause "nonpoint" water pollution. Wild land restrictions under the clean air legislation were generally not significant but threatened to augment under efforts to prevent air quality deterioration in rural areas. The new Federal Environmental Pesticide Control Act called into question a few chemicals which were important in forest and range management and which were thought or determined to be hazardous to human health. Finally, special legislation passed to protect certain wildlife, including threatened and endangered species, was the source of another series of novel concerns confronting forest and range managers for the first time.

The new environmental laws were not adopted in a vacuum but were surrounded by related developments of significance to forest and range policy. These included government reorganization to respond better to the expanded federal involvement in regulating activities affecting the environment. A new federal superagency, the Department of Environment and Natural Resources, was seriously considered but never established. Instead, Congress created the Environmental Protection Agency to administer the air, water, pesticide, and other federal environmental control efforts. At the same time, the broad citizen suit provisions of the environmental laws led to citizen organizations instigating key court challenges to EPA's actions in implementing the mandated programs. In both air and water pollution, this spurt of litigation produced important changes which extended the acts' scope to wild land practices and suddenly threw foresters and EPA lawyers and engineers in the same conference room. Citizen legal tactics were motivated by fundamental questions regarding the competence of regulatory agencies and land managers alike and resulted in forest and range professionals having to incorporate new values and considerations into their traditional management decisions, plans, and philosophies.

Even in light of these formative developments, the relationship between forest and range management and the various facets of environmental protection is at present a nascent one. Many fewer issues have been resolved than remain to be decided. Moreover, if the past is any indication of the future, the environmental laws will grow more rather than less complex in their implementation, and litigation will play an important role in ensuring proper interpretation and enforcement. The most interesting developments in the field are surely yet to come.

REFERENCES CITED

American Forestry Association. *Workshops on Forest Practices and Water Quality.* Washington, D.C.: American Forestry Association, 1976.

Anderson, Frederick. *NEPA in the Courts.* Baltimore, Md.: Johns Hopkins Press, 1973.

Council on Environmental Quality. *Guidelines, Statements on Proposed Federal Actions Affecting the Environment.* 36 *Federal Register* 7724–29 (April 23, 1971).

———. *National Wildlife Law.* Washington, D.C.: Government Printing Office, 1977.

Haeussler, Frederick. "Forestry and the Water Law." 38 *Forest Farmer* 8 (1978).

Krivak, Joseph. "Best Management Practices to Control Nonpoint Source Pollution from Agriculture." 33 *Journal of Soil and Water Conservation* 161; 34 *Journal of Soil and Water Conservation* 67 (1978).

Miskovsky, Milan C., and Van Hook, Matthew B. "Regulation of Forestry Related Nonpoint Source Pollution Under the Federal Water Pollution Control Act Amendments of 1972." 9 *Natural Resources Lawyer* 646 (1976).

Proctor, John. "The Clean Air Act Amendments of 1970: Implications for Wildlands Management." In S. K. Fairfax, ed. *Legal Aspects of Wildlands Management,* Ann Arbor, Mich.: Natural Resources Law Monograph No. 1, 1977, pp. 51–72.

Quarles, John. *Cleaning Up America—An Insider's View of the Environmental Protection Agency.* Boston: Houghton Mifflin Company, 1976.

Train, Russell. "Forestry and Pollution—An Interview with Russell Train." 82 *American Forests* 20 (1976).

Whitaker, John. *Striking a Balance—Environment and Natural Resources Policy in the Nixon-Ford Years.* Washington, D.C.: American Enterprise Institute, 1976.

Chapter 10

Government Regulation of Private Lands in the Environmental Era

As public preoccupation with environmental quality and natural beauty grew in the 1960s and 1970s, private land management became the focus of sharpened scrutiny from Congress, environmental groups, state and local governments, and the general public. A strong movement emerged espousing direct federal control of private lands. Unlike the forest land regulation controversy of the 1920s, and 1930s, and 1940s, agitation for national land use planning in the early 1970s had a strongly urban bias. However, it also included rural problems such as suburban sprawl and the conversion of prime farmland to residential development and other nonagricultrual uses. In addition, the movement encompassed a widespread concern for unique and scenic environments; for aesthetic qualities along highways and in parks and recreation areas; and for fragile ecological areas such as wetlands, prairie potholes, sand dunes, and shorelines. The drive for comprehensive national legislation thus embraced a wide range of concerns shared by forest and range managers.

Despite broad visibility and support, the drive for national land use planning failed in the early 1970s, just as advocates of federal regulation were unable to move Congress to define federal forest practice controls during the earlier controversy. Federal involvement in private and local land use decisions continued to engender strong opposition. What the environmental era did produce, however, was a number of successful state-level efforts at land use regulation. The state laws surpassed any prior government involvement in the forest management and overall land use arena. The states in the 1970s pioneered powerful environmental protection and land use programs which prevailing political preference would not accept from federal authorities. These included "bottle bills" to control litter, statewide land use planning, and a few strong new state forest practices acts.*

The new regulations put particular pressure on nonindustrial private forests. At a time when increased productivity of these forests continued to be a major theme, the controls posed an additional cost for these small, financially marginal operations. In view of these considerations the overall policy approach toward nonindustrial forest owners has continued to be one of *incentive* rather than regulation. While Congress set nationwide standards for air and water pollution control, it reaffirmed its commitment to the small forest owner by rejuvenating a long standing cooperative approach through passage of the Forestry Incentives Program in 1973. Several states gave private owners further incentives, especially through property tax reforms. Property taxation was recognized as a singular program in forest management more than a century ago, and a maze of special state taxation measures was devised to relieve the forest property owner of what was commonly viewed as an unfair tax burden. While the majority of these measures failed to achieve their stated objectives, interest in the taxation issue was rekindled in the 1960s and 1970s because of escalating property values, land conversion, and an uneasy tension between destructive development and environmental preservation.

NATIONAL LAND USE PLANNING AND COASTAL ZONE MANAGEMENT

In the forestry field, federal regulation of management practices and land use has been a recurring policy issue since 1910. The environmental awareness of the 1960s and 1970s revived the federal land use control issue, but on a broader and more pervasive scale than the earlier forest practice controversies. The most recent land use debate arose out of the problems of haphazard metropolitan growth and the rapid conversion of open-space lands located on urban fringes through "suburban sprawl." By the 1960s, concerned citizens began to question rampant residential construction in the suburbs, unattractive highway strip development and other unwelcome disadvantages of urban growth. While air and water pollution and solid waste accumulaiton were most serious

---

*Throughout this chapter, the emphasis is on illustrating the nature and importance of state policies; no attempt is made to treat any one state or program exhaustively or definitively.

in the inner cities, it was clear that unplanned growth compounded these problems.

Congress responded to the environmental crisis by passing major regulatory statutes to control pollution. As discussed in Chapter 9, these statutes set performance standards and required state implementation plans which had an important, though indirect, effect on how land was used and developed. To most supporters of land use planning, the side effects of the pollution laws were not sufficient. A strong national movement surfaced urging Congress to pass legislation mandating comprehensive land use planning for all the states.

Despite this effort, land use control was still widely considered to be a function of local government and "home rule." Substantial opposition rallied against the "communistic threat" of pervasive "big government" control of local matters. The Land Use Policy and Planning Assistance Act of 1972 managed to pass the Senate in September, but no action was taken by the House. The following year the Senate passed essentially the same legislation, while the House defeated its Land Use Planning Act by 211 to 204 vote. Federal land use planing came that close to being a reality; however, once the legislation was defeated, support for the federal approach waned and largely dispersed.

Costal Zone Management

Although national land use planning advocates did not secure passage of their favored legislation, Congress provided for federal oversight of development in coastal areas by passing the Coastal Zone Management Act of 1972. This legislation has had minor impact on forest and range management, but it is an important precursor to the state land use planning efforts out of which several key forest practice acts have developed.

The call for some regulation of development in the coastal zone began in January 1969, with a report by the Commission of Marine Sciences, Engineering, and Resources. This report recommended legislation authorizing federal grants to establish state coastal zone authorities to manage coastal zone waters and adjacent lands. The report asserted that an important national interest was involved in coastal zone management and that critical and vulnerable coastal areas were being exploited or developed without due consideration of environmental values. The concept of administering federal grants to encourage state planning coincided with the views of the Nixon administration and legislation was soon drafted.

One of the first hurdles faced by the coastal zone program was one of jurisdiction: Which agency should administer the federal planning grants? This issue was settled with the creation in 1970 of the National Oceanic and Atmospheric Administration (NOAA) of the Department of Commerce, whose Office of Coastal Zone Management became the logical agency to implement the program. Congressional oversight authority was given to the Senate Commerce Committee and the House Merchant Marines and Fisheries Committee. Thus, neither the Department of the Interior nor the natural resource committees of Congress has had much control over the emerging coastal zone program.

The Coastal Zone Management Act (CZMA) was enacted in October, 1972. It paralleled the format adopted under section 208 of the Federal Water Pollution Control Act by granting funds to eligible states to develop and implement their own coastal zone strategies under broad federal guidelines. Although state participation was voluntary, most of the thirty-two eligible states have elected to participate. While early discussions surrounding the proposed coastal zone legislation rarely mentioned wild land resource impacts, the CZMA contains sufficiently broad authority to allow for state plans which could regulate forestry or even range management activities within or impacting on a defined coastal zone.

The federal planning guidelines required first that each participating state identify its coastal zone. Coastal zones generally included coastal waters and the lands beneath them as well as adjacent lands which could, if the state so chose, extend a considerable distance inland. The states could also prescribe permissible uses within the coastal zone and regulate any discharges or land uses which threatened to affect adversely coastal amenities. The states were also given broad authority to designate and develop special protective measures for coastal areas of "critical concern." Forestry or range interests could be affected by this provision to the extent that they fell within an ecologically critical area.

Private development in coastal areas was the focus of state attention under the CZMA. However, the CZMA typifies federal-state jurisdictional conflicts under many federal environmental statutes. Even though the CZMA explicitly excluded federal lands from state coastal zones, federal land management activities must abide by the "federal consistency" regulations of NOAA and make a significant effort to comply with federally approved state coastal zone plans and regulations. This regulation suggested the possibility that the states could interfere with the management of federal lands in the coastal zone. The problem was ameliorated somewhat by the 1976 amendments to the CZMA, which emphasized increased federal participation in the development of state coastal zone plans and improved coordination with states having considerable federal land within their coastal zones. Plainly, then, state coastal plans are not to interfere substantially with federal land management prerogatives.

The CZMA has not had widespread impact on the management of forests and other wild lands. Nevertheless, the CZMA is important because it provides yet another process under which wild land management activities must be reviewed and evaluated by state and federal planning authorities. It is unclear how well state coastal zone management programs will be coordinated with existing government regulatory programs under the clean air and water acts. Lack of such coordination could present difficult problems for public regulators and private land managers alike. Private forestry interests in the South are concerned that the strict requirements softened by 1977 amendments to the dredge and fill permit program under section 404 of the Federal Water Pollution Control Act may be revived in coastal areas under the developing state coastal zone programs. For example, the draft North Carolina coastal zone management plan restricts the construction of drainage ditches in the coastal zone. It is, therefore, to the advantage of land managers not only to participate in state coastal planning processes, but to determine how that process may interface with other existing and evolving environmental regulatory programs.

STATE COASTAL ZONE MANAGEMENT AND LAND USE PLANNING EFFORTS

Because strong federal land use controls were politically unacceptable in the 1970s, the federal Coastal Zone Management Act set the stage for the states to develop coastal protection programs to suit their individual needs. In addition, aside from the federal land use initiative, certain states realized that traditional local controls were inadequate to encourage well-managed growth and protect important environmental values of statewide interest. States also recognized that the federal government could not be relied upon to administer adequate protection measures. Growing federal interest in such programs as nuclear power plant siting and offshore oil and gas development posed a substantial threat to states eager to avoid the location of large federal development projects within their borders. All of these factors combined in the 1970s to enhance the emergence of the states as the primary actors and regulators in the land use arena.

Although over thirty eligible states elected to participate in the federal coastal zone management program, many states were slow to activate their programs and to submit their draft coastal zone plans. Three states, however, had their final coastal zone management plans approved by 1978. These states were Washington, California, and Oregon. In fact, Washington adopted its own Shoreline Management Act (SMA) in 1971. It mandated a broad planning effort whereby local governments were to prepare "master programs" for shoreline areas. Master programs were essentially land development plans formulated under guidelines issued by the state Department of Ecology (DOE). Local development planning was based on a permit system designed to regulate most proposed private development projects within the state's shoreline zone. Broad oversight of local planning and permit activities was reserved to the DOE, which could review and modify master programs. State authority was especially strong when applied to defined shoreline areas of statewide significance.

California's Coastal Zone Program

Although the state of Washington was the first to enact coastal zone management protection, California's program, initially the result of a popular referendum in 1972, is the most comprehensive. By 1975, California's population had tripled, over a period of thirty years, to total twenty million. Fully 85 percent of these twenty million lived within 30 miles of the state's 1100-mile-long coast. And the population within 5 miles of the coast was growing at a rate twice that occurring in the rest of the state. The institutional mechanisms for controlling or determining the nature of this growth were scattered among 200 coastal governmental and planning jurisdictions.

The referendum passed the California Coastal Zone Conservation Act of 1972, which declared that "the California coastal zone is a distinct and valuable natural resource" and that its "permanent protection . . . is a paramount concern to present and future residents of the state and nation." The act established six regional coastal commissions with permit authority. It also set up a state coastal zone agency charged with coordinating the regions in developing a state coastal plan and ensuring state coastal zone protection until a permanent act could be passed by the legislature.

The referendum plan was a temporary measure, but in 1976, the year in which the interim arrangements were to lapse, the California legislature adopted a permanent coastal act based on the 442-page state coastal zone plan published in December, 1975. The new act retained the basic regulatory and administrative structure devised in 1972: Broad state coastal zone policies were adopted which were to be followed by local plans subject to review by the regional commission and overview by the central state agency. Any coastal zone development requires local permit and is loosely defined to encompass any alteration in the intensities or density of land use. The state commission was also charged with designating "sensitive coastal resource areas" which, when approved by the legislature, would receive additional protection. While the new California act struck a balance between broad state regulation and the need to retain development control at the local level, it is still the most comprehensive in the nation.

Oregon's Land Use Law

Oregon, the third West Coast state in the forefront of coastal zone management, actually pioneered another, broader approach to land use regulation. Washington and California adopted comprehensive land use programs for their coastal areas, while other states such as Maine, New Jersey, and Georgia adopted more specialized laws to regulate facility site location or development in wetlands. Oregon, in contrast, followed the early lead set by Hawaii in 1961 and passed a land use law in 1973 which provided for comprehensive statewide planning. In general, Oregon is less densely developed than California, but it was still experiencing a rapid population growth which, in the mid-1970s, surpassed that of most other states. Oregonians earned a national reputation for taking action to enhance their state's environment and for jealously guarding the pristine and open character of Oregon's wild lands.

Oregon's land use law followed the familiar model of retaining development decisions at the local level but making them subject to compliance with state goals and guidelines and to review and modification by a strong state planning authority. The new state Land Conservation and Development Commission (LCDC) created by the act was also charged with setting state policy and asserting control over activities of statewide significance and with reviewing and recommending areas of critical state concern. The land use plans to be adopted by local units were to be comprehensive.

Land Use and Strip Mining in Wyoming

Similar legislation passed in Wyoming in 1975. The act created a new state Land Use Commission. This action was unique among predominantly rural states, many of which were dominated by conservative interests and resisted joining the state planning movement. Wyoming's decision to take action was prompted by widespread interest in energy development and strip mining for coal which, by the mid-1970s, had become a major federal policy concern. The state had good reason to be anxious over the potential impact of energy development on its water resources and grazing lands. Accordingly, the State Land Use Commission was charged with formulating state planning goals and guidelines whereby each county would prepare its own local land use plan. The commission's authority to identify areas of critical concern extended to a wide array of lands which could include range resources determined to be of "short- or long-term public interest . . . of more than local significance."

STATE ENVIRONMENTAL REORGANIZATION
AND POLICY ACTION

The barrage of special state environmental protection and resource conservation measures passed in the 1970s was as impressive and extensive as it was multifaceted. Some of the legislation was adopted in response to federal initiatives such as air and water pollution control, coastal zone management, and endangered species protection. The measures also encompassed many individual state concerns ranging from broad-scale land use control to wetland protection, floodplain regulation, energy facility siting, fish and wildlife protection, and strip mine reclamation. New modes of dealing with these problems were formulated during the environmental years and their implementation often required restructuring of state government administrative functions. As is typical of most state actions, a wide variety of different solutions was found and each state chose the particular scheme which best addressed its own perceived needs and political climate.

State Reorganizations

Some states, such as Minnesota and Washington, created agencies which, like the U.S. Environmental Protection Agency, were given responsibility for state pollution control programs. Other states, such as New York and New Jersey, created "superagencies" which consolidated state pollution and natural resource conservation programs. Vermont and Maine created environmental boards or commissions to administer statewide land use regulations. California, interestingly, provided a notable contrast to state consolidation efforts by continuing to rely on decentralized decision making. Although the state created a major Resources Agency in 1961, this move was not so much a structural reorganization as it was a measure to gather some seventeen independent agencies, boards, departments, and commissions together under one umbrella. The Resources Agency was also distinctive in that it contained units which exercised resource development as well as environmental protection functions.

"Little NEPAs"

Coincident with state movements to reorganize their governments and better to address environmental quality, resource conservation, and land use concerns during the 1970s was the passage in nearly half the states of legislation patterned on the 1969 National Environmental Policy Act. A majority of these states instituted comprehensive environmental impact statement requirements, while a few states opted to mandate EIS preparation for specific activities only —for example, water resource projects in Arizona. The salient impact of the state "little NEPAs" was that while they applied to projects undertaken by state agencies, many of the acts also were extended to cover private activities needing a government permit, lease, or license. Accordingly, "little NEPAs" had the capacity to affect the myriad projects and activities implemented at the local level and were important in determining how land and resource were actually used. However, despite this broad potential impact, only two states, California and Washington, aggressively pursued impact statement requirements for a wide range of state and private projects.

California's CEQA California again played the role of trend setter among the states by being the first to pass an environmental policy act. The California Environmental Quality Act (CEQA) of 1970 also had the most extensive impact of all the state statutes. CEQA, in fact, surpassed the federal NEPA in a number of its provisions. California's forcefulness was prompted by a recognized need for the state to take "a positive role in influencing population growth and distribution, land use patterns, and the control of environmental degradation" (State of California, Assembly Select Commtitee on Environmental Quality, 6).

Like NEPA, CEQA contains a broad declaration of environmental policy as well as the mandate that the state and most local agencies prepare an environmental impact report (EIR) for any project or activity having a significant effect on the environment. CEQA went beyond NEPA by requiring that the EIR consider mitigation measures which might be implemented to rectify potential adverse environmental impacts and by requiring the EIR to analyze the growth-inducing aspects of a proposed action. A centralized environmental impact review agency similar to the Council of Environmental Quality was not established. In 1972 amendments to the act, however, the State Resources Agency was given broad discretion to formulate guidelines for the implementation of CEQA.

The "Friends of Mammoth" Decision Like NEPA, CEQA was designed to be a procedural, rather than a substantive, measure, and no provision was made for the Resources Agency to reject an inadequate EIR. The real "teeth" of CEQA implementation lay in citizen resort to the courts. Accordingly, CEQA's real potential was not realized until the pivotal state supreme court case *Friends of Mammoth* v. *Board of County Supervisors of Mono County,* which in 1972 extended the EIR requirement to private developments, which could proceed only upon receipt of a state license or some other form of public permission. This ruling made CEQA, unlike NEPA, applicable to a vast array of private development projects. The statutes' procedural provisions were vastly increased in importance and thus became a critical device for local land use control. By 1975, 6000 EIRs per year were being written in California, the majority of which concerned private projects licensed by cities, counties, and the state. The *Mammoth* ruling also made private forest management activities susceptible to the EIR requirement, and eventually it engendered a heated, statewide controversy on the issue which is discussed below.

Washington's SEPA Washington's State Environmental Policy Act (SEPA) passed in 1971 and, along with CEQA, came to be recognized as one of the most effective "state NEPAs." Statistics of 1975 showed, however, that only 200 impact statements per year were being prepared under SEPA, as compared to 6000 written annually under CEQA (Environmental Law Reporter, 50017). SEPA was not being applied as widely on the local level as was CEQA in the post-*Mammoth* years. SEPA, in addition, was patterned closely on NEPA and did not contain the extra mitigation measure and growth inducement provisions contained in CEQA. In the 1974 amendment to SEPA, the state legislature created an independent Council on Environmental Policy (CEQ) which, like the federal CEQ, was charged with defining guidelines and adopting rules and regulations for impact statement implementation. The state council, however, differed from its federal counterpart in that it was to be provisional only; in June, 1976, it was to be abolished and its duties and functions transferred to the State Department of Ecology.

STATE FOREST PRACTICE LEGISLATION IN THE ENVIRONMENTAL ERA

State activity in the environmental decade reached an impressive height in the areas of forest practice regulation. Three states—California, Oregon, and Washington—led the way in the drive to minimize the adverse impacts of modern forestry activities on private timberlands. Several other states critically examined the forest practice legislation on their books. In a few states, such as Nevada and Massachusetts, the laws were strengthened; and in others, agitation for reform was substantial, if unsuccessful. Only in the South is there continuing lack of movement in legislation. However, even there the section 208 planning program has brought discussion of state regulation of forest practices into the region. It was on the Pacific Coast, however, that public concern over cutting activities found expression in strong regulations.

Early State Forest Practice Acts

The history of the forest practice regulation exhibits an interesting tension between the anticipated efficacy of federal regulation and the political acceptability of state regulation of private forestlands. From the 1920s on, while nationwide regulation was constantly debated and defeated, the federal threat prodded the states into action and motivated industry to accept state regulation in order to avoid federal rules. This was especially true in the 1930s and 1940s, when a rash of state forest practice acts was passed. The states thus emerged as major actors and as the principal force affecting activities on private lands.

In response to the specter of federal control, eleven states passed forest practice acts in the 1940s. These acts were confined to prescribing various cutting requirements and, on the whole, were not significantly more restrictive than their predecessors. Some of the acts, such as those passed by Vermont in 1945 and New York in 1946, were voluntary and offered complimentary state forestry assistance in return for owner compliance. Other states, such as

New Hampshire in its 1949 "Act Relating to Forest Conservation and Taxation," offered taxation incentives to owners following prescribed forestry practices. Many of the state forest property taxation laws, in fact, required that
specific practices be adopted before lands could become eligible for special tax
treatment.

By 1950, some type of forest practice legislation, whether compulsory or
voluntary, covered one-fifth of the commercial forestlands in the United States
in terms of volume of standing timber (American Forestry Association, 193).
Of all the acts passed, the strictest were in Oregon and Washington. These laws
were a direct outgrowth of the influence of the National Industrial Recovery
Act Lumber Code and resulted from timber industry interest in sounder
management. The acts set up administrative systems whereby each commercial operator was required to obtain a permit from the state forester. During
this same period, Washington was the site of the first major court case challenging the constitutionality of state forest practice regulation. In *State* v.
Dexter, the Washington Supreme Court upheld the 1945 state act as a reasonable exercise of state policy power which was justified by the need to conserve
natural resources in the public interest.

Nationwide, state concern over regulating forest practices diminished
during the 1950s. The conservatism of the Eisenhower years combined with
noticeable improvement in industrial forest management to make the need for
regulation seem less pressing. Furthermore, the cries of impending timber
famine had abated somewhat. In addition to better productivity records, one
index of improved management was the fact that industry was hiring increasing numbers of foresters and beginning to build up its own cadre of trained
professionals. During the 1950s, therefore, only two new states—Virginia and
North Carolina—passed forest practice acts. Both were basically seed tree
provisions, and the North Carolina statute was limited in applicability to only
two or three counties. The focus of forest practice regulation during the decade
was in the West, where Oregon and California instituted significant procedural
changes in strengthening their existing acts. Nevada in 1955 added a new
Forest Practice Act to supplement its 1903 seed tree law and, in so doing,
represented a growing trend toward requiring timber owners to obtain permits
for logging and land conversion activities.

State Programs in Forestry Education and Research

Education and research became major components of state forestry programs during this period. Forestry education has, in fact, always been primarily a state function, carried on almost exclusively at state universities and land
grant colleges throughout the nation. Only a few private institutions have ever
entered the field of forestry education, and none of those remaining, Duke,
Yale, and Harvard, has ever offered a complete undergraduate and graduate

program. After the Second World War, returning veterans caused the enrollment in forestry schools to jump 1128 percent between 1944 and 1946. That influx subsided, but numerous new institutions were chartered in the 1940s and 1950s (Dana and Johnson, Chap. 3).

The state role in research has also expanded since World War II, when state legislatures began appropriating significant funds for forestry research at the state schools. The 1962 McIntire-Stennis Cooperative Research Act further stimulated state investments in the area. The act defines a formula for allocating federal grants to match state funding of forestry research. The federal participation sometimes obscures the state role, but it is the backbone of research and education in forestry.

The environmental era has required that the educational offerings and research efforts diversify and expand anew to meet evolving public expectations of the profession. In the late 1960s and 1970s, forest management bore the brunt of the public attack for a variety of adverse impacts on aesthetics; natural beauty; wildlife habitat; and, perhaps most important, water quality. The clear cutting controversy on national forestlands enveloped all of these concerns and focused public wrath on forest management. Not only did the image of the Forest Service suffer, but the timber industry was identified as an obvious earth destroyer. Furthermore, even though the President's Advisory Panel on Timber and the Environment reported in 1973 that forest industry lands include some of the highest quality land for timber production and are generally intensively managed (PAPTE, 37), the ability of many small forest owners to make the extra investments necessary to manage their properties in environmentally sensitive ways was open to question.

Environmental Era Forest Practice Regulations

California, Oregon, and Washington passed new forest practice laws in the early 1970s which went well beyond the old acts. Their paramount concern was to protect environmental quality in the timber growing and harvesting processes. Rather than addressing purely silvicultural issues by such measures as not cutting trees under a certain diameter, the new laws imposed extensive requirements designed to guard against runoff and erosion, slope failure, water quality degradation, chemical pollution, and fish and wildlife habitat destruction. To a much greater extent than ever before, timber operators in those three states had to modify their activities in many ways to meet both the timber productivity and environmental quality goals of the era.

California Forest Practice Regulation Early Efforts   California's experience generally typifies similar actions taken by Oregon and Washington; however, the California act is more stringent. The forest practice controversy was, moreover, particularly heated due to renewed public interest in "saving the redwoods" in Humboldt and other northern California counties. California financed and built its state forestry organization starting in 1885. However, California has had virtually no system of state-owned forest lands. Furthermore, the state had made virtually no attempt to regulate private forest practices other than to adopt forest fire restrictions. In 1943, California appointed a State Forestry Study Committee. The committee submitted its comprehensive report on the forestry situation in California in 1945. It recommended state acquisition and the adoption of forest practices based on " 'the principle of [industry] self-regulation under state guidance and surveillance' " (Dana and Krueger, 193).

The committee's report and recommendations resulted in two significant acts providing for the acquisition, administration, and management of a state forest system and a Forest Practice Act. Typically, the Forest Practice Act focused on silviculture; its aim was to regulate cutting practices to achieve maximum sustainable productivity. The Forest Practice Act contained little regulatory punch because the rules adopted by the private owners were nonspecific and the act contained inadequate enforcement provisions. Furthermore, the State Division of Forestry lacked the necessary staff and financial resources to oversee adequately activities undertaken on California's 8.2 million acres of private timberland.

Between 1945 and 1971, public dissatisfaction with the deficiencies and loopholes of the California Forest Practice Act, coupled with growing environmental sensitivity, led to a number of amendments to strengthen the act. In 1957, enforcement was improved through the requirement that every timber operator obtain a permit from the State Forester before beginning to harvest. Failure to secure a permit constituted a misdemeanor, and violation of the forest practice rules was made grounds for revoking an owner's permission to operate. In 1963, the Division of Forestry gained even more enforcement authority, including the right to remedy violations and sue the owner for the expense incurred. Heightened public impatience with industry control of the regulatory process led, in 1970, to the addition of public representatives to the district forestry committees and the State Forestry Board. Finally, in 1971, the requirement that two-thirds of the industry ownership approve the forest practice rules was repealed; and the State Forester was given additional funds to correct violations.

Forest Practice Act Unconstitutional   In spite of these changes, controversy continued. Many believed the act was administered by the industry and totally ignored environmental protection. The fact that some California counties had adopted their own logging regulations was a persistent manifestation that the state program was not going far enough. Tension culminated in 1971 in the court case *Bayside Timber Company* v. *Board of Supervisors of San Mateo County.* The case concerned the fact that San Mateo County, the first county in the state to have instituted its own logging regulations in 1937, denied a harvesting permit to Bayside Timber Company in 1969. The timber company filed suit and won on the grounds that the 1945 state Forest Practice Act preempted the county's regulations. County citizens then appealed the decision, maintaining that such preemption was impossible since the 1945 act was unconstitutional. The California Court of Appeals agreed: The act's rule-making system was indeed unconstitutional, in large part because the district committees and State Forestry Board were industry-dominated and thus characterized by unacceptable conflict of interest (Stanford Environmental Law Society, 13–14).

The Z'berg-Nejedly Act   The *Bayside* decision forced the state legislature to adopt a new act in 1973. Known after its principal sponsors as the Z'berg-Nejedly Forest Practice Act, the new statute addressed all the criticisms of the 1945 act. Most important, it broadened the goals of the older legislation from timber productivity to include environmental quality. California's 1973 Forest Practice Act departed in other significant ways from the old system. First, it provides for a State Forestry Board dominated no longer by industry but including a majority (five) of "public" members. All members must have qualifications in fields watershed management, water quality, soil science, fish and wildlife, range management, forest economics, or land use planning. The board was required to divide the state into at least three districts, and a technical advisory committee with knowledge of forest, range, and environmental protection was provided for each district. The act also requires a majority of public members on the district technical advisory committees.

The 1973 act imposed conservation standards and provided that the board make rules to achieve them. The standards and rules covered a number of areas, including prevention and control of fire and soil erosion, water quality maintenance, and attainment of desired stocking levels. In all areas, the rules required adherence to specific practices designed to enhance timber production balanced with environmental objectives. For example, to prevent water quality degradation, stream crossings had to be kept to a minimum and generally had to utilize bridges or culverts; trees located within 50 feet of a water body had to be harvested with special care; road construction had to conform to specified standards; and vegetative stream protection zones were often required to be left along stream banks. Clear cuts were limited to certain maximum sizes in each district, and minimum standards of restocking were set by law. The new act retained the old permit system but instituted the additional mandatory measure that each harvesting operation be preceded by a plan prepared by a registered professional forester. The harvesting plan—a requirement unique to California and adopted by no other state—specifies logging and regeneration techniques as well as special steps taken to prevent erosion and protect water quality and scenic or ecologically fragile features. Each plan must be approved by the Department of Forestry before operations can begin. Violation of the act was a misdemeanor punishable by a stiff fine or imprisonment.

EPA and CEQA   As advanced as the new California Forest Practice Act was, particularly in its provision for approved timber harvesting plans, it still did not satisfy certain government officials and public interest groups concerned with environmental protection. In 1972, the famous *Mammoth* decision extended the California Environmental Quality Act to private projects and activities licensed by a government agency. This decision immediately brought into question the status of private forestry activities under the environmental impact report requirement of CEQA. Under the 1973 Forest Practice Act, the nature and impacts of private harvesting operations were already subject to examination under the timber harvesting plan, a document similar in many respects to an EIR. The CEQA implementation guidelines issued by the State Resources Agency in 1973 appeared to exempt harvesting operations from CEQA, an interpretation to which the State Attorney General objected (Trzyna and Jokela, 46). Furthermore, while it was the function of the State Forester to review timber harvesting plans, he did so according to rules promulgated by the State Forestry Board, which environmentalists suspected of being subverted by conservative, proindustry gubernatorial appointees (Forestry News, 239).

Uncertainty surrounding the applicability of CEQA to California's Forest Practice Act came to a head in January, 1975, when the Humboldt County Superior Court ruled that logging activities on private lands surrounding Redwood National Park were ecologically destructive and had to be analyzed under CEQA procedures. The decision created instant havoc, not just in the redwood region but throughout the state. Timber industry proponents vociferously and even violently expressed their objections to complying with both the Forest Practice Act and CEQA. After a desperate interim solution implemented by a harried state administration and the introduction of some nine remedial measures into the state legislature, an amendment to the 1973 act was adopted which exempted all timber harvesting plans effective prior to January 1, 1976, from the EIR requirement. Subsequent to this action, the State Secretary of Resources was given authority to declare the timber harvest planning process to be the "functional equivalent" of an EIR on the condition that the 1973 statute's environmental safeguards were judged to be adequate (Forestry News, 1976, 96). In other respects, California forest practice regulation remains subject to CEQA.

After the CEQA controversy, the environmental protection aspects of California's forest practice rules were substantially strengthened by further amendments. Interestingly, in Washington state, analogous confusion was more adroitly avoided by a 1975 amendment to the state's 1974 Forest Practices Act, which explicitly exempted most private forest management activities from the impact statement requirement of the 1971 SEPA. This same 1975 legislative activity provided certain exemptions to avoid confusing overlap between Washington's Shoreline Management Act of 1971 and state and private forestry operations affecting coastal areas.

Oregon: Putting It All Together   All of the modern elements of state concern with long-term forest productivity and environmental quality coalesced in Oregon in the 1970s. The state encompassed 30 million acres of forestland, 38 percent of which was privately owned, and contained one-fifth of the nation's volume of standing sawtimber. The forest products industry was yielding $2 billion annually, or one-eighth of the gross state product (Hostetter, 478). At the same time, Oregonians prided themselves on their state's environmental amenities.

By the late 1960s, Oregon was struggling with difficult problems arising from its divided preoccupations with timber productivity and environmental quality. In 1971, the state revamped its old forest practice legislation, on the books since 1941, and adopted a new act which compared with California's in terms of its strict environmental quality standards and emphasis on related nonsilvicultural concerns. Oregon also pioneered a sophisticated forest smoke control system to respond to heightened concerns about air quality in rural areas. This system, relying on advanced computer technology to integrate timberland burning schedules with weather forecasts and anticipated pollution effects, provided a model for other states to follow.

Most important, in 1978, forestry experts at Oregon State University predicted a timber shortage for the state by the year 2000. The state, to address growing uneasiness about future timber supplies, studied its forestry situation anew and recommended as one solution more intensive management of Forest Service and Bureau of Land Management lands in Oregon. The state also announced the need for increased state attention to the productivity of Oregon's 3.5 million acres of nonindustrial private forestland (NIPF). Accordingly, in March, 1978, the Governor established a special task force to consider alternatives for dealing with the NIPF problem in Oregon. Among the possible solutions suggested were public leasing of small woodlots and state taxes and other financial incentives to create an economic climate favorable to investment in improved NIPF productivity.

Oregon's activity on a wide variety of forest policy issues illustrates the developing strength and independence of state forestry programs. The federal government provided the primary impetus in the incentive, federal-state cooperative, and small forest management areas; but by the 1970s, certain key states were beginning to take the initiative. The passage of strict forest practice acts on the Pacific Coast between 1971 and 1974 reflected state ability to function in areas where federal efforts had failed.

THE PROBLEM OF NONINDUSTRIAL PRIVATE FORESTS: FEDERAL RESPONSE AND CURRENT DEBATE

Throughout American forestry history, professionals and legislators have been concerned about the different ownership classes of forestland. In the early years of forestry, policymakers concentrated on reserving the national forests in federal ownership and establishing the U.S. Forest Service. Once the federal system of forest reserves was organized, overcutting on private lands became a major concern of W. B. Greeley, Forest Service Chief during the 1920s. The financial crash of 1929 and the ensuing Depression foreclosed most opportunities for improved industrial forestry and aggravated the abandonment of cutover lands for failure to pay property taxes. It was not surprising, therefore, that private forestlands were identified in the 1933 Copeland report as the nation's foremost timber supply concern. The need for national industrial recovery during the Franklin D. Roosevelt administration focused continuing government concern on improving the performance of the nation's large private timber producers.

The increasing government attention to the problems of private forestry, the growing activity of national and regional forest products associations, the influence of the short-lived lumber code of the National Industrial Recovery Act, and the steadily improving economic conditions throughout the 1930s all combined to make industrial timberland management more respectable, responsible, and successful than it had been. At the close of World War II, with its tremendous demand for forest products, the timber industry emerged essentially in its modern form, which was at last fairly firmly committed to ensuring the continued productivity of large holdings of private forestlands. Needing new fields to conquer, forestry experts began to eye the performance of the small, nonindustrial private forests.

The Forest Service highlighted the small forest problem in its 1958 periodic report, *Timber Resources for America's Future,* which predicted that "there is no timber famine in the offing, but some shortages may be expected . . . " By the early 1970s, the agency predicted significant softwood shortages by the year 2000, assuming unchanging prices and intensity of management. Responding to these concerns, the President's Advisory Panel on Timber and the Environment reflected the broad consensus that achieving high productivity on nonindustrial private forests was a major forest policy goal for the years 1990–2020. President Jimmy Carter reiterated and reinforced this belief in his 1977 environmental message when he announced that " . . . the greatest challenge remaining to American forestry is to improve the condition and productivity of small, private forest holdings. . . ." (Clawson, 275).

Federal concern over NIPFs was only partially attributable to projected shortfalls of timber. NIPFs were also given special attention because of their alleged low productivity in comparison with public and industrial timberlands. NIPFs have been branded as the most mismanaged timberland ownership class in the United States. Experts studying this problem ascribed low NIPF productivity to a variety of factors arising from their small size. Forest Service statistics showed that NIPFs covered 296 million acres—a full 59 percent of the commercial forestland in the United States; however, the total acreage was broken into farm woodlands and miscellaneous private holdings, which averaged a mere 71 acres. The management of NIPFs was, consequently, scattered among several million separate parcels (Zivnuska, 232–233). The small size of the average NIPF posed a fundamental problem of forest economics. Small size meant that NIPF owners could not take advantage of the economics of scale which enabled larger landholders to make efficient and profitable investments in their industrial operations. Higher per-acre expenses and difficulties in obtaining easy access to credit discouraged many NIPF owners from making investments in restocking, stand improvement, favorable species conversion, and other forestry activities.

The timber productivity problem on NIPFs was associated not only with small size and economics of scale but also with the diverse objectives of the owners themselves. While roughly half of the NIPF acreage was in the hands of forest farmers since the mid-1950s, these owners had lost ground to the "miscellaneous" classification of small private landholders, which includes a nonuniform hodgepodge of individuals encompassing just about every occupation and life aspiration imaginable. Few, in fact, have any interest in the forest production capabilities of their properties. The suboptimal management on NIPFs was thus blamed on a combination of ignorance, lack of motivation, alternative ownership goals, inadequate financial ability, and short-time horizons on the part of most forest land owners.

Early Programs for NIPFs

This traditional diagnosis of the small forest problem resulted in a standard government response until the 1970s. The first major national controversy over private timberlands in the 1920s led not to federal regulation but to the cooperation-incentive approach established by the Clark-McNary Act of 1924 (see Ch. 5, pp. 126–129). Federal forestry involvement was extended beyond national forest boundaries not through rigid directive but by cost sharing with the states and technical assistance, information, and educational services to state agencies and private owners. The incentive approach was instituted specifically for forest farms in the Cooperative Farm Forestry Act of 1937.

This was repeated in 1950 with the passage of the Cooperative Forest Management Act, which extended the federal-state aid to the miscellaneous category of NIPF owners as well as to processors of primary forest products.

Because NIPFs were viewed from the national level as predominantly a productivity problem and because their low productivity was attributed to economic and motivational barriers, federal incentives were adopted as the appropriate policy to influence the use and management of small private forests. The incentive strategy was also attractive since it allowed congressional representatives to send federal funds into their respective districts. Regulation, in contrast, was not a promising means for garnering public support. Furthermore, most policymakers regarded regulation as overly burdensome to the small owner, who had enough other economic disincentives with which to contend.

The technical assistance, education, and research services offered under the Cooperative Farm Management (CFM) program were one basic incentive approach. Another major approach involved making direct financial outlays to farmers and NIPF owners to encourage the undertaking of certain desirable management practices. This direct financial alternative was first instituted through the Agricultural Conservation Program (ACP), created in response to the Depression and Dustbowl conditions under the Soil Conservation and Domestic Allotment Act of 1936. Administered by the Agricultural Stabilization and Conservation Service, ACP funds were used for two primary purposes —tree planting and timber stand improvement. The program is known as the Rural Environmental Assistance Program (REAP).

The experience of NIPF owners under the Agricultural Conservation Program indicates a basic problem confronted by forestry interests when they are subsumed under a broad-based agricultural conservation program. In the late 1960s and 1970s, ACP expenditures were only averaging about 1 cent per acre of NIPF land (Skok and Gregersen, 202), reflecting the difficulties which NIPF interests had competing with other agricultural concerns for available ACP funds. As a result, Congress enacted the new Forestry Incentives Program (FIP) under Title X of the Agriculture and Consumer Protection Act of 1973. Administratively, FIP was equally if not more complex than the Agricultural Conservation Program. The Agricultural Stabilization and Conservation service administered the program while the Forest Service maintained a technical oversight role and states and counties approved payments and worked directly with the landowners. Despite this involved arrangement, FIP gave small landowners a financial incentive program of their own for timber production purposes. Accordingly, ACP declined in importance as an incentive program in private forestry.

The creation of FIP in the midst of the environmental decade showed clearly that regardless of congressional preoccupation with regulation as the major method of achieving environmental quality goals, the incentive approach continued to be the preferred tool for encouraging enhanced productivity in the nation's nonindustrial private forests. By the middle of the decade, FIP combined with its predecessor, ACP; the Cooperative Farm Management program; and additional aid, such as that instituted under the cooperative Forest Pest Control Act of 1947 to offer a variety of technical, research, informational, management planning, and financial services to the small forest owner. Two new cooperative forestry bills were introduced during the Ninety-fifth Congress; and, while they did not pass, they reflected continued public support for the federal incentive approach.

Debate over NIPFs and FIPs

While support for NIPF incentives was sustained in Congress, a number of forestry and forest policy experts began to question seriously the federal approach to the NIPF problem and the very nature of the problem itself. Critics maintained first that NIPF incentive programs tended to have excessive per-acre costs, to be loosely defined, to be poorly coordinated and awkwardly administered, and failed to address elusive landowner goals and motivation. Cooperative incentive programs by their nature necessarily involved a variety of agencies at different government levels, but agency overlap in program implementation was viewed as the major problem in delivery of services to NIPFs (Sedjo and Ostermeier, p. 33). Regarding the availability of incentive resources to small forest owners, the President's Advisory Panel on Timber and the Environment reached the dismal conclusion that "the present level of assistance has no significant effect on the intensity of forest practice" on NIPFs. Responding to these and other problems, President Carter questioned the programs in his 1977 environmental message and "asked . . . the Secretary of Agriculture to undertake a Comprehensive study of the Cooperative Forestry Program" (Glascock, 450).

Other contemporary students pointed out that NIPFs were *not* unproductive, as was so commonly thought. One prominent resource expert compared NIPFs with industrial timberlands on a state-by-state basis and concluded that their productivities were actually comparable. NIPFs were making significant contributions to national timber supplies in the 1970s and were especially productive in timber-boom regions of the South (Clawson, 4). Second, Forest Service projections of future timber shortages were open to challenge. Critics of contemporary Forest Service projections maintain that the agency ignores future price rises which would balance supply and demand in the last decades of the present century. In addition, the critics emphasized that any future timber shortage which does arise will occur in the softwood category. This limits the future productivity contribution of NIPFs, which are overloaded with hardwoods and deficiently stocked in softwood species.

Other factors also caused critics to challenge the federal reliance on future NIPF productivity to meet national timber supply goals. NIPF owners have diverse goals which often do not include timber harvesting. Many NIPFs are held for recreational, scenic, sentimental, or speculative property investment purposes. No amount of federal proselytizing on the virtues of forest management can persuade an owner with firm alternative goals to make investments for timber productivity. On the other hand observers of NIPF owner behavior have suggested that, if there really is good money to be made in forestry investments, the average NIPF owner will be among the first to invest. This reasoning suggests that if tree farming is profitable, NIPF owners will manage their lands accordingly; if it is not profitable, massive federal incentive programs are not going to change anything.

These alternative views on the NIPF problem began to be circulated in the 1970s and reflected both an interest in valuing forestlands for outputs other than timber production as well as a need to reasses basic and long-standing assumptions underlying the national timber supply problem. Experts could not agree on the nature and possibility of a projected timber famine, on the overall presence or lack of productivity, on small forest properties, on the efficacy of existing federal incentive programs, or on the relative merits of other approaches which might be implemented to accomplish the same goal. Uncertainty over these problems prevailed in the 1970s, but preoccupation with NIPF productivity persisted and incentives ruled the day.

STATE TAXATION OF PRIVATE FOREST PROPERTIES

In general, incentive programs for nonindustrial private forests can be classified into three major types: cost sharing in various forest management practices, the direct provision of technical and educational services, and the institution of certain fiscal policies to create a more favorable climate for small forest investment. The first two incentive types were pioneered by the federal government, implemented through state and local cooperation, and typified by the Cooperative Farm Management Program and, most recently, the FIP. The third type of incentive—fiscal policy—was activated at the federal level by changes in forestry income taxation procedures which have already been discussed in Chapter 7.

It was the states, however, which took the lead in another important area of fiscal incentive policy—property taxation. State activity was predicated on the belief that burdensome property taxes added one more cost which, at least in small forestry operations, was often a disincentive to invest. While forest property taxation was recognized as a problem as early as 1870, the issue was revived with special implications in the 1970s.

The revenues derived from property taxation have always been the major source of income for state and local government. Property taxation policy is made at the state level and implemented by county assessors and other local tax officials. Each state has formulated its taxation system to suit its own particular needs, and many different tax schemes thus exist. In general, however, property taxes are determined on an *ad valorem* basis based on the market value of the property. The process of taxation involves *assessing* (estimating the dollar value of the property, which may or may not equal the fair market value), *setting the tax rate* according to the anticipated revenue needed and the sum of individual assessments, and *collecting* and *providing for delinquency* or failure to pay (Gregory, 192–193).

The classic formulation of the forest taxation problem was made by Fred R. Fairchild, Professor of Political Economy at Yale in the 1908 report of President T. Roosevelt's National Conservation Commission. According to Fairchild, forest property taxation was inequitable because of inherent time lags. Forest property owners must pay taxes at least once a year while their property produces timber-related income only once every several years or, indeed, several decades. Theoretically, the perfect sustained yield forest produced income once every year and, thus, tax costs could be met; but forests did not produce income that frequently. The longer the income from the property was deferred, the more the tax discriminated against the forest owner. NIPF owners were especially hard pressed because of their low-level investments in forest management practices and the fact that they might only harvest their property once in a lifetime. Larger enterprises were also burdened, especially if they owned extensive backlogs of old-growth timber (Zivnuska, 251–252).

Onerous property taxes were a deterrent to sound forest management because they encouraged owners to liquidate their standing timber crop, often prematurely, as the most expeditious way to meet the tax bill. Furthermore, they discouraged investment in replanting—a cost which owners could not expect to receive returns on for many years. In the meantime, property taxes based on land value plus timber value would become due regularly regardless of the deferred nature of the income expected from the future management of the property for forestry purposes. Moreover, fire, disease, and insect infestation posed ever-present threats which, despite advances in their control, could wipe out a forestry investment before its anticipated periodic income could be realized.

Early State Forest Taxation Alternatives

As the specter of local and national timber famine loomed in the late nineteenth century, forestry professionals and government officials identified the property tax as an adverse influence on the holding and management of forestlands for long-term production. Furthermore, growing awareness of the hydrological and other benefits of forests stimulated interest in modifying the property tax to encourage tree planting and conservation in the plains states. The earliest techniques adopted by concerned state governments varied but generally fell into the categories of exemption, bounty, and rebate laws. These measures did not modify the property tax; they simply exempted certain classes of timber or forestland from it or offered financial rewards to owners planting trees. Although the first exemption law was passed in the Nebraska Territory in 1861, a better-known example was the Wisconsin Forest Tax Law of 1868. This act applied to "tree belts" of 5 acres or more, which were exempted from taxation until the trees grew to 12 feet in height. The Wisconsin measure also included a bounty feature which entitled owners to a tax rebate of $2 per acre after their trees exceeded the 12-foot limit (Solberg, 110).

A number of other states, mostly in the Midwest and Northeast, followed the lead of Nebraska and Wisconsin, adapting the exemption or rebate models to fit various ownership or management characteristics deserving special tax treatment. A few states, such as Indiana in 1899 and Iowa in 1906, chose to implement a fixed-assessment approach where the taxable value of certain forest properties was limited to a certain nominal figure, such as $1 per acre. Most of these special laws, however, were narrow and had limited effect. Certain of the laws were eventually repealed; some were amended, often repeatedly; and others were left on the books but were left unused.

The Yield Tax

Although states continued to experiment with variations on the exemption and fixed-assessment themes, an entirely new concept in forest property taxation became popular in the early 1900s. This concept, known as the yield tax, was attributed to an engineer and timber cruiser from Manistee, Michigan, named J. J. Hubbell.

The idea is relatively simple: As long as timber was growing on the land, it would not be taxed as real property. The land itself would be valued separately from the timber and taxed according to either normal or modified procedures. The tax on the timber would be treated more as an income than a property tax and would be collected as a certain percentage of stumpage value *at the time of harvest.* In this way, Hubbell solved the inherent time lag or income deferment problem. The bulk of the owner's tax would be paid when income from the forest property was realized.

The yield tax represents an attempt to satisfy two competing interests: those of the local taxing authority in ensuring adequate income and those of the forestry community and property owners in maintaining productive timberlands. Income is provided to local government by taxing the bare land; any resulting decrease in the tax base can be cushioned in various ways, such as the establishment of special state funds or other arrangements. Property owners benefit from the deferral of the timber tax until harvest, when they are best able to bear the tax. As a result, the temptation to cut prematurely is eliminated and the value of the property is enhanced for forest management use (Teeguarden, 816).

Michigan was the first state to adopt a yield tax in 1911. New York, Pennsylvania, Connecticut, Vermont, and ten other states followed rapidly.

Wisconsin turned to a yield tax in 1927 for tracts larger than 40 acres to supplement its existing exemption system. In general, the yield tax was quick to catch on in the East but was not widely accepted in the South and West until the 1920s and early 1930s. While state yield tax programs were usually optional, in 1931 Washington passed a mandatory yield tax.

The Fairchild Commission Report

In spite of the many states adopting special forest taxation measures, the severe economic conditions prevalent in rural America after World War I and during the Depression guaranteed that almost any tax would bankrupt small forestry operations. The "cut-and-get-out" approach to the public lands of early forestry days evolved in the 1920s and to wholesale abandonment of cutover private forestlands for failure to pay property taxes. Local governments desperate for funds increased the tax burden on the remaining property owners and thereby further accentuated tax delinquency.

In 1923, Congress responded by appointing the Senate Select Committee on Reforestation, chaired by Charles McNary of Oregon. As a result of the committee's studies, a comprehensive study of property taxation was authorized in the Clarke-McNary Act of 1924. Known as the Forest Taxation Inquiry, the study was chaired by the renowned authority Fred Fairchild. Its report, *Forest Taxation in the United States,* was published in 1935 and continues to be a basic reference in the field.

The Fairchild report did not recommend the yield tax because payment at harvest did not provide dependable revenue to local government. The inquiry, also rejecting exemption and rebate measures as unsatisfactory, proposed three novel alternatives which were based on alternations in assessment, the tax rate, and the timing of tax payments. The three altertives, termed "adjusted," "deferred," and "differential" timber taxes, were designed to address the needs of both property owners and local governments. They were so complicated and difficult that they were coolly received and never adopted by any state.

By the end of World War II, twenty-six states had some special forest taxation laws, approximately half of which were yield taxes. However, only a small fraction of eligible forestlands were classified under the available provisions. In many states, owners preferred to keep their properties under the general tax laws, often because special tax treatment was regarded as a liability against the property or variations in assessment actually made taxation under the old regime more favorable.

Taxes and Land Conversions

National interest in the forest taxation problem waned in the 1950s because of general prosperity and the low level of local property taxes. By the mid-1960s, however, the situation was changing. The new urban "explosion" and movement to the suburbs and rural fringe areas combined with inflation to escalate the assessed values of most land. The property tax problem became most acute around urban areas, where owners of prime agricultural and forest lands found it more profitable to sell to developers than to retain their properties as open space. Rising property valuations plus accelerated tax rates created an overall growth in the property tax which, by the 1970s, outpaced inflation (Zivnuska, 251–252).

Rising property taxes caused conversion and development of agricultural and wooded lands on the urban-rural fringe and became a concern to a public increasingly sensitized to environmental values. The statistics were certainly alarming; over 8 million acres of prime U.S. farmland were withdrawn from agricultural production and converted to other uses between 1967 and 1975 (CEQ, xii). Maryland, in 1956, was the first state to enact special legislation to deal with the property tax problem. California, in 1965, passed a Land Conversion Act which enabled counties to enter into long-term agreements with landowners whereby their property would be assessed at a lower, present-use value as long as it was not converted to uses incompatible with the defined character of "open space." Many other states in the 1960s and 1970s implemented comparable preferential assessment strategies to relieve open-space owners of the excessive burden of a property tax based on the development potential or full market value of their lands.

Many of the nation's private timberlands were located far enough from major metropolitan areas that their assessed values for taxation purposes were not directly affected by suburban development pressures. Still, land values were rising and stumpage prices jumped considerably in the late 1960s. Accordingly, the property tax again became a major cost in forestry operations. These financial pressures, combined with professional and environmentalist agitation for improved forest management, caused a number of states including Michigan, New York, and Wisconsin to reexamine their old special forest tax property laws. The major timber-producing states in the West, however, were the most active. Oregon, which already had a relatively successful yield tax scheme, held hearings to amend its legislation and California acted in 1976 (Ayer, 417).

Earlier in the twentieth century, California lagged behind taxation developments in other states. It did not even adopt an exemption law until 1926. Although the exemption provision endured and was applied to large acreages of private timberlands, it was criticized for encouraging clear cutting of older timber, for discouraging selection and uneven-aged logging, and for penalizing the owner leaving timber buffer strips for environmental protection purposes. These concerns led to adoption of a yield tax in 1976. In most respects, the new state law followed the traditional yield tax format of subjecting the bare land to the normal property tax while collecting an income-type tax on the forest products at harvest. The law was mandatory, however, and required all private lands within "timberland preserve zones" to be subject to the special tax classification system. As a result, California's law has been described as "more aggressive than the (yield tax) systems developed in most states" and is in the forefront of contemporary efforts to solve the forest property tax problem (Teeguarden, 819).

Challenge to Tax Oriented "Solutions"

In the 1970s, forest economists continue to challenge Fairchild's diagnosis of the forest taxation dilemma. Just as predictions of timber famine and diminishing small forest productivity led to federal-state incentive programs to aid the NIPF owner, many special state taxation schemes were predicated on the assumption tax incentives would encourage commercial forestry. Contemporary critics, however, have reevaluated the taxation issue and claim that if overall economic conditions are favorable and timber prices sufficiently high, the problem of taxation becomes insignificant. Critics also point out that the time bias of the forest property tax essentially disappears if one regards forest growth as accumulating value or income which is being *reinvested* rather than *deferred* (Klemperer, 651). Finally, the financial burden of the property tax may have an effect opposite that of causing owners to liquidate their timber; it may actually spur owners to reinvest in their forestry operations or to branch out into nontimber enterprises to realize the additional profit necessary to meet their rising tax bill.

Dissatisfaction with most state taxation systems, as well as professional disagreement over the nature of the problem and how to solve it, means that forest property taxation persists as an age-old and unresolved issue. Taxation reform at the federal level was a key issue in the Carter presidential campaign of 1976, and revitalized public interest in the subject has permeated all levels of government and has been adopted as an overriding concern of millions of individuals and private enterprises. Perhaps the only consensus is that timber taxation policy is just one aspect of the complex problem of stimulating reforestation and forestland productivity. The fate of the special forest property tax measures during the 1920s and 1930s illustrates how taxation policy alone cannot mitigate the ills of a faltering economy. In today's environmental era, a multifaceted approach to productivity problems, especially on nonindustrial private forests, must include tax reform along with improved credit availability, interest rates, stumpage prices, economies of scale, education, technical advice, incentives, research, and owner and public goals. Even more important than solutions, the problem being addressed must be properly identified and assessed. The property "taxpayers revolt" which came to the forefront of state politics in California and other states in 1978 sustained the conclusions of early Fairchild critics and showed that the structure of the tax was of less concern than the mode of its administration and the inflated costs of government service. The lessons of the past, therefore, may help not so much to indicate answers as to help us ask better questions.

SUMMARY

Concern for environmental quality in the 1960s and 1970s focused public attention on the use, management, and conversion of private lands. Reliance on government regulation became a more prominent means of controlling large-scale private development, including forestry operations. Land use regulation, however, was politically acceptable only at the state level. For smaller parcels of land, such as forest farms or private woodlots, the incentive approach was preferred and was implemented through both continuing federal assistance programs and revisions in state forest property taxation laws. A third major policy option for controlling private land—transfer from private to public ownership—was common in the early twentieth century; but the regulation and incentive approaches were the dominant mode of the 1970s.

During the environmental era, the general public and state and local government agencies sharpened their interest in private forestry activities. The minimization of environmental impacts in forestry became a concern on a par with, or even greater than, the more traditional problem of private land productivity. Public pressure to control undesirable environmental impacts led to the adoption in Oregon, California, and Washington of new statewide forest practice acts. The strictness of these acts far exceeded the requirements of their predecessors passed during the first major wave of state regulatory activity in the 1940s. The states accomplished a feat in this area which had eluded the federal government since the early 1900s. The three Pacific Coast states, in fact, provided a precedent for the federal government in 1974 when the EPA proposed a forest practice act based on the Pacific Coast models to be applicable nationwide for meeting the requirements of section 208 of the 1972 Federal Water Pollution Control Act (see Chapter 9).

State leadership in the forest practice arena was paralleled by state initiatives taken in other fields of environmental protection. In 1970, California passed what was soon recognized as the nation's strictest state environmental policy act. In 1975, this law became entangled with the requirements of the 1973 state Forest Practice Act and strengthened the latter's standards and rules. California also led the states in legislation passed to protect its coastal zone. Washington was in the forefront of this effort by virtue of its 1971 Shoreline Management Act. Oregon became famous for its clear achievements in coastal conservation, litter control, and comprehensive statewide land use planning. The federal government, in contrast, came close to adopting, but was never able to pass, an act requiring national land use planning.

Balanced against the period's preoccupation with environmental quality was a continuing concern with the productivity of the nation's private timberlands. This concern focused not so much on industrial holdings, which had come under increasingly improved management since the end of World War II. Rather, most forestry experts pinpointed the small nonindustrial private forests—covering over half of the country's commercial timberland but averaging under 100 acres per holding—as the long-term solution to the nation's projected timber shortfall. To motivate more efficient forest productivity on these lands, Congress instituted the Forestry Incentives Program in 1973. This reasserted the federal government's ongoing dedication to the concept of cooperative service rather than outright regulation.

The states, for their part, reevaluated their forest property taxation schemes which, although experimented with and modified since the late 1880s, still tended to act as a disincentive to investment in forestry, particularly for the small forest owner.

The strong state move to regulate management practices on private lands was confined to forests and did not extend to ranges. Most Western states had, over the years, adopted a variety of specific laws to regulate fencing, brush burning, and other private rangeland activities. By the 1970s, however, no state had a Rangelands Practice Act comparable to the comprehensive statutes passed to control private forestry on the Pacific Coast. So far as environmental quality and the nation's ranges were concerned, the public concentrated the bulk of its attention on the federal lands. Private rangelands came to the forefront of prevailing public policy concerns only in the context of their interrelationship with major federal activities, such as energy development and strip mining in Wyoming and neighboring states. In such cases, however, environmentalists worried more about how federal development would impair the use of private rangelands than about how private grazing activities were threatening the environment. Indeed, across the spectrum of resource areas of wilderness, minerals, wildlife, forests, and ranges, public interest in federal activities and federal lands was paramount, notwithstanding a strong, concomitant concern with the management and state regulation of private sector wild lands.

REFERENCES CITED

American Forestry Association. *The Progress of Forestry: 1945 to 1950*. Washington, D.C.: American Forestry, 1951.

Ayer, J. D. "Public Regulation of Private Forestry: A Survey and a Proposal." 10 *Harvard Journal on Legislation* 407 (1973).

Clawson, Marion. "Economic Timber Production Characteristics of Nonindustrial Private Forests in the United States: Discussion Paper." Cited in Roger Sedjo and David Ostermeier, *Policy Alternatives for Nonindustrial Private Forests*. Washington, D.C.: Society of American Foresters, 1978.

Dana, Samuel T., and Krueger, M. *California Lands: Ownership, Use, and Management.* Washington, D.C.: American Forestry Association, 1958.

————, and Johnson, Evert W. *Forestry Education In America Today and Tomorrow.* Washington, D. C.: Society of American Foresters, 1963.

Environmental Law Reporter. "The National Environmental Policy Act." 5 *ELR* 50005 (1975).

Fairchild, Fred R. *Forest Taxation in The United States.* Washington. D.C.: U.S. Government Printing Office, 1935.

Forestry News. "California Adopts New Forest Practice Act." 71 *Journal of Forestry* 238 (1973).

————. "California's Law Jam." 73 *Journal of Forestry* 238 (1975).

————. "California Forestry—Up the Redwood Creek." 74 *Journal of Forestry* 95 (1976).

Glascock, H. R., Jr. "The View from Here—Small-Forest Wood: Who Needs? Who Pays?" 75 *Journal of Forestry* 448 (1977).

————. "The View from Here—Greater Outputs from NIPFs: What Programs are Cost-Effective?" 76 *Journal of Forestry 268 (1978).*

Gregory, G. Robinson. *Forest Resource Economics.* New York: The Ronald Press Company, 1972.

Hostetter, R. D. "Oregon Will Surprise You!" 71 *Journal of Forestry* 474 (1973).

Klemperer, W. D. "Unmodified Forest Property Tax—Is It Fair?" 75 *Journal of Forestry* 650 (1977).

Sedjo, Robert A., and Ostermeier, David M. *Policy Alternatives for Nonindustrial Private Forests.* Washington, D.C.: Society of American Foresters, 1978.

Skok, R. A., and Gregersen, H. M. "Motivating Private Forestry: An Overview." 73 *Journal of Forestry* 202 (1975).

Solberg, E. D. *New Laws for New Forests: Wisconsin's Forest-Fire, Tax, Zoning, and County-Forest Laws in Operation.* Madison: University of Wisconsin Press, 1961.

Stanford Environmental Law Society. *California's Private Timberlands: Regulation, Taxation, Preservation.* Stanford, Cal.: Stanford Law School, 1973.

State of California, Assembly Select Committee on Environmental Quality. *Environmental Bill of Rights.* Sacramento: California State Assembly, 1970.

Teeguarden, Dennis E. "Transition to the Timber Yield Tax: The California Case." 74 *Journal of Forestry* 813 (1976).

Trzyna, T. C., and Jokela, A. W. *The California Environmental Quality Act: An Innovation in State and Local Decisionmaking.* Claremont, Cal.: Center for California Public Affairs, 1974.

U.S. Council on Environmental Quality. *Environmental Quality—1977: The Eighth Annual Report of the Council on Environmental Quality.* Washington, D.C.: Government Printing Office, 1977.

U.S. President's Advisory Panel on Timber and the Environment. *Final Report of the President's Advisory Panel on Timber and the Environment.* Washington, D.C.: Government Printing Office, 1973.

Zivnuska, John. "Forestry Investment for Multiple Uses Among Multiple Ownership Types." In Marion Clawson, ed., *Forest Policy for the Future: Conflict, Compromise, Consensus.* Washington, D.C.: Resources for the Future, 1974.

Chapter 11

Citizen Activism in Forest and Range Policy in the 1970s

The same citizen activism and concern for environmental quality that led to extensive pollution control and land use regulations was also decisive in the continuing redefinition of federal land management programs. Although the atmosphere in which all groups maneuvered was intense and politicized and mistrust of government endured, the policy debate proceeded largely without the street demonstrations which had characterized political action in the 1960s. Citizen activism was manifest in a continuing elaboration of the goals and values which merged in the 1960s and in the widespread public attention focused on resource issues. Litigation and legislation affecting forest and range policy made national headlines; while much was done, it is not clear what was accomplished. The main theme emerging from the activity of the 1970s is uncertainty in wild lands management. Resource management is no longer suffused with the clarity of purpose and sense of direction that made forestry a national crusade at the turn of the century.

Uncertainty stems first from diversification of the variables which must be weighed in land management decisions. Increased pressure from traditional user groups has been accompanied by numerous additional concerns and demands. Environmental quality, endangered species, historic and cultural preservation, and coastal zone protection programs have multiplied the demands of amenity-oriented forest and rangeland users. The traditional conflict between wilderness and timber production has been exacerbated by intensified pressures and extensive wilderness designation debates. Commodity production pressures have also been diversified, most notably by the energy crisis and the growing need to allocate land to minerals production while protecting surface resources. The major drought of the mid-1970s also focused new attention on wild lands as watersheds and the need to produce and protect water supplies. Competition over water allocation was sharpened by the growing demands of the urbanizing arid West and energy developers, and was further complicated by the Native American rights movement. Long-ignored treaty provisions have given rise to virtually inestimable Native American claims for both land and water. These traditional and emerging demands must all be balanced within constraints imposed by recognition of national policy goals in the areas of full employment, inflation control, the international balance of trade, and a host of other local and national concerns.

Uncertainty stems secondly from the increasingly complicated political arena in which forest and range policy is debated. Consensus on goals and priorities in wild lands policy has broken down, and assumptions which formed the bedrock of the renewable resource management professions are being broadly questioned from a number of diverse perspectives. In this atmosphere, industry and professional land managers are mistrusted, environmental groups are growing and uncompromising, and elected officials are unable to articulate standards for coherent land management programs. Citizen activism, the major force in land management policy in the 1970s, has significantly altered the decision-making process. Following the civil rights movement precedent, environmentalists successfully sought procedures for citizen review and participation in executive agency decision making. Program planning systems were significantly reformed under sustained pressure. Citizen activists also increasingly turned to the courts to vindicate their views. As was true in the shaping of environmental regulations, court proceedings have become a major avenue for defining land management priorities.

INTENSIFYING DEMAND AND DIVERSIFYING USES

Multiple-use management has long been a complex balancing process, but recently the problem has been compounded. Demand for the traditional goods is increasing, and more and different goods are demanded. Increased use strains the land's capabilities and requires increasingly adroit compromises which will never satisfy everyone. Moveover, these demands require land managers to deal with new issues, not all of which are within the purview of professional land management competence.

Mining and Mineral Development

Forest and range managers have traditionally ignored subsurface values. In the private sector, mineralized land is not managed for multiple use; it is simply mined. This was also true, until recently, for public land because public land laws emphasize mineral development as the highest use of the land. In addition to the law, both forest and range managers are trained to focus on renewable surface resources and tend not to think about managing or replenishing non-renewable resources.

Attention is now focused on minerals management for several reasons. First, the energy crisis of the early 1970s made it politically necessary and economically feasible to exploit domestic energy minerals, and much of our mineral wealth is on the public lands. Second, mining can have severe environmental and aesthetic consequences and concerns many. Finally, several new statutes have given land managing agencies the authority to control the surface disturbances associated with mining.

Attempts to Control Hard Rock Mining   The basic law of hard rock mining, as discussed above (see pp. 27) promotes mineral development. The 1872 act makes no reference to minimizing or mitigating surface disturbances associated with mining operations, and efforts to modify the law to include such provisions have been unavailing. However, during the mid-1970s, increased mining and pressure from environmentalists encouraged both the Forest Service and BLM to reread their authorities, as suggested by NEPA, in the light of national goals for environmental protection. The Forest Service has no authority over the mineral resources on the national forests; the Department of the Interior retains all control over the nation's mineral estate, most of which is exercised by the BLM and the U.S. Geological Survey. However, the Forest Service is responsible for the management of surface resources. Accordingly, in December, 1973, the Forest Service proposed regulations to minimize the impact of hard rock mining on those surface resources.

Under the regulations, the forest supervisor can require an operation plan specifying measures to be taken to reduce surface damage and reclaim the site. Performance bonds reflecting the cost of reclamation can be required. The Forest Service approves plans, and it may require modifications. Periodic inspections are conducted to assure compliance (Glascock, 162). Public response to the proposal was intense and criticism was heated; however, the regulations were adopted on September 1, 1974. BLM proposed similar regulations in December, 1976, but they were withdrawn by the newly elected Carter administration following violent attacks. The Forest Service regulations, however, remain in force in spite of storms of protest and lawsuits from the mining industry.

Developments in the Coal Program   BLM did, however, succeed in its efforts to reinterpret the Mineral Leasing Act of 1920. The Secretary of the Interior always had authority to write restrictions "in the public interest" into the leases; NEPA and the controversy surrounding coal and phosphate mining encouraged Interior officials to include environmental protection requirements. This policy change occurred for two reasons. First, a departmentwide review of the coal-leasing program in the early 1970s revealed major problems, particularly that millions of acres were under coal leases being held for speculative purposes, waiting for the price of coal to go up. The Secretary of the Interior stopped all coal leasing until a program could be developed which would promote actual mining while curbing speculation and environmentally unsound practices. Second, the Secretary faced decisions on two phosphate leases in especially sensitive environments—the Osceola and Los Padres National Forests—and sought a way to deny leases.

In response to these problems, key statutory terms of the Mineral Leasing Act were redefined. To qualify for a preference-right lease under the act, a prospector had to "diligently develop" a deposit of "commercial quantity." A commercial quantity was interpreted to mean a deposit of such quality and size that the operator could show that working it would be profitable even when all the lease terms, including environmental protection requirements, were met. The new diligent development rules require lessees to begin mining promptly and continue mining steadily. If these requirements are not met, the department can cancel the lease. These new rules enable the BLM to cancel speculative leases and to condition new leases to protect the environment. In spite of opposition from the coal industry, Congress both confused and supported the department efforts by passing the Coal Leasing Act Amendments of 1975. The act accomplishes many of the same things as the Interior regulations in slightly different ways. By the end of 1976, requirements of the new act were incorporated into the new regulations.

Leasing did not occur, however, because of a lawsuit brought by environmentalists (*NRDC* v. *Hughes*) and the change in administrations. NRDC successfully challenged the adequacy of the environmental impact statement on the coal development program. Leasing was enjoined until NEPA requirements were met. Additional delay in leasing was caused by the Carter administration's efforts to review the entire controversial program again.

Although the NRDC case has been settled, two agencies recently created by Congress contribute to a continuation of confusion. A long-sought bill to control adverse effects of strip-mining operations was signed on August 3, 1977. It is complex legislation covering many controversial surface management issues such as surface owner consent, state enforcement authority, and coordination with EPA on air and water quality standards. In spite of the state focus of the enforcement provisions, a new agency in Interior—the Office of Surface Mining and Reclamation Enforcement (OSM)—has been established.

OSM both competes with and cooperates with the BLM and the existing minerals management structure. The entire program relies heavily on preparation and review of mining and reclamation plans, which largely duplicate the existing planning and EIS process.

The Department of Energy   The complex situation surrounding coal leasing was confounded immeasurably by a second agency created through Carter's energy reorganization—the Department of Energy. The Department of Energy regulates the "economic terms" of coal leases, controls competition within the industry, establishes diligent development requirements, and establishes production rates for the leases (2 *Public Land News* (5), 2–4). The BLM manages the leases, handles the mechanics, prepares the environmental impact statement, and controls withdrawals. The division of labor makes little sense. In the absence of a coal program and confronted by an aggressive single-use agency aimed at energy development, concern that the coal management will be severed from multiple-use land management seems justified. Uncertainty, confusion, and interagency conflict, which have characterized energy-minerals management since well before passage of the strip-mining and Energy Department legislation, has been intensified by this most recent reorganization.

Public land managers and both mineral and nonmineral users of the public lands are in a difficult position. The public lands will unquestionably be used to provide energy resources in future years. However, the institutional conflicts created in the name of reorganization prevent expeditious, environmentally sensitive energy-mineral planning and development. Given the degree of mineralization on the public lands and the importance of fuel-minerals management to the nation's future, serious ambiguity will confront all aspects of forest and range management; and minerals management will never again be ignored by forest and range managers.

New Aspects of Wilderness Management

Pressures to add extensive acreage to the national wilderness system constitute another new demand on the public lands—new in the sense of increased force and political organization. Mineral development prospects in many existing roadless areas have contributed to this pressure.

RARE I and the Conti Decision   The Forest Service has been concerned for many years that areas are sometimes added to the wilderness system in response to pressure to protect areas of only local significance. Under the 1964 Wilderness Act, it was contemplated that the Forest Service-administered component of the wilderness system would consist mainly of areas previously administered under the 1920s and 1950s regulations. However, the legislation was no barrier to other designations. As the wilderness idea became popular and recreational use increased, numerous areas were added which the Forest Service believed to be inadequately studied. In order to control the designation process, the Forest Service instituted its first roadless area study (RARE I). Relying heavily on the most extensive public involvement program in American history, the Forest Service concluded that of the 56 million acres inventoried, approximately 12 million acres warranted consideration for wilderness status. Both the Forest Service and concerned citizens and interest groups expended tremendous effort on the RARE I study, but it was unsuccessful. Preservationists criticized the Forest Service for leaving eastern national forests and national grasslands out of the inventory and for dropping 44 million acres from consideration on ill-defined grounds. The agency was vulnerable to the charge that its decisions were based on a definition of wilderness that was too "pure" or restrictive and thus minimized the potential wilderness designations.

A 1972 Sierra Club suit challenged the RARE I study on the ground that it was not accompanied by a satisfactory environmental impact statement. The litigation resulted in an out-of-court-settlement in which the Forest Service agreed not to alter any potential or de facto wilderness areas without preparing a land use plan and an EIS. This foreclosed many management activities on all 56 million identified roadless acres, pending the completion of the planning process. This action has made planning difficult for firms dependent on national forest resources. The implications of this decision have been complicated by the major changes in the Forest Service land use planning program mandated by legislation to be discussed in Chapter 12. Planning has not proceeded expeditiously.

The Eastern Wilderness Act   The exclusion of eastern lands from the RARE I study dramatized the Forest Service's belief that there were no wilderness areas in the East. This conclusion was politically unacceptable. In 1972, President Nixon ordered an accelerated review of eastern areas with wilderness potential. In January 1975, the Eastern Wilderness Act passed. It declares that the term "wilderness" is applicable in the East. No new land use category was established. All the provisions of the 1964 act are operable regarding seventeen areas Congress designated as appropriate for further study and sixteen "instant wilderness areas" extended immediate wilderness status by the new act.

Although the Forest Service was rebuked by Congress for taking an excessively purist view of what constitutes wilderness, the Eastern Wilderness Bill is problematic for wilderness advocates. It has taken some of the urgency out of the arguments in behalf of wilderness. If wilderness is a renewable rather than an irreplaceable resource, as the Eastern Wilderness Bill clearly implies, then the need to hurry to protect pristine areas is abated. If second growth, old farm sites, or abandoned mines are wilderness, then the assertion that what we fail to save now is gone forever is undermined.

The wilderness designation controversies are complicated further by the fact that the concept has changed considerably over the last fifty years. Aldo Leopold spoke originally in terms of setting aside an area of about 400,000 acres in each Western state, a unique place large enough to accommodate a two-week pack trip. In the 1930s, Bob Marshall recommended wilderness areas of 100,000 to 300,000 acres, but "tolerated" less than 100,000-acre designations (Gilligan, 84, 177, 194). The 1964 act calls for a minimum of 5000 roadless, untrammeled acres. The Eastern Wilderness Act flatly rejected a pure or literal interpretation of "untrammeled," but it does not supply clear standards to guide agency analysis of potential inclusions. Wilderness is, quite simply, what Congress says it is. Attempting to define and evaluate wilderness characteristics has become a risky and uncertain undertaking at best.

RARE II   Confronted with the withdrawal of 56 million acres resulting from the Conti decision, the timber industry joined the wilderness advocates in its long-standing efforts to have the Forest Service accelerate its wilderness review and complete the wilderness system. The industry was willing to risk losing some harvestable timber in order to clarify what would be available. Newly appointed officials in the Carter administration instituted RARE II in the late spring of 1977 to speed up land allocation. The massive national wilderness study and environmental impact statement was as much a response to industry pressure as it was a reflection of the new Assistant Secretary of Agriculture's Wilderness Society background. The goal was to inventory and evaluate all roadless areas and prepare an impact statement which would meet NEPA requirements and thereby protect wilderness areas and open nonwilderness roadless areas to multiple-use management.

The RARE II inventory was based on another massive public involvement effort, including 227 public meetings in the summer of 1977. Approximately 65.7 million roadless acres in 1920 areas were identified as having wilderness potential. The 700,000 acres freed by the normal land use planning process were reincluded as roadless areas in RARE II. Hence, all 56 million acres from RARE I were put back in the formal roadless area inventory, and another 10 million acres were added. Many of these areas were under 1000 acres with some, mostly islands, as small as 1 acre. At the time of the study, approximately 3.5 million additional acres of proposed wilderness were pending before Congress and another 15.7 million acres were already in the system, most of which were on the national forests (2–3 *Public Land News;* passim). These 84.9 million acres of wilderness and study areas constituted well over half of the total national forest acreage and were in addition to other categories of restricted use areas for recreation, wildlife habitat, scenic buffers, and so on. The impact on timber harvest was substantial (NFPA, passim); and the conflict with minerals management, particularly in the northern Rocky Mountains, was significant.

Although the RARE II study was instituted by wilderness advocates within the Carter administration, the aggregated RARE II data have not been helpful to the wilderness cause. Major congressional supporters of wilderness in both the House and Senate began actively promoting the idea of wilderness "*de*designations" as well as designations. In this altered atmosphere, preservationists are reconsidering the theory that the Forest Service should hurry to complete the wilderness system. (*Public Land Management,* May 18, 1978, p. 6.) The final EIS released in early 1979 was hotly criticized by preservationists for too-limited wilderness recommendations and won only conditional favor with industry.

RARE II posed further problems because it occurred simultaneously with the elaborate land use planning process mandated for the national forests and the continuing congressional designation of wilderness areas. The relationship among all these inventorying, planning, and designating activities has never been established. Many wilderness opponents argue that to have a special wilderness inventory undercuts ongoing multiple-use planning. Initiated in an attempt to resolve the impasse on management of 56 million acres of national forestland, RARE II added another layer of confusion to the process. The "final" action proposed by the Forest Service is not, of course, final, as wilderness designations require congressional action.

BLM Wilderness   The demand for wilderness has also affected the BLM. The 1964 Wilderness Act did not require any review of roadless areas managed by the BLM, although the BLM administratively designated several primitive areas after the legislation passed. In 1976, however, the Federal Land Policy and Management Act was enacted (see Chap. 12). It required the BLM to review, by 1991, all roadless areas of 5000 acres or more and all roadless islands with wilderness characteristics under its jurisdiction. Problematically, the statute directed the Secretary of the Interior to protect the wilderness qualities of all identified roadless areas with wilderness characteristics during the study period, while simultaneously allowing existing uses and mining activities to continue. The key issue in this statutorily mandated roadless inventory will be deciding not only which areas are roadless but which ones have "wilderness characteristics." The debate began when the BLM first presented its wilderness inventory methodology for public comment in the spring of 1978. The BLM also confronts the same difficulty as the Forest Service in coordinating wilderness inventory with overall land use planning.

New Conflicts: Native Claims and Alaska Lands

The traditional controversies concerning wilderness and mining do not, however, tell the whole story of the 1970s. Numerous new issues have emerged in the past decade which further complicate matters. Water quality, air quality, and endangered species protection have already been discussed. Technological changes in recreation also have complicated management. Snowmobiles, trail bikes, and other outdoor recreational vehicles have put increasing pressure on recreation facilities and conflict with other land use designations. These pressures have resulted in special regulations to control off-road vehicles on federal and many state lands.

Native American Rights Movement   Perhaps the most dramatic emergent claim on wild lands resources is the growing recognition of Native American treaty rights to land, water, fish, and wildlife resources. These ancient claims have gained new stature because of judicial recognition of wholesale fraud and injustice in a wide range of contracts and treaties with Indians. Because written treaties and contracts were white society's way of doing business, the courts treat any ambiguity arising in such agreements with all possible consideration to the Native Americans. Recently, numerous ambiguities have been exhumed and resolved in favor of the Native Americans. This extensive litigation has many complex and interesting ramifications, but for present purposes, three broad impacts are important.

First, Native American claims that they are exempt from state fish and game laws which infringe on hunting and fishing rights defined in land cession treaties are being recognized by more and more courts. Irrespective of the merits of the claim, to have a major user group exempt from regulation encourages serious conflict among users and threatens the integrity of many state fish and wildlife management schemes. Major litigation in Michigan, Oregon, and Washington has been decided in favor of the Indians.

Second, Native American claims to enormous, perhaps unlimited, quantities of water in the arid West will have important effects on future development in many areas. Water claims arise from basically two sources. First, many federal water developments were built ignoring or obliterating valid Native American claims to the land and the water or to hunting and fishing rights destroyed by the development. Their claims to the water or to compensation for the property illegally seized have been recognized throughout the country. A second and more complex source of water claims is the reserved water rights defined by the Supreme Court in 1908 in connection with Indian reservations. Although most treaties establishing reservations do not specifically mention water allocations, the Supreme Court reasoned that the reservation of the land implied reservation of sufficient water to achieve the purpose of the land reservation. The original intent of most Indian reservations was to develop self-sufficient agricultural societies on the reservations, thus supporting a right to water for agricultural purposes. There is, however, reason to believe that broader claims for water sufficient to make the reservations full-fledged participants in contemporary society will be upheld. The Native American claims supersede all water claims filed after the reservations were made. Because of these early priority dates, there is potential for serious disruption in the state water allocation systems.

Finally, Native Americans are making extensive claims to both public and private lands. Approximately five-eighths of the state of Maine—most of it unincorporated townships owned by major paper companies—has been claimed by the Passamaquoddy Indians. They based their allegations on the fact that Congress failed to approve the sale of land by the Indians to the state of Maine, as was required by the post—Revolutionary War Non-Intercourse Acts. Therefore, the sale was invalid and the title never passed. When the court agreed that the tribes had a good enough claim for the case to be heard on the merits, it set off a rash of similar claims throughout the East. In the West, Native American claims that whites simply usurped lands granted to the Indians by treaties appear to have validity. For example, the Shoshone Indians in Nevada are claiming that 86 percent of the public land in the state is theirs.

Irrespective of the merits of the issues raised by these claims, uncertainty results. It takes years, sometimes decades, to resolve the conflicts. In the interim, it is difficult to proceed with programs, investments, and management of the disrupted resources. Unfortunately, perhaps inevitably, such conflicts are frequently complicated by confrontations and violence.

Alaskan Native Claims   Critical as these claims are, however, they have been overshadowed by the Alaskan Native Claim Settlement Act. The Alaskan natives' claims do not grow out of violated treaty rights because the U.S. government has no treaty with the Alaskan natives. The 1867 treaty with Russia consummating the purchase of Alaska did not acknowledge native land rights at all. However, the statute which organized a civil government in Alaska in 1884 did recognize the natives' land claims. The "Organic Act" provided that no natives should be removed from their land. It only stated that a system by which the natives could obtain title to the land would be developed in subsequent legislation, which was not forthcoming. Thus, their claims were neither established nor extinguished.

When Alaska entered the Union in 1958, 99 percent of its 375 million acres were federally owned, mostly administered by the BLM. The Statehood Act provided that the state could select 103 million acres for itself over a twenty-five-year period. The state had selected one-fourth of its allotment when, in 1966, the Secretary of the Interior halted further transfers pending settlement of the native claims. Little action was taken until 1968, when

Atlantic Richfield struck oil on the North Slope and the native claims became a barrier to building the pipeline necessary to developing the oil industry.

The Alaskan Native Claims Settlement Act   The Alaskan Native Claim Settlement Act (ANCSA), passed in 1971, gives the Alaskan natives $462.5 million in grants, $500 million in mineral lease revenues, and 40 million acres of land. In order to make the land selections and administer their new wealth, the natives were organized into regional and village corporations. Existing parks, forests, and wildlife refuges were protected by the bill. The Secretary of the Interior also was authorized by section d(2) of the act to withdraw 80 million additional acres from state or native entry for national parks, forests, wildlife refuges, or utility corridors (*Congress and the Nation,* 753–754, 83). For about five years, the pipeline issue dominated the news from Alaska. However, after much litigation, the pipeline was built, brought on line, and, after a flurry of publicity surrounding the inevitable first few oil spills, forgotten. Alaska news began to come from Washington, D.C.

The d(2) Lands Debate   The ANCSA required the Secretary of the Interior to propose to Congress how he would proceed in selecting the 80 million acres which he could reserve under section d(2) of the act. Congress gave itself five years, until December, 1978, to act on the proposals. The maneuvering began in early 1977, when a consortium of environmental groups proposed 114.7 million acres of parks and wildlife refuges and 4 million acres of wild rivers in addition to 32.1 million acres of wilderness. This proposal was introduced as legislation by Representative Morris Udall. The administration proposal was fairly close to the Udall bill. Development interests in Alaska proffered a "fifth system approach" which would allow for joint federal-state administration of 45 to 55 million acres (2 *Public Land News* [8], 4). Congress failed to enact legislation by the deadline, and the Secretary of the Interior moved hastily to withdraw the proposed d(2) lands from entry in order to protect them until Congress passes the requisite legislation. Predictably, development interests in Alaska challenged the Secretary's actions in court, adding one more layer of conflict and confusion to an already complex situation. President Carter, by executive order, used the authority of the 1906 Antiquities Act to place 56 million acres in national monuments.

The original settlement of the native claims was testimony to the national feeling that original dealings with natives in the lower forty-eight were less than honorable. However, the allocation of the d(2) federal-interest lands is in many ways similar to the disposition era of the previous century. The federal land in Alaska is being allocated with inadequate regard for its quality as a resource. As a condition of statehood, 103 million acres were granted. Another 40 million acres went as a matter of social policy, not resource policy, to expiate our national guilt regarding Alaskan natives while simultaneously extinguishing their claims in order to facilitate the pipeline. Very little consideration was given to the cultural impact of thrusting responsibility for $1 billion and 40 million acres of land on an estimated 53,000 natives.

Regarding the d(2) land debates, the lack of data is particularly severe. On the basis of inadequate information regarding the people, the wildlife, mineralization, and vegetative cover, Congress and the President have allocated huge amounts of land in accordance with the dictates of pressure group politics. Little thought has been given to who will use the remote preserves or, more seriously, to how the final landholding pattern will affect management. As at the end of the disposition era, BLM is required to manage the scattered parcels of residuals. For all that has been learned in the last one hundred years about land use planning and the need for social, economic, and environmental impact assessment, the Alaska d(2) lands debate is the counterpoint. It serves as an important reminder that resource management is, at bottom, a political as much as a professional undertaking.

PUBLIC INVOLVEMENT AND LITIGATION: INCREASING COMPLEXITY IN THE FOREST AND RANGE POLICY PROCESS

The Alaska situation is particularly striking when juxtaposed with the complex land use decision-making process which evolved in the 1970s. Citizen activists effectively pressed for more extensive inventories and more open planning in the public land managing agencies. Both the Forest Service and BLM were overhauling their procedures in response to this force before the judicial elaboration of NEPA; however, the NEPA process symbolizes two major aspects of citizen access to decision making—public involvement and increased reliance on the courts. These procedures have complicated an already complex decision-making process.

Public Involvement

The citizen activism which has been so decisive in wild lands management has roots in both the protest movements of the 1960s and the traditions of the land management agencies. Citizen activists of a century ago called attention to numerous problems of public domain and public resource policies. Through their efforts, agencies were established and policies were defined which are still the nucleus of management programs. The Forest Service has always maintained an extensive program of public education and public contact and has benefited from well-organized and articulate public support. Similarly, the lack of public attention to BLM and public land needs and programs has been a cause of that agency's inability to perform basic range inventory and management functions.

Public involvement today differs dramatically from historical experience.

Earlier efforts supported agency programs. Old-line conservation groups, such as the American Forestry Association, the National Wildlife Federation, and the Audubon Society, gained influence within the agencies by cooperating, cajoling, and encouraging from the inside. In the 1970s, public involvement became more adversarial and new groups, such as Friends of the Earth and the Defenders of Wildlife, emerged. These groups have sought influence by sharply criticizing rather than cajoling the land management agencies. Many old conservation and outdoor clubs, such as the Sierra Club and the Izaak Walton League, also eschewed their quiet inside role for the active role of critics.

The Forest Service Program   The development of the Forest Service program planning process reflects the complications which public involvement, 1970s vintage, introduced to land management decision making. It grew from a response to the shattering conflict of the clear-cutting debate. Three agency publications, one issued in 1970 and two in 1971, typify the new planning process and its growing emphasis on public involvement.

In 1970, the Forest Service attempted to counter criticism that it was inappropriately overcommitted to timber management and clear cutting rather than multiple-use management by adopting a *Framework for the Future.* The agency defined a broad range of goals and policies to guide future action. The document is vague, and the goals are too general and diverse to be implemented. More significant, while never quite admitting major management errors, the agency reached out to the new and hostile groups, implying past errors by promising a "better balanced future." Publicly recognizing and responding to critics was the first step in the development of the agency's public involvement effort. It represents a significant step back from the view that the forester knows what is best for the forest and can do it without help.

The second publication in this series evinces a more developed concept of public involvement. *Timber Management for a Quality Environment,* published in 1971, goes beyond assertions of improved intentions and uses a question-and-answer format, photographs, a historical narrative, and a brief primer on harvest techniques to raise and respond to many of the issues posed by Forest Service critics. Why does the Forest Service insist on roading and harvesting in de facto wilderness areas? Is clear cutting practiced because the timber industry demands it or because it is cheap (*Timber Management for a Quality Environment,* 26–28)? Public involvement was expanded to mean informing people about what the agency was doing and why. These sincere but inadequate explanation efforts outraged many already angry citizens. Citizen activists sought power to influence decisions, not agency show-and-tell programs.

The Environmental Program for the Future (EPFF) was the third stage of Forest Service public involvement efforts. In it the agency attempted to translate the goals of the *Framework for the Future* into specific management programs tied to particular target dates and a five-year program budget. The EPFF was complemented and implemented by the introduction of the unit planning process. This process had three levels: regional, area, and unit. While national, regional, area, and unit plans have never meshed totally, the process is a significant agency response to intense public criticism. In the evolution of the unit planning process, the public involvement program reached its present configuration. The public was to participate in priority setting and land use planning rather than simply be accounted for or educated by agency personnel. This cooperative planning process explicitly attempted to overcome the timber bias of former "multiple-use" plans by inventorying and planning for all uses simultaneously. The plans begin by assessing land use capabilities rather than production requirements; the system emphasizes managing the land rather than using it to produce outputs (VTN Consolidated, Inc., 146). Full implementation of the program was short-circuited by major planning legislation, to be discussed in Chapter 12.

As described by the Forest Service, the new approach calls for "making plans responsive to the economic and social needs of the people involved," including both rural and urban populations, by involving the public in plan formulation, and in the continuing evolution of plans which will keep them responsive to change. The first step in this new phase of public involvement —to include the public in the decision-making process and to secure their advice in formulating land use plans—was taken by obtaining public reaction to the EPFF. The agency went to a great deal of effort to solicit and compile public comments on the new program and prepared a massive volume entitled *Public Comment on the EPFF* to herald the undertaking and publicize results.

NEPA, Public Involvement, and Land Use Planning   The evolving public involvement and planning developments were recast and redirected by the rise of NEPA as an important tool of environmental decision making. The initial response to NEPA in most agencies, including BLM and the Forest Service, was the assertion that their activities protected or enhanced the environment already. Several rounds of NEPA litigation broadened the applicability of the statute and clarified and specified the requirements of the evolving of the EIS process. Agencies realized that they would have to change their procedures to comply with the new requirements as elaborated by the Council on Environmental Quality Guidelines, various executive orders, and the proliferating case law. The Forest Service responded by incorporating the NEPA requirements into its new planning process.

The applicability of NEPA's action-forcing requirements to land management is, nevertheless, somewhat strained. The EIS provisions of NEPA are aimed best at government licenses or large construction projects such as dams, highways, and power generation facilities. In the context of such projects, the requirement to consider the alternatives and weigh all relevant costs, benefits, and impacts prior to taking action is not difficult. Applying these same concepts to program planning, such as Forest Service or BLM land use plans, is problematic. Land use and management activities are ongoing, and it is often difficult to analyze alternatives as if there were no existing commitments. It is particularly difficult to analyze "no action" alternatives; what does no action mean in the context of ten-year plans for continuing land management? The management agenda for long-term activities such as forest management cannot be assessed *de novo* at any particular point in time nor can it be reconsidered or significantly altered on ten-year cycles. Moreover, in a multi-tier planning system for units, areas, and regions, it is difficult to decide where the proposal for a "major federal action significantly affecting the human environment" occurs. Is the proposed action a unit plan which allocates general areas to a specified combination of uses which may, *if* funding becomes available, be implemented? If so, the specific activities required to implement the plan are so vague at that unit level that it is difficult to analyze the environmental impacts of any one of them, let alone their combined impact, and the impact of various combinations of alternatives. Is the overall regional plan the proposed action? The aggregated impacts certainly concern more people and will be more significant, but it is even more difficult to analyze the specific impacts of the aggregated proposals. On the other hand, EISs on every timber sale, grazing permit, trail marker, and culvert would be futile and burdensome for everyone.

The Forest Service and BLM resolved these issues in different ways. Both agencies, in accordance with the Council on Environmental Quality guidelines, provided for a formal analysis of each discrete project—the building of a fence, a timber sale, or a road repair. This environmental assessment report (EAR) analyzes the environmental impact of the specific activity and concludes either that an EIS is not required, a "negative determination," or that a full EIS is needed.

Both agencies must balance many uses on the same area, so both decided that in-depth analysis and public review at a more aggregated level was preferable in most cases. The Forest Service opted to fit NEPA requirements in at the unit level, but BLM decided that the more specific activity plans on specific resources—timber, grazing, coal—provided the appropriate focus for NEPA analysis. It is important to note that, because NEPA could be used to halt ongoing management programs, it altered the status of the planning reforms in both agencies. The new procedures were imposed under threat of court action rather than adopted voluntarily, and the threat of judicial involvement altered the public involvement process. CEQ guidelines required public involvement at every stage of agency deliberations, and the agencies were required not only to allow interested persons to comment on plans but also to solicit actively the participation of the "person in the street."

Public Involvement Problems and Promise   The hostility of some participants turned what had been a low-key, informal exchange of views into a threatening, quasi-judicial proceeding. Agency personnel were unsure of how to proceed and unfamiliar with the skills of small group dynamics, communications, and crowd control. The goals of dialogue and mutual education were threatened by the excessively formal style adopted by inexperienced land managers, who feared a lawsuit. Public involvement almost lost its potential for exchange of views and information and trust building. Sensitive to criticism that agency propaganda and presence at meetings colored or inhibited public comment, the Forest Service adopted a defensive "listening session" format in which agency personnel were merely to listen to the public while not speaking, explaining the issues, or discussing the options.

With experience among both the public and the agency, public involvement programs have become more sophisticated and generally more civil, with the more constructive workshop format predominating; but many problems remain.

First, there have simply been too many efforts to involve the public. Overinvolvement has been counterproductive. After the first or second unit plan-impact statement on a planning unit was filed, the proceedings became familiar, repetitious, and dull; and proliferation of involvement programs imposed unfair burdens on all participants, most particularly volunteer citizens groups.

Second, it is not at all clear how the agency should respond to and assess citizen input. The RARE I study reflects this difficulty. It was the most extensive public involvement effort in government history; however, it has been thoroughly criticized not because of inadequate public involvement but because the analysis of the public comment reflected agency biases, and the resulting recommendations were unacceptable to many participants. Evaluating public sentiments and using them in decision making is the most troubling aspect of the public involvement effort. It is difficult to devise a planning methodology that will give appropriate weights to site characteristics, budget constraints, competing goals, and public comment. Moreover, when public interest is keen and polarized, it is frequently impossible to respond to all public concerns.

Finally, the cost of generating, recording, and processing public comment is a problem. The costs are high and the means for utilizing the fruits of the effort are unclear, leading some to ask whether the agency effort is matched by the benefits.

In spite of these concerns, specific requirements for extensive public involvement appear in numerous critical forest and range management statutes. Although problematic, these requirements have already had significant impact on resource policy. The most obvious result of citizen activism is that the land managing agencies' constituencies—those interest groups which monitor, support, challenge, and in part depend on the agency—have diversified. It is hoped that this will enable the agencies to move flexibly in new and positive directions and lead to wiser programs responsive to more diverse needs. Moreover, although public involvement is frequently and appropriately thought of in terms of new access for new groups, it has required industry representatives to "go public" with their own lobbying efforts. When industry concerns were articulated quietly and among professionals and the environmentalists' concerns were voiced by developing public protests, it inevitably appeared that industry had no complaints and the environmentalists were being ignored. Public involvement has encouraged and required commondity industries to be more open about their criticism and problems. This provides better balance in public awareness of forest and range issues.

It will never be possible to draw a clear line indicating the proper balance between professional competence and public preference in resource decision making. However, the public involvement efforts of the 1960s and 1970s have forced professional managers to recognize that there is frequently a difference between the two and that both sources of guidance are legitimate and necessary. The precedent and the mechanisms for close agency-citizen deliberations have been established and accepted. Government managers are becoming accustomed to responding to challenges and aware of the broad range of public values and social concerns at issue in resource management. All of these developments complicate the job of the resource manager; however, it is not overly optimistic to hope that improved understanding of the issues will lead to improved dialogue and, ultimately, improved forest and range policy.

Litigation in Forest and Range Policy

Public involvement programs have evolved to the point of emphasizing cooperative discursive planning programs. However, the adversarial tone of court involvement underlies much of the discussion.

Opening the Courts to Environmental Litigants Critical changes in judicial procedures and doctrine during the late 1960s opened the courts to citizen activists during the 1970s. The cases they brought under NEPA and other statutes have affected budget processes, planning programs, wilderness policy, and the full range of forest and range management activities. The courts have not made management decisions; but by interpreting statutory mandates, they have forced change. Most major land managing agencies have been challenged by litigation during the 1970s and have been forced to reevaluate many of their programs. This litigation is exemplified by two cases, *Izaak Walton League* v. *Butz*—the so-called "Monangahela decision" on Forest Service timber management practices—and *NRDC* v. *Morton,* challenging BLM compliance with NEPA in the implementation of its grazing program.

It is important to note that litigation challenging federal and state land managing agencies only became a major policy factor after change in long-standing judicial doctrines designed to limit the role of the courts occurred in the late 1960s. Over the years, the courts, in order to limit their own role, developed numerous formal and informal guidelines regulating several elements of litigation: who can bring an action in a court, what issues the court will review, and what kinds of remedies the court can provide. The two most important concepts are "standing to sue" and "scope of judicial review."

Standing to Sue   Standing to sue, or the right of a citizen to be heard in court, is a concept which the courts use to determine whether or not a person bringing a suit is a legitimate plaintiff. Early environmentalists had difficulty meeting the "injury in fact" test which the courts used to define standing. Standing was denied unless the plaintiff's injury was an invasion of a legally protected right and peculiarly suffered by the litigant, as opposed to being borne by the public generally. The test was hard for environmentalists to meet because it emphasized clear, compensable economic harms to individuals rather than generally suffered environmental degradation. Citizen activists were frequently denied the opportunity to be heard in court because they had not been actually injured in the court's view.

Standing to sue was radically expanded starting in 1965. In *Scenic Hudson Preservation Conference* v. *Federal Power Commission* (FPC), a citizen's group was granted standing to sue the FPC for failing to consider damage to aesthetics, recreation, and fish habitat in the awarding of a license for a pumped storage project. In the famous Mineral King case (*Sierra Club* v. *Morton*), the Supreme Court, while denying the Sierra Club standing to sue to halt a ski development on a California national forest, in effect wrote a set of instructions for future litigants to use to gain standing. The essence of the doctrine is that members of the plaintiff organization must be alleged to use the area or resource in some way which would be adversely affected unless relief is granted.

Scope of Review   The courts' narrow view of its ability to review agency actions was a second major barrier to many litigants challenging government agencies. The courts generally deferred to agency expertise. This made it extremely difficult for a petitioner with standing to challenge agency actions successfully. Again, the *Scenic Hudson* case reflects the gradual evolution away from limited review of agency actions. In *Scenic Hudson,* the court looked at FPC's statutory responsibilities as a planning agency and found that they had not been met. Far from deferring to agency expertise in a complex factual situation, the court defined its own role broadly. While it reiterated the basic rule that the court could not substitute its own judgments for those of an agency, it found that it had the responsibility to determine whether the Federal Power Commission had properly discharged its statutory responsibilities. The judges decided that it had not. Thus, when NEPA and other environmental cases were brought in the early 1970s, the courts were ready to consider them.

NEPA Litigation and Land Managing Agencies   NEPA litigation involving land managing agencies has generally challenged the agency's decision to prepare or not prepare an EIS on a particular program or activity. Improvements in the planning process and better EIS rules from the courts and CEQ have resolved many of these issues today, but they caused considerable controversy at the time. For example, the previously discussed *Conti* decision involving wilderness policy and NEPA had a continuing effect on Forest Service land use planning and allocation.

NEPA has also been used in the budgetary process. In early 1974, the Sierra Club, the Natural Resources Defense Council, the Wilderness Society, and others sued the Forest Service for failure to prepare an environmental impact statement on its budget request for 1975 and 1976. Again, the court did not render a decision because the Forest Service agreed, in another out-of-court settlement, to prepare the Resource Planning Act and assessment as an EIS on the budget to meet the plaintiff's complaints. The impact of this settlement has had far less significance than the *Conti* decision, but the attempt to use the EIS process to influence agency actions is clear.

The "NRDC Grazing Case"   Perhaps the most dramatic NEPA litigation in terms of its overall impact on agency programs is the "NRDC grazing case," *NRDC* v. *Morton.* The Natural Resources Defense Council sued BLM for failing to prepare an EIS on the environmental effects of grazing while it continued to grant grazing permits. NRDC pointed out that BLM had completed no EIS on livestock grazing in the four years since NEPA had passed. BLM countered that, in accord with their planning procedures, they were doing environmental assessment reports on all individual permits, a national statement on the entire program, and would do EISs on specific areas as required.

It should be noted that when NEPA passed, BLM had fewer than 3000 full-time employees to manage 485 million acres of land and no budget or clear statutory authority to inventory resources. In fact, for the decade prior to 1974, when the suit was filed, real expenditures for range management activities by the bureau dropped dramatically in all states. Expenditures in Colorado, for example, declined by 50 percent (Box, et al, 21). Budget problems were probably related to the fact that Congress still had not committed itself to retaining and managing the lands. Thus the Bureau lacked the budget flexibility to permit the kind of planning and assessment required for EISs. Throughout the 1960s, the agency's range programs were, in fact, seriously strained by its attempts to diversify into a semblance of a multiple-use management agency.

Ironically, the problem of understaffing in the range management program was intensified when NEPA was passed and many range managers were reassigned to writing impact statements (Box, et al, 25). To Bureau planners, the site-specific EAR plus a programmatic EIS seemed to be the best way for BLM to meet NEPA requirements and the best way to achieve their program goals. To environmentalists unsympathetic with BLM's plight, the agency's failure to prepare EISs presented both a sure sign of bad intentions and an opportunity to halt grazing use of the public domain lands.

The court found the agency's EIS process inadequate. The court had little choice—no final impact statements had been prepared, and the draft program-matic EIS was clearly inadequate. However, the remedy provided by the court presents a number of critical problems for the Bureau and raises very serious questions about the role of the courts in this type of controversy. Because the judge really did not know very much about the issues at hand, he ordered the parties to try to agree on a schedule for EIS preparation. Failure to devise a schedule would oblige the judge to develop one. The Department of the Inte-rior lawyers handling the case for BLM reached an agreement with NRDC that became the court order. It required BLM to prepare 212 impact state-ments between 1975 and 1988. The larger number of impact statements was necessitated by the Bureau's emphasis on allotment management plans in its planning process (see pp. 308–309). Other aspects of the agreement were arrived at in negotiations between government lawyers and the Natural Re-sources Defense Council lawyers and largely ignored the Bureau's personnel and planning budget limitations. More important, ranchers, recreationists, wildlife managers, miners, and other interest groups were neither consulted nor involved in the negotiations. Future planning and budget priorities for the management of vast public resources were defined by government lawyers who know nothing about resource management in consultation with representatives of one narrow segment of users.

The Bureau has consistently been unable to meet the court schedule and the ever-changing standards for adequate EISs. The schedule was based on the assumption that existing data could be used; yet data have proved to be so inadequate that impact analysis could not be done without extensive new studies and inventories. Congress has repeatedly refused to appropriate supple-mental funds for meeting the inventory, analysis, printing, and public contact requirements of NEPA, and the court has been unwilling to allow deviation from the schedule in order to provide for accumulation of new data. BLM's budget is so small compared to its needs and tasks and its personnel is so limited that the court order has shifted the bureau's efforts from on-the-ground activities to planning and EIS preparation.

Although this reallocation of agency efforts is distressing to both Bureau personnel and those dependent on use of the public range, the litigation has focused attention on several important range management issues. Rest-rotation grazing and type conversion have not become household words like clear cutting, but the NRDC litigation has had the effect of focusing increased scrutiny on BLM range management practices.

Rest-Rotation Grazing   Rest-rotation grazing has been a recognized range management tool since early in the twentieth century. Although it is subject to numerous variations and modifications, the practice involves what the name suggests: concentrating the stock in one area while other areas, in rotation, rest. The basic assumption is that each area will get sufficient time between periods of concentrated use both to recover from the use and improve in overall quality. The practice became controversial in the 1970s. The EIS process forced the Bureau to discuss specific techniques for range management just when many tools—such as use of herbicides and planting of nonnative grasses—were being eliminated by environmental concerns and regulations. The Bureau seized, somewhat uncritically, on August L. ("Gus") Hormay's 1960 rest-rotation grazing research and adopted it as the major tool of range management efforts throughout the West. Range scientists and stock operators have argued that the system, while potentially of great benefit in some areas, should not be viewed as a panacea for management of the entire public range. The NRDC focused attention on weaknesses in the Bureau's reliance on rest-rotation systems.

Type Conversion and Nonnative Grasses   The issue of type conversion has also been highlighted in discussions engendered by the NRDC litigation. The Bureau has long sought to improve range quality by plantings. The process of removing unwanted vegetation and preparing seeding sites is controversial since it may involve herbicides, destruction of native vegetation, or threat of soil erosion. However, seeding with nonnative species also is frequently opposed, especially when it is done primarily or exclusively to benefit domestic livestock, because of possible harm to native wildlife populations or the natural diversity of the area. The NRDC litigation has raised questions regarding the degree to which the BLM is and ought to be relying on introduction of nonnative grasses and type conversions as management tools for the public range.

Although it is important and necessary that these questions regarding appropriate techniques are at last being heard, the circumstances surrounding the debate, limited though it may be, are unfortunate. On the one hand, the Bureau is pressed to increase productivity in all sectors: minerals, recreation, wilderness, wildlife, and forage for livestock. On the other, the Bureau encounters growing pressure from environmental groups to bar all livestock use from the public range. This conflict occurs at a time at which there is widespread public acceptance of the idea that the range is steadily deteriorating from overgrazing and mismanagement. Unfortunately, though there is insufficient historical trend data to prove the case either way, there is substantial evidence indicating the contrary, that range quality improved dramatically since passage of the Taylor Grazing Act (Box, 13–14).

The Bureau is in an especially unenviable position in this controversy. They have been saying for decades that they could not do an adequate job without support. The first blush of public attention has been focused on all the obvious inadequacies of BLM's underfunded efforts. To the extent that the discussion has encouraged the Bureau to reassess some of the debated techniques, and simultaneously encouraged Congress at last to provide the wherewithal necessary for effective range management, it has been worthwhile. If the controversy simply results in another vilification of the Bureau and further congressional reluctance to invest in BLM activities, then it will have been costly indeed.

The NRDC grazing case has simultaneously occasioned potentially dramatic changes in range management and raised more important issues about the role of lawyers and the courts in resource management than any environmental litigation in recent years. The whole process has, however, attracted relatively little comment or public attention. This is probably because BLM, its problems, and its programs continue to be invisible to the public generally. Both the public and resource professionals were also transfixed for much of the time the grazing case was evolving by the storm of activities surrounding the denouement of the clear-cutting controversy.

Clear Cutting Revisited   The clear cutting controversy which began in the early 1950s in West Virginia towns and valleys (see above, pp. 225–227) became a major national issue in the early 1970s. The Church Committee guidelines discussed in Chapter 8 were accepted by the Forest Service as an agency "action plan" to assure environmental protection in clear cutting. The Forest Service's discretion to select silvicultural techniques was not severely restricted, and the congressional guidelines could be used to defend its practices. The matter did not rest there, however. The West Virginians were still unsatisfied. The local chapter of the Izaak Walton League and the West Virginia Highlands Conservancy brought a suit to halt all commercial harvesting on the Monongahela National Forest. The suit, *Izaak Walton League* v. *Butz,* was not brought under NEPA. The plaintiffs alleged that Forest Service harvesting practices violated the Organic Act of 1897. Although many of the litigants took action because of their profound opposition to clear cutting, the case did not focus specifically on that practice. The Izaak Walton League charged that timber harvesting practices on three small timber sales on the Monongahela exceeded the authority granted in the 1897 act, which limited the agency to harvesting *mature* timber which had been *marked and designated* and was *cut and removed* from the forest under the supervision of an agent of the Secretary of Agriculture. Those old and unnoticed phrases in that much-praised statute came to haunt the Forest Service.

The judge consulted the dictionary to ascertain the plain meaning of the key words in the statute—"mature," "marked and designated," and "cut and removed"—and found the Forest Service timber harvest programs included cutting of immature, unmarked trees which were frequently not entirely removed from the forest and, therefore, violated the 1897 act. He enjoined the agency from further commercial cutting until their practices matched their authorities or Congress passed remedial legislation. Clear cutting was not banned by this decision. The court prohibited any further commercial harvesting.

As with every judicial finding, the injunction initially applied only to the three sales on the Monongahela National Forest. The decision did, however, attract the attention of Forest Service critics throughout the nation. Soon Monongahela-type cases were brought in district courts in South Carolina, Texas, Tennessee, Georgia, Alaska, and Oregon. Injunctions were issued in Alaska and Texas, and many feared it was only a matter of time before all national forest timber harvesting was halted. By the time the Fourth Circuit Court of Appeals upheld the original West Virginia District Court decision, wheels were already in motion to have the Organic Act amended.

Texas Committee on Natural Resources v. *Butz,* one of the Monongahela spin-off cases, is interesting because it represents a direct challenge to clear cutting. As part of a diverse complaint which included, among other things, the familiar Organic Act arguments, petitioners alleged that clear cutting, on its face, was a violation of the Multiple Use Sustained Yield Act. The district court judge granted a preliminary injunction after which the case, unlike the Monongahela one, went to trial during which evidence was introduced regarding the merits of clear cutting. The judge's opinion that clear cutting does violate the Multiple Use Act is based on his "Findings of Fact" which accompany the opinion. Noteworthy among these court-made findings are the following:

> **23a.**   Clearcutting results in increased fire hazard . . .
> **24.**   Clearcutting probably results in increased hazard from insects and diseases . . .
> **25.**   Clearcutting impairs the productivity of land . . .
> **27.**   Clearcutting impairs and reduces the amount of habitat essential to various species of wildlife . . .
> **30.**   Even-age management results in the liquidation of high quality timber while it is still in the period of greatest volume growth, which inevitably leads to a future scarcity of high quality wood.

The judge's certainty surprised most professional foresters, who are painfully aware of the intricacies, subtleties, and ambiguities surrounding even-age management. This ultimately proved a viable route to review of the decision. On appeal, the government attorneys pointed out that the judge's findings were based entirely on the facts as submitted by the Texas Committee on Natural Resources and its four experts. None of the four had any experience in southern pineries, two had absolutely no forestry experience whatsoever, and one was a journalist with a three-week course in tree cutting as his only qualification. In uncritically accepting the testimony of those experts while ignoring the government's witnesses, the judge gave insufficient weight to agency discretion and expertise, according to the government. Two years after the original injunction was granted, the appeals court lifted the ban on harvesting. The Supreme Court subsequently upheld the Court of Appeals, but the absurdity of the initial decision infuriated many professional foresters.

The Role of the Courts   Probably because legal tools have only recently been applied to land management, their role has been closely scrutinized, analyzed, and assessed. It is frequently implied that the presence of the courts is in some way improper. This is both erroneous and irrelevant. The courts require special study because their language, procedures, and concepts are unfamiliar to most land managers; but they are an integral and important part of the political process and will continue to play an important role in land management. As was seen in the Monongahela litigation, the courts provide a forum for airing questions which might never be heard in the more political, compromise-oriented congressional and executive branches (Fairfax and Achterman, passim). Clear cutting opponents, unsatisfied by the middle-of-the-road responses of the Forest Service and Congress, found another avenue for redress. Nonetheless, litigation is so expensive that both industry and environmentalists litigate only as a last resort. The environmental groups that can afford litigation are large and few in number. Indeed, environmental case law is a bit confusing because many of the key cases have similar or identical names because they have been instituted by one of two or three major groups against one of three government employees or agencies: NRDC, the Environmental Defense Fund (EDF), or the Sierra Club *versus* the Secretary of the Interior or Agriculture or the Environmental Protection Agency. The newly formed environmental litigation groups have succeeded spectacularly in pressing their claims and will continue to be major actors shaping forest and range policy. They do not, however, have unlimited resources and do not engage in frivolous or marginal litigation.

Some argue that the courts provide a fresh, outside look at resource issues. In the Monongahela case, most would agree that the courts filled this role well. However, a fresh look can be useless if uninformed. Lawyers do not know much about resource management, and their involvement sometimes imposes the worst limitations of the legal system on resource management. This was especially apparent in the Texas case. Moreover, working out a settlement may look like law to a lawyer, but it also should be a management decision. The courts and lawyers tend to think in terms of resolvable conflict. Sometimes, as in the NRDC grazing case, no clear solution exists. Judicial involvement, and pressing for a "settlement" in the disputed management programs, can have marginal or negative impact.

Judicial decisions are typically crude instruments, yes-or-no answers to allegations that specific statutes have been violated. As such, the courtroom is an inappropriate forum for devising a land use plan or setting land management priorities. Courts are very effective, however, at raising the political visibility of issues and forcing agency and legislative attention (Sax, chap. 6). Even this point must be tempered by the fact that neither Congress nor the agencies can long remain unresponsive to concerns of large numbers of citizens. The pace or nature of change may not be adequate to allay concerns. But, as was seen in the clear-cutting controversy, neither Congress nor the Forest Service was inactive; their actions simply did not satisfy everyone. The judiciary is only one part of our political process. The courts will always have a role; but they cannot provide leadership, consensus, or goals lacking elsewhere.

SUMMARY

The increasing diversity and intensity of demands for wild lands resources preordained that conflict would increase in forest and range policy. More users were competing for a share of a limited resource base. Although the participation program was to some extent forced on hesitant, nervous, land managers, public involvement constitutes an optimistic approach to this conflict. The process rests on the hopeful assumption that a better understanding of the conflict—the full diversity of values at stake and what the impacts of the various alternatives are on interested groups—will make it easier to reach optimal solutions. Litigation is frequently a sign that less formal and adversarial methods of conflict resolution have failed. Because of the expense involved, resort to the courts is generally perceived as a final and undesirable option. Litigation also has an optimistic component, however, to the extent that plaintiffs believe that the judges may find in the law a satisfactory solution to conflicts that had eluded the land managers.

This optimism is in part justified. The activism of the 1970s has indeed led to a fuller and more sympathetic evaluation of land use alternatives that received inadequate consideration in the past. Moreover, the process of confrontation, litigation, and negotiation is becoming familiar to all participants and, appropriately, less threatening to the professionalism of professional land managers. As sophistication develops, it will hopefully become easier to get on with the task of making and implementing the hard choices that confront the nation in resource management.

However, this possible settling down should not, probably could not, obscure the fact that the choices are indeed difficult. Ample, relevant data, full public comment, insightful judges and lawyers, and sensitive, competent land managers can only minimize frustration and error. The hard choices remain. There is conflict, not because participants are unreasonable or uninformed, but because they disagree profoundly on land management priorities. The complexity of the decision-making process is one result of the fundamental lack of consensus in forest and range policy.

REFERENCES CITED

Box, Thadis W. "The Arid Lands Revisited: 100 Years After John Wesley Powell." Address, 57th Annual Faculty Honor Lecture, Utah State University, Logan, Utah, n.d.

Box, Thadis W., Dwyer, Don D., and Wagner, Frederic H. "The Public Rangelands and Their Management: A Report to the President's Council on Environmental Quality." Mimeo, 1976, 1977.

Congressional Quarterly, Inc. *Congress and the Nation, III.* Washington, D.C.: Congressional Quarterly Service, 1973.

Fairfax, Sally K. and Gail L. Achterman. "The Monongahela Controversey and the Political Process." 75 *Journal of Forestry* 485 (1977).

Gilligan, James P. *The Development of Policy and Administration of Forest Service Wilderness and Primitive Areas in the United States.* Ph.D. dissertation, University of Michigan, 1953.

Glascock, Hardin. "Forestry News: USDA Proposes Regulation of Mining and Prospecting in National Forests." 72 *Journal of Forestry* 162 (1974).

National Forest Products Association. *Wilderness Withdrawals and Timber Supply.* Washington, September 12, 1977.

Public Land News. Washington, D.C.: Resources Publishing Co.

Sax, Joseph. *Defending the Environment.* New York: Alfred A. Knopf, Inc., 1970.

VTN Consolidated, Inc. *NEPA Process Study of the Forest Service and the Bureau of Land Management.* Irvine, Cal., 1973.

Chapter 12

Legislation in a Period of Uncertainty

The litigation and public involvement of programs of the 1960s and 1970s are more than ample testimony that resource management has emerged as an important and controversial social and political issue. It is no longer possible, if indeed it ever was, for land managers to feel secure in the assumption that they are apolitical professionals applying their skills to achieve publicly defined goals. Nor is it possible to assume, as many technically trained managers are frequently, perhaps understandably, inclined to do, that the priorities of their profession constitute an adequate approximation of society's priorities.

Resource management will never again be a relatively small and homogeneous field presided over by a loving, if irascible, patriarch. Both public and private land managing institutions have diversified. They employ anthropologists, sociologists, water pollution biologists, and a host of professionals from an ever-broadening spectrum of scientific and social scientific endeavor. This change is reflected in the constantly broadening curricula in resource management-oriented schools, in the pages of professional journals, and in the in-service training programs for practicing land managers. There are no longer any easily identified boundaries on what constitutes resource management expertise.

Nowhere is the emerging diversity and ambiguity which surrounds resource management better expressed than in the major Forest Service and BLM statutes which passed in the 1970s. Two major planning directives—the Forest and Rangelands Renewable Resources Planning Act of 1974 (RPA) and the National Forest Management Act of 1976 (NFMA)—mandate extensive additions to the process defined by the Forest Service in connection with its own reform effort, *Environmental Program for the Future,* and the NEPA process. The Bureau of Land Management, after thirty years without basic authority for management activities, finally achieved legislative recognition, also through a planning-oriented statute, the Federal Land Policy and Management Act (FLPMA). These legislative achievements are important, but the ultimate meaning is unclear because Congress did not identify priorities.

Typically, in the United States, citizens expect Congress to debate issues, define compromises, and establish parameters to guide public policy. Unfortunately, even if obliged to act by a court-created crisis or intense public pressure, Congress is sometimes unable to act coherently or consistently or to reflect a national consensus in legislative enactments. Although Congress was pressed frequently during the 1970s to legislate on aspects of renewable and nonrenewable resources management, its work generally reflects rather than resolves the divisions of the time. In the heat of debate about appropriate land management methodologies and goals, Congress temporized. This strategy suits Congress as an institution; it is structured to produce compromise rather than bold new policy directions. It is also probably appropriate to contemporary needs. The crisis in forest and range management was caused by irreconcilable differences. Congress listened, reviewed, studied, provided a forum for all sides of the issues, and in the end decided not to decide.

The major characteristic of the initial 1970s legislation is that it defines procedures rather than goals or substance. It tells land managing agencies to weigh all factors but does not set priorities among them. If this approach was the best that could be hoped for, it still creates a great deal of uncertainty. Layers of review and procedures were added to the already confusing pastiche of agency planning programs, CEQ guidelines, and state and federal environmental quality regulations.

Defined by vague mandates to plan and consult, agency programs are subject to challenge and litigation. As in the environmental regulation field, the time-consuming process of regulation writing, lobbying, litigating, and amending will determine the basic ground rules. For those whose livelihood depends on forest and range resources, this uncertainty is particularly nettlesome, though endless rounds of confusing procedural discussions and public meetings cannot be satisfactory to anyone concerned with any aspect of wild land management.

Three general characteristics of the procedures established by the new legislation contribute to the uncertainty which is increasingly a part of public land management. First, the statutes reassert congressional authority over the public lands. The definition of extensive and explicit congressional responsibilities is not unusual, but the legislative process is slow and cumbersome. Congress has not accomplished many of the tasks it assigned itself. Second, all the legislation strongly supports public involvement. In lieu of telling the agencies what to do, Congress told them to consult the public. This failure to guide explicitly places the agencies in the role of umpire between interest groups. Political decision making has always been a part of public resource management, protests from foresters that were merely using scientific tools to achieve public goals notwithstanding. However, the degree to which land managers are mandated to play a political broker role is unprecedented—and frequently uncomfortable. Lacking clear congressional directions to guide their priorities, federal land managers are vulnerable to criticism from all sides, including Congress. Finally, the vague and often conflicting provisions of key sections of the principal statues amount to an invitation to litigation.

The challenge of the 1970s and beyond is to learn to deal with this ambiguity. Clarity cannot be expected in forest and range policy at a time when social values, the economy, the world energy supply, and so many other factors which increasingly press against renewable resource management are in constant flux.

THE FOREST AND RANGE RENEWABLE RESOURCES ACT OF 1974

The RPA occasioned the first comprehensive legislative reconsideration of the Forest Service's mission since the early 1900s. Although the measure enjoyed wide support and popular acclaim when enacted, it originated in one of the most divisive issues in land management. Industry pressure for more attention to timber management was augmented by growing criticism from economists concerning the inefficient allocation of public resources in national forest management. A very complex planning process resulted from the congressional attempt to balance industry needs with environmentalists' criticisms of the Forest Service.

In 1969, timber prices increased so dramatically as to become the focus of much congressional concern. Although the precipitous rise was probably due as much to a dock workers' strike, export of wood products to Japan, and climatic factors as to timber supplies available from the national forests (*Congress and the Nation,* 770), the timber industry seized the opportunity to focus congressional attention on its need for a steady supply. Throughout the 1960s, as land was removed from commodity production by wilderness, trail, park, habitat, and other restricted-use designations, the explicit and implicit promise was made that greater funding would be available for more intensive management of the remaining high-quality timber sites. Such increased funding was not forthcoming; and management intensity has been, in fact, curtailed by the environmental regulations discussed in Chapter 9. After 1969, numerous versions of a "Timber Supply Act" were debated annually but were unacceptable to environmentalists. The only provision of the industry bills which survived, a requirement that the Secretary prepare a national plan for all resources, was nearly unanimously supported.

Industry was not alone in pressing for a major redirection of Forest Service priorities. Forest economists argued that efficient utilization of public funds and resources required changed management (Clawson, passim). Many of these arguments were contained in the 1973 report of the President's Advisory Panel on Timber and the Environment, established by President Nixon to make recommendations to ameliorate the growing conflict between timber and environmental values. Three of the panel's recommendations were notable in this context: (1) that the harvesting of national forest timber on western lands should be expanded substantially, increasing the rate of old growth cut by 50 to 100 percent; (2) that investment in forest management should be made in accord with sound economic concepts so that expenditures and investments be related to anticipated returns; and (3) that commercial forestlands not in wilderness or other restricted-use categories should be designated for timber production (PAPTE, 3–5). The advisory panel also recommended a massive long-range plan for nationwide forest development vaguely suggestive of the provisions of the act which passed a year later. Predictably, the panel's report was not well received; the political climate was not right for concepts which appeared supportive of industry or timber harvesting, and association with President Nixon in 1975 was not an asset due to Watergate-related tensions. The report was dismissed as an industry effort. However, Congress was responsive to the panel's criticism of the basis of Forest Service expenditures since it, too, was seeking mechanisms for assuring budget accountability. Environmentalists also supported the report's budget-related recommendations as a way further to influence agency action. Although the pressure behind the Resources Planning Act was initiated by industry, when the bill evolved into a planning and resource policy statute, environmentalists supported it.

RPA Provisions and Implications

The 1974 legislation directs the Forest Service to assess resource needs and capabilities, define alternatives, and recommend a program of management and investment as a basis for its budget requests. The agency is required to prepare and publish an updated *Program* every five years and an updated *Assessment* every ten years. The *Program,* according to an out-of-court agreement with the Sierra Club is treated as an EIS. The Resources Planning Act also required the President to submit the program and a policy statement for national forest management to Congress; Congress must either accept or modify the President's program, after which the President must defend any subsequent budget requests which deviate from approved policy. This was a clear attempt by Congress to achieve two goals: first, to curtail presidential impoundment of funds allocated for reforestation and other purposes and, second, to force the Forest Service to tie their budget requests to a clear set of management goals based on long-range projections of demand, supply, and productivity in all ownership categories.

The Forest Service, long frustrated in attempts to get increased budget requests through the executive branch, viewed the Resources Planning Act as an opportunity to take its needs directly to Congress and the people. They believed that, once a program and goals had been approved, the President would be obligated to provide funding. They downplayed the congressional oversight and review aspects of the RPA program and were, apparently, not alarmed by the heavy emphases on cost-benefit analysis of investment alternatives. Therefore, although the Resources Planning Act was enacted shortly before the agency's long-range planning and budget effort, *Environmental Planning for the Future,* was unveiled, Forest Service officials welcomed the legislation. The RPA authorized agency expenditures of up to $20 million for the preparation of the *Program* and *Assessment.* This was the first congressional action in recognition of the tremendous costs involved in each extensive planning and public involvement effort.

The Resources Planning Act was an overwhelming expression of faith in the utility of accumulating and analyzing data. The RPA assumed that, with more information about the impacts of management programs, timber and other commodity needs can be better balanced with amenity and environmental quality values. Unfortunately, data and analysis cannot eliminate fundamental conflicts in goals and perceptions. Moreover, even if data and methodologies were adequate to define the trade-offs involved, they cannot make decisions.

RPA Compliance

The first RPA *Program* and *Assessment* documents were prepared quickly and presented to the President in December, 1975. Although the Forest Service had recently completed its *Environmental Program for the Future*—an ostensibly similar exercise—the specific date requirements of the *Assessment* were too extensive to achieve in so short a time. The documents represented a good effort under the circumstances but had a number of fundamental flaws. Most obviously, the *Program* was prepared simultaneously with the *Assessment* and was, therefore, not based on it. Thus, although a staggering number of alternatives were analyzed, the resource base was not treated as a limiting factor on outputs. The agency's basic position was that the more money they were granted, the more of everything they could produce. Management intensity and its returns were related only to investment levels, not to land capabilities. Second, in assessing management options, the Forest Service only varied investment levels. None of the assumptions behind the traditional investment program were varied. Specifically, the agency did not analyze the cost of commitments to maximizing growth on all acres or to gradual utilization of old growth. Third, the *Program* was not an additive compilation of unit, area, and regional plans. National goals were not tied to site-specific activities. Finally, the national forest management program is not related to other land-ownership programs. The Forest Service cannot proceed in a vacuum, refusing to relate its goals to those of the states, other federal agencies, and the private sector. These inadequacies were apparent and became the focus of considerable comment and criticism (Hyde; Manthy; Vaux, passim).

Other barriers to the Forests Service's hopes for the new planning process as a route to bigger budgets were institutional rather than substantive. The Office of Management and Budget (OMB), the major budget oversight operative in the White House, delayed release of the Resources Planning Act documents and held its own public involvement and review sessions. Only after the President intervened were the reports released. Even then, the President did not take strong action; President Ford did not want to foreclose future budgetary options with a clear statement of priorities which Congress would make binding. His bland policy statement issued March 2, 1976, merely emphasized dispersed recreation and the need to keep the Forest Service budget in balance with other national priorities.

Congressional Response to RPA

Congress itself did not act for over a year. The workload of Congress and its general lassitude is such that it responds to crises better than to the ongoing day-to-day requirements of oversight. In the summer of 1977, two years after the Resources Planning Act draft documents appeared, the House Forests Subcommittee held hearings. Its report, reflecting statements from nearly 200 interested persons, generally directed the agency to do a better and more thorough job in preparing the next set of documents—especially in public involvement. This advice came about four months after the Forest Service unveiled its plans for preparing the *Assessment* and *Program* due in 1979 and 1980.

The RPA has resulted, these problems notwithstanding, in increased Forest Service appropriations. The President's 1977 proposed budget was $500 million below the RPA *Program,* and the House and Senate both made substantial additions. The final bill provided for an appropriation of approximately $250 million over President Carter's proposal—about 85 percent of RPA levels. The war between the White House and Congress on spending continued, however, as Carter allowed the Forest Service to spend all it could *provided* that personnel ceilings imposed by the President were not violated. Thus, 1977 action on the fiscal 1978 budget did not fully reward Forest Service hopes for more money under RPA. Congress was frustrated in its battle with the President over budget control. The 1978 budget process was similar; Forest Service programs were funded at 81 percent of Resources Planning Act levels (2 *Public Lands News,* passim).

Beneath the averages, some programs were less well funded. The wildlife program was only funded at 60 percent of the proposed program. The National Wildlife Federation filed an unsuccessful suit complaining that President Carter and the OMB failed to supply a written statement explining deviations from the *Program,* as required by RPA. The litigation reflects some of the limitations in the Resources Planning Act's budget-related provisoins.

It is also apparent that the RPA process has vastly complicated the paperwork inherent in agency planning and budgeting. Moreover, the agency has avoided thus far discussing the costs of its assumptions about investments of public resources, but this will become more difficult as the system is refined. For the present, a major, if unanticipated, result of the process is that it gives interest groups new targets to attack. If the goals emerge as important program standards or guides, the timber interests will gain legitimization of their use of Forest Service land and resources; wilderness advocates will probably lose considerable acreage of *de facto* wilderness. The RPA goal of 25 to 30 million acres in wilderness, if honored, would bar from the system most of the areas assessed in the RARE II inventory. The real impact of the Resources Planning Act will not be known or felt until planning, budgeting, and litigation under the 1974 act have progressed further and until the amendments to the act, passed in connection with the Monongahela litigation, are implemented and reviewed by the courts.

NFMA: The Sorcerer's Apprentice of National Forest Policy

Congress was aware of the West Virginia District Court's 1973 decision during the debate on the RPA. The Forest Service did not think the situation serious enough to require legislation and stalled Senator Hubert Humphrey's efforts to use the RPA to amend the 1897 act. The aftermath of Monongahela, the government's loss of the appeal and related litigation, soon required congressional action. The National Forest Management Act, passed in October, 1976, was unusual in a number of respects. It was major legislation passed in a presidential election year—a period normally reserved for avoiding contentious issues. It passed with remarkable speed. Finally, it made substantial additions to the Resources Planning Act, which was still in its embryonic stages of implementation. It passed primarily because there was consensus about the need to reverse the courts' Monongahela decisions legislatively. The Forest Service and the timber industry would have been satisfied with a one-paragraph bill amending the 1897 act to correct the disputed phrases. A broad coalition of environmentalists were unwilling to see their hard-won court victories disappear entirely. A major battle ensued which is striking because the number of major issues debated did not prevent unusually speedy congressional action. Virtually every issue discussed was raised by the environmental groups. Interestingly, almost all of the debate concerned timber management techniques; mining, grazing, recreation, wildlife, and watershed management were scarcely mentioned. The major issue was clear cutting; however, a whole series of other intensive forest management practices was also reviewed.

The discussion focused generally on the question of how much discretion administrative agencies should have to manage public resources. The environmentalists generally supported a bill sponsored by Senator Jennings Randolph of West Virginia which circumscibed or eliminated a variety of management techniques. The industry generally supported a bill introduced by Senator Humphrey which was less restrictive. President Ford did not want to take a position on many of the issues involved in the controversy. The administration, hence, the Forest Service, made no suggestions of its own; it only commented on alternatives being weighed by Congress. The Society of American Foresters participated actively in the debates, advising congressional committees on technical aspects of the various proposals. This participation signaled a new era in professional attention to political and social aspects of forest policy.

Key Provisions of the NFMA

The bill that passed reflects the general contours of the Humphrey bill. It is largely directed toward achieving increased regulation of forest management by amending the planning process defined in the Resources Planning Act. The key section of the National Forest Management Act directs the Secretary to consider certain points and issues in writing regulations. This leaves definition of the most specific provisions to the discretion of the Secretary and the Forest Service. However, the Randolph proposals raised a number of critical forest management issues which required congressional attention. Sections dealing with nondeclining evenflow, species diversity, rotation age, clear cutting, and marginal lands were heatedly debated. The final bill addresses these subjects with highly qualified phrases, allowing exemptions and alterations to be defined in regulations. However, with the exception of clear cutting, these were new issues to general public debate over forest policy; and the legislation promises that they will be fully aired in subsequent rule making and litigation. In addition to those intensely problematic confrontations, the legislation makes a number of small but significant additions and corrections to Forest Service authority.

Major Issues Unresolved   Five major topics were raised in Senator Randolph's bill. Congress noted the issues but did not resolve them. All but one are treated in section 6, which gave the Secretary two years to develop regulations defining standards and guidelines for national forest planning. The new regulations must be reflected in all plans by 1985. All of the language on clear cutting, rotation age, marginal lands, and species diversity is pursuant to the requirement that the Secretary promulgate regulations. It is, however, consistently qualified by such phrases as "to the degree practicable," "to meet multiple-use objectives," and "considering pertinent factors." Congress has not given directions; it has left the Secretary almost total discretion. Most of these issues will not be resolved until the courts decide whether the Secretary's exercise of this descretion has been reasonable. A brief look at the language of section 6 illustrates the ambiguities of the National Forest Management Act.

Clear cutting   Congress wrote a modified version of the Church guidelines into section 6(g), (3), and (F) of the NFMA. Clear cutting is to be used only where

(1) it is determined to be the optimum method . . . to meet the objectives and requirements of the relevant land management plan; . . .. (iii) cut(s) . . . are blended to the extent possible with the terrain; (iv) there are established according to geographic areas, forest types or other suitable classifications the maximum size limits for areas to be cut in one harvest operation . . . and (v) such cuts are carried out in a manner consistant with the protection of soil, watershed, fish, wildlife, recreation and aesthetic resources, and the regeneration of the timber resource.

By providing guidelines for clear cutting, Congress also specifically authorized it. Moreover, salvage cuts are specifically exempted from the acre limitations, and the 25-acre limitation of the Church guidelines was dropped in favor of establishing suitable classifications for size limits. Apparently, the long clear cutting debate was resolved in favor of qualified agency discretion.

Species Diversity   Section 6(g), (3), and (B) deals with the related issue of species diversity. It calls for regulations specifying guidelines which

(B) provide for diversity of plant and animal communities based on the suitability and capability of the specific land area in order to meet overall multiple-use objectives, and within the multiple-use objectives of a land management plan adopted pursuant to this section, provide, where appropriate, to the degree practicable, for steps to be taken to preserve the diversity of tree species similar to that existing in the region controlled by the plan

Leaving aside the "where appropriate, to the degree practicable" language, this section is still inconclusive. Pressures to curtail intensive management, species conversions, and alleged monocultures and maintain genetic variability are clear. It is also clear, however, that Congress tried to respond to that pressure without seriously hampering timber production. The result is confusing. Southeastern pineries, apparently the major target of environmentalists' concern, are probably not even touched by the section as pine "monocultures" are characteristic of the region in nature as well as in managed stands.

Marginal Lands   The marginal lands issue is treated in section 6(k). Congress amended the Resources Planning Act to require the Secretary to include consideration of the specified factors in the planning process. The section requires the Secretary to identify lands " . . . which are not suited for timber production, considering physical, economic, and other factors to the extent feasible, as determined by the Secretary, and shall assure that except for salvage sales or sales necessitated to protect other multiple-use values, no timber harvesting shall occur on such lands for a period of 10 years. . . ." The marginal lands category is subject to review every ten years. This provision is a mass of conditions and exceptions. It goes to the heart of a major criticism —voiced by environmentalists, industry representatives, the Bolle report, the President's Advisory Panel on Timber and the Environment, and economists outside the Forest Service—that the Forest Service was not serving public interest by trying to practice forestry on every acre of land. Industry is probably more interested in having areas designated *for* timber management than in having marginal lands removed, but it is also interested in having the Forest Service make its timber management investments on high-quality sites. Environmentalists have long urged that harvesting be eliminated from fragile sites which cannot be regenerated. The Forest Service is, however, mentally bound by the assumptions and philosophies taken directly from land-scarce eighteenth-century Germany, where managing every available acre probably made sense.

Rotation Age   The rotation age language in section 6(m) is not much more effective. Harkening back to the original litigation, in which plaintiffs complained that the Forest Service was cutting immature trees, the Randolph Bill required extended rotation periods. The NFMA does not, however, speak clearly to the issue. Section 6(m) directs the Secretary to establish

> . . . standards to insure that, prior to harvest, stands of trees throughout the National Forest System shall generally have reached the culmination of mean-annual increment of growth (calculated on the basis of cubic measurement or other methods of calculation at the discretion of the Secretary); Provided that these standards shall not preclude the use of sound silvicultural practices. . . .

The section also provides for salvage and sanitation cuts and exceptions to the standards "after consideration has been given to the multiple uses of the forests. . . ." The greatest variability in this section comes not from the qualifiers, provisos, and exceptions but from the discretion given the Secretary to choose methods for calculating the mean annual increment. It has been estimated, for example, that rotation age for ponderosa pine on site class 120 varies from 39 to 107 years, depending on the unit of measurement employed and the utilization standards assumed (Zivnuska, passim).

Enough has been said about these four major points in section 6 to indicate that the matters are far from resolved. A major contribution of the Randolph Bill was that it raised all of these issues, and Congress probably did well—given the broad ramifications of these issues—to avoid imposing hasty or premature conclusions.

Nondeclining Even Flow The ambiguities in section 6 were overshadowed by the controversy surrounding the nondecling even flow (NDEF) provisions in section 11. The basic concept is relatively uncomplicated, but it raises several emotional forestry issues related to the German roots of resource management and the ideological commitments of public forestry. Nondeclining even flow is a distinctly regional issue of importance in the Pacific Northwest and the northern Rocky Mountain West, where old-growth timber still exists in commercial quantities. If these regions' timber economies or local mills are adversely affected by the outcome of the NDEF-old-growth debate, the bulk of future industry development will shift to the Southeast and other areas where old-growth management is not an issue. This possibility threatens to rekindle the regional rivalries of previous decades and is sure to be a major forest management issue of the 1980s and 1990s.

Nondeclining even flow refers to the commitment of most state forest managers, the BLM, and the Forest Service to schedule harvests in such a way that the yield is sustainable in perpetuity without downward variation. The policy was adopted formally by the BLM in 1970 and by the Forest Service in 1973; but the basic ideas have been an article of the faith for foresters for nearly two centuries. NDEF is the most conservative possible formulation of sustained yield forestry. The sustained yield provisions which were so uncontroversial during debate on the Multiple Use Sustained Yield Act of 1960 require "the achievement and maintenance in perpetuity of a high-level or regular periodic output of the various renewable resources of the national forests without impairment of the productivity of the land." The NDEF concept of sustained yield does not allow for flexibility in achieving a high-level output or for flexibility inherent in calculating the output over regular periods. NDEF allows for flexibility only in an upward direction and only when increases can be maintained in perpetuity. NDEF is based on the rather crude concept, "cut equals growth." It is rigidified further by the requirement that every year's cut forevermore will not decline and will be equal to growth achievable under present conditions. This system of harvest scheduling does not permit consideration of changes in harvest technology and wood utilization, price, supply from other landownerships, or public values regarding forestlands. It is a straight and unvarying physical volume measurement.

The Forest Service justified this rigid commitment primarily because of its responsibility to maintain economic stability in timber-dependent communities. The Forest Service reasoned that productivity on a managed forest will never equal the output achievable during the conversion period when the old growth's several-centuries-long head start is being liquidated. In order to avoid a collapse in supply at the end of the conversion period, they concluded that it was necessary to minimize the distorting effect of the old growth on present flow by limiting present harvests to what will be the allowable cut from future managed forests. They estimate future cut on the basis of present conditions and technologies. This constraint limits present allowable cut and extends the conversion period to 175 to 200 years.

The sustainable yield from a managed forest of well-stocked stands which include a preponderance of thrifty, rapidly growing trees is obviously much greater than the sustainable yield from an unmanaged forest which may include poor stocking and a great deal of land effectively removed from production because it is occupied by trees that are not growing at all. However, if the old growth is harvested and the resulting yield is projected as part of productivity which will be sustainable in subsequent rotations, a falsely exaggerated picture of the long-term sustainable yield results. Dealing with the old growth during the period of converting to a managed forest is obviously an important problem, and it is at the heart of the NDEF controversy.

The Forest Service's nondeclining even flow policy is a commitment to the most gradual allowable transition to a managed forest and a very slow harvest of the old growth. Because yield can never decline, a slight short-term rise in yield resulting from an accelerated removal of old growth is not allowed. Therefore, the utilization of old growth will cover both present annual growth plus harvest of stock accumulated in the old-growth timber.

Mindful of the destructive boom-and-bust cycles which accompanied nineteenth-century forestry, the Forest Service argued that the NDEF policy was necessary to assure community stability. Their analysis assumes, first, that stability is an accepted goal, as opposed to, for example, growth, diversification, or reorientation of a community's economic base; second, that the Forest Service has a mandate and a capacity to contribute to that goal; and, third, that even flows of timber volumes from federal lands contribute to that goal.

None of these assumptions—the validity of the goal, the mandate, or the capacity to achieve it—is broadly accepted as a working assumption. Far more serious, however, the NDEF commitment will never produce an even flow in an area unless all suppliers are bound by the same commitment or the Forest Service is the only supplier. If, for example, Forest Service cut remains constant while timber available from industry lands declines, the result is not a stable supply to local mills but the very declining flow the agency ostensibly seeks to avoid. The Forest Service commitment is especially troubling in the Northwest, where there is strong indication that flow from industry lands will decline sharply until the turn of the century. On its face, then, the NDEF is rigid, conservative, and justifiable only if numerous highly questionable assumptions are granted. Why the controversy then?

The NDEF policy has many ardent supporters. Their enthusiasm stems primarily from desire to slow or halt the harvest of old-growth forests. Environmentalists and preservationists argue that the old growth should remain untouched in wilderness preserves or be harvested slowly to prevent harm to the ecosystem.

Nobody is advocating a rapid liquidation of the old growth, which would swamp mill capacities and produce a glut in the timber and wood products market. However, the timber industry generally opposes nondeclining even flow as an artificial restriction on both present and future productivity on the national forests. They want the old growth utilized and replaced with more productive managed stands with a higher sustainable yield. They also favor basing present cut calculations on the anticipated increases in future yield.

Economists argue further that the nondeclining even flow leads to the misallocation of public resources. Valuable public stocks are left to rot, burn, and be destroyed by insects at an annual rate of 6 billion bf. Mortality is approximately half the present annual allowable cut. Moreover, unproductive areas are being maintained, as such, rather than replaced with growing trees.

Economists also argue that NDEF appeals to the Forest Service because it perpetuates an anomalous situation in which the agency can show artificially high returns to their timber management budget requests. The "allowable cut effect" (ACE) creates this situation. By combining an old-growth area with a poorly stocked area in a planning unit, the Forest Service is able to inflate artificially the return on an investment in the poorly stocked area. This is done by using the present value of the old growth released for harvest by investment as the basis for calculating the return to the investment. For example, if you harvest an acre of old growth and invest $35 in site preparation and replanting, you can make the investment appear worthwhile indeed if you assess return to the $35 on the basis of the sale price of the harvested acre of old growth. Economists argue that the future value of the future growth resulting from the investment is a sounder and more typical basis for calculating investment returns. Nevertheless, in order to make the system function, the Forest Service needs to maintain the long-term reserve of old growth to continue to enhance the apparent value of investment in timber management. Through the NDEF policy, the old growth is held "hostage" to gain higher appropriations (Popovich, 696).

NDEF and NFMA   During the debate on the National Forest Management Act, Congress heard testimony from advocates on every side of this issue. The Forest Service and preservationists sought a legislative mandate requiring continued adherence to the nondeclining even flow policy. Industry representatives and many economists opposed it. Congressional reaction is probably reflective of confusion created by the conflicting testimony of experts and uncertainty regarding the difference between nondeclining even flow and sustained yield. Unclear, controversial statutory language resulted. The opening lines of section II appear rather decisive: "The Secretary of Agriculture shall limit the sale of timber from each national forest to a quantity equal to or less than a quantity which can be removed from such forest annually in perpetuity on a sustained yield basis." That would seem to endorse the Forest Service position, although some flexibility might be introduced by referencing the sustained yield definition in the 1960 act (see above, p. 202). However, the familiar qualifiers muddy matters considerably. Salvage cuts and sanitation harvesting are exempted from the coverage of the provision, and departures from the schedule for any decade may be permitted in order to meet multiple-use objectives. Moreover, the amount sold in any year can vary within decades as long as the average meets the schedule.

Regulation Writing   Congress anticipated that the process of writing regulations would resolve the statutory ambiguities discussed above. The Administrative Procedures Act (APA) established the ground rules which direct all regulation writing. It required agencies to clarify broad statutory mandates, such as those found in the National Forest Management Act, through regulations which would apprise their own personnel and other interested persons of how the agency has interpreted its authority and how it plans to comply with the statute. The APA also required agencies to notify the public when regulation writing or rule making was in progress and to give people an opportunity to comment on the proposed rules. After an adequate period to receive and assess the comments—usually not less than ninety days except in emergencies—the agency may publish final rules, which have the force of law. Normally, the notice and proposed rules are published in the *Federal Register*. However, agencies typically seek broader public comment, and *Federal Register* publication is increasingly viewed by the Forest Service as a minimum requirement. Moreover, the NFMA, in a unique departure from customary APA notice-and-comment rule-making procedures, made detailed provisions for a committee of scientists to review the technical feasibility of rules promulgated under the act. This body is without precedent in administrative law. After public involvement, the final rules are promulgated. In addition to promulgating rules, the Forest Service is required to assume that the manual complies with the new rules. By 1985, land use plans must reflect NFMA standards established in the 1976 act.

Litigation further clarifies the rules after they have been adopted and implemented. Any agency action taken under the rules can be challenged, typically on one or all of three grounds. Litigants can charge, first, that either the action or the rules justifying the action was not authorized by the statute; second, that the rule or action was an abuse of the discretion granted in the statute, that is, it was arbitrary and capricious—usually defined to mean it was undertaken without sufficient information or evidence; or, third, that proper procedures were not followed in developing the rule or taking the action. Procedural complaints are usually frequent under statutes, such as RPA-NFMA, which established a complex process for planning. There are, for example, many specific public involvement requirements in the act. Unlike Forest Service defined planning programs, which are agency procedures rather than regulations with force of law, departures from the prescribed format may justify an injunction.

Litigants complaining that the Secretary has misinterpreted or abused the discretion in the act must prove that the way the Secretary proceeded was clearly not allowed by the statute. Given the extreme ambiguity of all of the sections discussed above, it is easy to imagine numerous possible interpretations, but it is difficult to see how any Forest Service interpretation made with full public participation and the advice of the committee of scientists would be disallowed. On the other hand, a lot of people thought they knew what the 1897 Organic Act said until a judge in West Virginia found new and plain meanings in old forgotten words. The NFMA will be the basis of lawsuits well into the twenty-first century.

There are advantages in having major aspects of national forest management publicly debated, but there are also costs involved in the snail-like pace of piecemeal resolutions. The viability of many businesses, communities, and individual careers is at issue; yet it is impossible to count on clarity in the law, the process, or the timber supply for several decades. Almost every section of this act has the potential for becoming the Monongahela of the 1980s or 1990s. Moreover, it is not reasonable to assume that the courts' interpretation of the regulations will end matters. Congress may enact new legislation at any time, altering or supplementing the provisions of RPA-NFMA.

Interdisciplinary Planning The interdisciplinary planning focus of RPA-NFMA has been inadequately addressed due to the tremendous public attention focused on the timber management provisions discussed above. However, the growing emphasis on the interdisciplinary team (IDT) approach is a significant factor in the future of the land managing agencies and professions.

The 1974 Resource Planning Act directed that the Forest Service use "a systematic interdisciplinary approach to achieve integrated consideration of physical, biological, economic and other sciences" in its planning. This mandate was specified further by the National Forest Management Act. Section 6(f) required that each national forest plan be prepared by an "interdisciplinary team." Other provisions suggest the broad scope of congressional intent. For example, clear cutting can be used only where the Secretary of Agriculture has concluded an interdisciplinary assessment of the "potential environmental, biological, esthetic, engineering and economic impacts" of each advertised sale.

This language is an expansion of concepts initially articulated in the National Environmental Policy Act. It augers tremendous changes in the definition of land management skills and in the training of renewable resource managers. Challenged in the late 1960s and early 1970s by the environmental movement, many forestry schools changed from School of Forestry to School of Forestry and Environmental Studies. As the uses of wildlands continued to diversify, even this expansion has been insufficient. Interdisciplinary teams are established to recognize the physical aspects of the planning unit and, in addition, social, cultural, historic, aesthetic, economic, and other dimensions comprising the plan. Forest and range managers are required to recognize the perspectives of a variety of disciplines and to share decision-making authority with them. This has already affected job opportunities and hiring priorities in the field. Over the long term, these provisions have the potential to alter significantly the entire concept of resource management professionalism.

Minor Provisions   In addition to these intensely debated and potentially major provisions, a number of relatively minor unrelated items in the National Forest Management Act gave important direction to the Forest Service. They also illustrate how, once major legislation is introduced, every affected interest group seeks to have its special concerns addressed. By accommodating their interests, legislators build support for the pending bill.

Section 3 of the NFMA amends the RPA and directs the Forest Service to include in the *Assessment* a report on additional fiber potential which could be achieved through greater utilization of dead and down trees, woods and mill wastes, and, through changes in contract provisions, sales systems and markets. Notably, the agency is also directed to study potential recycling of urban wood wastes and wood products.

The interests of states and counties were served by section 16, which changes the formula for distributing the states' share of timber revenues to 25 percent of gross rather than the 25 percent of net receipts. This means that the costs of roading and environmental protection are not deducted from the sales price before the states' take is calculated, thereby reducing long-standing state and county opposition to higher road standards and restrictive contract provisions. Section 14(i) assists small operators bidding for federal timber by providing them with the option of having the Forest Service build all permanent roads with an estimated cost of $20,000 or more.

A final example of these minor provisions was introduced by a single House member very late in the discussion of the bill. He was concerned about collusive bidding practices in timber purchases. Language hammered out in the House-Senate Conference Committee and never commented upon at the hearings provided that the Secretary should "take such action as he may deem appropriate to obviate collusive practices in bidding," including "requiring sealed bidding on all sales except where the Secretary deems otherwise by regulation." It is unclear why written bids are less conducive to collusive practices than auction. The message to the Forest Service was clear, however: Adopt regulations requiring sealed bidding. Small mill operators generally prefer oral auctions because they have limited supply alternatives and cannot afford to be shut out of needed sales by a one-shot written bidding system. They believe that oral bidding is vital to the economic stability of many small communities. Although aware of the concern, the Forest Service wrote preliminary regulations immediately which responded to the congressional demands providing for oral auction of 49 percent of the national forest timber volume tributary to a community. This caused the first major fight under the new act. It ended when Congress amended the act to eliminate the sealed bid "requirement."

Almost forgotten among the myriad of complex provisions in the NFMA is section 13. It simply repeals the problematic language in the 1897 Organic Act which gave rise to the litigation and subsequent legislation.

THE FEDERAL LAND POLICY AND MANAGEMENT ACT OF 1976

Important as NFMA may be, it was not the only, or even the most significant, federal land management bill considered by the Ninety-fourth Congress, nor was it the only one hurriedly passed in the waning days of the second session. More than thirty years after it was created by executive reorganization and charged with administering 3500 statutes and 485 million acres of land pending disposition, the BLM was legislatively established as an agency and authorized to inventory and manage the public domain lands. As of October 21, 1976, the public domain lands, in fact, ceased to exist. Formally declaring the nation's intention to retain and manage the public domain, Congress renamed virtually all areas administered by the BLM the "public lands."

Pressures Behind FLPMA

In seeking organic or authorizing legislation, the BLM was in a slightly different position than the Forest Service during the passage of the National Forest Management Act. Unlike the Forest Service, the bureau never had a comprehensive statute defining its mission and authorities. The BLM authority came from a collection of over 3500 public land laws. In view of the enormity of its tasks and the handicaps under which the bureau has long labored, it is especially unfortunate that, when the organic act passed, it did not stimulate an overdue flowering of the agency, its programs, and its public image. The statute answers many basic questions about the future of the public domain, but it reflects the same divisions and conflicts as the National Forest Management Act. Moreover, implementation of the act has been slowed by litigation and an unusually inexperienced new administration in Washington, D.C.

The major sustained pressure behind the bill was the Bureau itself. The Multiple Use and Sustained Yield Act of 1960 inspired the BLM to seek similar legislation. The Public Land Law Review Commission and the Classification and Multiple Use Act of 1964 gave reason to hope that the long-sought authorities would soon be granted. Over the years, the BLM tried numerous strategies. When efforts to secure comprehensive legislation failed, they proffered multiple-bill packages to be "piggy backed" together to form a management mandate (Senzel, passim). Nothing availed until 1976, when, in a dramatic race against the clock, widely divergent House and Senate versions of the bill were negotiated, force fit, and folded together. Four major issues which had dominated the discussion of the bill for the entire session were subjects of critical compromises in the final harried days.

Provisions of FLPMA

Law Enforcement   Law enforcement authority was a crucial and controversial question. Unlike other federal land managing agencies, the BLM had no authority to enforce its regulations on the public lands. The BLM officers encountering claim jumpers, cactus nappers, wild horse hunters, or petroglyph defacers had no alternative but to hope the offender would remain in place with evidence undisturbed until a local sheriff could be summoned to make the arrest. Many local police were unwilling to leave their regular assignments and chase long-since-departed criminals to enforce laws frequently unpopular among their local electorate. The BLM recognized that it could not get support from western representatives for an extensive BLM police force, but the congressionally preferred scheme of providing funds to contract for police protection with local officials was expensive and seemed no better than the existing system. Section 303, as finally written, provides full law enforcement authority for the BLM but requires that the bureau achieve "maximum feasible reliance upon local law enforcement officials in enforcing [federal] laws and regulations." Objections to this delegation of BLM authority to frequently hostile locals were assuaged somewhat by a section specifically authorizing a "uniformed desert ranger force" to protect the California Desert Conservation Area, which was of major concern.

Inclusion of the Forest Service   A second hotly debated issue was the insistence of the House subcommittee on including the Forest Service in the BLM bill. Several powerful members of Congress were determined to achieve a major reorganization and extend the authority of their Interior Committee into the Agriculture Committee's territory by writing a bill covering all federal multiple-use lands. The Senate, the Forest Service, the administration, the environmentalists, most affected industries, and almost everyone else involved objected strenuously. The House held out, however, and passed a bill which included the Forest Service in key sections dealing with the planning process, grazing fees, land acquisitions and exchanges, rights of way, withdrawals, and advisory boards. The Forest Service already had congressional direction on these points, and the new language only confused matters. Happily, the most troublesome references to Forest Service programs were deleted in the Conference Committee.

Withdrawals and Reservations   Congressional review of withdrawals was the third intensely debated issue. Reasserting its authority to manage the public lands, Congress sought to limit the President's authority to withdraw land unilaterally from mineral entry. The debate focused on the size of an area and the length of time for which a withdrawal could be made without congressional review. Interestingly, the same environmentalists who were insisting that Congress be involved in extensive and detailed instructions to the Forest Service on timber management strongly opposed congressional review of withdrawals. This is because Congress was at that time less likely to support the environmentalists' position on mining issues than on timber management questions.

Grazing Fees   The final issue was grazing fees. Ranchers have traditionally argued for a fee-setting formula that will include the cost of production or the cost of doing business. Varying the theme, they occasionally support two- or three-tiered formulas that would allow varying the fee according to the quality of the available forage. Competing interests urge a fair market value formula and oppose subsidies or guaranteed profits for the livestock operators. Historically, BLM has argued for fair market value fees. The bill, as it passed, included no statutory grazing fee and placed a yearlong moratorium on fee increases, pending a joint BLM-Forest Service study of the issue.

Given the number of years the Bureau struggled to achieve legislative recognition and a basic operating mandate, it is interesting to note that these four intensely debated issues are actually tangential to the major focus of the bill. As so frequently happens in Congress, long after the basic principles are agreed to, a major bill is delayed, sometimes for years, while competing groups dicker at the margins to protect their special interests.

Multiple-Use Management and Planning   The Federal Land Policy and Management Act bears numerous scars from its final days in Conference Committee. It is poorly organized, and numerous provisions include conflicting language as House and Senate versions of the bill were simply pasted together. It also reflects the same contemporary congressional themes as the National Forest Management Act: public involvement, consultation with state and local governments, congressional review and oversight, and decision making based on planning. Very few goals or priorities are defined; the BLM is authorized and required to plan extensively to manage the public lands on a "multiple use-sustained yield basis.

In spite of this vague mandate and some of the problematic sections discussed above, the new law does reflect enduring concerns and resolves a number of important questions. First, the Bureau was formally established by Congress. Its existence and mission are defined in law. Second, Congress finally declared the nation's intention to retain and manage the lands which had been held "pending disposition" for 200 years. Third, the law gives the BLM broad authority to achieve its new mission. The final section of the bill contains hundreds of "repealers"—a weeding out of the awkward collection of statutes which were the basis of the BLM's authority. Sifting through the list and figuring out what is gone and what remains will be a lengthy process. Several congressional delegations successfully protected their constituents' interests by retaining some outdated laws like the Desert Land Entry Act. Nonetheless, the repealers alone are a major achievement. The BLM has a clear administrative structure, modern real estate management tools, and a resource management system which did not exist prior to October, 1976 (Achterman, passim).

Most of the administrative structure for the newly established BLM is defined in Title III of the Federal Lands Policy and Management Act. The Bureau is established and the director of the BLM is made, for the first time, a presidential appointee requiring the advice and consent of the Senate. Many of the public involvement provisions, including appeals procedures, cooperation with state and local government, and rule-making requirements, are also included in Title III. Sections 304 and 305 of Title III give the Bureau authority to collect service charges and require reimbursement payments and cost recovery or performance bonds. Previously, the Bureau had no general authority to engage in such normal fiscal activities.

Much of the bill is devoted to giving the BLM modern real estate management tools. For example, before FLPMA passed, the Bureau was authorized to issue leases only in specific instances. If a situation seeming to call for a lease did not fit under the precise details of one of the special statutes authorizing leasing, the BLM could not proceed. The new law provides general authority for leasing, land exchanges, acquisition, and sales. All real estate transactions must be evaluated in the land use planning process and must protect the multiple-use value of the land. General authorities are, however, available to the Bureau for the first time.

Finally, FLPMA gives overall management guidance for the Bureau's resource management activities. The entire program must be carried out under the principles of multiple-use planning. There are, however, extensive provisions for single-use management programs which may create problems. These sections reflect congressional compromises with single-interest groups. After the act passed, all mining claimants were given three years to record their claims with BLM. Failure to notify the government of an existing claim will be, at the expiration of the time period, considered tantamount to abandonment. That this requirement is new in 1976 underscores the difficulties under which BLM has long operated.

Range management provisions in Title IV emphasize preserving ranchers' tenure on the public lands by requiring ten-year grazing permits in most circumstances and requiring two-year notification prior to cancellation of leases or permits. The wilderness provisions of the act are similarly problematic. The Bureau has already been sued for proceeding with a special wilderness study, which is explicitly required by section 603 of the act, apart from and in advance of the evaluation of the multiple uses of the lands at issue. BLM's efforts to avoid the kind of problems RARE I and RARE II have created for the Forest Service may be unavailing—wilderness is a controversial issue under the best of circumstances. However, the Bureau now has authority, which was previously lacking, to include wilderness as a component of its land use spectrum.

Implementation of FLPMA

As in the case of the National Forest Management Act, Congress required the Bureau to clarify the ambiguities of the act through rule making. The regulations required by FLPMA are even more extensive than those required by NFMA, and resort to litigation to refine the regulations, as noted above, began soon after the act passed. BLM is required to go through essentially the same procedures as the Forest Service and may also wind up back in Congress when disputes and confusion about the meaning of FLMPA become intolerable.

The Future of BLM

It is important to note, however, that the passage and implementation of FLPMA does not signal that the Bureau will now become an organization similar in style and professionalism to the Forest Service. One of the major differences is timing. The Forest Service was founded during a period in which technical competence and government efficiency were unquestioned values. The Forest Service became a paramilitary spit-and-polish outfit because the public allowed and demanded it. Today technical competence is everywhere balanced by an overriding concern with public involvement. Government agencies continue to be suspect in many circles. It seems unlikely that the Bureau will be allowed and encouraged to assert that its will is synonymous with the public interest the way the Forest Service did for over sixty years. Resource management, at the end of the twentieth century, is far too complex an undertaking affecting far too many diverse interests to allow BLM the hegemony which the Forest Service enjoyed.

More important, however, BLM manages resources which differ dramatically from those of the national forests, and this factor requires a different management style. The generalization that the Forest Service manages the trees and the BLM manages the grass is only partially accurate. The Forest Service manages a great deal of grazing land, both admixed in timberlands in the West and in the national grasslands reclaimed during the Depression from abused farmland (see above, pp. 146). The Bureau manages the mineral leasing program on the entire public domain, the submerged resources on the Outer Continental Shelf, and the valuable timber on the Oregon and California revested lands. Nevertheless, the majority of the BLM-administered land is low elevation and arid. Although there are many nongrazing values on these lands—particularly aesthetic and recreation resources and strippable coal— the bulk of the land is used for domestic stock and wildlife grazing. Especially regarding livestock management, the Bureau has difficulties that are vastly more complex than those confronting the Forest Service. Both the resource and the user are harder to manage than trees and loggers. Livestock cannot be directed by contract provisions the way a logger can. Confronted with ten-year permits, the Bureau has little discretion to withhold the resource from use. The resource itself is also dramatically different. Unlike trees, grasses vary considerably from year to year and even from day to day in arid regions. In some parts of the West, long-range planning based on inventory or productivity data is highly problematic. Forage productivity is more consistent where the water comes from relatively stable winter snows than from periodic rains; but even under the best of circumstances, it is an uncertain business. Allocating the extremely variable range resource among wildlife, wild horses and burros, and domestic livestock on a grazing allotment is an extremely difficult problem. The carrying capacity of most rangeland was allocated twenty to forty years before wildlife was even recognized as a legitimate concern. The Taylor Grazing Act made those lands grazing districts, and it will be an arduous process to bring all the newly authorized multiple uses into balance.

Problems with the resource and the livestock are exacerbated by the unavoidable fact that BLM has never and will never control the land it administers the way the Forest Service does. In 1978, BLM had approximately 7000 full-time employees and an annual budget of around $440 million to manage 451 million acres. Both the budget and the employee figures are, moreover, about twice what they were in 1974. This compares with the Forest Service's approximately 44,000 employees and $1190 million annual budget to manage approximately 187 million acres. BLM has roughly one-seventh the personnel, one-third the money, and four times the land of the Forest Service, plus all the mineral leasing and Outer Continental Shelf responsibilities. Even on the relatively well-funded O and C districts, BLM receives a third to a half of what the Forest Service gets to manage comparable resources.

Thus, BLM managers are thin on the ground. They must, therefore, rely extensively on the cooperation of land users to implement management programs. Such cooperation has not usually been forthcoming in the past. However, even in the most supportive atmosphere, there are major problems. In some states, BLM land is intermixed section by section with state land, permittee-owned land, and other private land. Because it is impossible to manage the sections separately, all must be managed according to the most restrictive scheme. BLM standards are significantly different than those typically pertaining to state allotments or the practices on the permittee's own land. For example, the grazing permittee on most state land is authorized to close the allotment to all hunters and recreationists. This is especially important to stock operators when beef prices rise and make cattle rustling profitable. BLM-administered lands must, however, remain open to hunters and recreationists. This is legitimate, given that it is a public resource; but it is difficult for a rancher to protect the stock and private land under such a scheme. Regulating the use of BLM-administered land requires extensive regulation of the rancher's own property. Ranchers willingly use the public resource, which may justify the regulation of their activities; but such regulation is not popular with many ranchers nor is it easy to achieve. Turning cattle from pasture to pasture may be simple in the East or Midwest; but, in the arid West, where grazing allotments sometimes exceed 500,000 acres with one head per four to ten sections, controlling stock is difficult and expensive.

Moreover, there are real and important differences of opinion among ranchers and between ranchers and BLM managers as to the proper citeria for managing the range. Livestock operators argue that they have the greatest stake in the sustained yield of their allotments and base properties. They cannot afford to destroy the range that feeds them. Moreover, many of the ranchers are in their third or fourth generation on the same land. They have been supporting themselves for over a century, in many instances, precisely by carefully managing the land on a sustained yield basis. They sincerely question the wisdom of sending a range manager fresh out of college to tell them about range conservation.

Because BLM is dependent upon the permittees for cooperation in implementing its management programs, these differences of opinion are critical. The land use planning focus of FLPMA may be an appropriate route for introducing national guidance into management of resources which evince a tremendous local and temporal variability. However, the rigid standards currently espoused by government and environmentalist lawyers conflict sharply with the political, economic, and ecological realities of range management. Moreover, the assumption, widely held in the East and elsewhere, that ranchers are land-grabbing earth rapers is not a productive approach to necessarily cooperative programs. Implementation of FLPMA's new directives will hopefully mark the beginning of a mutual education process which will lay to rest old caricatures that have too long stalked the range.

BLM's inability to "control" the range is exacerbated by extensive mineral claims and increasingly divided responsibility for energy-mineral management. One of the great achievements of FLPMA is the recordation requirement imposed on prospectors. The limited control implied by simple recordation underscores the extent to which BLM and its programs continue to be subject to interruption by the rights of mining operations. The existence of the new Department of Energy futher complicates mineral matters. How multiple-use land management will fare when confronted by the energy development mandate of the Department of Energy is not clear. However, as discussed above, when Congress divided the responsibility for leasing between the Interior and Energy departments, it further restricted BLM's ability to manage the land for which it is responsible.

Implementation of FLPMA would have been difficult in any case, but the first steps toward operations under the new act have been complicated by the requirements of the NRDC grazing case settlement. One-third of the 1977 budget was spent on assessment work (1 *Public Land News* (3), 7). BLM staffers estimate, moreover, that 40 percent to 60 percent of their time is spent in processing the papers required. Some of this effort is appropriate to compensate for the years when BLM had unclear inventory or planning authority; however, it is questionable whether such a radical shift to inventory and paperwork can be justified. Basic range improvement work has been halted on 6700 of 6902 allotment management units pending completion of the necessary EISs (1 *Public Land News* (3), 7). After waiting thirty years for comprehensive management authority, many BLM employees are frustrated by the new round of delays in their management programs.

More frustrating still, however, is the lack of support within the Department of the Interior for the revitalization of BLM. FLPMA was enacted in the closing days of the 1976 presidential election campaign, and BLM staffers were hopeful that a new administration plus the new statute would start great things for the Bureau. Unfortunately, few of Carter's appointments in the Department have shown signs of interest in or knowledge of the BLM. The new Secretary set the tone by alleging, in a number of well-publicized speeches made early in his tenure, that the Bureau had sold out to industry. During his administration, Secretary Andrus declared, "the Bureau of Livestock and Mining" would be altered into an environmentally sensitive land managing agency serving the whole public. This was just the kind of publicity and encouragement the Bureau did not need. Andrus followed his oratorical flourishes by delaying over a year in nominating a new director for BLM. Frank Gregg, the first director appointed under the new provisions, was not sworn in until February 1978. Meanwhile, major policy matters languished for up to eighteen months on high officials' desks without action. This has not been auspicious start for a new era in public land management. There are many factors which comprise a successful program. Frequently, intangible or uncontrollable factors, such as the attitude of administrative officials or an unfortunate lawsuit, can undo the boldest congressional initiative. FLPMA implementation and a clear understanding of its ramifications for public land management are probably at least a decade away.

This negative note may not be an appropriate conclusion to a discussion of BLM programs. There is some evidence that the fracas may have positive results. At the close of the 1978 legislative session, Congress passed the Omnibus Range Improvement or Roncalio Bill. The legislation authorizes $365 million over the next twenty years for range improvements and establishes guidelines whereby specified improvements may be exempted from the environmental assessments required by the NRDC grazing suit settlement. Any appropriations under the act will be subject to the budget and personnel restrictions imposed by the Carter administration's efforts to control inflation and reduce taxes. However, the authorization is, in itself, a unique commitment to range management. Perhaps more significantly, the bill also authorizes the Bureau to dispose humanely of wild and free roaming horses and burros. Under the protection afforded by the 1971 statutes, wild horse populations had expanded dramatically and were in many areas consuming all the available forage.

Some environmentalists opposed the bill because it adopted a grazing fee formula devised by a team of BLM and Forest Service economists established by the Federal Land Policy and Management Act. The formula, which is only effective until 1985 under terms of the bill, takes into account the cost of livestock production, the price of beef, and the value of the forage. Many groups, including the Bureau, have long supported a fair market value basis for setting grazing fees (3 *Public Land News* (20), 3–4). Debate over this issue has been a major rallying point in efforts to defeat range regulation management programs throughout the century. Whatever gains might accrue to a fair market value standard have probably been expended many times over in simply studying the issue. Although the cost of production index is indeed a subsidy to the permittees, most other users of the public lands—wilderness hikers, recreationists, hunters, fishers, miners, special permit holders of all sorts—are subsidized. Grazing fees have been the heart of too many controversies for too long and have distracted too much attention from the major problems of range allocation and management. It seems constructive and positive that this long-fought battle has been laid to rest, albeit temporarily.

SUMMARY

Even perfect legislation and hearty administrative support would not have prevented conflict and uncertainty in implementation of FLPMA. Uncertainty and conflict are characteristic of modern life generally and will continue to be major aspects of all land management activities. Forest and range policy was for many decades the primary domain of a fairly small, tightly knit group of government land management professionals. Occasional controversy or congressional activity did not alter the relatively serene story of progress in the science and application of land management techniques. The major break occurred during the Second World War. New values, new goals, and new actors have swirled around land management ever since. Beginning in the late 1960s, growing conflicts became confrontations; and the intensity of the civil rights and peace movements were manifest in increasing hostility about forest and range management.

There would be pleasing symmetry in concluding that two major bills of our bicentennial year, NFMA and FLPMA, resolve these conflicts and chart a clear course for another hundred years of progress. This did not and could not happen. The best we can hope is that FLPMA and RPA-NFMA have instituted procedures through which we can deal with conflicts which have only begun to emerge. Embracing a flexible planning framework for both BLM and the Forest Service, Congress has recognized that a great many issues surrounding forest and range mangement are themselves unfolding. The full impact of state programs implementing air quality, water quality, pesticide control, and other environmental quality regulations is yet to be seen. State regulation of private land use is increasing and may provide stimulus to further federal legislation. Energy use of wild lands in all ownership categories is bound to increase, and management techniques may soon be recast to account for energy efficiency even as they are now being retooled to achieve environmental quality.

If FLPMA and RPA-NFMA succeed, there is some basis for hoping that decision making may ultimately be simplified. At least the process may stabilize and become familiar. Surely, the integration of national and local land use planning and the linking of budget and land use planning is a sound step. However, the emergence of forest and range issues as important social questions and the number of competing interests which surround them doom any hope of returning to a quiet simple process. Competing groups will seek advantageous access to the process wherever it suits their interests. The steady push toward openness in government may subside, but the structures already in place assure that future planning will be subject to constant review and challenge.

In the end, careful planning and sensitivity to the trade-offs and impacts of management activities still will not make it possible to meet all the demands on forest and rangelands. At best, we have a process for assessing conflict and making decisions. Nothing can prevent the conflict or keep it from growing as public demands proliferate and compete. To succeed, land management professionals must recognize that they are part of a confusing policy arena, increasingly controversial, increasingly politicized, and increasingly uncertain. The object must be not to seek certainty, but to learn to live with complexity.

REFERENCES CITED

Achterman, Gail L. "Implementation of the BLM 'Organic Act.' " Address, Utah State Bar, Salt Lake City, October, 1977.

Clawson, Marion. "The National Forests." 191 *Science* 762 (February 20, 1976).

Congress and The Nation. Vol. IV. Washington, D.C.: Congressional Quarterly, Inc., 1977.

Hyde, William F. "Resources Planning Act: Critique and Alternative Approach." 74 *Journal of Forestry* 282 (1976).

Manthy, Robert. "Resource Planning Act: Forest Policy." 74 *Journal of Forestry* 280 (1976).

Popovich, Luke. "Harvest Schedules: Parts I and II." 74 *Journal of Forestry* 634 (September, 1976) and 695 (October, 1976).

President's Advisory Panel on Timber and the Environment. *Report.* Washington, D.C.: Government Printing Office, 1973.

Public Lands News, 1975–present.

Senzel, Irving. "Genesis of a Law: Parts I and II." 84 *American Forests* 30 (January, 1978) and 32 (February, 1978).

Teeguarden, Dennis E. "Developing Regulations to Implement the National Forest Management Act of 1976." Address, Western Timber Association Annual Meeting, San Francisco, March, 1978.

Vaux, Henry J. "Problems in Legislating Federal Forest Policy." In Dennis Le Master and Luke Popovich, eds., *Crises in Federal Land Management.* Washington, D.C.: Society of American Foresters, 1977.

Zivnuska, John. "Timber Harvesting and Land Use Planning Under the National Forest Management Act of 1976." Address, Meeting of the Committee of Scientists, Denver, August, 1977.

Chronological Summary of Important Events in the Development of Colonial and Federal Policies Relating to Forest and Range Policy

This summary includes only the major features of the events listed. Items of particular interest from the standpoint of forest and range policy are treated at greater length in the text.

1609

First shipment of masts from the colonies was sent from Virginia to England.

1626

Plymouth Colony forbade the selling or transportation of timber out of the colony without the approval of the governor and council.

1631

First commercial sawmill in the colonies was probably established at Berwick, Maine. (Claim of a sawmill at York, Maine, in 1623 is poorly substantiated.)

1631

Massachusetts Bay Colony forbade the burning of any ground prior to March 1.
Subsequent legislation in Massachusetts and other colonies forbade burning at other
times and specifically recognized damage by fire not only to timber but also to young
growth, soil, and domestic stock.

1651

First of the Navigation Acts attempting to limit English and colonial trade to ships of
English registry and to channel raw materials from the colonies to England to pay for
British manufactures was passed.

1668

Massachusetts reserved for the public all white pine trees fit for masts in certain parts
of the town of Exeter.

1681

William Penn provided that for every 5 acres of forest cleared 1 acre should be kept
in trees.

1691

William and Mary in a new charter creating the Province of Massachusetts Bay forbade
the cutting, without permission of the British government, of all trees 24 inches or more
in diameter at 12 inches from the ground growing on land not theretofore granted to
a private person, under penalty of £100. This became known as the Broad Arrow policy
because of the practice of marking trees reserved under it for the use of the Crown with
the broad arrow of sovereignty.

1704

Bounties were offered for naval stores and masts shipped to England, and these items
were put on the enumerated list under the Navigation Acts. The law also placed a
penalty on injuring pitch pine through fire or cutting.

1705

The British Parliament prohibited the felling of all "Pitch Pine and Tar Trees" less than
12 inches in diameter and not growing on private property in the various colonies.

1708

New Hampshire enacted legislation embodying the British Broad Arrow policy of 1691.

1711

Broad Arrow policy was extended to include all white pine trees fit for masts 24 inches or more in diameter at 12 inches from the ground, and not private property, anywhere in New England, New York, and New Jersey. A penalty of £5 was provided for unlawfully marking any tree with the broad arrow.

1721

Broad Arrow policy was broadened to forbid the cutting of any white pine trees not growing within a township, from Nova Scotia to New Jersey, under penalties ranging from £5 to £50.

1729

Broad Arrow policy was reenacted with somewhat stricter provisions as to what constituted private land and with better machinery for enforcement and was extended to every part of America which belonged to Great Britain or should thereafter be acquired. It remained in effect in this form until the Revolution. The act also reduced somewhat the bounties on naval stores provided by the act of 1704.

1739

Massachusetts undertook to check the encroachment of sand dunes at Truro and on Plumb Island in Ipswich Bay by regulating timber cutting, grazing, and burning. Later acts applied to other parts of Cape Cod.

1743

New York authorized anyone to call for help in fighting forest fires in certain counties.

1744

Massachusetts authorized groups of five or more owners in the town of Ipswich to apply for the establishment of a common woods. If two-thirds of the proprietors within the proposed limits approved, all of the lands involved became subject to the joint control and management of the proprietors.

1752

Connecticut forbade appropriation by others than their owners of logs and other forest products being floated down the Connecticut River. This action was followed by similar legislation in other colonies and states, which led to abandonment of the English common law that only tidal streams are navigable and substitution therefore of the doctrine that any stream which will float a log or boat is navigable and consequently a public highway.

1772

New York forbade the bringing to Albany for fuel of more than six pieces of wood per load under 6 inches in diameter at the large end for pine and under 4 inches for other species.

1776

Continental Congress offered land bounties to deserters from the enemy army and to soldiers who should serve throughout the war.

1780

Continental Congress resolved that lands ceded to the United States should be used for the common benefit of all the states.

1781

New York ceded its western lands to the federal government. Virginia, Massachusetts, Connecticut, South Carolina, North Carolina, and Georgia presently followed suit, the last cession being made by Georgia in 1802. The 233 million acres included in these cessions started the public domain.

1783

Massachusetts passed an act substantially equivalent to the Broad Arrow policy of the British.

1785

Ordinance of May 20 provided for the rectangular system of survey of the public lands. After survey, the lands were to be sold at auction for cash to the highest bidder at not less than $1 per acre. Sections 8, 11, 26, and 29 were reserved for later disposal by the government, and section 16 for common-school purposes. Reservation was also made of one-third of all gold, silver, lead, and copper mines to be sold or otherwise disposed of as Congress should direct.

1787

Ordinance of April 21 provided that one-third of the sale price of public lands should be paid immediately and the balance in three months.

1788

First patent to public land was issued by the government on March 4.

1789

Constitution provided (Art. 4, Sec. 3) that "the Congress shall have Power to dispose of and make all needful Rules and Regulations respecting the Territory or other Property belonging to the United States." This provision has been repeatedly interpreted by the Supreme Court (14 Peters 526, 13 Wallace 92, and other cases) as giving Congress complete control over the public domain.

1796

Congress provided for a Surveyor General and gave directions for applying the rectangular system of survey adopted in 1785. Sales were to be made at auction to the highest bidder, with a minimum price of $2 per acre, payable in full within one year. All navigable streams within the territory covered by the act were declared to be public highways.

1799

Congress appropriated $200,000 for the purchase of timber or of lands on which timber suitable for purposes of naval construction was growing and for the perservation of such timber for future uses.

1802–1803

Acts providing for organization of the state of Ohio granted section 16 in each township to the state for school purposes. Ohio was also granted 3 percent of the net proceeds from all sales of public lands within the state for the construction of roads, and 5 percent of the net proceeds was to be used by Congress for the construction of roads leading to and through the state. In return, Ohio agreed to exempt from taxation all land sold by the government for five years from the date of sale.

1803

Louisiana Purchase added 523 million acres to the public domain.

1804

Congress reduces the minimum area of public lands offered for sale to a quarter section (160 acres). The minimum price of $2 per acre was retained, but no interest was to be charged on deferred payments unless they became delinquent. Section 16 in each township and all salt springs were reserved for educational purposes, but the other four sections near the center of each township previously reserved were now to be sold.

1807

Act of March 3 forbade anyone to settle on or occupy the public lands until authorized by law. The President was authorized to direct the marshal to remove trespassers and to take such other measures and to use such military force as necessary for the purpose.

Lead mines in Indiana Territory reserved for future disposal and authorized the President to lease such mines for terms not exceeding five years.

1811–1812

Acts admitting Louisiana to the Union granted the state 5 percent of the net proceeds from the sale of public lands for the construction of roads and levees. Lands sold by the government were to be exempt from taxation for five years, and lands belonging to nonresident citizens were never to be taxed higher than those belonging to residents.

1812

General Land Office established in the Treasury Department.

1816

Act of April 19 admitting Indiana to the Union, in addition to the usual provisions concerning school lands and exemption from taxation, reserved 5 percent of the net proceeds from the sale of public lands for the construction of public roads and canals; of this amount, three-fifths was to be spent by the state and two-fifths by Congress for the construction of roads leading to the state. An additional township, to be designated by the President, was reserved for a seminary of learning.

1817

Secretary of the Navy authorized to reserve from sale public lands containing live oak and red cedar for "the sole purpose of supplying timber for the navy of the United States." Administration of the reserves was under the Navy Department.

1819

Florida purchase adds 43 million acres to the public domain.

1820

Act of April 24 provided that public lands should thereafter be offered at public sale to the highest bidder in half-quarter sections (80 acres); reduced the minimum price to $1.25 per acre; and required full payment at the time of sale. Private sale (at not less than the minimum price) of lands unsold at public auction was authorized.

1821

Attorney General ruled that under the act of 1807 timber trespassers on public lands could be removed by military force and subjected to fine and imprisonment.

1823

Ohio granted a right of way 120 feet wide, together with a strip of land 1 mile in width on each side, to aid in the construction of a wagon road from the lower rapids of the Miami River to the western boundary of the Connecticut Western Reserve. The road was to be completed in four years, and none of the land was to be sold for less than $1.25 per acre.

1824

Army Corps of Engineers assigned responsibility for the handling of internal improvements, including improvement of rivers and harbors. The first act dealing only with rivers and harbors was passed in 1826.

1827

Illinois and Indiana granted land for canal construction equal to one-half of five sections in width on each side of proposed canals in the two states, reserving each alternate section to the United States. The canals were to be free public highways for the use of the United States.

President authorized to take proper measures to preserve the live oak timber growing on the lands of the United States and to reserve from sale public lands which contain timber valuable for naval purposes.

1828

Naval Appropriations Act appropriated not more than $10,000 for the purchase of lands necessary to provide a supply of live oak and other timber for the Navy. This was for the Santa Rosa naval timber reserve and experiment station.

Henry M. Brackenridge, in a letter to Secretary Southard of the Navy Department, discussed the culture of live oak in one of the first American papers on silviculture.

Alabama granted 400,000 acres for improvement of navigation on the Tennessee River to be sold at the minimum price charged for public lands. Subsequent grants for river improvement were made to Wisconsin and Iowa in 1846.

1830

Preemption rights granted for one year to settlers on the public lands. Such settlers, on proof of settlement or improvement, might purchase not more than 160 acres on payment of the minimum price of $1.25 per acre; but the act was not to delay the regular sale of any of the public lands, and preemption rights were not transferable. Temporary preemption laws were also enacted in 1832, 1833, 1838, and 1840. Numerous laws relating to preemption in restricted localities and for specified purposes had been passed prior to 1830.

1831

Fine imposed of not less than three times the value of the timber and imprisonment for not more than twelve months (1) on anyone who should unlawfully cut or remove any live oak, red cedar, or other timber from lands reserved or purchased for the use of the Navy and (2) on anyone who should cut or remove any live oak, red cedar, or other timber from any other lands of the United States without written authorization or with intent to export it or use it for any other purpose than for the Navy of the United States.

1832

Minimum size of tracts offered at private sale reduced to 40 acres.

Hot springs in Arkansas reserved from entry, together with four sections of land surrounding them, for future disposal by the United States.

Last of the laws providing relief for settlers who had purchased lands under the credit system passed.

1835

From 1835 on, Congress frequently granted to railroads a free right of way through public lands. The privilege was made general in 1852.

1836

Specie Circular of July 11 required local land officials to accept only gold and silver in payment for public land, except for actual settlers buying not more than 320 acres.

1841

Act of September 4 covered three important points:

1. It granted 10 percent of the net proceeds from the sale of public lands in Ohio, Indiana, Illinois, Alabama, Missouri, Mississippi, Louisiana, Arkansas, and Michigan to the state concerned. The balance was to be distributed quarterly to the states, the District of Columbia, and the territories of Wisconsin, Iowa, and Florida for use as the legislatures might direct. Distribution was, however, to cease in case of war, if the minimum price of public lands was increased above $1.25 per acre (except in alternate sections), or if the duties fixed by the act of March 2, 1833, were raised above 20 percent.

2. For purposes of internal improvement 500,000 acres were granted to each of the nine states named above and to such new states as might later be admitted to the Union. Grants already received from the federal government were to be deducted from this figure. The lands were to be disposed of by the states for not less than $1.25 per acre and the proceeds used only for internal improvements.

3. The preemption privilege was made general by providing that every head of a family, widow, or single man over twenty-one years of age who was a citizen of the United States or had declared his intention to become a citizen could settle upon and purchase at the minimum price of $1.25 per acre not more than 160 acres of surveyed, nonmineral, unoccupied, and unreserved public lands, subject to certain restrictions. Preemptors must inhabit and improve the land and must swear that the land was being taken up for their own exclusive use and benefit. Final proof of settlement and habitation had to be made within one year of the date of settlement, but preemption was not to delay the regular sale of any of the public lands of the United States.

1842

A forerunner of the Homestead Act offered to donate lands in Florida to actual settlers in lots of 160 acres up to a grand total of 200,000 acres.

Distribution to the states of proceeds from the sale of public lands was suspended and never resumed.

1843

The Senate asked the Secretary of the Navy for any evidence "that depredations of a most ruinous kind are being daily committed on the navy timber."

Reservations of live oak lands in Louisiana opened to settlement. The last disposal of these reservations was made in 1923.

1845

Joint Resolution of March 1 consented to the annexation of Texas, which had been an independent republic since 1836, with the provision that it should retain control of its public lands.

1846

Treaty of June 15 with Great Britain confirmed the claim of the United States to some 181 million acres of territory embracing the present states of Oregon, Washington, and Idaho, and parts of Montana and Wyoming and defined the northern boundary of the territory.

Public sale of reserved lead mines in Illinois, Arkansas, Wisconsin, and Iowa at not less than $2.50 per acre authorized.

Commissioner of the General Land Office authorized to sell isolated or disconnected tracts of unoffered lands without the formality of a proclamation by the President.

Grant of public lands to Wisconsin for the construction of the Wisconsin-Fox River Canal, inaugurated the policy of charging the "double minimum" price of $2.50 per acre for land in the alternate sections retained by the government.

1847

All states admitted to the Union prior to 1820 authorized to tax all public lands from and after the day of their sale, provided that lands belonging to citizens living outside the states were never to be taxed higher than those belonging to persons residing therein.

1847

Lake Superior district in Michigan and the Chippewa land district in Wisconsin established for purposes of mineral survey and authorized sale in quarter sections, after six months' notice, of lands containing copper, lead, or other valuable ores at a minimum price of $5 per acre.

1848

Treaty with Mexico added 335 million acres to the public domain.

Beginning with the act establishing the territorial government of Oregon, sections 16 and 36 in each township were reserved for school purposes.

American Association for the Advancement of Science organized.

1849

Swampland Grant Act granted to Louisiana all of the swamp and overflowed lands in that state unfit for cultivation, with the proviso that the proceeds should be used exclusively, as far as necessary, for the construction of levees and drains.

Department of the Interior created. Secretary has responsibility for administering the public lands (except reservations administered by another department, such as the naval-timber reserves). The new department acquired the General Land Office, Indian Affairs, and the Patent Office (in which the government's agricultural services were then carried on) by transfer from the Treasury Department, War Department, and State Department, respectively.

1850

Seventy-nine million acres added to the public domain by purchase from Texas.

The first of the railroad land grants, granted to the states of Illinois, Alabama, and Mississippi, to aid in the construction of the Illinois Central Railroad (which was privately built): (1) a right of way not over 200 feet wide; (2) free use of construction material, such as earth, stone, and timber; and (3) every alternate section of land designated by even numbers of six sections in width on each side of the road, with the right to make lieu selections in place of alienated lands to a distance of not more than 15 miles from the road. The alternate sections retained by the government were to be sold at not less than $2.50 per acre. Property and troops of the United States were at all time to be transported over the railroad free of charge, and the mails at such rates as Congress might fix.

1850

Alabama, Arkansas, California, Florida, Illinois, Indiana, Iowa, Michigan, Mississippi, Missouri, Ohio, and Wisconsin granted all of the swamp and overflowed lands in those states, under conditions similar to those contained in the grant to Louisiana.

Special agents were appointed, probably for the first time, to suppress timber trespass on the public lands generally.

1852

Railroads already chartered or to be chartered within ten years granted free right of way through public lands together with free use of timber and other construction materials.

1853

Sale of red cedar lands in Alabama that had been reserved for naval purposes in 1817 authorized.

Gadsden Purchase of December 30 added 19 million acres to the public domain.

1854

Graduation Act reduced the price of land according to the time it had been on the market, with a minimum of 12.5 cents per acre after thirty years. The act did not apply to alternate sections in grants made for internal improvements or to mineral lands held at more than $1.25 per acre. Purchasers had to swear that they were acquiring the land for their own use and for the purpose of actual settlement and cultivation.

1855

Responsibility for prevention of timber trespass was transferred from special agents to the local land offices.

1860

Provisions of the swampland grants extended to Minnesota and Oregon.

1862

Department of Agriculture (not of cabinet rank), headed by a Commissioner of Agriculture, established.

1862

Homestead Act of authorized any person who was head of a family or over twenty-one years of age, and who was a citizen of the United States or had declared an intention to become such, to enter upon not more than 160 acres of unappropriated land subject to preemption and sale at a minimum price of $1.25 per acre, or not more than 80 acres subject to sale at a minimum price of $2.50 per acre. Free patent could then be secured by the settler for his exclusive use and benefit on proof that he had resided upon or cultivated the land for five years, provided that if he should actually change his residence during that period or should abandon the land for more than six months at any one time, it was to revert to the government. Commutation, or purchase of the land at its regular price, was possible at any time after six months from the date of filing.

Preemption Act extended to unsurveyed lands in all the public land states and territories and repealed the Graduation Act of 1854.

Union Pacific and Central Pacific railroads granted alternate, odd-numbered sections of land for 10 miles on each side of the road. This distance was increased to 20 miles in 1864. Mineral lands were not included, but the amendments in 1864 excluded coal and iron land from this category. Government mails, troops, and supplies were to be transported at fair and reasonable rates. Three years after completion of the roads any lands remaining were to be subject to preemption by settlers and sold to them for not more than $1.25 per acre. The price of the sections retained by the government was not increased.

Morrill Act granted to each state 30,000 acres of nonmineral public land (with minimum price of $1.25 per acre) for each senator and representative to which it was entitled under the census of 1860. The proceeds were to be invested in a permanent fund and the interest used for the establishment of colleges of agriculture and the mechanic arts. States without public lands were given an equivalent amount of scrip, purchasers of which were not to take up more than a million acres in any one state.

1864

Man and Nature by George Perkins Marsh published.

Yosemite Valley and the Mariposa Big Tree Grove granted to California to be held forever "for public use, resort, and recreation."

Act of July 1 provided for the sale of coal lands in the public domain at auction at a minimum price of $20 per acre.

Northern Pacific Railroad granted alternate, odd-numbered sections of nonmineral land for 40 miles on each side of the road in the territories traversed, and half that amount in the states. Lieu lands could be selected within 10 miles of the outer limit of the primary grant. The price of the alternate sections retained by the government was raised to $2.50 per acre. Five years after completion of the road, the railroad was required to sell all unmortgaged lands still in its possession for not more than $2.50 per acre. Transportation of government mails, troops, and supplies was to be furnished under regulations imposed by Congress.

1866

All lands in Alabama, Mississippi, Louisiana, Arkansas, and Florida withdrawn from disposal except under the Homestead Act.

California and Oregon Railroad Company granted alternate, odd-numbered sections of nonmineral public land to a distance of 20 miles on each side of the road. Property and troops of the United States were to be transported without charge.

Congress declares that mineral lands of the public domain, both surveyed and unsurveyed, should be free and open to exploration and occupation by citizens of the United States or those who had declared their intention to become citizens. Lode mines could be purchased for $5 per acre if the claimant had occupied them according to local mining rules and had expended as much as $1000 in labor and improvements.

Right of way for the construction of ditches and canals across public lands granted to persons having rights to the use of water for mining, agricultural, manufacturing, or other purposes.

Grants made to the Atlantic and Pacific Railroad (now the Atchison, Topeka, and Santa Fe) and to the Southern Pacific Railroad similar in amount to the grant to the Northern Pacific Railroad.

1867

Alaska purchased from Russia, adding 365 million acres to the public domain.

1869

To aid in the construction of a military wagon road from Coos Bay to Roseburg, Oregon granted the odd-numbered sections of nonmineral land to 6 miles on each side of the road, which was to be a public highway for the free transportation of property, troops, and mails of the United States.

John Wesley Powell explores the Colorado River.

1870

Act provides for the sale of placer mines at $2.50 per acre in tracts not exceeding 160 acres.

1871

Joint Resolution of February 9 authorized the President to appoint a civil officer of the government as Commissioner of Fish and Fisheries to study problems relating to the conservation of the food fishes of the coast and lakes of the United States. Deficiency Appropriations Act of May 18 appropriated $3500 for the work.

$5000 appropriated for the fiscal year 1872 for the protection of timberlands in naval timber reservations. The last appropriation for this purpose was for the fiscal year 1876.

The last railroad land grant, to the Texas Pacific Railroad Company, made March 3.

1872

Yellowstone National Park reserved "as a public park or pleasuring-ground for the benefit and enjoyment of the people."

Arbor Day was first celebrated in Nebraska on April 10 at the instance of J. Sterling Morton, later Secretary of Agriculture.

Mineral lands constituted as a distinct class and their survey and sale provided for at $2.50 per acre for placer mines and at $5 per acre for lode mines.

$10,000 appropriated for the protection of public timberlands in general from trespass and fraud.

1873

Lands containing iron, coal, or any other minerals in Michigan, Wisconsin, and Minnesota excluded from the provisions of the Mineral Act of 1872 and opened them to exploration and purchase as before the passage of that act.

Timber Culture Act offered to donate 160 acres of public land to any person who would plant 40 acres to trees, not more than 12 feet apart each way (302 per acre), and keep them in a growing and healthy condition by cultivation for a period of ten years. Any homesteader who should, at the end of three years, submit satisfactory proof of having had under cultivation for two years 1 acre of trees for each 16 acres in his homestead claim was entitled to receive a patent at once, the planting and cultivation of the trees being accepted in lieu of the additional two years' residence required by the Homestead Act of 1862.

American Association for the Advancement of Science passed a resolution favoring the creation of federal and state forestry commissions and appointed a committee with Franklin B. Hough as chairman to follow the matter up.

1874

Timber Culture Act amended by limiting it to heads of families or persons over twenty-one years of age who were citizens or had declared their intentions to become citizens and by reducing the period of cultivation to eight years. A person entering a quarter section had to plow 10 acres the first year, 10 acres the second year, and 20 acres the third year, and to plant 10 acres the second year, 10 acres the third year, and 20 acres the fourth year, with proportional acres for smaller claims.

Land grant railroads allowed to make lieu selections for land found to be in the possession of actual settlers.

President Grant in a special message to Congress called attention to the urgent need for forest protection and transmitted a draft of proposed legislation on the subject.

Report by William H. Brewer of Yale University, *The Woodlands and Forest Systems of the United States,* was published in the "Statistical Atlas of the Ninth Census."

1875

Railroads granted free rights of way through public lands and the use of timber and other materials for construction purposes.

1875

The American Forestry Association was organized.

1876

Timber Culture Act amended by extending for one year the period during which cultivation and planting must be accomplished for each year that the trees were destroyed by grasshoppers or other inevitable causes. Planting of seeds, nuts, and cuttings was declared to constitute compliance with the law.

A rider on the Appropriations Act of August 15 appropriated $2000 for the employment by the Commissioner of Agriculture of an expert to study and report upon forest conditions. Franklin B. Hough was appointed.

A forest reserve bill was introduced by Representative Fort of Illinois but received no action.

Appalachian Mountain Club founded as major New England hiking and conservation group.

1877

Act provided that saline lands which had been reserved for granting to the states on their admission to the Union were to be examined and offered for sale at public auction at not less than $1.25 per acre if found to be actually saline.

1877

Entomological Commission established in the Department of the Interior. It was transferred to the Department of Agriculture in 1881.

Desert Land Act provided for the sale in eleven Western states and territories of 640 acres of nontimber, nonmineral land unfit for cultivation without irrigation to any settler who would irrigate it within three years after filing. A payment of 25 cents per acre was to be made at the time of filing and $1 per acre at time of final proof.

The system of special agents to check timber trespass on the public domain was revived and expanded under Carl Schurz, Secretary of the Interior, and J. A. Williamson, Commissioner of the General Land Office.

1878

John Wesley Powell's *Report on the Lands of the Arid Region of the United States* published.

Free Timber Act provided that residents of Colorado, Nevada, New Mexico, Arizona, Utah, Wyoming, Dakota, Idaho, or Montana might cut timber on public mineral lands for building, agricultural, mining, or other domestic purposes, subject to such regulations as the Secretary of the Interior might prescribe. This privilege was later extended in acts of 1891, 1893, and 1901.

Timber and Stone Act provided for the sale in Washington, Oregon, California, and Nevada of 160 acres of surveyed, nonmineral land, chiefly valuable for timber or stone and unfit for cultivation, which had not been offered at public sale, for not less than $2.50 per acre. The purchaser had to swear that the land was being acquired solely for his own use and benefit. In 1892 the provisions of this act were extended to all the public land states. In the states concerned, the act also forbade the unlawful cutting or wanton destruction of timber on any public lands or its removal for export or other disposal; granted permission to miners and farmers to clear land and to use such timber as necessary for improvements; relieved trespassers who had not exported the timber from the United States from further prosecution on payment of $2.50 per acre for the timber; and directed that all moneys collected should be covered into the Treasury of the United States.

Congress reduced the area to be planted under the Timber Culture Act to not less than one-sixteenth of the amount entered for areas of not less than 40 acres. The number of trees to be planted was increased to 2700 per acre, of which 675 had to be living at the time of final proof. An extension of one year in the cultivation and planting was allowed for each year the trees were destroyed by grasshoppers or drought.

1879

Sundry Civil Appropriations Act of March 3 created both the Geological Survey and the Public Land Commission. A preliminary report by the commission, submitted in 1880, offered a proposal for the classification of the public lands and recommended sale of timber without the land and formulated a number of concepts which continue to be the core of government conservation programs.

United States Circuit Court (5 Dillon 405) ruled that the trespass acts of 1831 and 1859 did not apply to Indian reservations, since these are not "lands of the United States."

1880

Timber trespassers on the public lands prior to March 1, 1979 relieved from both civil and criminal prosecution on payment of $1.25 per acre.

1881

The forestry work started by Hough in 1876 was organized as a separate division under the Commissioner of Agriculture.

1882

American Forestry Congress met in Cincinnati in April, absorbed Dr. Warder's American Forestry Association in August, and in 1889 assumed that name.

F. B. Hough started the *American Journal of Forestry,* which ran from October, 1882, to September, 1883.

1884

Alaskan "Organic Act" established civil government, with schools and federal courts, for Alaska and provided that native land claims would be treated in subsequent legislation.

1885

Act of February 25 forbade fencing of the public domain and authorized the destruction of illegal enclosures.

Funds "for the promotion of economic ornithology" by the Entomological Division included in Agricultural Appropriations Act.

1886

Division of Economic Ornithology and Mammalogy in the Department of Agriculture established.

1886

Congress gave forestry statutory recognition as a distinct division of the Department of Agriculture. Bernhard E. Fernow took charge.

1887

Hatch Act provided for financial assistance to states in the establishment of agricultural experiment stations.

Boone and Crockett Club, major sports organization which included most early conservation leaders among its members, founded.

1888

At John Wesley Powell's urging, Congress provided for a survey of the public lands suitable for irrigation and directed that all lands selected as sites for reservoirs, canals, and ditches and all lands thereby made susceptible of irrigation should be withdrawn from entry. Powell was in charge.

1889

Act provided for the cession to the government of lands in the Chippewa Indian Reservation in Minnesota and for the sale of land and timber under government supervision, with the proceeds going into a permanent fund for the benefit of the tribe.

President authorized to permit Indians to cut and sell dead timber on Indian reservations, provided the timber had not been intentionally killed.

Department of Agriculture, headed by the Secretary of Agriculture, got cabinet rank.

President authorized to reserve the land containing the Casa Grande Ruin in Arizona, which thus became the first prehistoric site reservation.

1890

Powell went too far, and Congress repealed that part of the 1888 act relating to the withdrawal from entry of irrigable lands and of sites for canals and ditches, but permitted the continued withdrawal of sites for reservoirs. The act also forbade anyone to acquire title to a grand total of more than 320 acres of public land, thus cutting in half the amount previously available under the Desert Land Act of 1877.

Second Morrill Act provided for additional assistance to land-grant colleges out of proceeds from the sale of the public lands. An amendment in 1903 provided that in case these proceeds were insufficient to meet the amount appropriated, it should be paid from the Treasury.

1890

Big Tree National Park set apart as a public park, or pleasuring ground.

Act of Congress forfeited and restored to the public domain all land in grants adjacent to the uncompleted sections of railroads to which grants had been made.

Yosemite National Park and General Grant National Park set apart "as forest reservations."

1891

Act of Congress repealed the Timber Culture Act and the Preemption Act; put a stop to auction sales of public lands except isolated tracts and abandoned military and other reservations; tightened up the requirements for improvement and cultivation under the Desert Land Act of 1877, and extended it to include Colorado; did not allow commutation under the Homestead Act of 1862 until fourteen months after filing; limited the time within which suit to annul patent might be brought; restricted withdrawals for reservoir sites to the area actually needed for that purpose; authorized rights of way for irrigation canals and drainage ditches through public lands and reservations; provided that in any criminal or civil prosecution for trespass on the public lands in any of the Rocky Mountain states or territories except Arizona and New Mexico and in the district of Alaska, it should be a defense if the timber had been cut for use in such state or territory by a resident thereof for agricultural, mining, manufacturing, or domestic purposes and had not been transported out of the same, and authorized the Secretary of the Interior to make rules and regulations for the carrying out of this provision; and empowered the President to set aside as forest reserves public lands covered with timber or undergrowth, whether of commercial value or not. The last provision (Sec. 24) was added by the conference committee and is often referred to as the Forest Reserve Act.

President Harrison on March 30 proclaimed the Yellowstone Forest Reserve.

1892

The Timber and Stone Act extended to all of the public land states.

Sierra Club founded under leadership of John Muir to promote enjoyment and protection of Sierra Nevada Mountains.

1893

Free Timber Act as amended in 1891 extended to New Mexico and Arizona.

1894

Congress prohibited the hunting of birds or wild animals in Yellowstone National Park, but permitted fishing with hook and line. It also authorized the Secretary of the Interior to make rules and regulations for the management and care of the park, "especially for the preservation from injury or spoiliation of all timber, mineral deposits, natural curiosities, or wonderful objects"; for the protection of birds and animals from capture or destruction; and for the control of fishing.

Cary Act authorized the donation to states having desert lands (or to their assigns) of not more than 1 million acres each which they should cause to be settled, irrigated, and in part cultivated within ten years. Not more than 160 acres was to be sold or disposed of to any one person. Subsequent amendments made it possible for the states to obtain a total of 14 million acres, of which only about 600,000 acres has actually been granted.

1895

Division of Agricultural Soils established in the Department of Agriculture. Research relating to soils had been authorized in 1894.

1896

At the request of Secretary of the Interior Hoke Smith, the National Academy of Sciences appointed a special committee to investigate the forest reserve situation and recommended a national forestry policy.

United States Supreme Court decision on March 2 in case of *Geer* v. *Connecticut* (161 U.S. 519) confirmed the right of the states to protect their wildlife.

Division of Biological Survey established in the Department of Agriculture.

1897

Appropriations bill rider specified the purposes for which forest reserves might be established and provided for their protection and administration. Commonly known as "Organic Act."

A Division of Geography and Forestry was established in the Geological Survey to handle surveying and mapping of the forest reserves and to collect data on their resources.

1898

Homestead laws extended to Alaska, with the proviso that no homestead should exceed 80 acres. It also authorized the Secretary of the Interior to sell timber on the public lands in Alaska for use in the district, and to grant free use of timber for specified purposes. Export of pulpwood and wood pulp was authorized in 1905 and of birch timber in 1920.

1898

First appropriation ($75,000) for protection and administration of the forest reserves made July 1.

Gifford Pinchot succeeded Fernow as chief of the Division of Forestry.

1899

Secretary of the Interior authorized to lease ground near or adjacent to mineral, medicinal, or other springs in forest reserves for the erection of sanitariums or hotels, under such regulations as he might prescribe. All receipts were to be covered into a special fund to be expended in the care of public forest reservations.

Mt. Rainier National Park established.

Persons connected with the administration and protection of forest reserves directed by Congress to assist so far as practicable in the enforcement of state fish and game laws.

Appalachian National Park Association was organized in North Carolina in November.

1900

Lacey Act prohibited the importation of any foreign wild animal or bird except under special permit from the Department of Agriculture and specifically prohibited the importation of the mongoose, fruit bat, English sparrow, starling, and such other birds or animals as the Secretary of Agriculture may declare injurious to the interest of agriculture or horticulture. It also prohibited the interstate transportation of wild animals or birds taken or possessed in violation of the laws of the state from which or to which they were shipped.

The sum of $5000 appropriated for investigating forest conditions in the Appalachians with a view to purchasing land for forest reserves.

Sundry Civil Appropriations Act of June 6 limited lieu selections under the 1897 act to vacant, nonmineral, surveyed public lands subject to homestead entry.

Society of American Foresters organized.

1901

City of San Francisco applies for permit for reservoir in Hetch Hetchy Valley.

1901

Congress authorized the Secretary of the Interior to grant rights of way through forest reserves for canals and ditches, dams and reservoirs, electrical lines, and other purposes, revocable at the discretion of the Secretary.

Agricultural Appropriations Act of March 2 changed the Division of Forestry in the Department of Agriculture to the Bureau of Forestry.

Agricultural Appropriations Act of March 2 created the Bureau of Soils in place of the Division of Soils, which had been established in the Department of Agriculture in 1895.

Provisions of the Free Timber Act of 1878, as amended in 1891 and 1893 extended to California, Oregon, and Washington.

A Forestry Division was created in the General Land Office in the Department of the Interior under Filibert Roth.

1902

Newlands Act created the "reclamation fund" out of receipts from the sale and disposal of public lands in certain states west of the Mississippi River; authorized the Secretary of the Interior to construct irrigation works and to withdraw irrigable lands from entry; and provided for the homesteading of irrigated lands and their sale at a price estimated to return to the reclamation fund the cost of construction.

1903

Department of Commerce and Labor established incorporating the Commission of Fish and Fisheries, thereafter known as the Bureau of Fisheries.

Second Public Lands Commission appointed by President Roosevelt and submitted reports in 1904 and 1905. These reports made recommendations similar to the 1879 commission's, with a Pinchot/Roosevelt emphasis.

President Roosevelt set aside Pelican Island, Florida, as the first federal wildlife refuge.

1904

Kinkaid Act increased the size of homesteads in western Nebraska to 640 acres of nonirrigable land and required the construction of permanent improvements to the extent of not less than $1.25 per acre.

1905

National Audubon Society organized.

1905

President authorized to set aside areas in the Wichita Forest Reserve, Oklahoma, for the protection of game animals and birds. The refuge was transferred to the Bureau of Biological Survey by presidential proclamation in 1936.

Transfer Act of February 1 (1) transferred the administration of the forest reserves from the Secretary of the Interior to the Secretary of Agriculture; (2) covered all receipts from the forest reserves for a period of five years into a special fund to be available, until expended, as the Secretary of Agriculture might direct, for the protection, administration, improvement, and extension of the reserves; (3) provided that forest supervisors and rangers should be selected, when practicable, from the states or territories in which the reserves were located; (4) authorized the export of pulpwood and wood pulp from Alaska; and (5) granted rights of way for dams, ditches, and flumes across the reserves for various purposes under regulations prescribed by the Secretary of the Interior and subject to state laws.

Any officer of the United States authorized to arrest without process, any person taken in the act of violating the regulations relating to forest reserves and national parks.

Agricultural Appropriations Act of March 3 permitted timber on forest reserves to be exported from the state or territory (including Alaska) in which cut except in the Black Hills (South Dakota) and Idaho. This provision was made general in 1913.

Name of the Bureau of Forestry changed to Forest Service, effective July 1. It also repealed the provisions of the act of February 6, 1905, authorizing forest and park officers to arrest without process any person taken in the act of violating the laws and regulations relating to forest reserves and national parks.

Lieu land provision of the Organic Act of 1897 repealed but the perfecting of valid selections already made was permitted.

1906

President Roosevelt began withdrawal of coal and oil lands for purposes of examination and classification.

Beginning January 1, a charge was made for the first time for grazing on the forest reserves.

Act authorized the Secretary of the Interior to lease for a period of not more than ten years any surplus power developed in connection with an irrigation project, giving preference to municipal purposes.

1906

Antiquities Act forbade anyone without proper authority to appropriate, excavate, injure, or destroy any historic or prehistoric ruin or monument or any object of antiquity on lands owned or controlled by the government of the United States. It also authorized the President to establish by proclamation national monuments for the preservation of features of historic, prehistoric, and scientific interest, under administration of the department already having jurisdiction over the land in question. The area reserved must be as small as compatible with the proper care and management of the objects to be preserved.

Forest Homestead Act authorized the Secretary of Agriculture to open for entry, through the Secretary of the Interior, forest reserve lands chiefly valuable for agriculture which were not needed for public purposes and which in his judgment might be occupied without injury to the forest. Each tract was to be surveyed by metes and bounds and must not exceed 160 acres in area or 1 mile in length. Commutation was not allowed.

Joint Resolution of June 11 accepted recession by California of the lands in the Yosemite Valley and the Mariposa Big Tree Grove granted to it in 1864 for use as a state park.

Agricultural Appropriations Act of June 30 provided that 10 percent of all money received from the forest reserves during any fiscal year, including 1906, was to be turned over to the states or territories for the benefit of the public schools and public roads of the counties in which the reserves were located, but not to the extent of more than 40 percent of their income from other sources. It also forbade unrestricted spending after June 30, 1908, from the special fund set up in 1905.

1906–1907

Senate and House of Representatives passed separate but similar resolutions requesting the Bureau of Corporations to investigate the lumber industry.

1907

Appropriations Act of March 4 changed "forest reserves" to "national forests"; permitted the export of national forest timber from the state or territory in which cut, except from the Black Hills National Forest, South Dakota; forbade the further creation or enlargement of national forests except by act of Congress in Washington, Oregon, Montana, Idaho, Wyoming, and Colorado; abolished the special fund established in 1905; increased Forest Service appropriations by $1,000,000; required the Forest Service to submit to Congress annually a classified and detailed report of receipts and estimate of expenditures; and raised the Forester's salary from $3500 to $5000; appropriated $25,000 for survey of lands in the Appalachian and White Mountains in connection with their proposed purchase for national forests.

1907

On March 14, President Roosevelt appointed the Inland Waterways Commission, with Representative Burton of Ohio as chairman.

Public Lands Convention at Denver in June gave occasion for much criticism of the Forest Service.

1908

Cooperative agreement of January 22 between the Secretary of the Interior and the Secretary of Agriculture gave the Forest Service supervision over the handling of timber on Indian reservations.

U.S. Supreme Court developed Winter's Doctrine, finding federal water reservations implicit in federal land reservations (*United States* v. *Winters,* 207 U.S. 564).

Joint Resolution of April 30 authorized the Attorney General to start proceedings looking to the forfeiture of the lands granted to aid in the construction of the Oregon and California Railroad and the Coos Bay Wagon Road.

First Conference of Governors, called by President Roosevelt, met May 13 to 15 in Washington, D.C. A National Conservation Commission was appointed, with Pinchot as chairman.

Agricultural Appropriations Act of May 23 increased payment to the states for benefit of county schools and roads increased to 25 percent of the gross receipts from national forests, eliminated the 40 percent limitation, and made the legislation permanent. It also directed such officials of the Forest Service as might be designated by the Secretary of Agriculture to aid in the enforcement of state laws relating to stock, forest fire control, and fish and game protection, and to aid other federal bureaus in the performance of their duties.

An area of 12,800 acres reserved (increased in 1909 to 20,000 acres) to establish a permanent National Bison Range in the Flathead Indian Reservation in Montana.

Minnesota National Forest created out of lands covered by the Morris Act of 1902, with appropriate compensation to the Indians. It also increased from 5 to 10 percent the amount of merchantable pine timber that must be reserved in future sales outside of the "ten sections," in which the forester was permitted to use such methods of cutting as he thought wise.

First federal forest experiment station was established at Fort Valley, near Flagstaff, Arizona.

1908

Regional organization of the Forest Service was put into effect on December 1.

1909

Western Forestry and Conservation Association was organized.

Treaty of January 11 between the United States and Great Britain established the International Joint Commission and provided for the utilization and development of the boundary waters between the United States and Canada.

Report of National Conservation Commission was transmitted to Congress by President Roosevelt on January 22, with a request for an appropriation of at least $50,000 to meet the expenses of the commission, which Congress denied.

North American Conservation Conference, attended by official representatives of the United States, Canada, Newfoundland, and Mexico, was held on February 18 in Washington.

Enlarged Homestead Act made it possible to acquire homesteads of 320 acres in Arizona, Colorado, Montana, Nevada, New Mexico, Oregon, Utah, Washington, and Wyoming. Idaho (1910), California (1912), North Dakota (1912), Kansas (1915), and South Dakota (1915) were later added to the list. The lands entered must be nonmineral, nonirrigable, and contain no merchantable timber. Commutation was not allowed.

Commissioner of Indian Affairs authorized to manage the timber on Indian reservations. It resulted on July 17, 1909, in termination of the 1908 agreement with the Forest Service, and in February, 1910, in the establishment in the Office of Indian Affairs of an Indian Forest Service (later Forestry Branch of the Indian Service) under Jay P. Kinney.

National Waterways Commission created, consisting of twelve members of Congress, to conduct investigations and to make recommendations pertaining to water transportation and the improvement of waterways.

Persons who in good faith had entered coal lands under the nonmineral laws authorized to obtain patent thereto subject to reservation of the coal to the United States.

Sundry Civil Appropriations Act of March 4 prohibited the use of any public money for compensation or expenses of any commission, council, board, or other similar body not authorized by law or the detail of personal services from any federal agency to such body.

First National Conservation Congress was held at Seattle, Washington, August 26 to 28.

1909

Organization of National Conservation Association, with Charles W. Eliot of Harvard University as president, was announced on September 15.

1910

Ballinger-Pinchot controversy led on January 7 to the dismissal of Gifford Pinchot as Forester and O. W. Price as Associate Forester. They were succeeded by H. S. Graves and A. F. Potter.

Bureau of Mines established in the Department of the Interior.

Act authorized entry of coal lands under the agricultural land laws but with retention of mineral rights by the government.

Pickett Act authorized the President to withdraw temporarily public lands from entry and reserve them for specified purposes, such withdrawals or reservations to remain in force until revoked by him or by Congress. It also provided that all withdrawn lands shall be open to exploration, occupation, and purchase for all minerals other than coal, oil, gas, and phosphates.

Act extended to Indian reservations the penalties provided by the act of February 24, 1897, for failing to extinguish fires built in or near any forest, timber, or other inflammable material upon the public domain. It also provided for the sale and management of timber on Indian reservations (except in Minnesota and Wisconsin) and on certain Indian allotments, for the benefit of the Indians, under regulations prescribed by the Secretary of the Interior.

Forest Products Laboratory was established at Madison, Wisconsin, in cooperation with the University of Wisconsin.

1911

Treaty of February 7 between the United States and Great Britain provided for the protection and preservation of fur seals, including the prohibition of pelagic sealing.

Sale of surplus water from an irrigation project for use on lands outside the project authorized.

Weeks Law (1) authorized the enactment of interstate compacts for the conservation of forests and the water supply; (2) appropriated $200,000 to enable the Secretary of Agriculture to cooperate with any state which had provided by law for a system of forest fire protection; and (3) appropriated $1 million for the fiscal year 1910 and $2 million for each succeeding fiscal year until June 30, 1915, for use in the examination, survey, and acquisition by the government of lands located on the headwaters of navigable streams. It also created a National Forest Reservation Commission to pass upon lands approved for purchase and to fix the price at which purchases shall be made and provided for the protection and administration of acquired lands.

The head of the department having jurisdiction over public lands, national forests, and reservations of the United States authorized to grant rights of way for transmission, telephone, and telegraph lines for a period not exceeding fifty years.

U.S. Supreme Court held that Congress has the constitutional right (1) to reserve portions of the public domain as national forests; (2) to delegate to the Secretary of Agriculture administrative authority to make rules and regulations for their occupancy and use; and (3) to prescribe penalties for the violation of such regulations. It also confirmed the right of the Secretary of Agriculture to charge fees for grazing permits and ruled that state fencing laws gave no right willfully to drive one's stock upon the land of another (*United States* v. *Grimaud*).

1911–1914

Bureau of Corporations submitted a comprehensive report on the lumber industry in four parts.

1912

Commissioner of the General Land Office authorized to sell on application of adjoining landowners at public auction at not less than $1.25 per acre tracts containing not more than 160 acres of public land which is mountainous or too rough for cultivation, whether isolated or not.

Coal lands opened for selection by the states and for sale as isolated tracts, with reservation to the United States of the coal in such lands.

Congress reduced to three years the length of residence necessary to obtain patent under the Homestead Act and set up certain minimum cultivation requirements. Commutation was allowed after fourteen months of actual residence.

Agricultural Appropriations Act of August 10 (1) directed the Secretary of Agriculture to select, classify, and segregate all lands that may be opened to settlement and entry under the homestead laws applicable to national forests; (2) authorized and directed the Secretary to sell timber at actual cost to homestead settlers and farmers for their domestic use; and (3) made 10 percent of the gross receipts from national forests available for expenditure by the Secretary of Agriculture for the construction of roads and trails within national forests. The latter provision was made permanent in 1913.

1912

Settlement of suit authorized against forty-six defendants who had bought Oregon and California Railroad grant lands by forfeiture of the lands to the government with privilege of repurchase by the defendants at $2.50 per acre. All of these cases were settled by 1919.

Act of August 24 provided that all lands withdrawn by the President under the Pickett Act of 1910 should at all times be open to exploration, discovery, occupation, and purchase under the mining laws of the United States, so far as these applied to metalliferous minerals. It also added California to the list of states within which national forests cannot be created or enlarged except by act of Congress.

1913

Agricultural Appropriations Act of March 4 permitted timber cut on any national forest to be exported from the state or territory in which cut.

Weeks-McLean Act declared all migratory game and insectivorous birds to be within the custody and protection of the government of the United States and forbade their destruction or capture contrary to regulations prescribed by the Secretary of Agriculture. This provision was declared unconstitutional and was superseded in 1918 by the Migratory Bird Treaty Act.

National Forest Reservation Commission authorized to acquire lands subject to rights of way, easements, and reservations which the Secretary of Agriculture believes will not interfere with the use of the lands so encumbered.

Act of March 4 authorized the Secretary of the Interior to sell any timber on public lands outside of national forests which had been killed or seriously damaged by fire prior to passage of the act.

Act of September 30 authorized the President to prescribe the methods of opening to entry public lands thereafter excluded from national forests or released from withdrawals.

San Francisco granted the authority to construct a reservoir in the Hetch Hetchy Valley in the Yosemite National Park to supply the city with water.

1914

Smith-Lever Act provided for cooperative agricultural extension work between the U.S. Department of Agriculture and the land grant colleges.

Agricultural Appropriations Act of June 30 increased from 5 to 25 percent the payment of states of the gross receipts from lands acquired under the Weeks Act of 1911.

1914

Congress stopped the sale of coal lands in Alaska previously authorized; directed the reservation of certain lands; and provided for the leasing of unreserved coal lands.

1915

Branch of Research was established in the U.S. Forest Service.

Agricultural Appropriations Act of March 4 authorized the Secretary of Agriculture to grant permits for summer homes, hotels, stores, or other structures needed for recreation or public convenience in national forests in tracts of not more than 5 acres and for periods of not more than thirty years.

U.S. Supreme Court, in *United States* v. *Midwest Oil Co.,* affirmed the right of the President to withdraw public lands from entry without specific authorization from Congress.

U.S. Supreme Court reversed on technical grounds a 1913 decision of the Federal District Court for Oregon forfeiting to the government the Oregon and California Railroad grant lands, but enjoined their further disposal by the railroad pending action by Congress (*Oregon and California Railroad Co.* v. *U.S.*).

1916

Chamberlain-Ferris Act revested in the United States title to the unsold lands in the grant to the Oregon and California Railroad Company (Southern Pacific) and provided for their classification and disposition.

A sum of $11 million a year appropriated for ten years for the construction of roads and trails within or partly within national forests when necessary for the use and development of their resources. Additional appropriations of $3 million a year for the same purpose were made for the fiscal years 1919, 1920, and 1921.

Agricultural Appropriations Act of August 11 authorized the Secretary of Agriculture to require purchasers of national forest stumpage to make deposits adequate to cover the cost of disposing of brush and other debris resulting from cutting operations. The proviso authorizing return to the purchaser of any deposit in excess of the amount actually required for the work was repealed in 1950. The act also authorized the Secretary, under general regulations prescribed by him to permit the prospecting, development, and utilization of the mineral resources of lands acquired under the Weeks Act of 1911.

President authorized to establish refuges for the protection of game animals, birds, or fish on any lands purchased under the Weeks Act of 1911.

1916

Convention of August 16 between the United States and Great Britain provided for the protection by the United States and Canada of migratory game birds, migratory insectivorous birds, and certain other migratory nongame birds.

National Park Service created in the Department of Interior, defined the purposes for which national parks may be established, and authorized the Secretary of the Interior to make such rules and regulations as he may deem necessary for their proper use and management. Grazing was authorized when in the judgment of the Secretary it will not be detrimental to the primary purpose for which the park, monument, or other reservation was established.

Stockraising Homestead Act authorized the Secretary of the Interior to open for entry under the homestead laws not more than 640 acres per person of public lands the surface of which is chiefly valuable for grazing and raising forage crops, which do not contain merchantable timber, are not susceptible of irrigation from any known source of water supply, and are of such a character that 640 acres are reasonably required for the support of a family. Instead of cultivation, the entryman must make permanent improvements to the extent of $1.25 per acre. Commutation was not allowed. All of the coal and other minerals were reserved to the United States and made subject to disposal under the coal and mineral land laws. Lands containing water holes and other bodies of water needed or used by the public for watering purposes were not to be designated, but might be reserved under the act of 1910 and held open for public use. The Secretary of the Interior could also withdraw from entry lands needed to ensure access by the public to watering places and needed for use in the movement of stock to summer and winter ranges or to shipping points.

1917

United States Supreme Court upheld the constitutionality of the act of June 9, 1916, revesting in the United States title to the lands granted to the Oregon and California Railroad (*Oregon and California Railroad Co.* v. *U.S.*).

1918

Secretary of the Interior authorized to exchange revested Oregon and California Railroad lands for lands of equal value in private ownership within or contiguous to the former limits of the grant.

Migratory Bird Treaty Act of July 3 effectuated the convention of August 16, 1916, with Great Britain and authorized the Secretary of Agriculture, subject to the approval of the President, to promulgate regulations for the protection of the migratory birds covered by the convention.

1919

A movement was started by H.S. Graves, Chief of the Forest Service and by F. E. Olmsted as president and Gifford Pinchot as chairman of a Committee for the Application of Forestry of the Society of American Foresters, to bring about public control of cutting on private forest lands.

Suit against the Southern Oregon Company settled by staute providing for reconveyance to the United States of the remaining lands in the 1869 grant to aid in the construction of the Coos Bay Wagon Road, with payment by the government of delinquent taxes and of $232,463.07 to the company. The reconveyed lands were to be classified and disposed of as provided in the act of June 9, 1916, relating to revested O. and C. lands. After reimbursement of the government for these items, 25 percent of the gross receipts from the reconveyed lands was to be paid to the counties for schools and permanent improvements.

National Parks and Conservation Association founded to support newly formed National Park Service.

1920

Mineral Leasing Act of 1920 provided for the leasing of deposits of coal, phosphate, sodium, oil, oil shale, or gas, and authorized the Secretary of the Interior to reserve the right to sell, lease, or otherwise dispose of the surface of lands embraced in such leases if not necessary for the use of the lessee. Lessees pay both an annual rental and a royalty per unit of the mineral removed. Of the amount received, 52 ½ percent was allocated to the reclamation fund, 37 ½ percent to the states for the construction of roads or the support of education, and 10 percent to the Treasury of the United States. The act applied to national forests created from the original public domain, but not to national forests acquired under the Weeks Act of 1911, to national parks, to game refuges, or to military or naval reservations.

United States Surpreme Court, in *Missouri* v. *Holland* confirmed the constitutionality of the Migratory Bird Treaty Act of July 3, 1918.

Capper report on timber depletion, lumber prices, lumber exports, and concentration of timber ownership was transmitted to the Senate on June 1 in response to Senate Resolution 311.

Secretary of the Interior authorized to sell timber on revested Oregon and California Railroad lands and on reconveyed Coos Bay Wagon Road lands classified as power sites, and to exchange reconveyed Coos Bay Wagon Road lands for lands in private ownership.

Federal Power Commission consisting of the Secretary of War, Secretary of the Interior, and Secretary of Agriculture created with authority to issue licenses for a period not exceeding fifty years "for the development and improvement of navigation, and for the development, transmission, and utilization of power across, along, from or in any part of the navigable waters of the United States, or upon any part of the public lands and reservations of the United States (including the territories), or for the purpose of utilizing the surplus water or water power from any Government dam."

1921

Congress prohibited the issuance of permits, licenses, or leases for the development of water in existing national parks or national monuments without specific authority of Congress and repealed that part of the Federal Power Act of 1920 authorizing the issuance of such licenses by the Federal Power Commission. Act of August 26, 1935 redefined "reservations" so as to exclude national parks and national monuments, made congressional approval necessary for parks and monuments created after as well as before 1921.

Colorado River Compact approved. Congress authorized Arizona, California, Colorado, Nevada, New Mexico, Utah, and Wyoming to enter into a compact for the disposition and apportionment of the waters of the Colorado River.

Federal Highway Act started the practice of appropriating funds specifically for the construction of "forest-development roads" and "forest highways." Cooperation with states was authorized but not required.

Establishment of eastern forest experiment stations began.

1922

General Exchange Act authorized the Secretary of Agriculture (through the Secretary of the Interior) to exchange surveyed, nonmineral land or timber in national forests established from the public domain for privately owned or state land of equal value within national forests in the same state.

Agricultural Appropriations Act of May 11 made the first appropriation ($10,000) for the improvement of public campgrounds in national forests, with special reference to protection of the public health and prevention of forest fires.

Colorado River Compact allocating waters of Colorado River signed by all concerned states except Arizona.

1923

Last of the naval timber reserves restored (about 3000 acres in Louisiana) to the public domain.

Convention of March 2 between the United States and Great Britain prohibited fishing for halibut in the North Pacific Ocean between November 16 and February 15 and established an International Fisheries Commission consisting of two representatives of each government to conduct studies and make recommendations for the preservation and development of the halibut fishery.

Provisions of the Enlarged Homestead Act of 1909 extended to homestead entries in national forests under certain conditions.

1924

President Coolidge convened a National Conference on Outdoor Recreation.

Rachford report, prepared by the Forest Service as a result of a four-year study of the grazing situation, recommended substantial increases in national forest grazing fees.

First national forest wilderness area designated on Gila National Forest at urging of Aldo Leopold.

Secretary of the Interior authorized to reserve fishing areas in any of the waters of Alaska over which the United States has jurisdiction, and within such areas to establish closed seasons during which fishing can be limited or prohibited as he may prescribe.

Clarke-McNary Act authorized appropriations to enable the Secretary of Agriculture to cooperate in forest fire control with states meeting prescribed standards, in the growing and distribution of planting stock to farmers, and in promoting the efficient management of farm woodlots and shelterbelts; authorized the purchase of lands anywhere on the watersheds of navigable streams and for timber production as well as stream flow protection; authorized acceptance of gifts to be added to the national forests; authorized the Secretary of Agriculture to report to Congress such unreserved public timberlands as in his judgment should be added to the national foerests; and authorized the creation of military and naval reserves as national forests, without interference with their use for military and naval purposes.

A National Conference on Utilization of Forest Products, called by the Secretary of Agriculture, was held in Washington, November 19 to 20.

1925

A system of ten-year permits for grazing on western national forests was put into effect by the Forest Service on January 1.

Alaska Game Law created the Alaska Game Commission of five members and authorized the Secretary of Agriculture, upon consultation with or recommendation from the commission, to adopt regulations governing the taking of animals and the issuance of hunting and trapping licenses.

1925

General Exchange Act of 1922 amended to permit either party to an exchange to make reservations of timber, minerals, or easements, the values of which shall be considered in determining the values of the exchanged lands, provided that such reservations shall be subject to the tax laws of the states concerned.

Act of March 3 included watersheds from which water is secured for domestic use or irrigation among the lands on which the federal government can cooperate with states in control of forest fires under section 2 of the Clarke-McNary Act of 1924.

Act of March 3 authorized the exchange of land or timber for land within the exterior boundaries of national forests acquired under the Weeks Act of 1911 or the Clarke-McNary Act of 1924, on an equal–value basis.

1926

Export of timber lawfully cut on any national forest, or on the public lands in Alaska, authorized if the supply of timber for local use will not be endangered thereby.

Secretary of Agriculture authorized to cooperate with the territories and other possessions in studies of forest taxation and forest insurance and in reforestation and woodlot management, under the Clarke-McNary Act of 1924, on the same terms as with the states.

First World Forestry Congress was held in Rome, Italy, April 29 to May 5.

Period for repayment of construction charges in irrigation projects increased to forty years (from ten years in 1902 and twenty years in 1914); provided that repayment contracts on new projects should be made only with water users' organizations; and limited to 160 irrigable acres the area in single ownership that might receive water in an irrigation project.

Recreation and Public Purposes Act passed. Secretary of the Interior authorized to make available to states, counties, or municipalities, by exchange, sale, or lease, unreserved, nonmineral public lands classified by him as chiefly valuable for recreational purposes.

Creation of or additions to national forests in Arizona and New Mexico except by act of Congress forbidden.

Provision made for paying to the counties containing revested Oregon and California Railroad lands the equivalent of the taxes that would have been paid from 1915 to 1926 inclusive, if the lands had remained privately owned and taxable. Taxes were to be computed on the basis of 1915 assessed values and the rate of taxation prevailing in each of the counties involved. After 1926, payments were to be continued on the same basis until all charges against the "Oregon and California land-grant fund" (including back and current payments in lieu of taxes) had been liquidated and the fund showed a credit balance available for distribution under the 1916 act.

1927

States permitted to acquire title to school sections that are mineral in character, subject to certain restrictions and reservations.

Secretary of the Interior authorized to lease public lands containing salts of potassium (potash) under the general provisions of the Mineral Leasing Act of 1920 and repealed the prior act of October 2, 1917.

Secretary of the Interior authorized to establish grazing districts on unreserved public lands in Alaska and to promulgate rules and regulations for their administration. Net receipts from leases, which may run up to twenty years, are paid to the territory for public education and roads.

A Conference on Commercial Forestry was held at Chicago, Illinois, November 16 to 17, under the sponsorship of the Chamber of Commerce of the United States.

1928

McNary-Woodruff Act authorized appropriation of $2 million in 1928–1929, of $3 million in 1929–1930, and of $3 million in 1930–1931 for the purchase of land under the Weeks Act of 1911 and the Clarke-McNary Act of 1924. Not more than 1 million acres of land was to be purchased in any one state primarily for timber production.

Act of June 9, 1916, amended to require the cutting and removal of any timber sold on revested Oregon and California Railroad lands under such rules and regulations as might be prescribed by the Secretary of the Interior.

McSweeney-McNary Act authorized a comprehensive ten-year program of research in all phases of forestry and range management, including a timber survey, with an annual appropriation amounting to $3,625,000 by the end of the period, and thereafter such amounts as needed to carry out the provisions of the act.

Society of American Foresters appointed a committee on forest policy to review the regulation situation and make recommendations to the society.

Boulder Canyon Project Act called for the construction of works for the protection and development of the Colorado River Basin and authorized the states concerned to enter into supplemental contracts for the development of the Colorado River.

1929

Forest Service adopted L-20 regulations which provide for the designation and protection of "primitive" areas. This is the first agency–wide wilderness program.

Migratory Bird Conservation Act (Norbeck-Andersen Act) established the Migratory Bird Conservation Commission and authorized a continuing program for the acquisition of migratory bird reservations, subject to the consent of the state concerned.

1930

Appropriation of $50,000 authorized to enable the President to appoint a commission to study and report on the conservation and administration of the public domain.

On April 15 the Forestry Branch of the Bureau of Indian Affairs was given responsibility for the handling of grazing on rangelands in Indian reservations. A grazing policy was put into effect on July 1, 1931.

Convention of May 26 between the United States and Canada for the protection and promotion of the sockeye salmon fishery of the Fraser River system established an International Pacific Salmon Fisheries Commission to conduct investigations and to promulgate regulations governing the taking of sockeye salmon in certain specified waters.

Knutson-Vandenberg Act of June 9 authorized appropriation not to exceed $400,000 a year by the fiscal year 1934 for reforestation activities on the national forests and provided that additional charges could be made in timber sales to provide a special fund for reforestation or silvicultural improvement of the cutover area included in the timber sale.

Shipstead-Nolan Act withdrew from entry all public land north of Township 60 North in Cook and Lake counties, Minnesota; required the Forest Service to conserve for recreational use the natural beauty of all lakes and streams within this region (chiefly in the Superior National Forest); and provided that there should be no further alteration of the natural water level of any lake or stream within the region without further act of Congress.

President Hoover on December 6 appointed a Timber Conservation Board to study the economic problem of overproduction in the forest industries. The board made a thorough study of the situation, with special reference to overproduction in the lumber industry, but issued no comprehensive report.

A nationwide forest survey was initiated under authority of the McSweeney-McNary Act of 1928.

1931

Society of American Foresters Committee on Forest Policy submitted a comprehensive report, including endorsement of the principle of public control of cutting on private lands. The report was adopted by the society by a large majority in a referendum vote. The majority favored state rather than federal control.

On January 16 the Committee on the Conservation and Administration of the Public Domain (appointed by President Hoover in 1930) submitted a report recommending that all portions of the unreserved and unappropriated public domain be placed under responsible administration for the conservation of its natural resources; that areas which are chiefly valuable for the production of forage and which can be effectively conserved and administered by the states containing them be granted to the states which will accept them; and that the President be authorized to consolidate the executive agencies dealing with the administration and disposition of the public domain, the administration of national reservations, and the conservation of natural resources.

Joint Resolution of February 20 authorized the Secretary of Agriculture to cooperate with the territories in forest fire protection under the Clarke-McNary Act of 1924 on the same terms as with the states.

Multilateral international convention of September 24 prohibited the taking or killing of right whales; required full utilization of the carcasses of baleens or whalebone whales; and provided for the communication of statistical information regarding all whaling operations to the International Bureau for Whaling Statistics at Oslo, Norway.

A National Conference on Land Utilization was held in Chicago, Illinois, November 19 to 21, at the call of the Secretary of Agriculture and the Association of Land-Grant Colleges and Universities.

1932

Federation of Western Outdoor Clubs organized.

1933

A National Plan for American Forestry, known as the Copeland report, was submitted to the Senate on March 27 by the Secretary of Agriculture. It made two main recommendations: a large extension of public ownership and more intensive management of all publicly owned lands.

Executive order of April 5 established the Office of Emergency Conservation Work as an independent agency for the dual purpose of relieving unemployment and promoting conservation of natural resources. It was popularly known as the Civilian Conservation Corps.

1933

Agricultural Adjustment Act provided in detail for relieving the acute economic emergency in agriculture.

Federal Emergency Relief Act and subsequent amendments provided funds for the relief of unemployment which were used in part for forestry and other conservations activities.

Tennessee Valley Authority, which includes many phases of conservation in its activities, created.

President Roosevelt by executive order, under authority of the Reorganization Act of March 3, 1933, placed all national monuments, the National Capital parks, and national military parks under the administration of the Interior Department.

National Industrial Recovery Act (NIRA) attempted to promote economic recovery by a wide variety of measures, including codes of fair competition, an extensive public works program, and subsistence homesteads. The Code of Fair Competition for the Lumber and Timber Products Industries, approved August 21, led to the adoption (March 23, 1934) of a Forest Conservation Code which required the various divisions of the industry to formulate and enforce rules of forest practice.

On July 20, the Administrator of Public Works appointed the National Planning Board.

Soil Erosion Service was established in the Department of the Interior on August 25 under authority of National Industrial Recovery Act.

1934

Shelterbelt Project (Prairie States Forestry Project) was started with emergency funds administered by the Forest Service.

President authorized, upon recommendation of the Secretary of Agriculture and the Secretary of Commerce and with the approval of legislatures of the states concerned, to establish fish and game sanctuaries or refuges in national forests.

Coordination Act authorized the Secretary of Agriculture and the Secretary of Commerce to cooperate with federal, state, and other agencies in developing a nationwide program of wildlife conservation and rehabilitation; to study the effect of water pollution on wildlife and to recommend remedial measures; and to prepare plans for the maintenance of an adequate supply of wildlife on public lands, Indian reservations, and unallotted Indian lands. It also provided for use for wildlife purposes of water impounded by the Bureau of Reclamation or otherwise and for facilitating the migration of fish in connection with the construction of any future dam by the federal government or under federal permit.

Migratory Bird Hunting Stamp Act of March 16 required takers of migratory water-flow to buy a $1 federal hunting stamp, good for one year, and made the proceeds available for the acquisition and management of migratory waterfowl refuges and for the conduct of research.

Taylor Grazing Act authorized the Secretary of the Interior to establish not more than 80 million acres of grazing districts in the unreserved public domain (exlusive of Alaska) and to make rules and regulations for their occupancy and use. The act contained specific provisions with respect to mineral resources, hunting and fishing, homestead entry, and the lease of isolated tracts to owners of contiguous lands. Receipts were allocated as follows: 25 percent, when appropriated by Congress, for the construction, purchase, or maintenance of range improvements; 50 percent to the counties in which the districts are located; and 25 percent to the United States Treasury. The act also increased to 760 acres the size of isolated tracts that could be offered for sale and authorized the Secretary of the Interior to sell not more than 160 acres of land that is mountainous or too rough for cultivation, whether isolated or not, to adjoining owners.

President Roosevelt moved to implement Taylor Grazing Act by withdrawing all land in twelve Western States from homestead entry. The withdrawal was extended to all lower forty-eight states in 1935.

Executive order of June 30 created the Quetico-Superior Committee to advise with federal and other agencies concerning the wilderness sanctuary in the Rainy Lake and Pigeon River watersheds in Minnesota.

1935

Soil Conservation Act of April 27 declared it to be the policy of Congress to provide permanently for the control and prevention of soil erosion, delegated activities relating to soil erosion to the Secretary of Agriculture, and established the Soil Conservation Service in the Department of Agriculture. The latter succeeded the Soil Erosion Service which had been set up in the Department of the Interior in 1933 under the National Industrial Recovery Act and transferred to the Department of Agriculture by executive order in March, 1935.

Resettlement Administration was established by executive order of April 30. In 1936, it was transferred to the Department of Agriculture, and in 1937, it was changed to the Farm Security Administration.

1935

U.S. Supreme Court invalidated the National Industrial Recovery Act on grounds that it involved an unconstitutional delegation of legislative power, exceeded the power of Congress to regulate interstate commerce, and invaded the powers reserved exclusively to the states. The Court's action automatically nullified the lumber industry code and the rules of forest practice adopted thereunder (*Schechter Poultry Corp.* v. *United States*).

Act of June 15 authorized the addition to wildlife refuges of land acquired by exchange of (1) land, timber, or other materials in wildlife refuges or (2) of unreserved nonmineral public lands, in both cases on an equal-value basis. It also authorized payment to the counties, for the benefit of schools and roads, of 25 percent of the gross receipts from wildlife refuges.

Bankhead-Jones Act authorized an annual appropriation increasing from $1 to $5 million for conduct by the Secretary of Agriculture and by the agricultural experiment stations of research into laws and principles underlying basic problems of agriculture in its broadest aspects. The act also authorized appropriations for the further development of cooperative agricultural extension work and the more complete endowment and support of land grant colleges.

A Forest Service report entitled *National Pulp and Paper Requirements in Relation to Forest Conservation* (Hale report) was transmitted to the Senate on July 12 in response to Senate Resolution 205.

Antiquities Act authorized the Secretary of the Interior to acquire and administer historic sites and buildings and established an Advisory Board on National Parks, Historic Sites, Buildings, and Monuments.

Appropriation of receipts from the Uinta and Wasatch National Forests in Utah for the purchase of lands therein was authorized. Similar provisions were enacted with respect to the Cache National Forest in Utah, the San Bernardino and Cleveland National Forest in California, the Nevada and Toiyabe National Forests in Nevada, the Ozark and Ouachita National Forests in Arkansas, the Angeles National Forest in California, and the Sequoia National Forest in California.

The Wilderness Society organized.

Fulmer Act authorized an appropriation of $5 million for the purchase by the federal government of lands to be administered as state forests under plans of management satisfactory to the Secretary of Agriculture. Congress has never appropriated funds to put the act into operation.

1936

U.S. Surpreme Court (297 U.S. 1) declared unconstitutional the agricultural adjustments parts of the Agricultural Adjustment Act of 1935, dealing chiefly with acreage
allotments, benefit payments, and processing taxes, on the ground that they invaded
powers reserved to the states (*United States* v. *Butler*).

Convention of February 7 between the United States and Mexico provided for the
protection by the United States and Mexico of migratory game and nongame birds and
for the control of transportation between the two countres of migratory birds and game
mammals, dead or alive.

Soil Conservation and Domestic Allotment Act attempted to attain the objectives of
the Agricultural Adjustment Act of 1933 by authorizing the Secretary of Agriculture
to make benefit payments to farmers as a soil conservation measure. "Parity payments"
were also authorized in order to make the purchasing power of the farmer comparable
to that existing in 1909 to 1914.

A comprehensive report by the Forest Service entitled *The Western Range* was transmitted to the Senate on April 28 in response to Senate Resolution 199. The document
was highly critical of the Department of the Interior.

Whaling Treaty Act provided for effectuation of the multilateral convention of 1931
for the regulation of whaling, including authorization of the Secretary of the Treasury
and the Secretary of Commerce to make the necessary regulations for the control of
whaling.

McSweeney-McNary Act of 1928 amended to authorize the establishment of the Great
Plains Forest Experiment Station.

On June 16 the Division of Forestry and Grazing in the Bureau of Indian Affairs was
given charge of all matters relating to wildlife management on Indian reservations.

Flood Control Act of 1936 recognized the fact that flood control on navigable waters
or their tributaries is a proper activity of the federal government, in cooperation with
the states and their political subdivisions. It provided that thereafter federal investigations and improvements of rivers and other waterways for flood control and allied
purposes should be under the jurisdiction of the War Department, and federal investigations of watersheds and measures for runoff and water flow retardation and soil
erosion prevention on watersheds under the jurisdiction of the Department of Agriculture. The act authorized interstate flood control compacts and authorized a long list
of projects for prosecution by the Army Engineers. Amendments in 1937 and 1938
authorized additional surveys and examinations at specific localities and directed the
Secretary of Agriculture to make runoff and erosion surveys on all watersheds specified

for flood control surveys by the Secretary of War. The 1937 act also authorized the Secretary of Agriculture to impose such conditions as he might deem necessary in prosecuting measures for retarding runoff and preventing erosion on nonfederal lands.

The Park, Parkways and Recreation Act authorized Park Service to make a comprehensive study, other than on lands under the jurisdiction of the Department of Agriculture, of the public park, parkway, and recreational area programs of the United States and of the several states and political subdivisions thereof, and of the lands chiefly valuable as such areas, and to cooperate with the states and their political subdivisions in planning such areas. It also authorized the states to enter into interstate compacts for the establishment and development of park, parkway, and recreational areas, subject to the approval of the state legislatures and of Congress.

Taylor Grazing Act amendments increased the maximum allowable area of grazing districts to 142 million acres. Exchange of lands with states was authorized on either an equal-value or equal-area basis. The President was authorized, with the advice and consent of the Senate, to select a Director of Grazing; and the Secretary of the Interior was authorized to appoint such assistant directors and other employees as necessary to administer the act, provided that every appointee must have been for one year a bona fide citizen or resident of the state in which he is to serve.

Second World Forestry Congress was held in Budapest, Hungary, September 10 to 14.

An "upstream engineering" conference called by President Roosevelt was held in Washington, September 22 to 23, to emphasize the importance of this phase of flood and erosion control.

Presidential proclamation of November 27 abolished the Wichita National Forest in Oklahoma and placed the Wichita Mountains Wildlife Refuge under the administration of the Bureau of Biological Survey.

National Wildlife Federation organized.

1937

Disaster Loan Corporation created to make such loans as it may determine to be necessary because of floods or other catastrophes. Funds were provided by the corporation in connection with the Northeastern timber-salvage work of the Forest Service. It was dissolved and its functions transferred to the Reconstruction Finance Corporation in 1945.

Cooperative Farm Forestry Act (Norris-Doxey Act) of May 18 authorized an annual appropriation of $2,500,000 for the promotion of farm forestry in cooperation with the states. The first appropriation ($300,000) was for the fiscal year 1940.

1937

Civilian Conservation Corps officially established as the official successor to the Emergency Conservation Work; provided in detail for its administration; authorized the use of ten hours a week for educational and vocational training on a voluntary basis; and extended its life to June 30, 1940. In 1939 the C.C.C. was continued through June 30, 1943. Subsequent acts extended its life through June 30, 1944.

Bankhead-Jones Farm Tenant Act of July 22 provided for loans to farm tenants, for rehabilitation loans, and for the retirement and rehabilitation of submarginal agricultural lands. Acquired lands could be sold, exchanged, leased, or otherwise disposed of, under specified conditions, one of which was the reservation of an undivided three-fourths interest in all coal, oil, gas, and other minerals. The Secretary was also authorized to cooperate with federal, state, and other public agencies in developing plans for a program of land conservation and land utilization.

Water Facilities Act provided for the development by the Secretary of Agriculture of facilities for water storage and utilization in the arid and semiarid regions.

Act provided for reclassification of the lands of the revested Oregon and California Railroad and the reconveyed Coos Bay Wagon Road grants and for sustained-yield management by the Secretary of Interior of those classified as timberlands. The Secretary was authorized to establish sustained-yield forest units for the support of dependent communities and local industries and to make cooperative agreements with other federal agencies, with state agencies, and with private forest owners to secure coordinated administration. Lands chiefly valuable for agriculture could be opened to homestead entry or sale under the terms of the Taylor Grazing Act of 1934. Receipts from O. and C. lands were to be distributed as follows: 50 percent to the counties immediately concerned, an additional 25 percent to the counties permanently after satisfying reimbursable federal charges against the lands, and 25 percent for administration in such amounts as appropriated by Congress.

Wildlife Restoration Act (Pittman-Robertson Act) authorized the setting apart of the tax on firearms, shells, and cartridges in the "federal aid to wildlife restoration fund" to be used for cooperation with the states in approved wildlife restoration projects up to 75 percent of the total cost of the projects. Each cooperating state must pass legislation for the conservation of wildlife, including a prohibition against the diversion of license fees paid by hunters for any other purpose than the administration of its fish and game department.

The Wildlife Society organized.

1938

Agricultural Adjustment Act provided in great detail for benefit and parity payments to farmers, stressed the idea of the "ever-normal granary," and inaugurated federal crop insurance for wheat through the creation of the Federal Crop Insurance Corporation under control of the Secretary of Agriculture. The act also provided for the establishment by the Department of Agriculture of four regional laboratories for the conduct of investigations relating to the industrial use of farm products. These were located at Philadelphia, Pennsylvania, Peoria, Illinois, New Orleans, Louisiana, and Albany, California.

Secretary of Commerce authorized to establish salmon-cultural stations in the Columbia River Basin; to conduct investigations; and to install devices for improving feeding and spawning conditions in order to protect migratory fish from irrigation projects.

Congress authorized the Secretary of the Interior to sell or lease not more than 5 acres of certain public lands, outside of Alaska, which he may classify as chiefly valuable as home, cabin, health, convalescent, recreational, or business sites, subject to a reservation to the United States of all oil, gas, and other mineral deposits. Regulations under the act provide for leases of not more than five years.

Concurrent Resolution of June 14 created a Joint Congressional Committee on Forestry to study the present and prospective situation with respect to the forest land of the United States and to make a report and recommendations by April 1, 1939. The time limit was later extended to April 1, 1941. The report was presented March 24, 1941.

Secretary of the Interior authorized to lease at rates determined by him any state, county, or private land chiefly valuable for grazing within the exterior boundaries of a grazing district. Such leases are to run for not more than ten years, and the fees paid for grazing privileges on the leased lands shall not be less than the rental paid by the Unites States for them. All moneys received in the administration of leased lands are made available, when appropriated by Congress, for the leasing of lands under this act, and shall not be distributed to the states as are other receipts.

Olympic National Park established and President is authorized, after eight months, to add national forest or other lands to the park, provided the total area of the park shall not exceed 898,292 acres.

1939

Forest Service adopts U-regulations defining wilderness, wild, and recreation areas on the national forests.

Reorganization Plan No. I of April 25 approved by Congress on June 7 to take effect July 1, established the National Resources Planning Board in the Executive Office of the President by transfer and consolidation of the National Resources Committee and the Federal Employment Stabilization Office in the Department of Commerce.

1939

Reorganization Plan No. II of May 9 transferred the Bureau of Fisheries from the Department of Commerce, and the Bureau of Biological Survey from the Department of Agriculture, to the Department of the Interior, and made the Secretary of the Interior chairman of the Migratory Bird Conservation Commission.

Department of the Interior Appropriations Act of May 10 made the first appropriation ($37,500) for the prevention and suppression of fires on the public domain in Alaska.

Congress provides for payments to Coos County and Douglas County, Oregon, in lieu of taxes on reconveyed Coos Bay Wagon Road lands on the basis of the appraised value of the lands and the current rate of taxation, provided that payments during any ten-year period shall not exceed 75 percent of the receipts from the reconveyed lands. Not more than 25 percent of the receipts was made available, when appropriated by Congress, for administration of the lands.

Taylor Grazing Act amendments provided for the establishment within each grazing district of an advisory board of five to twelve local stock operators elected by the users of the range but appointed by the Secretary of the Interior, who may also on his own initiative appoint on wildlife member on each board. Each advisory board shall offer advice on application for grazing permits and on all other matters affecting the administration of the Taylor Grazing Act. Except in an emergency the Secretary of the Interior shall request the advice of the advisory board prior to the promulgation of any rules and regulations affecting the district.

Act of July 20 restored to the President authority to establish national forests in Montana.

Act of July 31 authorized the Secretary of the Interior to exchange revested Oregon and California Railroad lands and reconveyed Coos Bay Wagon Road lands for lands of equal value in private, state, or county ownership within or contiguous to the former limits of the grants; and repealed the previous acts relating to such exchanges.

Reclamation Project Act effected various reforms in existing reclamation legislation; authorized the sale of electric power or lease of power privileges for periods of not more than forty years, at such rates as would cover an appropriate share of the cost of operation and maintenance as well as the construction investment, with preference to municipalities and other public corporations or agencies; and specified the basis of payment for the various kinds of benefits provided by multipurpose reclamation projects.

Office of Director of Forestry was established in the Department of the Interior to coordinate the forestry work of the department.

1940

Forest Outings, a comprehensive report on forest recreation, was published by the Forest Service.

Reorganization Plan No. III of April 2 consolidated the Bureau of Fisheries and the Bureau of Biological Survey into the Fish and Wildlife Service.

Lea Act provided for federal cooperation in the protection of forest lands from white pine blister rust, irrespective of ownership, provided that on state or private lands federal expenditures must be at least matched by state or local authorities or by individuals or organizations.

Act of May 28 authorized the President, on the basis of a cooperative agreement between the Secretary of Agriculture and the municipality concerned, to withdraw national forest lands from which a municipality obtains its water supply from all forms of location, entry, or appropriation. The Secretary of Agriculture may prescribe such rules and regulations as he considers necessary for adequate protection of the watershed.

Convention between the United States and other American republics committed the signatory powers to take appropriate steps for the protection of nature and the preservation of wildlife in their respective countries.

U.S. Supreme Court, in *United States* v. *Appalachian Electric Power Company* (311 U.S. 377), held that a waterway constitutes "navigable water of the United States" if it can be made available for navigation by the construction of improvements, whether such improvements have actually been made or even authorized; and that a navigable waterway of the United States does not lose its character because its use for interstate commerce has lessened or ceased. The Court also stated that navigation is only a part of interstate commerce and that "flood protection, watershed development, recovery of the cost of improvements through utilization of power are likewise parts of commerce control."

1941

Forest Lands of the United States, report of the Joint Committee on Forestry established in 1938, was submitted to Congress on March 24.

U.S. Supreme Court, in *Oklahoma* v. *Atkinson Company*, stated that "it is clear that Congress may exercise its control over the non-navigable stretches of a river in order to preserve or promote commerce on the navigable portions" and added that "the power of flood control extends to the tributaries of navigable streams."

Congress extended to all lands owned by, leased by, or under the jurisdiction of the United States, including Indian lands and lands in process of acquisition, the penalties (somewhat modified) for setting and for failing to extinguish fires in or near any timber, underbrush, grass, or other inflammable material.

1942

Executive order of April 12 delegated to the Secretary of the Interior authority to make withdrawals and restorations of public lands.

1942–1943

A series of bills required liquidation of the C.C.C. as quickly as possible but not later than June 30, 1944. Liquidation of most of the personnel was accomplished by August 15, 1942.

1943

Forest Products Research Society was organized on January 3.

National Resources Planning Board abolished effective August 31, except for such administrative action as required to wind up its affairs by January 1, 1944.

The American Forestry Association undertook a Forest Resources Appraisal, a three-year inventory of the nation's forest resources.

1944

Treaty of February 3 between the United States and Mexico established the International Boundary and Water Commission and provided for the allocation of the flow of the Rio Grande River and the Colorado River, the construction of dams, and other purposes.

Sustained-Yield Forest Management Act of March 29 authorized the Secretary of Agriculture and/or the Secretary of the Interior to establish cooperative sustained-yield units consisting of federal forest land and private forest land or federal sustained-yield units consisting only of federal forest land, when in their judgment the maintenance of stable communities is primarily dependent upon federal stumpage and when such maintenance cannot be secured through usual timber sale procedures. Provision is made for the sale of federal stumpage to cooperating landowners or to responsible purchasers within communities dependent on federal stumpage, without competitive bidding at prices not less than the appraised value of the timber.

Clarke-McNary Act of 1924 amended to authorize annual increases in the appropriation for cooperative forest fire protection with the states and for studies of tax laws and forest fire insurance up to a maximum of $9 million for the fiscal year 1948 and thereafter.

1944

Annual appropriation of $750,000 authorized to complete the initial survey of forest resources inaugurated by the McSweeney-McNary Act of 1928, with the stipulation that total appropriations for this purpose should not exceed $6,500,000. An additional appropriation of $250,000 annually was authorized to keep the survey current.

Department of Agriculture Organic Act of September 21, among many other administrative provisions, authorized the Secretary of Agriculture to pay rewards for information leading to arrest and conviction for violating laws and regulations relating to fires in or near national forests or for the unlawful taking of, or injury to, government property. It also authorized an annual expenditure during the existing emergency of not more than $1 million for cooperative forest fire protection under the Clarke-McNary Act of 1924 without requiring an equal expenditure by state and private owners.

Act of September 27 authorized the Secretary of the Interior to dispose of sand, stone, gravel, vegetation, and timber or other forest products on unreserved public lands during the period of hostilities. This authority terminated on December 31, 1946, but was restored by the permanent and more comprehensive act of July 31, 1947.

Flood Control Act provided that thereafter federal investigations and improvements of rivers and waterways for flood control and allied purposes should be under the jurisdiction the War Department, and that federal investigations of watersheds and measures for runoff and water flow retardation and soil erosion prevention on watersheds should be under the jurisdiction of the Secretary of Agriculture.

1945

Presidential proclamation of September 28 stated that the United States regards the natural resources in the continental shelf as subject to its jurisdiction and control without thereby affecting the free and unimpeded navigation of the high seas above the continental shelf.

The Soil Conservation Society of America organized.

Presidential proclamation of September 28 stated that the United States regards it as proper, without affecting the freedom of navigation, to establish conservation zones in part of the high seas contiguous to its coasts, in which fishing activities shall be subject to the regulation and control of the United States, either alone or in cooperation with other nations.

The United States on October 16 signed the Constitution of the Food and Agriculture Organization of the United Nations. "Agriculture" was defined as including fisheries, marine products, forestry, and primary forest products.

1946

Reorganization Plan No. 3 of May 16 consolidated the General Land Office and the Grazing Service to form the Bureau of Land Management in the Department of the Interior. Simultaneously, the Grazing Service budget was cut by 80 percent, resulting in the "McCarren Leaves" when most Grazing Service personnel were fired or paid by the advisory boards.

Act of July 24 amended the Wildlife Restoration Act of 1937 by limiting the apportionment of funds to any one state to not less than ½ percent and not more than 5 percent of the total amount apportioned, and by permitting the use of not more than 25 percent of the federal apportionment for maintenance of completed wildlife restoration projects.

Joint Resolution of August 8 directed the Fish and Wildlife Service to prosecute investigations, experiments, and a vigorous program for the elimination of the sea lamprey from the Great Lakes.

Act of August 14 strengthened the Coordination Act of 1934 by authorizing the Secretary of the Interior, through the Fish and Wildlife Service, to provide assistance to, and cooperate with, federal, state, and public or private agencies and organizations in the development, protection, and rehabilitation of wildlife resources of the United States.

An American Forest Congress was held October 9 to 11 in Washington, D.C., under the sponsorship of the American Forestry Association. The directors of the association subsequently drafted a detailed program which was overwhelmingly adopted early in 1947 by a referendum vote of the membership.

The Nature Conservancy organized to promote preservation of threatened ecosystems through private purchase of land.

On December 9, the Secretary of the Interior delegated to the Commissioner of Indian Affairs authority to approve sales of timber from Indian lands up to 40,000 M board feet and to adjust stumpage prices on these sales.

The Forest Service, in December, issued the first of six reappraisal reports, based on its nationwide reappraisal project conducted in 1945 and 1946.

Local research centers were organized for the first time under the Southern and the Southeastern Forest Experiment Stations.

1947

McCarran Subcommittee Report attacking Grazing Service published.

1947

Forest Pest Control Act of June 25 declared it to be the policy of the government to protect all forest lands irrespective of ownership from destructive forest insect pests and diseases. It authorized the Secretary of Agriculture either directly or in cooperation with other federal agencies, state and local agencies, and private concerns and individuals to conduct surveys to detect infestations and to determine and carry out control measures against incipient, potential, or emergency outbreaks.

Commission on Organization of the Executive Branch of the Government (Hoover Commission) established to make recommendations to promote economy, efficiency, and improved service in the executive branch of the government.

Secretary of the Interior authorized to dispose of sand, stone, gravel, clay, timber, and other materials on public lands exclusive of national forests, national parks, national monuments, and Indian lands. Material exceeding $1000 in appraised value must be sold at public auction. Receipts are disposed of in the same manner as receipts from the sale of public lands.

Interior Department Appropriations Act amended the Taylor Grazing Act of 1934 to authorize the Secretary of the Interior in fixing fees for the grazing of livestock in grazing districts to "take into account the extent to which such districts yield public benefits over and above those accruing to the users of the forage for livestock purposes." Such fees were thereafter to consist of (1) a grazing fee, $12\frac{1}{2}$ percent of which is distributed to the states for the benefit of the counties in which the grazing districts are located, and (2) a range improvement fee which, when appropriated by Congress, is available for the construction, purchase, or maintenance of range improvements. Of the receipts from public lands not in grazing districts which are leased for grazing under section 15 of the Taylor Grazing Act, 25 percent is available, when appropriated by Congress, for range improvements, and 50 percent is distributed to the states for the benefit of the counties. Of the receipts from grazing districts on ceded Indian lands, $33\frac{1}{3}$ percent is distributed to the states for the benefit of the counties, and the remaining $66\frac{2}{3}$ percent is deposited to the credit of the Indians.

Mineral Leasing Act for Acquired Lands authorized the Secretary of the Interior to lease acquired lands containing deposits of coal, phosphate, oil, oil shale, gas, sodium, potassium, and sulfur under the provisions of the mineral leasing laws, with the consent of the head of the department having jurisdiction over the lands and subject to such conditions as he may prescribe.

1948

Barrett Committee investigation of Forest Service grazing programs took place.

Use and occupancy of national forest lands in Alaska permitted for purposes of residence, recreation, public convenience, education, industry, agriculture, and commerce for periods not exceeding thirty years and in tracts not exceeding 80 acres. Lands so leased are not subject to disposal or leasing under the mining laws.

Oregon and California Railroad lands and the reconveyed Coos Bay Wagon Road lands, except power sites, reopened to exploration, location, entry and disposition under the general mining laws.

Secretary of Agriculture established the National Forest Board of Review, the name of which was changed in 1950 to National Forest Advisory Council.

Transfer of certain real property controlled but no longer needed by federal agencies authorized (1) to the states for wildlife conservation purposes other than for migratory birds or (2) to the Secretary of the Interior if the property has particular value in carrying out the national migratory bird management program.

Appropriations not to exceed a total of $500,000 authorized for the purpose of acquiring certain specified lands in Cook, Lake, and St. Louis counties in the Superior National Forest, Minnesota, the development or exploitation of which might impair the unique qualities and natural features of the remaining wilderness canoe country. It also directed payment of the counties, in lieu of the usual 25 percent of gross receipts, of 0.75 percent of the fair appraised value of the land in the area covered by the act, as determined by the Secretary of Agriculture at ten-year intervals.

Water Pollution Control Act (Taft-Barkley Act) provided for technical and financial cooperation by the federal government with states and municipalities in the formulation and execution of programs for the abatement of stream pollution. Necessary appropriations were authorized for the five-year period ending June 30, 1953.

The Society for Range Management organized.

1949

First of the reports of the Commission on Organization of the Executive Branch of the Government (Hoover Commission) was sent to Congress on February 5.

Convention of February 8 between the United States and ten other countries (T.I.A.S. 2089) established the International Commission for the Northwest Atlantic Fisheries, with authority to conduct investigations and to promulgate regulations for the taking of fish in the Northwest Atlantic Ocean.

Third International Forestry Congress was held at Helsinki, Finland, July 10 to 20.

United Nations Scientific Conference on the Conservation and Utilization of Resources was held at Lake Success, New York, August 17 to September 6. An International Technical Conference on the Protection of Nature was held simultaneously.

1949

Congress provided for the sale at public auction of public land in Alaska not within national parks, monuments, forests, Indian lands, or military reservations which have been classified by the Secretary of the Interior as suitable for industrial or commercial purposes, including the construction of housing, in tracts not to exceed 160 acres, to any bidder who furnishes satisfactory proof that he has bona fide intentions and the means to develop the tract for the intended use.

Anderson-Mansfield Reforestation and Revegetation Act authorized a schedule of appropriations for the reforestation and revegetation of the forest and range lands of the national forests. "It is the declared policy of the Congress to accelerate and provide a continuing basis for the needed reforestation and revegetation of national forestlands and other lands under administration or control of the Forest Service".

Clarke-McNary Act amended by authorizing (1) annual increases in the appropriation for cooperative forest fire protection with the states up to a maximum of $20,000,000 for the fiscal year 1955 and thereafter; (2) annual increases in the appropriation for cooperation with the states in providing planting stock for farmers and others up to a maximum of $2,500,000 for the fiscal year 1953 and thereafter; and (3) an annual appropriation of $500,000 for cooperation with the land-grant colleges or other suitable state agencies in educating farmers in the management of forest lands and in harvesting, utilizing, and marketing the products thereof.

U.S. Supreme Court on November 7 affirms decision of the Washington Supreme Court that a Washington law of 1945 providing for the control of cutting on privately owned forest lands is constitutional.

Southern Regional Education Compact was ratified by the legislatures of ten states. Coordination of teaching and research in forestry has been attempted under the compact.

1950

Reorganization Plan No. 3 of March 13 transferred to the Secretary of the Interior, with two exceptions, all functions of all agencies and employees of the department; authorized the Secretary to effect such organization of the department as he deemed appropriate; and added an assistant secretary and an administrative assistant secretary to the department.

Granger-Thye Act "to facilitate and simplify the work of the Forest Service," broadened the authority granted the Secretary of Agriculture by the act of March 3, 1925, to accept contributions for administration, protection, improvement, reforestation, and other work on nonfederal lands within or near national forests; provided for sales and exchanges of nursery stock with public agencies; authorized the lease, protection, and management of public and private range land intermingled with or adjacent to national forest land; made available, when appropriated by Congress, an amount equivalent to 2 cents per animal-month for sheep and 10 cents per animal-month for other kinds of livestock under permit on a national forest for range improvements on that forest; provided for the organization of local advisory boards on petition of a majority of the grazing permittees on a national forest; authorized the Secretary of Agriculture to issue permits for the grazing of livestock on national forests for periods not exceeding ten years and renewals thereof; and repealed the provision of the Weeks Act of 1911 limiting contributions to counties to 40 percent of their income from other sources.

National Science Foundation established "to promote the progress of science" and for other purposes.

Fish Restoration and Management Act (Dingell-Johnson Act) authorized the annual appropriation of an amount equivalent to the revenue from the tax on fishing rods, creels, reels, and artificial lures, baits, and flies, to be used for cooperation with the states in fish restoration and management projects up to 75 percent of the total cost of the projects.

Cooperative Forest Management Act authorized an annual appropriation of $2,500,000 to enable the Secretary of Agriculture to cooperate with state foresters in providing technical services to private forest landowners and operators and to processors of primary forest products. The Cooperative Farm Forestry Act of 1937 was repealed effective June 30, 1951.

A Water Policy for the American People, the first volume of a three-volume report of the President's Water Resources Policy Commission (Cooke Commission), was transmitted to the President on December 11.

President Truman's "Point Four" proposed a cooperative program for aid in the development of economically undeveloped areas of the world.

The Society of American Foresters celebrated its Golden Anniversary and published a comprehensive history of forestry in the United States during the previous fifty years.

Airports Bill authorized Secretary of the Interior to recommend building of airports to promote use and management of national parks and monuments and to convey lands to build needed airports.

1952

Resources for Freedom, report of the President's Materials Policy Commission (Paley Commission), was transmitted to the President on June 2.

Interior Department Appropriations Act of July 9 made the appropriation for access roads to O. and C. lands deductible from the 75 percent of gross receipts payable to the counties.

1952

Financial authorizations approved by the Water Pollution Control Act of 1948 extended to June 30, 1956.

Budget Bureau Circular A-47, outlining restrictive criteria for evaluating water projects, adopted. Taxes foregone as result of project must be included as a cost, and only direct benefits were to be calculated. Power benefits were not to be included unless power produced was cheaper than next cheapest alternative.

Secretary of Agriculture appointed a Forest Research Advisory Committee under authority of the Agricultural Research and Marketing Act of August 14, 1946.

1953

Reorganization Plan No. 2 of March 25 transferred to the Secretary of Agriculture, with certain specified exceptions, all functions of all agencies and employees of the department; authorized the Secretary to effect such organization of the department as he deemed appropriate; and added two assistant secretaries and an administrative assistant secretary to the department.

Submerged Lands Act of May 22 confirmed and established the titles of the states to lands beneath navigable waters within state boundaries and to the natural resources within such lands and waters; provided for the use and control of such lands and resources; and confirmed the jurisdiction and control of the United States over the natural resources of the seabed of the continental shelf seaward of state boundaries.

Commission on Organization of the Executive Branch of the Government (Second Hoover Commission) established.

Commission on Intergovernmental Relations (Kestenbaum Commission), one of the committees which dealt with federal-state relations in the field of natural resources, established.

Agricultural Appropriations Act appropriated $5 million to conduct studies and carry out preventive measures for the protection of watersheds under the provisions of the Soil Conservation Act of 1935.

Act of August 7 provided for the jurisdiction of the United States over the submerged lands of the outer continental shelf and authorized the Secretary of the Interior to lease such lands for certain purposes.

A National Advisory Committee on Weather Control established to study and evaluate public and private experiments in weather modification.

1953

The Federal Reserve Act amended to authorize national banks to make loans secured by first liens up to 40 percent of their appraised value "upon forest tracts which are properly managed in all respects." Loans may not be made for more than two years, except that they may be made for ten years under a mortgage providing for their amortization at a rate of not less than 10 percent a year.

Fourth American Forest Congress was held October 29 to 31 in Washington, D.C., under the sponsorship of the American Forestry Association. Following the Congress, "A Program for American Forestry" was formulated by the directors and in 1954 was approved by the membership of the association.

1953–1954

Numerous bills providing for recognition of grazing permittees' "rights" on public lands or sale of allotments to permittees defeated in Congress.

1954

Atomic Energy Commission established, forbidding government competition with commercial nuclear electric power industry and requiring an AEC license from all operators.

President Eisenhower on May 26 established a Cabinet Committee on Water Resources policy consisting of the Secretaries of the Interior (chairman), Agriculture, Commerce, Army, and Health, Education, and Welfare, and the chairman of the Federal Power Commission.

Limitation of 142 million acres on the total area that might be included in grazing districts removed.

Act declared the controverted Oregon and California Railroad lands in the indemnity strip to be O. and C. lands shall continue to be administered as national forest lands, and the receipts from which shall be disposed of as provided in the act of August 28, 1937. In order to facilitate administration and accounting, the Secretary of Agriculture was authorized to designate in each county an area of national forest land of substantially equal value, revenues from which shall be disposed of under the 1937 act. The Secretary of the Interior and the Secretary of Agriculture were also directed to block up national forest and intermingled and adjacent O. and C. lands, exclusive of those in the indemnity strip, by exchange of administrative jurisdiction on approximately an equal-value (and so far as practicable an equal-area) basis.

Southeastern Interstate Forest Fire Protection Compact established "to promote effective prevention and control of forest fires in the Southeastern region of the United States." It applied to Alabama, Florida, Georgia, Kentucky, Mississippi, North

Carolina, South Carolina, Tennessee, Virginia, and West Virginia, and to any contiguous state on approval by the legislature of each member state.

Secretary of Interior recommended in favor of Echo Park Dam in Dinosaur National Monument Dam, setting off major public movement in opposition.

Internal Revenue Code authorized farmers to deduct expenditures for soil or water conservation or for the prevention of erosion, up to 25 percent of gross income in computing federal income taxes.

Controversy over reclassification of Three Sisters Primitive Area in Oregon led preservation groups to seek legislative action to protect wilderness.

Small Watersheds Act initiated extensive new program in which the Soil Conservation Service and Local groups would cooperate in flood and soil erosion prevention programs. Popularly known as the "Small Watersheds Act," the program provided for funding and construction of projects in small watersheds.

A National Watershed Congress was held in Washington, D.C., December 6 to 7.

After fifty years of discussion, the Saint Lawrence Seaway, linking the Great Lakes with the Atlantic Ocean, was authorized.

1955

The Surgeon General of the Public Health Service authorized to cooperate with other agencies in providing research and technical assistance relating to the control of air pollution.

Materials Disposal Act amended by adding common pumice, pumicite, and cinders to the materials specified in that act, and authorized the disposal of all such materials on both unreserved and reserved public lands except national parks, national monuments, and Indian lands by the secretary of the department having jurisdiction over the lands in question. It also provided that on unpatented claims subsequently located, the United States shall have the right to dispose of the timber and other nonmineral surface resources, provided that such disposal shall not endanger or materially interfere with mining operations; and it established a procedure whereby the right to the use of timber and other surface resources on existing, inactive mining claims may be canceled or waived.

U.S. Supreme Court ruled, in Pelton Dam case (*F.P.C.* v. *Oregon,*), that the federal government has jurisdiction over unappropriated, nonnavigable waters arising from or flowing over reserved federal lands. This defeat for state water control raised fears of federal jurisdiction over western waters.

1955

National Park Service identified sixteen choice coastal recreation/park sites in study, *Our Vanishing Shoreline,* undertaken with donated funds.

Mining Claims Rights Restoration Act authorized development of mineral resources on public lands withdrawn or reserved by the United States for power production purposes subject to oversight of the Secretary of Interior.

Air Pollution Control Act authorized federal program in air pollution research and training.

1956

Fish and Wildlife Act reorganized the Fish and Wildlife Service into Bureau of Sport Fisheries and Wildlife and Bureau of Commercial Fisheries.

"Mission '66" undertaken by National Park Service.

Federal Water Pollution Control Act Amendments provided funding for water pollution control programs on state and federal levels and created Water Pollution Control Advisory Board.

Great Plains Conservation Program authorized Secretary of Agriculture to enter into contractual relations with Great Plains farmers and ranchers in counties susceptible to severe soil erosion. The program's objective was to encourage new soil and water conservation techniques in Great Plains region.

Agricultural Act initiated new federal/state reforestation program on public and private lands, authorizing aid to farmers converting farmland to forest land.

Al Sarena mining scandal, prompted by alleged Department of Interior improprieties in issuing questionable mining patent for valuable timberland, becomes partisan issue.

Upper Colorado River Project authorized deleting controversial Echo Park Dam but including large multipurpose dam program consisting of four major and eleven smaller dams.

1957

"Operation Outdoors" undertaken by Forest Service.

Deferred Grazing Program commenced payments to stock owners engaged in deferred grazing scheme. The act stipulated payments equal to fair rental value for grazing use of land withheld, and allowed payments to ranchers on nonfederal lands proclaimed major disaster areas in times of drought.

1958

Seneca Indians lose effort to block construction of Kinzua Dam in Pennsylvania on grounds that dam would flood lands protected by a 1754 treaty (*Seneca Indians* v. *Brucker*).

Fish and Wildlife Coordination Act amended the Watershed Protection and Flood Prevention Act of 1954 to require executive level interagency consultation in developing integrated wildlife conservation watershed improvement plans. Also provided for interagency cooperation to ensure the protection of fish and wildlife in construction or operation of water resource projects.

Pesticide Research Act authorized investigations of pesticide impact on fish and wildlife.

National Outdoor Recreation Resources Review Commission (ORRRC) established by Congress.

"Timber Resources For America's Future" published by Forest Service, emphasizing the importance of private holdings in Eastern and Southern regions.

Alaska Statehood Act admitted Alaska to Union and granted new state authority to select 102.9 million acres over twenty five years.

1959

Minute Man Historical Park Act authorized first expenditure of public revenues for national park land acquisition.

"Pacific Coast Recreation Area Survey," prepared by National Park Service, recommended establishment of five state and five national parks.

"A Program for the National Forests" promulgated by Secretary of Agriculture, a long-range plan based on Timber Resources Review publication of previous year.

Criminal sanctions for water pollution impacting horses and burros on public lands authorized by Congress.

1960

Multiple Use Sustained Yield Act authorized Secretary of Agriculture to "develop and administer the renewable surface resources of the national forests for multiple use and sustained yield of the several products and services obtained therefrom." Stipulated as multiple uses were outdoor recreation, range, timber, water, and wildlife and fish. Finally, the multiple uses were qualified as being supplemental to, but not in derogation of, the purposes for which the national forests were established as set forth in act of June 4, 1897.

1960

"Our Fourth Shore," a National Park Service Study of Great Lakes shoreline recreation opportunities, recommended five new national parks.

Public Land Administration Act authorized BLM to engage in cooperative management agreements for use and development of public lands.

Amendments to Mineral Leasing Act of 1920 authorized raise in yearly minimum rentals on oil and gas leases, and development of cooperative plans to operate oil and gas reserves for conservation purposes.

"National Grasslands" established by decree of Secretary of Agriculture announcing formal policy for management of 3.8 million acres of national forest land.

Congress instructed U.S. Army Corp of Engineers to manage its reservoir areas for maintenance of adequate timber supplies through sustained yield programs, reforestation, and related conservation practices.

BLM launched "Project 2012."

1961

President Kennedy declared national goal of putting a man on the moon by the end of the decade.

Land Application Moritorium imposed for eighteen months by Interior Secretary Udall. BLM prohibited from accepting new applications for nonmining disposition of public lands until backlog processed.

"Development Program for the National Forests" promulgated by Kennedy administration based on 1959 program.

Wetlands Loan Program authorized $105 million loans to purchase wetlands for waterfowl habitat.

Cape Cod National Seashore Act authorized first national park to be acquired primarily through purchase/condemnation.

Agriculture Act authorized Secretary of Agriculture to make/insure loans to associations and private farmers for purposes of promoting land and water development, use, and conservation.

Delaware River Basin Compact established commission to oversee interstate use.

1961

Amendments to Federal Water Pollution Control Act strengthened enforcement provisions, increased authorization for sewage treatment plant construction grants, and authorized inclusion of pollution control or abatement as benefit of federal dam projects.

Hawaii Land Use Planning Act enacted two years after statehood granted.

McIntire-Stennis Cooperative Research Act authorized Secretary of Agriculture to undertake coordinated program in forestry, range, and related research.

Food and Agricultural Act amended the Soil Conservation and Domestic Allotment Act of 1936 to authorize ongoing federal administration of the Agricultural Conservation Program (ACP).

Final reports of Outdoor Recreation Resources Review Commission released.

Rachel Carson's *Silent Spring* published, calling attention to environmental impact of pesticides.

Point Reyes National Seashore authorized by Congress, but allows ranch and dairy operations to continue and permits 50-year amortization period for summer residence property.

Bureau of Sport Fisheries and Wildlife receives first authorization for recreation facilities.

One-year suspension of Jones Act authorized to permit use of foreign ships in transport of timber. Subsequent suspension renewal attempt in 1963 failed.

Forestry Research Act authorized Secretary of Agriculture to provide 50 percent matching funds for forestry research at land grant colleges, agricultural experiment stations, and state-supported graduate programs in forestry.

Relief authorized to occupants of invalid, unoccupied mining claims which served as principal residences for prescribed period.

Omnibus River and Harbor and Flood Control Act constituted massive appropriation for navigation and flood control projects to be implemented by Secretary of Army under direction of the Chief of Engineers.

Creation of Bureau of Outdoor Recreation in Department of Interior by secretarial order.

1963

In *Arizona* v. *California*, the United States Supreme Court approved for the first time allocation of water to non-Indian federal reservations under the reserved rights doctrine.

Outdoor Recreation Cooperation Act amended the 1936 Recreation Study Act and authorized Secretary of Interior to formulate a nationwide outdoor recreation plan. Technical assistance to states, recreation research, and new duties to Bureau of Outdoor Recreation also approved.

Bureau of Outdoor Recreation Act constituted the organic act for newly formed Bureau of Outdoor Recreation (Interior Department), created to provide technical planning services in the recreation field.

Clean Air Act authorized HEW to monitor air pollution violations.

Congress authorized Secretary of Interior to prepare national plan for outdoor recreation and to provide technical assistance for the promotion of regional and interagency cooperation.

1964

Congress authorized $15 million payment to Seneca Indians displaced by Kinzua Dam.

Land and Water Conservation Fund—consisting of motorboat fuel taxes, user fees, and limited appropriated monies—authorized to provide federal grants to aid states in planning for, acquiring, and developing land and water areas and facilities for recreation purposes.

BLM received its first appropriation ($700,000) for general recreation purposes.

Wilderness Act established National Wilderness Preservation System to be composed of federally owned lands designated by Congress as "wilderness areas." The Secretary of Agriculture was specifically charged with responsibility for reviewing all Forest Service primitive areas for their wilderness suitability and recommending candidate areas to President within ten years.

Classification and Multiple Use Act required Secretary of Interior to develop regulations for determining whether public lands should be disposed of or retained under federal management. Lands classified for sale or disposal were to be processed within two years of date of classification.

1965

Water Quality Act required states to establish and enforce water quality standards for interstate waters within their boundaries. Also authorized Department of Health, Education and Welfare to set standards in absence of appropriate state action.

White House Conference on Natural Beauty convened by President Johnson.

Highway Beautification Act established broad range of programs affecting billboards, junkyards, and strip development along federally funded highways, heralding new federal policy on aesthetic conservation.

Water Resources Planning Act authorized Federal Water Resources Council to coordinate water resources planning and policy.

Appalachian Regional Development Act authorized study to propose framework for federal involvement in stripmining regulation and authorized $1.1 billion in aid to twelve economically depressed states.

November blackout in northeastern states leaves New York City without electricity for eight to thirteen hours and focuses attention on energy matters.

In *Scenic Hudson Preservation Conference* v. *Federal Power Commission*, the Second Circuit Court of Appeals affirmed standing of plaintiffs to sue to protect aesthetic values. Established requirement that F.P.C. actively seek information on impacts and alternatives to proposed license.

Anadromous Fish Conservation Act authorized the Secretary of Interior to enter into cooperative agreements with states for purpose of enhancing anadromous fishery resources threatened by water resource developments.

Solid Waste Disposal Act provided technical and financial assistance to state and local governments and interstate agencies in the planning, development, and conduct of solid waste disposal programs.

River and Harbors and Flood Control Act authorized additional allocations to provide uniform policies with respect to recreation, fish, and wildlife impacts of federal multiple-purpose water resource projects.

Title III of Bankhead Jones Farm Tenant Act amended to include recreation.

1966

National Wildlife Refuge System Administration Act consolidated into one new National Wildlife Refuge System the various wildlife refuges, ranges, and management areas existing under Interior Department jurisdiction.

1966

National Historic Preservation Act declared national policy that "the historical and cultural foundations of the nation should be preserved as a living part of our community life and development in order to give a sense of orientation to the American people." To this end, the act established a national register of historic sites, structures, and objects; a grants-in-aid program to the states; and a matching-fund program to aid the National Trust for Historic Preservation chartered by Congress in 1949.

Seagrant College Act, an analog to land grant college concept, enacted to develop technology of aquaculture and exploitation of ocean resources.

Wildlife Protection Act authorized Secretary of Interior to acquire habitat of seventy–five species of birds and mammals threatened with extinction.

Secretary of Interior Udall put freeze on state selection of Alaskan acreage due to conflict with native land claims.

Clean Water Restoration Act authorized federal funding for flood control purposes on navigable rivers or their tributaries.

Executive Reorganization Plan No. 2 and Amendments to Federal Water Pollution Act transferred water pollution function from Department of Health, Education and Welfare to Department of the Interior.

Fur Seal Act prohibited taking of fur seals within U.S. territorial waters or by U.S. citizens in north Pacific Ocean.

1967

Air Quality Act gave Department of Health, Education and Welfare authority to oversee establishment of state air quality standards and implementation plans. Also empowered HEW to designate atmospheric areas and air quality control regions. The act instituted for the first time national standards for automobile emmissions.

National Park Foundation created, replacing National Park Trust Fund Board, to encourage charitable gifts to National Park Service for the advancement of its conservation activities.

1968

Wild and Scenic Rivers Act established a national system to preserve wild and scenic rivers which were to be authorized for inclusion by Congress or designated and administered by state through which they flowed. Three-tiered system of classification created: wild, scenic, and recreational. Criteria for inclusion in the system were established for each classification category.

1968

National Trail System Act created a national trail system based on three trail categories: state and metropolitan trails, national recreation trails, and national scenic trails. Provided for "instant" designation of Appalachian and Pacific Crest trails and for study of fourteen other trails for possible inclusion in the system.

Zero Population Growth (ZPG) organized.

Atlantic Richfield Company strikes oil in commercial quantities on North Slope of Alaska. Trans-Alaskan pipeline venture subsequently formed to transport oil from drilling sites to port of Valdez.

North Cascades Complex Act created North Cascades National Park as well as Ross Lake and Lake Chelan National Recreation Areas.

Redwood National Park Act set aside 58,000 acres in northern California coastal region for preservation of *Sequoia sempervirens* redwoods. Most expensive national park land acquisition program in history.

LWCF amended to allow appropriation from general revenues to support fund and to allocate up to $200 million annually from outer continental shelf oil and gas leasing to LWCF.

1969

Santa Barbara oil spill covers 800 square miles with a thick oil slick and focuses national attention on oil pollution.

Friends of the Earth organized.

Endangered Species Conservation Act prohibited importation of endangered species of fish or wildlife into the United States and proscribed "interstate shipment of reptiles, amphibians, and other wildlife taken contrary to state law."

"Stratton" [Marine Science] Commission report urges creation of NOAA (National Oceanic and Atmospheric Administration) to consolidate twenty-two bureaus in nine federal departments responsible for ocean policy matters.

National Conservation Bill of Rights introduced in House of Representatives proposing an amendment to the U.S. Constitution relating to natural resources conservation and natural beauty of the United States.

1970

National Environmental Policy Act of 1969 signed on New Year's Day, heralding the commencement of the "environmental decade." NEPA required every federal agency to prepare and circulate an environmental impact statement (EIS) "on proposals for legislation and other major federal actions significantly affecting the quality of the human environment." The act also created the federal Council of Environmental Quality (CEQ) in the Executive Office of the President to advise the President on matters of environmental quality and to review agency compliance with the act.

Natural Resources Defense Council organized.

Jet port in Everglades halted by White House order.

Executive Reorganization Plans Nos. 3 and 4 created Environmental Protection Agency (EPA) and the National Oceanic and Atmospheric Administration (NOAA). EPA delegated authority for water quality, air quality, pesticide, radiological, and solid waste functions while NOAA assigned existing federal programs in marine resource management under Secretary of Commerce.

Air Quality Act authorized EPA to set primary and secondary air quality standards and to foster development of state plans to implement standards.

Earth Day celebrated April 22.

Bolle report, *A University Looks at the Forest Service,* published. This evaluation of Forest Service practices in Bitterroot National Forest prompted national debate on clear cutting.

California Environmental Quality Act enacted incorporating many features of the federal model.

Executive Order 11574 (December 23) provided guidelines for administration of Refuse Act permit program.

Resource Recovery Act amended Solid Waste Disposal Act to provide additional assistance for development of resource recovery systems and improved solid waste disposal facilities.

Delaware River Basin Commission amended Comprehensive Plan to levy penalties against municipalities for continuing pollutant discharge.

Geothermal Resources Act empowered Secretary of Interior to issue leases for geothermal resources on public lands.

1970

In *Environmental Defense Fund* v. *Hardin*, judicial concept of standing expanded with determination that biological harm to people and other living things, resulting from Secretary of Agriculture's failure to suspend use of DDT, was sufficient to grant judicial review.

National Materials Policy Act created commission to develop national materials policy with the objective of promoting more efficient use of present resources and technology.

1971

Report of Public Land Law Review Commission issued, generating considerable controversy concerning its commodity and disposition orientation.

Calvert Cliffs Coordinating Committee v. *AEC* established the importance of the EIS and judicial review in the environmental reform movement. Construction of proposed nuclear facility enjoined pending preparation of an adequate EIS.

Congress refused to appropriate additional funds for development of SST (supersonic transport). Environmental hazards created by plane cited as congressional justification.

"Framework for the Future," calling for more balance in Forest Service Programs, adopted by Forest Service as goal statement.

Alaskan Native Claims Settlement Act facilitated building of Trans-Alaska pipeline by resolving native land claims. Law provided that approximately 53,000 Eskimos, Aleuts, and Indians would receive $462.5 million in federal grants, $500 million in federal and state mineral revenues, and 22 million acres of land outside TAPS corridor. Secretary of Interior authorized to withold 80 million acres of national interest lands from state and native selection.

Federal Communications Commission challenged in *Friends of the Earth* v. *FCC* on its refusal to hold that TV spots advertising big cars and leaded gasolines present one side of a controversial issue of public importance, raising Fairness Doctrine implications.

Coal-leasing moratorium imposed by Secretary of Interior after analysis revealed that most leaseholders were not producing coal. Massive reassessment of coal program triggered by this action.

Hunting from Aircraft Act prohibited hunting bald eagles, golden eagles, and wolves from helicopters, in response to public outrage over practice.

RARE I (Roadless Area Review and Evaluation) undertaken by the Forest Service to identify potential wilderness areas.

1971

The United States Supreme Court in *Citizen to Preserve Overton Park* v. *Volpe* by declaring that courts must adhere to rigorous standard for judicial review of administration decisions in environmental matters, advanced the "substantial inquiry" or hard look doctrine which has become central tenet of administrative and environmental law.

"Church Guidelines" for clear cutting published after Senate Subcommittee on Public Lands investigation of national forest harvest techniques. Guidelines immediately adopted as clear cutting policy by Forest Service.

Wild and Free Roaming Horse and Burro Act directed Secretary of Interior to manage and protect such animals from "capture, branding, harassment, or death," and to maintain for them specific sanctuaries on the public lands. Both BLM and Forest Service required to protect fedral populations on public lands.

Washington State Environmental Policy and Shoreline Management Acts Passed.

Oregon Forest Practice Act enacted.

1972

Marine Mammals Protection Act imposed moratorium on killing and importing of most marine mammals.

Coastal Zone Management Act authorized $186 million in grants to states for cooperative planning to protect coastal areas.

United Nations Stockholm Conference on the Human Enviroment concluded that all states are responsible for damage to environment of other states or international areas, and established "Earthwatch" program to monitor environmental indicators.

Federal Environmental Pesticide Control Act substantially amended 1947 Federal Insecticide, Fungicide, and Rodenticide Act, which had been administered by Department of Agriculture until transferred to EPA in 1970 reorganization.

Sierra Club v. *Butz* declared that all areas contiguous to a wilderness or primitive area must be protected as wilderness pending congressional actions on inclusion of area in wilderness system.

Noise Control Act charged EPA with responsibility to set emission standards for all major noise sources. Noise control programs were to be formulated and administered by the states under EPA supervision.

Bald and Golden Eagle Protection Act established criminal penalties for taking or possession of bald and golden eagles.

1972

Federal Water Pollution Control Act Amendments enacted, despite presidential veto, mandating complex set of state programs to meet EPA water quality standards and implementation of point and nonpoint source water pollution controls.

Executive Order 11643 (February 8) directed heads of all federal agencies to ban use of any chemical toxicant on federal lands against predatory animals when secondary harm could occur to human or other animals.

Executive Order 11644 (February 8) instructed agency and department heads to issue regulations controlling the use of off-road vehicles on public lands.

Forest Service published "Environmental Program for the Future" (EPFF) and initiated unit planning process.

Indians occupy Washington offices of the Bureau of Indian Affairs for one week to publicize demands that property rights granted them by treaties be recognized.

Oregon's Minimum Deposit Act (Ch. 745, Oregon Laws of 1971), commonly known as the "bottle bill," went into effect. First state act directed against popular use of disposable beverage containers.

Sierra Club v. *Ruckelshaus* held that administrator's duty to implement a policy of "no significant deterioration" under the Clean Air Act is nondiscretionary.

Florida Environmental Land and Water Management Act enacted, serving as model of major state land use legislation.

In *Friends of Mammoth* v. *Mono City* California Supreme Court dictated NEPA compliance for private activities "for which a government permit of other entitlement of use is necessary."

California Coastal Zone Commission created by Proposition 20, a public initiative calling for controlled coastal growth through increased environmental protection.

Sierra Club v. *Morton*, also known as the "Mineral King" case, clarified "standing" criteria in environmental litigation initiated by reformers acting as "private attorney generals." Justice W. Douglas's frequently cited dissenting opinion posed question of tree's right to sue on own behalf.

NRDC v. *Morton* established "rule of reason" standard for NEPA requirement of EIS discussion of "alternatives to the proposed action."

Volunteers in National Forests Program authorized Secretary of Agriculture to recruit and train volunteers to assist in Forest Service activities.

1973

Endangered Species Act established federal procedures for identification and protection of endangered plants and animals in their critical habitats. Declared broad prohibiting against taking, hunting, harming, or harassing listed species, and was intended, in large part, through cooperative federal and state efforts, to restore endangered populations to a level where protection no longer necessary.

Federal District Court decision in *West Virginia Division of Izaak Walton League* v. *Butz* commenced litigation phase of Monogahela controversy with ruling that Forest Service harvesting practices violate 1917 Organic Act.

Trans-Alaska Pipeline authorized by Congress in statute which removed 50-foot limit on rights-of-way across public lands and exempted TAPS from further litigation of NEPA requirements.

Arab oil embargo prompted 400 percent increase in cost of foreign oil and intense public concern for energy supplies.

Speed limit lowered to 55 mph on national highways.

Agricultural and Consumer Protection Act created under Title X of Forestry Incentives Program (FIP) to authorize financial assistance through long-term contracts with owners of nonindustrial private forest lands. Funds provided for tree planting and timber stand improvement to enhance productivity of nation's small private forests.

"Convention on International Trade in Endangered Species of Wild Fauna and Florida" established international treaty between United States and numerous nations to regulate trade strictly in threatened plant and animal species.

President's Advisory Panel on Timber and the Environment (PAPTE) report called for sounder financial management of national forests.

National Land Use Planning Bills rejected by Congress.

Executive Order 11752 issued, concerning prevention, control, and abatement of environmental pollution at federal facilities.

California Forest Practice Act enacted, outlining State Forestry Board authority in timber harvesting matters.

The Court of Appeals for D.C. Circuit upheld, in all respects, EPA's cancellation of virtually all remaining registrations for DDT in *Environmental Defense Fund* v. *Environmental Protection Agency*.

1973

Scientists' Institute for Public Information v. *AEC* held that NEPA required EIS for research and development program aimed at commercializing the Liquid Metal Fast Breeder Reactor, affirming NEPA's technology assessment function.

1974

Energy Reorganization Act created the Energy Research and Development Administration (ERDA), replacing the Atomic Energy Commission and centralizing energy programs from EPA, Interior, and other federal departments.

Federal Energy Administration created to consolidate federal energy management functions in face of fuel crisis.

Eastern Wilderness Act extended 1964 Wilderness Act to eastern third of nation, adding sixteen new areas to the system.

Forest and Rangeland Renewable Resources Planning Act directed Forest Service to undertake long-range planning to ensure adequate timber supply and maintenance of environmental quality. Forest Service required to prepare a decennial assessment of renewable resource supply and demand and update management program at five-year intervals.

Safe Drinking Water Act authorized EPA to promulgate national primary drinking water regulations specifying permissible contaminant levels or mandating adoption of specific treatment techniques. The states were given major enforcement responsibilities to be carried out under regulations and plans approved by the federal EPA.

"Conti decision," an out-of-court settlement of a Sierra Club suit brought against Forest Service for failure to prepare an EIS or RARE I, prohibited alternation of any de facto wilderness pending completion of land use planning process.

Justice Douglas, sitting as Circuit Justice, issued opinion in *Warm Springs Task Force* v. *Gribble* which stayed further work on Warm Springs Dam project in Sonoma County, California, confirming in dictum the central role of the CEQ as administrator of NEPA.

NRDC v. *Morton* confirmed applicability of NEPA to livestock grazing permit program of the Bureau of Land Management, Department of Interior.

Washington State Forest Practices Act enacted.

1975

Environmental Protection Agency regulations designated all federal lands as class II for air quality purposes.

1975

Initial "Monongahela" decision upheld by Fourth Circuit Court of Appeals, setting stage for legislative remedy of 1897 act inadequacies (*Zaak Walton League* v. *Butz*).

Executive Order 11870 (July 18) pertaining to "Animal Damage Control on Federal Lands" amended the first order promulgated to address problem in 1972 and allowed for the experimental use of sodium cyanide in federal predator control research programs.

I *NRDC* v. *Train,* District of Columbia Court of Appeals accepted theory that the citizen suit provisions of the environmental laws do not provide the exclusive bases of jurisdiction.

Wyoming Statewide Planning Law enacted.

In *Joint Tribal Council of the Passamaquoddy Tribe* v. *Morton* trust relationship between United States and tribal signatories to Nonintercourse Act established in land conveyancy matters.

In a major setback for public interest litigation, United States Supreme Court in *Alyeska Pipeline Service Co.* v. *Wilderness Society* held that only Congress, not the courts, can authorize exception to "American rule" that attorney's fees cannot ordinarily be recovered by a prevailing party from a losing party.

1976

National Forest Management Act repealed language of 1897 act which prompted Monongahela litigation, extensively amended the RPA planning process, and provoked controversy on nondeclining even flow and other key aspects of intensive management. Act also mandated greater public participation in Forest Service decision making and authorized $200 million annually for reforestation work.

Resource Conservation and Recovery Act also known as Solid Waste Bill, established new Office of Solid Waste within EPA to provide technical and financial assistance to states and localities for development and implementation of solid waste management plans.

In *Minnesota Public Interest Research Group* v. *Butz* (II), a statutory assurance that Boundary Waters Canoe Area be administered so as to protect its "primitive" character, interpreted to prohibit commercial exploitation of virgin timber within protected area.

Federal Land Policy and Management Act established the Bureau of Land Management, authorized multiple-use management of public lands, and declared government policy of retaining public lands in federal ownership.

Federal Coal Leasing Amendments enacted despite presidential veto, stipulated competitive bidding on all tracts and eliminated preference right leasing. Comprehensive land use planning requirements and strict bidding procedures outlined in act.

U.S. Supreme Court interpreted, in *Kleppe* v. *New Mexico*, the Wild and Free Roaming Horse and Burro Act to require federal rather than state control of wildlife on public lands. This interpretation has potential to alter traditional federal/state roles in wildlife management.

U.S. Supreme Court limited application of NEPA's EIS requirements by ruling in *Kleppe* v. *Sierra Club* that Interior Department need not prepare regional EIS on northern Great Plains coal program.

Teton Dam disaster occurs when a Bureau of Reclamation dam on Teton River breaks, killing eight people. This tragedy, clearly a result of engineering error, prompted reevaluation of structural approach to water development.

National Park Service Mining Regulation Act 1901) halted mineral entry in certain national parks and monuments by authorizing Secretary of Interior to proscribe regulations as deemed necessary to preserve the parks. Valid existing rights were not extinguished by the bill.

Forest Service canceled contract with Champion International Plywood Company to sell 8.75 bbf over fifty years in Alaska. This sale had been mired in litigation for many years.

Alpine Lakes Wilderness Bill established 392,000 acre area in central Cascade Mountains of Washington.

Energy Minerals Activity Recommendation System unveiled by Interior Department for competitive coal leasing on the public lands.

Park Services Administration Act raised uniform allowance, revised law enforcement authority, and authorized Park Service to recommend twelve new parks annually on land under any jurisdiction.

Payments-in-Lieu Act granted counties $120 million annually for public lands in their jurisdiction.

1976

Proposed reform of "range code," Department of the Interior regulations for range management and leasing, published in *Federal Register.*

Omnibus Wilderness Act designated nineteen wilderness areas in thirteen states.

Natural Defenses Council, Inc. v. *Arcata National Corporation* held that California Environmental Quality Act applied to harvesting of timber, requiring preparation of environmental impact report.

Executive Order 11917 (June 2) on Animal Damage Control on Public Lands amended prior executive decree to allow for limited operational use of sodium cyanide in federal programs on public lands.

Controversial Kaiparowits coal-fired power project proposed for southern Utah dropped by Southern California Edison after conflict with air quality maintenance area requirements (AQMAs) and unfavorable economic projections.

California Coastal Zone Management Act approved, establishing Coastal Zone Conservation Commission as permanent agency and providing administrative framework for preservation of coastal ecology.

Cappaert v. *United States* held that reservation doctrine does not apply to groundwater.

1977

RARE II, a second roadless area review, undertaken by Forest Service in an effort to speed up designation.

Clean Air Amendments established three classes of air quality maintenance areas. International parks, wilderness areas over 5000 acres, and national parks over 6000 acres included in designation permitting no designation of air quality.

Surface Mining Reclamation Act created Office of Strip Mining (OSM) in the Department of the Interior to oversee planning and review requirements of complex legislation.

Amendments to FWPCA exempted "normal silvicultural practices" from dredge and fill requirements of act in addition to changing name to "Clean Water Act" and giving EPA authority to grant case-by-case extensions to compliance deadline for adoption of best practicable control technology to select industrial dischargers.

1977

Executive Orders 11988–90 (May 25) addressed federal role in floodplain maintenance, use of off-road vehicles on public lands, and wetlands preservation, respectively. Unified federal policies and procedures sought in each area.

In *Dupont* v. *Train*, United States Supreme Court resolved series of inconsistent decisions among the circuits by upholding EPA's authority under § 301 of FWPCA to issue uniform effluent limitations.

Soil and Water Resources Conservation Act set forth objectives and guidelines for new soil and water conservation program under auspices of Soil Conservation Service of Department of Agriculture.

1978

Endangered American Wilderness Act designated largest single addition in wilderness system, totaling 1.3 million acres in ten western states.

Sealed bids provision of National Forest Management Act repealed.

Toxic Substances Control Act extended federal regulation of chemicals to include premarket testing of potentially dangerous substances.

Redwoods National Park extension approved, adding 48,000 acres of private land to park. Bill allocated $40 million for retraining of forest workers displaced by the controversial addition.

In *Tennessee Valley Authority* v. *Hill* U.S. Supreme Court interpreted Endangered Species Act to require that $100 million federal project be terminated because it would extinguish the endangered snail darter, a small fish found only in that part of Little Tennessee River to be flooded by the dam.

Congress passed amendment to Endangered Species Act which modifies act's rigid mandate in favor of allowing exemptions in specific cases, determined by a special cabinet-level committee.

U.S. Supreme Court in *Philadelphia* v. *New Jersey* struck down a 1974 New Jersey statute which prohibited liquid and solid waste from being transported into the sate for disposal.

In *California* v. *United States* the U.S. Supreme Court read §8 of Reclamation Act of 1902 to require federal agencies constructing reclamation projects to comply with state-imposed limitations on the use of project waters, striking new balance in federal-state tension over western water rights. On the same day, in *United States* v. *New Mexico,* Court declared that federal reservations of land from public domain do not by implication include reservations of waters flowing through or alongside such lands except for minimum amount of water essential to specific purposes for which land was reserved.

The U.S. Supreme Court unanimously held in *Vermont Yankee Nuclear Power Corp.* v. *Natural Resources Defense Council* that judicial authority to review agency rulemaking where licensing proceedings have been afforded the minimum procedural privileges afforded by the Administrative Procedure Act is limited in the absence of "extremely compelling circumstances."

NRDC v. *Hughes* confirmed mandatory, nondiscretionary duty pursuant to NEPA to consider fully all environmental impacts of and alternatives to a new federal coal leasing program prior to an administrative decision to adopt and implement it.

1979

President Carter's reorganiztion plan, including a Department of Natural Resources and a shift of the Forest Service out of the Department of Agriculture, dies during the discussion stage.

John McGuire retires as Chief of the Forest Service and is replaced by Max Peterson.

BIBILIOGRAPHIC ESSAY

Scholars tend to have strong feelings of personal kinship with books. This probably explains why they opt for university life rather than cabinet making (though I am surprised to learn how many of my colleagues are secretly and not-so-secretly dreaming about forsaking the former for the latter). It also may explain why there are so many bibliographies on so many subjects and at such length. What follows is probably available with more polish and analytic focus elsewhere. It is a rough and brief attempt to expand the references cited at the end of each chapter into a usable guide to the basic literature in the field. Its chief virtue is perhaps its brevity. It is simply an attempt to introduce the reader to the most useful starting points on most of the subjects covered in the previous pages. I am assuming that readers who have gotten this far knew very little when they began and now seek further references on specific topics for research or general information purposes. I make no pretense that this is an inclusive listing of references available. All this does is to point to the basic materials where the pertinent citations can be found.

In selecting items to include, I have adopted several reasonable criteria which relate to the scholarly purposes of the bibliography and have departed from them frequently in order to bring my own personal favorites into full view. Following the "places to start" theme, I have omitted references which are not readily available, including most government documents and publications. I have emphasized materials which have extensive footnotes and bibliographies to provide a third tier of sources for the enthusiast. I have also tried to include as many of the "classics" as possible. Usually, these oft-cited and relied-upon analyses have become classic because they are superb —lucid, exciting, well written, accurate, and useful. Several have, unfortunately, proven to be dangerously wrong. I have so noted with, perhaps, a trace of inappropriate gusto. Hell hath no fury to match a truth seeker misled.

These reasonable criteria guide the first four sections, which are arranged as follows: (1) a selected listing of "do not start withouts"—many classics and other materials which provide a broad introduction to American land and attitudes toward it, (2) a brief discussion of materials available regarding current issues, (3) bibliographies which are useful to the reader starting research in this general area, and (4) a list of useful references on selected specific topics. In all of these listings, I have included some materials which might seem to the initiated to be too obvious to be worth mentioning. However, I am frequently reminded that what is obvious to a professional researcher is less so to someone who is just starting out. Conversely, it is probably also true that I have omitted many references which others might consider essential. With apologies, I reiterate that feelings of personal kinship are involved.

The final categories reflect my own predilections a bit more thoroughly. I have reserved doctoral dissertations for special discussion. They are not readily available and are frequently simply awful. Like the child with the little curl, however, when they are good they are absolutely marvelous. I have also segregated a number of "the whole truth about"—yellow journalism exposés—into a separate category. Many of these lusty volumes provide color and insight into controversies that are meaningless without an understanding of the passion they have generated. They are not, however, scholarly materials. Finally, saving the best for last, I have devised a category of personal favorites: scholarly gems which are slightly off the beaten path but so exquisite and thought-provoking as to merit special mention somewhere.

GENERAL WORKS

Do not Start Without

Students of the general subject of forest and range policy should begin their search of this literature with an overall understanding of the land, its history, and its relationship to people, politics, and government.

An impressive consensus has emerged that, if you are going to read one book in this area, it should be Wallace Stegner's *Beyond the Hundreth Meridan: John Wesley Powell and the Second Opening of the West* (Houghton Mifflin, 1953). The story of Powell's career is a vibrant introduction to both physical and political realities which dominated critical decades in nineteenth-century resource policy. A broader gauged introduction to the general topic of the American people and land is Bernard De Voto's trilogy, *Course of Empire, Across the Wide Missouri,* and *Year of Decision: 1846* (Houghton Mifflin, 1952, 1947, and 1943, respectively). The first book begins with the Moors crossing the Straits of Gibralter from Africa into Spain, and the last concludes with a confluence of major and minor events in 1846. Although the sweep of the volumes is vast, the focus is such that the reader can, in relatively few pages, begin to get a feeling for the diversity of people, ideas, and happenings which have molded contemporary attitudes toward land and land management. Conveniently, Stegner takes up approximately where De Voto leaves off, creating a broad-brush portrait—increasingly finely etched as it approaches the twentieth century—of the context of American resource policy.

Two more specific but equally stimulating volumes are Samuel P. Hays's *Conservation and the Gospel of Efficiency* (Harvard University Press, 1959) and Roderick Nash's *Wilderness and the American Mind* (Yale University Press, 1968). Hays's study brings the progressive conservation movement within the range of comprehension and places the forestry crusade of Pinchot and Roosevelt into the context of other resource programs and its broader intellectual impulses. Nash's scholarship is perhaps less impressive than Hays's, in part because Nash retraces much of the ground Hans Huth charted in *Nature and the American* (University of California Press, 1957), and in part because of its clear advocacy orientation. However, the focus on conflicting American attitudes toward the natural world and the introduction to the broad intellectual heritage of the contemporary preservation movement is most valuable.

Two final and even more specifically relevant volumes round out this collection of essential first steps. Paul Wallace Gates's *History of Public Land Law Development* (U.S. Government Printing Office, 1968) is without doubt the most useful single reference in the general area of American land policy. Not designed to enthrall the casual reader, it nevertheless tells the story of the public lands in minute detail without sacrificing readability, analytic coherence, and zest. Gates is one of our most prolific and insightful public land historians; and this volume, done for the Public Land Law Review Commission, is without peer. It is also, unfortunately, out of print. Write your congressperson immediately and urge that funds be allocated to reprint this invaluable volume. Failing that, it is available in most libraries.

E. Louise Peffer's *The Closing of the Public Domain* (Stanford University Press, 1951) is also out of print, but it has been recirculated by Arno Press, which has recycled many valuable classics in the field. Peffer's study of the Taylor Grazing Act is an excellent and totally necessary introduction to what has been for many the quiet corner of renewable resource management—range policy. For style, readability, and scholarship, Peffer's great work is difficult to match. I am not the only person I know who is in this field today because they fell in love with Peffer's masterpiece.

These eight books will put anyone on firm footing for dealing with almost any specific aspect of forest and range policy. Their utility is enhanced considerably, moreover, by extensive references. The bibliographies and footnotes will sate all but the truly intrepid.

Current Issues

Current events are frequently difficult to deal with. Generally, there is less that is reliable and insightful written about them, and recent controversies are apt to be mired in trivia and bias. Fortunately, there are numerous sources which alleviate these problems somewhat for students of forest and range policy.

In February 1976, the Resources Publishing Company (1010 Vermont Avenue N.W., Washington, D.C., 20005) began issuing the biweekly *Public Land News.* Covering a broad range of legislation, litigation regulation, and other activities affecting wild lands management, this new periodical is a reliable, evenhanded, thorough, and invaluable source of news. Viewed retrospectively, back issues provide a rapid synopsis of the development of major issues and, coincidentally, valuable insight to the two steps forward-one step back aspects of negotiating public policy. The *Conservation News,* published by the National Wildlife Federation (1412 16th Street N.W., Washington, D.C., 20036), is equally timely. Although it concentrates heavily on Washington and congressional activities, it is free; *Public Land News* is $95 per year.

Another excellent starting point for slightly less contemporary issues is *Congress and the Nation,* an occasional compendium of congressional activities which gives extensive and useful coverage to environmental and resource issues. Presently consisting of four volumes (Volume I, 1945–1964; Volume II, 1965–1968; Volume III, 1970–1972; and Volume IV, 1973–1976), this Congressional Quarterly, Inc. publication (1414 22d Street N.W., Washington, D.C., 20037) provides brief but thorough background on most major issues and access to congressional documents in the form of relevant bill numbers, dates, reports, and so forth. The same corporation also publishes *Congressional Quarterly* and a growing collection of related items which provide excellent jumping-off places on most major and some minor resource issues. Well indexed, they are a good first step for research in federal government documents.

Periodicals and journals also provide an excellent source of information on contemporary attitudes toward policy issues. *American Forests* and *Journal of Forestry* are both published monthly. Neither is devoted wholly to policy issues, but both are excellent sources of leads and information. *American Forests* is published by the American Forestry Association and reflects the eclectic interests of its membership. It has been published as *American Forestry, American Forests and Forest Life,* or *American Forests* since 1896. The *Journal of Forestry* is the publication of the Society of American Foresters. It has been published since 1902, and its utility as a policy reference varies considerably over time. It is always fascinating, however, to flip through ancient issues just to see how things were and how they have changed.

Rangeman's Journal is the policy-oriented publication of the Society for Range Management. The articles are generally brief but frequently useful. The *Journal of Soil and Water Conservation* is a consistently valuable source of articles in that professional realm. Finally, the *Natural Resources Journal,* published at the University of New Mexico, School of Law, frequently contains excellent articles of interest to students of forest and range policy. Most of the above journals are indexed annually and can be rapidly perused. In addition, the Public Affairs Information Service and the Index to Legal Periodicals give access to major social science and legal periodicals, which frequently contain articles of interest. Students should not be put off by law reviews. Articles are frequently too technical to be meaningful to nonlawyers, but the same is true of any professional literature. In my experience, law review articles are much more apt to be useful to nonlawyers than political scientists' or economists' articles are to those outside those professions.

Many interest groups have journals which provide special insight into their positions on policy issues. *The Living Wilderness* (The Wilderness Society), the *Sierra Club Bulletin, National Parks and Conservation Magazine* (originally *National Parks Magazine*), and *Audubon* contain useful articles on specific topics and provide over time an indication of evolving concerns in the environmental arena. *American Cattle Producer, National Wool Grower,* and *American Lumberman* are all worth consulting with reference to particular issues or eras.

Four books provide excellent background in the diverse events of the 1970s which are "current" at present writing. John Whitaker's *Striking A Balance* (AEI-Hoover Institute, 1976) and John Quarles's *Cleaning Up America* (Houghton Mifflin, 1976) are both highly readable and informative first-person accounts of Washington, D.C., environmental politics of the 1970s. Whitaker was Undersecretary of Interior, whereas Quarles was Chief Legal Officer for the Environmental Protection Agency, so the former is generally more relevant to the present topic than the latter. The two complement each other nicely, however, and provide a good basis of understanding the "environmental decade." A third contribution in the same area, *Land Use Controls in the United States,* has been prepared by the Natural Resources Defense Council (Dial Press, 1977). It has an explicit advocacy orientation but nevertheless succeeds in providing a very useful introduction to the land use implications of recent environmental legislation. It can be read in part in lieu of and in part as an introduction to *Federal Environmental Law,* edited by E. Dolgin and T. Guilbert (Environmental Law Institute for West Publishing Company, 1974) which, although already somewhat dated, constitutes an invaluable background in environmental law in the 1970s. Especially noteworthy is Frederick Anderson's chapter on the National Environmental Policy Act (NEPA)—a briefer and more useful study than his widely relied upon book on the same subject, *NEPA in the Courts* (Johns Hopkins Press for Resources for the Future, 1973).

Two very current topics deserve special mention because there is a plethora of literature available and one clearly outstanding source in both areas. On the subject of nonindustrial private forests, Robert A. Sedjo and David M. Ostermeier compiled *Policy Alternatives for Nonindustrial Private Forests* from a workshop on that subject held by the Society of American Foresters in 1977. It is a brief guide to the issues and the literature and is available from the Society.

On the equally flooded field of nondeclining even flow, readers are encouraged to consult the *Journal of Forestry* for articles and references. If you can obtain a copy, however, *Timber Harvest Policies on the O and C Lands,* prepared by R. Nelson and L. Pugliaresi for the Office of Policy Analysis in the Department of the Interior in March, 1977, is an excellent and easily overlooked brief introduction to the complex topic and literature.

Bibliographies

There are a number of bibliographies which constitute a useful research starting point. In June 1976, the Agricultural History Center of the University of California at Davis (Gerald Ogden, compiler) issued *The United States Forest Service: A Historical Bibliography, 1876–1972.* Almost everything one could seek is included. Ronald J. Fall's bibliography, *North American Forest and Conservation History* (ABC Clio Press for the Forest History Society, 1977) is more comprehensive and, therefore, even more valuable. For those with an unquenchable thirst for knowledge or a desire to do research in primary materials, Richard Davis has contributed *North American Forest History: A Guide to Archives and Manuscripts in the United States and Canada* (ABC Clio Press for Forest History Society, 1977). These three invaluable works plus the bibliographies in Gates, Peffer, Stegner, and De Voto should key the reader into almost everything available.

BRIEF INTRODUCTIONS TO SPECIFIC ISSUES
Public Domain Histories

Gates's study mentioned above is the most recent, hence the most useful for many purposes. Several earlier public domain histories are excellent, however, and provide a different analytical focus and a different set of references and footnotes. Thomas C. Donaldson wrote the first comprehensive study in 1880 for the First Public Land Commission. It was issued as *The Public Domain: Its History and Statistics* and reissued four years later as *The Public Domain: Its History with Statistics.* George M. Stephenson's *The Political History of the Public Lands from 1840 to 1862* was first published in 1917 and reissued in 1967 (Russell and Russell). It provides a detailed history of sectional influences of public land policies from the preemption period to the Homestead Act. Benjamin Hibbard's *A History of the Public Land Policies* (Macmillan, 1924) was the standard reference for several decades. It is comprehensive and useful but requires caution: errors in detail and a pervasive bias in favor of the wisdom of the progressive era mar the volume. Roy M. Robbins's *Our Landed Heritage* (Princeton University Press, 1942) is also comprehensive, more focused on policy debates, and less turgid stylistically. Gates and Peffer are better for openers, but those in search of different details and analyses will not be disappointed.

Vernon Carstensen has collected some of the major monographs on the topic in *The Public Lands* (University of Wisconsin Press, 1962). This useful volume puts some minute detail on the more general histories, introduces some of the scholarly disputes regarding the public lands, and contains extensive bibliographical materials. Marion Clawson and Burnell Held's *The Federal Lands: Their Use and Management* (Johns Hopkins Press for Resources for the Future, 1957) provides a valuable admixture of public land history, policy considerations, and economic anaysis. Though dated, it is a valuable introduction; and Clawson's more recent *The Federal Lands Since 1956: Recent Trends in Use and Management* (Johns Hopkins Press for Resources for the Future, 1965) is also useful. Charles McKinley's *Uncle Sam in the Pacific Northwest* (University of California Press, 1952) is a superb, comprehensive, and well-documented study of the Columbia River in regional resource development. It covers all federal agencies. Finally, for both scholarly monographs and valuable local color, the *Journal of Forest History* is an excellent and useful reference (Forest History Society, 109 Coral Street, Santa Cruz, CA, 95060).

Forest Service and the National Forests Generally

The Forest Service and the national forests are the subject of varied attention and analysis. Two familiar and much-cited references, John Ise's *The United Staes Forest Policy* (Yale University Press, 1920) and Jenks Cameron's *The Development of Governmental Forest Control in the United States* (Johns Hopkins Press, 1928) are invaluable and comprehensive introductions to the subject matter. Cameron offers more useful and extensive citations and his analysis is not characterized by the same degree of vitriol and bias that pervades the Ise book. Both are however, unduly uncritical of the Pinchot-progressive approach to conservation and should be relied upon with caution. Andrew Denny Rogers's study, *Bernhard Edward Fernow* (Princeton University Press, 1951) is an impressive biography of the life and works of our first professional forester. Fernow's reputation has suffered, and his considerable accomplishments have been underrated, at the hands of Pinchot and his devotees. Rogers's book is a necessary antidote to the general tendency to equate forestry with Pinchot and the Forest Service.

Robert Marshall, best known as the wilderness enthusiast of the 1930s, penned a fascinating tract, *The People's Forests* (Harrison, Smith, and Robert Haas, 1933), advocating a national forest purchase and management scheme similar to the 1933 National Plan for Forests (Copeland Report), of which he was principal author. Marshall's writings (see also *The Social Management of American Forests,* League for Industrial Democracy, 1930) are important reminders of the socialist strain in the early forestry profession. More typically, Gifford Pinchot's autobiography, *Breaking New Ground* (Harcourt, Brace, 1947), is a vigorous and indispensable but self-serving and occasionally wildly inaccurate report on the forestry crusade from its self-styled epicenter. William Greeley's *Forests and Men* (Doubleday, 1951) covers some of the same period with a significantly different perspective. Greeley's more reflective approach gives important insight into early controversies, especially when juxtaposed with Pinchot and Ise. Luther Gulick's *American Forest Policy* (Duell, Sloan, and Pearce, 1951) is an early analysis of the public administration aspects of the Forest Service and an excellent exemplar of that field's continuing fascination with the esprit and efficiency of the agency.

Herbert Kaufman's *Forest Ranger: A Study in Administrative Behavior* (Johns Hopkins Press, 1960) is a classic social science approach to Forest Service commitment and cohesion. In any analysis of the Forest Service, Kaufman's conclusions must be reckoned with. Charles Reich's *Bureaucracy and the Forests* (An Occasional Paper for the Center for the Study of Democratic Institutions, 1962) takes a less positive view of Forest Service (and other land-managing agencies) esprit, arguing that they are high-handed and unresponsive technocrats who serve professional values rather than the public interest.

Bernard Frank's *Our National Forests* (University of Oklahoma Press, 1955) and Arthur Carhart's *The National Forests* (Alfred A. Knopf, 1959) are among the better examples of a minor literary genre: books with similar or identical titles which tell the "Forest Service story" in more or less the same way, moderately to extremely awestruck and devotional. Carhart's observations are especially worth noting due to his gruff, flatfooted style and his long and significant participation in the policies of which he writes.

Michael Frome's contributions to the Forest Service story collection are interesting because, as the author evolves from a travel writer to a wilderness advocate, his assessment of the Forest Service becomes more critical. See especially *Whose Woods These Are* (Doubleday, 1962), *The National Forests of America* (Putnam, 1968, "with" Orville Freeman), *The Forest Service* (Praeger, 1971), and *The Battle for the Wilderness* (Praeger, 1974). The most recent volumes are even further and more interesting departures from the established saga mold. Glen O. Robinson's *The Forest Service: A Study in Public Land Management* (Johns Hopkins Press for Resources for the Future, 1975) compacts the traditional history into several succinct and analytically focused chapters and proceeds to a timely and significant discussion of major policy issues in Forest Service functional areas. Robinson's background as a lawyer and newcomer to the field has given him a fresh analytic view of the traditional subject matters. Historian Harold K. Steen brings an equally productive perspective to *The Forest Service: A History* (University of Washington Press, 1976, 1977). Although much of the ground he covers is familiar, it is not the predictable paean from Pinchot enthusiasts and Forest Service devotees. The references in Robinson's and Steen's efforts are useful, extensive, and also fresh. The critical analytic perspective on policy issues, perhaps lacking in Steen, is amply accounted for in Marion Clawson's *Forests for Whom and for What* (Johns Hopkins Press for Resources for the Future, 1975). Neither methodologically nor conceptually overwhelming, the book nonetheless provides a systematic framework for raising and dealing with basic issues that underlie present conflict over Forest Service policies. Finally, William Shands and Robert Healy headed a Conservation Foundation team which produced *The Lands Nobody Wanted,* an inquiry into the frequently overlooked eastern national forests (Conservation Foundation, 1977). The book is formatted in a semi-stream-of-consciousness fashion, capitalizing on interviews with interested persons throughout the region. Although less rigorous than one might like and inadequately documented for present purposes, it is nevertheless an interesting and useful study.

The Bureau of Land Management (BLM) and Its Antecedents

Although the Bureau has been largely ignored by Congress and the public, some of the best writing in the resource policy field has concerned management of the public domain lands. Peffer's *Closing of the Public Domain* has already been noted. Two additional outstanding studies were published in 1960. Philip Foss's *Politics and Grass* (Greenwood Press, 1960) is widely read, widely relied upon, quite vigorous, and perhaps a bit overwrought study of stock operators' domination of Bureau personnel, budget, and programs. More scholarly, less familiar, but equally outstanding is Wesley Calef's *Private Grazing and Public Lands* (University of Chicago Press, 1960). A brief but useful introduction to the public domain, the Taylor Grazing Act, and the modes of stock industry operation is followed through six case studies. Calef's conclusions are dated, but his observations are a necessary background to an understanding of current issues. The major defect of both books is inadequate bibliographic and reference material. This has been partially remedied by Marion Clawson's *The Bureau of Land Management* (Praeger, 1971). As a former director of the Bureau, Clawson has a unique understanding of Bureau problems. Although dated, it is an excellent reference, unlike many in the Praeger series.

National Park Service

There seems to be fewer books written about the Park Service than the Forest Service (or the BLM, interestingly); those that are available tend toward travelogues or breathless adorations of our unique contribution to world conservation thought. John Muir's *Our National Parks* (Houghton Mifflin) is available in numerous editions beginning in 1901. The same is true of Robert Sterling Yard's *The Book of the National Parks*

(Scribner's, 1919) and Freeman Tilden's *The National Parks—What They Mean to You and Me* (Alfred A Knopf, 1951, 1970. Tilden has given similar treatment to state parks.) These volumes are most interesting as evidence of evolving attitudes about the parks and their place in American life. Horace Albright's *Oh, Ranger!,* written with Frank Taylor (Stanford University Press, 1928), is a folksy story of life as a ranger. It is not analytically focused but reveals, nevertheless, much about agency policy in the eyes of one of the creators of the Park Service. John Ise's *Our National Park Policy— A Critical History* (Johns Hopkins University Press for Resources for the Future, 1961) is oriented toward history of individual parks and the movement to get them established. It is heavy on the local color, in many ways a long thank-you note to the early park boosters for their efforts. It also discusses the dominant themes of each National Park Service director, but still manages to fall more into the adoration than the analysis category. Perhaps, it is a good place to start, but it does not get you very far. William C. Everhart's *National Park Service* (Praeger, 1972) gives a clearer picture of some of the problems and conflicts in park management but still lacks detachment, rigor, and systematic assessment. Ronald F. Lee cannot be faulted on the same grounds. Though uncritical, *The Family Tree of the National Park Service* (Eastern National Park and Monument Association, 1972) was intended merely to catalog all the administrative types within the service and explain how they came about. His is a valuable reference for that limited purpose. Any of several editions of *Steve Mather of the National Parks,* by Robert Shankland (Alfred A. Knopf, 1951), is probably the best starting point on the Park Service. Shankland's account is clearly biased in favor of Mather and the parks, but it is an excellent and useful volume nonetheless—chock full of references and footnotes.

Soil Conservation Service

The Soil Conservation Service is, perhaps surprisingly, also better treated analytically than the Park Service. Hugh Bennet, first crusading director of the SCS, wrote a predictable *This Land We Defend* (Longmans, Green, 1942). It conveys the basics of soil conservation policy and programs and reminds one and all that Gifford Pinchot was only the first and the best of the self-occupied, messianic conservationists. Two 1965 Resources for the Future books (Johns Hopkins Press)—*Governing Soil Conservation: Thirty Years of the New Decentralization,* by Robert Morgan, and *Soil Conservation in Perspective,* by Marion Clawson and Burnell Held—have a more analytic focus. Clawson and Held concentrate on the economics of soil conservation, while Morgan is more concerned with coordination of the vast federal and state programs in the area.

Miscellaneous Other Agencies

Two books of Praeger Publishers—*The Bureau of Reclamation,* by William E. Warne (1973) and *The Bureau of Outdoor Recreation,* by Edwin M. Fitch and John Shanklin (1970)—are among the least helpful in their series on federal agencies. Both are written by Bureau employees. The Bureau of Outdoor Recreation (BOR) has ceased to exist, and public attitudes toward BuRec have altered significantly. Both volumes have the clang of hucksterism. It is probably better to ignore the BOR and rely on the pertinent sections of Hays and Gates for reclamation. Norris L. Hundley's *Water and the West* (University of California Press, 1975) is superb but narrowly focused on the Colorado

River Compact. Erwin Cooper's *Aqueduct Empire* (Arthur H. Clark Company, 1965) is thorough but journalistic, inadequately documented, and confined to California. *Uncle Sam in the Pacific Northwest,* discussed above, is also relevant to the reclamation topic. These are not my fields, obviously, but I have found little to lure me into them, either.

Forestry Profession

One book is so excellent and useful that it will suffice to fill the whole category. That is fortunate, because there is little else available but Henry Clepper's *Professional Forestry in the United States* (Johns Hopkins Press for Resources for the Future, 1971). Clepper was personally involved in most of the issues he discusses, but he remains, nevertheless, admirably evenhanded, engaging, and informative throughout. The book is useful in its entirety but has special merit as a source of references on major issues within the profession. It is especially good on topics like the evolution of industrial forestry, the development of the multiple-use concept, the regulation dispute, and other major themes in the profession that are less forthrightly treated in other places. I hesitate to mention my other favorite in this area, both because it is narrow and difficult to obtain and because it reveals me completely as an incurable and thoroughgoing bibliogrubber. However, I found *Forests for the Future: The Story of Sustained Yield as Told in the Diaries and Papers of David T. Mason, 1907–1950,* edited by Rodney C. Loehr (Minnesota Historical Society, 1952), to be mistitled but totally engrossing. The volume is most valuable for its insights into the forest products industry and the NIRA regulations of the 1930s, but the whole thing has such verisimilitude that I felt like I was reading a good novel.

Range Policy

Peffer, Gates, Calef, and Foss are the obvious references in this category, but several others merit attention. Ernest Osgood's *The Day of the Cattleman* has long been considered the classic study of the livestock industry. Originally published in 1929, it was reissued (University of Minnesota Press, 1954) to meet continuing demand. It has excellent references and remains valuable and difficult to obtain. *Bankers and Cattlemen,* by Gene M. Gressley (Alfred A. Knopf, 1966), focuses on the sources of capitalization in the cattle industry, 1870–1900. The book says less about fraud, corruption, and chicanery than one might anticipate and is an important introduction to an inadequately understood topic. Finally, *Hoofprints on Forest Ranges: The Early Years of National Forest Range Management* (Naylor Company, 1963) is the only apparent reference on that critical topic. Because it is the only book available, one might wish it were more scholarly. However, it is not intended to be so; even without references, Paul Robert's chatty and unsystematic recollections are insightful, useful, and totally enjoyable.

Recreation

There is surprisingly little useful treatment of recreation policy outside of indexed journals. The Outdoor Recreation Resources Review Commission (ORRRC) reports occupied the field in the early 1960s and very little else has been done. Jeanne Nienaber and Aaron Wildavsky used recreation as the focus of their budget analysis, *The Budgeting and Analysis of Federal Recreation Programs* (Basic Books, 1971). While interesting and useful, it is not a basic reference in the field. Many doctoral dissertations are available, however, and students are encouraged to consult *Dissertation Abstracts.*

Wilderness

The wilderness literature is also surprisingly limited. Nash seems, like the ORRRC, to have so occupied the field that others have not entered. This is an area, however, in which numerous interest groups have made available considerable journal- and book-length material. Again, moreover, dissertations abound.

Wildlife

The Council on Environmental Quality issued a volume prepared by Michael Bean, *The Evolution of National Wildlife Law* (U.S. Government Printing Office, 1977), which is an admirable if primarily legalistic treatment of the development of wildlife policy in America. James B. Trefethen's *An American Crusade for Wildlife* (Boone and Crockett Club, 1975) is too uncritical, incomplete, and inadequately documented to be a really good first step, but it does provide an interesting sweep of federal policy.

DOCTORAL DISSERTATIONS

Fortunately, many of the gaps above are filled by excellent doctoral dissertations, most of which can be located through *Dissertation Abstracts* in the reference room of most libraries and then either borrowed from the degree-granting institutions or purchased from University Microfilms in Ann Arbor, Michigan.

James P. Gilligan's *The Development of Policy and Administration of Forest Service Primitive and Wilderness Areas in the Western United States* (University of Michigan, Ann Arbor, 1953) is the best single source on the subject available. Several subsequent treatments of the Wilderness Act fail to achieve Gilligan's high standard of balanced scholarship. People seriously interested in wilderness policy simply cannot begin without Gilligan. Similarly indispensable is Donald Cates's study, *Recreation in the U.S. Forest Service* (Stanford University, 1963). A bit overlong, perhaps, it thoroughly documents and analyzes a very important and overlooked aspect of Forest Service development. Perforce, there is some overlap with the Gilligan thesis, but both are really necessary to the serious student of either topic. The references in both are exhaustive, a real feast for the specialist.

Three final gems in the forestry area should underscore the basic point that dissertations are valuable research tools. Joseph Miller has as firm a grasp on the pre-Roosevelt conservation movement as anyone writing in the field. His *Congress and the Origins of Conservation: Natural Resource Policies, 1865–1900* (University of Minnesota, 1973) is absolutely first-rate and invaluable. Herbert Kirkland's *The American Forest, 1864–1898: A Trend Toward Conservation* (Florida State University, 1971) covers similar ground with a forest emphasis. Together the two works constitute a devastating assault on much of the Ise-originated analysis of early forest history. With no particular reverence for Pinchot or the Forest Service, they have a much clearer picture of pre-1900 activities than most. They have contributed new perspectives on the forest reserve legislation in the 1890s and the dispositive and long underrated contributions of Bernhard Fernow. The final leaf in this triptych is *A History of Conservation in the Pacific Northwest, 1891–1913,* by Lawrence Rakestraw (University of Washington, 1955). This work should not be overlooked as being of merely regional interest. Rakestraw's analysis of early forest reservations is an invaluable contribution to expanded understanding of the crucial decade of the 1890s, and his findings should be part of the reassessment of the Ise approach to forest reserves and western attitudes to them. These three nuggets make me want to have my own dissertation recalled.

EXPOSÉS

Renewable resource land management has never achieved the status of the meatpacking industry in the muckraking genre, but numerous alarmist tracts have played an important part in its history. Land frauds chronicled in S. A. D. Puter's *Looters of the Public Domain* (Portland Printing House, 1908) contributed fuel to the charges of corruption in the Department of the Interior aired in the Ballinger-Pinchot controversy. George Ahern's broadsides, *Deforested America* (Senate Document 216, 70th Congress, 2d. Session, 1929) and *Forest Bankruptcy in America* (Green Lamp League, 1933), were part of another Pinchot dust-up aimed at securing extensive increases in federal forest ownership and regulation of private forests. Recently, a number of similar volumes have constituted an important part of more familiar controversies.

Bernard De Voto's *The Easy Chair* (Houghton Mifflin, 1955) is a collection of essays, many of which focus on the livestock industry's proposals for disposition of the grazing districts. It probably ranks as the high-water mark of modern conservation vitriol. K. Ross O'Toole's *The Rape of the Great Plains: Northwest America, Cattle, and Coal* (Little, Brown, 1976) is an equally unfettered expression of anger and pain from a similarly talented western historian on approximately the same subject. These volumes are not in the slightest bit confusing; the authors are quite clear as to their goals. William Voigt's *Public Grazing Lands: Use and Misuse by Industry and Government* (Rutgers University Press, 1976) is misleading. Although written by an ostensibly reasonable but clearly identified advocate, the volume relies heavily on biased sources. It is a classic case of believing the man who would be (but was not) chosen king in assessing the king's virtues and policies. The book is useful but seriously unreliable.

Three recent items in the forestry field also deserve mention. The Sierra Club "Battle Book" by Nancy Wood, *Clearcut: The Deforestation of America* (Ballantine Books, 1971), and Jack Shepherd's *The Forest Killers: The Destruction of the American Wilderness* (Weybright and Tally, 1975) can be described as rather uncomplicated diatribes. *The Last Stand,* prepared by Daniel B. Barney (Grossman Publishers, 1974) for The Ralph Nader Study Group is the best of its kind, but it is still not particularly accurate. These volumes are, nonetheless, important. They indicate the passions which are aroused and with which public policymakers must contend. Moreover, they should explain to resource managers the enormity of the sins attributed to them by many and the degree to which popular acceptance of their professions has been eroded. Finally, if there is among some citizens a feeling that they encounter inappropriate resentment from their public servants, they should dwell on these broadsides and consider whether some officials' attitudes might be understandable, if not justified. Although not always a contribution to the debate, these exposés are part of it and must be accounted for. Generally, however, the books are angry, inaccurate, badly documented, humorless, and unpleasant.

GEMS

Finally, there are a number of works which lack the sweep of most of the volumes and are therefore not particularly good places to start. However, the authors have examined particular facets of resource policy with such supreme skill that their books have aesthetic merit and should, among other things, serve as exemplars of that exacting art of scholarship whereby the specific case analysis achieves general relevance. Sherry Olson has focused the watchmaker's glass on essential assumptions underlying the timber famine theory of the late nineteenth and early twentieth centuries and thereby cast critical doubts on many of the most durable tenets of American renewable resource management. Her brief but incisive book, *The Depletion Myth: A History of Railroad Use of Timber* (Harvard University Press, 1971), may not sound like a spellbinder, but is is absolutely gripping. Ashley Schiff's *Fire and Water: Scientific Heresy in the Forest Service* (Harvard University Press, 1962) is a similarly devastating argument concerning early Forest Service policy on fire and water research. Finally, *Order Upon the Land* (Oxford University Press, 1976), Hildegard Binder Johnson's treatment of the rectangular survey, its origins, and its ramifications for land management, is a superb and invigorating assessment of land concepts so fundamental that their enormous impact is frequently overlooked. All three of these books are stimulating, challenging, and creative, not only in the ingenuity and precision of their authors but hopefully in the sparks that their rethinking of first principles generates.

Index of Abbreviations
or
a Brief Guide to the Alphabet Soup of Resource Policy

AAA	American Automobile Association
AAAS	American Association for the Advancement of Science
ACE	"allowable cut effect"
ACP	Agricultural Conservation Program
AFA	American Forestry Association
ANCSA	Alaskan Native Claim Settlement Act
APA	Administrative Procedures Act
BHC	benezine hexachloride
BLM	Bureau of Land Management
BMPs	Best Management Practices
BOR	Bureau of Outdoor Recreation
CCC	Civilian Conservation Corps
CEQ	Council on Environmental Quality
CEQA	California Environmental Quality Act
CFM	Cooperative Farm Management Program
DENR	Department of Environment and Natural Resources
DNR	Department of Natural Resources

EDF   Environmental Defense Fund
EIS   Environmental Impact Statement
EPA   Environmental Protection Agency
EPFF   Environmental Program for the Future
FEPCA   Federal Environmental Pesticide Control Act
FIFRA   Federal Insecticide, Fungicide and Rodenticide Act
FLPMA   Federal Land Policy Management Act
FPC   Federal Power Commission
FWPCA   Federal Water Pollution Control Act
"4L"   Loyal Legion of Loggers and Lumbermen
GLO   General Land Office
HEW   Health, Education and Welfare, Department of
"K-V"   programs and funding under the Knutson-Vandenberg Act
LCDC   Land Conservation and Development Commission (Oregon)
LWCF   Land and Water Conservation Fund
NDEF   nondeclining even flow
NEPA   National Environmental Policy Act
NFMA   National Forest Management Act
NIPF   nonindustrial private forest
NIRA   National Industrial Recovery Act
NOAA   National Oceanic and Atmospheric Administration
NPDES   National Pollution Discharge Elimination System
NRDC   National Resource Defense Council
OCS   Outer Continental Shelf
OMB   Office of Management and Budget
ORRRC   Outdoor Recreation Resources Review Commission
PLLRC   Public Land Law Review Commission
"PR funds"   money for state wildlife programs under Pittman-Robertson Act
PSD   prevention of significant deterioration
REA   Rural Electrification Administration
REAP   Rural Environmental Assistance Program
RPA   Forest and Rangelands Renewable Resources Planning Act
RPAR   Rebuttable Presumption Against Registration
SAF   Society of American Foresters
SCS   Soil Conservation Service
SEPA   State Environmental Policy Act (Washington)
SES   Soil Erosion Service
TGA   Taylor Grazing Act
TVA   Tennessee Valley Authority
USGS   United States Geological Survey

Index